Handbook of
International Psychology

Handbook of
International Psychology

Edited by
Michael J. Stevens and Danny Wedding

Brunner-Routledge
Taylor & Francis Group
NEW YORK AND HOVE

Published in 2004 by
Brunner-Routledge
270 Madison Avenue
New York, NY 10016
www.brunner-routledge.com

Published in Great Britain by
Brunner-Routledge
27 Church Road
Hove, East Sussex
BN3 2FA
www.brunner-routledge.co.uk

Brunner-Routledge is an imprint of the Taylor & Francis Group.
Printed in the United States of America on acid-free paper.

10 9 8 7 6 5 4 3 2 1

Library of Congress Cataloging-in-Publication Data

Handbook of international psychology / Michael J. Stevens and Danny Wedding, editors.
        p. cm.
   Includes bibliographical references and index.
   ISBN 0-415-94612-3 (hardback)
   1. psychology.   I.   Stevens, Michael J., 1954-   II.   Wedding, Danny.
   III. Title.
BF121.H2115 2004
150'.9—dc22

                                                                    2004000334

Dedication

For Beverly Elaine Stevens, my loving wife,
with appreciation for her encouragement throughout this project
and for her support of my life as an academic. MJS

For Sara Jane Serot, with gratitude for her patience
with my peripatetic ways. DW

Contents

Foreword

In recent years, there has been a renewed focus on connecting countries around the world through international psychology. There is growing cultural and ethnic diversity in many countries, and this, along with the increasing globalization of the world economy, has led to a focus on international cooperation among nations. Over the past few decades, several international conferences and congresses related to psychology have been held in different parts of the developed and developing world. Cities and communities all over the world are becoming increasingly diverse, and this diversity has led to a need for increased awareness of multiculturalism and the importance of international psychology.

Research in the social sciences, as well as in other sciences, is recognizing cultural factors and realizing the importance of cross-cultural and cross-ethnic comparisons in studies. Nations are beginning to realize how much more they can learn from one another by sharing ideas and working together toward international cooperation. Psychological explanations for events and people's behavior must be understood in relation to the context and the sociocultural world in which people are immersed.

The *Handbook of International Psychology* provides an opportunity to educate readers about international perspectives by giving the unique perspectives of several different areas of the world. This book will likely encourage communication among members of the international community through its promotion of awareness of global issues and perspectives. The *Handbook* is a collection that can be read and referred to continuously in the coming years. The knowledge that it provides will serve as a major resource internationally for psychologists, scientists, and graduate and undergraduate students, as well as educators. The editors are to be admired for producing a work that will certainly prove to be an essential guidebook in the coming years.

The publication of this volume represents the current work of the best thinkers in the field of international psychology. It builds on a foundation of prior knowledge, while also moving forward to discuss the evolving characteristics of psychology worldwide. It investigates concerns of global significance, societal transformation and national development, and international psychology organizations, as well as the future of international psychology. The chapters in this volume are extremely interesting and provide information in such a way that the field of international psychology can be proud of its accomplishments thus far, while at the same time feeling prepared and excited to face the challenges that lie ahead.

The selection of the areas of the world included in this book is an excellent representation of the growth of psychology internationally in both the scientific and professional realms. After much consideration, 27 countries from nine regions across six continents were selected. These countries include Iran, Japan, Nigeria, Poland, and Thailand, as well as the United States, just to name a few. The careful consideration and thought that went into the selection of the countries chosen for this volume are reflected in the breadth of coverage and perspectives that are included. This makes this volume even more priceless because it depicts such a wide range of diversity through its inclusion of such distinct regions of the world.

In addition, all of the authors chosen to contribute to this book are among the most knowledgeable and notable in the field of international psychology. All of the authors are native to the country they write about, making them the most educated about that particular country. Overall, this group of authors is very distinguished, as well as recognized internationally.

Although this volume may not include every issue pertaining to the field of international psychology, it goes far beyond simply providing information and research findings relevant to international studies. Instead, the *Handbook* describes the beginnings of international psychology and its course of development over time, and offers the various perspectives of different countries on the growth and progress of psychology as an international profession and science. This collection is not merely a series of papers written by psychologists concerned about the importance of the growth of international psychology; rather, it is a collection of unique perspectives about international psychology. Each author brings his or her own special expertise, viewpoint, and background to the field of international psychology. These chapters emphasize how much progress has been made, while at the same time focusing on how much work society and science has yet to do.

The discussion of the growth in psychology highlights the increase in the number of psychologists working worldwide over the last decade, as well as the lack of growth in many underdeveloped and developing countries. The varying definitions of psychology as a profession and a science across the world are discussed. The impact of psychology organizations, the proliferation of scientific and applied specialties, and the increase in education and training in these specialties are highlighted and discussed in depth in this volume.

Recent advances in communications technology are an important component to the *Handbook*, as now more than ever technology has allowed for a major increase in communication among various nations by allowing connections to be made so quickly and easily. This volume also includes an in-depth discussion of multicultural issues and how they are related to international psychology. In summary, the *Handbook* includes the perspective from each author on what American psychology can gain through a greater understanding of the characteristics of psychology worldwide.

The hope for peace and understanding among the many countries of the world can only begin through the acceptance of diversity and the striving to spread knowledge of different cultures globally. Although there have been cross-cultural volumes compiled to compare and contrast the cultures of the world, this is the first *Handbook of International Psychology*, and therefore most definitely a groundbreaking work within the field of psychology, as well as outside it. This reference work is itself a landmark in the study of international psychology and will be of still increasing significance as time goes on. The topics that are presented here are of enduring importance, and the perspectives represented are unique as well as significant to the field.

Florence L. Denmark, Ph.D.
Robert Scott Pace Distinguished Research
Professor, Pace University

Preface

As American psychology faces the challenges of the 21st century, it is determined to become more inclusive by internationalizing its base of scientific knowledge and applied skills. This commitment reflects the cultural and ethnic diversity of populations worldwide, global economic and political interdependence, and sophisticated telecommunications (Mays, Rubin, Sabourin, & Walker, 1996). The internationalizing of psychology also rests on the premise that the science and practice of American psychology must become less parochial and more responsive if it is to help solve problems of living that have no borders, such as overpopulation, pollution, poverty, and violence (Mays et al., 1996).

However, American psychologists "have been notorious for their absence from the major debates of the past 20 years" (Gergen, 2001, p. 811). Much of this neglect is because American psychology's traditional focus on individual behavior and small-group process is ill suited for addressing societal, national, and global phenomena that have, in part, a psychological basis. Moreover, the fact that American psychology has isolated itself from other social sciences accounts for its limited capacity to understand phenomena that are highly contextual in nature. For example, intergroup conflict is rooted in a complex matrix of economics, history, politics, and religion, as well as psychology (Stevens, 2002).

The primary reason for American psychology's limited applicability internationally is its reductionistic orientation. The reductionistic basis for most psychological theory, research, and practice fails to identify mechanisms by which cultural, economic, political, and religious variables mediate or moderate the complexities of human functioning and experience (Stevens, 2002). The psychological vision of the modern, industrial world called for the separation of individuals from those communities that had shaped and defined them. Psychology sought to understand this isolated individual whose actions and interactions were hypothesized to fashion the structure and dynamics of larger social formations including community, society, and nation (Sampson, 1989).

Reductionistic psychology also makes claim to an objectivity that supersedes cultural boundaries and to a universally applicable investigative methodology (Gergen, 2001; Gergen, Gulerce, Lock, & Misra, 1996). However, empirical tests of hypotheses about a rational, self-contained individual often fail to capture the "local truth" about people who are born and reared in non-Western cultures (Gergen et al., 1996). It is bad science and practice, and ethnocentric as well, to assume automatically that paradigms conceived by American psychologists can be applied successfully to different cultures.

Growing awareness that the world is becoming an interdependent network of individuals, communities, and nations, coupled with recognition of the culture-bound nature of the discipline and profession, are prompting the transformation of American psychology. Theories of the person and psychological explanations of unusual events (e.g., terrorism) are becoming more sensitive to the sociocultural world in which people live and events take place (Gergen, 1996, 2001; Sampson, 1989). Likewise, the modernist tradition of individualism is giving way to a postmodern framework. Within this postmodern paradigm, the conception of the individual has been reconstructed as relational and as constituted by his or her sociocultural milieu (Gergen, 1996, 2001; Gergen et al., 1996). Consequently, the study of the individual adopts nonreductionistic approaches that preserve the unity of the person and the context in which he or she is embedded.

Our rationale for the *Handbook of International Psychology* is simple. We seek to inform American readers about the discipline and profession of psychology as constituted and evolving in distinct regions of the world. We believe that an authoritative understanding of human functioning and experience, particularly its considerable variability, must rest on an appreciation of the contextual, as well as individual and universal, variables that directly or indirectly, separately or interactively, determine what we do and who we

are. To this end, The *Handbook* serves to reduce the isolation and parochialism of American psychology by exposing the reader to international perspectives on psychology of which he or she would otherwise be ignorant. We hope that the *Handbook* will contribute to international awareness and understanding and facilitate international dialogue and collaboration.

Draguns (2001) reminds us that American psychology continues to disregard the conceptual, empirical, and practical contributions to psychology of other countries, especially non-English-speaking countries. There is virtually no English-language market for foreign scholarship that does not conform to the American taste for the abstract and reductionistic, yet such scholarship has a profound influence on theory building, investigative methodologies, and applied practice worldwide. Few American university libraries subscribe to foreign journals and, where they do, they are typically not widely read by American psychologists and psychology students. Likewise, translations of publications of potential interest are virtually nonexistent. Compounding matters is the fact that the literature on international psychology is highly scattered. Thus, for American psychologists regardless of specialty, psychology students at all levels, and the interested public, there are few opportunities to study developments in psychology in other countries or to become acquainted with the cultural, economic, historical, political, and religious forces that shape psychology in those countries. *Handbook of International Psychology* represents a special opportunity to inform American readers about the foci and contributions of psychology in different regions of the world in order to expand their conceptual, methodological, and practical perspectives.

Many foreign students have earned graduate degrees in psychology from American universities and have returned to their native countries as psychologists. Little is known about their accomplishments as scholars and practitioners. What have these psychologists found useful in terms of their American training? How have they blended their preparation with the psychology of their homelands? What do they have to say about psychology in their countries that can inform American psychologists and psychology students? Specifically, how can their perspectives promote further growth in the theory, research, and practice of American psychology? Answers to these questions might yield valuable insights for our readers.

In addition, for many, attendance at international conferences, where the exchange of ideas and fruitful interaction often occur, is prohibitively expensive and time consuming. Relatively few American psychologists and fewer psychology students are able to participate in such meetings. The *Handbook of International Psychology* is a vehicle to promote communication across borders and to provide a global view of psychology for those who have had limited access to it.

The *Handbook of International Psychology* builds on a proud tradition: the *International Handbook of Psychology* (Gilgen & Gilgen, 1987) and *International Psychology: Views from Around the World* (Sexton & Hogan, 1992). These books are now over a decade old, and we believed it was time for another comprehensive review of international psychology.

The 1990s witnessed an explosion of interest in international psychology. Two illustrations are the appearance in 1996 in the *American Psychologist* of a special section devoted to developments and issues in international psychology and the establishment in 1997 of the Division of International Psychology by the American Psychological Association (APA). Of course, the terrorist attacks on the World Trade Center and the Pentagon on September 11, 2001, fueled interest in international psychology, as evidenced by the official statements of prominent leaders of the American Psychological Association (e.g., former CEO Raymond Fowler and Past President Philip Zimbardo). Beyond its timeliness, we were encouraged to edit the *Handbook* because the Sexton and Hogan volume, its predecessor (Sexton & Misiak, 1976), and the Gilgen and Gilgen book received so many favorable reviews as the major source of information in English on international psychology and the internationalizing of psychology. We believe that the *Handbook* will follow in the tradition of its predecessors by becoming the definitive publication in the field.

To achieve a panoramic vista of international psychology, we developed a fine-grained chapter outline with a detailed list of topics that we hoped would yield a balanced, yet comprehensive, description of psychology as a discipline and profession within each of the countries we included. We invited our authors to prepare a chapter, approximately 20 pages in length and organized in four parts: an overview of psychology, the education and training of psychologists, the scope of psychological practice, and future challenges and prospects. Within each section, we asked authors to respond to at least 10 highly focused questions covering a wide range of topics. For example, in the overview, we requested descriptions of the history of psychology, formal organizations that represent psychologists, and the status of psychologists relative to allied professionals. In the section on education and training, we requested descriptions of undergraduate and graduate curricula, pedagogical methods and tools, and requirements for practice. In the section on practice, we inquired about the work of psychologists in various settings, prominent conceptual, methodological, and technical approaches, and legal and ethical guidelines and regulations. In the final section on the future of psychology, we solicited information on opportunities and obstacles facing psychology, controversial issues being debated (e.g., psychologists' political and social activism), the public's view of psychology, and what American psychologists can learn from the discipline and profession of psychology in the authors' countries. Each chapter also contains a biographical sketch of the author(s) and a list of the most influential literature on psychology that had been published in the country being discussed. These lists were necessarily subjective, and many authors found it difficult to choose the top 10 or so publications in psychology that originated in their country. However, when pressed, almost all authors acknowledged that making these selections was a useful heuristic exercise.

We did not permit significant variation in the content and organization of each chapter because of the importance of maintaining consistency and coherence throughout the book. Consequently, we worked closely with authors to ensure adherence to the basic chapter outline. However, we recognized that, owing to the peculiarities of psychology in other countries, it would not be possible for authors to respond meaningfully to every question contained within each section of the chapter outline, or give equal weight to such

distinct aspects of psychology as academia, professional practice, and governance. Because cultural, economic, political, religious, and social differences among countries contribute to the diversity of their national psychologies, we allowed for a degree of flexibility within the standard chapter format. We also believed that some limited variability in structure would be less off-putting to the reader attempting to digest several chapters in one sitting. However, we insisted that substantial departures from the chapter outline be justified. As will become evident, each chapter conforms to a relatively uniform schema, yet each is stamped by the cultural context and status of psychology in the authors' countries as well as the authors' unique presentational style.

In selecting countries for inclusion in the *Handbook of International Psychology*, we identified three countries each in nine distinct regions of the world whose national psychologies are well established scientifically and professionally, are reappearing after a period of political oppression, or are emerging forces. We were also guided in our selection of representative countries by the goals of minimizing redundancy and presenting less well-known psychologies. After dozens of discussions, hundreds of e-mail messages, and more than a few false starts, we selected 27 countries from nine regions across six continents:

AFRICA:	Kenya, Nigeria, South Africa
NORTH AMERICA:	Canada, Mexico, United States
SOUTH AMERICA:	Argentina, Brazil, Colombia
EAST ASIA:	People's Republic of China, Japan, Singapore
SOUTH ASIA:	India, Pakistan, Thailand

EAST EUROPE: Poland, Russia, Turkey
WEST EUROPE: Germany, Spain, United
                           Kingdom
MIDDLE EAST: Egypt, Iran, Israel
PACIFIC RIM: Australia, Indonesia,
                           Philippines

The selection of countries is representative of distinct regions of the world, and the list incorporates considerable diversity in terms of the developmental maturity of national psychologies. For example, psychology in the United Kingdom has a seasoned scientific tradition whereas psychology in Thailand has a nascent practical orientation. Similarly, much is known about psychology in the United States and West Europe, whereas much less is known about psychology elsewhere, such as the People's Republic of China, where psychology reflects a synthesis of Confucian, Marxist, and Western philosophies, or India, a country whose psychology is increasingly blending Hindu with Western paradigms. Some countries have a long history of academic and professional psychology, such as Germany, whereas others are relative newcomers, such as Singapore. Finally, psychology in some countries is marked by uninterrupted evolution whereas the discipline and profession in other nations have been dislocated by massive and unprecedented macro-social change, such as the Islamic revolution in Iran, the fall of communism in Poland, and the transition from a dictatorship in Spain.

After the final list of countries was selected, we invited a group of prominent psychologists who resided in their homelands to contribute chapters on the psychology of their respective countries. We were guided in making these invitations by the recommendations of our advisory board.

We asked those unable to undertake the project to recommend esteemed colleagues.

When it was not possible to recruit a resident psychologist to prepare a chapter, we sought the most knowledgeable author(s), reared and educated in his or her native land, but residing elsewhere. The final set of authors includes dozens of distinguished psychologists, many of whom are internationally recognized.

Another restriction on the selection of authors was the requirement that chapters had to be written in English. We did this to avoid errors in translation and defray the expense of translating manuscripts. We asked authors to review the standard chapter outline and justify any substantial modifications to the format based on the nature and cultural context of psychology in their country. In only one or two instances were any changes negotiated with respect to the chapter content and organization. We then asked authors to submit an initial draft, which we and our editorial assistants reviewed. Our feedback to authors consisted of comments and suggestions aimed at making manuscripts more readable, eliminating potential sources of misinterpretation, and including overlooked or underemphasized material. We reexamined the revisions our authors made before approving their chapters for publication; multiple revisions were often necessary before we gave final approval to a manuscript.

The *Handbook of International Psychology* could not have succeeded without the untiring efforts of many to whom we owe a debt of gratitude. We thank the Board of the Division of International Psychology of the American Psychological Association, which initially inspired and encouraged our work on the *Handbook*. We were most gratified to recruit a distinguished editorial advisory board, led by Dr. Florence Denmark, past president of both the Division of International Psychology and the American Psychological Association. We also wish to thank Drs. Rubén Ardila, John Hogan, Brigitte Khoury, Anthony Marsella, Elizabeth Nair, Charles Spielberger, and Harold Takooshian, all of whom served skillfully as members of the advisory board. We also owe a tremendous debt of thanks to our editorial assistants, Vicki Eichhorn and Stephanie Steinman, who provided thoughtful critiques of chapter drafts and invaluable clerical assistance. Vicki worked late many evenings in order to make sure the *Handbook* manuscript was delivered on time. Of course, we deeply appreciate the authors for their expertise and devotion in preparing chapters. We also thank our editors at Brunner/Routledge, especially Dr. George Zimmar and Shannon Vargo, for their guidance and support in preparing this volume, particularly in making the many details related to publication so manageable. Finally, we appreciate the long-suffering patience of our respective spouses, who tolerated the many weekends and evenings we gave up to edit the *Handbook of International Psychology*.

Michael J. Stevens   **Danny Wedding**
Normal, Illinois   *St. Louis, Missouri*

mjsteven@ilstu.edu   *weddingd@mimh.edu*

REFERENCES

Draguns, J. (2001). Toward a truly international psychology: Beyond English only. *American Psychologist, 56,* 1019–1030.

Gergen, K. J. (1996). Theory under threat: Social construction and identity politics. In C. Tolman, F. Cherry, R. Van Hezewijk, & I. Lubeck (Eds.), *Problems of theoretical psychology* (pp. 13–23). North York, ON, Canada: Captus Press.

Gergen, K. J. (2001). Psychological science in a postmodern context. *American Psychologist, 56,* 803–813.

Gergen, K. J., Gulerce, A., Lock, A., & Misra, G. (1996). Psychological science in cultural context. *American Psychologist, 51,* 496–503.

Gilgen, A. R., & Gilgen, C. K. (Eds.). (1987). *International handbook of psychology.* New York: Greenwood.

Mays, V. M., Rubin, J., Sabourin, M., & Walker, L. (1996). Moving toward a global psychology: Changing theories and practice to meet the needs of a changing world. *American Psychologist, 51,* 485–487.

Sampson, E. E. (1989). The challenge of social change for psychology: Globalization and psychology's theory of the person. *American Psychologist, 44,* 914–921.

Sexton, V. S., & Hogan, J. D. (Eds.). (1992). *International psychology: Views from around the world.* Lincoln, NE: University of Nebraska Press.

Sexton, V. S., & Misiak, H. (Eds.). (1976). *Psychology around the world.* Monterey, CA: Brooks/Cole.

Stevens, M. J. (2002). The interplay of psychology and societal transformation. *International Journal of Group Tensions, 31,* 5–30.

Contributors

Ramadan A. Ahmed, Ph.D.
Department of Psychology
Meoufia University
Giza, Egypt

Rubén Ardila, Ph.D.
National University of Colombia
Bogota, Colombia

Tatiana Balachova, Ph.D.
Center on Child Abuse and Neglect
Department of Pediatrics
University of Oklahoma Medical Sciences
Center
Oklahoma City, Oklahoma, United States

Blanche Barnes, Ph.D.
Professor of Clinical Psychology (Retired)
Department of Psychology
SNDT University
Mumbai, India

Behrooz Birashk, Ph.D.
Department of Clinical Psychology
Tehran Psychiatric Institute
University of Tehran
Tehran, Iran

Hale Bolak Boratav, Ph.D.
Department of Psychology
Bilgi University
Sisli-Istanbul, Turkey

Florence L. Denmark, Ph.D.
Psychology Department
Pace University
New York, New York, United States

Lutz H. Eckensberger, Ph.D.
Deutsches Institut Für Internationale
Pädagogische Forschang (DIPF)
Frankfurt am Main, Germany

James T. Gire, Ph.D.
Department of Psychology
Virginia Military Institute
Lexington, Virginia, United States

Raymond D. Fowler, Ph.D.
Former CEO
American Psychological Association
Washington, D.C., United States

Yolanda García-Rodríguez, Ph.D.
Complutense University of Madrid
Madrid, Spain

Alison F. Garton, D.Phil.
School of Psychology
Edith Cowan University
Joondalup, Western Australia

William Gomes, Ph.D.
Universidade Federal do Rio Grande do Sul
Porto Alegre, Brazil

Irena Heszen-Niejodek, Ph.D.
Department of Health Psychology
Warsaw School of Social Psychology
Warsaw, Poland

Claudio S. Hutz, Ph.D.
Universidade Federal do Rio Grande do Sul
Instituto de Psicologia
Porto Alegre, Brazil

Galina Isurina, Ph.D.
St. Petersburg State University
St. Petersburg, Russia

Rebecca Jacoby, Ph.D.
Medical Psychology Graduate Program
The Academic College of Tel Aviv-Yaffo
Tel Aviv, Israel

Hugo Klappenbach, Ph.D.
Faculdad de Ciencias Humanas
Universidad Nacional de San Luis
San Luis, Argentina

June W. Koinange, M.A.
Lifespring Counseling and Training Center
Nairobi, Kenya

Sheldon Levy, Ph.D.
Brown University Medical School
Providence, Rhode Island, United States

Ingrid C. Lunt, Ph.D.
Institute of Education
University of London
London, England

Sherri McCarthy, Ph.D.
Northern Arizona University
Flagstaff, Arizona, United States

Cristina Jayme Montiel, Ph.D.
Department of Psychology
Ateneo de Manila University
Manila, Philippines

Elizabeth Nair, Ph.D.
National University of Singapore
Department of Social Work and Psychology
Singapore

Russ Newman, Ph.D., J.D.
Practice Directorate
American Psychological Association
Washington, D.C., United States

Kanako Otsui, M.A.
Kwansei Gakuin University
Nishinomiya City, Japan

Ingrid Plath, Ph.D.
Deutsches Institut für Internationale
Pädagogische Forschung (DIPF)
Frankfurt am Main, Germany

José M. Prieto, Ph.D.
Department of Individual Differences and
Work Psychology
Faculty of Psychology
Complutense University of Madrid
Madrid, Spain

Nosheen Khan Rahman, Ph.D.
Center for Clinical Psychology
University of the Punjab
Lahore, Pakistan

Pierre L.-J. Ritchie, Ph.D.
School of Psychology
University of Ottawa
Ontario, Canada

Michel E. Sabourin, Ph.D.
Department of Psychology
University of Montréal
Montréal, Canada

Juan José Sánchez-Sosa, Ph.D.
Parques del Pedregal
Mexico City, Mexico

Sarlito W. Sarwono, Ph.D.
Faculty of Psychology
University of Indonesia
Depok, Indonesia

Graham B. Stead, Ph.D.
Department of Psychology
University of Port Elizabeth, Vista Campus
Port Elizabeth, South Africa

Stephanie R. Steinman, M.A.
Department of Psychology
Illinois State University
Normal, Illinois, United States

Junko Tanaka-Matsumi, Ph.D.
Kwansei Gakuin University
Nishinomiya City, Japan

Sombat Tapanya, Ph.D.
Department of Psychiatry
Faculty of Medicine
Chiang Mai University
Bangkok, Thailand

Lota A. Teh, Ph.D.
Ateneo de Manila University
Manila, Philippines

Larissa Tsvetkova, Ph.D.
Center on Child Abuse and Neglect
St. Petersburg State University
St. Petersburg, Russia

Ludvig I. Wasserman, Ph.D.
The Bekhterev Institute
St. Petersburg, Russia

Yufang Yang, Ph.D.
Institute of Psychology
Chinese Academy of Sciences
Beijing, China

CHAPTER 1

International Psychology: An Overview

MICHAEL J. STEVENS AND DANNY WEDDING

1.1 INTRODUCTION

In this chapter, we introduce the specialty of international psychology. We begin by defining international psychology and distinguishing it from cross-cultural psychology and ethnic studies. We then examine two sources for the emergence and growth of international psychology: economic and political change and the limited utility of Western psychology as applied to complex and contextual global issues. We also survey five global concerns of contemporary significance that have given impetus to international psychology: intergroup conflict, societal transformation and national development, threats to the natural environment, physical and mental health needs, and the struggles of disempowered groups. Next, we describe the mission and activities of scientific and professional organizations that represent international psychology and the interface between international psychology and policy-making entities, specifically, the United Nations and World Health

Organization. We then address the future of international psychology, particularly trends toward greater unity and curriculum development. We conclude by linking our overview of international psychology to the objectives and foci of the *Handbook of International Psychology.*

1.2 DEFINITION OF INTERNATIONAL PSYCHOLOGY

International psychology can be defined in terms of its mission and the domain of scientific knowledge and professional practice that it subsumes. The chief aim of international psychology is to promote communication and collaboration among psychologists worldwide in the areas of teaching, research, practice, and public service. More precisely, the goals of international psychology are to promote international understanding and goodwill among people with similar interests from different

1

national and cultural backgrounds, to monitor psychology's cultural dependence, to capacity-build through transnational research and practice, and to facilitate the development of an international curriculum (Pawlik & d'Ydewalle, 1996; Sabourin, 2001). Mechanisms for enhancing communication and collaboration include organizations that represent the interests of international psychologists, regional and international conferences, journals that publish literature on international psychology, international exchange programs, and Internet resources. One index of the desire of psychologists to communicate and collaborate internationally is the proliferation of international organizations and journals, which we describe later. Clearly, the goals of international psychology are timely, given the complexities of an increasingly interdependent and rapidly changing world.

Beyond its mission of enhancing communication and collaboration, international psychology includes the application of psychology to an array of problems that have no borders. Among the more urgent international problems are terrorism, globalization's weakening of nation-states, global warming, HIV/AIDS, and traffic in women and children. Innovative conceptual models, investigative methodologies, and intervention strategies are needed to understand, study, and influence these problems. Moreover, because these problems are rooted in a complex matrix of culture, economics, history, politics, psychology, and religion, a comprehensive approach to their explanation and solution requires both a multidisciplinary and transnational framework. International psychology has already added creativity and vitality to the scientific and professional responses to global problems.

In contrast to international psychology, cross-cultural psychology can be defined as the study of culture's effects on human functioning. It involves comparing different cultural groups whose members share distinct perceptions and experiences that determine identifiable patterns of behavior (Jing, 2000). Cross-cultural psychology is a feature of international psychology (e.g., international psychologists devise models, conduct research, and intervene within a cultural context).

Ethnic studies is another specialty that overlaps with, but does not duplicate, international psychology. It entails investigating ethnic minority issues and applying psychological knowledge and techniques to those issues. Unlike cross-cultural psychology, which compares the impact of different cultures, ethnic studies emphasizes the impact of minority status on an ethnic group within a single culture. Ethnic studies is also essential to international psychology (e.g., international psychologists are interested in intergroup relations). Clearly, the emphasis of international psychology on scientific and professional communication and collaboration gives it a process focus, and its attention to global issues gives it a broader scope than either cross-cultural psychology or ethnic studies.

1.3 DISSATISFACTION WITH WESTERN PSYCHOLOGY

Dissatisfaction with Western psychology has contributed to the increased prominence of international psychology. Two sources for this dissatisfaction are the emergence of economic and political systems in the developing world that are more person-centered and the limited utility of psychological paradigms imported from the West.

The U.S. has 100,000–150,000 psychologists, approximately 20–25% of the world's psychologists (Rosenzweig, 1999). These estimates are inexact due to the lack of international agreement on criteria for using the title of psychologist. There is consensus, however, that the proportion of American psychologists will shrink because psychology worldwide is rapidly expanding (Rosenzweig). The expansion of psychology can be attributed to a rise in the number of countries whose economic and political systems depend on the role of the individual within society (Jing, 2000; Rosenzweig). Various forms of free-market democracy that fuel industrialization have also precipitated demands for psychology as a science and profession. For example, the link between economic and human development and the growth of psychology is manifested by the interest shown by governments, business and industry, and the general population in psychology as a means of enhancing national achievement and personal well-being. These trends are shifting the spotlight away from Western psychology to emerging psychologies that mirror the worldviews of developing countries and regions; they are also compelling Western psychologists to engage in dialogue with their psychology colleagues around the world.

Western psychology has proven somewhat useful when applied transnationally. For example, Bandura (2002) illustrated how efficacy expectations are not limited to judgments about personal capabilities, but are complemented by perceptions of collective efficacy. Collective efficacy consists of shared beliefs in a group's ability to produce desired outcomes through collective action. It reflects more than the sum of individual efficacy expectations; it embodies the interactive dynamics of a group. Collective efficacy is also situationally, historically, and culturally constituted, meaning that the specific, agentic group behavior it mediates reflects the multiple contexts in which it occurs. One contemporary expression of collective efficacy is the extent to which countries affected by globalization make transnational systems work more effectively for them.

Western psychology's focus on intra- and interpersonal causation has more typically yielded incomplete accounts of phenomena constituted in the non-Western world. The limited transnational usefulness of Western psychology is based on three paradigmatic criticisms (Gergen, 2001; Prilleltensky & Fox, 1997). First, because Western psychology is relatively decontextualized, psychologists often fail to appreciate the significance of the domains in which human functioning is embedded. Second, Western psychology leans toward reductionism; as a result, psychologists frequently dismantle the unity that provides a more accurate, complete, and meaningful view of psychological phenomenon. Finally, Western psychology can be hegemonic and oppressive, increasing the risk of ethnocentric science and practice.

Although psychology has a growing global presence, its characteristics remain diverse and are intimately connected to the history and culture of a country or region. Indigenous psychologies, which emerge from enduring social and cultural traditions, offer worldviews that resist imported perspectives. Indigenous psychology is defined as behavioral science and practice rooted in the realities of a particular society and culture (Sinha, 1997). For example, although psychology was introduced to Asia by the West, its contemporary forms reveal elements of Buddhism (e.g., spiritual practices that cultivate serenity and enlightenment) and Confucianism (e.g., the role of education in creating social harmony) (Jing, 2000; Walsh, 2000). Likewise, liberation psychology in Latin America is grounded in the awakening of social consciousness and the realignment of imported theory, research, and practice with the lives of people whom psychology has a responsibility to serve (Comas-Díaz, 2000; Comas-Díaz, Lykes, & Alarcón, 1998). Dissident Argentine psychologists demedicalized psychoanalysis and integrated elements of Marxism to form a socially relevant praxis that melds intrapsychic and class struggles. These examples reveal how psychology has not only resisted, but also challenged the hegemony of Western psychology in order to restore contextual validity to the discipline and profession (Gergen, 2001; Sinha, 1997).

International psychology is an antidote to the uncritical application of Western psychology. By questioning claims of objectivity that supersede culture and a universally applicable investigative methodology, international psychology affirms the necessity of constructing meaningful understanding and applications based on a constitutive view of human functioning (Gergen, 2001; Sinha, 1997). It is sensitive, knowledgeable, and skilled in terms of psychological conceptualizations, methods of acquiring knowledge, and strategies for change. Furthermore, in acknowledging psychology's history and capacity to unwittingly support institutions that maintain oppressive values, international psychology takes responsibility for being value-laden and identifies itself, in part, as a force for justice and human

welfare (Prilleltensky & Fox, 1997; Staub & Green, 1992). By advancing values to the position of figure in the gestalt that is psychology, international psychology promotes less esoteric science and practice. International psychology will continue to respond to calls for solutions to pressing global concerns that include intergroup conflict, national transformation and development, threats to the natural environment, physical and mental health needs, and the struggles of disempowered groups.

1.4 CONCERNS OF GLOBAL SIGNIFICANCE

1.4.1 Intergroup Conflict

Millions suffer under conditions of systemic violence that exist at various levels, including the family, community, society, or region. The late 1990s witnessed an explosion in intergroup violence as evidenced by numerous conflicts, the most extreme of which reached genocidal proportions in Bosnia and Rwanda (Mays, Bullock, Rosenzweig, & Wessells, 1998). A fundamental challenge for psychology is to transform systems of violence into cultures of peace, thus ending psychological, physical, and structural violence and creating conditions and processes that foster individual and collective well-being and growth (Wessells, 2000).

International psychology offers perspectives and tools for understanding and resolving intergroup conflict. International psychology recognizes the need to adopt a multidisciplinary perspective, to consider the interplay between macro-level institutions and micro-level processes, and to generate solutions based on local strengths and resources that are sensitive to diversity (Mays et al., 1998).

The worldviews of groups serve to facilitate or inhibit violent conflict. These worldviews consist of enduring ways of collectively understanding past, present, and anticipated events; such understanding mediates collective emotion and action. Collective worldviews can be dangerous because they are assumed to be true by a significant number of group members and because they are the bedrock of identification and socialization within a culture. Regrettably, collective worldviews contain distortions that are seldom questioned by group members; such biases include the selective recall of a group's history or the embellishment of historical narratives. Collective worldviews may trigger intergroup conflict when they supersede an objective evaluation of the intentions of others and limit opportunities for cooperation. Eidelson and Eidelson (2003) identify five collective worldviews that either promote or constrain intergroup conflict: superiority, injustice, vulnerability, distrust, and helplessness. Shared beliefs about superiority imply an in-group bias that can justify violent preservation of a group's social advantage, restoration of its usurped status, and purification of its membership, as well as interfere with intergroup reconciliation. The collective worldview of injustice strengthens a group's conviction that it has legitimate grievances against another group. Such convictions, real or perceived, heighten allegiance to the group, target an out-group as responsible, and mobilize violence (e.g., the Serbian belief of being unjustly denied respect as defenders of Europe). A group's belief in its vulnerability rests on perceptions of threat that heighten solidarity and precipitate hostility toward the source of threat.

Ethnic competition theory suggests that the increased mixing of people in contemporary urban societies enflames intergroup competition that may evoke ethnic identification; this contrasts with Allport's hypothesis that increased contact between groups will lead them to appreciate their similarities. Some groups engage in preemptive violence to preserve their integrity, and extreme threats to group survival can produce intractable conflict (e.g., the Middle East) or genocide (e.g., Rwanda). More subtle threats, such as the diluting of language and tradition through assimilation and globalization, can also prompt violence. Collective distrust occurs when one group believes that another group harbors ominous intentions. Such distrust forms the core of out-group stereotypes and can reach paranoid levels, as in the collective delusion of persecution, justification of hostility toward an alleged persecutory group, and unwillingness to examine evidence for entrenched suspicions. Finally, unlike superiority, injustice, vulnerability, and distrust, a group's sense of helplessness inhibits its expression of intergroup conflict. Such beliefs lead to an attributional style in which a group explains its inferior status as enduring, pervasive, and due to inherent weaknesses. Advantaged groups may exploit helpless groups by further convincing them of their unworthiness to share in society's rights and privileges.

Approaches to studying intergroup conflict include the examination of competing worldviews in a multidisciplinary context, separation of overlapping from independent elements of collective worldviews, identification of variables that harden or soften collective worldviews, and delineation of the relationship between individual and collective worldviews (Eidelson & Eidelson, 2003). Research on the aftermath of intergroup conflict often entails analyses of the testimony of survivors of violence and how adversarial groups maintain or revise interpretations of their relations (Mays et al., 1998); consideration of how individuals and communities come to terms with personal and collective loss and trauma gives a practical focus to this research. Indigenous approaches, such as liberation discourse, permit the rescue of cultural identity from survivors and the creation of a future. Such methods require that psychologists think culturally when working with those affected by intergroup conflict to discover alternative understandings of their suffering (Comas-Díaz et al., 1998).

In general, building cultures of tolerance and peace entails lowering the degree to which groups in conflict perceive each other as threats (Sullivan & Transue, 1999; Wessells, 2000); it also involves applying what can be learned from naturally occurring "outbreaks" of peace, as in the Baltic states where positive intergroup attitudes appear linked to a common history, language, and religion. The Middle East and Northern Ireland offer examples of psychological contributions to the reduction of group tension and violence. Rouhana and Bar-Tal (1998) describe a problem-solving workshop for high-ranking Israelis and Palestinians intended to foster an ethos of peace. The workshop provides a setting and rules for constructive engagement geared toward mutual problem-solving. Though time-consuming, such deep-rooted conflict requires sustained and facilitated interaction in order to build trust and empathy, examine competing beliefs about group

relations, and explore joint visions of peace. In Northern Ireland, realistic group-conflict theory has inspired government initiatives to reform an educational system that, unwittingly, has maintained group tensions by segregating Catholic and Protestant children (Cairns & Darby, 1998). Based on the hypothesis that contact between conflicting groups diminishes intergroup misunderstanding, the Education for Mutual Understanding and Cultural Heritage program designed a common curriculum that encourages Catholic and Protestant schools to establish contact between their pupils.

1.4.2 Societal Transformation and National Development

Societal transformation and the struggle for national development unleash tremendous social problems that exact a staggering personal and collective toll. Societal transformation is a massive and complex phenomenon that has cultural, economic, familial, institutional, personal, and religious dimensions. As a society undergoes transformation, virtually all aspects of social living become fluid and have uncertain outcomes. Established routines are interrupted, accustomed ways of thinking and acting are challenged, familiar social hierarchies collapse, and possibilities that could not have been foreseen become realities (e.g., homelessness, self-determination) (Stevens, 2002). Examples of societal transformation and national development can be found in countries that have survived distinct forms of oppression and struggle to realize their chosen economic, political, and social destiny: East European countries that endured communism, Latin American countries that have been oppressed by military dictatorships, and African countries that suffered racial autocracy. The causes, processes, and outcomes of societal transformation are also observable as developing countries encounter globalization.

International psychology can facilitate societal transformation and national development (Stevens, 2002). It supports these phenomena as legitimate domains of inquiry, and it endorses a multidimensional, multidisciplinary, and culturally sensitive framework for understanding, studying, and intervening in such macrosocial change. It encourages communication and collaboration among psychologists with different expertise from around the world on societal transformation and national development.

Social reducton theory (Moghaddam & Harré, 1996) examines the flip side of societal transformation and stability, and attempts to explain why political revolutions are often followed by a return to a regime similar to that which the revolution was intended to overthrow. A social reducton is a unit of analysis that subsumes local meaning structures and derivative social interactions that take place in daily life. Social reducton systems include family, village, and culture. Harré (2002) describes a social reducton as follows:

> A reduction is a minute social practice, so small, so insignificant that it is far too small for parliaments and committees of peasants and workers to bother about. A reducton is how we shake hands, who sits where art the table, how we pass in the street, and so on which seem to be the highly resistant bits of the social world that keep on keeping on, thereby reproducing the old regime. (p. 21)

Social reducton theory holds that local identity and behavior are resistant to imposed change (e.g., economic policies and legislative initiatives) and, when such change occurs, it is likely to be modest. Stable social orders that withstand top-down change are found wherever social reductons are so entrenched they are taken for granted. Social reducton systems are maintained by carriers (e.g., myths, traditions) that are culturally embedded. Carriers represent valued features of culture and include symbols such as flags. Carriers also include cognitive constructions, such as stereotypes about individuals based on their group membership (e.g., all Americans are seen by some Muslims as infidels). Social reducton theory has been applied to France, Iran, Japan, and Russia with the consistent finding that societal transformation is curtailed by the resilience of elementary normative practices (Moghaddam & Harré, 1996).

Methods for studying societal transformation and national development take many forms, including analog experiments, simulations, surveys, case studies, and field studies. The focus of such research is often on shifting public opinion and values as a country evolves from one economic and political paradigm to another. For example, transnational research indicates that democracies require citizens to tolerate the political participation of those who advocate unpopular views. Such tolerance is influenced by a commitment to democratic values, the degree of threat perceived in others, and personality (Sullivan & Transue, 1999; Wessells, 2000).

Psychologists concerned about the adverse effects of societal transformation and national development are frequently called upon to consult with governments and nongovernmental organizations (NGOs) on ways to strengthen public institutions and administrative processes tied to economic and political progress (e.g., ethical government), collaborate in building community-based programs that engage citizens (e.g., volunteerism), and respond to the needs of individuals who are impaired or at risk due to past and present societal conditions (e.g., restoring interpersonal trust) (Sullivan & Transue, 1999; Wessells, 2000). Many strategies for national development derive from research on social capital that underscores the importance of norms of reciprocity, civic virtues, and interpersonal trust in enhancing political involvement. Recently, the International Association for the Evaluation of Educational Achievement conducted a transnational study of how effectively educational programs have promoted civic attitudes, knowledge, and participation among students in developing democracies. The study's assumptions were that civic education involves interaction between attitudes and knowledge and requires the use of multiple pedagogical approaches. Students with the most civic knowledge were most likely to participate in civic activities, and schools and youth organizations that modeled democratic practices were most effective in promoting civic knowledge and participation (Torney-Purta, Lehmann, Oswald, & Schulz, 2001). Given these results, coupled with teachers' support for civic education, it is important that international psychologists design school curricula and activities (e.g., student councils) that deepen the values of responsible citizenship.

1.4.3 The Natural Environment

Human behavior has transformed the natural environment on a global scale. Burning fossils fuels, clearing forests, manufacturing and consuming chemical products, farming marginal lands, and overpopulation have all had a deleterious effect on the environment. Sadly, terms such as *dead zone* and *global warming* have been added to the transnational vernacular. Environmental change is global because many changes are co-occurring (e.g., in the atmosphere, ocean, and ecosystem), environmental systems connect and interact across the earth, and localized changes can accumulate to the point of having widespread impact (e.g., acid rain, deforestation).

International psychology is relevant to global environmental change because environmental problems are sociobehavioral and because their magnitude and severity threaten human welfare (Vlek, 2000; Winter, 2000). As is true of international psychology, environmental psychology views human action from multiple levels, including individual, communal, and institutional. Global environmental problems have challenged environmental psychologists to supplement theories and practices of traditional specialties (e.g., applied behavioral analysis and experimental social psychology) with the concepts and methods of less familiar subfields (e.g., engineering and organizational psychology). Both natural and social scientists will have to collaborate in the multidisciplinary response to global environmental change. Progress will require integrating psychological concepts of environmental action with economic concepts of decision-making, engineering concepts of energy use, political concepts of policy analysis, and sociological concepts of mobilization (Vlek, 2000; Winter, 2000).

Specific challenges for international psychology include analyzing, understanding, and explaining behavior that produces global environmental change, reducing barriers to the adoption of technologies and practices that mitigate such change, and facilitating support for pro-environmental policies (Vlek, 2000). Behavioral approaches are best represented by applied behavioral analysis; social psychological models center on altruism, attitudes, and dissonance; cognitive models emphasize the application of information processing to such targets as environmental risk assessment. For example, contingent administration of rebates and raffle tickets can increase the frequency of bus-riding, litter clean-up, and the lowering of thermostats (Winter, 2000).

Of course, psychology alone cannot provide comprehensive explanations and solutions for environmental problems. Moreover, some argue that Western psychology itself is at odds with the environment because it legitimizes a worldview that separates the individual from the environment and derives from an exploitative orientation toward the natural world (Vlek, 2000). If so, psychology may be colluding with economic and political systems that degrade the environment vis-à-vis their individualistic versus communal orientation, emphasis on efficiency versus justice, and tendency toward proximal versus distal thinking. International psychologists have sought to balance the polarities of this *commons dilemma* by developing educational materials and methods that raise consciousness and increase collective self-regulation, by partnering with organizations to invest in conservation, and by consulting with government to regulate and enforce environmentally responsible action.

1.4.4 Physical and Mental Health

Health psychology emerged in the 1970s partly in response to changing patterns of illness and death in industrialized countries. Cancer, heart disease, stroke, and accidents replaced infectious diseases as leading causes of death. Lifestyle choices such as drinking, overeating, smoking, and underexercising were linked to these changes. In the developing world, evidence of the adverse impact of globalization on the physical and mental health of individuals, especially in non-Western, collectivist societies, is growing. For example, the claim that eating disorders are culture-bound has been challenged by recent transnational research. Lee and Lee (1996) found that body dissatisfaction and eating disorders among Chinese adolescent females in Hong Kong were predicted by family conflict and the lack of family cohesion. The heightened exposure of these women to Western culture may partially explain these trends; specifically, eating disorders may be mediated by traditional communal structures weakened by globalization. In the underdeveloped world, millions suffer the physical and psychological toll of economic oppression, including child mortality, infectious disease, malnutrition, harsh living and work conditions, and limited access to education and health care as well as political oppression, including fear, social isolation, and trauma.

International psychology is closely tied to the study and treatment of physical and mental illness. First, health and clinical psychology are international because they are specialties within various regional and international psychological organizations. Second, there are many regional and international health and clinical psychology organizations with links to academic and professional psychology in the developed and developing world. Third, the number of international journals in health and clinical psychology is increasing, thereby enhancing the likelihood of international communication and collaboration among psychologists. Fourth, like international psychology itself, health and clinical psychology is multidisciplinary. Illness is multidetermined, and it is embedded in economic, environmental, political, and social contexts. Given their focus on ameliorating and preventing illness and disability and on promoting health, it is clear that health and clinical psychology must incorporate findings from education, medicine, public health, and sociology. Finally, some diseases have reached global proportions, most notably HIV/AIDS.

HIV/AIDS is having devastating effects at various levels, from personal to regional. Historical, political, social, and cultural factors have contributed to this pandemic and reflect the multidetermined character of the illness and the multidisciplinary responses it demands. The case of South Africa illustrates these points. By 2010, approximately 50% of the black population and 6% of the white population of South Africa will be HIV-positive (de lay Rey, 2002). Beyond the adverse health consequences of internecine wars, cross-border migration and transport, and a fragile healthcare infrastructure, indigenous values and traditions unwittingly escalate rates of infection and the difficulties of managing the disease. For example, Africans often attribute illness to the malevolent power of another person or group. Effective treatment can occur only after a cosmological explanation for the malady is identified and a shaman administers sacred rites. In addition to high-risk cultural practices (e.g., sexual initiation rites, evidence of fertility prior to marriage), some Africans do not distinguish life from death. Because death unites people with ancestral spirits, past and present become fused and there is less motivation to avoid contracting a fatal illness.

Western psychology has been ethnocentric in its attempt to establish universal dimensions of mental illness. Widespread problems in one part of the world may occur infrequently elsewhere (e.g., competitive achievement striving) and myths that one culture deems valid may be considered superstitions in others (e.g., imperfect parenting causes psychopathology). Western psychology has also overlooked contextual factors that cause and maintain mental illness. International psychology is becoming more sensitive and knowledgeable about the constitutive dimensions of people's lives. These changes in perspective are due partly to demands that scientific and professional psychology be accountable (Rosenzweig, 1999; Staub & Green, 1992). In the U.S., for example, demands for accountability have led to the identification of empirically supported treatments. However, few investigations outside of the Western world have confirmed the transnational relevance of these treatments.

Non-Western demands for accountability are more radical, often entailing the overhaul of imported theories of, and therapies for, psychopathology. Radical transformations typically presume a connection between mental health, human rights, and the struggle against injustice. Rather than seeking organic causes for mental illness and prescribing medications or hypothesizing about faulty learning and applying corrective therapies (e.g., behavior modification), international psychologists most often support a view of mental illness as the product of a confluence of oppressive sociocultural forces (e.g., discrimination, poverty, trauma). Rather than pathologize, international psychologists typically reframe disordered functioning as adaptive accommodation to pathological conditions (Comas-Díaz, 2000). An example of the medicalization of a sociopolitical problem is the diagnosis of symptoms produced by the machinery of oppression (e.g., torture) as posttraumatic stress disorder. Such diagnoses reflect the inappropriate application of an individualistic, decontextualized, and ethnocentric taxonomy.

International psychologists also hold that remediation and prevention are possible when therapeutic goals include social justice and equality, and treatment incorporates activism and advocacy. They employ conventional, innovative, and indigenous methods (e.g., bearing witness, attitudinal healing programs) to raise individual and collective awareness of how oppression affects mental health. Furthermore, they work to transform alienation into affirmation, empowerment, solidarity, and commitment to social action. International psychologists have formed organizations such as Psychologists for Social Responsibility to educate the public on policies and practices that adversely affect their lives and to lobby their professions to address human rights and social justice.

1.4.5 Disempowered Groups

Due to an increasingly sophisticated telecommunications infrastructure, most of the industrial and developing world is aware of the suffering of disempowered groups. Two such groups, women and children, have been important foci for international psychology.

Daily broadcasts report news about traffic in women, female genital mutilation, and honor killings in which young women who have been raped or seen in the company of men other than family members are killed to avenge the dishonor to the family. Other reports describe the trauma of entire communities of women who were raped in the course of ethnic conflict. This occurred in Bosnia and Rwanda, where rape was used as a way to inflict personal and collective shame for generations. There also are frequent reports of trafficking in children, who are also exploited for labor and sex. Shocking, too, is news about children conscripted to serve as combatants in ethnic civil wars. For example, in Sierra Leone, boys and girls have been threatened with execution unless they take up arms and participate in atrocities against civilian opponents.

International psychology has long been involved in women's issues, including domestic violence. Globally, one third of women in intimate relationships have been beaten, forced into sex, and/or abused emotionally (Walker, 1999). In addition to causing physical injury, domestic violence increases women's risk of chronic disability, unintended pregnancy, adverse pregnancy outcomes, sexually transmitted diseases, substance abuse, depression, and suicide. Notwithstanding transnational variability, women's susceptibility to violence appears related to a complex interaction among unequal gender norms, conservative religious values, attitudes that tolerate violence, poverty, weak political and civil institutions, state-sponsored violence, and migration. In Russia, for example, the rising incidence of domestic violence covaries with national economic and political deterioration. Although recent laws protecting women have been enacted in Latin American countries, the actual implementation of legal safeguards has been slow. In Israel, the challenges of integrating immigrants during an economic downturn, along with regional hostilities, has increased both domestic violence and teenage prostitution. As with other significant global concerns, the multidimensional and multidisciplinary nature of domestic violence calls for the sustained involvement of international psychology. International psychologists have designed ecological programs to heal and empower battered women recovering from violence as well as programs for batterers wanting to stop perpetrating violence against women. In 1994, an action program emerged from the U.N.-sponsored International Conference on Population and Development, which demanded rights-based, integrative interventions to combat domestic violence worldwide, in addition to rape, trafficking in women, harmful indigenous practices, and gender inequality in economic, legal, political, and social spheres. International psychologists have also collaborated on campaigns to educate the public about the link between violence against women and other health and social concerns and to resocialize men and women whose attitudes support domestic violence.

It is especially tragic that 300,000 children in over 80 countries have participated in armed conflicts (Smith, 2001). They serve as cooks, porters, prostitutes, spies, and soldiers. Many more children witness violence, including lethal violence against their families, friends, and communities. In a war-ravaged country, no aspect of a child's life is untouched by war (Hussain, 2002). Among the more devastating effects are chronic malnutrition, infectious disease, and psychological trauma; other consequences include hopelessness and desensitization to violence. In addition, children associated with armies are often discriminated against because of their participation in war (e.g., prevented from returning to school); marginalizing these children only sows the seeds of future violence. International psychologists are ideally situated to share their knowledge about different cultural values and cosmologies with governments and NGOs and to cooperate with other relief professionals and indigenous healers. International psychologists have recommended holistic interventions for children of war that integrate psychological, economic, political, and spiritual elements. Specific interventions include reconstructing families, integrating child-soldiers into society through education and vocational training, providing support for adults and caregivers, and building the capacities of communities to heal and create a better future.

1.4.6 International Psychological Organizations

We now describe the mission and activities of scientific and professional organizations that represent international psychology and the interface between these organizations and international policy-making entities, specifically the U.N. and World Health Organization (WHO). Separately and together, international psychological organizations promote the aims of international psychology: communication and collaboration among psychologists worldwide and the application of psychology to significant global concerns.

There are at least 250 regional and international psychological associations; some are small and specialized, whereas others are large and encompass many specialties (Pawlik & d'Ydewalle, 1996; Sabourin, 2001). For example, the International Test Commission (ITC; http://www.intestcom.org/) is an association of national psychological associations, test commissions, test publishers, and other organizations committed to effective testing and assessment policies and to the development, evaluation, and proper use of psychometric instruments. The proliferation of these organizations reflects the desire of psychologists to communicate and collaborate on issues of global import. Four psychological organizations are especially important: the International Association of Applied Psychology (IAAP), the International Council of Psychologists (ICP), the International Union of Psychological Science (IUPsyS), and the Division of International Psychology of the American Psychological Association (APA52).

The IAAP (http://www.iaapsy.org/) was founded in 1920 as the Association International de Psychotechnique and is the oldest international psychological association. The IAAP has more than 2,000 members from over 70 countries. Its goals are worldwide dialogue between psychologists who teach, conduct research, and practice the various fields of applied psychology. The IAAP has 13 divisions, some in specialties that often are absent from North American psychology (e.g., the psychology of national development, traffic and transportation psychology), as well as standing committees and task forces that respond to ongoing, recurrent, and situational matters of importance to the association. Since 1974, congresses have been convened every 4 years at venues across the globe. The IAAP also hosts regional conferences to benefit younger psychologists and colleagues from developing countries who may not be able to attend world congresses. The IAAP has cooperative ties to the ICP and IUPsyS, and has NGO status at the U.N. Educational, Scientific, and Cultural Organization (UNESCO) and the WHO. The IAAP also publishes *Applied Psychology: An International Review.*

The ICP (http://icpsych.tripod.com/) was founded in 1941 in the U.S. as the National Council of Women Psychologists to assist in the war effort. The current mission of the ICP is to advance scientific psychology and its global application. To this end, the ICP serves to strengthen international bonds between psychologists. Psychologists from over 80 countries are members. The ICP has several standing committees (e.g., long-range planning), professional concerns committees (e.g., peace), interest groups (e.g., cross-cultural issues and research), liaisons to national and international psychological organizations (e.g., International Organization for the Study of Group Tensions), and area chairs (i.e., country representatives who further the aims of the ICP in specified geographical areas). The ICP has NGO status at the U.N. Economic and Social Council (ECOSOC). The ICP hosts thematic annual conventions and publishes the *International Psychologist.*

The IUPsyS (http://www.iupsys.org) was founded in 1951 as the International Union of Scientific Psychology, having evolved from international congresses that began in 1889. The IUPsyS is recognized as the international voice of psychology because it is an umbrella organization and because it encompasses all specialties of the discipline and profession. The IUPsyS has no individual members; rather, it is composed of national psychological organizations. At present, the IUPsyS has members from 68 countries, representing over 500,000 psychologists. Membership includes most industrial nations, many developing nations, and countries classified by the U.N. as least developed (e.g., Bangladesh, Uganda). The IUPsyS fosters the global development and exchange of psychological science, whether biological or social, normal or abnormal, pure or applied. It contributes to the exchange of ideas and data and scholars and students, and to networking international and national organizations on matters of shared interest. The IUPsyS belongs to two major international scientific organizations: the International Social Science Council and International Council of Science. Through membership in these multidisciplinary organizations, the IUPsyS participates in research of global significance. The IUPsyS also has NGO status with the U.N. ECOSOC, UNESCO, and WHO. Finally, the IUPsyS has affiliations with 12 regional and international psychological organizations (e.g., the IAAP) and ties to psychological associations with narrow foci (e.g., the ITC). These ties permit the IUPsyS to lend its expertise to various global concerns, such as immunization and prenatal care, adult literacy, and capacity-building. The IUPsyS hosts the International Congress of Psychology quadrennially and publishes both the *International Journal of Psychology* and *Psychology: IUPsyS Global Resource*, a CD-ROM devoted to the concerns and needs of international psychologists.

The APA's Division of International Psychology (APA52; http://orgs.tamu-commerce.edu/div52/) was founded in 1997 in response to the complex needs of an increasingly interdependent and rapidly changing world and the urgency of understanding the multicultural and multidisciplinary dimensions of that world. APA52 serves psychologists interested in collaborating with colleagues from around the world in the teaching, research, and practice of psychology. Its activities include facilitating transnational research, informing psychologists about assessment and treatment practices worldwide, and encouraging psychologists to visit their counterparts in other countries in order to attend conferences, give lectures and workshops, and pursue advanced training or employment. APA52 has seven standing committees and 14 ad hoc committees that have specific charges related to the goals of the division. For example, the Committee for International Liaisons maintains a list and listserv of psychologists who represent 74 countries for the purpose of facilitating international communication. This committee also maintains the Web-based International Psychology Information Clearinghouse, a compendium of information intended to stimulate international collaboration in teaching, research, practice, and public service. This resource contains over 200 entries on careers in international psychology, opportunities in academic and research settings, opportunities in clinical and service agencies, funding for research, support for conferences, travel support, awards, resources for American psychology students, and resources for foreign psychologists and psychology students. Recently, a Web technology was introduced to enhance communication and collaboration among psychologists worldwide. Psychat.org permits the conversion of text to and from languages, and is now linked to the APA52 web site. E-mail messages, short documents, and web sites can be converted into any of the available languages. The site also features real-time online chat in which one can write text in one language and send it in another. APA52 also contributes an annual program of international scholarship and discourse to APA's annual meetings and publishes the *International Psychology Reporter*.

The American Psychological Association (APA; http://www.apa.org) has a long commitment to international psychology. In 1929, the APA dedicated its annual convention to hosting the Ninth International Congress of Psychology. In 1944, the APA established the Committee on International Relations in Psychology (CIRP; http://www.apa.org/international/cirp-desc.html). Operating out of the APA's Office of International Affairs, CIRP disseminates psychological information, supports exchange programs, promotes attendance at international meetings (e.g., the International Scientific Meetings Support Fund), and seeks ties to international organizations (e.g., the WHO). CIRP has facilitated the APA's global agenda by assisting psychologists from abroad to acquire scholarly and professional materials (e.g., the Journal Donations Program), advising them on how to publish in American journals (e.g., the Editorial Mentoring Program), and coordinating national conferences with meetings of international psychological associations. CIRP also encourages efforts to internationalize the psychology curriculum (e.g., the Disaster Management, Humanitarian Relations, and International Peacekeeping programs at the University of Hawaii). CIRP also monitors international cases that involve the abuse of psychological knowledge and methods, and the infringement of psychologists' rights. CIRP publishes *Psychology International*.

Psychological associations also play an important role at the United Nations (U.N.; http://www.un.org/) as NGOs. As we have shown, psychological knowledge and skills are essential to understanding and solving contemporary global problems. NGOs fulfill the charter of the U.N. by working for peace and security, economic and social advancement, and the promotion of human rights. With the assistance of the U.N.'s Department of Public Information, NGOs have drawn attention to global concerns, disseminated information, suggested interventions, monitored international agreements, and mobilized public support for U.N. initiatives. The shared goals of the U.N. and psychological NGOs include raising global consciousness and nurturing cooperative networks. Representatives from psychological NGOs attend U.N. briefings and consult with committees, units, and divisions that might benefit from their expertise. For example, the ICP plays an important role in the U.N. Children's Fund's Committee on the Girl Child, formed in response to the plight of females worldwide, and established the U.N. Committee on the Family. IUPsyS members participate on the Committee on Health and Mental Health and have worked on several UNESCO-sponsored projects (e.g., identifying the psychological dimensions of global change). The APA became an accredited NGO at the U.N. in 2001, and brings a psychological perspective to many U.N. policies and programs, including aging, child welfare, education, gender equality, human rights, racism, social justice, and violence. It has initiated, coordinated, or contributed to several U.N. caucuses (e.g., Child Rights Caucus), committees (e.g., aging, family), forums (e.g., indigenous issues), and task forces (e.g., children and HIV/AIDS), and has started to examine the impact the U.N. Declaration of Human Rights on economic development, environmental protection, and human rights. The International Working Group on Traumatic Stress, a multidisciplinary task force that has consultative status with the U.N. ECOSOC, has constructed guidelines for responding to humanitarian crises. The guidelines emphasize trauma intervention with various populations (e.g., child combatants, refugees, victims of natural disasters) in developing countries without a strong mental health infrastructure. The guidelines identify programs that can be implemented at different levels (e.g., societal, community, individual) and those that vary in scope (e.g., social policy, public education, coordination of services, capacity-building, counseling, self-help).

Like the U.N., many international psychological organizations have NGO status or less formal ties with the World Health Organization (WHO; http://www.who.int/en/). The mission of the WHO is to assist all peoples to attain the highest possible level of health. To fulfill its mission, the WHO directs and coordinates work in international health in concert with the U.N., specialized agencies, governmental heath administrations, and professional organizations. It encourages collaboration among scientific and professional groups on research related to illness and health and on training healthcare providers. The WHO also focuses on global mental health. In 2001, the WHO reported that 450 million people worldwide suffer from psychological and neurological disorders (World Health Organization, 2001). Major depression is the leading cause of disability and ranks fourth among the 10 leading contributors to the global disease burden; 70 million suffer from alcoholism and 24 million from schizophrenia. The WHO stressed that mental health is crucial to the well-being of individuals, societies, and countries, and should not be neglected. To this end, the WHO made 10

mental health recommendations that could be adapted to the needs and resources of each country; many are relevant for psychologists, including educating the public, conducting research, and involving families and community. Sensitive to the vast differences in resources among countries, the WHO has delineated three levels within which to enact its recommendations: (a) underdeveloped countries (e.g., transferring the mentally ill out of prisons), (b) developing countries (e.g., integrating custodial patients into the general health care system), and (c) developed countries (e.g., establishing community facilities that offer comprehensive mental health coverage). The WHO also sponsors collaborative centers in which national institutions form an international network to direct activities that support the WHO's international mental health agenda. Collaborative centers collect and disseminate information, educate and train healthcare workers, and design, deliver, and evaluate services. Finally, the WHO partners with civil society organizations and NGOs with overlapping health-related goals and programs.

1.5 THE FUTURE OF INTERNATIONAL PSYCHOLOGY

International psychology works to increase communication and collaboration among psychologists worldwide and respond to significant global concerns. To date, international psychology has made impressive strides toward fulfilling its mission, yet much remains to be accomplished. What is the agenda for international psychology as the 21st century unfolds?

First, the time is ripe for greater unity within international psychology. The integration of international psychological organizations has already begun (Pawlik & d'Ydewalle, 1996; Sabourin, 2001). For example, officers of the IAAP and IUPsyS meet yearly to coordinate existing relationships and identify new areas of cooperation, and the IAAP and ICP coordinate advanced research training seminars for psychologists in developing countries. Some have suggested a more complete merger of these complementary organizations. The benefits of a more unified international psychology include a stronger voice, pooled resources, and greater efficiency in carrying out projects that address various global problems. Increased coordination might also lead to development of a mechanism for data archiving and sharing that would advance psychological science and bring greater coherence to transnational research.

Second, curricula that are relevant to the preparation of competent international psychologists are being developed (Marsella, 1998). Most international psychologists are not trained in the specialty and embrace it from virtually every corner of the discipline and profession. Their talents and enthusiasm notwithstanding, there is a need for international psychologists who have been academically prepared and clinically trained with conceptual models, investigative methodologies, and practical interventions based on multidisciplinary and transnational foundations that are global in scope, relevant, applicable, and culturally appropriate. Recently, the APA began to address the pedagogical needs of 21st-century psychology through one of its Partnerships Programs. One project, "Teaching a World Psychology: International Dialogues," assembles world leaders in secondary and tertiary education in

psychology in order to internationalize the curriculum. In 2001, the APA convened representatives of its divisions, national credentialing organizations, and national education and training organizations for an educational leadership conference. The conference identified several issues relevant to the preparation of international psychologists that the APA's Board of Educational Affairs will review. Of overarching importance is a multidisciplinary approach to understanding, investigating, and intervening in global concerns, and the necessity of developing interprofessional knowledge, skills, and attitudes to ensure effective collaboration. Recommendations for internationalizing the psychology curriculum included expanding exchange programs, reinstituting a language requirement, evaluating the applicability of theories and research methods to global phenomena, and training in nontraditional approaches and settings (Belar, Nelson, & Wasik, 2003). These recommendations echo Marsella's (1998) earlier call for a curriculum that raises awareness of the ethnocentric bias of current training, emphasizes nonlinear, systems models of human functioning, and employs naturalistic and qualitative methods of inquiry and data analysis.

Other approaches to internationalizing the curriculum, still awaiting implementation, involve intensive, postgraduate preparation in specific target areas, such as intergroup conflict. Recently, a task force designed a yearlong curriculum in response to the 1997 Initiative on Ethnopolitical Warfare, proposed jointly by the American and Canadian Psychological Associations. This curriculum includes eight didactic areas: cross-cultural knowledge and perspectives, conflict analysis, violence prevention, conflict resolution, traumatic stress, psychosocial programs, intervention design, and peace-building and reconciliation. An internship follows to provide supervised international field experiences.

Finally, for international psychology to advance as a specialty, it must continue to demonstrate its relevance (Rosenzweig, 1999; Staub & Green, 1992). International psychologists and psychological organizations must show why their science and practice merit financial and public support. Specifically, international psychologists must test their conceptual models, evaluate their technical applications, and disseminate evidence that their theories and practices address significant global concerns. The development of international psychology also requires a renewed commitment to the value of social responsibility in teaching, research, practice, and public service. Social responsibility "is not simply about caring for the other outside of oneself; it means to be concerned for one's self in the other" (Staub & Green, 1992, p. 12).

1.6 CONCLUSION

We conclude our overview of international psychology by identifying links between this specialty and the chapters on national psychologies that follow. As stated in the Preface, our rationale for the *Handbook of International Psychology* is to inform readers about the discipline and profession of psychology as constituted and evolving in distinct countries and regions of the world. Each chapter describes the general background, education and training, scope of psychological practice, and future of psychology in 27

countries. Although our list of countries may seem incomplete and idiosyncratic, we believed that an in-depth presentation of each country was required. This decision necessarily limited the number and range of countries we included in the book.

If the mission of international psychology is to enhance communication and collaboration, then it is essential that psychologists and psychology students become familiar with theory, research, and practice in many lands. We believe that readers of the *Handbook* will become better equipped to engage their counterparts abroad in informed discourse and establish collegial relationships that will address significant global concerns. Information about the multidisciplinary and organizational links of national psychological organizations will also stimulate international communication and collaboration.

International psychology is a disciplinary and professional specialty that targets a variety of phenomena that have no borders. We reviewed several pressing global concerns, including intergroup conflict, societal transformation and national development, threats to the natural environment, physical and mental health needs, and the struggles of disempowered groups. These problems and their solutions require appreciation of the complex interplay of culture, economics, history, politics, and religion; in other words, a multidisciplinary and transnational perspective. Contributors to the *Handbook* have been conscientious about articulating the contextual dimensions of their country's psychology. For example, readers will become acquainted with controversial issues that psychologists are debating across the globe, particularly those related to politics and culture. They will discover how well the psychologies of other countries balance imported, Western features with indigenous elements that reflect circumstances that are relevant to those countries. They will learn about alternative paradigms for constructing theory, conducting research, and applying interventions. As a result, readers will better understand the multifactorial causes of and diverse possibilities for addressing global concerns as manifested in specific countries.

The future of international psychology will surely include greater unity among scientists and practitioners worldwide, and more specialized didactic and applied preparation of international psychologists. We hope that readers of the *Handbook* will become more involved internationally through their national psychological associations as well as through regional and international psychological organizations. In addition, we hope they will become better informed about opportunities for international partnership and mechanisms for global interface. Their increased involvement will reflect an expanding vista that invites psychologists to fulfill the goals of a socially responsible psychology. A new generation of leaders within international psychology will strengthen ties among psychological associations that have an international agenda and embolden psychology's role in addressing global issues through international policy-making entities. These leaders will support the refinement of educational and training materials to ensure the preparation of international psychologists who will have greater competencies than their predecessors. Readers of the *Handbook* will become familiar with psychology curricula that may be less specialized, but more externally valid. They will learn about relatively unknown specialties, such as transportation psychology and disaster mental health. They will learn about alternative forms of treatment, different modalities of service delivery, and diverse ethics codes. Finally, they will learn about an influential literature that is often not available through conventional databases.

In our concluding chapter, we offer a synthesis of the 27 national psychologies presented in the *Handbook*. In our synthesis, we examine three distinct and significant trends in psychology worldwide: some were identified in previous handbooks (see Gilgen & Gilgen, 1987; Sexton & Hogan, 1992), some have changed since the publication of those books, and some are more recent. These trends include the growth of psychology as a discipline and profession, the feminization of psychology, and the emergence of new paradigms. We conclude our synthesis by reflecting on what American psychologists can learn about theory, research, practice, and training in psychology from their international colleagues.

REFERENCES

Bandura, A. (2002). Social cognitive theory in cultural context. *Applied psychology: An International Review, 51,* 269–290.

Belar, C. D., Nelson, P. D., & Wasik, B. H. (2003). Rethinking education in psychology and psychology in education: The inaugural Educational Leadership Conference. *American Psychologist, 58,* 678–684.

Cairns, E., & Darby, J. (1998). The conflict in Northern Ireland: Causes, consequences, and controls. *American Psychologist, 53,* 754–760.

Comas-Díaz, L. (2000). An ethnopolitical approach to working with people of color. *American Psychologist, 55,* 1319–1325.

Comas-Díaz, L., Lykes, M. B., & Alarcón, R. D. (1998). Ethnic conflict and the psychology of liberation in Guatemala, Peru, and Puerto Rico. *American Psychologist, 53,* 778–792.

de la Rey, R. P. (2002, August). Management of HIV and AIDS: A South African perspective. In M. J. Stevens (Chair), *Psychology's response to global health issues.* Symposium conducted at the meeting of the American Psychological Association, Chicago, IL.

Eidelson, R. J., & Eidelson. J. I. (2003). Dangerous ideas: Five beliefs that propel groups toward conflict. *American Psychologist, 58,* 182–192.

Gergen, K. J. (2001). Psychological science in a postmodern context. *American Psychologist, 56,* 803–813.

Gilgen, A. R., & Gilgen, C. K. (Eds.). (1987). *International handbook of psychology.* New York: Greenwood Press.

Harré, R. (2002). Social reality and the myth of social structure. *European Journal of Social Theory, 5,* 111–123.

Hussain, S. A. (2002). *Hope for the children: Lessons from Bosnia.* Columbia, MO: International Medical and Educational Trust.

Jing, Q. (2000). International psychology. In K. Pawlik & M. R. Rosenzweig (Eds.), *The international handbook of psychology* (pp. 570–584). Thousand Oaks, CA: Sage.

Lee, A. M., & Lee, S. (1996). Distorted eating and its psychosocial correlates among Chinese adolescent females. *International Journal of Eating Disorders, 20,* 177–183.

Marsella, A. J. (1998). Toward a global-community psychology: Meeting the needs of a changing world. *American Psychologist, 53,* 1282–1291.

Mays, V. M., Bullock, M., Rosenzweig, M. R., & Wessells, M. (1998). Ethnic conflict: Global challenges and psychological perspectives. *American Psychologist, 53,* 737–742.

Moghaddam, F. M., & Harré, R. (1996). Psychological limits to political revolutions: An application of social reducton theory. In E. Hasselberg, L. Martienssen, & F. Radtke (Eds.), *Der dialogbegriff am ende des 20 jahrhunderts* [The concept of dialogue at the end of the 20th century] (pp. 230–240). Berlin: Hegel Institute.

Pawlik, K., & d'Ydewalle, G. (1996). Psychology and the global commons: Perspectives of international psychology. *American Psychologist, 51,* 488-495.

Prilleltensky, I., & Fox, D. (1997). Introducing critical psychology: Values, assumptions, and the status quo. In D. Fox & I. Prilleltensky (Eds.), *Critical psychology: An introduction* (pp. 3–20). Thousand Oaks, CA: Sage.

Rosenzweig, M. R. (1999). Continuity and change in the development of psychology around the world. *American Psychologist, 53,* 252-259.

Rouhana, N. N., & Bar-Tal, D. (1998). Psychological dynamics of intractable ethnonational conflict: The Israeli-Palestinian case. *American Psychologist, 53,* 761-770.

Sabourin, M. (2001). International psychology: Is the whole greater than the sum of its parts? *Canadian Psychology, 42,* 74-81.

Sexton, V. S., & Hogan, J. D. (Eds.). (1992). *International psychology: Views from around the world.* Lincoln, NE: University of Nebraska Press.

Sinha, D. (1997). Indigenizing psychology. In J. W. Berry, Y. H. Poortinga, & J. Pandey (Eds.), *Handbook of cross-cultural psychology: Vol. 1. Theory and method* (2nd ed., pp. 129–169). Boston: Allyn and Bacon.

Smith, D. (2001). Children in the heat of war. *Monitor on Psychology, 32,* 29–31.

Staub, S., & Green, P. (1992). Introduction: Toward a socially responsible psychology. In S. Staub & P. Green (Eds.), *Psychology and social responsibility: Facing global challenges* (pp. 3–14). New York: New York University Press.

Stevens, M. J. (2002). The interplay of psychology and societal transformation. *International Journal of Group Tensions, 31,* 5–30.

Sullivan, J. L., & Transue, J. E. (1999). The psychological underpinnings of democracy: A selective review of research on political tolerance, interpersonal trust, and social capital. *Annual Review of Psychology, 50,* 625–650.

Torney-Purta, J., Lehmann, R., Oswald, H., & Schulz, W. (2001). *Citizenship and education in twenty-eight countries: Civic knowledge and engagement at age fourteen.* Amsterdam: International Association for the Evaluation of Educational Achievement.

Vlek, C. (2000). Essential psychology for environmental policy making. *International Journal of Psychology, 35,* 153–167.

Walker, L. E. (1999). Psychology and domestic violence around the world. *American Psychologist, 54,* 21–29.

Walsh, R. (2000). Asian psychotherapies. In R. J. Corsini & D. Wedding (Eds.), *Current psychotherapies* (pp. 407–444). Itasca, IL: Peacock.

Wessells, M. G. (2000). Contributions of psychology of peace and nonviolent conflict resolution. In K. Pawlik & M. R. Rosenzweig (Eds.), *The interna-*

tional handbook of psychology (pp. 526–533). Thousand Oaks, CA: Sage.

Winter, D. D. N. (2000). Some big ideas for some big problems. *American Psychologist, 55,* 516–522.

World Health Organization (WHO). (2001). *The World Health Report: 2001.* Geneva: Author.

Political Map of the World, June 2003

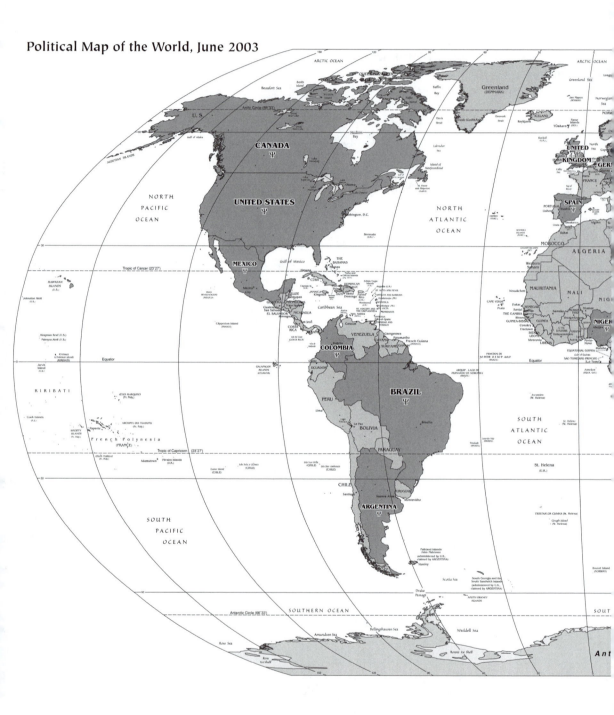

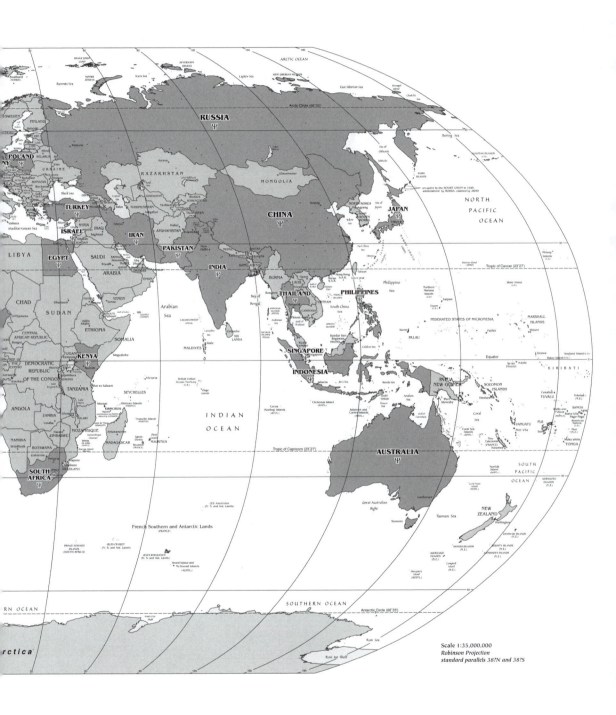

Scale 1:35,000,000
Robinson Projection
standard parallels 38?N and 38?S

CHAPTER 2

Psychology in Kenya

JUNE W. KOINANGE

June W. Koinange has a B.A. in psychology and an M.A. in counseling psychology from the United States International University–Africa in Nairobi, Kenya. She has established her own practice, Lifespring Counseling and Training Center (LCTC), where the main focus is on psychological interventions in stress and trauma management and marriage and family counseling, as well as youth-related issues and challenges. LCTC has been contracted to provide workplace and outreach psychosocial care and support services for specific U.N. staff undergoing cumulative and traumatic stress. Koinange has also worked as a stress counselor for staff members of UNICEF/Operation Lifeline in the Sudan. She is a founding member and chairperson of the Kenya Psychological Association.

June Koinange has published several articles and presented papers at various workshops and conferences. These include "Psychosocial Consequences and Implication of Female Genital Mutilation (FGM)
and the Role and Function of Education in Eradicating FGM" at the UNICEF National FGM Symposium in Nairobi. She has also published "Psychology Strides Forward in Kenya" in Psychology International, *a publication of the American Psychological Association's Office of International Affairs.*

2.1 OVERVIEW

In many African countries, mental health has long been a major concern. This concern is heightened by critical events characteristic of Africa, such as corruption, political turmoil, poverty, the refugee situation, and lack of water and other basic necessities of life; the list is endless. All of these factors add up to exert tremendous pressures on the African family, generally, and the individual, in particular. In most cases, when physical and psychological needs compete, the physical are addressed at the expense of the psychological.

Experts in the fields of education, medicine, psychology, and sociology share a common concern over the alarming level of stress that both the young and the old in Africa experience in their daily activities. The cumulative effects of these pressures are myriad and often negative, including anxiety, depression, hysteria, paranoia, and schizophrenia. Many of the victims of these pressures also end up abusing alcohol and drugs, enacting gender-based violence, engaging in promiscuous sex, and even committing suicide.

Psychology, as it is known today, is fairly new to Kenya. Historically, traditional medicine men and healers practiced caring interventions in local communities. They focused on psychosocial and spiritual matters in addition to physical ailments. Given this cultural tradition, the introduction of applied psychology into the community was received initially with skepticism or denial. This attitude is rapidly changing due to the intensification of problems caused by corruption, HIV/AIDS, poverty, and the general inefficiency of the social service system. These realities underscore the urgent need for psychosocial interventions (Koinange, 2001).

It is estimated that there are approximately 3,000 psychologists and professional counselors (with counselors outnumbering psychologists) in Kenya, which has a population of about 30.5 million. There are three groups of mental health providers in Kenya: the first group is psychologists who have master's degrees in counseling, clinical or research; the second group is that of professional counselors who have a bachelor's degree either in psychology or other related disciplines, such as sociology, nursing, or education, and a master's degree in counseling. In this second group of professional counselors, there are those who do not have a degree, but have done extensive training in focused areas of interest such as HIV/AIDS counseling. The third group consists of counselors with very limited training in psychology. Inclusion of these different professional groups is important in understanding the scope and future of psychology in Kenya. In this chapter, I will refer mainly to the first and second group of mental health providers.

Most psychologists and professional counselors were trained in the U.K., in North America, or at Kenyan universities. Most psychologists and professional counselors are concentrated in urban areas due to the opportunities that are available and the nature of their work. This makes it difficult for the majority of rural Kenyans to access mental health services from professionals when needed. In addition to the fact that the proportion of psychologists and professional counselors to the population is low, most psychologists and counselors opt to seek employment at universities or in human-resources departments in organizations, rather than practice psychotherapy. The current data show that most psychologists work as university professors, counseling and guidance counselors in schools, counselors on the staff of NGOs and U.N. agencies, such as the U.N. Office in Nairobi, U.N.–World Food Program, and the U.N. High Commission for Refugees (Koinange & Asakhulu, 2003). Psychologists and professional counselors are also attached to human resources departments in prisons and hospitals.

Psychologists and professional counselors do not pursue careers in social services because remuneration for psychotherapy in Kenya is generally not quite relative to the workload and in comparison to what others are paid in similar occupations. Only those who manage to secure jobs with international NGOs and U.N. agencies in Kenya receive salaries that are commensurate with their workload and qualifications. Most of these organizations and agencies hire psychologists and professional counselors who have master's degrees and above. Another reason that so few psychologists and professional counselors choose to offer psychotherapy may be that Kenya has no national, regional, or local governing body to regulate professional practice, specifically through a code of ethics or guidelines for the provision of services. As it stands today, the profession is at risk for abuses to occur. However, there are by laws and ethical guidelines put forth by individual psychological and counseling associations to regulate the conduct and professional practices of their own members. Members pay membership and subscription fees to join these associations. There are benefits to this arrangement because members have a common code of ethics to follow; they share information and education on various issues of concern to their professional practice; they have a stronger voice when it comes to advocacy and creating awareness of certain areas such as HIV/AIDS; and they have a registered body to support them in case of legal problems with clients and the courts.

Furthermore, it is likely that antagonistic feelings between some psychologists, professional counselors, and psychiatrists may cause some would-be practitioners not to venture into psychotherapy and social services. There are three categories of psychiatrists encountered by psychologists and professional counselors: the first group consists of those who highly appreciate the practice of psychotherapy and see this function as complementing their work. The second group does not see the need of dealing with psychological issues; to those in this group, psychotherapy is very secondary to medical assistance. The third group seems to feel professionally threatened by competent psychologists. This third group is the one that tends to be antagonistic (Koinange & Asakhulu, 2003). This situation is not unique to Kenya, of course.

Although Kenya has psychological associations such as the Kenya Psychological Association (KPsyA), the Kenya Counselors Association, the Kenya Association of Professional Counselors, and the Kenya Association of Christian Counselors, these entities do not possess the power to effect changes due to lack of legislation that regulates training in and the practice of psychotherapy. Yet, many Kenyans have suffered from traumatic incidents that require expert psychosocial interventions (e.g., traffic accidents, HIV/AIDS, natural disasters, forced migration, substance abuse, teen pregnancy, terrorist attacks, tribal clashes and wars, and unemployment).

Awareness of the limited availability of psychological services has recently penetrated the Kenyan community through the media's reporting on various disasters that have struck Kenya, such as the 1997 El Niño rains, the 1998 terrorist bomb blast, the Kenya Airways crash off Abidjan in Ivory Coast in 2000, and the ongoing HIV/AIDS scourge. Formal and informal programs for counselors have been organized to help religious and community leaders acquire the counseling skills necessary to assist victims of these disasters. Through conferences, seminars, and workshops on urgent issues facing the country, psychologists and professional counselors are reaching out to communities in order to raise awareness of the usefulness of counseling in helping those in need cope more effectively.

On July 15, 2002, the KPsyA presented to the Constitution of Kenya Review Commission (CKRC) a paper on psychosocial issues of national significance, among them the need for a "Psychology General" at the policy-making level. The paper outlined the association's corporate voice on the specific issue of mental health, which it strongly believes is a basic human right, and on general issues affecting the science, practice, and training in psychology in Kenya.

Other key recommendations presented to the Commission included a new constitution that would guarantee the right to mental health by explicitly acknowledging mental health as a basic human right, not merely a derivative of the right to life as presently guaranteed under Section 70 of the Constitution. It would explicitly provide for a constitutional office (e.g., a Psychology General) to be held by a person fully conversant with the science and profession of psychology, whose portfolio would subsume matters pertaining to the provision of mental health care for the nation; explicitly provide administrative and legal structures within which such a constitutional office can function; and establish a trust fund through which free mental health services would be offered to needy citizens.

The new constitution would also guarantee the right to means of earning a livelihood by protecting the right to form trade unions and workers associations for all cadres of employed persons; protecting the right to hold any job anywhere, the only criteria being merit; and providing for the right to family benefits, including allowances for maternity and spousal leave, and expanding benefits for dependants to aged members of the extended family.

The constitution would also guarantee the right to own or have access to land and property by providing for equal access to land for men and women; protecting communal rights to land (e.g., in pastoral communities); and simplifying procedures for the transfer of land and property.

Finally, the constitution would guarantee the right of vulnerable groups that need special care and provision by identifying vulnerable groups, such as women and children, physically disabled and mentally retarded persons, refugees and displaced persons, street children, and unwed mothers; providing affirmative action programs for vulnerable groups (e.g., setting aside a number of slots for them to be nominated into Parliament); and providing for the automatic national implementation of international treaties that provide for the rights of vulnerable groups.

Clearly, many of the recommendations of the KPsyA to the CKRC are in the form of changes to existing social policy. However, such changes would have psychosocial benefits for Kenyans. For example, guaranteeing the right to earn a livelihood as well as the right to own land and property should curb maladaptive social behavior, such as corruption, crime, and promiscuity, which are of great concern to psychologists and professional counselors. The presentation of this document to the CKRC was made in the hope that a meaningful and ongoing dialogue would begin between psychologists and the Kenyan government, one that would evolve into a partnership to serve the needs of the people more efficiently and effectively. At this point in time, KPsyA is waiting for feedback from CKRC. The CKRC still has much to do before completing its work and handing over a completed document to Parliament.

2.2 EDUCATION AND TRAINING

Kenya has 6 public and 11 private universities. Seven of the private universities are fully accredited by the Commission for Higher Education, a body that is charged with the responsibility of inspecting institutions of higher learning for purposes of maintaining standards. The other four private universities are partially accredited.

During the 1960s and early 1970s, Europeans, many of whom were missionaries, introduced formal education to Kenya, including psychology (Okatcha, Omar, & Kariuki, 1989). Most university lecturers in psychology at the time were educated and trained in the U.K. or North America. Even then, the study of psychology at Kenyan universities was offered as part of the required core curriculum for a bachelor's degree in education (B.Ed.). In other words, the psychology that was taught was limited to educational psychology. A course in educational psychology was offered in one semester only, during the entire 3-year degree program (Kithuka, 1985).

In the last decade, the number of psychology courses offered to B.Ed. students has increased significantly. In fact, some universities now offer degree programs in psychology (see Table 2.1). For example, the United States International University–Africa, a private university established 30 years ago, spearheaded high-quality degree programs leading to a bachelor of arts in psychology and a master of arts in counseling psychology. The university's vice chancellor, Dr. Frieda Brown, is a clinical psychologist whose accomplishments have contributed to the department of psychology's reputation for academic excellence.

Master's degrees at most universities require coursework, a thesis involving a supervised research project, and a practicum or supervised field placement. Most universities in Kenya do not have master's or doctoral programs, but there are plans to develop them in the near future.

As indicated in Table 2.1, universities that require educational psychology for students who plan on careers in teaching, such as Egerton, Kabarak, Kenyatta, Maseno, and Moi, offer less than 10 psychology units. These units include or address in less comprehensive ways an introduction to psychology, developmental psychology, human behavior and learning, guidance and counseling, research methods and statistics, and tests and measurements (Koinange & Asakhulu, 2003). A few universities offer undergraduate programs in guidance and counseling so that students can graduate with a bachelor's degree in counseling.

Many universities also have initiated graduate programs that culminate either in a master's diploma or certificate; these programs aim to train guidance and counseling personnel. A few doctoral programs in educational psychology are available, as can be seen from Table 2.1. Many teachers have taken a few courses in psychology, but obviously cannot be considered to be psychologists. It is evident from Table 2.1 that it is difficult for the universities to mount doctoral programs in psychology because the country lacks qualified faculty in the discipline to train and supervise such advanced graduate students. Overall, considerably more work must be done in

TABLE 2.1
Education and Training in Psychology at Kenyan Universities

University	College(s)	Department(s)	Bachelor's/Diploma		Master's and Postgraduate Diploma		Ph.D.
			Units	Students	Units	Students	Students
Baraton[*]	Education	Curriculum	6	3			
	Arts and Social Sciences	Guidance and Counseling	16	20			
Catholic[*]	Sciences	Education	5	470			
Daystar[*]	Arts	Community Development	55	150	48	—	
Egerton[x]	Education and Human Resources	Educational Psychology	8	450	36	12	
Kabarak[*]	Education	Educational Psychology	4	—			
Kenyatta[x]	Education and Human Resources	Educational Psychology	4	1500	10	25	2
		Guidance and Counseling			14	18	
	Education	Educational Psychology	4	600	10	—	
Maseno[x]	Arts and Social Sciences	Education	3	600			
Methodist[*]	Sciences	Counseling	52	6			
	Education	Educational Psychology	5	600	9	9	
Moi[x]	Education	Psychology	48	1,055	15	—	
Nairobi[x]	Social Science	Education	5	—			
	Arts and Social Science	Psychiatry	4	—			
USIU–A[*]	Sciences	Psychology	78	80	58	30	

Note. [x] = public universities. [*] = private universities. — = not yet started.

From "Assessment of the Development and Status of the Discipline of Psychology in the Institutions of Higher Education in Kenya," by J. W. Koinange and N. M. Asakhulu, 2003.

Kenya to produce psychology majors at all levels.

Universities that offer counseling psychology or educational psychology typically have their own distinctive units that are determined by departmental committees, approved by the university senate, and recognized by the Commission for Higher Education. At some universities, these units are offered as a psychology major or psychology minor or both. Students who major in psychology take more units than those who take psychology minors. At these universities, the departments of psychology and departments of guidance and counseling are housed in colleges of education and are chaired by a professor who may or may not have had training in psychology.

The number of psychology majors at most universities is small relative to other majors, ranging from 6 to 50 students per graduating class. The percentage of undergraduates studying psychology (mainly educational psychology) is much higher than that of graduate students. At this point in time, there are no psychology majors at the master's level except at the United States International University–Africa. Master's programs at universities like Kenyatta University are in educational psychology.

The conceptual perspectives and research methodologies in psychology tend to be integrative. For undergraduates, both theory and practice are emphasized whereas theory, research, and practice are combined at the graduate level. Qualitative as well as quantitative investigative methodologies are used, with one or the other methodology emphasized, depending on the particular focus of a department. These theories and methodologies reflect the sociocultural and political undercurrents in contemporary Kenya to some degree because students' research is tailored to solving Kenyan-related problems and challenges.

Standards and practices for the profession of psychology are changing due to the Kenyan government's need for counseling programs to remedy school-related problems. For example, through the Teachers Service Commission, the government is currently negotiating with Methodist University to train counseling students in a distinct school subject along with counseling in order to enhance quality of education and services in schools. This university is producing graduates with B.Ed. degrees as well as bachelor's in counseling, who will eventually be employed by the school system. Egerton University is running a graduate diploma in counseling with plans underway to start a certificate course in counseling for social workers. Daystar University has established a psychology major that will evolve into a master's program in counseling. The Daystar master's program will attempt to integrate psychology with African culture and a Christian perspective. Meanwhile, at the United States International University–Africa, there are plans for a much needed doctoral program in community counseling.

Kenyatta University has well-trained lecturers in the discipline of psychology, with one in cognitive psychology, one in experimental psychology, and three in research and tests and measurements.

The growing demand for education and training in psychology has prompted departments of psychology to consider expanding the number and type of programs they offer. This is due to an acute need for competent practitioners to respond to the psychosocial impact of such contemporary concerns as addiction, child abuse, HIV/AIDS, poverty, and intergroup conflict. As noted, many have plans to establish degree programs at the master's and doctoral levels in branches of applied psychology.

At present, apart from a few doctoral students in education-related doctoral studies at Kenyatta University, there are no doctoral students in clinical or counseling psychology in Kenyan universities. The trend has been for such students to take their degrees in Europe or the U.S., particularly with the availability of grants and sponsorships. Those who are unable to leave the country due to financial constraints compete for limited openings at Kenyatta University, attempt to acquire a Ph.D. through distance learning, or try to meet the stringent conditions set by the Ministry of Education in order to qualify for a scholarship or loan. This is very frustrating for many master's degree holders who would like to further their education.

Most of the psychology taught at public and private universities is imported from the West, mainly from Europe and the U.S. This knowledge, however, is contextualized (i.e., made socioculturally relevant and comprehensible) in order to fit the Kenyan situation. Though imported, Western theories, research, and practices are useful in framing the structure and organization of programs and in providing opportunities for cross-cultural comparisons. There is some local psychological literature, but this is generally not rigorous enough for academic purposes, and Kenyan psychologists have tended to rely on Western scholarship. Paradoxically, this disciplinary dependency on the West has left Kenyan academics without access to books and materials because of their

expense. Even if they are successful at procuring the latest publications, these are of limited utility, as they must first be refitted to Kenyan society and culture. Occasionally, a lack of cultural sensitivity brings about confusion because many theories and techniques borrowed from the West do not adequately address local realities. Disciplinary and professional dependence can lead to the uncritical adoption of a Western perspective, which may inadvertently weaken initiatives to developing a distinctly Kenyan approach to psychological theory, research, practice, and pedagogy. However, the importing of Western psychology allows for the sharing of some universal principles, thereby adding to the local body of knowledge and skills.

Resources available to facilitate education and training at universities include textbooks (mostly foreign), indigenous literature, journals, videos, computer hardware and software, the Internet (though very expensive), distance-learning modules, and lecturers' notes and research materials. However, though available, these resources are very limited at some universities. Universities try to recommend books that are no more than 5 years old. However, both new and old books are used depending on the subject being taught. In addition to the influential publications cited at the end of this chapter, several books that complement the university curriculum in psychology include Ballenger's *The Curious Researcher: A Guide to Writing Research Papers* (1998), Erickson's *Identity, Youth and Crisis* (1968), Furniss' *The Multi-professional Handbook of Child Sexual Abuse: Integrated Management, Therapy and Legal Intervention* (1995), Kelvin's *Educational Psychology* (1983), and Mouly's *Psychology for Effective Teaching* (1968).

Although the degrees conferred by universities are general, bachelor's degree holders and those with post-graduate certificates are currently allowed to work as volunteers at counseling and testing clinics and in the schools. However, they are not permitted to establish their own practices or clinics unless they obtain further training.

The minimum requirement for one to practice educational psychology or lecture in the subject at an institution of higher learning is the master's in education (M.Ed.) or master's in counseling psychology (available at the United States International University–Africa). Interestingly, because the United States International University–Africa has such high standards for education and training, it has the local authority to license graduates of its master's degree program in counseling psychology, the only one of its kind in Kenya.

On average, faculty and staff teaching psychology-related courses at Kenyan universities are distributed in the following academic ranks:

Professors: Typically one faculty member who received training abroad, usually in the U.S.
Lecturers with doctorates: Typically three, two of whom received some international training, usually in Europe and North America
Lecturers with master's degrees: Typically four, most of whom were trained in Kenya

Most psychology faculty are Kenyan. Most of them are employed full-time, although some professors with a master's degree lecture on a part-time basis. There is a dramatic shortage of full-time lecturers in psychology, hence the need to hire part-timers. Occasionally, there are a few visiting academic or practicing psychologists from other countries who come to Kenya to teach for short periods of time (e.g., one semester to two years).

Collaboration with foreign psychologists has helped establish transnational cooperation in exploring culturally different models, methods, and interventions. For example, it has helped prevent replications of research that are not culturally appropriate to Kenya or, conversely, has helped us avoid "re-inventing the wheel." For example, by consulting with a number of foreign psychologists, the Trauma Response Organization was able to carry out research on the 1998 terrorist bomb blast in Kenya that claimed infant victims. More broadly, the KPsyA, the American Psychological Association (APA), and the U.N. collaborate on a number of applied research projects.

There is a significant difference between public and private universities in their remuneration for faculty and staff. Private universities tend to offer better salaries and benefits, including smaller classes and better instructional resources. Although faculty seem to be satisfied with their lot in terms of Kenyan standards, local remuneration falls far below international levels. At public universities, faculty experience the pressure of teaching very large classes with few facilities to make their instruction more "student-friendly." Salaries at public universities are significantly below that at private universities.

The criteria for admission to public universities require applicants to have a minimum of a Certificate of Secondary Education (a 4-year high-school education) with an average grade of "B" or "B+." Students must also have selected psychology or education in their three-course choices when completing their application form. For most private universities, the criteria for admission to psychology is a Certificate of Secondary School Education with a good pass, or a Certificate of Advance Level of Secondary School Education (another 2 years of study after high school). For those private universities just now offering psychology or counseling and guidance programs, the undergraduate admission standard is slightly lower. This lower standard is likely to compromise admission standards generally, as universities compete for applicants. However, because there are more students seeking to enroll in psychology or counseling and guidance at private universities than there are spaces available, applicants are also required to complete written essays, which are evaluated for verbal and analytical aptitude prior to admission.

Requirements for graduate admission at private universities include a bachelor's degree in the behavioral sciences and a GPA of at least 2.5. Those without a behavioral sciences background must take several undergraduate courses in psychology before qualifying for admission. Some of the more prestigious private universities (e.g., the United States International University–Africa) require all graduate applicants to take Graduate Record Examination from recognized centers in Nairobi. Privately sponsored students wishing to enroll in graduate programs at public universities must have a good pass in advanced secondary school education; a diploma from a recognized college; a higher diploma in a social science at the graduate level or at the primary-teacher level; and 5 year's work experience. The entrance requirements to master's degree programs in educational psychology at public universities include second-class honors and above (equivalent to a GPA 3.5); for master's programs in guidance and counseling, second-class honors lower division and above are required (equivalent to a GPA of 3.0).

Limited financial support for students at universities is available, but students must meet several criteria in order to qualify. These criteria include: an assessment made by the Higher Education Loans Board (HELB) on the basis of information provided by the student. HELB assists students in public universities by giving them loans. This is in addition to a subsidy of 70% of the total fees that the government pays across the board for all students at public universities. A student can qualify for up to $525 as well as a scholarship of $100. The HELB has extended its loan program to most private universities, but it does not subsidize education at a specified amount or percentage. Most universities have a work-study program that specifically targets financially challenged students who are performing well in their studies; the Rattansi Trust Fund supports only undergraduates from poor families and only provides tuition money. Graduate scholarships are available to graduate students who demonstrate a high level of achievement in their program of study. For example, at the United States International University–Africa, eligible students must have a minimum GPA of 3.2. At public universities, students must have received an "A" in at least eight of ten master's units completed and must have been awarded first-class honors (equivalent to GPA 3.9) at the bachelor's level. Scholarships such as the Dosh Scholars Fund are available to assist students, especially at Maseno University.

2.3 SCOPE OF PSYCHOLOGICAL PRACTICE

The study of psychology, especially in the specialty of counseling, has become very popular in Kenya. As a result, even those with little expertise or poor qualifications have opened offices where they deliver psychosocial interventions in the hope of earning money. The lack of standardized ethical guidelines that govern the practice of psychology and the failure to regulate the profession through legislation have contributed to considerable professional misconduct.

On average, there are between two and four psychologists and professional counselors employed per institution or organization. However, in most cases, they are part of a team working with other mental health professionals, such as psychiatrists, social workers, guidance counselors, HIV/AIDS counselors, and others calling themselves counselors. In a few organizations, there are psychologists whereas in others, social workers are employed. The work done by psychologists and professional counselors tends to emphasize community-oriented counseling for individuals and groups. The range of services typically offered to a community are counseling services for clients and staff; sharing knowledge and skills through workshops for staff at institutions for the community on such topics as capacity-building, conflict management, disaster management, stress management, and team-building; and predeployment and postdeployment briefings, especially in preparing for, and returning from, a mission (e.g., the armed forces). Some critical incidence stress debriefing takes place but contextualized to the sociocultural background of those being debriefed. To make critical incidence stress debriefing relevant to Kenya, instructions are modified so that clients are asked to share their stories "whole" about what they saw, heard, thought, and felt without a break in the narrative. This is because Africans generally love to tell stories. Hence, it is virtually impossible for an African to report on each aspect of a traumatic event separately and sequentially; the unity of observations and reactions cannot be broken.

Other services include preparing written resources for peer-support volunteers, conducting research on counseling, engaging in community service (e.g., raising awareness of HIV/AIDS via radio and TV programs and political engagement to eradicate female genital mutilation), staffing telephone hotlines, and undertaking compassion projects (e.g., helping to pay school fees for students from very poor families and starting sustainable micro-income-generating projects for women groups and youth groups), conducting outreach activities (e.g., assessment of patients' standard of living and social conditions), and making referrals to specialists.

These mental health professionals also network with human-resources departments to assess the welfare of staff. Some also carry out psychological research on relevant social issues, such as the causes of school disruption and unrest, drug use and abuse among students, ways to manage community stress caused by HIV/AIDS, and why female genital mutilation (FGM) continues to be practiced.

In Kenya, several ethnic groups practice FGM. Psychologists and professional counselors have responded to this practice by facilitating counseling interventions for women who have undergone the genital cut or who fear the act and its consequences. Psychologists and professional counselors are also involved in anti-FGM consciousness-raising and advocacy programs within communities with the assistance of the media. Finally, psychologists and professional counselors research the effects of FGM on attitudinal and behavioral dimensions of female sexuality.

The number of psychologists employed by most institutions and organizations is small compared to physicians, psychiatrists, psychiatric nurses, and social workers. These other health professionals are employed in large numbers depending on the setting. In hospitals, for example, health professionals are in high demand. On average, there are 10 social workers for every psychologist. This is because fewer funds are allocated for psychological services, and it is often assumed that such services can be performed easily by a social worker. In addition, the relative dearth of professional psychologists in Kenya has meant that few such personnel are available for recruitment by various service agencies. Finally, many highly qualified psychologists have elected to establish solo or small group practices.

It is clear that there is a serious shortage of psychologists relative to the demand for services. As institutions and organizations that offer psychological services begin to expand into underdeveloped regions of the country, this shortage of psychologists is felt even more acutely. For example, the Kenya Association of Professional Counselors (this is an organization, not an association as the name implies) currently has branches in only two major towns, Kisumu and Mombasa, besides their headquarters in Nairobi. World Vision–Africa Relief Office, an international NGO, strongly

encourages professionalism in all of its activities and, unlike other agencies, only assigns psychological tasks to qualified psychologists. This appears to be the exception, however, because of the formidable unmet need for psychological services.

Hospitals in Kenya also need more psychologists to tend to the psychological needs of their patients. At the Aga Khan Hospital, professional psychologists are so respected by the administration that some doctors and nurses have enrolled in graduate programs in psychology. Hospital administrators who have been exposed to psychology have a positive view of its contribution to the welfare of clients and employees alike. In some quarters, however, there is still controversy about psychology's benefits. Some claim that psychology as practiced today is not suitable to Kenyan culture. Both public and private universities in Kenya have responded to this call by renewing their efforts to teach psychology in a culturally informed manner.

Psychologists and professional counselors in the public sector do not consider themselves to be adequately reimbursed for their services due to limited resources available for public employees.

The Internet and the World Wide Web offer psychologists and professional counselors access to unlimited knowledge. Although this service is extensively used, it is very expensive to maintain, especially for students. This service is available at universities, hospitals, schools, and national and international organizations where psychologists work. Through this information super-highway, psychologists are becoming better informed about the mission and activities of psychological associations in other countries. The Internet and World Wide Web are being used extensively for the purposes of reviewing published research and for networking with international psychologists and organizations that represent various specialties in psychology. This mode of communication also enables institutions to monitor disasters and emergencies, and to respond immediately, especially in zones of violent conflict.

Kenyan psychologists have many opportunities for international partnership by participating in various mechanisms for global interface (e.g., attending conferences worldwide). This is a potential boon to psychology because it exposes them to new information in research and applied psychology. However, due to limited financial ability, many forego the chances available to them.

Institutions often network with both local and international agencies. For example, Lifespring Counseling and Training Center, which employs psychologists, is contracted with several U.N. agencies (e.g., Habitat, UNICEF, UNON) to offer psychosocial services to their staff in Kenya. Also, Lifespring psychologists facilitate psychological interventions for several local and international NGOs based in Kenya, such as stress management. Over time, Lifespring psychologists have been sent on international missions as consultants under contract from and on behalf of World Vision International, UNICEF, and UNON. Lifespring is also heavily involved in the affairs of KPsyA.

More broadly, the KPsyA and the APA are currently involved in collaborative efforts, whereby KPsyA and the APA are exploring a possible partnership to build the capacity of NGOs in Sub-Sahara Africa to develop, implement, and evaluate programs geared toward HIV prevention and AIDS orphans. Kenya and Uganda have been selected as the pilot locations to start this partnership. The first visit by APA representatives to Kenya will be in early 2004, and will be a landmark event in the history of the KPsyA and of Kenya itself.

Amani Counseling and Training Center offers diplomas in counseling in liaison with the University College of Cork, Ireland. The two have an exchange program: Students from Cork visit Amani and receive supervized field experiences in Kenya, while staff from Amani visit Cork and take advanced coursework in Ireland. The Kenya Association of Professional Counselors and Durham University in the U.K. have a mutually beneficial research and training relationship. While Durham University is rich in theory and research traditions, the Kenya Association of Professional Counselors can offer technical expertise based on tested local applications. By consulting with a number of foreign psychologists, the Trauma Response Organization was able to carry out research on infant survivors of the 1998 terrorist bombblast in Kenya.

In addition, many local and regional organizations affiliate with national and international associations; for example, the KPsyA is affiliated with the APA. Some members of KPsyA are individual members of APA, and also of the Association of American Christian Counselors, British Psychological Society, and International Society for Traumatic Studies.

Kenyan psychologists are encouraged to continue their education. There are many opportunities to pursue continuing education through universities, hospitals, psychological associations, the U.N., and NGOs. Typically, limited allowances are provided that enable psychologists to attend conferences, seminars, and workshops at the national and international level in order to obtain further training. For example, U.N. stress counselors hold conferences and workshops each year in different parts of the world. These counselors are invited to present papers on various psychological topics that are relevant for the countries where they are stationed.

As previously stated, Kenya has no national, regional, or local entity that regulates professional psychology through legal statute. However, there are by-laws and ethical guidelines put forth by individual psychological and counseling associations that attempt to constrain the unethical psychological practice of their own members. These guidelines have been adopted from the West. As a result, many psychologists and professional counselors refer to the ethical guidelines published by the APA and British Psychological Society, among others. However, these guidelines are routinely reviewed by the individual associations for their suitability at mid-year and annual meetings. Likewise, the NGO Council, which is a consortium of NGOs, provides and updates legal and ethical guidelines that regulate the counseling activities of providers within NGO organizations. Regrettably, because no legislation currently exists to govern the professional practice of psychology, the lack of such legislation has had a negative impact on the effectiveness of psychological and counseling associations in Kenya. For example, other professional associations, such as those for accountants, architects, and lawyers, are recognized by Parliament and have established strong working relationships with the government. To be a force for change in Kenya, psychological and

counseling associations must create a similar partnership with the national government.

2.4 FUTURE CHALLENGES AND PROSPECTS

The discipline of psychology faces a number of challenges in terms of education and training as well as professional practice. With regard to education and training, universities tend to have a narrow perspective of psychology. Only counseling and educational psychology are offered. Hence, there is a need to develop a more diversified faculty capable of offering courses in other specialties of the discipline. Kenya's Commission for Higher Education takes inordinately long to commission proposed programs, psychology being a case in point; a more rapid review process is needed.

There is a grave shortage of instructional resources, such as current textbooks and journals, and scientific literature is not available or easily accessible at some universities. Likewise, Internet services are exceedingly expensive for most universities, costing up to $0.13 per minute, which is high by Kenyan standards.

Many students who want to pursue degrees in psychology suffer from financial hardships, and more scholarships to support these students are needed.

The professional practice of psychology in Kenya has been constrained by a number of issues, such as the lack of legislation governing the standards of training in psychology and a licensing board to regulate professional practice, and irregular funding to maintain the viability of institutions and organizations, which may explain why so few work in these settings. At the Agha Khan Hospital, psychologists are currently responsible for two caseloads of patients; there is short supply of competent and experienced psychologists and professional counselors. As stated in the overview, many counselors are not adequately equipped to respond effectively to more severe psychosocial crises that arise in the community. As a result, there is mistrust in certain quarters about the profession.

A market is not readily available to psychologists or professional counselors. They must become proactive and inform the government and public of their potential contribution to the well-being of Kenyan society. For example, there is a widespread belief that psychological concerns can be adequately addressed within the family or by society; this assumption needs to be challenged. Moreover, the general public is not well-informed about the nature and range of psychological services. For example, more than 85% of Kenyans are Christians (National Council for Population and Development, 1998). Some Christians believe that spiritual matters encompass psychological issues and, hence, prefer to address these issues with ministers and fellow believers, as well as through the reading of scripture. These Christians do not view counseling as an option for the solution or management of their psychological problems.

Psychologists and professional counselors are still trying to find their sociopolitical role in the country. An example of such a role might be to work with the newly elected democratic government to alleviate corruption by nurturing honesty among the population. This role, among others, has not been appreciated either by the govern-ment or society, perhaps because neither fully understands the work of psychologists and professional counselors. As a result, the government does not recognize, let alone consult with psychologists at policy-making levels. The public, too, is not fully aware of the benefits of psychosocial support services, although its awareness at this point in time is greater than ever before.

In addition, psychologists and professional counselors are faced with a wide range of issues and concerns in their daily practice. Key among these issues is the relevance of currently used theories and techniques within the sociocultural context of Kenya. How can cultural and religious traditions be integrated into the discipline and profession of psychology without compromising its fundamental identity or corpus of knowledge? At a more basic level, there are questions surrounding the role and responsibilities of psychologists, how these differ from professional counselors and social workers, and how various allied health professionals can coordinate the delivery of services in distinct health-care settings. Of course, the limited scope of education and training along with the absence of ethical guidelines and legal standards make it difficult for psychologists to practice competently, particularly in a country facing so many psychosocial challenges.

If the discipline and profession of psychology are to serve Kenya more effectively, they must address a number of issues. A code of ethical principles and conduct at the national level as well as legislation designed to regulate training and professional practice must be formed. More meetings of psychological associations should be arranged at which researchers and practitioners can share information and offer each other support. Not only should associations encourage membership, but they should also offer journals and newsletters, along the lines of *Psychology Beat*, published by the KPsyA. Associations must also function as a bridge between government and universities in setting standards and monitoring the quality of education and training.

Universities should expand their course offerings to include clinical psychology, industrial–organizational psychology, psychometric assessment, research design and statistical analysis, and theories of learning and personality, as well as advanced courses in program evaluation and psychotherapeutic methods. Campus-based clinics need to be developed, like those at the United States International University–Africa and Daystar University, which would serve as practicum training sites as well as offer counseling services to the general public. In addition to coursework, universities should expand the number of certificates, diplomas, and degree programs.

Affordable Internet services for psychologists and psychology students must become a priority. Through the information super-highway, psychologists and psychology students will have access to contemporary literature on psychological theory, research, and practice as well as have opportunities to liaise with psychologists in other countries via their professional associations. Information technology will have an increasingly important role to play in ensuring that Kenyan psychologists are prepared to meet the challenges of the 21st century.

The future of psychology looks optimistic. With a new government having formed in December, 2002, and still blazing with energy and a renewed vision

for positive change, the future of psychology can only be better.

REFERENCES

Kithuka, M. (1985). *Content and structure of teacher education programs in selected teacher education institutions.* Unpublished master's thesis, University of Ibadan, Ibadan, Nigeria.

Koinange, J. W. (2001). Psychology strides forward in Kenya. *Psychology International, 12,* 1–3.

Koinange, J. W., & Asakhulu, N. M. (2003). *Assessment of the development and status of the discipline of psychology in the institutions of higher education in Kenya.* Unpublished manuscript.

National Council for Population and Development. (1998). *Demographic and health survey.* Calverton, MD: Macro International.

Okatcha, F. M., Omar, I. M., & Kariuki, P. W. (1989). *Teaching and psychological research.* Nairobi: Eastern and Southern Africa Publishers.

IMPORTANT PUBLICATIONS

Bali, S. K., & Ingule, F. O. (1988). *Psychology: Educational statistics.* Nairobi: University of Nairobi Press.

Bugguss, M. (2002). *A date with Jesus.* Nairobi: Creative.

Gichinga, E. M. (1999). *Basic counseling skills.* Nairobi: Faith Communications.

Gichinga, E. M. (2003). *Pre-marital counseling: A counseling guide.* Makuyu, Kenya: Don Bosco Printing Press.

Kiminyo, D. M. (1992). *Child development.* Nairobi: Educational Research.

Koinange, J. W. (2001). Psychology strides forward in Kenya. *Psychology International, 12,* 1–3.

Munavi, K. M. (1988). *Education: General psychology.* Nairobi: University of Nairobi Press.

Mwiria, K., & Wamahiu, S. P. (1995). *Issues in educational research in Africa.* Nairobi: East African Educational.

Ndirangu, M. J. (2000). *Youth in danger: A handbook for teachers, students, parents, pastors, and community workers.* Nairobi,: Uzima Press.

Okatcha, F. M., Omar, I., & Kariuki, P. W. (1989). *Teaching and psychological research.* Nairobi: Eastern and Southern Africa Publishers.

Talitwala, E. (2002). *When death strikes: A counseling guide.* Nairobi: Uzima Press.

CHAPTER 3

Psychology in Nigeria: Origins, Current Status and Future

JAMES T. GIRE

James T. Gire received a bachelor's degree from the University of Jos, a master's from the London School of Economics, and a doctorate in experimental psychology from McMaster University, Canada. He is currently a professor of psychology (colonel) in the Department of Psychology and Philosophy at the Virginia Military Institute. His research interests are in the areas of adult development and aging, cross-cultural social psychology, and substance use and misuse, especially alcohol and tobacco. He has published articles in more than half a dozen peer-review journals, including the Canadian Journal of Behavioral Science, Journal of Social Psychology, Psychology of Addictive Behaviors, *and* Substance Use and Misuse. *He also has published a book with Frank Eyetsemitan on adult development and aging in the developing world through Greenwood/Praeger. He is the immediate past president of the Virginia Social Science Association and*

current editor of the Virginia Social Science Journal.

3.1 OVERVIEW

Psychology is relatively new to Nigeria, as it is to most other countries in the developing world. Initial efforts at establishing psychology in Nigeria began with the offering of psychology courses in departments of education at the few universities in the country. The main areas of psychology covered in these departments and colleges of education were counseling and educational psychology. In fact, some of the earliest psychologists in Nigeria were British-educated professors who specialized in psychology or were exposed to the discipline during their training. Psychology is said to have officially started as an academic discipline in 1964 when the first department of psychology was established at the University of Nigeria, Nsukka, with 16 students and two lecturers (Olomolaiye, 1985).

Not surprisingly, given its antecedents in Nigeria, psychology emerged from a department of education. It may have taken even longer for this first department to become established had it not been for a fortuitous convergence of two academics: J. O. Anowi and Carl Frost. Anowi was a developmental psychologist teaching at the department of education and a tireless advocate for the establishment of an independent department of psychology. Frost, a psychologist from Michigan State University, was deputy vice chancellor (vice president) of the University of Nigeria at the time (Uzoka, 1989). Counseling and educational psychology continue to be popular areas of specialization in faculties and colleges of education in Nigeria. However, beginning with the first department, psychology's identity in Nigeria has been that of a social science discipline (Obot & Gire, 1995).

Five years later, in 1969 a second department was opened at the University of Lagos where, for some years, a number of psychology courses had been offered in the core sciences. Three more departments of psychology were established in the 1970s at the universities of Jos and Ibadan (1976), and the then University of Ife (now Obafemi Awolowo University) in 1977. In addition, the University of Benin offered a master's degree in clinical psychology at the department of psychiatry in 1975. There was a lull in the growth of departments from the late 1970s through the 1980s until a surge in the establishment of new universities in Nigeria led to the creation of more departments of psychology. From a modest number of 13 universities in the early 1980s, Nigeria today has 49 universities, 6 of which are owned by private entities that were finally allowed to operate universities in the late 1990s. The federal and state governments claim ownership of the remaining 43 universities. In addition, there are 15 colleges of education that award bachelor's degrees, mainly in education (Joint Admissions and Matriculation Board [JAMB], 2002). There are 19 departments of psychology in Nigerian universities), each of which offers a bachelor's degree in psychology, and about half that number offer graduate programs, especially at the master's level. The program at the University of Benin is specifically designed to train graduate students in psychology and to provide psychological services in hospital settings through the department of mental health.

Despite what appears to be a steady growth in the number of established departments of psychology in Nigeria, the discipline has not kept pace with the rapid expansion by other social sciences. Almost all of the liberal arts and science universities in Nigeria have departments of economics, political science, and sociology as a matter of course. It is encouraging that a number of universities have recently expressed interest in establishing new departments of psychology; however, these efforts are sometimes hampered by the cost of equipping the mandatory psychology laboratory, procedural delays, and by the lack of qualified staff (Obot, 1996).

In 1988, in a survey of student admissions and staffing at the quarter-century mark of the existence of psychology in Nigeria, Uzoka (1989) found that there were only 837 undergraduates, 113 graduate students, and 67 lecturers in all departments of psychology that year. By 1988, six of the seven departments in existence at the time had awarded bachelor's degrees to 2,034 candidates. The average number of faculty was approximately 10 per department, most of whom had received their degrees from European and North American universities. It is imperative that an adequate appraisal of the development of psychology in Nigeria deal with growth, not only in terms of the number of independent psychology departments but also on the functional status of psychologists actively engaged in various domains of professional practice.

There are very few psychologists in Nigeria. It is difficult to arrive at a realistic estimate of the number of psychologists for a variety of reasons. Obot (1996) put the number of psychologists in active practice in Nigeria at "several hundred." In a recent survey of a sample of psychology lecturers and graduate students of psychology at Nigerian universities, Gire (2003) obtained a figure ranging from 720 to 40,000. The estimate of 40,000 psychologists was an outlier and is most certainly incorrect. When that was removed from the estimate, the next highest number was 12,000, also represented by only one respondent. Aside from the two outliers, none of the other estimates was higher than 7,000. Thus, it is safe to conclude that there could not be more than a few thousand active psychologists in Nigeria. This is a small number in a country with an estimated population of 120 million. Even at the optimistic number of 7,000, it means that there are about 58 psychologists per 100,000 citizens, an overwhelming number of whom work in major urban centers. Two factors mainly account for the difficulty in estimating the number of psychologists in Nigeria. The first is that it is difficult to define who qualifies to hold

the title of psychologist. Second, there is no statutory body responsible for regulating psychology as a profession.

The Nigerian Psychological Association (NPA) is the body that represents the professional interests of psychologists. This body was founded in 1984 with the merger of the Nigerian Psychological Society, which had a high proportion of its membership from departments and colleges of education, and the Nigerian Association of Psychologists, founded by a dissident group of "real" psychologists (i.e., those with bachelor's and graduate degrees in psychology). Thus, there seemed to be some disagreement between people who regarded themselves as psychologists. However, this appeared to have been resolved with the creation of the NPA. At the inaugural meeting that unified the two associations, a new constitution was adopted. Full membership in the NPA is now open only to those "with at least a master's degree or equivalent from recognized universities" (Nigerian Psychological Association [NPA], 1984, p. 4). Even though the association resolved to hold annual meetings at which papers are presented and the association's business is discussed, there are some years in which no convention is held. The association also publishes the *Nigerian Journal of Psychology* (Obot & Gire, 1995).

Aside from this umbrella organization, associations have been formed that aim to bring together professionals in various specializations of psychology. These are analogous to most of the divisions of the American Psychological Association (APA), without the kind of central coordination provided by the APA. Notable among these are the Nigerian Association of Clinical Psychologists, the Nigerian

Association of Industrial-Organization Psychologists, the Environment and Behavior Association, and the Association of Educational Psychologists. Unfortunately, some of these associations are inactive for lengthy periods of time.

Psychologists work in concert with a number of other professionals, particularly physicians and psychiatrists. This is because, outside of academia, psychologists in Nigeria are most likely to be found in the psychiatric departments of major federal and state hospitals and teaching hospitals. There are many more physicians than psychologists in Nigeria, and the influence of the former is undoubtedly enhanced by the fact that medicine has a greater social recognition as a legitimate profession. On average, physicians in hospital settings earn up to three times more than psychologists due to the separate pay structure for medical personnel (i.e., physicians, pharmacists, and nurses). Thus, workers with a degree in psychology, especially if they lack graduate-level training, earn less than nurses. In university settings, psychiatrists also earn more than psychologists because the salaries of psychiatrists come from two sources: the university and the federal or state ministries of health, which support the teaching hospitals in which psychiatrists and other medical faculty are affiliated. The number of psychologists may be closer to that of psychiatrists, but the spread of psychologists across other spheres in society gives psychiatrists an advantage in both numbers and status. Given the small number of psychologists and the fact that psychology has yet to establish a foothold as a viable profession, psychologists are spread thin across many domains, and their visibility and impact are thereby minimized. Outside of hospital settings, psychologists enjoy a status comparable to their counterparts in other disciplines. This matter will be addressed more comprehensively in the section on psychological practice.

3.2 EDUCATION AND TRAINING

Undergraduate training in all academic disciplines in Nigeria is controlled and regulated by the National Universities Commission, and psychology is not an exception. Admission into a university to study psychology requires at least a credit (a credit would be the equivalent of at least a *C* or higher in the American system) in English language and biology, credits in at least three other subjects, and passing the mathematics section of the General Certificate of Education examination, which is equivalent to the external exams taken by high-school seniors in the U.S. (e.g., the ACT or SAT, advanced placement tests). The psychology curriculum, adopted during the 1991–1992 academic year, is highly quantitative and is geared toward graduate education and practical application upon completion of the bachelor's degree. The early 1990s also marked the beginning of the process of accrediting departments. What the new curriculum did was to introduce reasonably uniform standards for undergraduate education in Nigeria. For example, a psychology laboratory with a predetermined list of equipment is required by every department of psychology. This is a difficult condition to fulfill and few departments have what would qualify as a functional laboratory. This requirement also presents another problem: it does not provide the flexibility to make the frequent technical improvements that are necessary for a department to avoid being saddled with obsolete equipment.

Students begin their freshman year in psychology with 12 credit hours and are required to take up to 30 credits hours in each of the three remaining years. Table 3.1 contains an example of the range of courses offered in the 1997–1998 Undergraduate Handbook of the University of Ibadan. The curricula is comparable across the universities in Nigeria. The main area where there could be a noticeable departure between courses offered at the University of Ibadan and other psychology departments is in physiological psychology. Universities such as Lagos have courses in neuropsychology, an area that is not well represented in the Table. In addition to psychology courses, students are expected to take external elec-tives from at least two departments within the college, which includes departments of economics, geography, political science, and sociology.

Every functioning psychology depart-ment is supposed to be equipped with a psychology laboratory. Because the required list of laboratory equipment was drawn up many years ago, some items have questionable pedagogical value in prepar-ing students to engage in contemporary social-science research. A list of some of the equipment and tests in the laboratory at the University of Ibadan include: Pursuit Rotor Test, O'Connor Finger Dexterity Test, O'Connor Tweezer Test, Purdue Pegboard Test, Grooved Pegboard Test, Minnesota Manual Dexterity Test, Depth Perception Test, memory drum, portable two-field, color mixer, mirror tracer, one-

TABLE 3.1
Number of Psychology Courses Offered in a Typical Undergraduate Curriculum

First-Year Courses	Second-Year Courses	Third-Year Courses	Fourth-Year Courses
Introduction to Psycho-Biological Bases of Behavior	Learning Processes	Psychological Aspects of Disability	Correctional Psychology
Introduction to Personality	Abnormal Psychology	Psychology of Substance Abuse	Psychology of Adolescence
Quantitative Methods in Psychology	Developmental Psychology	Child Psychopathology	Psychological Testing and Test Construction
History of Experimental Psychology	Social Psychology	Statistical Methods in Psychology	Clinical Psychology II
	Physiological Psychology I	Clinical Psychology	Practicum in Psychotherapy
	General Experimental Psychology	Personality Assessment	Medical Psychology
	Personality Theories of Deception	Language and Thought	Social Perception
	Social Psychology of Race and Ethnic Group Relations	Psychology of Women	Psychology of Union Management Relations
	Industrial and Personnel Psychology	Research in Social Psychology	Attitudes
		Psychology of Social Work and Social Welfare	Psychological Aspects of Leadership
		Group Dynamics	Organizational Psychology
		Consumer Psychology	Honors Project
		Motivation in the World of Work	

Note. From the *Department of Psychology Undergraduate Handbook* (University of Ibadan, Nigeria, 1997).

way mirror, galvanic skin response meter, and audio biofeedback machine (University of Ibadan, 1997). Thus, in terms of the sheer volume of course offerings, psychology undergraduates are exposed to more courses and practical aspects of the discipline than their counterparts in other social and behavioral sciences at other Nigerian universities.

Whereas undergraduate training has been streamlined, graduate training in psychology is more variable. There are significant differences in requirements for admission as well as in the content of courses. Committees within each department are responsible for determining the curriculum for advanced degrees in most of the traditional specializations in psychology. However, all programs contain a core of course requirements and practical experiences. Based on a review of programs in several departments, most show general agreement in the objectives of graduate training in psychology: to develop a cadre of well-trained psychologists for careers in professional psychology, to train researchers in psychological science, and to contribute to the national development of Nigeria.

Classroom lectures are the primary method of teaching psychology at the undergraduate level. Due to funding problems, many departments do not have the technological tools that are readily available in the developed world. However, resourceful professors still incorporate some audio-visual aids and class demonstrations in their classes. The typical undergraduate class is fairly large; it is not uncommon to find in excess of 100 students in first- and second-year classes.

Most professors use textbooks as the main source for class materials. There are very few books written by Nigerian psychologists and for the Nigerian market. Whenever possible, professors adopt books written by psychologists, especially those from the U.S., that have international student editions. Due to funding problems at most universities, there are very few current journals. From time to time, however, certain departments obtain a journal grant from the APA. For example, the University of Jos was awarded such a grant a number of years ago whereby the department received 5-year subscriptions to flagship journals of the APA, including the *Journal of Personality and Social Psychology* and *Psychological Bulletin*. Other departments have also benefited from journal grants. Based on the unmet needs of other departments across the country, recipient departments generously share these resources with their colleagues elsewhere.

The most basic requirement for acceptance into a graduate program in psychology is a bachelor's degree in the subject, although one department makes an allowance for applicants with degrees in other disciplines who may "only be admitted as occasional students in the first instance. Such candidates will be required to make up the deficiency by [taking] prescribed courses in psychology" (University of Lagos, n.d., p. 2). Many candidates without a bachelor's degree in psychology are physicians who seek a master's degree in clinical psychology; others are those with bachelor's degrees from business schools who pursue graduate studies in industrial–organizational psychology. Some departments have instituted graduate diploma programs mainly for candidates from other disciplines as a means of preparing them for graduate work in psychology.

Although graduate programs have been established in most specialties of psychology and are officially listed by departments as operational, the dearth of qualified faculty has rendered many graduate programs inactive. In fact, in colleges of social sciences, psychology tends to have the least number of graduate students. The duration of master's programs is one or two years depending on the area of study. Programs in clinical psychology require an additional 6-month supervised internship. In industrial–organizational psychology, students are required to participate in a field experience as part of their training (Obot, 1996).

Only a handful of graduate students are enrolled in doctoral programs. Doctoral study in psychology is the most varied across departments. Requirements for admission into Ph.D. programs at Nigerian universities have increasingly integrated British and American traditions. For many years, no coursework was required of students enrolled in doctoral programs. All a student needed to do was carry out and successfully defend a research project under the direction of a faculty member or committee of the faculty in that student's department. In some cases, a student was also required to present seminars during his or her first few years in the program. Much has changed of late. Today, many departments include coursework in the doctoral curriculum. This shift has come about because of the greater diversity in the training of faculty and the need to produce well-rounded scientist-practitioners (Obot & Gire, 1995).

3.3 SCOPE OF PSYCHOLOGICAL PRACTICE

At present, the scope of psychological practice in Nigeria remains limited. At a superficial level, it appears as if the low impact of psychology is due to the scarcity of professional psychologists and, hence, the lack of available psychological services. However, the problem is much more fundamental and may be the result of the perceived irrelevance of psychology by the general population. Viewed in historical terms, this circumstance is not peculiar to Nigeria. Even in Europe and the U.S., where the synthesis between psychology and society has become a reality, this was not always the case. Soon after its foundation, psychology had an image problem, partly because of its roots in philosophy and its link with pseudosciences such as phrenology, and from both "association with the occult and practices of spiritualism, and from the influx of psychoanalytic theory" (Benjamin, 1986, p. 945). Given this context, the public was unaware of the scientific basis for this new discipline. Psychologists, in turn, were concerned about "the public's equation of psychology with clairvoyance, mind reading, and spiritualism" (Benjamin, 1986, p. 941). In order to modify this public image, the APA undertook extensive public campaigns in newspapers, magazines, and popular books, as well as public exhibitions to modify the public's perception of the discipline and profession.

Medicine is one of the few areas in which psychological services have had an impact in Nigeria. However, in the Nigerian case, psychology today appears to be caught in the transition between its initial establishment and full acceptance. This is partly due to the fact that infectious and parasitic diseases still predominate as major causes of death. For example, even though tremendous progress has been made in recent years, the infant mortality rate is 81 per 1000 live births, life expectancy is 50 years, expenditures on health are below optimal levels, the ratio of health care workers to the population is low, and nutritional requirements for both mother and child are grossly inadequate (World Health Organization, 1999). At the same time, there is a growing concern over the so-called diseases of civilization. In the last two decades, diseases such as cancer, cirrhosis of the liver, heart disease, hypertension, mental illness, and accidents have contributed significantly to morbidity and mortality (Osuntokun, 1987). These health problems involve lifestyle issues that clearly have a psychological base.

Not surprisingly, one of the important areas in which Nigerian psychologists are providing professional services is in health care. Two health-related areas in which psychologists are involved heavily are in the training of medical students and the provision of mental health services. Obot (1988) conducted a survey of the participation of social scientists in all 12 universities that operated a medical college at the time. He found that all but 10 of 12 schools had at least one social scientist on its faculty. Of particular interest is the level of involvement of psychologists. Of the 19 social scientists that were appointed to medical schools, 10 were psychologists. These psychologists were hired mainly into departments of community health and social medicine and into psychiatry and mental health. In terms of the relative amount of time spent in different activities, Obot's survey showed that psychologists spent 33.8% of their time teaching, 25.0% delivering clinical health care, 18.8% conducting both basic and applied research, 17.0% consulting, and 5.5% on administration. The specific courses that psychologists taught in these schools included introductory psychology, medical psychology, sociocultural

factors in health and disease, social epidemiology, special topics in mental health, and statistics. The time allotted to teaching courses was generally believed to be inadequate and limited to the preclinical years of medical education (Obot, 1988).

Although a few psychologists are involved in medical education, these individuals have not yet attained equality with their physician colleagues. The two main problems reported by psychologists in the Obot (1988) study were perceived inequality with their medical colleagues and a belief that medical administrators were not interested in or appreciative of their work. An encouraging finding was the perception that students did show interest in the contribution of the psychologists. Interestingly, despite these problems, almost all the psychologists reported that they could have worked in traditional psychology departments within the university. They chose instead to work in medical schools because of the perceived opportunity to do research, receive high salaries, engage in clinical practice, and interact with other health professionals.

Outside of colleges and schools of medicine, a relatively large number of psychologists in the health care sector work at general medical and psychiatric hospitals. A noticeable proportion of them also work with other mental health professionals as psychotherapists and counselors. It is difficult to estimate the number of psychologists working in medical and psychiatric hospitals because there has been no survey of psychologists working in these settings. As stated earlier, there are no established procedures for licensing and certification; therefore, arriving at an estimate other than through survey research is very challenging. Private clinical practice is still rare, although there is an increasing demand for psychological services, especially in large urban centers.

Unfortunately, there has been little improvement in the employment of psychologists in the health care sector since the surveys of the late 1980s. The only encouraging development in recent years is the increasing mention by policy makers of the role of psychology in both physical and mental health. Even here, no significant progress has been made to modify the observation by Uzoka (1989), who stated, "It is a sad commentary on the nature of our national life that ministers will declare their recognition of psychological factors in physical and emotional illness, yet, at the stage of policy evolution or implementation, restricted interests are permitted to hijack national planning and thus eliminate meaningful and fruitful contributions to the programmes" (p. 98).

One area in which psychologists were surprisingly absent for many years, but seem to be making advances of late, is in substance-abuse research and treatment. Substance abuse has become a major health and social problem in Nigeria, and is now viewed by government as a major impediment to national development. Many social scientists, with psychologists at the forefront, argue that the phenomenal rise in alcohol and other drug problems in Nigeria is linked to rapid social change (Obot & Gire, 1995). Consequently, the problem is receiving the attention of many professionals, especially psychologists, psychiatrists, and other social scientists who are concerned with the welfare of Nigerians, particularly youth. A group of social scientists at the University of Jos established the Centre for Research and Information on Substance Abuse with the aim of disseminating information on substance-related problems. Today, that center is registered in both Nigeria and the U.S. as a nonprofit organization and is the leading source of information on substance abuse in Africa. To provide an outlet for research, the center also publishes a peer-reviewed journal, *African Journal of Drug and Alcohol Studies*, and other informational brochures and pamphlets.

Another area in which psychology has been introduced is political mobilization. One of the persistent problems of national development in Nigeria has been the inability to build and sustain political structures. Nigeria has been under civil rule for only 13 of its 43 years as a sovereign nation. After several failed attempts at democratic governance, many Nigerians have come to regard political instability as the major cause of economic underdevelopment. On this, even the military leaders were in agreement. Thus, in 1986, the military government set up a political bureau to, among other things, "review Nigeria's political history and identify the basic problems which have led to our failure in the past and suggest ways of resolving and coping with these problems" (Federal Republic of Nigeria, 1987, p. 11). The significance of this development was that, for the first time in the history of Nigeria, psychologists played a visible role in addressing a national issue. This was manifested in at least two ways. First, a psychologist was one of the 17 members of the bureau and was expected to provide input from a psychological perspective. Second, the NPA was one of the bodies invited and sponsored by the bureau to provide professional insights and expertise on the psychological variables involved in political participation. At the resulting conference that was organized on the "Roots and Nature of Alienation and the Perception of Politics in Nigeria," psychologists in Nigeria were invited to present their views, which were later incorporated into the final report to the bureau.

Unfortunately, the prevailing opinion among psychologists was that their contributions did not receive the attention they deserved in the final report. However, the mere recognition that attitudes and values of political leaders and other person variables are important in understanding political behavior created a noticeable impact and introduced the concept of attitude change into Nigerian political discourse (Obot & Gire, 1995). For example, in a 1989 speech to a cross-section of influential political and business leaders, President Babangida declared, "Our dilemma today is that... structural changes are yet to be matched with behavioral changes. This means that we need democratic attitudes to match democratic structures" (Babangida, 1989, p. 9). The president proceeded to challenge scholars to conduct studies that are "committed to eliciting the content of democratic beliefs among Nigerians from various demographic groups" (Babangida, 1989, p. 10). Furthermore, in a speech to the NPA later that same year, Babangida called upon psychologists to make available data on the prevalent attitudes of Nigerians in order to help planners make informed decisions. Thus, although there still are only a handful of Nigerian psychologists working in the political realm, the recognition of psychology's relevance to politics has led to psychologists becoming involved in the Center for Democratic Studies that was created within the executive branch of government. A doctoral-level psychologist works at the center.

A few psychologists can be found in industrial settings such as personnel offices. There are also psychologists working in research centers engaged in research on a diverse array of issues (Obot, 1996). A few psychologists can also be found in the armed forces (including the Nigerian Defense Academy), in schools, and in prisons (Gire, 2003). Psychologists have begun to complain that nonpsychologists are being assigned to perform services in different settings that require psychological expertise due to the mistaken assumption that services provided by psychologists could be capably performed by almost any person with a decent education.

Finally, in addition to the scope of psychological services, it is also interesting to sketch a personal profile of who practices psychology in Nigeria. In a survey conducted during the 1994 annual meeting of the NPA to assess the problems experienced by psychologists in their daily work, the organizers distributed questionnaires to all those in attendance and who had maintained membership in the association at the time of the meeting. Of the more than 20 participants, only one was female, a finding that accurately represents the situation in Nigeria. Most of the respondents were between 35–54 years of age and were in intermediate faculty positions at universities. A majority of respondents had doctoral degrees; only five were master's level psychologists. The average number of years of work in psychology was 12, almost all of which were spent in teaching and research. These findings suggest that a majority of Nigerian psychologists are employed by universities, where they are required to teach, conduct research, and, in the case of clinicians, deliver treatment at the university hospital. Thus, the prototype of a Nigerian psychologist is that of a mid-level male academic/practitioner with an advanced degree and many years of experience. Though their numbers do not compare favorably with their counterparts in the developed world, the people who practice psychology in Nigeria appear to be highly qualified in their fields, and most of these have received at least part of their training in Europe or North America.

There appear to be two main impediments to the practice of psychology in Nigeria. The first is the absence of clear and established ethical guidelines that would regulate the activities of psychologists. Fortunately, a member of the executive committee of the NPA has indicated that a committee has been named and charged with the task of developing an ethical code. The other impediment is related to the dearth of locally developed theories that would guide both research and practice. Failing that, the "imported" theories ought at least to have been validated and deemed appropriate for the Nigerian context. Unfortunately, this has not been done. Thus, there is a preponderance of "foreign," largely American, theories that are uncritically applied to dramatically different contexts and settings. This issue should be of concern to both Nigerian psychologists and the developed world in general.

The developing world constitutes approximately three-fourths of the entire world. If one of psychology's goals is to establish so-called universal laws of behavior, it is imperative that psychologists address the matter of external validity because these laws may not apply to areas of the world that lie outside their range of convenience. This task provides a golden opportunity for mutually beneficial collaboration between Nigerian psychologists and their counterparts in Europe and North America to extend the applicability of theories and interventions developed in the heavily industrialized world. Of course, Nigerian and other psychologists in the developing world must also begin to construct indigenous theories, methodologies, and practices.

3.4 FUTURE CHALLENGES AND PROSPECTS

The future looks bright for psychology in Nigeria. This view is based on a number of factors, three of the most pertinent of which are societal need, a growing acceptance and positive view of psychology, and advances in information technology. Nigeria is a developing country with an estimated population of 120 million that is undergoing rapid social change. The military regime had begun to appreciate the need for psychological services 15 years ago. With the transition to democracy that occurred in 1999 and an increasingly complex economy, the need for psychological expertise is even more acute. However, the number of practicing psychologists in Nigeria is grossly inadequate. This need creates an opportunity for psychologists not only to increase their numbers, but also to tailor their skills to the most appropriate needs of society. Areas in which psychologists are poised to make an impact include the legal system (including prisons), community development, business organizations, and responding to individual needs through private practice.

The other opportunity that Nigerian psychologists must capitalize upon is the public's image of psychology. In a survey, Obot (1993) found that respondents generally viewed psychology positively. "Most respondents associated psychologists with testing, behavioral research and the solution of minor 'problems of living,' but not the treatment of mental illness. A strong belief in the popular notion that psychologists 'read people's minds' was also displayed" (p. 1). Although some myths such as the ability to read minds need to be dispelled, the acceptance that psychologists provide solutions to problems of living suggests that the public might respond positively to psychological services if they became available. Thus, people with psychological skills appear to have a large base of potential clients who think positively about the information and assistance psychologists are able to offer to them.

This positive image of psychologists is not limited to the general public. As stated earlier, some of the problems experienced by psychologists who are attached to medical schools were based on their perceptions of status inequality and the lack of interest in their services by their medical counterparts. Based on the belief that the successful application of psychological knowledge within the legal system would be dependent on attorneys and other legal professionals, Ojiji and Alaedu (1995) conducted a survey of attorneys to gauge their knowledge about and attitudes toward psychology, and their willingness to involve psychologists in the administration of justice. They found that lawyers had a broad knowledge and generally favorable attitudes toward psychologists. Furthermore, 80% of those surveyed expressed readiness to work with psychologists in judicial administration. With members of the legal profession showing a readiness to partner with psychologists,

Nigerian psychologists have good prospects of making inroads into this vital segment of society.

The other opportunity for the growth of psychology involves the enormous possibilities brought about by advances in technology generally, but especially in information technology. The Internet and World Wide Web made it possible to instantly access information that was hitherto very difficult to obtain. This has implications for the acquisition of knowledge, the exchange of ideas, and interaction with a vast network of colleagues from around the globe. Many texts, including journals, are now available online and, even though these come at a cost, with the assistance from some colleagues with greater resources, more information is reaching students and colleagues in less affluent societies. Technology also opens opportunities for peer consultation and mentoring. The author currently maintains such a relationship with a handful of colleagues in Nigeria. These new technologies and the opportunities for communication they provide are bound to increase the breadth and depth of collaborations, and raise the quality of professional knowledge and skills of Nigerian psychologists.

Despite these prospects, psychologists must contend with enormous challenges so that this potential is realized. One of the most important of these is the availability of personnel. Nigeria's economic decline, coupled with several years of political instability brought about by, at times, repressive military regimes, have led many highly qualified psychologists to leave Nigeria for better opportunities abroad, a phenomenon popularly referred to as the "brain drain." Even those who remained have been hobbled by the frequent closures of universities occasioned by the government's unwillingness to provide adequate funding for education. This has contributed to at least two pressing concerns. The few professional psychologists who provided services are no longer there, with the consequence that even fewer people can benefit from psychological services. More striking is the fact that, because these same psychologists were teaching at universities, their departure has curtailed the ability of universities to increase the numbers of both undergraduate and graduate students. Thus, there has been no significant increase in psychologists at a time when the need for their talents has grown substantially. The chance of realizing the opportunities identified earlier depend heavily on reversing this trend.

In addition, psychologists need to make a strong case for the value and role of psychology in the everyday experience and well-being of citizens. By themselves, the government and public are not likely to comprehend the many ways in which psychology can be of value to different facets of society. The NPA needs to take on this challenge and embark upon an extensive and sustained campaign to promote psychology as a discipline and profession that is relevant to the nation's well-being. This absence of strong professional advocacy has cost psychologists in the past; for example, assignments for which psychologists are suited have been given to political scientists. Uzoka (1989) called for the establishment of a psychologists' lobby to pressure and influence governments at the state and national levels, but this has yet to produce the desired outcomes.

Closely tied to the issue of advocacy for psychology is the need to create a career structure and job classification for psychol-

ogists. A profession or discipline is said to have a career structure when there is a clear hierarchy and an identifiable path for upward mobility to which members can aspire. A person just starting work as a welfare officer may begin as Welfare Officer II, could be promoted to the position of Welfare Officer I, then Senior Welfare Officer, and, ultimately, may be named Director of Welfare. Psychologists do not have this structure. When a psychologist is hired, his or her career fortunes are at the mercy of whoever may be in charge of the department in question, and, thus, may have an uncertain and frustrating vocational future. A structure similar to the one described above can provide a realistic level of aspiration and a realizable goal of fulfilled professional participation. Within clinical psychology, efforts have been undertaken that yielded meetings between the Nigerian Association of Clinical Psychologists and the minister of health. The goal was to place psychologists in government and industry in positions in which they would enjoy a fair salary relative to their counterparts in other professions. Lacking such a structure, few psychologists will be keen on contributing their expertise through jobs with the government or in industry due to the lack of defined opportunities for advancement.

One challenge to Nigerian psychology that has recently appeared, but which relates to the issue of contextual relevance, is the introduction of Sharia law in some of the northern states of Nigeria. When rigorously enforced, Sharia law discourages the interaction between men and women, especially if these exchanges are not formalized within a strict kinship network. As stated earlier, there are very few psychologists in Nigeria, but these few happen to be predominantly male. Restricting male–female interactions, as may be required by Sharia law, could potentially limit the delivery of much needed psychological service to a large segment of the population. Nigerian psychologists must find creative ways of providing these services without violating the religious convictions of their constituents.

Another challenge for Nigerian psychology is the need for a culturally relevant body of knowledge. Knowledge flows from experts, and where there are few experts or where poor training predominates, growth in knowledge is stymied. Uzoka (1989) considers the lack of guiding philosophies or theories in research as the most serious indictment of psychology in Nigeria. He argues that Nigerian psychology has been too dependent on Western models: "We have made no sustained efforts to put forward coherent philosophical or theoretical points of view that are Nigerian or, indeed, African. We have accepted the Western dogmas as final commentaries on man and the human condition" (Uzoka, 1989, p. 108). The problem that Uzoka identifies is not peculiar to psychology. The influence of Western paradigms have constricted other social sciences, but they have responded to this concern more systematically than has psychology.

The main point is not that Western concepts and methods should be avoided entirely. However, the uncritical acceptance of concepts and methods without testing their validity or appropriateness to the Nigerian situation is unacceptable. Thus, aside from carrying out new research, Nigerian psychologists should replicate existing research findings in order to determine whether they can be generalized in the Nigerian context. This effort should include the restandardization of most psychometric

tests. The lack of a culturally relevant knowledge base is, perhaps, responsible for the absence of books and monographs by Nigerian psychologists that have had a major impact in Nigeria. The only publication that has made a significant contribution is the edited book by Okpara (1985), *Psychological Strategies for National Development*. Interestingly, although this book was published by the NPA, its circulation is limited. Thus, for psychologists to fulfill the enormous potential that lies ahead, commitment to, and support for, research is critical.

This is at the core of the Nigerian challenge. If psychological knowledge is not deemed to be relevant to the developmental needs of the country, its growth will be stunted. Nigerian psychology must find a balance between maintaining its ties with mainstream psychology and addressing problems peculiar to its immediate situation. This is not an easy challenge and is aptly captured in the analysis by Bloom (1982):

> Psychology as a profession is exceptionally threatening: it is based upon the universalistic study of people. Yet its subject matter is immediately obvious... It is a rival for the demotic analysis of behavior. It cannot be safely ignored because it implicitly and overtly indicates the deficiencies of everyday "psychologizing." Yet, it also runs the risk of appearing aloof, irrelevant and elitist because it has to distance itself in order to function. Psychology is therefore caught in a politically difficult conflict: Either it is professionally distant and is regarded as indifferent to the problems of a developing society, or it is regarded as a dangerous rival for everyday phenomenology of social life. (p. 144)

Clearly, psychology has many contributions to make to Nigerian society. It is poised to experience phenomenal growth in the next quarter century. To do so, psychologists must come to terms with the seemingly conflicting roles of scientist and social change agent in a nation that is in dire need of a unifying sense of direction and purpose. Psychologists also need to increase the number and quality of professionals by improving and expanding departments of psychology, collaborating with their counterparts in other parts of the world, advocating for a career structure, and becoming ardent advocates of the potential that psychology holds for Nigeria.

REFERENCES

Babangida, I. B. (1989, July 17). Our dilemma. [Speech delivered at the second annual Guardian Lecture]. *The Guardian*, pp. 9–10.

Benjamin, L. T. (1986). Why don't they understand us? A history of psychology's public image. *American Psychologist, 41,* 941–946.

Bloom, L. (1982). Applying psychology in the Third World. *Bulletin of the British Psychological Society, 35,* 143–146.

Federal Republic of Nigeria. (1987). *Report of the Political Bureau*. Lagos: Author.

Gire, J. T. (2003). *A preliminary survey of the status of psychology in Nigeria*. Unpublished manuscript.

Joint Admissions and Matriculation Board (2002*). Guidelines for admissions to first degree courses in Nigerian universities 2003/2004 session*. Abuja, Nigeria: Author.

Nigerian Psychological Association. (1984). *The constitution of the Nigerian Psychological Association*. Lagos, Nigeria: Author.

Obot, I. S. (1988). Social science and medical education in Nigeria. *Social Science and Medicine, 26,* 1191–1196.

Obot, I. S. (1993). What do they think of us? The public image of psychology and psychologists in Nigeria. *Nigerian Journal of Basic and Applied Psychology, 3,* 1–9.

Obot, I. S. (1996). Country profile: Nigeria. *Psychology International, 7,* 4–5.

Obot, I. S., & Gire, J. T. (1995). Psychology and national development. *Nigerian Journal of Basic and Applied Psychology, 4,* 20–31.

Ojiji, O. O., & Alaedu, U. D. (1995). Nigerian psychology and the legal profession: Do they need each other? *Nigerian Journal of Basic and Applied Psychology, 4,* 10–19.

Okpara, E. (Ed.). (1985). *Psychological strategies for national development*. Enugu, Nigeria: Nigerian Psychological Association.

Olomolaiye, F. (1985). What psychology has to offer Nigeria now. In E. Okpara (Ed.), *Psychological strategies for development* (pp. 341–351). Enugu, Nigeria: Nigerian Psychological Association.

Oshuntokun, B. O. (1987). *The health of the public servant and Nigeria's destiny*. Distinguished lecture (series no. 3) presented at the National Institute for Policy and Strategic Studies, Kuru, Nigeria.

University of Ibadan. (1997). *Department of psychology undergraduate handbook*. Ibadan, Nigeria: Author.

University of Lagos (n.d.). *Requirements for admission into post-graduate studies in psychology*. Unpublished manuscript, University of Lagos.

Uzoka, A. F. (1989). Twenty five years of professional psychology in Nigeria. *Journal of Basic and Applied Psychology, 2,* 93–115.

World Health Organization (1999). *The world health report 1999: Making a difference*. Geneva: Author.

IMPORTANT PUBLICATIONS

Durojaiye, M. O. A. (1972). *Psychological guidance of the school child*. Ibadan, Nigeria: Evans Press.

Erinosho, O. A., & Bell, N. W. (Eds.). (1982). *Mental health in Africa*. Ibadan, Nigeria: Ibadan University Press.

Kalu, A. U., & Osinbajo, Y. (Eds.). (1990). *Narcotics: Law and policy in Nigeria*. Lagos: Federal Ministry of Justice.

Obot, I. S. (Ed.). (1993). *Epidemiology and control of substance abuse in Nigeria*. Jos, Nigeria: CRISA.

Obot, I. S., & Ibanga, A. J. (Eds.). (2000). *Perspectives on drugs and society*. Jos, Nigeria: CRISA.

Okpara, E. (Ed.). (1985). *Psychological strategies for national development*. Enugu, Nigeria: Nigerian Psychological Association.

Omotosho, J. A. (1991). *Learning disabilities and learning problems: The role of teachers, parents, and counselors*. Ilorin, Nigeria: University of Ilorin Press.

Onwuzurike, C. A., & Enekwechi, E. (Eds.). (1984). *Clinical psychology and the Nigerian society*. Jos, Nigeria: Nigerian Association of Clinical Psychology.

Peltzer, K., & Ebigbo, P. (Eds.). (1989). *Clinical psychology in Africa*. Eschborn, Germany: Fachbuchhandlung für Psychologie.

Uzoka, A. F., & Awaritefe, A. (Eds.). (1985). *Mental health priorities in Nigeria*. Nsukka, Nigeria: University of Nigeria, Department of Psychology.

Wilson, E. (1986). *Psychology and society*. Ife, Nigeria: Nigerian Psychological Association.

CHAPTER 4

Psychology in South Africa

GRAHAM B. STEAD

Graham B. Stead began his career as a high school teacher–counselor and obtained his Ph.D. in psychology in 1989. He is a full professor and a registered psychologist currently teaching research methods, statistics, and career psychology at the University of Port Elizabeth (Vista Campus). He has presented over 50 papers at international and national conferences, and he is the author of 50 articles and book chapters that have been published in South Africa, the United States, Europe, and Australia. Graham Stead has coedited Career Psychology in the South African Context *and coauthored* Planning, Designing, and Reporting Research. *Dr. Stead is also the South African liaison for Division 52 (International Psychology) of the American Psychological Association.*

4.1 OVERVIEW

Psychology in South Africa has its roots in European and American psychologies, and yet the issues it confronts are largely embedded in African histories and contexts. This tension between (a) relying on foreign practices and adapting these practices or (b) developing new ones indigenous to the South African context continues to be debated in various psychological forums. South African psychology must be part of, and utilize appropriate knowledge from, the international psychological community. Yet, it also needs to ground its practices, research, and policies in local realities and knowledge. Psychological approaches in South Africa are variegated with no single school of thought or therapy commanding center stage. Psychologists continue to search for, and provide meaningful solutions to, South Africa's social problems with a focus on social justice. However, South African psychology has been "absorbed in introspective self-criticism and plagued by self-doubts about the progress it has made" (Louw, 1992, p. 352) and continues in this vein, notwithstanding its achievements. The genesis of such self-criticism may partly be understood by examining the history of psychology in South Africa.

The seeds of psychology in South Africa were possibly planted circa 1916 when intelligence tests were used to identify mentally retarded students. A few years later psychology was studied at the universities of Stellenbosch (1917), Cape Town (1920), and Rhodes (1923). In 1927, the architect of apartheid, H. F. Verwoerd, became the first professor of applied psychology at the University of Stellenbosch. During the 1920s and 1930s, mental testing was prolific. During this time, research into racial differences in terms of mental abilities was explored (Claassen, 1997; Foster, 1993). The lower performance of Blacks relative to Whites was generally attributed to heredity or environmental deprivation (e.g., poverty, culture, and education) or both. This dovetailed with the prevailing mood of Afrikaner nationalism, which eventually led to the National Party coming to power in 1948 and implementing its policy of apartheid. Unfortunately, this ideology of racial separateness later came to influence the thinking of psychologists and psychological associations.

In 1948 the South African Psychological Association (SAPA) was established. An Indian person applied for SAPA membership in 1956 and this conflicted with South African racial segregation policies at the time. After much debate among SAPA members, it was decided that the applicant be admitted. This caused a split in SAPA, which had become a multiracial association, and in 1962 the Psychological Association of South Africa (PIRSA) was formed (Louw, 1987). PIRSA subscribed to racial segregation, with psychological research on racial differences sustaining its stance. Its members were White and largely Afrikaans-speaking. In 1977, an agreement of cooperation between SAPA and PIRSA was negotiated, resulting in joint conferences being hosted and the joint launch of the *South African Journal of Psychology* (Nicholas, 1990). In 1974 the registration of psychologists became compulsory and the Professional Board for Psychology was formed under the auspices of the South African Medical and Dental Council. Eventually, the rift between SAPA and PIRSA was healed, possibly due to the government's softening position towards apartheid. The two associations then disbanded, and in 1983 the Psychological Association of South Africa (PASA) was formed (Louw, 1987; Stead, 2002). Although PASA did not overtly support apartheid, it was perceived by many psychologists as doing so because of its unwillingness both to challenge apartheid policies that included detentions, torture, and discrimination and to promote mental health for all South Africans.

It fell upon the Organization of Appropriate Social Services in South Africa (OASSSA), which was established in 1983, to provide mental health and social services for those suffering under apartheid and for those who did not have access to such services (Flisher, Skinner, Lazarus, & Louw, 1993). OASSSA worked across disciplines (e.g., psychology, psychiatry, and social work) and also provided a forum to protest against the delivery of inadequate social services to the majority of South Africans. Thus, OASSSA was closely associated with antiapartheid movements but disbanded in 1992 before a new democratic government assumed power (Louw & van Hoorn, 1997). In 1994 PASA ceased to exist and was replaced by the Psychological

Society of South Africa (PsySSA) in the hope that the latter would be viewed as more representative of psychologists. An important aim of PsySSA is the promotion of psychology as a science and as a profession. On July 31, 2001, PsySSA had 1,180 members (Psychological Society of South Africa Executive, 2001), which was far short of the approximately 5,000 psychologists in South Africa. This discrepancy could be partly due to the historical skepticism of psychologists toward professional organizations (Stead, 2002). PsySSA has forged international links, which PASA struggled to achieve. For example, a bilateral agreement exists between PsySSA and the American Psychological Association to advance the interests of psychology such as promoting scholarship programs to attract Black psychology students.

Although the commencement of apartheid is associated with the National Party assuming political power in 1948, racial issues have always been part of South Africa's history since the 17th century. Indeed, the politics and history of a country are often intimately related to the development of psychology in that country (Stevens, 2002). The testing movement was very prominent in South African psychology until the early 1990s, and it will be described briefly as one example of the close links between psychology and political developments in South Africa. Louw and van Hoorn (1997) pointed out that in the 1920s scientists were generally unanimous in their view of the importance of racial segregation. This was partly responsible for the rapid construction of cognitive ability tests, although test development also accelerated in Europe and the U.S. during this time. Psychological testing was used to provide solutions to difficult political prob-

lems such as justifying segregation on the basis of racial differences in mental test scores. Psychologists also employed testing to solve the "poor White" political problem of the 1920s and 1930s in an attempt to improve their education and free them from poverty. From the 1950s on, psychological tests were used to compare the ability scores of ethnic groups, notably English- and Afrikaans-speaking Whites. With the government's political desire to include persons of mixed racial ancestry and Indians, but not Blacks, in parliament in the 1980s, existing psychological tests were examined for their utility in relation to these groups (Claassen, 1997). Comparable norms had to be developed, and issues surrounding the fairness of these tests were fiercely debated (Abrahams, 2001). Psychological testing was also conducted in organizations, and in the 1980s the use of different tests for different racial groups became problematic.

With a democratically elected government assuming power in 1994, psychological testing has since focused on fairness and overcoming bias. This was partly in reaction to the Employment Equity Act (1998) which states that employees can be psychometrically assessed only if the test scores are reliable and valid, they can be fairly applied to all employees, and they are not biased toward an employee or group. As few tests meet these requirements, one wonders what "unbiased" alternatives to testing are in place to assess employees. This remains a troublesome issue that has not been adequately addressed by industry or antitesting lobbyists. The political implications of testing and its potential for abuse continue to be debated. The political histories of psychological testing in South Africa have ensured that it remains a sensitive issue.

4.2 EDUCATION AND TRAINING

The Professional Board for Psychology exercises authority in terms of all matters relating to psychologists and registered counselors. Their mission is also to promote standards of psychological education and training in South Africa and maintain and enhance the dignity of the psychological profession (Professional Board for Psychology, 2003a). Psychologists generally complete a 3-year undergraduate degree with psychology as a major, a 1-year honors degree in psychology, and a master's degree in psychology. In certain departments, students are required to obtain at least 60% for 3-year coursework in psychology to be considered for acceptance into honors degree psychology programs. Entry into such programs can be highly competitive. Students with an honors degree in psychology may become registered counselors if they complete additional requirements. However, the undergraduate programs are being replaced in some departments by a 4-year bachelor's degree in psychology (registered counselor) (Professional Board for Psychology, 2001b).

The scope of the registered counselor is the competent application of structured and formalized short-term interventions at the preventative level. The core competencies include psychological assessment (e.g., general screening and identification of symptoms for referral), psychological intervention (e.g., short-term counseling, psychoeducation), referral expertise, the ability to conduct a research project, policy and standards implementation, project implementation and management, and practice management. The registered counselor must also have completed 200 hr of supervised practical training and a 6-month practicum that may run concurrently with the degree. Registered counselors may register for no more than two practice areas, which include psychometrics, HIV and AIDS counseling, trauma counseling, career counseling, sport counseling, and primary mental health, among others (Professional Board for Psychology, 2001a). However, registered counselors are not permitted to register for independent practice, but may be employed in the public sector or in nongovernmental organizations (Professional Board for Psychology, 2003b).

The coursework and training of psychologists occur at almost all of South Africa's universities. There are no objective indicators of which university departments offer outstanding training. Undergraduate degrees generally comprise about four to five first-year subjects, three second-year subjects, and two third-year majors. Although prospective psychologists study psychology at all year levels, a general curriculum is followed that might include, for example, anthropology, geography, history, languages, mathematics, philosophy, political science, or sociology. Major fields of psychology are also studied during the first and second year; second year subjects may also be taken during the first year of study. Psychology courses at the undergraduate level vary between universities but generally focus on introductory psychology (in the first year), developmental psychology, social psychology, personality, psychopathology, assessment, counseling, and research methods. Although psychology students are encouraged to study social science courses (e.g., anthropology, sociology, or social work), they are not required subjects for being admitted into honors or master's programs. The curriculum for an honors degree in psychology varies between universities and is specific to departments' foci and lecturers' skills. Each honors degree includes a variety of courses such as developmental psychology, social psychology, neuropsychology, psychopathology, assessment, counseling and psychotherapy, career psychology, community psychology, health psychology, research methods, statistics, and a research project.

The methods of instruction at undergraduate and honors levels include lectures, tutorials, supervision by a psychologist, invited addresses from prominent psychologists, and visits to outpatient clinics, psychiatric hospitals, and schools. Students are required to complete written projects that involve gathering information from psychologists employed outside of universities such as psychologists working in clinics, industry, and private practice. At the honors level, students may also gain experience in group-therapy workshops, observing children in natural settings, and conducting research.

Psychologists in South Africa are registered with the Professional Board for Psychology on completion of an MA degree in psychology and an internship. Registration permits them to use the title "psychologist" and binds them to the professional code of ethics. There are four registration categories: counseling, educational, clinical, and industrial. Those previously registered as research psychologists will continue to be registered with the Professional Board for Psychology. There have been extensive discussions between university departments and the Professional Board regarding the replacement of the structured master's program with a structured doctoral program for the purpose of registration as a psychol-

ogist. However, doctoral programs in psychology have been deferred indefinitely as of August 2003, pending the Minister of Education's forthcoming National Academic Policy.

Admissions criteria for master's programs vary widely between psychology departments and may require candidates to possess a minimum grade for honors in psychology, complete a battery of psychological tests to determine their suitability for the program, role-play counseling sessions, and be interviewed by faculty. Master's courses for registration as a psychologist typically include counseling and psychotherapy, research methods and statistics, assessment (including neuropsychological assessment), family therapy, professional psychology, psychodiagnostics, and a thesis. Generally, members of the department and an examiner external to the university evaluate the thesis. The registration category will also depend on the additional courses presented. For example, advanced career psychology and advanced neuropsychology might be offered as part of the counseling psychology and clinical psychology courses, respectively. The coursework is typically completed in one year; thereafter, the student completes a yearlong internship with a training site accredited by the Professional Board for Psychology. Clinical psychologists recently have been required to complete an additional year of community service at an approved institution, excluding the year-long internship.

The methods of instruction at the master's level include lectures, but students also are required to take an active role in class by delivering lectures or workshops on a topic. Thus, the focus is more on active participation involving experiential learning and group work. Practical activities occur to a greater extent than in undergraduate and honors-level courses. During their first year of master's study, students are generally required to assume a caseload. The scientist–practitioner model is employed in most psychology departments. In fact, students applying for grants from the Human Sciences Research Council will be considered for such grants only if their university ensures that 50% of the master's coursework comprises research.

Although psychology departments generally require a Ph.D. candidate to complete only a dissertation, certain departments offer a Ph.D. degree that also includes coursework. For example, the University of Pretoria and Rhodes University in Grahamstown offer Ph.D. degrees in psychotherapy with the latter university including coursework in phenomenology and hermeneutics, psychoanalysis and analytical psychology, and a dissertation, among other requirements.

Psychologists are now required to comply with a system of continuing professional development (CPD). All psychologists must obtain a minimum of 25 CPD points in each subsequent year to retain their registration with the Professional Board for Psychology. One participation hour equals one CPD point. CPD points can be obtained through individual activities (e.g., studying reputable journals), small-group activities (e.g., lectures, workshops), or organizational activities (e.g., conferences). The presentation of papers and symposia at conferences and writing of articles and books also earn CPD points (e.g., four CPD points for a short paper of up to 15 min, 15 points for an edited book) (Professional Board for Psychology, 2002).

There are various sources that offer financial support for deserving students in degree programs in psychology. The National Research Foundation (NRF) is the primary funding source. The NRF was established in 1999 and serves to develop students' research capabilities. It also supports basic and applied research projects in psychology and other disciplines. Current and completed research projects funded by the NRF can be found at http://star.nrf.ac.za/index.html.

In 2000, there were 7,047 diplomas and certificates awarded in health care and health sciences; 4,046 in the social sciences (excluding psychology); 19,196 in business, commerce, and management sciences; 4,400 in psychology at universities, technikons (i.e., tertiary institutions that focus on vocational training), and teacher or agricultural training colleges. Psychology training for registration is offered only at universities, although undergraduate psychology courses are offered at some technikons. The ratio of White to Black psychology graduates was 1:1 as opposed to 1:2 for the social sciences (South African Institute of Race Relations, 2002). According to the Health Professions Council of South Africa (2003), as of February 20, 2003, for a population of 44.5 million people, there were 5,437 psychologists (approximately 12 psychologists per 100,000 people), 31,012 medical doctors and specialists, and 522 psychiatrists. Specifically, 36% of psychologists identified their primary specialization as clinical, 22% as counseling, 21% as educational, 17% as industrial, and 4% as research. The majority of psychologists received their registration training in South Africa with 2.1% obtaining it in a foreign country.

The majority of psychologists were in Gauteng province (49.4%), followed by the Western Cape (21.7%) and Kwazulu-Natal provinces (10.6%). In addition, 60% of psychologists were female; 7% were Black and 79% White, although the latter two racial statistics could be inaccurate as the racial identities of 51% of psychologists were unknown. However, the marked discrepancy between the percentages of Black and White psychologists highlights the urgent need to train more Black psychologists.

There has been a 57% growth in the number of registered psychologists in the past decade. Whiteford, van Zyl, Simkins, and Hall (1999) provided estimates for the growth of various occupations from 1998 to 2003. They stated that during this period less than 250 psychologist positions would need to be filled and that the growth in demand for psychologists would be between 5% to 10%, as opposed to 10% to 15% for the medical profession (including psychiatrists) and less than 5% for social workers. There is a documented need for more psychologists because, as mentioned, there are only 12 psychologists per 100,000 people. Ironically, employment opportunities do not reflect this need.

There are two psychology journals that specifically focus on psychological issues in South Africa. The *South African Journal of Psychology* is published four times a year and is the most important psychological publication. *Psychology in Society* is published at least three times a year and focuses on articles that promote a sociohistorical and critical-theory perspective to psychological theory and practice in the South African context. The *Journal of Psychology in Africa* accepts South African manuscripts, as well as those from African countries south of the Sahara, the Caribbean, and Afro-Latin America. It is published biannually in Germany. The lack of sufficient publication outlets for psychologists results in much South African research being published in journals in the Europe and the United States.

4.3 SCOPE OF PSYCHOLOGICAL PRACTICE

Historically, the major psychotherapeutic approaches were cognitive–behavioral therapy and psychoanalysis. Well-known South African proponents of the former included Joseph Wolpe, Stanley Rachman, and Arnold Lazarus, although they continued their careers outside South Africa. According to Knight (2002), the dominant psychotherapeutic approach currently taught at South African universities follows the psychodynamic model. Those practicing psychotherapy generally refer to themselves as psychologists or psychiatrists but seldom as psychotherapists. One does not register as a psychotherapist with the Health Professions Council of South Africa. Phenomenological, behavioral, cognitive, humanistic, and postmodern approaches are also taught at various training institutions and are employed by psychologists in their private practices.

Although psychological approaches found in Europe and the U.S. are practiced in South Africa, there have been calls for indigenization (i.e., theories and techniques are taken from elsewhere and adapted to suit the context in which they are applied) and for indigenous psychologies (i.e., knowledge developed in a country and not imported form elsewhere) (Seedat, 1997; Stead & Watson, 1999) to play a greater role in the development of psychology in South Africa. Stead and Watson (2002) argued that much of career psychology (and by implication, psychology in general) is contextually bound, in that many psychological findings are not easily generalizable to other cultures. They added that psychology is also contextually blind in the sense that personal factors have often taken precedence over contextual factors in psychological research. They stated that psychological theories, constructs, and instruments should either be adapted from other psychologies or developed indigenously or both in preference to exporting them without evaluating them sufficiently. The purpose is to utilize mainstream psychological approaches, wherever appropriate, as well as those developed and adapted in the South African context. Many psychologists wish to utilize African ethnopsychologies and Euro-American psychologies, but do not want indigenous psychology to become as "parochial and ethnocentric as mainstream psychology is at present" (Nsamenang, 1995, p. 737). Dawes (1998) concisely summed it up by stating that "… an African psychology should draw on both local and external knowledge systems. But in wishing to call itself a psychology, it needs to be guided by the conventions for psychological activity which exist in the various corners of the discipline" (p. 4).

Psychologists in South Africa practice in various work places that include business organizations, correctional services, government institutions, the military, psychiatric hospitals, research organizations, schools, and student counseling centers. Four such workplaces will be described briefly: psychiatric hospitals, student counseling centers, schools, and research organizations. In psychiatric hospitals, psychologists generally work in association with other professionals such as psychiatrists, social workers,

and nurses. A team approach is generally utilized and decisions regarding, for example, patients' diagnoses, medication, psychotherapies, and discharge are made in consultation with the professional team rather than by one professional. Psychologists may not prescribe medication although it is common for psychiatrists to discuss patients' medication with psychologists and nurses.

Psychologists are also employed at student counseling centers at universities. The core competencies required of psychologists at a student counseling center in Port Elizabeth were as follows: academic development, student development, career development, wellness, peer helping, assessment, research, resource development, counseling and therapy, and consultation and advocacy. During 2002, the primary forms of psychological intervention at this center were career counseling (14.6% of all cases), study and academic difficulties (14.0%), financial concerns (13.2%), course information and registration (10.3%), family problems (6.2%), and interpersonal problems (4.4%). Psychologists were also expected to conduct group counseling and life-skills training, and liaise with parents, administration, and student councils.

Psychologists are being employed by a small but growing number of schools, although school counselors or guidance teachers with undergraduate or honors degrees in psychology largely occupy such posts. Although the psychologist must work closely with teachers and the school principal, ethical standards prevent the psychologist from disclosing client data to teachers without the client's permission. Therefore, the psychologist in a school tends to discuss client issues with other school psychologists working in the same locality. The role of the psychologist or school counselor can be a difficult one, particularly if the psychologist is expected to teach school subjects as well as counsel students. As expected, sensitive issues regarding the demarcation of roles often arise.

Some research organizations focus primarily on marketing, whereas others emphasize investigations of social problems. An example of the latter is the Human Sciences Research Council (HSRC), which was established in 1968. The HSRC employs psychologists and is the largest social science research organization in Africa. It is monitored by a ministerially appointed council and conducts psychological research into problems related to child, youth, and family development; social aspects of HIV and AIDS and health; and assessment technology. Psychologists at the HSRC often conduct national surveys on social science topics using both quantitative and qualitative research methods.

In an interesting study limited in its generalizability, Viljoen, Beukes, and Louw (1999) sent a survey on professional issues to 61 psychologists who completed their training as psychologists at the University of the Free State from 1990 to 1996. They found that of the participants, 43.3% were in private practice full-time and 13.3% part-time, 33.3% were employed in the public sector (of which 15% were in the Department of Education, 6.6% in the South African National Defense Force, and 5% in the Department of Correctional Services), 18.3% were in academic institutions, and 3.4% in nongovernmental organizations.

Richter et al. (1998) reported that in their analyses of the advertisements of three major weekly newspapers in South Africa for psychology graduates, only 11% required a psychologist for the post, the majority requesting the applicants to possess degrees in psychology or the social sciences. The five most commonly requested skills were training and teaching (59% of advertisements), administration and management (37%), research (35%), data analysis (27%), and labor and industrial relations (24%), with counseling/group facilitation (20%) being only seventh on the list. As they pointed out, some of these requirements were either inadequately covered or omitted from undergraduate psychology programs. Richter et al. concluded that there were few jobs available for the professional psychologist and that this influenced many psychologists to enter private practice. Thus, psychology is not firmly entrenched in the public sector or in the community. Clearly it is the intention for registered counselors to practice largely in disadvantaged communities and utilize their skills in, for example, preventative healthcare and psychoeducation. There is an urgent need for such community services to be provided, but there is no clear indication who will employ registered counselors in sufficiently large numbers for such services to be provided.

One project to bring psychology to rural communities is the Phelophepa (greek for "good, clean health") Train that began in 1994. Psychology students travel on the train and stop at various rural areas providing primary care psychological services to local communities, including screening, psychoeducation, and counseling. As Wilson, Richter, Durrheim, Surendorff, and Asafo-Agyei (1999) point out, the elitist nature of the profession and its urban base are likely to be maintained unless psychology positions come with adequate salaries.

The profession of psychology in South Africa is committed to addressing these concerns, but whether psychology will become firmly entrenched in the public sector remains to be seen.

Psychologists attained legal status after the promulgation of Act 56 of 1974 (Government Gazette, 1974). However, this Act did not provide comprehensive ethical guidelines for psychologists. Various ethical guidelines subsequently appeared in the form of books and articles, and through professional associations (Louw, 1997; Wassenaar, 1998). This resulted in much confusion among psychologists, particularly regarding the powers of the ethics committee of PASA and the Professional Board. Indeed, between 1991 and 1994, the PASA ethics committee was the only point of reference for ethical issues, and there was a close liaison between them and the Professional Board. By 1992, the Professional Board decided to update all regulations regarding health professionals in South Africa and draft regulations became available for commentary (Wassenaar, 1998). The new Professional Board for Psychology was elected in 1994 and is the highest authority on ethical matters, having the sole power to suspend psychologists or strike them from the register should they violate ethical regulations. Therefore, it has the statutory mandate of protecting the public from professional misconduct. The Professional Board's Ethical Code of Professional Conduct was adopted in 1999 and, in part, utilized the ethics codes of the American Psychological Association, the Association of State and Provincial Boards of Psychology, (U.S. and Canada) the Canadian Psychological Association, and PsySSA. The ethical code comprises the following sections: professional competence; professional relations; confidentiality, privacy, and records; fees and financial arrangements; assessment activities; therapeutic activities; psycho-legal activities; advertising and other public statement activities; teaching, training, and supervision; research and publication; and resolving ethical issues.

Scherrer, Louw, and Möller (2002) provided an account of ethical complaints against psychologists from 1990 to 1999. The chief complaints were psychologists neglecting to register with the HPCSA in a given year (21.3%); fraudulent billing (16%), unprofessional or inaccurate psychological reports (13.1%); incompetence (12.9%) (e.g., offering a diagnosis before a thorough assessment), improper conduct (11.5%) (e.g., sexual relations with a client), and breach of confidentiality (6%).

4.4 FUTURE CHALLENGES AND PROSPECTS

Prior to 1985, psychological research in South Africa was overwhelmingly quantitative and positivistic and focused largely on White samples, thus reflecting the political views of the time. Such positivistic and "apolitical" research (which ironically was quite political) declined somewhat after 1985 (Durrheim & Mokeki, 1997), and it became more common for psychologists to acknowledge the political nature of their work and to comment on political injustices. Although positivistic and quantitative research projects continue to dominate, their influence has decreased somewhat in the past 20 years. Stead (2002) categorized articles and short discussions in the *South African Journal of Psychology* and reported that the percentage of qualitative articles in relation to the total number of articles increased from 9% (1990 to 1994) to 23.1% (1995 to 1999). In turn, quantitative articles decreased from 57.7% to 50% during the same time periods. Current trends suggest that there will be a continuing interest in qualitative research approaches, as they do not require participants to be "test literate" as is the case with conventional surveys and questionnaires composed of dichotomous and Likert-type scales. As there are 11 official languages in South Africa, it is difficult for researchers to ensure that all participants understand their questionnaires. Research among Black samples has increased considerably in the past decade, and this is expected to continue.

Previous commentaries on South African psychology (Biesheuvel, 1976; Louw, 1992) have reflected on the emphasis placed on test construction and development, and cross-cultural assessment in psychology. Since 1990, there has been less focus on psychometric testing, with the HSRC not as involved in developing new and updating old measures as they were in the past. Test development can be costly and time-consuming, and psychometric expertise in psychology departments is probably not as prevalent as may be desired. There is an urgent need for new psychometric measures to be constructed, existing measures to be updated, and foreign measures to be adapted wherever appropriate.

As psychologists acknowledged their silent complicity with apartheid and also recognized the political nature of their practice and research, they became more involved in advocacy and social justice issues. An examination of special issues in the *South African Journal of Psychology* over the past decade serves to underscore

this point and indicates some research directions that interest South African psychologists. The special issues included HIV and AIDS, race and prejudice, health psychology, Black scholarship, gender issues, postmodern perspectives, qualitative methods, and the Truth and Reconciliation Commission (which was designed to reveal past abuses of human rights and provide reparations to apartheid victims). Such topics also reflect the interest that South African psychologists have in solving community and societal problems, and in understanding people in these contexts. These trends are bound to continue. For example, Hook (2002) reflected on the necessity of South African psychologists to be less insular and more open to historical and sociopolitical South African contexts when considering pathology. He argued that, although South African psychologists inherited diagnostic systems from Europe and the United States, unique contexts "exceed those categories of 'disorder'" (p. 34). He contended that pathology should not be viewed as exclusively individualistic or essentialist because it cannot be separated from the ways psychologists talk about it, understand it, and respond to it. It is the re-examining and deconstructing of the mainstream and positivist views of psychology that is an important facet of South African psychology.

Community psychology will probably continue to be prominent in South Africa. Swartz and Gibson (2001) emphasized new ways of approaching community issues, including community participation in research, going beyond the consulting room or the laboratory, and utilizing community-based interventions. Knowledge is democratized and subjective. Such research has a political goal of removing oppression and enabling disempowered communities to take control of their destinies. Examples of such research in South Africa include the work of van Vlaenderen (1999) and Gilbert (1997). Given this sociopolitical conflict, psychology in South Africa generally is less modulative (i.e., where one reacts to social change, assists people to cope, and seeks to maintain the social order) than generative (i.e., proactive in relation to transformation) (Moghaddam, 1990). However, although the focus of South African psychology is on research having explicit sociopolitical connotations, it has yet to become multidisciplinary in focus. Researchers in psychology network nationally and internationally, but seldom conduct research with members of other disciplines. Such multidisciplinary collaboration has the potential to enrich psychology and provide deeper insights into the social problems facing the country.

There remain calls for indigenous healing practices to be integrated into the health system. These practices include *sangomas* (i.e., diviners), herbalists, and faith healers, among others. According to Bodibe and Sodi (1997), 80% of Black South Africans consulted traditional healers in 1997, which either reflects preferences for such treatment or the dearth of medical practitioners, particularly in rural areas. However, demands by traditional healers to be included in the health system have been resisted by some psychologists and medical practitioners on the grounds of insufficient scientific support for the efficacy of their treatments. Although no legislation has been passed to accord indigenous healers equal status in mainstream health, debates surrounding the issue continue.

There is little information on public attitudes toward psychologists. Using a sample from the Eastern Cape, Stones (1996) reported that psychiatric patients and service providers had confidence in psychiatric treatment and that psychologists were less confident than the general public in the efficacy of psychological and psychiatric treatment. However, Stones found that the general public and medical practitioners had insufficient knowledge about mental illness and that the people in his sample would prefer to confide in friends than in psychologists if they were distressed. It would appear that psychology in South Africa could be better marketed in terms of the services offered and that psychological services remain unavailable to most South Africans. Lupuwana, Simbayi, and Elkonin (1999) found that, of a sample of Black people in Port Elizabeth, 53% were not aware of psychologists and only 10% of those who were aware had consulted a psychologist. Leach, Akhurst, and Basson (2003) believed that this might be due in part to the general mistrust Blacks have of Whites. They stated that psychology needs to be perceived as being relevant to Black communities and not merely an extension of the oppressive philosophies and interventions of the apartheid era. In addition, many White psychologists do not speak a Black language, of which there are nine, and those working in traditional and rural communities must often engage translators.

In conclusion, political developments and psychology are intertwined in South Africa. Psychology in South Africa does not operate in an objective, neutral, and apolitical social vacuum. The political transformation that occurred in South Africa in 1994, when a democratic government assumed power, has also been reflected in the transformation of psychology in South Africa during the past decade.

Change and renewal bring their own uncertainties, insecurities, failed dreams, hopes, ideals, and successes. They also bring creative insights, new perspectives, and demanding challenges for South African psychologists. Psychologists in South Africa will continue striving to make meaningful contributions to improving the well-being of all South Africans.

ACKNOWLEDGMENTS

The author acknowledges the helpful comments of Professor Donna E. Schultheiss and Professor Christopher R. Stones on an earlier draft of this chapter.

REFERENCES

Abrahams, F. (2001). The use and abuse of psychological testing in industry: An overview. In C. R. Stones (Ed.), *Socio-political and psychological perspectives on South Africa* (pp. 197–214). New York: Nova Science.

Biesheuvel, S. (1976). South Africa. In V. S. Sexton & H. Misiak (Eds.), *Psychology around the world* (pp. 357–369). Monterey, CA: Brooks/Cole.

Bodibe, R. C., & Sodi, T. (1997). Indigenous healing. In D. Foster, M. Freeman, & Y. Pillay (Eds.), *Mental health policy issues for South Africa* (pp. 181–192). Pinelands, South Africa: Multimedia.

Claassen, N. C. W. (1997). Cultural differences, politics, and test bias in South Africa. *European Review of Applied Psychology, 47,* 297–307.

Dawes, A. (1998). Africanization of psychology: Identities and continents. *Psychology in Society, 23,* 4–16.

Durrheim, K., & Mokeki, S. (1997). Race and relevance: A content analysis of the South African Journal of Psychology. *South African Journal of Psychology, 27,* 206–213.

Employment Equity Act, 55, Republic of South Africa Parliament, §§ 2–293–305 (1998).

Flisher, A. J., Skinner, D., Lazarus, S., & Louw, J. (1993). Organizing mental health workers on the basis of politics and service: The case of the Organization of Appropriate Social Services in South Africa. In L. J. Nicholas (Ed.), *Psychology and oppression: Critiques and proposals* (pp. 236–245). Johannesburg: Skotaville.

Foster, D. (1993). On racism: Virulent mythologies and fragile threads. In L. J. Nicholas (Ed.), *Psychology and oppression: Critiques and proposals* (pp. 55–80). Johannesburg: Skotaville.

Gilbert, A. (1997). Small voices against the wind: Local knowledge and social transformation. *Peace and Conflict: Journal of Peace Psychology, 3,* 275–292.

Government Gazette. (1974). *Law on doctors, dentists, and supplementary health professions, No. 56 of 1974.* Pretoria, South Africa: Government Printer.

Health Professions Council of South Africa. (2003). *Number of registered psychologists, psychiatrists and medical practitioners per category* [Data file]. Available from Health Professions Council of South Africa Web site, http://www.hpcsa.co.za

Hook, D. (2002). Special feature: Critical contexts of pathology. *South African Journal of Psychology, 32,* 34–36.

Knight, Z. (2002). South Africa. In A. Pritz (Ed.), *Globalized psychotherapy* (pp. 593–609). Vienna: Facultas Universitätsverlag.

Leach, M. M., Akhurst, J., & Basson, C. (2003). Counseling psychology in South Africa: Current political and professional challenges and future promise. *Counseling Psychologist, 31,* 619–640.

Louw, D. A. (1995). Psychology in South Africa: Old problems and new challenges. *World Psychology, 1,* 69–82.

Louw, J. (1987). From separation to division: The origins of two psychological associations in South Africa. *Journal of the History of the Behavioral Sciences, 23,* 341–352.

Louw, J. (1992). South Africa. In V. S. Sexton & J. D. Hogan (Eds.), *International psychology. Views from around the world* (pp. 352–363). London: University of Nebraska Press.

Louw, J. (1997). Regulating professional conduct. Part I: Codes of ethics of national psychology associations in South Africa. *South African Journal of Psychology, 27,* 183–188.

Louw, J., & van Hoorn, W. (1997). Psychology, conflict, and peace in South Africa: Historical notes. *Peace and Conflict: Journal of Peace Psychology, 3*, 233–243.

Lupuwana, B. W., Simbayi, L. C., & Elkonin, D. (1999). Psychological services in the Black community of Port Elizabeth in South Africa: Assessment of awareness, attitudes, practices, and needs. *Journal of Psychology in Africa, 9*, 25–57.

Moghaddam, F. M. (1990). Modulative and generative orientations in psychology. Implications for psychology in the three worlds. *Journal of Social Issues, 46*, 21–41.

Nicholas, L. J. (1990). The response of South African professional psychology associations to apartheid. *Journal of the History of the Behavioral Sciences, 26*, 58–63.

Nsamenang, A. B. (1995). Factors influencing the development of psychology in sub–Saharan Africa. *International Journal of Psychology, 30*, 729–739.

Professional Board for Psychology. (2001a, March). *Professional Board for Psychology Policy on Roles, Registration/Licensing, Training, and Education within the Professional Field of Psychology.* Pretoria: Health Professions Council of South Africa.

Professional Board for Psychology. (2001b, April). *Letter addressed to those registered with the Professional Board for Psychology.* Pretoria: Health Professions Council of South Africa.

Professional Board for Psychology. (2002, May). *Continuing professional development. Guidelines for psychologists and registered counselors* (Form 222). Pretoria: Health Professions Council of South Africa.

Professional Board for Psychology. (2003a). *Mission and mandate.* Retrieved March 25, 2003, from http://www.hpcsa.co.za/professional-boards/Psychology/Mission%20and%20Mandate.html

Professional Board for Psychology. (2003b, September). *Practice framework for psychology.* Pretorias: South Africa: Health Professions Council of South Africa.

Psychological Society of South Africa Executive. (2001). 2001 annual report. *PsyTalk, 3*, 8–15.

Richter, L. M., Griesel, R. D., Durrheim, K., Wilson, M., Surendorff, N., & Asafo-Agyei, L. (1998). Employment opportunities for psychology graduates in South Africa: A contemporary analysis.

South African Journal of Psychology, 28, 1–7.

Scherrer, R., Louw, D. A., & Möller, A. T. (2002). Ethical complaints and disciplinary action against South African psychologists. *South African Journal of Psychology, 32*, 54–64.

Seedat, M. (1997). The quest for liberatory psychology. *South African Journal of Psychology, 27*, 261–270.

South African Institute of Race Relations. (2002, November). *Fast Facts, 11*, 1–12.

Stead, G. B. (2002). The transformation of psychology in a post-apartheid South Africa: An overview. *International Journal of Group Tensions, 31*, 79–102.

Stead, G. B., & Watson, M. B. (1999). Indigenization of career psychology in South Africa. In G. B. Stead & M. B. Watson (Eds.), *Career psychology in the South African context* (pp. 214–225). Pretoria: J. L. van Schaik.

Stead, G. B., & Watson, M. B. (2002). Contextualising career psychology in South Africa: Bringing it all back home. *Journal of Psychology in Africa, 12*, 147–160.

Stevens, M. J. (2002). The interplay of psychology and societal transformation. *International Journal of Group Tensions, 31*, 5–30.

Stones, C. R. (1996). Attitudes towards psychology, psychiatry and mental illness in the central Eastern Cape of South Africa. *South African Journal of Psychology, 26*, 221–225.

Stones, C. R. (Ed.). (2001). *Socio-political and psychological perspectives on South Africa.* New York: Nova Science.

Swartz, L., & Gibson, K. (2001). The 'old' versus the 'new' in South African psychology: The quest for appropriate change. In M. Seedat, N. Duncan, & S. Lazarus (Eds.), *Community psychology. Theory, method, and practice* (pp. 37–50). Cape Town: Oxford University Press.

van Vlaenderen, H. (1999). Problem solving: A process of reaching common understanding and consensus. *South African Journal of Psychology, 29*, 166–177.

Viljoen, D. J., Beukes, R. B. I., & Louw, D. A. (1999). An evaluation of the training of psychologists at the University of the Free State. *South African Journal of Psychology, 29*, 201–208.

Wassenaar, D. (1998). A history of ethical codes in South African psychology: An insider's view. *South African Journal of Psychology, 28*, 135–145.

Whiteford, A., van Zyl, E., Simkins, C., & Hall, E.

(1999). *SA labor market trends and future workforce needs: 1998–2003.* Pretoria: Human Sciences Research Council.

Wilson, N. M., Richter, L. M., Durrheim, K., Surendorff, N., & Asafo-Agyei, L. (1999). Professional psychology: Where are we headed? *South African Journal of Psychology, 29,* 184–190.

IMPORTANT PUBLICATIONS

Biesheuvel, S. (1991). Neutrality, relevance and accountability in psychological research and practice in South Africa. *South African Journal of Psychology, 21,* 131–140.

Dawes, A. (1998). Africanization of psychology: Identities and continents. *Psychology in Society, 23,* 4–16.

Foster, D., Freeman, M., & Pillay (Eds). (1997). *Mental health policy issues for South Africa.* Pinelands, South Africa: Multimedia.

Holdstock, T. L. (1981). Psychology in South Africa belongs to the colonial era: Arrogance or ignorance? *South African Journal of Psychology, 11,* 123–129.

Manganyi, N. C. (1973). *Being black in the world.* Braamfontein, South Africa: SPRO/CAS/Ravan.

Stones, C. R. (Ed.). (2001). *Socio-political and psychological perspectives on South Africa.* New York: Nova Science.

Straker, G. (1992). *Faces in the revolution.* Cape Town: David Philip.

Swartz, L. (1998). *Culture and mental health: A southern African view.* Cape Town: Oxford University Press.

CHAPTER 5

Psychology in Canada

PIERRE L.-J. RITCHIE AND MICHEL E. SABOURIN

Pierre L.-J. Ritchie was raised in rural Quebec and educated at McGill University and Duke University (Ph.D., clinical psychology, 1975). Since 1980, he has taught at the University of Ottawa where he is responsible for clinical training in Canada's only fully bilingual clinical psychology program. He is currently an associate editor for the International Journal of Psychology. *Ritchie has been a leader in organized psychology for a quarter century, holding offices in Canada, the United States, and internationally. He is currently executive director of the Canadian Register of Health Service Providers in Psychology and secretary-general of the International Union of Psychological Science (IUPsyS), which he also serves as main representative in the area of psychology to the World Health Organization.*

Pierre Ritchie has received a number of awards, among them the CPA Award for Distinguished Contributions to the International Development of Psychology, the Award for Excellence in Clinical Training

of the Canadian Council of Professional Psychology Programs, and a Presidential Citation from the APA.

Michel E. Sabourin is a lifelong resident of Montreal. He received a classical education before completing a Ph.D. at the University of Montreal, where he has been a member of the faculty since 1970. From 1988 to 1992, Sabourin was the editor of the International Journal of Psychology.

Michel Sabourin served twice as full-time president of the Quebec College of Psychologists. Between these terms, he was the president of the CPA. He is now in his third term as the treasurer of the IUPsyS, for which he is also main representative as a psychologist to the U.N. Secretariat as well as to the U.N.'s Economic and Social Council.

The recipient of several awards as well as a Fellow of both the CPA and APA, Sabourin was the recipient of the CPA Award for Distinguished Contributions to the International Development of Psychology and the APA's Karl H. Heiser Presidential

Award for his contribution to professional psychology.

5.1 OVERVIEW

Psychology in Canada is as old as its universities. Its origins can be traced to the first courses offered in mental and moral philosophy in the colleges long before the creation of the Canadian Confederation by the British North America Act in 1867 (Wright & Myers, 1982). These courses were heavily influenced by the Scottish "common sense" school of philosophical thought, brought to the country by the well-educated and influential Scots immigrants often considered to have largely moulded the values of English Canada (Wright & Myers). However, in French-speaking lower Canada (now Quebec), known during the colonial period as New France before it became a British colony in 1763, it was customary to send promising (and wealthy) young French-speaking adults to train in European universities. Because the Protestant British were suspicious of the strong influence of the Roman Catholic clergy in Quebec, for nearly another century all efforts to create a French language university in Quebec were doomed to failure. Hence, the major French-speaking Quebec universities began to develop only in the middle of the 19th century. Ironically, the antecedents of Francophone university education began in Ontario earlier in the 19th century at what is now the University of Ottawa.

Two very different traditions guided the initial development of psychology in Canada. The French educational model of pre-Napoleonic France characterized French Canada's educational orientation with the omnipresent philosophical tradition of Thomas Aquinas. The British tradition, noted above, determined the approach of English Canada's universities. Even today, remnants of these differences are still visible (Granger, 1993). Today, however, with the large influx of immigrants from all over the world, Canada also prides itself as being a multicultural and open society. The two national origins of Canada, coupled with strong influences from the U.S. in the second half of the 20th century, have subtly influenced the development of psychology and have given it unique characteristics (Adair, Paivio, & Ritchie, 1996).

In spite of the strong experimental psychology tradition that characterized the early development of psychology in English Canada, applied psychology was dominant in Canada between the two World Wars. Surprisingly, little research was actually conducted during this period. Wright and Myers (1982) identified three probable determinants of this situation: "First, having so recently gained recognition as an independent discipline, there was a felt urgency to demonstrate that psychology could be used to solve practical problems. Second, following the first great war, there were urgent demands for help from the social sciences .... Thirdly, there was little or no money for basic research. There were, however, funds for applied research" (p. 16). Both World Wars were instrumental in developing tests related to the selection and training of the service personnel, and this experience undoubtedly influenced the development of ability and personality testing (Adair et al., 1996).

During and immediately after World War II, sources of funding for basic research again became available, largely through the efforts of the Canadian

Psychological Association (CPA) that had been created in 1939, "primarily in response to the desire of its members to ensure that their expertise was used appropriately and effectively in the war effort" (Wright & Myers, 1982, p. 17). After the war, there was renewed emphasis on basic research in English Canadian universities. In stark contrast to the American Psychological Association (APA) during the same era, the CPA decided not to espouse the development of professional psychology; rather, it endorsed a return to the lab and to the classroom. This tendency culminated years later in the First National Conference on Training for Research in Psychology, held in 1960 (Bernhardt, 1961).

Notwithstanding the stance of organized psychology's national body, other psychologists were concerned with psychology's responsibility to society through applications of psychological expertise in clinics, hospitals, schools, and industry. This prompted the development of provincial and, later, territorial associations of psychology that became the main agents for the evolution of modern professional psychology in Canada. The Ontario Psychological Association was the first one, founded in 1948. However, unlike the U.S., there was no formal connection between the CPA and the provincial associations. In the absence of national policies and standards, professional psychology was to evolve far less coherently and less cohesively in Canada. Nonetheless, their advocacy led to licensure laws being adopted in all provinces and one of the territories over a 30-year period beginning with Ontario in 1960. Ironically, five provincial associations are affiliated with the APA, while no mechanism exists for affiliating with the CPA, except through an umbrella organiza-

tion, the Council of Provincial Associations of Psychologists (CPAP) that was recently invited to appoint a member to the CPA Board of Directors. The invitation was declined, with CPAP preferring to maintain a liaison status.

A series of national conferences over a 30-year period attempted to identify remedies for this situation. Thus, in 1965, another national conference was convened to deal with the training for professional practice (Webster, 1967). With very few exceptions, there was strong consensus favoring the scientist–practitioner model of training along the lines of the American (Boulder) model. In 1984, a conference examined the "state of the discipline" by focusing concurrently on education, research, and service delivery (Ritchie, Hogan, & Hogan, 1988). Finally, in 1994, another national conference, held in Mississauga, Ontario, was devoted entirely to professional psychology (Dobson & King, 1995). This conference dealt with professional psychology's current preoccupations and tried to delineate its future goals. In particular, it sought to legitimize a more market-oriented focus for applied research, education, and training, as well as for service delivery.

The 1984 and 1994 conferences reflect an important shift in the CPA. Beginning in the mid-1970s and accelerating in the 1980s, the CPA reversed its earlier decision and embraced professional psychology. In part, this resulted from the academic community's recognition that allying itself with the professional community would strengthen its advocacy efforts through a more visible link with responses to immediate efforts to enhance the well-being of Canadians. Consequently, the CPA now strives to serve the educational, professional, and research communities of Canadian psychology. This was conceptualized as a structural–functional approach to the unity of psychology (Ritchie & Sabourin, 1992). Despite the CPA's eventual commitment to professional psychology, only about one third of licensed psychologists are CPA members. The organization continues to be hampered in meeting its ambitious mission to represent all parts of the Canadian psychological community. The greatest problem is insufficient resources resulting from the failure to recruit a critical mass of members.

As in the U.S., some members of the academic community were dissatisfied with the CPA's growing attention to professional issues in the 1980s. They created the Canadian Society for Brain, Behavior, and Cognitive Science. It has maintained a base of several hundred psychological scientists.

To complete the picture of organized psychology at the national level, the profession's only national credentialing body, the Canadian Register of Health Service Providers in Psychology (CRHSPP), was legally incorporated in 1985 to identify for private and public sector bodies (e.g., government agencies and insurance companies), as well as for the general public, those practitioners who met basic requirements of education, training, and experience to qualify as health service providers in psychology.

In statistical terms, there are approximately 14,000 psychologists in Canada, of whom some 7,000 are in Quebec. With a total population heading toward 35 million, the ratio of psychologists per population is approximately one psychologist for every 2,000 Canadians. This number is somewhat misleading as there are great disparities in the distribution of psychologists, with the majority concentrated in the large metropolitan areas of the largest provinces. Average salaries also vary considerably across the provinces and territories, and in relation to the locus of practice (e.g., urban–rural) and type of services rendered. Over time, private practice tends to become more lucrative than institutional practice. The upper range of academic salaries is greater than that in service settings although the reverse occurs at the earlier stage of careers. Psychologists practicing in industrial–organizational or work psychology, as well as those providing privately funded legal expertise, usually have a higher income. Average salaries are thus misleading. However, income ranges from approximately $40,000 CAD ($30,600 USD) for early-career practitioners to in excess of $100,000 CAD ($76,500 USD) for more experienced psychologists, with some psychologists in private practice and a few in academia earning well above these amounts.

5.2 EDUCATION AND TRAINING

The first known course in psychology was taught in 1838 at Dalhousie University. After this initial effort, only sporadic repetitions of this course were offered in the next quarter century. The teaching of psychology really began on a continuing basis in the early 1850s at both McGill University and the University of Toronto. The first textbooks in psychology in Canada were both published in 1885: William Lyall's *The Intellect, the Emotions, and the Moral Nature* and John Clark Murray's *Handbook of Psychology.*

Psychology was taught as philosophy in all higher educational institutions well into the 20th century, thus defining this period as the prescientific era. The first modern psychologist appointed to a faculty in Canada was James Mark Baldwin at the University of Toronto in 1889. Trained at Leipzig in the Wundt tradition, he established the first psychological laboratory and initiated its first program of experimental research and its first curriculum in experimental psychology. A few years later, in 1893, a German named August Kirschmann, who had studied with Wundt, succeeded Baldwin (who had accepted an invitation from Princeton University) as head of the psychology laboratory. A friend of E. B. Titchener, he was among those who promoted the creation of the Society of Experimental Psychology. Two of his graduate students were destined to play important roles in the development of Canadian psychology: E. A. Bott and R. B. Liddy. Bott was active for 40 years at the University of Toronto, while Liddy spent his career at the University of Western Ontario. Only in the 1920s were the first autonomous psychology departments in Canada established at McGill (1924) and Toronto (1926), foreshadowing modern Canadian psychology. Other departments would not be created until the 1940s.

In French Canada, the initial development of academic psychology was essentially limited to the University of Ottawa, a bilingual institution, and the University of Montreal. During the 19th century, they both offered psychology as a relatively undifferentiated aspect of philosophy. Independent "institutes" of psychology were established at Ottawa (in 1941) and at Montreal (in 1942), and both institutes initially fostered a Roman Catholic outlook. This was before separate departments were established at most of the English Canadian universities, with the exception of McGill and Toronto. It is noteworthy that modest experimental psychology laboratories were only established in the 1940s at the University of Ottawa and not until the 1950s at the University of Montreal. Furthermore, at the French Canadian universities, the early emphasis was more clearly focused on applied psychology, particularly the clinical and counseling branches.

The intervening half-century has substantially reduced the disparities in education and training between English and French Canadian universities, both the older and the newer institutions, and all Canadian departments now offer strong programs in both scientific and applied psychology. Most English Canadian departments offering clinical psychology programs have received either CPA or APA accreditation. More recently, Quebec's French language universities have begun seeking such accreditation.

There is a strong commitment to public education in Canada. Virtually all colleges and universities are publicly funded, complemented by endowments, grants, and tuition. French-language postsecondary education (i.e., colleges and universities) is concentrated in Quebec, with other large-scale French-language universities found only in New Brunswick and Ontario. Endowments are more common in English Canadian universities; this is a relatively recent phenomenon in Quebec universities. The amount of tuition for postsecondary education varies from province to province; it is somewhat lower in Quebec universities (mandated at $1,700 CAD, or $1,300 USD) and ranging up to $7,000 CAD ($5,360 USD), with the median being approximately $4,200 CAD ($3,215 USD).

There are some differences in programs and curriculum. In Quebec, it takes 11 years to complete the primary (6 years) and secondary (5 years) levels. Once this is accomplished, and before entering a university undergraduate program in psychology, 2 years must be spent at the college level. These 2 years constitute a preparatory and transition phase for further studies at the university level. In the rest of Canada, students typically enter university directly after 12 years (7 years of primary and 5 years of secondary education).

At the undergraduate level, there are two possibilities: either an Honors Baccalaureate (3 years in Quebec or 4 years elsewhere) or a major in psychology. Unlike American undergraduate education, here the focus is on psychology courses, especially in the honors programs. An Honors Baccalaureate has become the norm for admission to graduate studies. However, admission to honors programs is highly competitive; for example, in 2003 at the University of Montreal, there were over 800 applications for 205 available admissions. Psychology is also a very popular subject for students in other programs, often comprising the most subscribed courses across departments. Hence, undergraduate courses provide much exposure for the discipline to all university-educated Canadians.

At the graduate level, the focus is becoming more exclusively doctoral. Those departments that have retained master's degree programs typically use them as entry points for their doctoral programs. The majority of graduate students at the doctoral level are in scientist–practitioner programs, especially in clinical psychol-ogy. Admission to these programs is also highly competitive with applications far exceeding available places, often by a ratio of 30:1 or more. In English Canada, as in the U.S., students often enter graduate programs at universities other than those where their undergraduate degrees were received. In contrast, in French Canada, it is common for students to do both undergraduate and graduate studies at the same university. This is probably due to the smaller number of potential universities and to cultural factors, especially comfort in English, even though Francophones are more common than Anglophones. Only a few terminal master's degree programs remain. In Quebec, all universities have abolished their terminal professionally oriented masters' programs in response to the new admissions criteria adopted by the Quebec's regulatory body for psychology that will require a competency-based doctoral degree.

The typical doctoral degree is the Ph.D. However, in Quebec, three universities offer professional doctoral degrees, the D.Ps. or Psy.D. The duration ranges from 4 years for professional doctorates to 6 or 7 years for the Ph.D., including an internship for professional and scientist–practitioner programs in both cases. None of the English Canadian universities currently offers a professional doctoral degree although several are currently considering such a development. There are no professional schools of psychology awarding degrees, except through extension programs of American universities. In these instances, the degree is awarded in the U.S. without sanction from Canadian education regulatory authorities.

In both English- and French-language comprehensive universities, the most important goals are to advance knowledge by promoting strong research programs and to obtain support for doing so through grants from federal and provincial agencies. At comprehensive universities, a secondary goal is to provide education and training in the professional branches of psychology. A smaller number of universities, which provide mainly undergraduate education, focus more on the quality of teaching.

Outside the university setting, continuing education and specialized training in different therapeutic approaches are offered to the psychological practitioner by private groups or trainers. This training does not lead to a recognized diploma. Provincial associations and regulatory bodies, as well as the CPA and CRHSPP, also offer continuing education, usually through workshops.

5.3 SCOPE OF PSYCHOLOGICAL PRACTICE

Psychology in Canada is now regulated in all 10 provinces as well as in two of the three territories, the exception being the Yukon Territory where the number of resident psychologists has rarely, if ever, exceeded single digit numbers. The first Psychology Act was enacted in Ontario in 1960. It took more than 30 years before Prince Edward Island became the last province to pass legislation governing the practice of psychology. Canada's system of regulating psychology is largely similar to that in the U.S., so much so that all the regulatory bodies of psychology in the two countries are linked through a common umbrella organization, the Association of State and

Provincial Psychology Regulatory Boards (ASPPB). The regulation of professions is the responsibility of the respective provinces and territories. Hence, there is separate legislation in each jurisdiction, and entry requirements for admission to the profession vary across provinces and territories (see http://www.cpa.ca/ licensing.html for entry requirements). This led to noteworthy differences that restricted the mobility of psychologists. Nonetheless, as described below, there has been progress within the profession and legislatively that allows psychology to better meet the needs of Canadian society.

A major breakthrough in resolving impediments to mobility was accomplished by the Mutual Recognition Agreement (MRA), signed by all of Canada's regulatory bodies of psychology in 2001 and implemented in 2003. The MRA was preceded by 5 years of intense deliberation and negotiation in which CPA and CRHSPP participated. This process was precipitated by the Agreement on Internal Trade (AIT), adopted by the federal government and all provincial and territorial governments in 1995, with the objective of reducing barriers to the internal movement of goods, supplies, and services. The impetus for the AIT followed from the provisions of several international free-trade agreements, most notably the North American Free Trade Agreement, which had the effect of making external trade less restrictive than such activities across Canadian jurisdictions. One of the principal components of the AIT was to mandate a competency-based approach to professional regulation. The regulatory bodies of all professions were charged with developing such a system.

The MRA established five core competencies to be attained by all persons seeking admission to the profession in any jurisdiction. They include ethics and standards, evaluation and diagnosis, interpersonal relations, intervention and consultation, and research. The MRA defines each competency and delineates the knowledge and skills to be attained. For example, research competency is defined in terms of the capacity to apply current methodology. It does not require the ability to generate new knowledge, typically associated with the criteria for obtaining a doctorate. This means that persons seeking a professional doctoral degree (e.g., D.Ps., Psy.D.) are equally eligible for licensure. The MRA also provides improved mechanisms to enhance the mobility of psychologists already admitted to practice. For example, psychologists who hold the credential provided by the CRHSPP are eligible to be treated on an expedited basis if they wish to gain licensure in another Canadian jurisdiction. The MRA is regarded as one of the most important accomplishments of Canadian psychology in the past half-century. Although a number of implementation details remain to be resolved, the prospect of a national standard for the practice of psychology in Canada is now at hand.

The regulatory system for Canadian psychology has been evolving rapidly in the past decade. Its fundamental mandate is protection of the public by controlling admission to the profession, adjudicating complaints and, where necessary, disciplining psychologists, and establishing criteria for maintaining licensure. Among the main features found increasingly across jurisdictions are (a) self-governance, whereby licensed psychologists themselves elect peers to the board of directors or council of the regulatory body, complemented by substantial public representation through persons typically named to the boards of directors by the respective provincial or territorial governments; (b) defined scopes of practice that establish the parameters for the professional practice of psychology; and (c) requirements for sustaining competence. The latter may include traditional continuing education, but may also contain other features such as self-directed learning programs. Greater controversy is likely to occur in the determination of scopes of practice. Where they are descriptive and nonexclusive, it is often easier to have them adopted legislatively. However, when they include "controlled" activities such as diagnosis, vigorous advocacy is typically required to succeed. The Examination for the Professional Practice of Psychology developed and administered by the ASPPB is compulsory, albeit with different criteria for passing, in all regulated provinces and territories except Quebec. In every jurisdiction, it is also possible for those holding foreign diplomas to have their credentials examined and potentially recognized as equivalent for licensure.

The overlap among the areas or branches of professional psychology (e.g., clinical, counseling, forensic, industrial–organizational–work, neuropsychology, rehabilitation, school) has been a conundrum for Canadian professionals for many years, as it has been in the U.S. and some other countries. A call to reduce overlap and for graduate programs to concentrate on truly specialized areas of skills and competencies was made almost 15 years ago (Service et al., 1989), but definitive action has yet to occur.

The absence of clearly defined specialties and the generic nature of professional recognition created a particular problem in the area of health service delivery, in that the proper identification of those duly trained to offer health-related services cannot be assumed from the generic title. In the early 1980s, this ambiguity was increasingly hampering advocacy efforts to improve access to, and recognition of, the value of psychological health services. This prompted the Council of Provincial Associations of Psychology (CPAP) to establish the Canadian Register of Health Service Providers in Psychology (CRHSPP) in 1985. The purpose was to credential individual psychologists who meet the criteria for education, training, and experience for recognition as a heath service provider. Thus, it became possible, without a system for recognizing specialization, to distinguish a particular category of psychologists, the health service provider. A few years later, in 1991, the value of CRHSPP was confirmed, as its credential provided the means for psychological health services to be exempted from the Goods and Service Tax in federal legislation then being created. This also had the effect of prompting similar exemptions in provincial and territorial tax laws. This achievement had resulted from the most extensive advocacy effort ever mounted by Canadian psychology (Sabourin, 1991).

The CPA has been the main organization leading the development of national ethical guidelines. The Code of Ethics for Psychologists (Canadian Psychological Association, 2001) was first published by the CPA in 1985 and subsequently revised in 1991 and 2001. Prior to this time, the code of ethics of the APA was used in most parts of Canada. However, differences in cultural and economic orientations between the two countries led to the development of the Canadian code. In addition to its impact in Canada, psychologists in numerous other countries have regarded it as innovative. It has provided inspiration to the current ethical codes in countries as diverse as Ireland and South Africa. The code has four core principles (respect for the dignity of persons, responsible caring, integrity in relationships, responsibility to society), each framed by a statement that makes explicit its ethical basis. Each principle is elaborated by specific standards, totaling 173 that are operationally oriented. The Canadian code is anchored in an ethical decision-making approach, contributing to its functionality. In addition to the CPA, 11 of the 12 provinces and territories in which psychology is regulated have adopted the Canadian code of ethics. The exception is Quebec. Within the Canadian federation, Quebec was allowed to retain its civil code system of law for areas of responsibility allocated to it by the Canadian constitution. All other jurisdictions and the federal component of the country's legal and judicial framework use the common law system. As a result, all professional codes of ethics used for regulatory purposes in Quebec must adhere to certain particulars that preclude the adoption of an external code. However, proposed revisions to the regulatory code of ethics for Quebec psychologists reflect many of the features of the Canadian code of ethics for psychologists.

Canada has a rich tradition of research across the full spectrum of psychological science. Adair et al. (1996) reviewed the various sectors in detail. Of particular note are contributions to the neurosciences and neuropsychology. There are also areas that are distinctively Canadian, especially research on bilingualism and cross-cultural psychology. The former has made unique contributions to the understanding of language and communication, whereas the latter has examined both English–French issues, characteristics of First Nations' peoples, and the experience of more recently arrived ethnic groups.

In the realm of professional psychology, research and practice mirror the experience of the U.S. and other economically advantaged countries. All the major orientations are practiced in Canada, and Canadian psychologists have made outstanding contributions to all major orientations used by psychologists in many other countries. They have also benefited from research conducted elsewhere. In recent years, cognitive–behavior therapy has been gaining ground, along with interpersonal and systemic approaches. Nonetheless, experiential–humanistic and psychodynamic orientations continue to be utilized. Cutting across specific theoretical approaches, clinical health psychology is becoming an increasingly important organizing framework for the delivery of psychological services in both public and private sectors.

There is also increasing attention to developing evidence-based practices (Hunsley, Dobson, Johnston, & Mikhail, 1999). While reservations remain about adopting narrow, orthodox, "empirically supported" treatments, current public policy and private sector decision-makers clearly favor approaches and disciplines that can demonstrate their efficacy and efficiency. Although this has prompted a shift toward more short-term approaches, it has led to greater accountability in making the case for longer-term interventions. The phenomenon of evidence-based practice has been addressed more pragmatically in Canada than in the U.S., as illustrated by the leadership taken by the Canadian Register, which has made a significant investment to enable its registrants to become

familiar with the principles and methods of evidence-based practice. This has led to an educational package that is disseminated to all registrants, a workshop offered in partnership with provincial and territorial organizations, and an innovative on-line consultation service.

As a clinical discipline, psychology is emerging as a predominantly health care profession. Ritchie and Edwards (1998) provide a comprehensive review of Canada's health care system and its implications for the practice of psychology as a health care profession. Constitutionally, the provinces and territories are responsible for health. However, due to the peculiarities of Canada's constitutional regime, the federal government is unfettered in its spending power. Hence, under the authority of the Canada Health Act, the federal government offers financial incentives to the provinces and territories in order to achieve comparable publicly funded health services across the country. Currently, about 70% of psychological services in Canada are funded through the public sector, whereas some 30% is funded through the private sector. In the past decade, there has been a shift of about 5% of aggregate healthcare spending from the public to the private sector. The largest influence has been cutbacks generated by the commitment of the federal and all provincial and territorial governments to reduce their budgetary deficits substantially. This has meant fewer positions in traditional settings such as hospitals and publicly funded agencies. In some parts of the country, notably Quebec, the volume of newly admitted practitioners has also been a contributing factor to the upward trend in private practice. However, some of this is also due to the typical profile of psychologists, whose primary work setting is a publicly funded facility, and who engage in private practice as a secondary form of employment. Psychologists are found in virtually all settings in which health services are provided.

Within the public sector, psychologists practice in hospitals of all types (i.e., general, psychiatric, rehabilitation, and university teaching hospitals) and a variety of clinics and agencies. A small number receive public funds to practice in multidisciplinary settings with family physicians and nurses, and they are reimbursed by nontraditional payment mechanisms. In the private sector, the typical setting is a private practice office that may take the form of a solo or group practice. The latter may be composed of other psychologists or a mix of providers from several health disciplines.

In both sectors, the mix of assessment, diagnosis, consultation, and treatment varies with the characteristics of the setting and the particular population being served. Consistent with their mandate, psychologists working in acute care hospitals are likely to do more comprehensive diagnostic work-ups than in the typical community setting where treatment is likely to be the main focus. However, there is considerable variance in practice patterns, which make such generalizations difficult. For example, in rural and remote communities with more limited access to psychological services, a different mix of diagnostic work and treatment may prevail than in the urban communities of southern Canada where there is greater possibility to specialize and concentrate expertise more narrowly.

One factor transcends public and private sectors, as well as demographic and geographic characteristics. Although Canadian psychologists continue to make important contributions to services asso-

ciated with traditional mental health, they now intervene frequently with persons presenting with the full range of health problems (Arnett, 2001). Of particular importance, psychologists are identified as primary care as well as tertiary care providers. Hence, while anxiety and mood disorders remain the modal diagnostic entities, they are now likely to be addressed as problems associated with cardiovascular disorders rather than as exclusively psychiatric. This is prompting changes in patterns of service delivery. For example, family physicians and nurses are more likely to be the primary referral sources rather than psychiatrists.

Psychologists also provide services in a wide variety of other settings. In these settings, the traditional public–private distinction is becoming more blurred. For example, a publicly funded community agency may secure psychological services by either hiring a psychologist, who becomes an employee of the setting, or it may contract with a private practitioner to provide services either at the agency or at the psychologist's own office, with a number of possible payment mechanisms. Psychologists also offer clinical services in a range of social service agencies, such as those serving children in need of protection and their families.

Canadian psychologists have a long history of working in school systems across the range of primary, secondary, and university education. At all levels, the great majority of psychological services provided in educational settings is publicly funded. However, some psychologists in private practice specialize in learning assessments and delivering focused remedial programs.

Forensic psychology has grown considerably in the past two decades, reflecting

Canada's general adherence to a rehabilitation model of criminal justice compared to the retributive approach found in some other countries. There was some attenuation of this orientation during the past decade in conjunction with a conservative orientation to public finance, as noted above. Nonetheless, the federal government, which is constitutionally responsible for legislating the criminal code, continues to have more psychologists working in the criminal justice system than in any other branch of the federal government.

Canadian psychologists made important contributions while serving in the armed forces during World War II. However, in subsequent decades, there have been relatively few psychologists working in the armed services, although these psychologists do provide an impressive range of clinical and organizational services, as well as engage in applied research. In recent years, psychologists have treated service men and women presenting with problems that are associated with Canada's major contribution to U.N. peacekeeping activities overseas.

Although a small cohort of industrial–organizational psychologists have worked principally in the private sector for more than a half-century, there is renewed interest in workplace health. This has prompted consideration of how best to apply psychological expertise in clinical health to the workplace. This goes beyond the provision of direct services for psychological disorders in conjunction with employee assistance programs or as part of extended health programs that are provided a benefit of employment. The more recent focus involves teaching managers and senior executives to respond more effectively to the psychological problems of their employees and maximize performance in a knowledge-based economy.

5.4 FUTURE CHALLENGES AND PROSPECTS

Canadian psychology has grown dramatically in the past half-century. Its academic core has expanded considerably, and psychology remains one of the most popular subjects at the undergraduate level. Admission to its graduate programs is highly competitive, especially in all areas associated with professional psychology. As a science, research productivity has increased steadily with pioneering work in the foundational areas, the neurosciences, and the applied research that is recognized internationally. Psychology is the only discipline eligible for funding from all three of Canada's major funding agencies: the Medical Research Council, Natural Sciences and Engineering Research Council, and Social Sciences and Humanities Research Council. In the professional realm, more than 10,000 psychologists contribute to Canadian society as practitioners. Psychology has also been legitimized as a health care profession through legislation, publicly funded programs, and private sector endeavors. This has been possible because Canadian psychology has retained its capacity to manage its remarkable diversity. The vibrancy of Canadian psychology and its pertinence to the country will depend on its capacity to mirror core Canadian values. It is sometimes difficult for Canadians themselves, let alone colleagues and observers from elsewhere, to make sense of the paradox of Canadian life. It incorporates a collective desire to maintain decency and integrity, expressed as a strong adherence to basic principles of human rights, coupled with a concurrent espousal of compromise and pragmatism as a means of achieving goals and resolving seemingly intractable differences.

The future of Canadian psychology is bright. As an academically based science, psychology is well positioned to contribute to an increasingly knowledge-based economy. It will continue to be a bulwark of undergraduate education. In particular, its tradition of combining rigorous intellectual preparation in the natural as well as social sciences enables it to play a lead role in the postsecondary education of Canadians. Indeed, psychology has a great capacity to foster the integration of technologically oriented knowledge and skills with those generated from a social science perspective. Whether they are engaged at the frontiers of artificial intelligence and neuro-imaging, reforming the healthcare system to be sustainable in an increasingly aged society, or creating a more culturally cosmopolitan society, Canadian psychological scientists will play a seminal role.

Despite this bright overall future, professional psychologists in Canada face daunting challenges. The reality is that the vast majority of practitioners provide their services within a broadly construed clinical and population-health framework. Nonetheless, there will be varying emphasis on the degree to which the focus is more clinical and molecular (i.e., on individuals, couples, and families) versus collective and social (i.e., on demographically defined groups and the larger community).

At one end of the continuum will be psychologists with a community or counseling background, working in a variety of community settings to address the range of personal and social phenomena experienced by people coping with changes in family life, workplace stressors, and community transition as the ethnic and racial composition of Canadian society evolves. Hence, there will be a need for psychologists with strong community psychology and applied social psychology backgrounds. This extends to traditional service areas such as the criminal justice system. These psychologists will bridge strong methodological skills in applied research (e.g., needs assessment and program evaluation) with a practical problem-solving approach to individual and collective needs. It is also possible that some of the problem-resolution principles and methods found in the traditional First Nations' cultures will better inform Canadian psychology. The First Nations have been reconstituting themselves as viable cultures after centuries of oppression. As this evolves, a greater synthesis may be possible in which psychologists could play a major role. If this occurs, Canada might again offer an example of how modern society can build a sustainable collectivity founded in diversity.

In the more traditionally clinical health domain, two dimensions are likely to be important. First, in many industrial countries, the fiscal burden of a largely publicly funded health care system is compelling re-evaluation and prompting reforms. This has been true in Canada, with numerous national, provincial, and territorial reviews commissioned in the past decade. The Canadian public has made its voice felt in public hearings and through the media. Second, Canadians are consistent and clear about their sense of entitlement to a mainly publicly funded health care system; it is the only area of government spending for which they are willing to pay more taxes, and they are increasingly impatient about the failure to find the political will to create solutions that are more permanent. In the interim, the prospect of an increasingly aged society looms ever larger as the post–World War II baby-boomers approach the point at which their aging will generate inevitable new pressures on the viability of the Canadian healthcare system.

Unfortunately, Canadian psychology has had only modest success at the national, provincial, and territorial levels in effecting legislative and policy changes in ways that increase the public's access to the profession. This results from entrenched prerogatives accorded other professions: historically, professional privilege has been anchored in the gatekeeper role granted to physicians; more recently, nurses and nurse practitioners have also assumed a larger place. Psychology itself has contributed to the problem by traditionally defining itself as a mental health profession. Recently though, psychology has identified itself as a broad based health care profession, an identity that has been increasingly recognized. Whether this recognition can be translated into public policy and legislative change is one of the most important questions of the coming decade.

Canadian psychologists will continue to participate actively in the globalization of the discipline and the profession. To an important degree, Canadian psychological scientists are already experiencing the benefits of opportunities provided by the Internet and World Wide Web. Canada is a leader in such technology, and all psychological scientists in Canada are active consumers. Some are also involved in its creative adaptation to the needs of science.

At the professional level, the focus has been more on regional activities. For example, Canadian psychologists as well as the CPA, CPAP, and CRHSPP have provided sustained participation to the Trilateral Forum on Professional Psychology in North America that brings together the leadership and senior psychologists of Canada, Mexico, and the U.S. Among the topics to which Canadian psychologists have made particular contributions are competencies essential for practice and the development of a North American metacode of ethics.

Canadian psychologists also have a long tradition of contributing to the leadership of the main global organization embracing both academic and professional dimensions, the International Union of Psychological Science (IUPsyS). There has been at least one Canadian officer of IUPsyS for more than a half-century; Canadians have twice assumed the post of the editor of the *International Journal of Psychology*; and, currently, Canadian psychologists are the IUPsyS' main representatives to the U.N. Secretariat and Economic and Social Council, and to the World Health Organization. Canadian psychologists have also been in key leadership positions in the Interamerican Society of Psychology. They have also been active contributors to international and regional congresses of psychology. Canadian psychology and psychologists can be expected to maintain support for international psychology in the 21st century.

Canadian psychology has enjoyed a unique relationship with American psychology for many decades. Prior to World War II, the relationships of individual psychologists, especially in the academic world, were more likely to have been with

British and European French-language colleagues than with their American neighbors. In the past half-century, there has been a steady increase in exchanges with American colleagues. In the scientific realm, there is no fundamental distinction between the two countries except for certain foci on distinctive social and demographic characteristics. The two national unitary organizations, the CPA and the APA, probably enjoy the closest relationship of any two national psychology organizations. This is exemplified in the Joint Memorandum on Accreditation, which provides for joint accreditation of professional psychology programs and internships that seek concurrent accreditation in both countries.

Canadians have profited from American experience in advocacy efforts to achieve licensure. The establishment of the CRHSPP borrowed considerably from the National Register; core functions operate very similarly, albeit with different models of governance. As this example suggests, professional change is rarely a matter of simply adopting American models. Canadian constitutional realities, culture, history, and political tradition compel thoughtful adaptation, even when the incorporation of an American approach is possible. One example is prescriptive authority. The prescription privilege is the centerpiece for national advocacy of professional psychology in the U.S., and it is a high priority area for the APA. Yet, while Canadian psychologists followed the debate among American psychologists with interest and are reasonably informed about recent progress, none of the Canadian psychological organizations has made it a priority. Indeed, the policy objective has not even been the object of much debate,

let alone adopted as a goal. Some leaders of American psychology have been puzzled, even shocked, by this fact, suggesting that it represents a failure of leadership. Such views are only possible when the characteristics that distinguish Canadian psychology from American psychology are unknown. Regrettably, only a small number of leaders of American psychology have become well-informed about Canadian psychology. It may well be that Canadian psychologists will decide to seek inclusion of prescription privileges in psychology's scope of practice. If it does, it will, unquestionably, profit once more from prior American experience.

At present, there are other priorities for improving Canadian psychology's capacity to contribute to Canadian society. Some of these issues include reform of Canada's health care system (especially primary care and specialized tertiary care), securing adequate funding to maintain Canadian psychological science's preeminence in basic and applied research, enhancing non-traditional community interventions and population-health initiatives, sustaining psychology's presence in the primary and secondary school systems and in the criminal justice system, supporting private practitioners to make their practices evidence-based and enabling them to offer their services in new settings, and contributing to Canada's continuing evolution as a peaceful, multicultural, and cosmopolitan society. These endeavors will likely be complemented by a sustained commitment to the international development of psychology. This will include, but not be limited to, dealing with the opportunities and risks of economically driven globalization. It will also address the challenges of a world in which peaceful solutions to conflict resolution are ever necessary. In this respect, Canadian psychologists can be expected to reflect values that are typically regarded as Canadian hallmarks: informed debate and negotiation, perseverance in the face of adversity, and principled compromise.

REFERENCES

Adair, J. G., Paivio, A., & Ritchie, P. (1996). Psychology in Canada. *Annual Review of Psychology, 47,* 341–370.

Arnett, J. (2001). Clinical and health psychology: Future directions. *Canadian Psychology, 42,* 38–48.

Bernhardt, K. S. (1961). *Training for research in psychology: The Canadian Opinicon Conference.* Toronto: University of Toronto Press.

Canadian Psychological Association. (2001). *Companion manual to the code of ethics* (3rd ed.). Ottawa: Author.

Dobson, K. S., & King, M. C. (1995). *The Mississauga conference on professional psychology in Canada.* Ottawa: Canadian Psychological Association.

Granger, L. (1993). The union of regulatory and fraternal roles: The professional corporation model of regulation. In K. S. Dobson & D. J. G. Dobson (Eds.), *Professional psychology in Canada* (pp. 225–243). Toronto: Hogrefe & Huber.

Hunsley, J., Dobson, K., Johnston, C., & Mikhail, S. (1999). Empirically supported treatments in psychology: Implications for Canadian professional psychology. *Canadian Psychology, 40,* 289–319.

Ritchie, P., & Sabourin, M. (1992). Sous un même toit (Under the same roof): Canada's functional-structural approach to the unity of psychology. *International Journal of Psychology, 27,* 311–325.

Ritchie, P. L.-J., & Edwards, H. P. (1998). National health policies in Canada and the practice of clinical psychology. In A. Bellack, M. Hersen, & A. Wiens (Eds.), *Comprehensive clinical psychology: Professional issues* (Vol. 2, pp. 377–391). New York: Pergamon.

Ritchie, P. L.-J., Hogan, T. P., & Hogan, T. V. (Eds.). (1988). *Psychology in Canada: The state of the discipline, 1984.* Ottawa: Canadian Psychological Association.

Sabourin, M. (1991). Faire reconnaître la psychologie sur la scène politique: L'approche TPS (tractations, planification, stratégie) [Advocating psychology in the public forum: The GST approach (guile, strategy, timing)]. *Canadian Psychology, 32,* 3–15.

Service, J., Sabourin, M., Catano, V. M., Day, V., Hayes, C., & MacDonald, G. W. (1989). *Report of the CPA/CPAP task force on specialty designation.* Ottawa: Canadian Psychological Association.

Webster, E. C. (Ed.). (1967). *The Couchiching Conference on Professional Psychology in Canada.* Montreal: Canadian Psychological Association.

Wright, M. J., & Myers, C. R. (1982). *History of academic psychology in Canada.* Toronto: Hogrefe.

IMPORTANT PUBLICATION

Danziger, K. (1990). *Constructing the subject: Historical origins of psychological research.* New York: Cambridge University Press.

Dobson, K., & Dobson, D. (Eds). (1993). *Professional psychology in Canada.* Toronto: Hogrefe & Huber.

Endler, N. S., & Magnusson, D. (1976). Toward an interactional psychology of personality. *Psychological Bulletin, 83,* 956–974.

Gardner, R. C., & Kalin, R. (1981). *A Canadian social psychology of ethnic relations.* Toronto: Methuen.

Hebb, D. O., (1949). *The organization of behavior.* New York: Wiley.

Meichenbaum, D. (1977). *Cognitive-behavior modification.* New York: Plenum.

Melzack, R. (1993). Pain: past, present, and future. *Canadian Journal of Psychology, 47,* 617–629.

Milner, B. (1980). Complementary functional specializations of the human cerebral hemispheres. In R. Levi-Montalcini (Ed.), *Nerve cells, transmitters, and behavior* (pp. 601–625). Vatican City: Pontifical Academy of Science.

Reynolds, A. G. (Ed.). (1991). *Bilinguilism, multiculturalism, and second language learning: The McGill Conference in honor of Wallace E. Lambert*. Hillsdale, NJ: Erlbaum.

Tulving, E. (1983). *Elements of episodic memory*. New York: Oxford University Press.

CHAPTER 6

Psychology in Mexico: Recent Developments and Perspective

JUAN JOSÉ SÁNCHEZ-SOSA

Juan José Sánchez-Sosa obtained his licentiate *in psychology degree from Mexico's National University (1970), and his M.A. (1975) and Ph.D. (1983) in the United States from the University of Kansas. He is a full-time faculty member at National University and has served as a member of doctoral dissertation defense committees by invitation in Spain, Switzerland, and the United States.*

Juan Sánchez-Sosa is author or editor of six books and some 60 articles and chapters on educational, health, and professional psychology, and was editor of the Mexican Journal of Behavior Analysis. *He has served on the review boards of numerous international journals.*

Past president of the Mexican Psychological Society, the Mexican College of Psychologists, and the International Society of Clinical Psychology, he is currently secretary general of the Union of Latin American Universities, vice-president of the International Union of Psychological Sciences, and president of the Division of Clinical and Community Psychology of the International Association of Applied Psychology.

6.1 OVERVIEW

It has been said that psychology in Mexico has a long past but a relatively recent history. Indeed, although its beginnings date back to the late 19th century when courses were first taught at universities, psychology as a well-established profession with its own disciplinary identity originated in the first few decades of the 20th century. As in most other Latin American countries, Mexican psychology was born within its main universities. Even though the University of Mexico was founded in 1551, disciplines other than architecture, law, medicine, mining (engineering), and theology offered courses centuries later. Formal courses in psychology, first taught by Ezequiel Chavez in 1896 at Mexico's National University (UNAM), gave clear evidence of the establishment of psychology (Sánchez Sosa & Valderrama-Iturbe, 2001).

Modern psychology developed in Europe and the United States in the last third of the 19th century, and psychology established itself in Latin America during the last decade of that century, influenced simultaneously by the academic and intellectual ferment in both Europe and the United States. The primary influences that helped to shape psychology in Mexico were English positivism (e.g., the writings of Herbert Spencer and John Stuart Mill) and German psychology (especially Wilhelm Wundt and, later, Kurt Koffka, Wolfgang Köhler, and Kurt Lewin). Other important early influences arose from the psychoanalytic perspective of Sigmund Freud and the work of French clinical and experimental psychologists such as Alfred Binet, Jean Charcot, and Théodule Ribot. Also, French social psychologists, including Gustave Le Bon and Gabriel Tarde, and the Geneva school scholars Edouard Claparede and Gabriel Compayre were historical sources for the early development of Mexican psychology.

Mexican psychology was also influenced by U.S. psychologists, especially by Edward Titchener's interpretation of structuralism (i.e., the belief that all mental experience could be understood as a combination of simple elements or events). Shortly after, the work of James Baldwin and Columbia's functionalistic school became widely known and adopted. Functionalism focuses on the acts and functions of the mind rather than on its internal contents. The influence of various pioneers of U.S. psychology in the fields of psychological assessment and the experimental analysis of behavior progressively added to a mosaic that was simultaneously being influenced by neurology and psychiatry (Sanchez-Sosa & Valderrama-Iturbe, 2001).

Contemporary Mexican psychology has been shaped by the rapid expansion of experimentation, inductive theory construction, psychological testing, and statistical methods—the axes of modern scientific psychology. This expansion started during the early 1960s at the College of Psychology of the School of Philosophy and Letters of UNAM. After a contentious period in which professors and students representing the two main general approaches to psychology (psychodynamic and experimental) competed for supremacy, the College separated from the School of Philosophy and Letters, becoming the School of Psychology in 1973. This was, perhaps, the first such school in Latin America to offer a doctoral degree exclusively in psychology.

Data obtained from the Office for the Regulation of the Professions of Mexico's Ministry of Education reveal that approximately 64,000 licenses for psychologists have been issued since 1945 (Direccion General de Profesiones, 2003). However, there are no reliable data available on how many psychologists are currently practicing. Recent estimates from the Mexican Psychological Society (2003) suggest that roughly half of those who practice do so in fields related to clinical or health psychology. Some 10–15% work in an industrial–organizational setting, and another 10–15% are employed in school settings. The remainder is made up mainly of academicians and researchers in universities and other higher education and research institutions. A few psychologists practice in emerging applied fields such as forensic psychology. Approximately 95% of Mexico's psychologists practice in urban areas. These figures constitute approximations because accurate record keeping is a relatively recent development in many Mexican institutions, public and private.

Although there is a long historical tradition of scientific and professional societies in Mexico (the first two psychological societies in Latin America were founded in 1907 in Mexico and in 1908 in Argentina), scientific and professional organizations tend to attract relatively few individuals, except, perhaps, in the fields of accounting, architecture, engineering, and law (Sanchez-Sosa & Valderrama-Iturbe, 2001). There are generally two types of organizations: societies and *colegios* (colleges). Societies are usually scientific or disciplinary in nature whereas *colegios* tend to function more as professional guilds. The two main organizations serving psychology are the Mexican Psychological Society (MPS; founded in 1950) and the Mexican College of Psychologists (MCP; founded in 1985).

These two organizations are perceived by Mexican psychologists as complementary rather than as competitive, and they have worked closely together since the MCP was founded. The MPS holds an annual convention and publishes the *Mexican Journal of Psychology*. The MCP holds a biannual convention and publishes its proceedings as books. Although Mexican regulatory laws for the professions give more weight to *colegios*, nearly all government administrations since the 1970s have consulted both organizations regarding professional-practice regulations and pub-

lic policy whenever behavior is identified as a significant part of a problem or its solution. This consulting trend by federal and state administrations has become more frequent and formal in the last decade, and delegates from both organizations hold seats on commissions for health and education.

Another important organization is the National Council for Research and Education in Psychology (CNEIP), composed of 80 department chairs and deans of schools of psychology. About half of CNEIP members represent public universities, and the other half are from private universities. With over 300 university programs training professional psychologists in Mexico, the council only represents about 25% of all departments or schools of psychology currently active in Mexico; however, it is still the largest association of its kind. It includes the leading training programs in psychology in Mexico. In addition, the council supports the publication of two journals: *Teaching and Research in Psychology* (*Ensenanza e Investigacion en Psicologia*) and *Psychology and Health* (*Psicologia y Salud*).

Other psychological organizations tend to be more specialized. The oldest and most prominent include the Mexican Society of Behavior Analysis (SMAC), the Mexican Society of Clinical Psychology, and two associations of social psychologists founded along different methodological and theoretical lines. These societies usually organize congresses on a relatively regular basis, but only SMAC and the Mexican Association of Social Psychology actually publish well-established journals.

In general, salaries for psychologists in the public sector are lower than those of some other professionals. In the health sector, for example, a psychologist at Mexico's Institute for Social Security (a nationwide healthcare system) makes about 30% less than a physician and about 10% less than a registered nurse. In this system, a psychologist's salary is about that of a social worker. Although relationships between psychologists and these other professionals depend greatly on the nature of the services they offer and their respective responsibilities, physicians are considered the persons in charge of health teams in hospital settings and community health centers. Psychologists have been inching their way toward comparable recognition with psychiatrists. This is in part because evidence-based psychological treatments for emotional problems have evolved more quickly than those of traditional clinical psychiatry despite the constant introduction of new medications. There has not been any push to promote prescription privileges for psychologists in Mexico, and it does not look like this will change any time soon.

On the other hand, if the number and type of articles published are an indicator, research is an area where psychologists have had at least as much success as psychiatrists. The number of research articles jointly published by psychologists and psychiatrists is on the rise, and this provides evidence of improving professional relationships.

6.2 EDUCATION AND TRAINING

As in other parts of the world, interest in psychology in Latin America originated in other professions such as education, law, and medicine. The success of early applications of psychological expertise and the country's need for professionally trained psychologists soon led to the foundation of university-level programs in psychology. Many institutes of applied psychology later became schools whose primary purpose was to educate and train psychologists. Thus, seminal and isolated courses gradually evolved into fully developed university curricula. In 1937, Ezequiel Chavez formally proposed the establishment of master's and doctoral degree programs in psychology at UNAM. In time, these degrees evolved into the professional degree program that leads to licensure, currently termed *licenciatura*.

The structure of the Mexican educational system can be traced almost directly to the French system that was adopted by the Mexican government during the last decade of the 19th and first decade of the 20th centuries. After kindergarten and 1–2 years of preelementary education ending by age six, children attend elementary school for 6 years, followed by 3 years of high school and 3 years toward the bachelor's degree, thus completing a 12-year pre-university cycle. In Mexico, the terms "undergraduate" and "graduate," as used in the United States, are not relevant because after the bachelor's degree is awarded at about age 18, students enter universities to pursue professional degrees.

A typical B.A. curriculum is six semesters in duration, and includes such subjects as anthropology, biology, physics, chemistry, cybernetics (or informatics) and computing, economics, environmental design, modern foreign languages, Greek and Latin, geography, art, health sciences, history, Mexican law, literature, mathematics including calculus, philosophy, political sciences, introductory psychology, and statistics. Many of these subjects are actually taught across semesters; therefore, it is common to find such courses as Physics III, Biology IV, and so on.

Once they have completed their B.A., students who go on to become professional psychologists are admitted to either a public or private university to study psychology exclusively. Depending on a variety of factors such as student demand, facilities, and faculty, schools or departments (especially at public universities) require applicants to pass an entrance examination. All programs, public or private, file their admissions criteria with the Ministry for Education. Most public universities, as well as highly prestigious private universities, also require that applicants to professional training programs in psychology complete several bachelors-level courses in the natural sciences at their pre-university institutions.

Students enter the university for professional training at around 18 or 19 years of age. Most programs in professional psychology require 5–6 years of coursework as well as laboratory experiences and practica that are exclusively devoted to psychology. The last portion of this cycle involves either the completion of a thesis or a supervised practicum at an external training site; sometimes both are required. Part of this practicum, referred to as social service, is mandatory for all professions that require university training, and usually requires 500–1000 h of service. Usually, the thesis is publicly defended before a faculty committee composed of at least three professors. Most programs that train professional psychologists are housed in either a school of psychology or a department of psychology that is part of a larger school. Schools of psychology are normally headed by a dean and may have various departments that represent distinct specialties in psy-

chology. Departments, however, are not empowered to issue diplomas (i.e., professional titles).

Some professional schools in other disciplines have massive numbers of students (e.g., UNAM's medical school has some 10,000 students and the school of business administration has over 15,000). For logistical reasons, these schools have replaced the thesis requirement with an objective, multiple-choice examination of approximately 500 questions. Although this trend has recently started in psychology, nearly all schools have retained both options for programs that lead to a professional license.

During the first 3 years, the typical professional licensing degree in psychology requires coursework and laboratory experience in subjects such as the biological bases of behavior, perception, cognitive processes, emotion, learning, motivation, sensation, research methodology, statistics, test construction, and theories and systems of psychology. The last 2 to 3 years of training require courses and experience in assessment as well as training in the development and implementation of intervention strategies. The thematic areas covered usually include clinical and health problems, counseling, school performance, job performance, interpersonal relations, community psychology, and ethics. The basic structure of many professional programs tends to resemble those called "combined" or "integrated" in the United States (see Beutler & Fisher, 1994). Teaching formats vary, but lectures are widely used in introductory level courses. The typical class size at this level at many public universities is around 45 students. Class size decreases and other formats including seminars and study groups are more widely used as students progress through their programs.

The oldest, best established, and most prominent professional training psychology programs in public universities include those at UNAM and the state universities of Baja California, Guadalajara, Nuevo Leon, Sonora, Veracruz, and Yucatan. Private universities with good professional training programs in psychology include Anahuac, Iberoamericana, Latinoamericana, and del Valle de Mexico, among others. Practically all psychologists at the licensure degree level are trained in Mexico. Approximately half of psychologists wishing to become advanced researchers and specialized instructors seek graduate degrees abroad, mainly in Belgium, Canada, France, Spain, and the U.S.

In the last 15 years, Mexico has become a relatively well-connected and well-equipped country with access to high-speed computers and digital telecommunications, and with widespread use of the Internet. Higher educational institutions have shared in this progress, although there is still wide variability across universities in the access students have to computers and the Internet. Globalization has made access to books and scientific journals easier, but it has not reduced the cost of this access.

Starting in the early 1970s, several well-established publishing houses in Latin America and Spain (e.g., Trillas, Aguilar, Manual Moderno, and Plaza y Valdes) quickly responded to the growing demand for psychology textbooks written in Spanish, especially in Mexico, Colombia, and Peru. By the early 1980s, many of the textbooks commonly used in the United Staes had been translated into Spanish and were routinely used to teach psychology students, especially during the first half of professional level programs. This trend,

however, has not made significant inroads into the second half of professional training or to postgraduate training, primarily due to the increasing tendency to recruit and admit students who can read English.

It should be noted that nearly half of all students admitted to public university programs that lead to a license to practice psychology drop out before completing their third year of study. Follow-up data on dropouts reveal that the main reasons for leaving the university include a scarcity of financial resources and a need to cope with life's transitions (e.g., starting a family, relocating to find employment). Institutional funding for students at the professional training level is rare in Mexico. Funding agencies tend to target students in programs that are dedicated to training highly specialized instructors at the master's level and researchers at the Ph.D. level. These funding sources are highly competitive, and only postgraduate university programs listed by the National Council for Science and Technology as "Programs of Excellence" can expect all their admitted students to receive a scholarship for the duration of their studies. Students in these programs who fail to graduate must reimburse all scholarship money received; however, those students who manage to graduate can have their student loans fully repaid if they are fortunate enough to be hired by a public higher education institution.

Once psychologists receive a professional diploma from an accredited university program, they can register in either a state or federal registry office for the regulation of professions. This process leads to a nationally valid permanent license called *cedula profesional*, which can be revoked by either the Ministry of Education or a judge in case of improper or illegal professional conduct. Thus, *licenciatura* is the name of the academic diploma and *cedula* is the actual government-registered license. At present, there is legislation being drafted that will make all professional licenses valid for a 5-year period with a requirement that psychologists meet various conditions before their license will be renewed. Consistent with their European origins and tradition, master's programs are regarded as the appropriate training venue for those students who intend to become instructors, whereas doctoral programs are almost exclusively devoted to training researchers. Most doctoral degrees require at least 9 years of academic preparation including the *licenciatura.*

Another intermediate university title, viewed as a postgraduate degree by some universities, is called a specialty or specialization diploma. This diploma can be earned after completing the licensing degree and does not require a master's degree. For professions such as medicine, this degree is mandatory if a general practitioner wants to practice a medical specialty. Although specialization diplomas are also available in psychology, taking anywhere between 1and 3 years to complete, very few universities actually offer them.

Recently, journal articles have addressed the professional education needs of psychologists in Mexico, covering topics like the importance of methodology in the training of school psychologists, the need to link theory and practice in training experts on mental retardation, strategies to relate basic and applied knowledge in psychology, and training and professional deficits and ways to overcome them (e.g., reorganizing university psychology curricula) (Ribes, 1989). Other related issues include formalizing the accreditation of

programs and professional certification, supporting research groups, and reinforcing scientific and professional associations.

Professional or postgraduate programs in psychology get accredited mainly through one of two mechanisms. In the case of public universities, most of which are well-established, specially appointed committees of experts develop professional programs (often modeled after either UNAM's or other prestigious Mexican or foreign institutions). After approval by a school's technical council, these programs are submitted to the pertinent university council or senate for final approval, and then registered with the corresponding state or federal higher education authorities. Many public universities have the word *autonomous* in their name, which means that they can legally develop and implement academic programs through their own university structures without interference or influence by the state or federal governments, despite the fact that their funding comes from government sources.

The second mechanism was established, in principle, for the regulation of private universities. In this system, plans for a new program, or substantial modification of an already accredited one, are sent to the Ministry of Education, which turns it over to a formally established committee. In the case of programs that train health service providers in a field such as psychology, the committee is composed of representatives from the Ministry of Education and Ministry of Health, plus delegates from the main national scientific and professional associations and colleges of the discipline in question. If the program meets the standards of quality in terms of its curriculum, equipment and facilities, and faculty, the committee makes a formal recommendation to the Ministry of Education to issue a certificate that officially recognizes the program. It is important to note that if a private university has not received such a certificate, its graduates cannot obtain the professional license, or *cedula*, necessary to practice.

The current criteria used by this committee are virtually identical to those used by American Psychological Association and Canadian Psychological Association. Only a few years ago, more lenient criteria led to the annual accreditation of approximately 5 to 10 new psychology programs; since the adoption of new procedures and criteria, the rate of approval for new programs has slowed to about one every 2 years. In addition, committees in the health professions have recommended that accreditation should remain valid for only 5 years with a new review necessary for reaccreditation.

Mexican laws allow nearly anyone to establish facilities where instruction can be offered in any field at almost any level of sophistication. Thus, in principle, any institution meeting the minimal criteria to call itself a university or training institute could offer psychology courses and issue diplomas upon graduation. However, if the program in question is not accredited, their graduates cannot obtain a license, or *cedula*, to practice the profession legally.

6.3 SCOPE OF PSYCHOLOGICAL PRACTICE

Psychology in Mexico is currently regarded as a dual discipline with links to both the natural sciences and the social sciences. Psychologists' identification with the natu-

ral sciences results from the proximity of their field disciplines like neurology and physiology, which lead to specialties such as neuropsychology. Psychology has been allied with the social sciences beginning in the 1960s when Mexican psychologists responded to social needs with actuarial, epidemiological, and psychometric data.

Until the late 1960s, both academics and practitioners identified primarily with the psychodynamic model, which was the dominant conceptual and methodological perspective in Mexican psychology. However, the dominance of this model has gradually and substantially eroded. At UNAM, for example, there was a clear shift from orthodox psychoanalysis toward the more culturally relevant views of Erich Fromm. The 1970s also witnessed a burgeoning of experimental psychology in Mexico, including work ranging from animal research within the behavior analytic tradition to novel applications of psychological testing and innovations in statistical methods. More recently, applied psychology has shifted toward evidence-based forms of cognitive–behavioral interventions. In school psychology, the Piagetian approach still prevails. Industrial–organizational psychologists have been less influenced by psychological research, tending, rather, to adopt concepts and approaches developed in schools of business and in the business community.

Sometimes, new theories, methodologies, and interventions reflect sociocultural or sociopolitical undercurrents in Mexico; at other times, they merely reflect popular or political views held by cohesive groups of psychologists. An example of this was the rather idiosyncratic position held in the 1970s and 1980s at some influential departments and schools of psychology by psychoanalytically oriented professors with a strong Marxist orientation. These academics believed that any psychological approach that deviated from the positions espoused by Freud and Marx was either unscientific or suspiciously in line with the hegemonic interests associated with the practice of psychology in capitalist countries (e.g., behaviorism). The recent evolution of Mexican psychology has shown, however, that there are competent as well as incompetent researchers and practitioners associated with every ideological approach to psychology.

The current status of Mexican psychology reflects, for better or worse, the long-term consequences of its fragmented and frequently contentious early development. New theoretical and methodological traditions evolved and gathered advocates, mainly at universities; these advocates formed insular groups that were defined in terms of ideology rather than science. Although this trend has diminished greatly in the last decade, one can still notice subtle expressions of this pernicious tradition in Mexican psychology.

The status and role of Mexican psychologists in relation to other disciplines has changed significantly in the past 10 years. In the health sector, for example, although physicians still have higher status and salaries than psychologists, there are now defined and respected professional roles for psychologists that are clearly differentiated from those for physicians. In the past, it would be unusual to find psychologists caring for patients with chronic diseases (e.g., diabetes, hypertension) or working alongside physicians, nurses, and social workers in major hospitals. However, it is gradually becoming commonplace for psychologists to work in these settings, helping patients adhere to therapeutic regimens,

cope with the side effects of medication, or manage chronic pain. Mexican psychologists who work in hospitals also consult with other health care professionals to improve caregiver–patient interactions.

Although Mexican psychologists have worked in psychiatric hospitals for over two decades, their historical role consisted of providing little more than psychological testing. Due in part to the growing stature and prestige of research psychologists at the Mexican Institute of Psychiatry and at other mental health institutions, the professional roles of these psychologists have gradually expanded to include other professional responsibilities such as psychotherapy.

Psychologists working in schools still provide mainly assessment services and occasionally treat children or adolescents with learning difficulties. They have achieved modest success in such areas as increasing the quality of teaching, improving the curricula, and offering study and test-taking skills. Industrial–organizational psychologists are involved in personnel selection and job training. Ironically, in contrast to other settings in which psychologists are being given increased administrative responsibilities (e.g., becoming university presidents or vice-ministers for education), professional psychologists still have limited access to management-level positions in healthcare organizations. Psychologists frequently compete with educators for positions in schools, and industrial–organizational psychologists compete with business administrators for positions in industry.

The most widely accepted set of ethical guidelines for Mexican psychologists is contained in the *Ethical Code of the Psychologist* (*Codigo Etico del Psicólogo*)

(Mexican Psychological Society, 2002). This code was developed in three successive editions by the MPS, beginning in the early 1980s. The revisions were based on a nationwide survey of recent ethical dilemmas actually encountered by Mexican psychologists. Much of the conceptual and methodological work underlying the new code grew out of collaboration with the Canadian Register of Health Service Providers in Psychology. Also, some concepts and organizational experiences presented during the annual meetings of the Forum of Professional Psychology of North America served as sources for revisions. The Forum, which first met in 1994, began as a series of informal meetings aimed at promoting mutual knowledge in the main aspects of professional psychology (e.g., education and training, licensing and professional practice, ethics and professional regulations) in Mexico, Canada, and the United States. Annual meetings are attended by leading psychologists with responsibilities in these areas.

The inauguration of Mexico's National Council for Science and Technology (*CoNaCyT*) in the early 1970s set the stage for the exponential growth of psychological research. In addition, UNAM, Mexico's oldest and most influential university, also created peer review committees and began to fund research projects. At UNAM's three campuses, psychology is awarded approximately 45% of all research funding targeted for the social sciences. In addition, psychologists have been awarded research funding from other committees including those that oversee biology and medicine. Psychology also receives the largest proportion of CoNaCyT funding in the social sciences. Before the establishment of these two systems, funding for research was very

scarce and came mainly from universities, private groups, and foundations. Some collaborative research projects were also funded by foreign universities or foundations, often in the United States.

In order to promote scientific research, the Mexican government provides supplemental salaries to those scientists at public and private academic and research institutions who show sustained high quality scholarship as evidenced by journal and book publications. These supplements range from one half to two times a professor's customary monthly salary. Young researchers usually enter the system as a "candidate" immediately after obtaining their doctorate and progress through four successive levels. Thus, candidates who keep publishing at a sustained rate and good quality (for 3 years), will get promoted to level I, then to level II, and then III. Finally, a researcher with a lifelong contribution to research in an area is promoted to emeritus level. This incentive system has been extremely successful in promoting research.

A few psychology journals in Mexico publish most of the research produced by Mexican psychologists. Perhaps the most influential of these is the *Mexican Journal of Psychology*, one of the few Latin American journals that have appeared uninterrupted for the last 20 years. Published by the MPS, it has outlasted many journals that either published a few initial volumes and failed or disappeared for long periods of time, only to reappear under a new title. Other periodicals feature mainly conference proceedings, but pretend to be peer-reviewed publications (Hernandez-Guzman, Montero, & Carrillo, 2002).

Other journals with stable production schedules and relatively consistent peer review procedures include the *Mexican Journal of Behavior Analysis* (*Revista Mexicana de Análisis de la Conducta*), *Acta Comportamentalia,* the *Latin Journal of Thought and Language* (*Revista Latina de Pensamiento y Lenguaje*), the *Journal of the National Council for Research and Teaching in Psychology (Ensenanza e Investigacion en Psicologia)*, and *Psychology and Health* (*Psicología y Salud*). Another journal, although not exclusively psychological in its focus, that meets high editorial and procedural standards is *Mental Health* (*Salud Mental*) published by the National Institute of Psychiatry. Approximately 30–40% of the articles in this journal are written by psychologists. Scientific journals edited in developing countries tend to suffer from chronic lack of financial support, and journal editors frequently carry out administrative and clerical tasks in addition to their editing responsibilities.

The rate of submissions to major psychology journals in Mexico has been growing steadily as has the quality of accepted manuscripts. Double-blind editorial reviews by two or more well-known researchers have yielded high quality feedback for authors and, in turn, the publication of strong manuscripts. Educating reviewers on reviewing is becoming a priority in Mexico as a scientific tradition in publishing solidifies. Special guidelines have been developed by the MPS to help reviewers reach reasonable editorial decisions and communicate them in a constructive fashion to authors.

Although several Mexican journals publish articles in either Spanish or English, most include articles only in Spanish or in Spanish and other Latin languages (mainly French, Italian, and Portu-guese). In one sense, this constricts the widespread dissemination of Mexican psychological research in the predominantly English language mainstream of the scientific world. However, although publishing in Spanish may be a necessity for authors with only partial command of written English, numerous Mexican authors view publishing in Spanish as a matter of pride. For many years, Spanish was a widely used scientific language, and it has only recently lost ground to the hegemony of English in the scientific and academic world.

Approximately 85% of all research is carried out in higher education or health service institutions, many of them located in Mexico City. UNAM alone accounts for approximately 60% of all research published by Mexican psychologists.

The following are a few of Mexico's most significant research centers: UNAM, the Association for Psychoanalytical Psychotherapy (*Asociación de Psicoterapia Psicoanalítica*), the Center for studies in Rural Development (*Centro de Estudios de Desarrollo Rural*), the Ibero-American University (*Universidad Iberoamericana*), the Mexican Social Security Institute (*Instituto Mexicano del Seguro Social*), the Ministry of Health (*Secretaría de Salud*), the Monterrey Institute of Technology and Advanced Studies (*Instituto Tecnológico de Estudios Superiores de Monterrey*), the National Institute of Perinatology (*Instituto Nacional de Perinatología*), the National Institute of Psychiatry (*Instituto Mexicano de Psiquiatría*), and the National Institute of Neurology and Neurosurgery (*Instituto Nacional de Neurología y Neurocirugía*).

Other important research institutions located outside of Mexico City, include the autonomous universities at Baja California (*Universidad Autónoma de Baja California*),

Guadalajara (*Universidad Autónoma de Guadalajara*), Mexico State (*Universidad Autónoma del Estado de México, Toluca*), Morelos State (*Universidad Autónoma del Estado de Morelos*), Tlaxcala (*Universidad Autónoma de Tlaxcala*), and Veracruz (*Universidad Veracruzana*). The University of the Americas (*Universidad de las Américas, Puebla*), University of Guadalajara (*Universidad de Guadalajara*), University of Sonora (*Universidad de Sonora*), and Tuxtla Gutierrez Institute of Technology (*Instituto Tecnológico de Tuxtla Gutiérrez*) are also well known.

6.4 FUTURE CHALLENGES AND PROSPECTS

Psychology in Mexico is currently a well-established scientific discipline and profession. The future will very likely involve dealing with a series of challenges mainly stemming from Mexico's socioeconomic conditions and from the pressures associated with a trend toward conceiving education, science, technology, and professional services as mere commercial products.

As has been the case in most Latin American countries, the recovery and development of the Mexican economy has been slower than expected. A recent political transition ended the 70-year rule by a single political party and greatly reduced capricious spending and corruption; however, funding for public universities continues to be limited, and positions for psychologists are difficult to find and are often underfunded. It is still expensive and difficult to secure the best facilities, equipment, faculty salaries, and so on, and many schools of psychology, both public and private, struggle to make ends meet. Underemployment of psychologists usually means that they sometimes are hired to perform tasks that are only partially related to their professional expertise. This situation is occasionally aggravated when foreign and multinational companies bring their own psychologists to Mexico, often disguised as "consultants."

Mexico's economic problems may end up indirectly affecting the quality of psychologists' education and training as a result of limited access to contemporary scientific and technological information. In sharp contrast to the expectation that global technological developments such as digital telecommunications and the Internet would facilitate access to scientific information, the increasing commercialization of electronic publishing has kept online journals as out of reach as ever. The increasing costs of books, journals (online and traditional), and other publications in psychology belie the promise that emerging technologies once held for developing countries.

The education of consumers, politicians, and the media is another short-term priority. Although most people with at least high school education have a reasonable knowledge of what psychologists do, Mexican psychologists still have to tackle public misconceptions of their science and profession. Such distortions are engendered mainly from ignorance and misrepresentations of the profession by the media. In addition, a recent onslaught of impostors offering services to relieve human suffering is making life more difficult for legitimate Mexican psychologists. Although the terms *psychology* and *psychologist* are protected by law, terms such as *therapy* and *therapist* are not, and consumers are frequently deceived.

Another growing problem appears to be a direct outcome of globalization. There are suddenly many online "universities" and "institutes" of very dubious quality that offer easy diplomas in numerous fields related to psychology. These businesses frequently require nothing more than a high school diploma as a condition for entry, and practically nothing is known of their actual academic infrastructure or training standards.

On the other hand, despite years of implementation and attempts to correct unfair practices, it has become evident that regional trade agreements like the North American Free Trade Agreement (NAFTA) have worked against the mobility of Mexican professionals. Although the worst examples of this probably have occurred in such professions as architecture and engineering, psychology has not fared much better. Notwithstanding almost 10 years of mostly well-intentioned efforts by key representatives of psychology from Mexico, Canada, and the United States, progress on professional mobility and the mutual recognition of professional licenses still seems quite distant. This appears to be the case despite good progress on such matters as comparable education and ethical guidelines, as well as improvements in accreditation and regulatory control on the Mexican side.

Most treaties include sections on the exchange of services that are directly or indirectly linked to professional practice. In the case of NAFTA, these sections include a prima facie description of educational systems in order to facilitate their comparison. One unfortunate aspect of the NAFTA negotiations involved a blatant translational (or conceptual) error that equated Mexico's license-eligible degrees

with B.A. degrees in English-speaking Canada and the United States. The NAFTA translators probably responded to the simple sequence of academic degrees in the three countries and found nothing in the Mexican educational system that corresponded directly with an M.A. or a Ph.D. in Canada or the United States (Sanchez-Sosa, 2002).

If free trade agreements and professional mobility, including the mutual recognition of licenses, is done on the basis of the mere *names* of diplomas or titles, it becomes clear that psychologists from Latin American countries (and also from European countries such as France, Germany, Italy, and Spain) are likely to be automatically excluded from the ranks of fully qualified psychologists, and will be denied professional opportunities. The regulating authorities in Canada and the United States must address the issue of equivalence of training if they hope to avoid discriminatory practices.

This, of course, does not mean that a Mexican licensing degree and a Canadian or U.S. doctoral degree are necessarily equivalent. In fact, during annual meetings of the Forum for Professional Psychology in North America, it was the Mexican group that pointed out serious weaknesses in the licensing requirements and promoted immediate modifications (Sanchez-Sosa & Hernandez-Guzman, 1996). Among other problems, the supervised practicum experience during the final stages of training is not as systematic and as prolonged as those in Canada and the United States. In addition, until 1996, accreditation criteria and standards were practically nonexistent in Mexico.

Furthermore, until 1998, Mexican ethical standards and guidelines had not been revised and updated for over a decade (Hernández-Guzmán & Ritchie, 2001; Mexican Psychological Society, 2002). Finally, terminal internships or residences established to fine-tune professional skills under supervision have only recently become an integral part of Mexican training programs. Coursework and laboratory classes as well as some basic aspects of practica, however, have remained virtually identical to those in Canada and the United States for decades, at least at the main Mexican universities.

In conclusion, Mexican psychology is alive and well, but is still grappling with numerous unfinished tasks and a somewhat uncertain future. Ironically, this uncertainty barely relates to the quality and commitment of Mexican psychologists; instead, it appears related to socioeconomic conditions, including some of the problems associated with globalization. In this context, the support of psychologists and psychological organizations from developed countries, especially in North America, has been a collegial expression of goodwill. However, only sustained commitment and lucid judgment on the part of Mexican psychologists and their organizations are likely to reduce professional uncertainty and stabilize Mexico's academic and scientific foundation well into the 21st century.

REFERENCES

Beutler, L. E., & Fisher, D. (1994). Combined specialty training in counseling, clinical, and school psychology: An idea whose time has returned. *Professional Psychology: Research and Practice, 25,* 62–69.

Dirección General de Profesiones, Subdirección de Colegios Profesionales (2003). Total de profesionistas registrados en la carrera de psicologia de 1945 al 18 Noviembre, 2003.

Hernandez-Guzman, L., Montero, L. L. M., & Carrillo, M. O. (2002). Latin American productivity from 1990 to 1998, in the *Mexican Journal of Psychology. International Journal of Group Tensions, 31,* 317–337.

Hernández-Guzmán, L., & Ritchie, P. L. J. (2001). Hacia la transformación y actualización empíricas del código ético de los psicólogos mexicanos [Toward the transformation and updating of the ethics code of Mexican psychologists]. *Revista Mexicana de Psicología, 18,* 347–357.

Mexican Psychological Society. (2002). *Codigo etico del psicologo* [Code of ethics of psychologists]. Mexico City: Trillas.

Mexican Psychological Society. (2003, November 6). *Informe de avance del Inventario Nacional de Conocimientos y Habilidades en Psicología* [Progress report on the National Inventory of Knowledge and Skills in Psychology]. Trabajo presentado en la X reunión del Consejo Tecnico para la Normatividad del Psicólogo y del Psicoterapeuta en el Area de la Salud [Paper presented at the 10th meeting of the Technical Council for Normativity of Psychologists and Psychotherapists in the Health Area]. Mexico City, Mexico.

Ribes, E. (1989). La psicología: Algunas reflexiones sobre su qué, su cómo, su porqué, y su para qué [Psychology: Some reflections on its what, its how, its why and its what for]. In J. Urbina-Soria (Ed.), *El psicologo: Formacion, ejercicio profesional y prospectiva* [The psychologist: Education, professional practice, and prospective] (pp. 847–860). Mexico City: National University Press.

Sanchez-Sosa, J. J. (2002). Globalizacion, practica profesional transnacional y certificacion [Globalization, transnational professional practice, and certification]. In G. Vazquez (Ed.), *Ensenanza, ejercicio y regulacion de la profesion: Psicología* [Teaching, practice, and professional regulation: Psychology] (pp. 43–64). Mexico City: National College of Psychologists and UNAM School of Psychology.

Sánchez-Sosa, J. J., & Hernández-Guzmán, L. (1996). La formación en servicio del psicólogo aplicado: El reto de la congruencia ciencia-profesión [The in-service training of the applied psychologist: The case of science-profession congruence]. *Enseñanza e Investigación en Psicología, 1,* 211–221.

Sánchez Sosa, J. J., & Valderrama-Iturbe, P. (2001). Psychology in Latin America: Historical reflections and perspectives. *International Journal of Psychology, 36,* 384–394.

IMPORTANT PUBLICATIONS

Alcaraz-Romero, V. M., & Martinez-Casas, R. (1994). Algunos elementos para la formulación de una teoría del lenguaje [Some elements for the formulation of a theory of language]. *Revista Latina de Pensamiento y Lenguaje, 2,* 57–104.

Bruner, C. A., & Vargas, I. (1994). The activity of rats in a swimming situation as a function of water temperature. *Physiology and Behavior, 55,* 21–28.

Corral-Verdugo, V. (1997). Dual "realities" of conservation behavior: Self-reports vs. observations of re-use and recycling behavior. *Journal of Environmental Psychology, 17,* 135–145.

Corsi-Cabrera, M., Miro, E., del Rio-Portilla, Y., Perez-Garci, E., Villanueva, Y., & Guevara, M. A. (2003). Rapid eye movement sleep dreaming is characterized by uncoupled EEG activity between frontal and perceptual cortical regions. *Brain and Cognition, 51,* 337–345.

De los Ríos, J. L., & Sánchez-Sosa, J. J. (2002). Well-being and medical recovery in the critical care unit: The role of the nurse-patient interaction. *Salud Mental, 25,* 21–31.

Diaz-Guerrero, R. (2003). *Bajo las garras de la cultura: Psicología del Mexicano* [Under the clutches of culture: Psychology of the Mexican]. Mexico City: Trillas.

Díaz-Loving, R. (1998). Contributions of Mexican ethnopsychology to the resolution of the etic-emic dilemma in personality. *Journal of Cross-Cultural Psychology, 28,* 104–118.

Hernandez-Guzman, L., Gonzalez, S., & Lopez, F. (2002). Effect of guided imagery on children's social performance. *Behavioral and Cognitive Psychotherapy, 30,* 471–483.

Medina-Mora, M. E., Borges, G., & Villatoro, J. (2000). The measurement of drinking patterns and consequences in Mexico. *Journal of Substance Abuse, 12*(1, 2), 183–196.

Ostrosky-Solis, F., Ardila, A., & Rosselli, M. (1999). NEUROPSI: A brief neuropsychological test battery in Spanish with norms by age and educational level. *Journal of the International Neuropsychological Society, 5,* 413–433.

Pick, S., Poortinga, Y. H., & Givaudan, M. (2003). Integrating intervention theory and strategy in culture-sensitive health promotion programs. *Professional Psychology: Research and Practice, 34,* 422–429.

Prado-Alcala, R. A. (1995). Serial and parallel processing during memory consolidation. In J. L. McGaugh, F. Bermudez-Rattoni, & R. A. Prado-Alcala (Eds.), *Plasticity in the central nervous system: Learning and memory* (pp. 57–65). Mahwah, NJ: Erlbaum.

Reyes-Lagunes, I. (2001). Aportaciones a la medición de la personalidad en México. [Contributions to personality assessment in Mexico]. In N. Calleja & G. Gomez-Perezmitre (Eds.), *Social Psychology: Research and applications in Mexico* (pp. 69–99). Mexico City: Fondo de Cultura Economica.

Ribes-Inesta, E. (2000). Instructions, rules, and abstraction: A misconstrued relation. *Behavior and Philosophy, 28*(1, 2), 41–55.

CHAPTER 7

Psychology in the United States

RAYMOND D. FOWLER AND RUSS NEWMAN

Raymond D. Fowler received his Ph.D. in psychology with a specialization in clinical psychology from Pennsylvania State University in 1957 and joined the faculty of the University of Alabama at Tuscaloosa, where he remained until 1987 when he was appointed professor emeritus. He served as department chairperson at Alabama from 1965 to 1983 and at the University of Tennessee in Knoxville from 1987 to 1989. He has contributed to research literature in psychology with articles, books, chapters, and other publications, especially in the areas of substance abuse, criminal behavior, and personality assessment.

Raymond Fowler has been an active participant in national and international psychological organizations for over 30 years. After serving 4 years as treasurer of the American Psychological Association, he became its 97th president in 1988 and subsequently served as its executive vice president and chief executive officer from 1989 to 2002. He is currently treasurer of the International Association of Applied Psychology.

Russ Newman received his Ph.D. in psychology with a specialization in clinical psychology from Kent State University in 1979 and joined the staff of Harding Hospital where he was staff psychologist and director of clinical psychology training until 1986. He received his law degree from Capital University Law School in 1987.

From 1986 to the present, Russ Newman has been employed by the American Psychological Association, first as assistant executive director of legal and regulatory affairs and since 1993 as executive director for professional practice. He is responsible for promoting the association's multifaceted agenda on behalf of practicing psychologists. He manages a variety of activities involving legislative advocacy, legal initiatives and efforts to shape the evolving health care market, and a nationwide public education campaign to enhance the value of psychological services. He has written and spoken extensively on professional and policy issues in psychology.

7.1 OVERVIEW

Even before psychology began to emerge as a formal discipline, the American public showed a great interest in psychological matters. In the early 19th century, practitioners, under various titles such as phrenologist, graphologist, and mental healer, were available to provide a diagnosis and treatment for a host of psychological ills (Benjamin, DeLeon, Freedheim, & VandenBos, 2003). Psychology courses were well established in colleges and universities by the mid-19th century, often with such titles as "Intellectual Philosophy" and "Mental Science," which were later replaced by the term *psychology* (Cadwallader, 1992).

Scientific psychology began to develop in the United States toward the close of the 19th century. William James, influenced by the emergence of scientific psychology in Europe, established a demonstration laboratory of psychology at Harvard in 1875, and the world's first Ph.D. in psychology was granted at Harvard in 1878 to Granville Stanley Hall (Cadwallader, 1992). When Wilhelm Wundt established the first experimental psychology laboratory at the University of Leipzig in 1879, students from the United States and other countries came to study with Wundt. Hall, who had studied with James and Wundt, established the first U.S. experimental psychology laboratory the following year. In the 1890s, other Americans, returning from their studies in Germany, founded laboratories at universities across the country (Hilgard, 1987). By 1904, there were 49 laboratories in colleges and universities in the United States, and psychology had become an accepted part of the curriculum throughout the country (Fuchs & Milar, 2003).

Nearly all of the psychologists in the early years were experimental psychologists, but some were also interested in the application of psychology to human problems. Lightner Witmer, a doctoral student of Wundt, established the first psychological clinic at the University of Pennsylvania in 1896, and is credited with being the father of both clinical and school psychology. Walter Dill Scott pioneered the application of psychology to the problems of business and industry. The mental-testing movement, largely initiated by James McKeen Cattell, a Wundt Ph.D., increased the visibility of psychologists in the United States and helped to open the doors for applied psychologists to schools, clinics, hospitals, and businesses.

In July 1892, G. S. Hall, by then president of the new Clark University, met with a small group of professors from U.S. and Canadian universities to organize the American Psychological Association (APA), and in December, 1892, the first APA convention was held in Philadelphia (Napoli, 1941). The founding of the APA represented the first time that psychologists in any country had organized themselves as a national association. Membership in the APA was open to all of North America, and has always included members from Canada and Mexico. The Canadian Psychological Association was established in 1938, and a national association was established in Mexico in 1953 (Pickren & Fowler, 2003).

By the year 2003, there were at least 80 national psychological associations, but the APA continues to be by far the largest. The APA's post–World War II growth was explosive. From 1945 to 2000, the APA's membership grew over 2000%, from 4,183 to 88,500 members, with an additional 70,500 affiliates, including students and international psychologists. Since 1945, the APA has had a central office in Washington,

DC, with an executive officer and a staff that has grown over the years to over 400. The APA's scientific journals include most of the premier journals in psychology, and APA Books publishes over 50 scholarly books each year. PsycINFO, the APA's database, covers the world's literature in psychology, and contains abstracts of books, book chapters, dissertations, and articles from more than 1,800 journals published worldwide. The annual APA conventions attract 12,000 to 20,000 members from the U.S. and around the world. Most U.S. psychologists are members of the APA; several thousand psychologists who live in other countries are also members.

Scientific psychology was well established in most U.S. universities for decades before programs were developed to train applied psychologists, and before applied psychology began to emerge as a profession. Psychologists were called upon to assist in personnel selection in World War I, but prior to 1941, psychology had little public recognition as a helping profession.

World War II marked a major shift in how Americans viewed mental disorders and the need for psychological services. Recognition of the psychological disorders that prevented military service and the psychological aspects of battlefield breakdowns increased the demand for services in the military and by the Veteran's Administration after the war. Veterans of World War II, their education supported by funding from the federal government, entered clinical psychology graduate programs in great numbers. The number of professional psychologists increased rapidly in the decades following World War II, and that growth, though less rapid, continues.

The APA was organized to promote psychology as a science, but from its inception there have been a number of organizations formed by members and others who felt that APA was not addressing the issues about which they were most concerned. In the first half of the 20th century, when the APA devoted little attention to applied psychology, several alternative organizations were established to promote those interests. In 1948, the APA reorganized through a merger with some of those organizations, and the mission statement of the association broadened to include promotion of professional interests as well as science.

More recently, psychologists who felt that the APA convention was not sufficiently scientific established the Psychonomic Society in 1960. The society currently has approximately 2,000 members and publishes six experimental psychology journals. A group of academic psychologists who believed the APA focused too much on practitioner-related issues established the American Psychological Society (APS) in 1988. The two organizations competed for academic members during the early years of the APS, but that competition has diminished over the years. At the present time, the APS has about 8,000 members, many of whom are also members of the APA.

Tensions between academic and practitioner psychologists have been a fact of life in the United States for over 100 years. The two groups have different perspectives, goals, and orientations. The APA seeks to reduce those tensions by providing four directorates that focus on the needs of members primarily oriented to science, practice, education, and the public interest, respectively. Many of the APA's divisions and governance groups include broad representation of scientists and practitioners.

There are several hundred psychological organizations in the United States (see Pickren & Fowler, 2003 and VandenBos, 1989). The APA alone includes over 100 semiautonomous organizations: 55 APA divisions (i.e., interest groups devoted to subareas of psychology such as clinical, experimental, social) and 60 state, provincial, and territorial associations that are separately incorporated but affiliated with the APA. All of these groups have their own officers and, in most cases, executive directors and administrative staff and offices.

A number of other organizations not affiliated with the APA perform specific functions or represent specialized interests, especially for applied psychologists. For example, the National Register of Health Care Providers in Psychology provides a listing of psychologists qualified to practice professionally. The Association of State and Provincial Psychology Boards helps to coordinate the separate licensing boards in the United States and Canada. Credentialing organizations include the American Board of Professional Psychology, the Association of Psychology Post-Doctoral and Internship Centers, the American Psychological Association Practice Organization's College of Professional Psychology, among many others. Specialty organizations, of which there are many, include the Society for Personality Assessment and the National Academy of Neuropsychology, the Association for the Advancement of Behavior Therapy, the Society of Psychologists in Management, and the American Association of Correctional Psychology. Psychology organizations exist for a number of ethnic groups including Hispanic, American Indian, African American, and Asian American.

Scientific and professional associations in the U.S. have no direct formal ties with the federal government, but the APA maintains liaisons with most relevant federal agencies. The APA actively advocates on behalf of psychology with the legislative and executive branches of the U.S. government, and even with the judicial branch, to some extent, as an amicus curiae or "friend of the court," providing testimony in cases that are relevant to psychology. The APA sometimes applies for and receives grants and contracts from federal agencies to carry out research and other projects.

7.2 EDUCATION AND TRAINING

Education and training in psychology takes place at several levels. Many high schools have courses in psychology, and, at the undergraduate level, psychology is one of the most popular elective courses. Most college students take at least one psychology course, and it is a required course at many colleges and universities. A great many students choose psychology as a major, especially women, who constitute more than two-thirds of undergraduate psychology majors.

Graduate work in psychology occurs primarily in colleges and universities, and in professional schools. Here, too, women represent the majority of students, a fairly recent trend in the U.S. Most university departments have a diverse faculty representing the major areas of psychology such as social, developmental, cognitive, clinical, and so forth. In larger departments, these faculty members may be organized into specialty areas. Most doctoral departments have a clearly defined clinical program and many have several other applied program areas with distinctive course requirements as well as programs in the traditional research areas.

Professional schools are set up primarily to provide education and training in applied psychology. Most professional schools have a clinical program, and some have programs in other specialties such as school, counseling, and organizational psychology. Professional schools usually grant the Doctor of Psychology (Psy.D.) degree although some also offer the Ph.D. These programs typically expect their graduates to understand the research literature and how it applies to practice, but usually do not expect them to conduct formal experimental research.

Typically, psychology departments in state and private universities have a chairperson who administers the department and reports to a dean. Most professional schools are headed by a dean, and some have a president. Some professional schools are affiliated with universities or medical schools, but most are freestanding private institutions.

There are no national admissions criteria for undergraduate or graduate study in psychology in the United States. At the undergraduate level, most colleges and universities set their own admission criteria based on high-school grades, tests such as the Scholastic Aptitude Test, and various other criteria, including extracurricular activities. Undergraduate admissions criteria vary greatly and tend to be much higher in the elite universities.

At the graduate level, each university department and professional school sets its own admission standards. The Graduate Record Examination is frequently used as a factor in admissions along with under-

graduate grades, recommendations, experience in research, and, sometimes, paid or volunteer experience in human services.

Most students in university graduate programs get some financial support during the period of their graduate training. The sources of support include teaching and research assistantships, scholarships, and training stipends through the U.S. Veteran's Administration and other federal agencies.

Professional schools tend to attract somewhat older students, many of whom have already been working in psychology-related settings, sometimes at the master's level. Because most professional schools do not have state or federal support and must support themselves through student fees, the tuition tends to be higher than for university programs, and opportunities for financial aid are more limited. Some students work part-time to support themselves through their programs, and students in professional school are more likely to graduate with substantial debt than are students in university programs.

Graduate education is broadly dispersed in the United States. There are several hundred psychology graduate programs in university departments, professional schools, and medical schools. About half of the new doctorates in psychology are in clinical psychology, and another 25% are in other health-provider areas such as counseling, school, and health psychology. Of the new graduates, 25% come from research subfields including developmental, social/personality, cognitive, experimental, neuroscience/physiological/biological, and industrial–organizational psychology (American Psychological Association Committee on Accreditation, 2002).

For over 50 years, the APA has administered an accreditation program for professional programs in clinical, counseling, and school psychology. There is no accreditation program for the research subfields. Accreditation is voluntary, but most doctoral programs in universities and professional schools seek accreditation. Students who graduate from programs that are not accredited have more difficulty obtaining internships, postdoctoral training, licensure, and employment.

To be accredited, programs must be able to demonstrate that students receive a comprehensive education in the relevant areas. Accreditation bodies permit considerable flexibility to programs that appear to be meeting their stated goals and turning out well-trained students.

There is no nationally accepted curriculum in psychology at the bachelor's, master's, or doctoral level. It is generally agreed that the science and practice of psychology rest upon a broad foundation that includes many domains of knowledge. At the graduate level, accreditation requires that a program has and implements a clear and coherent curriculum that enables students in health-service provider areas to acquire competence in a number of these domains, including the breadth of scientific psychology, its research methods, and its applications. Most programs attempt to achieve a balance between breadth and depth, and try to assure that graduates acquire broad knowledge about psychology as well as specialized skills (American Psychological Association Committee on Accreditation, 2000). Undergraduate programs focus on breadth, and specialization occurs mostly at the graduate level.

In 2003, there were 351 accredited doctoral programs in professional psychology, 13% in professional schools, 53% in university psychology departments, and 34%

in other settings. Each year, about 2,000 students graduate from accredited programs, about half of those from professional schools (American Psychological Association Committee on Accreditation, 2002). Many students from around the world come to the United States for their graduate work, but relatively few U.S. students go outside of the country for graduate training.

In addition to a supervised practicum experience, students in professional psychology typically have a 1-year internship toward the end of their doctoral study. These internships are independent of the doctoral programs and usually take place in hospitals, clinics, medical schools, or other relevant facilities. Some of the oldest and largest internship programs are offered by the Veterans Administration and Department of Defense through the Army, Navy, and Air Force. The APA accredits 466 internship programs (American Psychological Association Committee on Accreditation, 2002). Some graduates also spend one or more years in postdoctoral programs, and the APA recently initiated an accreditation program for those facilities, as well.

There is no widely accepted system to rank graduate programs in psychology or to identify outstanding programs, although some popular magazines publish lists and rankings based on surveys. The elite private and state supported programs are usually of high quality, but many good programs exist in less prestigious universities and professional schools. In general, the accreditation process assures that accredited programs are functioning competently.

Instruction at the undergraduate level uses the classroom format, and class size can range from over 500 in some introductory classes to less than 10 in more advanced courses; there are often opportunities for independent study and supervised research. Some applied courses exist at the undergraduate level but most focus on theory and research.

Graduate programs rest on the academic foundation established at the undergraduate level. In graduate school, there is much more emphasis on direct experience in conducting research, and in learning and practicing applied skills. Most psychology graduate students have access to all of the books, research equipment, tests, computer facilities, research databases, and Internet resources they need for graduate work.

7.3 PSYCHOLOGICAL SCIENCE IN THE UNITED STATES

In the early days of psychology, most research was carried out by individual faculty members in colleges and universities, often with little if any support from the institution. Some psychological laboratories were developed solely for demonstrations, and the research conducted by faculty members was often done primarily to demonstrate research techniques to students. Most departments were small with only a few students and usually were not differentiated into specialty areas. Faculty members and students interacted with each other and most students took similar courses. Students and faculty members each had their special research interests, but training was relatively generic, and most thought of themselves as general psychologists.

In the period that followed World War II, departments grew rapidly and often divided into specialty areas such as social, developmental, and clinical psychology. These specialty areas form clusters of faculty members and students who work together and are less likely to interact with others across the discipline. Students and faculty members tend to identify with their specialty area and most think of themselves as social psychologists, cognitive psychologists, neuroscientists, and so forth, rather than as general psychologists.

Moving from individual researchers to research groups has facilitated the ability to carry out studies that take place on a large scale and over a long time. It is not unusual for a single faculty member to have an active research laboratory with several graduate and postgraduate students engaged in related research and paid through research grants from federal, state, or private organizations. This way of organizing research decreases the level of information exchange across areas, but it also results in more systematic research and very high research productivity.

Research in psychology takes place in a number of settings in the United States, including agencies of the federal government, especially the National Institutes of Health, the Department of Defense (including the military branches), the Center for Disease Control, and the U.S. Veteran's Administration; the private sector (including business, the pharmaceutical industry, and independent research organizations); and medical facilities including medical schools, hospitals, and medical research organizations.

These, and many more facilities and organizations, employ or contract with psychologists to conduct research, but the largest cadre of researchers are still in the universities and university-based research centers. Most faculty members in higher education are expected to conduct research, especially in departments that have graduate programs. Research and the supervision of student research represent a major part of the workload of faculty members, especially those in doctoral departments, and salary, promotion, and tenure depend upon the quality and quantity of research produced. Faculty members who have especially active research programs tend to attract graduate students and grant funding to support the research. One result of the strong emphasis on research productivity is that many faculty members show limited interest in teaching, because teaching quality has little effect on advancement.

Like the discipline of psychology, psychological research covers an immense span of concerns from brain research at the cellular level to surveys of large populations and everything in between. There is hardly an area of psychology in which active research is not being conducted and published, often in highly specialized journals. An overview of the broad scope of psychological research is not possible in the limited space available, but some trends may be mentioned. In a recent paper on the status of psychological research presented at the European Congress of Psychology (2003), APA president Robert Sternberg (2003) described four broad areas that are particularly active. The first he refers to as *human nature*: how we think and perceive the world and how that affects everything we do from parenting to social interactions to risk assessment to intuition. The second is *human potential*: how to assess and evaluate different patterns of aptitude and ability, and the neural plasticity model of intelligence. The third is the *human brain*: how imaging technologies are helping to map the brain; memory training for Alzhe-

imer's patients; and cognitive functions in schizophrenic patients. The fourth is *quality of life*: positive psychology; building strengths, rather than correcting weakness; wisdom through the lifespan; and how the mind influences health, happiness, and longevity.

These four areas are just a sample of some areas of research that have gained much more attention recently. Of course, thousands of studies are still being done in the other traditional areas of psychology with animals, humans, and social groups. There has never been a time of higher research productivity or a time when the results of psychological research were more widely disseminated to, and understood by, the public.

7.4 SCOPE OF PSYCHOLOGICAL PRACTICE

There are well over 100,000 doctoral level psychologists in the United States (the exact number is difficult to determine because different agencies use different criteria to define the profession). It is estimated that approximately 20% of psychologists are in academic positions, teaching and conducting research. The remainder work in a number of subfields, a few of which include developmental, educational, forensic, organizational, engineering, cognitive, quantitative and assessment, social, sports, neuropsychology, rehabilitation, school, and counseling and clinical psychology. The latter two, clinical and counseling psychology, are somewhat familiar to the public. The remaining subfields, research shows, are unfamiliar to most people.

The diversity of psychologists' roles has increased dramatically over the last generation. For example, media psychologists were pioneers in studying the effects television has on its viewers, especially children, and they are currently in the forefront of studying the effects of the Internet. Sports psychologists work with athletes to help them improve their performance and to deal with the stress and fear of failure that often accompany competition. Psychologists in the workplace help businesses select employees, train them, and keep them healthy and efficient. Educational psychologists study the effectiveness of teaching and learning. Forensic psychologists provide expert testimony in the courtroom. These are only a few of the subfields in which psychologists are employed.

Approximately 50–60% of psychologists are licensed to practice, primarily in the health-service provider areas. (American Psychological Association Research Office, 2003). Psychologists are now involved in providing care in a broad array of settings, including independent practice, managed care, hospitals, mental health centers, community clinics, nursing homes, schools, university counseling centers, correctional facilities, and in the workplace. The services that psychologists provide go far beyond traditional individual psychotherapy and assessment, and include prevention, primary health care, community, systems, and organizational interventions.

According to a year 2000 density study of mental health practitioners, of those licensed psychologists who are clinically active or trained to provide health services, there are just over 28 psychologists for every 100,000 population in the country (West et al., 2001). In terms of the distribution of psychologists throughout the United States, that study found that psychologists ranged from a low of 4.9 per 100,000 population in Mississippi to a high of 78 per 100,000 in Vermont. Throughout the country, the density of psychologists was greater than the density for psychiatrists (West et al.). As with virtually all mental health professionals and most other professionals, psychologists are less likely to be found in rural areas.

A comparison of the number of psychologists to professionals in other disciplines who provide mental health services finds psychologists roughly in the middle, with clinically trained social workers (192,814) and professional counselors (108,000) having greater numbers, while marriage and family therapists (44,000), psychiatrists (40,731), and psychiatric nurses (17,318) all have smaller numbers than psychologists (West et al., 2001). Psychology has far more doctoral-level providers than the other professions.

Salaries for psychologists vary depending on the setting in which service is being provided and the psychologists' years of experience. According to a survey published in the October 2000 issue of *Psychotherapy Finances*, psychologists' median income was $80,000. By setting, median salaries range from $45,000 in university/college counseling centers for psychologists with 5–9 years' experience to over $100,000 for psychologists in medical-psychological group practice with more than 20 years' experience (American Psychological Association Research Office, 2003). By comparison, incomes for professional counselors, marriage and family therapists, and social workers surveyed by *Psychotherapy Finances* were $47,350, $59,405, and $61,164, respectively. According to the Association of American

Medical Colleges (2003), compensation for psychiatrists ranges from $99,000 to $160,337, with an average income of $145,470.

Specific state statutes and regulations govern the practice of psychology. In each of the states, the District of Columbia, and the U.S. territories, a psychology licensing law exists that establishes a board of psychological examiners, controls the use of the title "psychologist," defines the practice of psychology, establishes qualifications and procedures for licensure, and, typically, prohibits those without a license from engaging in the practice of psychology.

Although there is some variability among the jurisdictions, psychology licensing laws are relatively consistent and follow the recommendations of either the APA (1987) Model Act for State Licensure of Psychologists or the Model Act for Licensure of Psychologists promulgated by the Association of State and Provincial Psychology Boards (1992). With minor exceptions, licensing laws limit the independent practice of psychology to individuals who possess a doctoral degree in psychology from a recognized institution of higher education. Only two states, West Virginia and Vermont, allow the full independent practice of psychology for individuals who possess less than a doctoral degree in psychology. Licensing laws also typically require individuals to complete 2 years of supervised professional experience, including both a predoctoral internship and postdoctoral supervised experience. Forty-two states require ongoing continuing education for an individual to retain the license once it has been awarded. Approximately half of the states requiring continuing education specify a portion of the continuing education content to include legal and ethical issues.

The licensed scope of psychological practice usually follows the definition set forth in the APA (1987) Model Act (p. 696):

> [The] Practice of psychology is defined as the observation, description, evaluation, interpretation, and modification of human behavior by the application of psychological principles, methods, and procedures, for the purpose of preventing or eliminating symptomatic, maladaptive, or undesired behavior and of enhancing interpersonal relationships, work and life adjustment, personal effectiveness, behavioral health, and mental health. The practice of psychology includes but is not limited to psychological testing and the evaluation or assessment of personal characteristics such as intelligence, personality, abilities, interests, aptitudes, and neuropsychological function, counseling, psychoanalysis, psychotherapy, hypnosis, biofeedback, and behavior analysis and therapy; diagnosis and treatment of mental and emotional disorder or disability, alcoholism and substance abuse, disorders of habit or conduct, as well as the psychological aspects of physical illness, accident, injury, or disability; and psychoeducational evaluation, therapy, or remediation and consultation.

Frequently, state licensing laws incorporate, by reference, the APA Ethical Principles of Psychologists and Code of Conduct (American Psychological Association, 2002), thereby rendering violations of the code of ethics to be violations of the licensing laws, as well. These ethical standards consist of enforceable rules for conduct as psychologists, and cover such areas as boundaries of competence, multiple relationships, conflicts of interest, confidentiality, advertising and other public statements, record keeping, informed consent to therapy, and sexual intimacies with clients. The 1992 version of the APA code of ethics was revised in 2002 and the revised ethics code went into effect on June 1,

2003. Apart from state licensing laws, the APA code of ethics is enforceable by the APA upon its members.

Psychologists moving from one state to another have historically needed to go through cumbersome procedures to become relicensed to practice in a new jurisdiction because licensure is governed on a state-by-state basis, and some variability of laws exists. More recently, however, certain mechanisms are being used to better facilitate mobility for psychologists. The Association of State and Provincial Psychology Boards has established an endorsement process, termed the Certificate of Professional Qualification (CPQ), to universally recognize individuals who have met a specified standard qualification in order to make relicensure a much simpler process. To date, 21 states and 6 Canadian provinces have recognized the CPQ, thereby agreeing to automatically accept CPQ holders' educational preparation, supervised experience, and examination performance for licensure. In 2003, 15 additional jurisdictions were in the process of implementing the CPQ (Association of State and Provincial Psychology Boards, 2003).

Two other mechanisms exist that help to facilitate mobility for psychologists. The National Register of Health Service Providers in Psychology maintains a credentials repository that allows it to facilitate mobility. In some states, psychologists who are listed in the national register are exempt from having to submit to licensing boards their official transcripts, confirmation of postdoctoral experience, and scores on the nationally standardized licensure examination. In addition, the specialty diploma awarded by the American Board of Professional Psychology can serve as a national recognition standard for reciprocity of licensure among jurisdictions.

In addition to the need for greater mobility for psychologists, the profession is also responding to the changing demographics of society. Increasing cultural diversity within the United States is a significant factor already influencing psychologists' practice and one that will continue to do so for years to come. The APA ethics code, Principle 2.01 on boundaries of competence, for example, has expressly included factors associated with culture as essential for ethical practice (American Psychological Association, 2002). Similarly, culture has specifically been added to Principle 3.01, which now prohibits unfair discrimination based on culture (American Psychological Association, 2002).

The growing recognition of changing demographics within the U.S. population as they relate to race, ethnicity, language, and age is leading to reexamination of assessment and intervention models, with an increasing emphasis on multicultural psychology (American Psychological Association Board of Professional Affairs, 2002). This development notwithstanding, the scientist–practitioner model continues to be the dominant conceptual framework within which psychologists train and practice. Some professional schools with less emphasis on research have developed an alternative "scholar–practitioner" model for training and practice.

With respect to theoretical frameworks that guide practice, a number of orientations are represented in the practicing psychology community. These include psychoanalytic, psychodynamic, interpersonal, humanistic, behavioral, and cognitive–behavioral. An overarching biopsychosocial model is sometimes used to describe the framework for evaluation and treatment undertaken by psychologists. This is particularly true when the practice of health psychology is focused on psychological interventions for medical populations and physical health conditions.

Although psychologists in individual practice devote considerable time to traditional mental health activities (e.g., individual psychotherapy and assessment, family and couples therapy, and group therapy), appropriately trained psychologists have been functioning well beyond the area of mental health, providing more comprehensive health services (Newman & Reed, 1996). Psychologists are increasingly directing their efforts toward understanding the psychosocial contributors to, and consequences of, physical disease. In turn, this has led to an increased focus on health promotion and disease prevention, as well as on the development of psychological and behavioral interventions for the treatment of various medical problems. This is in addition to the traditional work of health psychologists who have historically focused on the contributions of psychology to the understanding of health and illness, and of neuropsychologists who have long been interested in the study of brain–behavior relationships.

The settings in which psychologists deliver health and mental health services and the roles psychologists play have been greatly expanded. However, a year 2000 study of mental health practitioners and trainees found that by far the largest percentage (38%) of clinically trained psychologists identified their primary work setting as independent practice (West et al., 2001). The next most frequent setting was at a university or college (17%), followed by clinics (8%), nonpsychiatric hospitals (7%), mental health hospitals (4%), and elementary and secondary schools (4%).

Although the percentage of psychologists indicating hospitals as their primary employment setting is relatively small, the profession has made considerable progress during the last decade in being recognized as an independent provider in hospitals and other inpatient settings. Large, publicly funded healthcare programs like the U.S. Department of Defense's Civilian Health and Medical Program of the Uniformed Services and the Medicare program have put regulations in place recognizing psychologists as independent health professionals in hospitals. Seventeen states and the District of Columbia have specifically authorized hospital practice for psychologists, either by statute or by regulations. In some states, legal action by psychologists has been necessary to force implementation of laws intended to authorize their practice in hospitals.

Perhaps related to psychology's increased authority to practice in hospitals or perhaps because managed care has caused many seriously ill patients to be treated on an outpatient basis, psychology is becoming more involved in treating people with serious mental illness. In the past, psychology seemed more focused on treatments for less severe psychological problems (Stewart, Horn, Becker, & Kline, 1993). Currently, however, psychologists' understanding of people with serious mental illnesses and the treatments that are effective with this patient population are dramatically increasing (Coursey, Alford, & Safarjan, 1997). Psychologists' integrative and holistic approach to intervention makes them well-suited to treat persons with serious mental illnesses in the context of integrated mental health service systems.

U.S. psychologists are increasingly providing services within the schools at both secondary and postsecondary institutions. In secondary schools, school psychologists are the predominant psychological specialists, although clinical and counseling psychologists are also employed. The relatively large number of school psychologists is due in a significant part to state and federal regulations requiring school systems to use state-credentialed school psychologists to evaluate children suspected of having learning disabilities, serious emotional disturbances, and other handicapping conditions as defined by law. A majority of those school psychologists working in school settings are trained at the nondoctoral level, most often with a specialist degree or certificate of advanced study in school psychology. Nondoctoral level school psychologists are not permitted to practice independently outside of the school. In addition to assessment of children for handicapping conditions, psychologists in schools also engage in counseling, consulting, behavioral interventions, staff development, and program evaluation.

In postsecondary schools, counseling psychologists are the predominant psychological specialists. Delivery of psychological services to clients in university counseling centers is a major part of the work by psychologists in this setting. In addition, psychologists' work in university or college settings typically includes supervision of interns, teaching, research, and the development and implementation of campus-wide outreach programs.

The broad range of services offered by military psychologists is another illustration of psychologists' increasingly diverse activities. Typical activities of a military psychologist might include direct support of combat units and working in a medical center, training and supervising interns and residents. Command consultation may include assessments related to fitness for duty, security risk, selection for special assignments, and unit morale and cohesiveness, as well as program analysis and development.

Another well-established specialty area that has grown in recent years is the practice of psychology applied to organizational entities, especially in business settings. The practice modality of the specialty is primarily one of consultation and development support for organizations aimed at improving their effectiveness (American Board of Organizational and Business Consulting Psychology, 2002). Practice areas characteristic of the specialty include assessment, selection, placement and performance measurement, training and development (e.g., managerial development programs), organizational development (e.g., organizational change and change management), and consumer performance in complex person–machine systems (American Board of Organizational and Business Consulting Psychology, 2002). Industrial–organizational psychologists also provide research expertise in the workplace, including research design, data analysis, statistical models, and research on employee attitudes and behaviors as they relate to organizational performance (Society for Industrial and Organizational Psychology, n.d.).

The work of organizational and business consulting psychologists is distinguished from the delivery of psychological health services in the work place, such as within employee assistance programs (EAPs). Through EAPs, psychologists are providing health, mental health, and substance abuse treatments for employees. Not only are these services credited with improving employees' mental and physical health, but productivity increases and cost savings are also being attributed to the provision of these psychological services in the workplace (McDonnell Douglas Corporation and Alexander Consulting Group, 1989).

Perhaps the area in which psychologists' roles and activities are increasing most rapidly is in the general healthcare arena, with psychological services being increasingly delivered as a part of treatment for physical health disorders. This includes work in primary prevention of disease, not surprising because the U.S. Public Health Services has reported that lifestyle and behavioral factors constitute 7 of the top 10 leading health risk factors in the United States (cf. Brown et al., 2002). Work in the health arena also includes the integration of psychological services into the treatment of physical conditions, such as breast cancer, cardiovascular disease, diabetes, and asthma. Psychologists are increasingly working in collaboration with physicians, including family physicians and pediatricians, and as part of multidisciplinary pain management teams. It should be noted that psychologists also frequently work in collaboration with many nonphysician professionals, including social workers, clergy, physical therapists, and dentists.

7.5 GLOBALIZATION OF PSYCHOLOGY

Psychology began in the late 1800s as a very international discipline. International congresses were held before there were any national associations, and psychologists, especially in Europe and North America, shared information and students. After the formation of national associations, international psychology waned, but in recent years, with the increasing globalization of the world economy, there has been a renewed focus on international cooperation. The APA has played an active role in promoting the globalization of psychology. Through its Office of International Affairs, the APA maintains contact with most of the world's national and international associations, including 75 national psychological associations and over 70 multinational or international organizations. A newly established visitors' program permits representatives from other national associations, especially those in developing countries, to visit the APA central office and receive exposure to many of APA's activities. The APA has sponsored several international congresses, most recently the International Congress of Applied Psychology in 1998 at which the first World Forum of Psychology was convened. Through travel grants and information dissemination, The APA encourages its members to attend and participate in international meetings. For 15 years, the APA has applied for and received funds from the National Science Foundation for U.S. participants to attend major international congresses. At many international meetings, U.S. psychologists represent a substantial percentage of the participants.

In many ways, the APA is an international as well as a national psychological association. The Committee on International Relations in Psychology (CIRP), the APA's oldest committee, provides oversight to the APA's Office of International Affairs and has launched a major program to encourage the internationalization of psychology curricula. The APA's membership includes over 4,500 overseas members and international affiliates from 121 countries, all of whom receive APA publications and other information and many of whom attend the APA's annual conventions. The Office of International Affairs publishes a quarterly newsletter, *Psychology International*, which currently has a subscription base of 10,000 psychologists. A well-developed program in the international office supports the donation of thousands of books and journals from U.S. psychologists to libraries and research facilities in countries that need them. The APA is recognized as a nongovernmental organization (NGO) by the U.N. and maintains contact with various U.N. offices and with other NGOs through its U.N. representatives.

Although globalization trends, for the most part, are not yet explicitly reflected in this country's licensing laws, discussions on related issues are taking place. For example, the Trilateral Forum on Professional Issues, a joint effort of psychologists in Mexico, Canada, and the U.S., focuses on education, training, and credentialing issues in North America, and allows participants to discuss professional psychology in a global context. Trilateral meetings have also been held to discuss graduate education in psychology and standards of licensure, and the APA has actively participated.

7.6 FUTURE CHALLENGES AND PROSPECTS

Because of its popularity with students, it is likely that psychology as a discipline will continue to prosper for the foreseeable future. Psychology remains one of the most popular undergraduate majors, ranking second as the most common major on most campuses. Only about 5% of these gradu-

ates go on to earn a doctorate. Psychology graduates at the bachelor's level are not qualified for psychology positions, but they find employment in private and public businesses and agencies in such fields as social services, sales, personnel work, management, and computer science; some go on for graduate work in psychology or other professions. Graduates with a master's degree may work in psychological positions, typically under the supervision of doctoral-level psychologists, but usually are not permitted to enter independent practice as psychologists. Doctoral-level psychologists have a broad range of professional opportunities. Most psychologists find employment before or soon after graduation, or continue in post-doctoral training. The rate of unemployment in psychology in the U.S. is very low.

The continuing demand for psychology courses at the undergraduate level and the large number of students applying to graduate school suggest that psychology departments and professional schools will continue to grow and that academic positions will continue to be secure for the foreseeable future. The range of practice opportunities continues to expand, especially as more psychologists enter underserved areas such as geriatrics and underserved places such as rural America. Potential opportunities in the field of general health are likely to be far greater than in mental health in the future, and the increased recognition of psychology as a comprehensive health profession reflects a growing interest in applying psychological knowledge to the prevention and treatment of physical illnesses.

Some psychologists believe that there is an oversupply of practicing psychologists in the United States. To the extent that psychologists limit their practice to the traditional mental health arena, the concern is quite valid. However, as psychologists continue to diversify their practices beyond mental health, particularly into a more comprehensive health arena, many more employment opportunities will be available to psychologists.

Psychology practitioners are more vulnerable to economic forces than are academic psychologists. Most health and mental health care in the United Staes is administered through organizations set up to control health care costs (i.e., managed care). The trend over the last decade toward reducing benefits for mental health care has restricted growth in independent practice. Increasingly, managed care is being recognized as having caused more problems than it has solved, and many believe it will be replaced by other approaches in the future. Psychologists in public facilities are also affected by economic factors such as state and federal deficits that reduce the funding available for mental health care in hospitals, prisons, and mental health facilities.

Interestingly, a considerable body of research has demonstrated that when psychological interventions are integrated with physical health treatments, psychological services have the ability to reduce overall health costs, termed "medical cost offset" (e.g., Mumford, Schlesinger, Glass, Patrick, & Cuerdon, 1984). This would seem to make the use of psychological services particularly valuable in a time of limited economic resources. Unfortunately, mental health care services and their payment mechanisms have been typically segregated from physical health services and their payment mechanisms. The result has been a health care system in this country that has made it difficult, if not impossible, to actually track and account for medical cost offset even when it does occur. Changes to the financing structure of health care are necessary for psychology to play an optimal role. Recent changes to codes used for billing purposes that permit psychologists to be reimbursed for services to individuals without a mental health diagnosis are making it possible to use psychological interventions for the treatment of physical health disorders, such as diabetes, asthma, and cardiovascular disease.

The U.S. public has shown remarkable interest in psychology for a 100 years. Columns on psychology began to appear in newspapers and magazines in the early years of the 20th century. Books on psychology have been bestsellers for years, and psychologists are increasingly heard on the radio and on television. A national telephone survey conducted in 1995 by the APA (Penn and Schoen Associates, Inc., 1995) found that 45% of all respondents believed that psychologists generally help people with problems or offer counseling. In general, the public seems to view practicing psychologists as less threatening than psychiatrists, who are seen as dealing primarily with the severely disturbed.

For the past 7 years, the APA has conducted a focused public education campaign, called "Talk to Someone Who Can Help," intended to inform the general public about the value and availability of psychological services. Despite the widespread availability of information about mental health disorders, many people who need help remain uncertain where to find it, do not have sufficient insurance to cover mental health services or do not seek help because of the stigma still associated with mental health disorders. As a result, many people do not receive the treatment they need.

Health and mental health information is increasingly being sought out by consumers on the Internet. A Harris Poll (Taylor, 1999) found online information concerning depression to be among the most sought after topics on the World Wide Web. Health professionals, including psychologists, are also using the Internet for informational and research purposes. Most psychologists have access to the Internet, which allows them to access the research databases of the APA as well as the thousands of Web sites concerned with health and mental health. The APA Web site is one of the oldest in the U.S., and has a million "hits" per week by psychologists and members of the public in the United States and abroad. Some psychologists have begun providing services via the Internet, but such use is relatively limited and in the early stages at present. A survey of psychologists found only 2% of respondents had utilized the Internet or satellite technology in the delivery of health care (VandenBos & Williams, 2000). As more is learned through research and experience about the conditions under which Internet technology can facilitate the delivery of health care services and the methods that are most effective, more psychologists will be likely to incorporate information technologies into their practice.

Probably the most controversial issue currently being debated in the United States is the issue of prescription privileges for psychologists. The APA has officially endorsed the expansion of the psychologist's scope of practice to include prescribing medication by appropriately trained psychologists and has provided assistance to state psychological associations seeking prescription privileges. Psychologists in one state, New Mexico, and one territory, Guam, have enacted laws that authorize appropriately trained psychologists to prescribe. Over 30 other states have active advocacy programs underway.

One consequence of the movement toward prescriptive authority has been a sharp deterioration in relationships between psychology and psychiatry. While individual psychologists and psychiatrists may still work well together and in interdisciplinary teams, the American Psychiatric Association has devoted considerable resources to defeating the efforts of psychologists to achieve prescriptive authority. Organized psychiatry's current efforts are similar to those undertaken in the 1960s and 1970s, when psychologists advocated for authority to provide independent outpatient treatment, and in the 1980s when psychologists advocated for independent practice in hospitals. The majority of APA members appear to support the right of appropriately trained psychologists to prescribe, but some relatively small but outspoken groups of U.S. psychologists actively oppose prescription privileges. The issue is likely to continue to be controversial.

For many years, psychologists in the United States have worked cooperatively with other professional groups in a wide variety of settings. In many mental health facilities, psychologists work with psychiatrists, social workers, physicians, nurses, and other professionals to provide care for their patients. As psychologists move increasingly into the area of general health and primary care, such interdisciplinary work will be even more common.

In addition to the training, research, and practice done by psychologists, U.S. psychologists advocate for laws that promote services to the underserved, prohibit discrimination against citizens, and prevent violence and abuse. The APA takes public positions on social issues when psychological research is available to support those positions. As a professional association, the APA does not participate in elective politics, but many members do as individuals. Three psychologists now serve in the U.S. Congress, and many others serve in state legislatures.

For over a century, psychology has been a respected and growing discipline in the United States. A strong scientific base, established in the first half of the 20th century, gave rise to a vigorous profession with applications to mental health, general health, education, business and industry, and the military, among others. As the major psychological association, the APA has played an important role in bringing psychologists together, facilitating information exchange and promoting high scientific, professional, and ethical standards. U.S. psychologists have produced much of the world's literature in psychological science, and the APA has archived that and other relevant research in PsychINFO, the world's most extensive behavioral-science database. Professional psychologists have provided leadership in the development and promulgation of psychological interventions and have set a high standard for the provisions of psychological services. The science and profession of psychology have prospered in the United States and the prospects for the future look very good.

ACKNOWLEDGMENTS

For their invaluable assistance and consultation in the preparation of this chapter, the authors wish to express their appreciation to Cynthia D. Belar, Ph.D.; Geoffrey M. Reed, Ph.D.; Lynn Bufka, Ph.D.; Billie Hinnefeld, J.D., Ph.D.; Ron Palomares, Ph.D.; Debra L. Dunivin, Ph.D.; Sandra M. Fowler, M.A.; Jan Ciuccio; and Rochelle Jennings.

REFERENCES

American Board of Organizational and Business Consulting Psychology. (2002). *Examination manual for board certification in organizational and business consulting psychology.* Jefferson City, MO: Author.

American Psychological Association. (1987). Model act for state licensure of psychologists. *American Psychologist, 42,* 696–703.

American Psychological Association. (2002). Ethical principles of psychologists and code of conduct. *American Psychologist, 57,* 1060–1073.

American Psychological Association Board of Professional Affairs. (2002). *America's changing demographics.* Washington, DC: Author.

American Psychological Association Committee on Accreditation. (2002). *2001 annual report.* Washington, DC: American Psychological Association.

American Psychological Association Committee on Accreditation. (2000). *Book I: Guidelines and principles for accreditation in professional psychology and Book II: Accreditation operating procedures of the Committee on Accreditation.* Washington, DC: American Psychological Association.

American Psychological Association Research Office. (2003). *Salaries in psychology 2001: Report of the 2001 APA salary survey.* Washington, DC: American Psychological Association.

Association of American Medical Colleges. (n.d.). *Careers in medicine: Specialty information.* Retrieved April 19, 2003, from http://www.aamc.org/students/cim/pub_psychiatry.htm

Association of State and Provincial Psychology Boards. (1992). *Model act for licensure of psychologists*. Montgomery, AL: Author.

Association of State and Provincial Psychology Boards. (2003, March 24). *Jurisdictions currently accepting the CPQ*. Retrieved April 21, 2003, from http://www.asppb.org/mobility/states.htm

Benjamin, L. T., DeLeon, P. H., Freedheim, D. K., & VandenBos, G. R. (2003). Psychology as a profession. In I. B. Weiner (Series Ed.) & D. K. Freedheim (Vol. Ed.), *Handbook of psychology: Vol. 1. History of psychology* (pp. 27–45). New York: Wiley.

Brown, R. T., Freeman, W. S., Brown, R. A., Belar, C., Hersch, L., Hornyak, L. M., et al. (2002). The role of psychology in health care delivery. *Professional Psychology: Research and Practice, 33,* 536–545.

Cadwallader, T. C. (1992). The historical roots of the American Psychological Association. In R. B. Evans, V. S. Sexton, & T. C. Cadwallader (Eds.), *The American Psychological Association: A historical perspective* (pp. 3–41). Washington, DC: American Psychological Association.

Coursey, R. D., Alford, J., & Safarjan, B. (1997). Significant advances in understanding and treating serious mental illness. *Professional Psychology: Research and Practice, 28,* 205–216.

Fuchs, A. H., & Milar, K. S. (2003). Psychology as a science. In I. B. Weiner (Series Ed.) & D. K. Freedheim (Vol. Ed.), *Handbook of psychology: Vol. 1. History of psychology* (pp. 1–26). New York: Wiley.

Hilgard, E. R. (1987). *Psychology in America*. Orlando, FL: Harcourt Brace Jovanovich.

Is therapist income holding up? (2000, October). *Psychotherapy Finances, 26,* 6–7.

McDonnell Douglas Corporation and Alexander Consulting Group. (1989). *Employee assistance program financial offset study, 1985–1988*. Bridgeton, MO: Author.

Mumford, E., Schelesinger, H. J., Glass, G. V., Patrick, C., & Cuerdon, T. (1984). A new look at evidence about reduced cost of medical utilization following mental health treatment. *American Journal of Psychiatry, 141,* 1145–1158.

Napoli, D. S. (1941). *Architects of adjustment: The history of the psychological profession in the United States*. Port Washington, NY: Kennikat Press.

Newman R., & Reed, G. M. (1996). Psychology as a health care profession: Its evolution and future directions. In R. J. Resnick & R. H. Rosensky (Eds.), *Health psychology through the life span* (pp. 11–26). Washington, DC: American Psychological Association.

Penn and Schoen Associates. (1995). *Public opinion on mental health issues. Report to the American Psychological Association, Practice Directorate*. Washington, DC: Author.

Pickren, W. S., & Fowler, R. D. (2003). Professional organizations. In I. B. Weiner (Series Ed.) & D. K. Freedheim (Vol. Ed.), *Handbook of psychology: Vol. 1. History of psychology* (pp. 535–554). New York: Wiley.

Smith, D. (2001). North American psychologists unite. *Monitor on Psychology, 32,* 78.

Society for Industrial and Organizational Psychology. (n.d.). Building better organizations. *Industrial organizational psychology in the workplace*. Retrieved April 24, 2003, from http://www.slop.org/visibilitybrochure/memberbrochue.htm

Sternberg, R. J. (2003, July). *The status of psychological research in Europe and North America*. Paper presented at the VIII European Congress of Psychology, Vienna, Austria.

Stewart, J. A., Horn, D. L., Becker, J. M., & Kline, J. S. (1993). Post-doctoral training in severe mental illness: A model for trainee development. *Professional Psychology: Research and Practice, 24,* 286–292.

Taylor, H. (1999, August 2). *Explosive growth of "cyberchondriacs" continues*. Retrieved November 2, 2000, from http://www.harris-inter-active.com/harris_poll/index.asp

VandenBos, G. R. (1989). Loosely organized "organized psychology" *American Psychologist, 44,* 979–986.

VandenBos, G. R., & Williams, S. (2000). The Internet versus the telephone: What is telehealth anyway? *Professional Psychology: Research and Practice, 31,* 490–492.

West, J., Kohout, J., Pion, G. M., Wichershi, M. M., Vandivort-Warren, R. E., Palmiter, M. L., et al. (2001). Mental health practitioners and trainees. In R. W. Manderscheid & M. J. Henderson (Eds.), *Mental health, United States, 2000* (DHHS Publication No. (SMA) 01-3537, pp. 279–315). Washington, DC: Superintendent of Documents.

IMPORTANT PUBLICATIONS

Allport, G. W. (1927). Concepts of trait and personality. *Psychological Bulletin, 24,* 284–293.

Bandura, A. L. (1977). *Social learning theory.* Englewood Cliffs, NJ: Prentice Hall.

Boring, E. G. (1929). *A history of experimental psychology.* New York: Appleton-Century.

Dollard, J., & Miller, N. E. (1950). *Personality and psychotherapy: An analysis in terms of learning, thinking, and culture.* New York: McGraw-Hill.

Festinger, L. (1957). *A theory of cognitive dissonance.* Palo Alto, CA: Stanford University Press.

Hull, C. L. (1943). *Principles of behavior.* New York: Appleton-Century.

James, W. (1890). *Principles of psychology* (Vols. 1 & 2). New York: Holt.

Maslow, A. H. (1943). A theory of human motivation. *Psychological Review, 50,* 370–396.

Meehl, P. E. (1954). *Clinical versus statistical prediction: A theoretical analysis and a review of the evidence.* Minneapolis, MN: University of Minnesota Press.

Milgram, S. (1963). Behavioral study of obedience. *Journal of Abnormal and Social Psychology, 69,* 137–143.

Raimy, V. V. (Ed.). (1950). *Training in clinical psychology.* New York: Prentice Hall.

Rogers, C. R. (1951). *Client-centered therapy.* Boston: Houghton Mifflin.

Thorndike, E. L. (1911). *Animal intelligence.* New York: Macmillan.

Skinner, B. F. (1938). *Behavior of organisms: An experimental analysis.* New York: Appleton-Century.

Watson, J. B. (1913). Psychology as the behaviorist views it. *Psychological Review, 20,* 158–177.

CHAPTER 8

Psychology in Argentina

HUGO KLAPPENBACH

*Hugo Klapplenbach received his bacca-
laureate in psychology from the University of the Savior, and a doctorate in
history at Buenos Aires University. At
present, he is a professor at the National
University of San Luis and researcher at
National Council of Scientific and Technical Research.* He edits Cuadernos
Argentinos de Historia de la Psicología,
*co-chairs the Task Force on the History
of Psychology for the Interamerican
Society of Psychology, and serves as liaison to the Division of International Psychology of the American Psychological
Association. Hugo Klappenbach has
also served as chair of the undergraduate program in psychology at the
National University of San Luis, as member of the executive board of the Argentine Psychological Association, and as
member of the board of directors of the
Buenos Aires Psychological Association.
He has authored more than 80 works on
psychology, notably on the history of
psychology.*

8.1 OVERVIEW

Psychology in Argentina is quite different
from psychology in other parts of the
world, including other Latin American
countries. The literature related to this subject is abundant, but is published mainly in
Spanish, beginning with the pioneering
works of H. Piñero, J. Ingenieros, I. Fora-
dori, and R. Gotthelf, with important literature published during the 1970s through
the 1980s (Ardila, 1979; Gentile, 1989;
Papini, 1985; Vezzetti, 1988).

During the last decade, studies of
Argentine psychology have increased, not
only those about the history of the discipline and profession (Dagfal, 2000; Diez,
1994; Gentile, 1987; Klappenbach, 2000a;
Paolucci & Verdinelli, 1999; Sanz Ferramola, 2000; Vilanova, 2001), but also
those on the current status of Argentine psychology (Alonso, 1999; Vilanova, 1993).

At the same time, other literature has
analyzed Argentine psychology in the
context of Latin American psychology

generally (Ardila, 1986; Carpintero, 1993; di Doménico & Vilanova, 1999; Geuter & León, 1997; Klappenbach & Pavesi, 1994; Vilanova, 1993; Vilanova & di Doménico, 1999). Despite these many studies, the literature in English on Argentine psychology is limited to a few papers (Horas, 1981; Klappenbach, 1995; Kohan, 1992).

In Argentina, the science of psychology began during the last years of the 19th century. The first course in psychology was proposed in 1895 by Ernesto Weigel Muñoz, a lawyer at the College of Law and Social Sciences at Buenos Aires University, with Rodolfo Rivarola, also a lawyer, appointed as chair of psychology in 1901. One year later, a second chair in psychology was appointed in the College of Philosophy and Humanities, a physician Horacio Piñero (Klappenbach & Pavesi, 1994).

In those early years, several laboratories of experimental psychology were established. Victor Mercante founded a psycho-physiological laboratory in 1891 at San Juan, where he measured psychophysical phenomena using students as subjects (Paolucci & Verdinelli, 1999). In 1899 Piñero established a laboratory of experimental psychology at the National Central High School and another laboratory at the College of Philosophy and Humanities of Buenos Aires University in 1904; Piñero used both laboratories mainly for teaching. In 1905, at the National University of La Plata, Mercante organized an experimental psychology laboratory (Klappenbach, 1996). In 1906 Felix Kreuger, Wundt's disciple in Leipzig, formed an experimental psychology laboratory at the National Institute of High Professorship (Klappenbach, 1996). Thus, Piñero, Mercante, and Krueger, as well as José Ingenieros and Carlos Bunge,

were among the pioneers of Argentine psychology at the turn of the century (Vezzetti, 1988), a psychology that was heavily experimental and distinctly European in origins (Klappenbach & Pavesi, 1994).

It is important to underscore the differences in the objectives of those laboratories from the ones that had been developed in Germany. In Germany, a close relationship existed between experimental laboratories and German universities, both of which were dedicated to research activities (Dobson & Bruce, 1972). James McKeen Cattell, a well-known student of Wundt's, affirmed that those "university laboratories have the same ends as the University itself, the education of students and the advancement of knowledge" (Cattell, 1888, p. 37). In Argentina, on the contrary, Piñero pointed out that psychology laboratories served "to supplement the teaching of the course" (Piñero, 1902, p. 138). Second, when Piñero explained the genealogy of the scientific psychology that he introduced to Argentina, he highlighted the importance of Ribot and Charcot, and criticized Wundt for what he called excessive psychometrics (Piñero, 1903).

Piñero stated that, in Argentine psychology, the prestige of experimental method resulted from two factors. The first involved the popularization of the experimental method in Ribot's classic, *Contemporary German Psychology*. The second was the enormous impact of Bernard's *Introduction to the Study of Experimental Medicine* (Piñero, 1903). Bernard argued that experimentation was the culmination of scientific medicine, but along a continuum in which experimental medicine does not exclude clinical medicine; on the contrary, the former derives from the latter (Klappenbach, 1996).

In terms of the history of ideas, Argentina clearly had a cultural model in France. Many have noted pointed out the devotion of the intellectual elite to France (Jitrik, 1982). Piñero himself stated in an address at the Institut Général Psychologique at the Sorbonne, "intellectually, in fact we [Argentines] are French" (Piñero, 1903, p. 404). Thus, Argentina was dominated by the clinical characteristics of French psychology. For this reason, I prefer to label early Argentine psychology as clinical *and* experimental psychology (Klappenbach, 1996).

After 1916, a reorientation of in Argentine psychology occurred, known as the anti-positivistic movement. It was stimulated both by the visit of the Spanish philosopher Ortega y Gasset (Biagini, 1989) and by the writing of the constitution of the Novecentista Association. The platform of this organization emphasized the limits of psychophysical determinism and defined humans as free.

There were other important influences on Argentine psychology between 1916 and 1940. First, foreign psychologists and psychological ideas were infused into the country, and institutions dedicated to psychological specialties were founded. Second, there remained an ambiguous relationship between clinical and experimental psychology. That is, on the one hand, psychologists continued pointing to the limits of physiological psychology, yet maintained an interest in the physiological bases of psychopathology. Third, there was a transformation in how academic psychology was viewed in relation to philosophy, but not in the Wundtian view of psychology as an empirical precursor to philosophy. Rather, the philosophical underpinnings of psychology seemed to promote specu-

lation. Specifically, they promoted various self-reflective methods through which to identify the limits of sensory approaches to experience (Paolucci & Verdinelli, 1999).

During the 1940s, such psychology was legitimized at Argentine universities. In 1937 the Department of Philosophy was formed at the National University of Tucumán, in which the Spanish philosopher Manuel Morente taught a popular course, Introductory Lectures on Philosophy. Other outstanding members of the department were, Luis Farré, Risieri Frondizi, Manuel Houses, Rodolfo Mondolfo, Diego Pró, Eugenio Pucciarelli, Aníbal Reulet, and Juan Vázquez (Pró, 1981).

The National University of Tucumán and National University of Cuyo, while promoting the speculative psychology just described, also developed an applied psychology especially related to education and work. Indeed, the country's sociopolitical context did not encourage the development of speculative psychology; instead, economic conditions promoted psychometrics and guidance. This trend accelerated after the military coup of 1943.

The Peronist government (1946–1955) generated a new, urban working class that needed labor training. For example, the 1947 and 1953 5-year economic plans encouraged the centralization of business and industry, and had an important role in orienting young people to the labor force (Waldmann, 1981). In this context, professional guidance became regulated at the federal level with the Constitutional Reform of 1949. At the same time, the second 5-year plan included the objective of promoting learning and professional guidance in educational settings and the workplace. In the former, the second 5-year plan established that national economic and social policies should be implemented in diverse ways, including the "establishment of rational correlations between worker's aptitude and its occupation, in order to obtain the highest levels of productivity and of retribution" (República Argentina, 1953, p. 83). As a result, applied psychology found itself on a favorable course. It was challenged to address the lack of abilities and skills provided by educational institutions and the consequent low productivity in the workplace. There were also questions about the construction of suitable psychometric instruments to guide diagnoses and interventions. In this context, then, Argentine psychometrics and career guidance became indispensable (Klappenbach, 1995).

During this time, undergraduate programs were designed at universities. Examples included the program in psychometrics and guidance at the National University of Tucumán in 1950 (Klappenbach, 1995), the program created in 1950 at the University of Rosario that trains psychometric assistants (Gentile, 1989), and the undergraduate specialization in psychology organized at the National University of Cuyo in San Luis in 1953 (Klappenbach, 1995). Because the development of these programs was irregular, the first Argentine Congress of Psychology in 1954 recommended that they reorganize under the banner of psychology at national universities (Klappenbach, 1995).

After the coup that toppled the Perón government in 1955, the cultural, ideological, and political atmosphere at Argentine universities changed significantly (Terán, 1993). Nevertheless, as mandated by the 1954 Congress, undergraduate programs in psychology were organized at the six national universities in existence through

the 1950s: the universities at Buenos Aires, Córdoba, Cuyo, La Plata, Litoral, and Tucumán. Between 1959 and 1964, the first six private universities were created: Argentine University John F. Kennedy, Buenos Aires Free College of Psychology, Catholic University of Cordoba, University of the Argentine Social Museum, University of the North Santo Tomás de Aquino, and University of the Savior. Two provincial institutions were also established: Instituto de Ciencias de la Educación in Mar del Plata and the Facultad de Antropología Escolar in Mendoza. Ten years after the first Argentine Congress of Psychology, 13 undergraduate programs in psychology had been established.

Since the early 1960s, an important change occurred in Argentine psychology: the emergence of the first graduates in psychology at national and some private universities. This ended the so-called period of "psychology without psychologists" (Vilanova & di Doménico, 1999) and inaugurated a new era in which psychology became a profession, placing the debate about the role of psychologists at center stage.

During the 1960s, 1970s, and early 1980s, most psychologists believed that a psychologist was a psychoanalyst. Such beliefs did not exclude the wide range of fields in which psychologists could work. However, psychoanalysis was considered a theory, an investigatory method, and a therapy. In fact, the commonly held view was that psychologists could not follow a scientific model if they lacked preparation in psychoanalysis (Klappenbach, 2000b). There were other reflections, less frequently expressed, that criticized the psychoanalytic perspective. Some criticized university training because Argentine psychologists completed their studies in psychology without having a clear idea of their role and with a poor professional self-perception (Klappenbach, 2000b). The emphasis on clinical psychology and psychoanalytic practice also produced considerable conflict with psychiatrists. Psychologists went without any legal recognition of their degree and, hence, were considered psychiatric assistants. This was generally the case across the country.

In 1983, the president of the Federation of Psychologists of the Republic of Argentina (FePRA) pointed to the growing paradox: psychologists were being trained in psychoanalysis and psychotherapy, yet such practices were forbidden for psychologists by law (Avelluto, 1983). This legal dilemma changed after the assumption of a new democratic government in 1983. From then on, Argentine law gave complete recognition to the profession of psychology and provided a means for the regulation of psychological practice (Klappenbach, 2000a). In addition, efforts were made to develop an academic tradition based on empirical research in the various disciplinary specialties.

In 1976, one of the bloodiest military dictatorships in all Latin America was launched, and it governed illegally until 1983. The House of Representatives and the Senate were closed, students, intellectuals, trade-union leaders, and political opponents were jailed or made to disappear. State-sponsored terrorism left many dead, maimed, or missing. Between 12,000 and 30,000 persons are estimated to be missing, among them the presidents of the FePRA and Buenos Aires Psychologists Association, as well as 33 other psychologists (Sanz, 2000).

Since the restoration of democracy, a group of prominent psychologists work for or closely with Mothers of May Square, Grandmothers of May Square, and other human-rights organizations to assist victims of the military dictatorship and their relatives. In November 2003, the Mothers of May Square sponsored the second International Congress on Mental Health and Human Rights.

8.2 EDUCATION AND TRAINING

The university system in Argentina is quite different from that in the United States Before 1955, all universities were national or provincial, supported by federal or provincial public funds; private universities were not recognized. Shortly after the overthrow of the Perón's government, the military government decreed that private initiative may create free universities. A similar law was enacted in 1958 by the new democratic government after public debate about approval of private universities (Terán, 1993), leading to the founding of private and religious universities (Fanelli & Balán, 1994). Private universities have been established throughout Argentina, more than half in the last decade alone (Fanelli & Balán, 1994).

In 2000, there were 36 national universities, 42 private universities, and 1 provincial university. There were 1,290,583 university students: 1,124,044 students at national universities (87.09%) and 166,539 at private universities (12.90%) (Ministerio de Educación, Ciencia y Tecnología. Secretaría de Políticas Universitarias, 2002). There also were 5 national university institutes and 10 private university institutes. The "university institute" was designated in a 1995 federal law; whereas universities activities include many disciplines, university institutes focus on a single field of knowledge. In all, there are 94 university-related entities in Argentina (Ministerio de Educación, Ciencia y Tecnología. Secretaría de Políticas Universitarias, 2002).

National universities remain the most prestigious. Only in the last decade have private universities hired full-time professors dedicated to teaching and research. Most private universities lack research facilities, online databases with full-text access, comprehensive collections of scientific journals, and other material indispensable to maintaining high standards in teaching and research.

Federal law approved in 1995 grants considerable autonomy to universities, including the establishment of bylaws, administrative structure, the creation of undergraduate and graduate programs, and the disbursement of money. It also includes the appointment of faculty and staff, although at national universities appointments occur after an examination of the curriculum vitae of applicants and a lecture on a topic included in a course syllabus.

At national universities, the central authority is the university superior council (*Consejo Superior Universitario*), composed of representative professors, graduates, students, and administrators, with at least 50% professors and 30% students. Councils typically elect a rector or president. Universities are divided into different colleges or schools whose governing body is a directive council, also formed by professors, graduates, students, and administrators. Each directive council elects a college dean. Most colleges are composed of discrete academic departments.

Argentina's degree system also differs from that of the United States. In Argentina,

university degrees are not in arts or sciences, but in a specific scientific or professional field. That is, there are no majors leading to a bachelor's degree. Undergraduate programs center on a single field of knowledge or profession. In psychology, the university degree is termed *licenciatura en psicología* (graduate in psychology), or simply, *psicólogo* (psychologist). After the customary 5 or 6 years of study, the licenciatura is the entry requirement to practice in clinical, educational, and forensic settings, including private practice in psychotherapy. In a sense, the licenciatura is the first, last, and only university degree for the professional practice of psychology, as well as law and medicine. Of course, psychologists recognize their obligation to continue professional training after graduation.

Usually, training after the *licenciatura* does not end in a master's or doctorate, as neither is encouraged by universities. Such training is obtained through postgraduate courses, mostly at professional institutions, although the situation began to change in the last decade when the first master's degree was granted. Although it was possible to obtain a Ph.D. before 1990 at a few universities, not many psychologists have doctorates; a doctorate is not even mandatory for an academic career or promotion to full professor. The last report in 1997 about undergraduate psychology programs at national universities pointed out that of 3,729 faculty, only 46 (1.3%) held a doctorate (Asociación de Unidades Académicas de Psicología, 1998).

Out of the total, 11 psychology programs—near one-third—have an independent structure, with 10 constituted as colleges of psychology and the other as a school of psychology. Another three programs are also independently organized as colleges of psychology and related sciences. The remaining 16 programs are constituted within psychology departments housed in colleges not explicitly related to psychology (e.g., colleges of the arts and sciences, educational sciences, humanities, law and sciences, philosophy and arts, or sciences of health). Such variety might reflect the ambiguous nature of psychology: Psychology may be considered a human, social science, or natural science. But, it also mirrors the close relationship between Argentine psychology and the humanities. Most psychologists in Argentina would agree with Freud's view that scientific observation must be subordinated to poetic intuition because the observation of the mind merely repeats what poetry has already said.

As of 2003, there were 7 undergraduate programs in psychology at national universities and 23 such programs at private universities. Since 2000, specialized undergraduate programs in organizational psychology and social psychology were established at a national and private university, respectively. Over 43% of psychology programs are in Buenos Aires; 1 is at a national university and 12 are at private universities.

Since 1954, there have been 53,829 graduates in psychology: 37,012 (68.8%) from national universities and 16,817 (31.2%) from private universities; 35,524 (66.0%) graduate from programs in Buenos Aires (deans and chairs of psychology programs, personal communications, 2002–2003). In 2003, 11,623 psychology students were enrolled, with 8,518 (73.3%) at national universities and 3,105 (26.7%) at private universities (deans and chairs of psychology programs, personal communications, 2002–2003).

The 30 undergraduate psychology programs differ in their objectives, coursework, staffing, and infrastructure. Nevertheless, they have several commonalities:

1. Admission criteria to most programs are implicit (Sigal, 1998). There are neither examinations at the end of high school or at the beginning of college, nor are there any aptitude tests. The only prerequisite for entering a university is the high-school degree. Since 1995 people older than 25 years without a high-school diploma have been able to enroll at a university after taking an examination.

2. Since 1997, the government requires that all programs be at least 2,600 hr over a minimum of 4 years. National universities and most private universities have set their required hours at 3,000 hr over 5 years. Moreover, the National University of La Plata and National University of Rosario require 6 years of study. The National University of Cordoba and National University of San Luis, which have 5-year programs, also require a thesis, which can extend the degree to 6 years. Only undergraduate programs at new universities have 4-year programs.

3. Since 1985, psychologists' competencies and qualifications (*Licenciados en Psicologia*) have been established for all universities by the Ministry of Education and Justice. The evaluation covers graduates' qualifications to conduct research and engage in professional practice (see Table 8.1). The qualifications and competencies have been criticized (Klappenbach 2000a). They tend

TABLE 8.1

Psychologists' Degree Competencies and Qualifications

1. To study and explore psychological data across the different stages of individual development, embracing both normal and abnormal aspects.

2. To carry out psychological guidance and advice directed toward health promotion and illness prevention.

3. To carry out tasks of psychological diagnosis, prognosis, and follow-up.

4. To conduct psychotherapeutic treatments according different theoretical approaches.

5. To carry out tasks of psychological rehabilitation.

6. To develop and design psychological methods, techniques, and instruments.

7. To carry out vocational and occupational guidance.

8. To study, guide, and explain the interpersonal conflicts and intergroup conflicts in the context of the structure and dynamics of institutions.

9. To diagnose, care for, guide, and advise in all matters related to psychological aspects of educational work, and to the structure and dynamics of educational institutions and the social environment of such institutions.

10. To study, guide, and advise on the motivations and attitudes in the social and community environment.

11. To carry out assessments that allow for the understanding of the psychological characteristics of the worker for use in the selection, allocation, and development of workers.

12. To elaborate psychological profiles in different labor environments, taking into account the analysis of positions and tasks.

13. To detect psychological causes of work accidents, and to advise and carry out activities directed toward their prevention.

14. To carry out studies and promote preventive action toward the creation of the most favorable conditions for the reciprocal adaptation of humans and work.

15. To provide psychological advice within the criminal justice system, and to rehabilitate and evaluate prisoners, ex-prisoners, and their relatives.

16. To provide psychological advice and care for within the environment of civil or private law, adoption, children's custody, guardianship, divorce, and all matters concerning family law.

17. To participate, from a psychological perspective, in the planning, carrying out, and evaluation of plans and programs of health and social action.

18. To carry out actions directed toward the promotion of human rights and to study, advise, and operate on the psychological repercussions derived from the violation of those human rights.

19. To advise, from a psychological perspective, on the elaboration of juridical norms related with the different areas of psychology.

20. To carry out research on the different areas and fields of psychology.

Source: From "El título profesional de psicólogo en Argentina: Antecedentes históricos y situación actual [The psychologist degree in Argentina: Historical antecedents and current situation]," by H. Klappenbach, 2000a, *Revista Latinoamericana de Psicología, 32,* 2000, 419–446.

to describe the scope of psychological knowledge and skills required for mastery using imprecise terms. However, they are relatively balanced and cover community, educational, forensic, industrial–organizational, and social psychology (Klappenbach, 2000a). The competencies and qualifications have been invaluable in developing new undergraduate programs and modifying existing ones since the restoration of democracy, especially in the selection of obligatory and elective coursework (Asociación de Unidades Académicas de Psicología, 1998).

4. The generic title obtained upon graduation from any undergraduate program is psychologist or graduate in psychology, implying that a title-holder can work in any field of psychology. However, as noted earlier, two universities now offer specialized 4-year degrees, one in organizational psychology at the National University of La Rioja, and one in social psychology at the University of the High Studies Center in Mathematics. As in the 1990s, the development of shorter, specialized degree programs reflects national economic and social need (Fanelli & Balán, 1994).

5. All undergraduate programs emphasize a core curriculum that includes general psychology; up to three courses on the biology of human behavior; clinical psychology; one or two courses on developmental psychology (infancy and adolescence in particular); educational psychology; forensic psychology; history of psychology; one or two courses on psychological assessment; psychopathology; one or two courses on statistics; and anthropology or sociology.

6. One of the features of Argentine undergraduate psychology is the number of courses on systems of psychotherapy, especially psychoanalysis. In some programs, there are five-course sequences on psychoanalysis. Most programs typically require a course on current systems of psychotherapy and offer many courses on psychoanalysis (e.g., Freudian theory; the British psychoanalytic school represented by Bion, Fairburn, and Klein; and the French psychoanalytic or Lacanian school). Courses on psychoanalysis are not enough to explain the prevalence of psychoanalysis. Most undergraduate programs take a psychoanalytic approach toward all other courses (Piacente, 1998; Vilanova, 1993).

7. Psychology courses do not require textbooks, and texts are rarely used, even in introductory classes. Professors prefer to assign chapters from classic books or printed versions of their lectures.

8. Most undergraduate programs do not have well-stocked libraries (Asociación de Unidades Académicas de Psicología, 1998). Until 1997, only the library at the National University of San Luis had a complete set of *Psychological Abstracts* since 1927. It is also rare to access full-text articles from an online database service; in 1999, the National University of Tucumán was able to subscribe to *PsycInfo* and in 2002, the National University of La Plata procured a full-text online system.

9. Other material conditions are also poor, which does not promote quality education. Classrooms do not have the capacity to hold 500–1,000 students, yet enrollments of this size are not unusual. There are no laboratories or resources for practical training. Professors' salaries are often low.

Almost all national universities and the oldest private universities offered doctoral degrees in the 1960s and 1970s. Doctoral degrees entailed a personalized course of study ending with a dissertation. The three national universities that currently offer accredited doctoral degrees are the National University of Cordoba, National University of San Luis, and National University of Rosario. Besides these graduate psychology programs, a few Argentine universities maintain traditional graduate training in philosophy. There was little interest in graduate training in psychology until the 1990s. Rather, psychologists sought postgraduate training in hospitals or at so-called private educational institutions that were not accredited by a recognized authority. Such institutions are staffed by professional psychologists, most of them without graduate degrees, but with extensive professional experience in various fields.

With the expansion of Argentine higher education in the 1990s (Fanelli & Balan, 1994), many universities have added graduate programs. In 1995 the Federal Law of Superior Education established three forms of graduate study: master's, doctoral, and specialized programs. All were limited to universities and had to be accredited by the National Council of University Evaluation and Accreditation (CONEAU), established by the same law.

To evaluate and accredit graduate programs, the CONEAU established a peer-review system, which has been widely criticized. Universities are allowed to propose reviewers, although no one can evaluate a program in which he or she is a professor. Furthermore, there are few reviewers with graduate degrees and few experts in some fields. Clearly, the system is new and need improvement. In addition, although universities are obligated to evaluate their graduate programs, they are not forced to categorize them. Thus, some programs are accredited but not categorized, which add more confusion to the evaluation process. Nevertheless, through June 2003, the CONEAU accredited 34 graduate programs in psychology throughout Argentina, several of them highly respected and many categorized as *B* or *C*, while other programs have not been categorized. There are no graduate programs in psychology categorized as *A*, the highest standard (see Table 8.2).

Good graduate programs, like the master's program in educational psychology at Buenos Aires University, may not be accredited for various reasons: perhaps, it is a new program, or university authorities reject the accreditation process, arguing that it violates academic freedom. Conversely, some accredited graduate programs are weak, like those established at universities that lack undergraduate programs— that is, without a psychology faculty or without a tradition of teaching and research in psychology.

While graduate programs formerly consisted of professional training at an institution other than a university, some new graduate programs have been incorporated by universities. As noted before, although most professors in graduate programs did not hold a graduate degree, they had acquired considerable applied experience and prestige, and students in these programs earned graduate degrees. Some of these programs were well-established, such as four of the six accredited programs at the University of Business and Social Sciences, which were specialized professional training programs affiliated with the Psychologists' Association of Buenos Aires. In 1996 the University of Business and Social Sciences formed an agreement with the Association that those

TABLE 8.2
Accredited Graduate Programs in Psychology

Accred-ited	Graduate Program	University	Category[a]
2001	Doctoral Program in Psychology	National University of Cordoba	B
1999	Doctoral Program in Psychology	National University of San Luis	C
2000	Doctoral Program in Social Psychology	Argentine University John F. Kennedy	—
2000	Specialization Program in Clinical Psychology	Argentine University John F. Kennedy	—
2000	Specialization Program in the Problem of Improper Use of Drugs	University of Buenos Aires	C
1999	Specialization Program in Family Violence	University of Buenos Aires	C
1995	Master's Program in Clinical Psychology: Cognitive-Integrative Orientation	National University of San Luis	C
2002	Specialization Program in Psychology in Education	National University of Rosario	C
2000	Specialization Program in Clinical, Institutional, and Community Psychology	National University of Rosario	—
2001	Master's Program in Cognitive, Clinical Psychology	University of Belgrano	Project
2000	Master's Program in Psychoanalysis	Argentine University John F. Kennedy	—
1999	Master's Program in Family and Minority Psychology	Catholic University of Cuyo	—
2000	Master's Program in Theoretical Psychoanalysis	National University of San Luis	C
1999	Master's Program in Social Psychology	National University of Mar del Plata	C New
2000	Specialization Program in Psychoanalysis with Adolescents	University of Business and Social Sciences	—
2003	Specialization Program in Community Mental Health	National University of Lanus	Project
2001	Master's Program in Theoretical Foundations of Lacanian Psychoanalytical Clinic	National University of San Luis	C
2001	Master's Program Neuropsychology	National University of Cordoba	B New
1999	Master's Program in Psychoanalysis	University of Aconcagua	C
1999	Master's Program in Educational Psychology	National University of Tucumán	C New
2001	Master's Program in Managerial and Organizational Psychology	University of Belgrano	Project
1999	Master's Program in Preventive Psychology	National University of Catamarca	C New
2000	Master's Program in Systemic Psychotherapy	University of Aconcagua	—
1999	Doctoral Program in Psychology National	University of Rosario	Project
2000	Specialization Program in Psychoanalysis with Children	University of Business and Social Sciences	—
2000	Specialization Program in Forensic Psychology	University of Business and Social Sciences	—

TABLE 8.2
(Continued)

2001	Doctoral Program of University of Palermo in Psychology	University of Palermo	B New
2001	Master's Program in Helplessness Problems and Pathologies	University of Business and Social Sciences	—
2002	Specialization Program in the Psychoanalytic Approach to the Family and Couples	University of the High Studies Center in Mathematics	—
2002	Specialization Program in Treatment of Psychosomatic Pathologies	University of the High Studies Center in Mathematics	—
2000	Specialization Program in Mental Health Politics and Administration	University of Business and Social Sciences	—
2001	Doctoral Program in Psychology	University of Business and Social Sciences	—
2003	Master's Program in Family and Disability	University of the Argentine Social Museum	Project
2003	Specialization Program in Psychological Assessment and Diagnosis	University of the Savior	Project

Note. From "Posgrados acreditados. Área disciplinaria psicología," by Comisión Nacional de Evaluación y Acreditación Universitaria, 2003. Retrieved June 22, 2003, from http://www.coneau.gov.ar/posgrado/acredita/psicologia/psicologia.html
[a]The letters *B* and *C* refer to ratings of excellence that a university receives if it requests an evaluation. The term *project* refers to a program in the planning stage. *New* refers to a program that has yet to graduate students.

professional programs would be changed into graduate academic programs within a university environment (S. Chiarvetti, personal communication, March 22, 2002).

Interestingly, the CONEAU observed in its 2002 Report on Criteria for Accreditation, that graduate education in Argentina has developed largely outside of the university, through psychology organizations, like the FePRA, at provincial colleges or associations, in public hospitals, and even via private networks of psychologists who study together and offer peer supervision. The CONEAU's praise for extra-university graduate training was echoed by studies of Argentina's graduate education, which found it to have high standards, particularly in psychoanalysis (Barsky, 1997).

Professors at national universities are employed by those universities, not by the federal government; nevertheless, they are still public employees. It is possible to be employed by a national university at the rank of auxiliary teacher, chief of practical teaching, assistant professor, associate professor, or professor. The typical 12-month appointment of university professors is either for a limited period, as a temporary professor, or, after examination of the curriculum vitae and a lecture, as a tenure-track professor. Salaries are established by the federal government and are consistent within academic rank regardless of field of specialization. Until the economic crisis of 2002, the maximum monthly salary of a full-time professor with 20 years' experience was $1,800. Since 1995, each professor has been able to receive an additional monthly maximum of $1,000 for a successful program of research. However, since January 2002, salaries in real dollars have dropped to nearly a third of their value in 2001; thus, the most senior and productive psychology professors in Argentina earn only $900 monthly.

8.3 SCOPE OF PSYCHOLOGICAL PRACTICE

The clinical profile of a prototypic Argentine psychologist generates conflict with other health professionals, especially psychiatrists (Klappenbach, 2000a). In 1967, the president of the military dictatorship instituted the federal law that regulated medical practice. The law defined the role of psychologists as limited to assisting physicians. It stipulated that psychologists could practice only under the supervision of physicians specialized in psychiatry and only if they indicate that they are under supervision. Such legislation implied two restrictions for professional practice. The first was that it reduced all professional specialties in psychology to the clinical field. The second restriction was that it denied autonomy to clinical psychologists. These restrictions were contradictory to the psychotherapeutic training that psychologists receive not only in undergraduate programs, but also after graduation as residents in clinical psychology programs at psychiatric or general hospitals (Klappenbach, 2000a).

It is important to note that such restrictions are unlike those placed on master's-level graduates in some U.S. states (Dale, 1988). As was explained above, the first graduate level in Argentina (i.e., graduate in psychology or psychologist) is the level that qualifies one for professional practice, not only in psychological science. Yet, physicians at the first level are given the authority to practice psychotherapy, and Argentine law allows physicians to practice psychotherapy without undergoing any training in psychotherapy.

During the democratic period of 1973–1976, two provinces, Entre Rios and Rio Negro, enacted new laws on the professional practice of psychology that gave psychologists autonomy in different specialties, including that of psychotherapy (Klappenbach, 2000a). Provincial regulation of professional practice was tied to the constitutional guarantee that provinces reserve to themselves all the powers that are not explicitly delegated to the federal government by the constitution.

During the military dictatorship, psychologists' legal recognition began to deteriorate. For example, in 1980, the governor of Rio Negro province limited psychologists' professional autonomy by applying the same arguments as those in the 1967 federal law. He decreed that the provincial law gave psychologists autonomy in their functions only when it did not conflict with codified principles that regulate the practice of medicine, arguing that the psychologist should act only as a physician's assistant (Klappenbach, 2000a). In the same year, the Ministry of Education enacted a resolution on psychologists' university qualifications which again stated that in the field of medicine psychologists can work only as specialized physician's assistants. Such resolutions established that scope of a psychologist's practice includes neither the practice of psychoanalysis or psychotherapy nor prescribing psychotropics drugs (Ministerio de Cultura y Education de la Nation, 1980, cited in Klappenbach, 2000a).

After the Malvinas' war in 1982, Argentine psychology obtained important institutional recognition. In 1983, new laws on the professional practice of psychology were passed in four provinces: Catamarca, Salta, San Luis, and Tucumán. These laws coincided in three ways that please psychological associations. They (a) gave psychologists full autonomy, (b) recognized different specialties within professional practice, and (c) deemed clinicians to be qualified to offer psychotherapy independent of a supervising psychiatrist. Similar laws were passed between 1984 and 1986 in the provinces of Chaco, Chubut, Corrientes, Federal District (in Buenos Aires), Formosa, Jujuy, La Pampa, La Rioja, Mendoza, Neuquén, Provincia de Buenos Aires, San Juan, Santa Cruz, and Santa Fé (Klappenbach, 2000a). Two years after the democratic recovery, all provinces and districts in Argentina had legalized the professional practice of psychology, permitting psychologists to deliver psychotherapy independently of psychiatrists.

In 1993, there were 405 psychologists in Buenos Aires for every 100,000 inhabitants and 111 in the rest of the country (Alonso, 1994). In 1996, this proportion increased to 506 psychologists per 100,000 inhabitants (M. Alonso, personal communication, October 13, 1996).

In 1998, the number of psychologists was estimated at about 43,000, including licensed psychologists and unlicensed psychology graduates (Abramzón, Airoldi, Cadile, & Ferrero, 2001). The estimated growth rate of psychologists from 1992–1998 in the areas of health care and human resources was 34.4%.

The number of licensed psychologists is not identical to the number of psychologists engaged in professional practice, and there are only approximate data on the employment of psychologists. Information was gathered from psychological associations, colleges of psychology, and from each province of Argentina. Data from the provinces, where professional associations control licensure, do not indicate whether licensed psychologists are engaged in professional practice; likewise, provincially licensed psychologists may have moved to another province, or have died. It is also impossible to determine how many psychologists work without a license. Second, in some provinces that regulate licensure (e.g., San Luis), licensing boards are not specific to psychology, but cover all health professions. In such cases, the precise number of psychologists is difficult to determine.

Although the available data must be interpreted carefully, our own data correspond with those previously reported. Through June 2003, there were 55,817 psychologists in Argentina, which is about 155 psychologists per 100,000 inhabitants or 645 inhabitants per psychologist. Taking into account data from 1993, the growth rate for psychologists in the past 10 years is 123.46%. Nevertheless, the increase in psychology graduates in the last 10 years is nearly 53.0%. Differences between the growth of psychologists and psychology graduates can be attributed to methodological differences and the difficulty of obtaining the data from various sources, specifically data from Buenos Aires. The exact number of psychologists licensed in Buenos Aires is 32,976 psychologists. That is, one out of 83 citizens of Buenos Aires is a psychologist! In general, Argentina has the one of the highest proportion of psychologists per population in the world (Plotkin, 2001).

Regardless of their differences, all studies demonstrate that psychologists constitute an important professional group—the second largest professional group in health care. Only physicians, with a 1998 census of 108,000, exceeded the number of psychologists (Abramzón et al., 2001).

The number of Argentine psychologists who work in clinical settings is well-known. Of the psychologists who were members of the Buenos Aires Psychologists, Association 25 years ago, 43% worked in clinical settings, whereas another 49% worked both in clinical and nonclinical settings. Therefore, 92% of psychologists, at least in Buenos Aires, were involved in clinical work (Litvinoff & Gomel, 1975). More than a decade later, another study in Rosario, the second largest city in the country, revealed similar figures. Based on a questionnaire administrated to 633 psychologists, Gentile (1987) found that 87% worked principally in clinical settings, whereas 8.8% worked primarily in educational settings. Another 9.3% worked in clinical settings, but as secondary employment. That is, 96.3% of psychologists were engaged in clinical work (Gentile, 1987).

Most psychologists work in hospitals, mental health centers, and in private practice. The most dominant approach for the last 15 years in clinical psychology has been psychoanalysis, especially the Lacanian variant. "[S]ince the 1960s Argentina has become the world center for psychoanalysis," and psychoanalysis has inspired the way Argentines "talk and think" (Plotkin, 2003, p. 2). The experimental analysis of behavior is very limited, but cognitive and cognitive–integrative approaches increased in popularity in the past decade.

Another important field of practice is educational and vocational guidance. Psychologists work in schools, assisting not only children and teenagers, but also their parents and teachers.

Although industrial–organizational remains a neglected area, forensic psychology has increased since the return of democracy. Twenty years ago, forensic activities were limited to experts' reports required in trials. Now, forensic psychologists have a more active social agenda, particularly in advocating for and protecting the human rights of Argentine citizens.

Research is not a principal activity in Argentine psychology. In undergraduate programs at national universities, credit hours directly related to research make up less than 10% of the total credit hours required. Nevertheless, in the last two decades, psychological research has increased, especially at universities and research institutes. In 1994 the federal government created an incentive program to stimulate research by university professors through salary raises. Although the program was criticized, it promoted scholarly productivity. In 2000, the Ministry of Education, Science, and Technology, reported that there were 135 research projects in psychology at national universities on a variety of topics. There are now much stronger research teams at national universities, and also at the National Council for Scientific and Technical Research. Nearly 25 years ago, the typical career for a psychologist involved working at a public hospital or clinic; today, psychologists can pursue an academic career centered on teaching and research.

There have been psychological associations of significance in Argentina since the turn of the 20th century. The first psychological society in Latin America was the Argentine Society of Psychology, founded in 1908 by Ingenieros, Mercante, and Piñero, among others. This institution disappeared around 1914, but was reestablished by Mouchet in 1930 under the name of Buenos Aires Society of Psychology (Klappenbach & Pavesi, 1994).

During the 1960s, psychological associations were organized by the first psychologists who graduated from universities. The first was established in 1962 and called the Psychologists' Association of Rosario (A. Gentile, personal communication, September 24, 2000). Also in 1962, the Psychologists' Association of Buenos Aires was established (Klappenbach, 2000a). In 1963 the Psychologists' Association of La Plata was formed (Asociación de Psicólogos de La Plata, 1973). In 1971, members of psychological associations from Córdoba, La Plata, Mar del Plata, Mendoza, Rosario, Buenos Aires, Salta, San Luis, and Tucumán organized the Confederation of Psychologists of the Argentine Republic, which did not survive after military dictatorship.

After the Confederation disappeared, it was necessary to reorganize psychologists throughout the whole country (Perosio, 1977). In 1977 the current and most important psychological association in Argentina was established, the FePRA, which organizes psychological associations and colleges in virtually all of Argentina's provinces. To join the FePRA, a degree in psychology from national or private university (*licenciatura en psicología*) is required. The FePRA has been recognized as the official representative of Argentine professional psychology. It represents Argentine psychology in the Integrative Committee of Psychologists of the Mercosur and Associate Countries. The FePRA is also responsible for organizing many of Argentina's congresses of psychology.

In Argentina, many provincial administrations, including those in Buenos Aires

Province, Córdoba, Santa Fé, and Tucumán have delegates to professional associations of psychologists (called *colegios*), with some functions related to professional regulation, especially the control of licensure (the *matrícula profesional*) and ethical supervision of professional practice. Because psychologists are obliged to join such colleges in order to obtain licensure, they are true representatives. In other provinces such as Corrientes, Formosa, Mendoza, Rio Negro, San Luis, and Buenos Aires, the regulation of the profession is the responsibility of the public administration. In these circumstances, psychologists are not obliged to join psychological associations.

Other professional associations serve specific fields within professional psychology, among them the Association of Forensic Psychologists from the Argentina Republic. In general, members of these national organizations also belong to local psychological associations or colleges.

Today, there are several important scientific societies, particularly the Argentine Association of Behavioral Sciences. Since 1994, the Association has been the national representative to the International Union of Psychological Science (IUPsyS). Although membership in the Association requires merely scientific work in the behavioral sciences, and not a degree in psychology, most members are psychologists.

There are scientific societies in which membership requires a scientific activity in a psychological specialty, for example, the Argentine Association for Study and Research in Mental Diagnosis. In other so-called scientific societies, membership may depend on theoretical orientation. Psychoanalytic associations are the most visible but, recently, systems, humanistic, and cognitive societies have been organized. Although it is a regional organization, there has been a noticeable increase in Argentine psychologists joining the Interamerican Society of Psychology (SIP), a group that shares many characteristics of a scientific society (Alonso, 1999).

In departments and colleges of psychology at national universities, the most important organization is the Association of Academic Units of Psychology from Argentina and Uruguay (AUAPsi), organized in 1991. The AUAPsi has been responsible for the first comprehensive report on the state of education in psychology at national universities, with suggestions for future improvements. In May 2003, a similar organization was formed for departments and colleges of psychology at private universities—the Association of Academic Units of Psychology at Private Universities (AUAPri).

Although the organization of Argentine psychology is quite dispersed and varied, there is a single voice on certain matters, such as the importance of psychology as a regulated profession. For example, both associations of university psychology departments (units) have recently requested that the federal government include undergraduate psychology programs among so-called regulated university programs. Such programs are related to professions that interface directly with the public interest. It is worth mentioning that FePRA made the same request in 2002 (M. Molina, personal communication, November 27, 2002).

At the beginning of the 20th century, three psychological journals were published in Argentina: in 1902, Ingenieros founded *Archives on Psychiatry and Criminology*; in 1906, Mercante founded *Arch-*

ives on Pedagogy and Related Sciences; and in 1909, the Argentina Society of Psychology inaugurated the first psychological journal in Latin America, *Annals of Psychology*. Even without peer reviews, most articles in these journals were of high conceptual and empirical quality.

Today, there are many psychological journals, but only 45 are included in *Latindex Directory*, an online regional database of scientific journals in Latin America, the Caribbean, Spain, and Portugal. Some important journals are not in this database (including the *Argentine Review of clinical psychology*, abstracted in *PsycInfo*) although most of these have been recently created. Given the shaky economic climate, their future is uncertain. *PsycInfo* abstracts five Argentine journals, two of which are psychoanalytic: the *Argentine Review of Clinical Psychology* and *Psychoanalysis*. Another two are devoted to clinical subjects: *Psychiatric and Psychological Acts of Latin America* and *Argentine Review of Clinical Psychology*. Only one may be described as a general publication outlet, *Interdisciplinary Journal of Psychology and Related Sciences*.

The journals read by most psychologists tend to be professional, rather than scientific, and more resemble the newsletters of professional associations. Among them are *Psychology Today*, edited by Miguel Kohan since 1974, *Topia*, and *Systemic Approaches*.

As early as 1910, there was a psychological sciences section within the International Interamerican Congress of Sciences held in Buenos Aires. Nevertheless, the first Argentine Congress of Psychology convened in 1954 at the National University of Tucumán. It is especially significant because of the recommendation to organize undergraduate psychology programs at national universities (Klappenbach, 1995). This congress met irregularly, as some meetings were organized by universities, some by professional associations, and some by both, as in the case the most recent eleventh congress, organized by the FePRA and AUAPsi in 2003.

8.4 FUTURE CHALLENGES AND PROSPECTS

At present, Argentina is a country with political weaknesses. It has an oppressive debt and alarming economic indicators. According to the National Institute of Statistics and Census, in 2002 more than one-third of adults did not have a steady job; 17.8% we, unemployed while 19.9% we employed part time. More than half of the population (57.5%) lived in poverty and, in some regions, 71.5% were impoverished. In contrast, Argentina maintains a high standing in the arts and sciences, and the country has a culture that is rich and diverse, although increasingly dogmatic.

Improving psychology in Argentina requires changing those undergraduate programs whose theoretical perspective is limited to psychoanalysis, whose applied interest is exclusively clinical, and whose intellectual culture is often dogmatic (di Doménico & Vilanova, 1999; Piacente, 1998). It is also important to incorporate different theoretical perspectives, such as cognitive and humanistic psychology, and emphasize empirical research in various disciplinary specialties. At the same time, it is necessary to review the standards for undergraduate preparation and to improve material conditions, which would advance teaching and research. Specifically, access to electronic journals and databases are essential to the vitality of academic psychology.

At the turn of the century, the AUAPsi tried to improve academic training in psychology by inviting European professors to offer graduate courses. This practice let to a common framework for all departments of psychology in Argentina (Asociación de Unidades Académicas de Psicología, 1999). In some respects, this movement was analogous to the formation of conferences on graduate education in psychology sponsored by the American Psychological Association (APA) and the European Federation of Psychologists Association (1992) transnational training standards.

The improvement of undergraduate programs and material conditions has the potential of internationalizing Argentine psychology in Argentina, a movement that began 20 years ago. Many prominent psychologists with academic and professional experiences in European and North American countries returned to the country in 1983 after the military regime collapsed. As a result, Argentine psychology has become more receptive to the international scientific community. A growing number of psychologists have become international affiliates of the APA, members of the SIP, or members of other international societies in specialized fields. Furthermore, in 1995, Argentina became the country that had the most fellows of the SIP. In 1994, the AACC was accepted as the representative of Argentina to the IUPsyS. And, in terms of theoretical orientation, although psychoanalysis remains most prominent, cognitive psychology has become a vigorous alternative perspective both in scientific and practical psychology.

In terms of professional practice, psychology was recently included within the federal system that regulates all professions, which was introduced by the new law on higher education. The regulation of professions is one way to ensure comparability in the qualifications of psychologists throughout Argentina. At the same time, psychology as a regulated profession must have an improved system of licensure, and some mechanism for license renewal that is tied to continuing education.

In a similar vein, debates on ethical standards in the profession began a few years ago. For example, it has been frequently observed that psychologists must guarantee basic rights and dignity of persons (Ferrero, 2002; Hermosilla, 2000). The FePRA approved in 2000 its first code of ethics, which, although it is not as complete as that of the APA, demonstrates significantly more guarantees for the protection of human rights and dignity than was the case 10 years ago.

Last, it is interesting to note that the economic, political, and social crises that Argentina faces may limit many of the changes that need to take place in the future. However, these crises obligate psychologists to find innovative ways to advance the science and profession of psychology.

ACKNOWLEDGMENTS

I would like to thank my colleagues, without whose help this paper would not have been possible. Specifically, I am indebted to the deans and presidents from undergraduate programs in psychology at national and private universities, as well as to authorities and psychologists from professional associations and federations who contributed objective data to this paper.

REFERENCES

Abramzón, M., Airoldi, S., Cadile, M. C., & Ferrero, L. (2001). Argentina. Recursos humanos en salud [Argentina. Human resources in health]. In Observatorio de Recursos Humanos en Salud (Ed.), *Recursos humanos en salud en Argentina: 2001* [Human resources in health in Argentina: 2001] (pp. 15–60). Buenos Aires: Organización Panamericana de la Salud.

Alonso, M. (1994). Los psicólogos en la Argentina. Datos cuantitativos [Psychologists in Argentina: Quantitative data]. *Acta Psiquiátrica y Psicológica de América Latina, 40,* 50–55.

Alonso, M. (1999). Psicología en Argentina [Psychology in Argentina]. In M. Alonso & A. Eagly (Eds.), *Psicología en las Américas* [Psychology in the Americas] (pp. 25–45). Caracas: Sociedad Interamericana de Psicología.

Ardila, R. (1979). La psicología en Argentina: Pasado, presente y futuro [Psychology in Argentina: Past, present, and future]. *Revista Latinoamericana de Psicología, 11,* 77–91.

Ardila, R. (1986). *La psicología en América Latina: Pasado, presente y futuro* [Psychology in Latin America: Past, present, and future]. Buenos Aires: Siglo XXI.

Asociación de Psicólogos de La Plata. (1973). La Asociación de Psicólogos de La Plata. Historia y perspectivas [La Plata Psychologists Association: History and perspectives]. *Revista de Psicología, 6,* 125–130.

Asociación de Unidades Académicas de Psicología. (1998). *Programa de formación de especialistas en innovación curricular en psicología. Informe diagnóstico de la situación actual* [Circular inovation program, second report, common protocol. Diagnostic report on current status of undergraduate programs in psychology in Argentina]. Unpublished Report, Universidad de Buenos Aires, Argentina.

Asociación de Unidades Académicas de Psicología. (1999). *Informe de la segunda etapa del programa de innovacion curricular. Protocolo de acuerdo: Recomendaciones acerca de la formación universitaria en psicología en Argentina y Uruguay* [Circular inovation program, second report, common protocol. Recommendations on university education in psychology in Argentina and Uruguay]. Unpublished Report, Universidad de Buenos Aires, Argentina.

Avelluto, O. (1983). Los psicólogos y la(s) paradoja(s) de los 25 años de la psicología [Psychologists and the paradox of 25 years of psychology]. *Revista Argentina de Psicología, 34,* 45–53.

Barsky, O. (1997). *Los posgrados universitarios en la República Argentina* [Graduate programs in Argentine republic]. Buenos Aires: Troquel.

Biagini, H. (1989). *Filosofía americana e identidad* [American philosophy and identity]. Buenos Aires: Eudeba.

Carpintero, H. (1993). Relaciones entre España e Iberoamérica en el campo de la psicología [Spain and Iberoamerican relationships in the field of psychology]. *Interacción Social, 3,* 25–46.

Cattell, J. M. K. (1888). The psychological laboratory at Leipzig. *Mind, 13,* 37–51.

Dagfal, A. (2000). José Bleger y los inicios de una "psicología psicoanalítica" en la Argentina de los años sesenta [Jose Bleger and the beginnings of a psychoanalytical psychology in the Argentina of the 1960s]. *Revista Universitaria de Psicoanálisis, 2,* 139–167.

Dale, R. H. (1988). State psychological association, licensing criteria and the "master's issue." *Professional Psychology: Research and Practice, 19,* 589–593.

di Doménico, C., & Vilanova, A. (Eds.). (1999). *Formación de psicólogos en el Mercosur* [Psychologists education in the Mercosur]. Mar del Plata, Argentina: Universidad Nacional de Mar del Plata.

Dobson, V., & Bruce, D. (1972). The German university and the development of experimental psychology. *Journal of the History of the Behavioral Sciences, 8,* 204–207.

European Federation of Professional Psychologists Associations. (1992). *Optimal standards for professional training in psychology.* Brussels: Author.

Fanelli, A. M. G., & Balán, J. (1994). *Expansión de la oferta universitaria: Nuevas instituciones, nuevos programas* [University growth: New institutions, new programs]. Buenos Aires: Centro de Estudios de Estado y Sociedad.

Ferrero, A. (2002). Importancia de los derechos humanos en los códigos deontológicos de psicología en la Argentina [Importance of human rights in psychology codes of ethics in Argentina]. *Revista Argentina de Psicología, 45,* 33–41.

Gentile, A. (1987). Situación profesional de los psicólogos en Rosario [Professional status of psychologists in Rosario]. *Revista del Colegio, 2*(Suppl. 2).

Gentile, A. (1989). La carrera de psicólogo en Rosario y el proceso de profesionalización [Psychology undergraduate program in Rosario and the process of professionalization]. *Intercambios en Psicología, Psicoanálisis, Salud Mental, 1,* 12–13.

Geuter, U., & León, R. (1997). The emigration of European psychologists to Latin America. *Cuadernos Argentinos de Historia de la Psicología, 3,* 67–97.

Hermosilla, A. M. (2000). Psicología y Mercosur: La dimensión ética de la integración y antecedentes del debate en Argentina [Psychology and Mercosur: The ethical aspect of integration and antecedents of debate in Argentina]. *Fundamentos en Humanidades, 1,* 63–76.

Horas, P. (1981). Current status of psychology in Argentina. *Spanish Language Psychology, 1,* 357–364.

Jitrik, N. (1982). *El mundo del ochenta* [The world of 1880]. Buenos Aires: Centro Editor de América Latina.

Klappenbach, H. (1995). The process of psychology's professionalization in Argentina. *Revista de Historia de la Psicología, 16,* 1995, 97–110.

Klappenbach, H. (1996). Prólogo a la psicología experimental en la República Argentina de Horacio Piñero [Prologue to experimental psychology in the Argentine Republic by Horacio Piñero]. *Cuadernos Argentinos de Historia de la Psicología, 2,* 239–268.

Klappenbach, H. (2000a). El título profesional de psicólogo en Argentina: Antecedentes históricos y situación actual [The psychologists' degree in Argentina: Historical antecedents and current situation]. *Revista Latinoamericana de Psicología, 32,* 2000, 419–446.

Klappenbach, H. (2000b). El psicoanálisis en los debates sobre el rol del psicólogo. Argentina: 1960–1975 [Psychoanalysis and the debates on the role of the psychologist. Argentina: 1960–1975]. *Revista Universitaria de Psicoanálisis, 2,* 191–227.

Klappenbach, H., & Pavesi, P. (1994). Una historia de la psicología en Latinoamérica [A history of psychology in Latin America]. *Revista Latinoamericana de Psicología, 26,* 445–482.

Kohan, N. C. (1992). Argentina. In V. S. Sexton & J. Hogan (Eds.), *International psychology: Views from around the world* (pp. 8–12). Lincoln, NE: University of Nebraska Press.

Litvinoff, N., & Gomel, S. K. (1975). *El psicólogo y su profesión* [The psychologist and his profession]. Buenos Aires: Nueva Visión.

Ministerio de Educación, Ciencia y Tecnología. Secretaría de Políticas Universitarias. (2002). *Anuario 1999–2000 de estadísticas universitarias* [University statistical yearbook: 1999–2000]. Buenos Aires: Author.

Paolucci, C., & Verdinelli, S. (1999). La psicología en Argentina [Psychology in Argentina]. In C. Di Doménico & A. Vilanova (Eds.), *Formación de psicólogos en el Mercosur* [Formation of psychology in the Mercosur] (pp. 15–32). Mar del Plata, Argentina: Universidad Nacional de Mar del Plata.

Papini, M. (1985). Notas sobre la psicología experimental en la Argentina: Breve reseña historiográfica [Notes about experimental psychology in Argentina: Brief historiographic review]. *Revista de Historia de la Psicología, 6,* 213–226.

Perosio, B. (1977). Reorganización nacional de los psicólogos [National reorganization of psychologists]. *Gaceta Psicológica, 4,* 1.

Piacente, T. (1998). Psicoanálisis y formación académica en psicología [Psychoanalysis and academic education in psychology]. *Acta Psiquiátrica y Psicológica de América Latina, 44,* 278–284.

Piñero, H. G. (1902). Enseñanza actual de la psicología en Europa y América [Current teaching of psychology in Europe and America]. *Anales de la Universidad de Buenos Aires, 17,* 117–138.

Piñero, H. G. (1903). La psychologie expérimentale dans la République Argentine [Experimental psychology in the Argentine Republic]. *Revista de la Sociedad Médica, 11,* 403–416.

Plotkin, M. (2001). *Freud in the Pampas: The formation of a psychoanlytical culture in Argentina (1910–1983).* Palo Alto, CA: Stanford University Press.

Plotkin, M. (2003). Introduction. In M. Plotkin (Ed.), *Argentina on the couch: Psychiatry, state, and society, 1880 to the present* (pp. 1–22). Albuquerque, NM: University of New Mexico Press.

Pró, D. (1981). Los estudios filosóficos en el norte argentino [Philosophical studies in the north of Argentina]. *Cuyo, 14,* 137–141.

República Argentina. (1953). Ley No. 14.184 (Segundo Plan Quinquenal) [Law No. 14.184 (Second five-year plan)]. *Anales de Legislación Argentina, 13,* 79–203.

Sanz Ferramola, R. (2000). La psicología como ideología exótica en los oscuros años del proceso de desorganización nacional: 1975–1980 [Psychology as an exotic ideology in the obscure years of the process of national disorganization: 1975–1980]. *Fundamentos en Humanidades* (Universidad Nacional de San Luis), *1,* 43–62.

Sigal, V. (1998). El sistema de admisión a la universidad en la Argentina [The university entrance system in Argentina]. *La Universidad, 14,* 18–22.

Terán, O. (1993). *Nuestros años sesenta. La formación de la nueva izquierda intelectual Argentina. 1956–1966* [Our years 60. The shaping of the new Argentine intellectual left. 1956–1966] (3rd ed.). Buenos Aires: Ediciones El Cielo por Asalto.

Vezzetti, H. (1988). Estudio preliminar [Preliminary study]. In H. Vezzetti (Ed.), *El nacimiento de la psicología en la Argentina* [The birth of psychology in Argentina] (pp. 11–34). Buenos Aires: Puntosur.

Vilanova, A. (1993). La formación de psicólogos en Iberoamérica [Psychologists education in Iberoamerica]. *Acta Psiquiátrica y Psicológica de América Latina, 3,* 193–205.

Vilanova, A. (2001). *El carácter argentino. Los primeros diagnósticos* [The national character: The first diagnostics]. Mar del Plata, Argentina: Universidad Nacional de Mar del Plata.

Vilanova, A., & di Doménico, C. (1999). *La psicología en el Cono Sur. Datos para una historia* [Psychology in the Southern Cone: Data for a history]. Mar del Plata, Argentina: Universidad Nacional de Mar del Plata-Editorial Martín.

Waldmann, P. (1981). *El peronismo: 1943– 1955* [The peronism: 1943–1955]. Buenos Aires: Sudamericana.

IMPORTANT PUBLICATIONS

Alvarez, H. F. (2001). *Fundamentals of an integrated model of psychotherapy* (A. LaBruzza, Trans.). Northvale, NJ: Jason Aronson. (Original work published in 1992)

Bleger, J. (1963). *Psicología de la conducta* [Psychology of behavior]. Buenos Aires: Editorial Universitaria de Buenos Aires.

Bricht, S., Calvo, I., Calvo, M. T., Dimant, F., Pravaz, S., Troya, E., et al. (1973). *El rol del psicólogo* [The role of the psychologist]. Buenos Aires: Nueva Visión.

García, G. (1978). *La entrada del psicoanálisis en la Argentina. Obstáculos y perspectivas* [The beginnings of psychoanalysis in Argentina: Obstacles and perspectives]. Buenos Aires: Altazor.

Ingenieros, J. (1916). *Principios de Psicología* [Principles of psychology] (5th ed.). Buenos Aires: Talleres Gráficos Rosso.

Mouchet, E. (1941). *Percepción, instinto y razón. Contribuciones a una psicología vital* [Perception, instinct, and reason: Contributions toward a vital psychology]. Buenos Aires: Gil.

Pichon Rivière, E. (1971). *El proceso grupal. Del psicoanálisis a la psicología social.* [Group process: From psychoanalysis to social psychology]. Buenos Aires: Galerna.

Piñero, H. G. (Ed.). (1916). *Trabajos de psicología normal y patológica* [Works on normal and abnormal psychology]. Buenos Aires: Laboratorio de Psicología de la Facultad de Filosofía y Letras.

Vezzetti, H. (1996). *Aventuras de Freud en el país de los argentinos. De José Ingenieros a Enrique Pichon Rivière.* [Adventures of Freud in the country of Argentina: From José Ingenieros to Enrique Pichon Rivière]. Buenos Aires: Paidós.

Vilanova, A. (2003). *Discusión por la psicología* [Discussion about psychology]. Mar del Plata, Argentina: Universidad Nacional de Mar del Plata.

CHAPTER 9

Psychology in Brazil: The Road Behind and the Road Ahead

CLAUDIO S. HUTZ, SHERRI MCCARTHY, AND WILLIAM GOMES

Claudio S. Hutz received his B.A. in psychology from the University of Haifa in Israel and his M.A. and Ph.D. in the United States from the University of Iowa. He is a professor at the Institute of Psychology of Universidade Federal do Rio Grande do Sul, Brazil. He has served on the board of several scientific societies, and is a past president of the Brazilian National Association of Research and Graduate Studies in Psychology. Claudio Hutz also served on the Brazilian National Council of Sciences under the auspices of the Ministry of Education. His research interests include the social development of children and adolescents at risk, and the development of methods and techniques for the psychological assessment of such groups.

Sherri McCarthy received her B.A. in psychology, M.A. in special education, and Ph.D. in educational psychology at Arizona State University, and is a professor at Northern Arizona University-Yuma in the graduate counseling program. She is active in international psychology, serving as liaison to the APA's Council on International Relations in Psychology for Division 2 (Teaching of Psychology) and Division 52 (International Psychology). She also serves as the membership chair for Division 52 and for the International Council of Psychologists. For the Psychology Partnership Project, she also headed their global psychology project, and served on the organizing committee for the First International Conference on Psychology in Education in St. Petersburg in 2002. Sherri McCarthy was a Senior Fulbright Fellow in Russia in 2003, and recently was a visiting professor at Universidade Federal do Rio Grande do Sul, Brazil. Her research interests include adolescent psychology, psychology applied to issues in education and criminal justice, grief and bereavement counseling, substance abuse counseling, and the history of psychology.

William B. Gomes graduated with a B.A. in psychology from Universidade Católica de Pernambuco, Brazil. In the United States he received an M.A. in counseling and a Ph.D. in education from Southern Illinois University. He is a professor at the Institute of Psychology of Universidade Federal do Rio Grande do Sul, Brazil. He was a founder of the graduate program in psychology at Universidade Federal do Rio Grande do Sul, and founder and long-time editor of the journal Psicologia: Reflexão e Crítica. *William Gomes research interests include phenomenological psychology and the history of psychology. He has published on psychotherapy outcomes and adolescent psychology, has participated actively in scientific societies, and has served on committees that evaluate undergraduate and graduate programs in psychology.*

9.1 OVERVIEW

After the United States, Brazil has more psychologists than any other country in the world. Considering that the discipline was not formally recognized by the Brazilian government until 1962, this is quite an accomplishment. At that time, a law established the 5-year professional training program at universities that leads to licensure as a psychologist. Currently, over 140,000 licensed psychologists practice in this country of over 170 million people, with 900 Brazilian psychologists holding doctoral degrees. There is a growing demand for doctoral-level psychologists in Brazil. With more than 70,000 students now enrolled in degree programs that will result in licensure and at least 10,000 psychologists joining the work force per year, the profession is growing rapidly as Brazil enters the 21st century. If this trend continues, it is likely that Brazil may soon become the country with the most psychologists in the world.

The majority of psychologists in Brazil practice in urban areas. Community organizations operating in rural areas may have psychologists on staff, although few NGOs employ or otherwise engage the services of psychologists. Hospitals, industry, and social service agencies in rural areas do hire psychologists. Relatively few psychologists support themselves in private practices in their rural hometowns. The majority of Brazilian psychologists, however, are employed in or around large cities, most working at private clinics.

Psychology is a respected profession in this country, and this is reflected in the economics of psychology. Entry-level psychologists in Brazil receive salaries that are higher than those of other social service professionals with comparable years of education, including social workers, nurses, and public school teachers. It should be noted, however, that psychologists are still underpaid by American standards, many working for the equivalent of $10 or less per hour at the time of writing this chapter. Because the Brazilian economy is subject to considerable fluctuation, however, the average monthly wage computed in U.S. dollars also fluctuates considerably. Today, it would be around $500. Salaries are competitive and the job outlook is favorable.

Three types of associations in Brazil support professional activity in psychology. First, there are the 15 regional councils, which were created by the Brazilian Congress in 1971 to monitor professional practice, uphold ethical standards, and regulate the functions and responsibilities of Brazilian psychologists. Membership in a regional council requires practicing psychologists to pay an annual fee (about $50). The members of each regional council are elected by all registered psychologists, who also elect the members of the Federal Council of Psychology (voting is mandatory).

State and special interest associations have been organized to promote communication and collaboration among psychologists via scientific meetings, including conferences, congresses, seminars, and workshops. The association most closely related to graduate training is Associação Nacional de Pesquisa e Pós-Graduação em Psicologia (ANPEPP; National Association for Graduate Study and Research in Psychology). It was founded in 1983 to stimulate research in psychology by encouraging the training of researchers, financing of research, publication of scientific papers, and exchange of scholars among institutions. Membership is available to graduate programs only, each of which pays dues to the association. This association plays a key role in evaluating and accrediting every graduate psychology program in Brazil. Reviews of each program occur often, and accreditation is renewed on a 3-year cycle. Each program is awarded a rating of 0 to 5 (with bonuses given to outstanding programs, which allows for ratings of 6 or 7). Programs must score at 3 or above to be allowed to operate. Funding of programs is contingent upon evaluations, which has resulted in a merit system.

Finally, some psychologists in Brazil have organized regional syndicates, which are analogous to labor unions. Syndicates are supported by the payment of annual membership fees and strive to improve the salaries and working conditions of psychologists.

Although the three types of professional organizations noted above actively support psychology in Brazil, there is no national organization equivalent to the American Psychological Association, and no psychological association officially represents Brazil in the International Union of Psychological Sciences; at the time this chapter was written, a cooperative of all organizations was being developed to fulfill this role. Brazil was once represented at the International Union of Psychological Sciences by Associação Brasiliera Psicologia (Brazilian Psychological Association), but this organization no longer exists. It was founded by well-meaning psychologists, among them Franco Seminerio, an outstanding psychologist, but it was not representative of Brazilian psychology and ultimately disbanded. Sociedade Brasileira de Psicologia (Brazilian Psychological Society), an independent scientific entity, was created in 1971 as a local society at Universidade de São Paulo-Ribeirão Preto and achieved national status in 1991. It was invited to serve as Brazil's representative internationally some years ago, but declined. Although this society still hosts small annual conventions including symposia, papers, and debates in many areas of psychology, it is also not representative of Brazilian psychology any more because it could not adjust and adapt to the development of psychology in the country. Today, it has a few hundred members, most of them in São Paulo.

There are relatively few psychiatrists in Brazil, and nearly as many psychologists as M.D.s. Both psychologists and psychiatrists tend to embrace psychoanalytic theory, although a biopsychological orientation has been gaining strength since the 1980s. Prescription privileges are currently limited to M.D.s; psychiatrists are trained in medical schools and have prescription privileges, whereas psychologists do not. This situation is especially interesting in light of the history of psychology in Brazil. When psychology began as a professional practice in Brazil during the late 19th century, it was taught primarily by faculty in medical schools. This practice continued until the mid-20th century. Early psychological experiments were conducted in the medical school in Rio de Janeiro (Lourenço-Filho, 1955).

A second historical influence came from educational psychology. Psychological labs for testing students and training educators existed in special schools devoted to training Brazilian teachers. In fact, the first psychological lab in Brazil was planned in Paris by Brazilian physician Manoel Bomfim with the guidance of Alfred Binet. The lab was installed in a pedagogical institute in Rio de Janeiro in 1906 to evaluate new educational practices. Another experimental pedagogy lab was created in the normal school of São Paulo in 1914 under the direction of Italian psychologist Ugo Pizzoli. This lab could be considered the nucleus for the training of the first psychologists in São Paulo. The work of Hall and Dewey, traditional to educational psychology, was imported to Brazil after the American Civil War when several church groups established schools for training teachers. Thus, clinical and educational psychology comprised much of the early focus of the discipline. A third influence was forensic psychology; law faculties have historically taught psychology, from both legal and rehabilitative perspectives (Lourenço-Filho, 1955).

From colonial times on, psychology has been first taught as part of philosophy programs at Brazilian Jesuit schools (Massimi, 1990). The way for modern psychology was paved with the foundation of schools of law and medicine in 1827 and 1832 respectively, and with the organization of schools to train teachers in the second half of the 19th century (Lourenço-Filho, 1955). The first treatise on general psychology in Brazil was written in 1854 by Eduardo Ferreira França, a Paris-educated professor at the medical school of Bahia, and integrated the sensualist philosophy of Etienne Bonnot Condillac with the spiritualism of Maine de Biran. The first experimental research in psychology was conducted by Henrique Roxo in 1900. He wrote a doctoral dissertation on the duration of psychological acts, and defended it at the medical school of Rio de Janeiro. Roxo used a psychometric instrument developed by the Italian experimental psychologist Grabiele Buccola, and introduced psychology as a requisite science for psychiatry. Roxo's work was the first psychological experiment written in Portuguese; it appeared in Brazil at the same time that Ivan Pavlov was conducting his experiments in Russia (Pessotti, 1975).

Emil Kraepelin, former student of Wilhelm Wundt, extended the application of psychology in the medical field. He conducted experiments with psychiatric patients in laboratories established at hospitals (Hearnshaw, 1989). An important laboratory of this type was constructed in a hospital in Rio de Janeiro in 1923 (Centofanti, 1982; Penna, 1992). The laboratory, associated with the International Mental Hygiene Movement, operated until 1932. The equipment came from Paris and Leipzig. Polish psychologist Waclaw

Radecki, a former student of Édouard Claparède at the University of Geneva, directed the lab. This laboratory was geared toward psychological testing and personnel selection. It was the center at which psychologists in Rio de Janeiro were first trained.

Psychology attracted more public attention in Brazil in the 1930s, when educators from throughout the country were invited by the federal government to undertake a radical reform of Brazilian schools. The reform was encouraged by the publication of the first books on psychological testing during the 1920s (Alves, 1928, 1930; Medeiros-e-Albuquerque, 1924) and inspired by the functional psychology of Edouard Claparède at the University of Geneva and John Dewey at Columbia University (Lourenço-Filho, 1955). Anísio Teixeira, a former student of Dewey, directed the enterprise. Teixeira invited M. Lourenço-Filho to be the first director of the Institute of Education in the former Brazilian capital, Rio de Janeiro. Lourenço-Filho was the most important Brazilian psychologist of the first half of the 20th century. Under the influence of Claparède and Dewey he wrote a landmark treatise on functional education, conducted experiments on habits, developed psychological tests. He is also regarded as the first behaviorist in Brazil, utilizing Watson's theory and research (Pessotti, 1975).

The years between 1925 and 1935 were very important for psychology in Brazil. Prominent European psychologists Henri Piéron, Édouard Claparède, Wolfang Köhler, Theodore Simon, and Leon Walther visited the country to present seminars and install laboratories. Claparède's former student and assistant, Helena Anti-

poff, stayed in Brazil and developed a laboratory and training program for teachers in Belo Horizonte. Also during this time, some Brazilians went to the United States to study. For example, Noemy da Silverira Rudolfer went to Columbia University and studied with Edward Thorndike. Annita Cabral, a former student of both Rudolfer and Lourenço-Filho, received a scholarship to the New School of Social Research in New York in 1941 to study with Max Wertheimer (Campos, 2001).

As practices from educational psychology became more prominent among Brazilian psychologists, psychiatrists became increasingly interested in psychoanalysis. In fact, several Brazilian psychiatrists had direct correspondence with Freud during this time, most notably Durval Marcondes. The group organized the Brazilian Psychoanalytic Society in 1927 and began publishing a journal. European-trained analysts, referred by Ernest Jones began to practice and train here, attracting the attention of many prominent Brazilian artists and socialites. The first Brazilian-trained analysts began practicing in the mid-1930s.

During the 1940s, the number of professionals interested in psychology continued to grow. Most were attracted to educational reform and the application of psychological testing in schools. At the same time, Freud's work was growing in influence with Brazilian psychiatrists. They used some psychological lab techniques along with projective tests such as the Rorschach. They also integrated Freudian psychoanalytic techniques into psychotherapy. The application of psychology to training, personnel selection, and organizational behavior, first initiated by

Swiss engineer Roberto Manger during the 1920s, also burgeoned during this decade. This branch of psychology was used mainly in the Brazilian civil service, the military, and by the railroads, and culminated in the creation of the Institute for Personnel Selection and Guidance in Rio de Janeiro in 1947. Emilio Mira y Lopez, a Cuban psychiatrist trained in Spain, was invited to direct the institute (Rosas, 1992). This institute launched the first psychological journal in Brazil, *Arquivos Brasileiros de Psicologia*, in 1948, which is still published today.

A mix of European and North American influences combined with uniquely Brazilian developments to create the current diversity and dynamism that characterizes the discipline. Phenomenological and experimental orientations coexist, creating a lively and healthy scientific pluralism. This openness to different perspectives within psychology is a reflection of 21st-century Brazilian society. Modern Brazil is characterized by over a decade of modest economic growth, a popular socialist government that embraces democratic values and is willing to wage "war against hunger," and an atmosphere favoring open expression and critical thought.

9.2 EDUCATION AND TRAINING

After the introduction of psychology to teacher training schools, schools of medicine, and colleges of law in Brazil, the Brazilian government organized universities during the first half of the 20th century and began to regulate all existing professional schools, including those in dentistry, engineering, law, and medicine. Teacher training was assigned to faculties (i.e., colleges) of philosophy, sciences, and humanities. This was the birthplace of liberal arts in Brazil. The first liberal arts university was created in 1934 by the State of São Paulo. Later, psychology was housed in liberal arts.

Psychology theories and topics were first taught in professional schools, mostly in law and medicine. Professors, who were primarily self-educated in the discipline through independent reading and contact with psychologists from abroad, taught the courses. Later, during the 1950s, psychology professors tended to be drawn from the disciplines of education, medicine, and philosophy. These professors, like their predecessors in schools of law and medicine, acquired much of their knowledge of psychology through reading and international contacts with psychologists.

The first psychology degree programs in Brazil were established in the mid-1950s. Henrique Justo, an educator who later introduced client-centered psychotherapy in Brazil, and Bela Székely, a former student of Freud, began a program at Pontifícia Universidade Católica, Rio Grande do Sul, in 1953 (Gomes, Lhullier, & Leite, 1999). The same year, Hans Lipmann and Antonio Benko, the latter a European-trained psychologist teaching at Pontifícia Universidade Católica–Rio de Janeiro, began a program (Mancebo, 2001). Other programs followed, including one in 1958 at Universidade de Sao Paulo initiated by Annita Cabral. Then, in 1962 the government legislated the 5-year professional psychology program for licensure that is in existence today. All universities able to meet the accreditation guidelines of this program were allowed to offer a degree in professional psychology. The growth of psychology programs in universities was rapid, moving from 28 undergraduate and graduate programs in 1971 to over 100 in 1990 (Biaggio & Grinder, 1992), and to about 150 currently recognized in Brazil (a listing of accredited psychology undergraduate programs in Brazil can be obtained in http://www.abepsi.org.br/facul/frames/fr_facul-br.htm). In 1965 and 1968, legislative reform allowed graduate programs in psychology to grant master's and doctoral degrees. Prior to this, individuals with faculty appointments could obtain a graduate degree in psychology by writing a thesis. The few professionals in the country who were qualified to examine them served on their committees. During the 1960s, some professors recognized that graduate programs in psychology were able to flourish. Father Benko in Rio de Janeiro and Julian Stanley, then at the University of Wisconsin–Madison, helped six Brazilian graduate students to obtain scholarships and assistantships. Four of them joined Stanley at Wisconsin, one went to Belgium, and the other went to the University of California at Los Angeles. Graduate students from São Paulo attended the New School for Social Research in New York and Arizona State University, among other institutions. Subsequently, in the 1970s, the Brazilian Ministry of Education provided scholarships for faculty who were teaching psychology at public universities to obtain doctoral degrees. These scholars studied primarily in Europe and in the United States, and returned to Brazil to build graduate programs in a variety of specialties, including clinical, developmental, educational and cognitive, experimental, and physiological psychology. At the same time, Universidade de São Paulo was devel-

oping doctoral training and research programs in psychology.

We appear to be in a golden age for psychology programs in Brazil. Over 150 undergraduate psychology programs exist at Brazilian universities, all evaluated and accredited by the Brazilian Ministry of Education. There are also 44 graduate programs at this time, 19 of which offer Ph.D. degrees in psychology designed by faculty trained at some of the best universities in the United States and Europe. Faculty members work closely with small groups of carefully selected students who will have no difficulty entering the workplace after completing their degrees. Whether they are employed as academics or enter the private sector, they are expected to make significant contributions to Brazilian psychology.

The structure of psychology departments in Brazil is legislated by the federal government and evaluated, in cooperation with professional associations, by the Ministry of Education. The most rigorous and selective programs are within public universities, which attract the best faculty and most capable students. Depending upon the location and program reputation of a particular federal university, only the top 5%–25% of applicants are admitted.

The Catholic universities, where psychology programs began in the 1950s, are also extensive in Brazil. Psychology programs at Catholic universities are slightly less competitive than those at federal and state universities, but are generally quite strong. Students who attend Catholic universities must pay tuition. There are also many private universities that offer specialized programs in psychology. Although regulated by the Ministry of Education, their quality is inferior to that found in other systems; admission criteria are less stringent and tuition is more costly.

Liberal studies—courses such as mathematics, history, and literature that are typically required in U.S. undergraduate programs—are covered in high school, and mastery is tested by the Vestibular, a university entrance examination that all applicants must take to qualify for admission. Public and private universities with respected programs in psychology accept, on average, 1 in 25 applicants; only 1 in 40 applicants are accepted into programs at elite public universities. The acceptance rates at less rigorous private colleges with steep tuition rates are considerably higher. Coursework focuses almost exclusively on applied aspects of psychology. With the exception of a few supplemental classes in biology, philosophy, and sociology, students study psychology almost exclusively. This intensive preparation is the sole route to licensure. As in much of the world, Brazilian psychologists are prepared in a 5-year undergraduate program that includes two years of internship and extensive coursework in all areas of the discipline (e.g., biopsychology, clinical psychology, developmental psychology, health psychology, industrial–organizational psychology, and social psychology). Programs must follow national curricular guidelines (which are about to be approved), although some flexibility that produces difference areas of emphasis from program to program is permitted. Graduates of an accredited program may apply for licensure and then practice in any area for which they ethically feel prepared. Internships and programs that offer additional specialization often determine the domain of a psychologist's professional practice. Continuing education has not yet been mandated and

such requirements are not even under consideration.

Exam scores are of primary importance in admission to undergraduate programs. As in other parts of the world, there are systematic differences in how some groups perform on these exams. Even though Blacks were imported to Brazil as slaves and indigenous peoples have also been deprived of property and rights, and even though Brazilian children demonstrate performance deficits similar to those found in the United States (Hutz, 1988), no affirmative action programs are currently in place. The one exception is the State University of Rio de Janeiro, which, following state recommendations, recently attempted to adopt a racial quota system and adjust exam score based on ethnic affiliation. This practice is currently being challenged in the courts. The Brazilian population is far less racially divided than the population of most countries. Many native Brazilians can likely claim to be the direct descendents of Black, European, or indigenous Indian relatives. Marking a census form to indicate whether one is Black, White, or indigenous Indian is a very difficult exercise in this country, and such differences are artificial, at any rate, and socially imposed (Pena et al., 2003). Further, even activist groups representing Black and indigenous people in Brazil do not wish to see exam scores adjusted to reflect quotas, a practice which, in the long run, is likely to erode group esteem (McCarthy, 2002). Instead, they prefer to see the economic and social conditions corrected that originally led to the group differences in exam scores.

The faculty-to-student ratio in psychology programs is generally high, especially at the public universities. Small classes, cooperative-learning seminars, and extensive mentoring, characterize the best programs. The focus of undergraduate programs is on application and practice rather than research, however. Applied specializations are self-selected by the internship experiences that students choose. Research is typically introduced at the graduate level. This artificial separation is partially responsible for the current gulf between research and practice in Brazil, but it is being addressed. Iniciação Científica (Scientific Initiation), a program funded by federal and state agencies, supports research activities at the undergraduate level. The program engages students in research activities with graduate students and faculty mentors from their second year of study. Consequently, it is not unusual to see undergraduate students co-author works with graduate students and faculty. This program supports the current trend to include students in research at the beginning of their undergraduate preparation. If this trend continues to grow, future Brazilian psychologists will have a better understanding of the reciprocal relationship between research and practice.

Historically, graduate programs in Brazil were established by distinguished psychologists. In the 1960s Robert Berryman, Carolina Bori, and Fred Keller developed programs in the operant tradition at Universidade de Brasilia and at Universidade de São Paulo. Universidade de São Paulo is also known for its Freudian ties and Piagetian research program. The work of Arrigo Angelini, Anita Cabral, Nelson Rosamilha, and Dante Moreira Leite in educational, developmental, personality, and social psychology is also noteworthy there. Pontifícia Universidade Católica-São Paulo has good programs in clinical, educational, and social-critical historical psychology. Pontificia Universidade Católica-Rio de Janeiro is well known for the clinical psychology program and the work of Terezinha Carneiro in family therapy. Universidade Federal do Rio de Janeiro was first recognized for important studies in attribution, balance, and equity theory and, subsequently, won an international reputation in social psychology (Biaggio & Grinder, 1992); it is now recognized for its research on psychoanalysis. More recently, two strong graduate programs were established at the State University of Rio de Janeiro. An important program in cognitive–developmental psychology continues at Universidade de Pernambuco at Recife. This program was organized by Analucia Schliemann, now at the University of Massachussets, and Terezinha Carraher, now at Oxford University. At Universidade Federal do Rio Grande do Sul, Robert Grinder, former president of the American Psychological Association's (APA) Division of Educational Psychology and author of many textbooks on adolescent psychology, helped to establish outstanding graduate programs in adolescent development and theoretical psychology.

As previously mentioned, many faculty members were educated outside of Brazil. Brazilian graduate programs also have a tradition of placing students at public expense at key institutions outside of the country for their internships. Many Brazilian graduate students, for example, have completed internships at Yale, the Sorbonne, and other prestigious international universities. This model encourages the exchange of information and the internationalization of psychology. Because funding is determined by state as well as public agencies, however, graduate students at some Brazilian universities have a greater chance to study abroad. Funds to support educational programs fluctuate from year to year, depending upon the political leanings of elected officials.

Brazilian graduate programs have a considerable degree of interinstitutional interaction. It is customary to have at least one committee member for a graduate student thesis and dissertation from a university other than that which the student attends. Faculty from across the country visit each other often for thesis and dissertation defenses, as well as for seminars and program evaluations. This practice has led to a healthy, collegial exchange on a national level, and may expand to an international level as some faculty members have been invited to serve on dissertation committees at universities around the world.

Initially, most textbooks and materials used in psychology programs were translations into Portuguese from the works of such European psychologists as Binet, Claparède, Dumas, Freud, Janet, Piaget, Ribot, and Wallon, and American psychologists such as James and Warren (Penna, 1992). By the time the profession of psychology was officially established in 1962, Portuguese translations of texts by distinguished American psychologists such as Allport, Hilgard, Keller, Rogers, and Skinner were also available. The infusion of funds and the growth of graduate programs during the 1970s resulted in more translations of textbooks in various fields of psychology, most notably Bee and Mussen, Conger, and Kagan in developmental; Hall and Lindzey in personality; Klineberg and Krech, Crutchfield, and Ballachey in social; Siegel in statistics; and Anastasi and Cronbach in testing. Much of the material covered in American textbooks does not apply to Brazilian culture, however. Consequently, these texts are now seldom used (except for Anastasi and Cronbach). Recently, textbooks by Brazilian authors have become more commonplace, especially on psychoanalysis and social psychology. An early example of this was a book edited by Otto Klineberg, a Canadian psychologist educated in the United States at Columbia University and former professor at McGill University, who came to teach in a psychology program at Universidade de São Paulo. His edited book contained chapters on each of the major branches of psychology taught in Brazil (developmental, educational, psychoanalytic, social, etc.) written by leading Brazilian authors. A list of the 10 most important Brazilian textbooks relevant to the teaching and practice of psychology appears at the end of this chapter.

There is no consensus among faculty members or programs as to which textbooks to adopt. Many Brazilian professors and graduate students in psychology can read English, but economic conditions limit the availability of books on contemporary theory and research. Taxes, currency restrictions, and postal delays, combined with the irrelevance of many foreign textbooks to Brazilian society, deter professors and students from importing books and even journals. Also, because textbooks are thought to provide one-sided perspectives that tend to force students into a single mode of thinking and to discourage the development of individual interests, the preference is to use customized collections of original readings or reading lists from which students may select works of interest. This practice encourages critical thinking and an eclectic exposure to the discipline.

The increasing availability of online journals and e-books has revolutionized information access in Brazil, as in the rest of the world. Combined with Brazilian textbook writers who have summarized contemporary research from around the globe, information technology permits the unfettered study of cutting-edge international scholarship. At the moment, Brazilian academics, students, and psychologists are in tune with international developments in psychology as evidenced by the number of internships that students and faculty have completed at leading universities around the globe and the number of international publications cited in journal articles and dissertations.

Several states fund public education in Brazil. The State of São Paulo has a long tradition of providing the best funding for their state universities. Therefore, the state universities of São Paulo are among the best in the country. In other parts of Brazil, the best universities are federal universities. The federal government in Brazil regulates and funds public university programs and students do not pay tuition. In addition, the federal government regulates all professional programs in private schools, including those in psychology. At present, the government utilizes the input of psychologists and professional organizations in making and implementing educational policies; this seems to be an efficient and satisfactory model.

The Ministry of Education and the Brazilian National Research Council provide financial support for both education and research in psychology. The Ministry distributes funds to universities for faculty, space, supplies, secretarial services, and graduate assistantships and scholarships, but there is a general consensus that such

funding is not enough. However, the Conselho Nacional de Desenvolvimento Cientifico e Tecnologico (National Council of Scientific and Technological Development), a branch of the Ministry of Science, is the major source of research funds in Brazil. The Conselho awards research grants to individuals in the form of salary supplements and graduate student scholarships. It also furnishes money for the purchase of equipment, employment of research assistants, sponsorship of visiting scholars, and convening of scientific meetings.

9.3 SCOPE OF PSYCHOLOGICAL PRACTICE

Licensure in Brazil, as in all of Latin America and much of Europe, is granted after an intense and focused 5-year undergraduate program that includes a 2-year internship (Gilgen & Gilgen, 1987). In Brazil, the internship requires a minimum of 500 (usually 1,500) contact hours under close supervision, as well as an average of 20 hr per week of classroom contact during the first 3 years, followed by an average of at least 10 contact hours per week over the last two years of education. A graduate degree in psychology, without the requisite undergraduate degree, will not result in licensure; completion of the applied 5-year undergraduate program is all that is necessary.

The government, through the Federal Ministry of Education, works closely with various national psychological associations in establishing guidelines and in evaluating, accrediting, and overseeing psychology programs at universities that result in licensure. There are currently 15 major psychological associations in Brazil, and all interact more or less collegially. They have established a Forum of Entidades, which they hope will evolve into a single voice for Brazilian psychology. These organizations include:

1. Conselho Federal de Psicologia (Federal Council of Psychology)
2. Federação Nacional dos Psicólogos (National Federation of Psychologists—an association of state syndicates)
3. Associação Nacional de Pesquisa e Pós-Graduação em Psicologia (National Association of Graduate Programs in Psychology)
4. Associação Brasileira de Psicologia Social (Brazilian Association of Social Psychology)
5. Associação Brasileira de Psicologia Escolar e Educacional (Brazilian Association of School and Educational Psychology)
6. Instituto Brasileiro de Avaliação Psicológica (Brazilian Institute of Psychological Assessment)
7. Sociedade Brasileira de Psicologia Política (Brazilian Society of Political Psychology)
8. Sociedade Brasileira de Psicologia Organizacional e do Trabalho (Brazilian Society of Organizational and Work Psychology)
9. Associação Brasileira de Psicologia Jurídica (Brazilian Psychology and Law Association)
10. Associação Brasileira de Orientadores Profissionals (Brazilian Association for Vocational Guidance)
11. Associação Brasileira de Ensino de Psicologia (Brazilian Association for the Teaching of Psychology)
12. Sociedade Brasileira de Psicologia do Desenvolvimento (Brazilian Society of Developmental Psychology)
13. Sociedade Brasileira de Psicologia Hospitalar (Brazilian Society of Hospital Psychology)
14. Sociedade Brasileira de Rorscharch (Brazilian Rorschach Society)
15. Conselho Nacional de Entidades Estudantis de Psicologia (National Council of Psychology Students).

Upon completion of an accredited undergraduate psychology program, graduates are eligible for licensure by regional/state branches of the Federal Council of Psychology once they apply and pay a fee. The Federal Council of Psychologists is responsible for the licensure of psychologists. Licensure throughout Brazil is lifelong. Licenses are granted by each state, but the requirements are the same throughout the country. Psychologists must register in the particular state in which they reside, but may practice psychology anywhere in Brazil, provided they join the appropriate regional council, roughly akin to a state organization. Furthermore, there are no reciprocal agreements with other countries. Psychologists emigrating from another country to Brazil must have their transcripts evaluated by the Ministry of Education. Prior to becoming eligible for licensure, psychologists educated in other countries must remediate any deficiencies in coursework and complete an internship in Brazil.

There is a national code of ethics that psychologists are obliged to follow. The Federal Council of Psychology is also the entity responsible for establishing and maintaining professional ethics and for censuring and revoking licenses in cases of ethical violations.

Once psychologists have completed their training, registered, and received their license, they may begin to practice psychology. Churches, government research centers, hospitals, and clinics, police departments, prisons, schools, and social service agencies are all potential employers. Private practice is quite common. However, with the growing number of training programs and licensed professionals who enter practice, the market for private practitioners has become congested. Positions in community psychology, environmental psychology, health psychology, human resources, measurement, research, and teaching are plentiful and continue to increase. Private businesses and research centers are gradually beginning to employ psychologists as well. As in other countries, the typical duties of psychologists vary greatly according to the agency or specialty area in which they are employed. Psychologists may be involved in a variety of activities from screening candidates for job positions to assessing government policies for their potential effects on community well-being and providing grief counseling for nurses and hospital staff or working in prisons.

Sociocultural and sociohistorical conceptual orientations, somewhat similar to the perspectives of community and peace psychology in the United States, have been adopted by many Brazilian practitioners. These orientations, as with Vygotsky's social interactionism, emphasize the influence of environment and social conditions on human development and seek to improve individuals' psychological well-being and mental health in tandem with the economic, environmental, and social conditions that directly influence it. Brazilian psychologists also utilize cognitive–behavioral, humanistic and biological perspectives to varying degrees. Psychoanalytic theory and treatment remain widely popular, but this is changing.

Just as university programs have rapidly expanded over the last three decades, so, too, have publications in psychology that are relevant to the training of psychologists. Over 50 journals are published in Brazil, 30% of which are considered of to be of high quality, with editorial processes comparable to the best psychology journals in the world. The editorial committee of the branch of the Ministry of Education that evaluates graduate psychology programs periodically assesses the quality of Brazilian psychology journals. The criteria used include authorship, generalizability and utility of content, editorial standards, circulation, and quality of research. The top national and local Brazilian journals in psychology according to the most recent assessment (Yamamoto et al., 2002) appear in Tables 9.1 and 9.2.

Brazilian journals are generally published by universities rather than by professional associations or commercial companies. Journals are divided into three categories: international, national, and local. Whether a journal is considered national or local is determined by the affiliations of the authors whose work appears in the journal, as well as by its circulation and overall quality. International journals must show evidence of international circulation and authorship of papers. For example, a journal published by a university that has only local academicians and psychologists on the editorial board and features only the work of faculty and graduates students at that institution would

TABLE 9.1
Top Ten National Psychology Journals According to the Most Recent Evaluation by CAPES-ANPEPP

Title	Translation	Quality Rating
Psicologia: Reflexão e Crítica	Psychology: Critical Reflection	89
Estudos de Psicologia (UFRN)	Studies in Psychology	86
Psyche	Psyche	80
Arquivos Brasileiros de Psicologia	Brazilian Archives of Psychology	77
Interaçõoes	Interactions	76
Psicologia em Estudo	Psychological Studies	76
Psicologia: Teoria e Pesquisa	Psychology: Theory and Research	74
Revista Latinoamericana de Psicopathologia Fundamental	Latin America Journal of Basic Psychopathology	74
Psico	Psychology	73
Estudos de Psicologia (PUCCAMP)	Studies in Psychology	68

Note: CAPES is an agency of the Ministry of Education responsible for evaluating graduate programs. ANPEPP is the National Association of Graduate Programs in Psychology. Twenty-five journals were rated on a 0–100 point scale, with ratings ranging from 49 to 89. Detailed information about the assessment, criteria, and rating can be obtained at www.anpepp.org.br.

TABLE 9.2
Top Five Local Psychology Journals According to the Most Recent Evaluation by CAPES-ANPEPP

Title	Translation	Quality Rating
Ágora	Agora	58
Psicologia Clinica	Clinical Psychology	49
Cadernos de Psicanalise	Psychoanalysis Notebook	46
Tempo Psicanalitico	Psychoanalitic Time	44
Psicologia: Teoria e Practica	Psychology: Theory and Practice	42

Note: CAPES is an agency of the Ministry of Education responsible for evaluating graduate programs. ANPEPP is the National Association of Graduate Programs in Psychology. Twenty-five journals were rated on a 0–100 point scale, with ratings ranging from 10 to 58. Detailed information about the assessment, criteria, and rating can be obtained at www.anpepp.org.br.

clearly be considered local. Journals with wider readerships and more distinguished editorial boards from several geographic regions that attract and publish submissions from throughout Brazil (and elsewhere) are considered national. As journals develop or change over time, they often shift from one category to the other.

Journals in Brazil, like the rest of the discipline, are evolving rapidly. A major Brazilian journal, *Arquivos Brasileiros,* long respected in Brazilian psychology (Biaggio & Grinder, 1992), illustrates that the phenomenological preference for studies on subjectivity are still evident in Brazilian psychology. As late as 1996, 35% of the articles published in *Arquivos Brasileiros* did not have references; during the 1960s, as much as 50% of research in this journal had no references (Hutz & Adair, 1996). Many psychologists believe it is important to study local, socially relevant problems that arise from the direct observations and experiences of the researcher, and that such problems are unique to the specific environments in which they occur; theory and research from other countries and other times are not considered useful (Lane, 1994). The fact that, until recently, Latin American culture placed greater value on the humanities than on science may also partially explain this (Ardila, 1982). Today, however, all major Brazilian journals include references and feature articles based on research, often empirical in content and quantitatively analyzed.

9.4 FUTURE CHALLENGES AND PROSPECTS

Because of the manner in which psychology has evolved in Brazil, the relatively recent establishment of graduate programs, often by faculty who were educated abroad, and the use of electronic resources, psychology in Brazil is already quite international in substance and receptive to global trends. In addition, the job outlook for psychologists in Brazil is favorable, especially for those holding graduate degrees. Psychologists are integral and respected members of interdisciplinary teams in most Brazilian institutions and workplaces. Most Brazilians are as comfortable visiting a psychologist as they are a physician or dentist, and take advantage of available mental health opportunities. Churches, schools, and state agencies routinely make referrals to psychologists.

At the moment, the greatest challenge to Brazilian psychology is the integration of the discipline and profession of psychology. The Forum of organizations recently convened the first Brazilian Congress of Psychology in São Paulo in 2002, with the aim of uniting science and practice. Over 12,000 psychologists attended, making the congress comparable in size and scope to annual conventions of the APA. Although there is no tension between science and practice in Brazil, there is also little interaction between the two. Contributors to the more than 40 peer-reviewed journals of psychological research published in Brazil are mainly academicians and postgraduate researchers. Practicing psychologists seldom subscribe to or contribute to the research journals. Trying to unite practicing psychologists with the growing body of scientific research, for the benefit of both, is a goal of the Congress, and of the next century of psychology in Brazil. Research-based practice and practice-based research in psychology loom on the horizon here. The interactions among the organizations and the consultative role that these organizations have with the federal government (e.g., regulating the profession) bode well for the realization of the synthesis of science and practice.

The trend to blend undergraduate and graduate programs by involving undergraduates in research in cooperation with faculty and graduate students early in their training will also assist in accomplishing this synthesis.

Defining good research is another challenge. Brazil's strong European roots in psychoanalysis and phenomenology, coupled with the contemporary emphasis on programs in cognitive–experimental psychology that receive the Ministry of Education's strongest evaluations, guarantees that case studies and experimental design are likely to coexist for years to come, to the benefit of both perspectives (Gomes, 1998). Correspondingly, a variety of assessment tools are being developed, translated, and adapted for use by Brazilian psychologists (e.g., Alves, 2002; Kroeff, 1988; Nascimento & Figueirdo, 2002; Noronha & Alcheieri, 2002; Nunes & Hutz, 2002). Although instrumentation, investigative methodologies, and statistical analyses in Brazil compare favorably to those of other countries (see Primi, 2002), there is also a parallel emphasis on the development of qualitative approaches to psychological research (see Gomes, 1998).

Brazil is a rapidly developing country. Dedication to democratic principles, respect for diversity, and general optimism are leading Brazil into strong economic and social development in the 21st century. These larger societal trends are apparent in the development of Brazilian psychology. Brazilian society places great value on the quality of life of the individual and respect for human rights. This meshes well with the ideals of scientific and professional psychology and helps make the profession accepted and well-regarded throughout the country. In addition, Brazilians' humor, pragmatism, social consciousness, and the ability to adapt, born of past political experience with repression, enriches the creativity and critical thinking necessary for psychology's continued advancement.

Psychology is currently poised for entry into a "golden age," much like that experienced in the 1940s and 1950s in the United States, provided current economic, political, and social trends continue. The diversity of Brazilian culture allows for rich exploration of psychology in multicultural contexts. Already international in flavor, comfortable with information technology, efficient in its use of resources, collaborative in terms of mentoring relationships between faculty and students, and democratic in its approach to evaluation, graduate psychology programs in Brazil could perhaps serve as an alternative model for other countries as they develop programs. Current trends and conditions suggest that the progress of Brazilian psychology over the past decade will continue. The discipline and profession will have vital roles to play in ensuring the health and well-being of Brazilian society. Its practices will be tempered by scientific evidence and critical thought, reflecting the best traditions of psychology.

REFERENCES

Alves, I. (1928). *Teste individual de inteligencia* [Individual test of intelligence]. Bahia, Brazil: Graphicas da Luva.

Alves, I. (1930). *Os testes e a reorganização escolar* [Tests and school reorganization]. Bahia, Brazil: A Nova Graphica.

Alves, I. C. B. (2002). Instrumentos disponíveis no Brasil para avaliação da inteligência [Available testing on intelligence in Brazil]. In R. Primi (Ed.), *Temas em avaliação psicológica* [Themes on psychological assessment] (pp. 80–102). Campinas, Brazil: Instituto Brasileiro de Avaliação Psicológica.

Ardila, R. (1982). Psychology in Latin America today. *Annual Review of Psychology, 33,* 103–122.

Biaggio, A., & Grinder, R. (1992). Brazil. In V. S. Sexton & J. D. Hogan (Eds.), *International psychology: Views from around the world* (pp. 52–64). Lincoln, NE: University of Nebraska Press.

Campos, R. H. F. (Ed.). (2001). *Dicionário biográfico da psicologia no Brasil* [Biographic dictionary of psychology in Brazil]. Rio de Janeiro: Imago.

Centofanti, R. (1982). Radecki e a psicologia no Brasil [Radecki and psychology in Brazil]. *Psicologia: Ciência e Profissão, 3,* 3–50.

Gilgen A. R., & Gilgen, C. K. (Eds.). (1987). *International handbook of psychology.* New York: Greenwood Press.

Gomes, W. (1998). Apresentação: Fenomenologia e pesquisa em psicologia [Presentation: Phenomenology and research in psychology]. In W. Gomes (Ed.), *Fenomenologia e pesquisa em psicologia* [Phenomenology and research in psychology] (pp. 11–18). Porto Alegre, Brazil: Editora da Universidade Federal do Rio Grande do Sul.

Gomes, W. B., Lhullier, C., & Leite, L. O. (1999). Das primeiras disciplinas aos primeiros cursos de psicologia no Rio Grande do Sul [From the first courses to the first programs in psychology in Rio Grande do Sul]. In M. C. Guedes & R. H. F. Campos (Eds.), *Estudos em história da psicologia* [Studies in the history of psychology] (pp. 153–180). São Paulo: Editora da Pontifícia Universidade Católica de São Paulo.

Hearnshaw, L. S. (1989). *The shaping of modern psychology.* London: Routledge.

Hutz, C. (1988). Atitudes com relação e cor em criancas pré-escolares brancas, mulatas e negras [Color attitudes in White, Mulatto, and Black preschool children]. *Psicologia: Reflexão e Crítica, 3,* 32–37.

Hutz, C., & Adair, J. (1996). The use of references in Brazilian psychology journals reveals trends in thought and research. *International Journal of Psychology, 31,* 145–148.

Kroeff, P. (1988). Normas brasileiras para o teste de Bender [Brazilian norms to the Bender test]. *Psicologia: Reflexão e Crítica, 3,* 12–19.

Lane, S. (1994, May). *The social relevance of research and graduate study in Brazil.* Invited address delivered at the meeting of the Brazilian National Association for Research and Graduate Study, Caxambu, Brazil.

Lourenço-Filho, H. B. (1955). Psicologia no Brasil [Psychology in Brazil]. In F. Azevedo (Ed.), *Ciências no Brasil* [Sciences in Brazil] (pp. 263–296). São Paulo: Melhoramentos.

Mancebo, D. (2001). Hans Ludwig Lippmann. In R. H. F. Campos (Ed.). *Dicionário biográfico da psicologia no Brasil* [Biographic dictionary of psychology in Brazil] (pp. 207–209). Rio de Janeiro: Imago.

Massimi, M. (1990). História da psicologia brasileira: Da época colonial até 1934 [History of Brazilian psychology: From colonial times to 1934]. São Paulo: Editora da Universidade de São Paulo.

McCarthy, S. (2002). Preventing future terrorist activities among adolescents through global psychology. In C. Stout (Ed.), *The psychology of terrorism* (Vol. 4, pp. 131–156). New York: Greenwood Press.

Medeiros-e-Albuquerque, J. J. C. C. (1924). *Tests.* Rio de Janeiro: Livraria Alves.

Nascimento, E., & Figueiredo, V. (2002). A terceira edição das escalas Wechsler de inteligência [The third edition of the Weschsler scales of intelligence]. In R. Primi (Ed.), *Temas em avaliação psicológica* [Themes on psychological assessment] (pp. 61–79). Campinas, Brazil: Instituto Brasileiro de Avaliação Psicológica.

Noronha, A., & Alchieri, J. (2002). Reflexões sobre os instrumentos de avaliação psicológica [Thoughts about psychological assessment instruments]. In R. Primi (Ed.), *Temas em avaliação psicológica* [Themes on psychological assessment] (pp. 7–16). Campinas, Brazil: Instituto Brasileiro de Avaliação Psicológica.

Nunes, C., & Hutz, C. (2002). O modelo dos cinco grandes fatores de personalidade [The model of the big five personality factors]. In R. Primi (Ed.), *Temas em avaliação psicológica* [Themes on psychological assessment] (pp. 40–49). Campinas, Brazil: Instituto Brasileiro de Avaliação Psicológica.

Pena, S. D. J., Parra, F. C., Amado, R. C., Lambertucci, J. R., Rocha, J., & Antunes, C. M. (2003). Color and genomic ancestry in Brazilians. *Proceedings of the National Academy of Sciences, USA, 100,* 177–182.

Penna, A. G. (1992). *História da psicologia no Rio de Janeiro* [History of psychology in Rio de Janeiro]. Rio de Janeiro: Imago.

Pessotti, I. (1975). Dados para uma história da psicologia no Brasil [Data for a history of psychogy in Brazil]. *Psicologia, 1,* 1–14.

Primi, R. (Ed.). (2002). *Teams em avaliação Psicológica* [Themes on psychological assessment]. Campinas, Brazil: Instituto Brasileiro de Avaliação Psicológica.

Rosas, P. (1992). *Mira y López: 30 anos depois* [Mira y López: 30 years later]. São Paulo: Vetor.

Yamamoto, O., Menandro, P., Koller, S., LoBianco, A., Hutz, C. S., Bueno, J., et al. (2002). Evaluation of the Brazilian scientific journals in the area of psychology. *Ciência da Informação, 31,* 163–171.

IMPORTANT PUBLICATIONS

Biaggio, A. M. B. (1991). *Psicologia do desenvolvimento* [Developmental psychology] (10th ed.). Petrópolis, Brazil: Vozes.

Cunha, J. A. (Ed.). (2000). *Psicodiagnóstico.* [Psychodiagnosis] (5th ed.) Porto Alegre, Brazil: Artes Médicas.

Graeff, F. G., & Brandão, M. L. (1999). *Neurobiologia das doenças mentais* (5th ed.). [Neurobiology of mental illness]. São Paulo: Lemos.

Lane, S., & Codo, W. (1984). *Psicologia social: O homem em movimento.* [Social psychology: Man in movement]. São Paulo: Brasiliense.

Pasquali, L. (1997). *Psicometria: Teoria e aplicações* [Psychometrics: Theory and applications]. Brasília: Editora da Universidade de Brasília.

Patto, M. H. S. (1989). *Introdução à psicologia escolar.* [Introduction to school psychology]. São Paulo: Queiroz.

Ramozzi-Chiarottino, Z. (1972). *Piaget: Modelo e estrutura.* [Piaget: Model and structure]. Rio de Janeiro: Olympio Editora.

Rodrigues, A. (1973). *Psicologia social.* [Social psychology]. Petrópolis, Brazil: Vozes.

Van-Kolck, O. L. (1973). *Técnicas de exame psicológicos e suas aplicações no Brasil* [Techniques for psychological assessment and their applications in Brazil]. Petrópolis, Brazil: Vozes.

Yamamoto, O. H., & Gouveia, V. V. (Eds.). (2003). *Construindo a psicologia brasileira: Desafios da ciência e prática psicológica* [Constructing Brazilian psychology: Challenges for psychological science and practice]. São Paulo: Casa do Psicólogo.

CHAPTER 10

Psychology in Colombia: Development and Current Status

RUBÉN ARDILA

Rubén Ardila received his degree in psychology from the National University of Colombia (in Bogotá) and his Ph.D. at the University of Nebraska-Lincoln in experimental psychology. His research areas are the experimental analysis of behavior, psychobiology, and history of psychology. He has been chair of the psychology department at the National University of Colombia, chair of the psychology department at the University of the Andes, and director of the psychology graduate program at the University of St. Thomas.

Rubén Ardila has written 27 books and more than 250 scientific papers, published in several countries and in several languages. He has been visiting professor in Argentina, Germany, Puerto Rico, Spain, and the United States. He is also a member of the executive committee of the International Union of Psychological Science, and the International Council of Psychologists, and was president

of the Interamerican Society of Psychology. He is the founder and editor of the Latin American Journal of Psychology.

10.1 OVERVIEW

Colombia is located in northwestern South America, with coasts on the Atlantic (Caribbean Sea) and the Pacific oceans, and with the Amazon River to the south. The area encompasses 439,737 mi^2 (1,138,914 km^2). Colombia's natural resources include oil, coal, natural gas, most of the world's emeralds, fertile soil, and plenty of water. The climate is cool in the mountains where the majority of the population lives, and tropical on the coast and in the east. The population was 42 million in 2003; the literacy rate is 90.9%, and 71% of the people live in urban areas. Roman Catholics comprise 95% of the people, and the national language is Spanish.

The Human Development Index (HDI) was developed by the United Nations Development Program to serve as a composite measure of a country's health vis-à-vis other nations. The HDI is comprised of three key variables: life expectancy, knowledge (as measured by the adult literacy rate and school enrollment), and per capita gross domestic product. Colombia ranks 57th among 174 countries on the Human Development Index. Table 10.1 shows the main demographic indicators comparing Colombia and the rest of the world for the year 2000.

Colombia has a long tradition in education, above all in the humanities and in the arts. In the major cities there is an elite class with a high level of education; members of this class are very well-informed about what is happening in the world, particularly in politics, art, literature and economics.

A very good relationship with the United States and with Europe exists. There are many colleges and universities in Colombia, but these schools vary widely in quality. A university education is thought to help with social ascent, and it is clearly a status symbol.

The high value of education has caused the proliferation of universities, and within them there has been a proliferation of service and health programs such as medicine, law, business administration, and psychology.

Psychology in Colombia is a well-established discipline. It has a long tradition that goes back in a broad sense to the primitive inhabitants of the current territory of Colombia, and in the strict sense to the founding of the first professional program of psychology (i.e., a major in psychology) in 1947. At present, there are

TABLE 10.1

Demographic Indicators for the Year 2000

	Colombia	World
Population	38 million	6 million
Life Expectancy		
Males	70 years	62 years
Females	75 years	69 years
Total	72 years	67 years
Average Age	25 years	22 years
Fertility Rate per Woman	2.8	3.3
Annual per Capital Income	$1,600 USA	$3,610 USA
Literacy Rate	90.9%	87%
Percent Urban	71%	44%
Percent of Population Over 65	5%	7%

Note. Adapted from *Cuadro de la población mundial* [Table of the world population], by Population Reference Bureau, 2002, Washington, DC: Author; *La cátedra abierta en población 2000–2003.* [Open chair on population 2000–2003], by Wartenberg, L. (Ed.), 2003, Bogota, Colombia: Universidad Externado de Colombia.

12,000 graduated psychologists, 20,000 students of psychology, and 77 professional training programs. There are 43 psychologists per 100,000 people in Colombia.

The development of psychology in Colombia can be divided into five phases (Ardila, 1973, 1993):

Before the arrival of Europeans. In the territory that today is called Colombia, several cultures existed with medium levels of social and cultural development. They were not as advanced as the Mayas, Aztecs, or Incas. These early inhabitants of Colombia had clear ideas about behavior, the family, the raising of children, the soul, sexuality, the normal and the abnormal, and harmony among people. The study of the indigenous psychologies of Colombia is just beginning.

Following the arrival of the Spanish. After 1492, the philosophy of St. Thomas Aquinas was introduced, which included the study of the faculties of the soul. The Spanish colonial period lasted three centuries, during which many universities and centers of higher learning were created. There were scientific expeditions (led by Humboldt, La Condamine, Mutis, and other European scientists), which shed light on aspects of astronomy, botany, geography, zoology, and the behavior and social organization of several human groups.

In the 19th century. Many scientific advances were made in psychology. Some physicians wrote theses on psychological topics, educators carried out pedagogical innovations, and philosophers were concerned with studying perceptual and epistemological problems, the nature of the mind, and so forth.

The professionalization of psychology. This began in 1947 with the creation of the first professional training program at the National University of Colombia. It was founded by Mercedes Rodrigo (1891–1982), a Spanish immigrant who had left her country because of the Spanish Civil War: Rodrigo was invited to Colombia by the rector of the National University and arrived in 1939. She founded the Section of Psychotechnics and, in 1947, the Institute of Applied Psychology. She established the importance of psychometric investigation, adapting many psychological tests and creating new ones. She also made progress on the professional application of psychology to education and to the world of work. Rodrigo trained many collaborators and students.

When Rodrigo disembarked in Colombia, a certain research tradition in psychology already existed, as evidenced by the modest body of published work at the time. The applied work of Rodrigo was very important and fulfilled social needs that already existed in the family, community, schools, and industry. On November 20, 1947, she created the Institute of Applied Psychology for the purpose of training professional psychologists. It is relevant to point out that, at the time, the profession of psychologist did not exist in any country of South America.

Growth and consolidation. Psychology has grown considerably between 1952 (the year that the first psychologists in Colombia received their diploma) and today. Seventy-seven programs exist for professional training in psychology, among which 20 are graduate programs. All of the main cities of Colombia (Barranquilla, Bogotá, Bucaramanga, Cali, Cartagena, Manizales, Medellín, and Pereira) have psychology training programs.

The majority of psychologists live in large, metropolitan centers that have potential for the greatest development. Nevertheless, in recent years there has been a tendency to fill the existing shortage of psychologists in small towns. In general, however, psychology is a predominately urban profession.

The professional organization that represents psychology in Colombia is the Colombian Society of Psychology. Founded in 1979, it organizes and hosts the Colombian Congress of Psychology every 2 years, publishes a newsletter, serves as the voice of the profession in Colombia, represents the country before the International Union of Psychological Science, maintains a Code of Ethics (Sociedad

Colombiana de Psicología, 2000), and carries out many other activities to promote psychology as a science and profession.

Other organizations exist, dedicated to specific areas, including the Association for Behavior Analysis and Therapy, the Colombian Association of Clinical Psychologists and Psychotherapists, the Colombian Association of Neuropsychology, the Colombian Association of Social Psychology, the Society of Industrial–Organizational Psychologists, and the Society of Sport Psychologists. There is also an association of faculties (colleges) of psychology, the Colombian Association of Psychology Faculties. In general, these professional associations have good relationships with one another, and are complementary rather than competitive.

The professional associations serve psychologists in many ways. They defend the profession, support its inclusion in society, foster positive relationships with the government, and address problems associated with the recruitment and training of psychologists. These associations have multiple links with the government and with NGOs.

There is little tension between scientists and practitioners in Colombia. The status and role of psychologists are high vis-à-vis other disciplines. There was an obvious struggle for power between psychiatrists and psychologists a few decades ago; today, that struggle no longer exists. The salaries earned by psychologists are similar to earned by other Colombian professionals, but are very low by international standards. Some psychologists have several jobs in order to maintain a decent standard of living. However, other professionals also work multiple jobs, so this is not unique to psychology.

10.2 EDUCATION AND TRAINING

To enroll in a Colombian university, a student has to take a national exam (similar to the Scholastic Aptitude Test in the United States). It is an aptitude and knowledge test. This entrance examination includes abstract reasoning, verbal reasoning, knowledge of history, philosophy, mathematics, natural sciences, social sciences, etc. All high school graduates must take this state exam (called the ICFES national exam). In addition, some university careers (for instance, art and music) require special exams. The required score for admittance varies in each university and from program to program, but admissions criteria are generally very high across university programs. In the case of psychology programs, admissions criteria are especially high. Psychology students are highly selected and are among the best qualified in the whole country. Some universities (e.g., the National University of Colombia) enroll less than 10% of the candidates who apply for admission to psychology programs.

There are no scholarships available at the undergraduate level, although some students will qualify for financial aid. In contrast, at the graduate level, students often qualify for financial aid and grants, although less than the 50% of students qualify for scholarships.

At an organizational level, psychology programs are almost always embedded in a college of psychology (*Facultad de Psicología*), although a few universities have departments of psychology. The college structure usually allows more independence and autonomy than the department structure. The tendency in Colombia, and in the rest of Latin America and Spain as well, is for psychology to be studied in autonomous colleges that are part of universities. These universities can be public or private. The "professional school of psychology" model also exists in Colombia, but is more limited, and there are few professional schools independent from universities.

The most prestigious public universities that train psychologists are the National University of Colombia (established in 1947), the University of Valle–Cali (established in 1976), and the University of Antioquia–Medellín (established in 1977).

Many private universities also train psychologists. Some of them are excellent, whereas others are less than stellar. The private universities that offer the best psychology training programs include the University of the Andes, Javeriana University, Konrad Lorenz University, Autonomous University of Bucaramanga, Catholic University of Colombia, University of Manizales, University of the North (Barranquilla), University of St. Buenaventura (Medellín), and the University of St. Thomas.

The typical curriculum for undergraduate training lasts 5 years. It is very professionally oriented and very different from the typical undergraduate psychology curriculum in the United States (B.A. or B.S.). It is actually more similar to the professional training that is offered in various European countries, for example in Germany, Spain, and Sweden. During the 5 years of training, instruction in all areas of psychology is provided at a basic level (perception, cognition, learning, social psychology, research methodology), as

well as at an applied level (clinical psychology, community psychology, educational psychology, industrial–organizational, health psychology). In addition, students take courses in related disciplines (anthropology, biology, English, informatics, neuroscience, physiology, sociology, and statistics).

During the last three semesters, students focus on one area (i.e., clinical, educational, industrial–organizational, or sport psychology). Students also have a year of supervised practice and a graduation thesis. This thesis is typically very demanding, and it is intended to be an empirical contribution to the profession.

A generic degree in psychology is awarded at the undergraduate level. This degree is similar to the master's (M.A., M.S.) in the United States. No specialized degrees are offered at the undergraduate level.

In Colombia, the curriculum at the master's level is very specialized, and is also oriented toward scientific research. It is expected that a graduate student will master an area of psychology (e.g., forensic psychology) and go on to conduct scientific research in that area. Graduate programs are available in clinical psychology, behavior analysis, neuropsychology, educational psychology, industrial–organizational psychology, social psychology, forensic psychology, health psychology, family psychology, and cognitive psychology.

Doctoral programs in psychology do not exist in Colombia as of 2003, but there are advanced plans for the development of doctoral programs at two Colombian universities. Colombian psychologists with a Ph.D. or Psy.D. have most often received their advanced training in the United States,

Belgium, Mexico, Russia, or Spain. Out of the 12,000 psychologists working in Colombia, perhaps 300 hold an M.A. or a M.S., and 40 or 50 have a Ph.D. or Psy.D.

The pedagogic methods used in training programs in psychology are very broad, and include lectures, seminars, practicum, lab sessions, and fieldwork, among other techniques. The emphasis on theory, research, and practice varies across training programs at different universities in Colombia.

Students use a variety of resources in learning about psychology, including books written by Colombian psychologists, books translated from other languages (mainly from English by U.S. authors), international journals, journals edited in Colombia, indigenous and translated psychometric tests, hardware and software, audiovisual materials, etc. University libraries possess good collections of books and journals, primarily those published in the United States and Europe, but also from other Latin American nations (e.g., Argentina, Mexico).

A small percentage of psychologists receive their education and training outside Colombia, mostly in the United States, Spain, Canada, and Mexico.

The professional practice of psychology requires a degree in psychology and registration by the Secretary of Health. Licensing and certification are based on one's professional training. There are no formal requirements for continuing education, although many Colombian psychologists participate in conferences, seminars, and/or workshops. The major continuing-education event is the Colombian Congress of Psychology, which meets every 2 years.

10.3 SCOPE OF PSYCHOLOGICAL PRACTICE

The profession of psychology has been regulated by law in Colombia since 1983. However, this law is currently being revised. In addition, the Code of Ethics was updated in 2000 (Sociedad Colombiana de Psicología, 2000). It is a comprehensive code, and one that covers most situations, helping psychologists resolve the most vexing ethical dilemmas they encounter. The Code of Ethics was originally promulgated in 1974 (see Federación Colombiana de Psicología, 1974) and was revised and updated in 2000 to conform to changes in society and to new challenges that confront the profession.

The Code of Ethics has the following sections: professional competences, integrity, professional and scientific responsibility, social responsibility, respect for others, confidentiality, avoiding harm, interference in professional activity, delegation and supervision, fees and financial arrangements, advertising and professional promotion, therapeutic relationships, evaluation, assessment and diagnosis, scientific research, applications and social context, relationships with colleagues and other professionals, relationships with the society and the state, and disciplinary measures.

The training of psychologists is very rigorous, and high standards are set for professional practice. Psychology is considered to be a science of behavior, but this does not mean that the predominant paradigm is behaviorism. In fact, the vast majority of training programs offer instruction in all fields and in all approaches, including behaviorism, cognitive psychology, humanistic psychology, psychobiology, and psychodynamics. However, it is fair to state that the behavioral approach has had more influence in the profession than the other theoretical approaches.

Psychologists attempt to harmonize their practice with the traditions of the Colombian culture and with the sociopolitical undercurrents of the country. This is not always simple, especially in a varied and heterogeneous developing country like Colombia, a nation with multiple cultural traditions. Some traditional approaches have been adapted to Colombian culture and society.

Colombian psychology has tried to be original, although at first it tended to mimic or reproduce foreign models, as has probably occurred in all countries of the region (see Alarcón, 1997, 2002). Most new psychological ideas came from the United States, England, France, and Germany. Experimental psychology came from Germany. The ideas of Piaget came from the French-speaking world. Psychoanalysis came from several sources, including the Argentina, France, and the United States.

Original psychological research has been carried out by Colombian psychologists. Theories have been postulated (e.g., the experimental synthesis of behavior; see Alarcón [1997] for a description of the theory), books have been written, psychological tests have been constructed, and important studies have been conducted in cognitive development, comparative psychology, the experimental analysis of behavior, and social psychology. Models of clinical intervention and new procedures in educational psychology also have been proposed.

In spite of the leadership that Colombian psychology currently occupies in Latin America, there is a long way to go. Colombian psychology maintains a delicate balance between (a) the use of psychological theories and techniques of the developed world and (b) the formulation of original proposals for a "local" psychology. In Colombia, psychologists are still grappling with the a dimension that is taken very seriously in the developing world. This issue refers to the universality of psychological laws, in contrast to the "indigenous" approach that is relative to particular cultures and epochs. Psychology in Colombia is more Western oriented, and scientific principles are accepted as universal and not necessarily unique to the people or the culture of Colombia.

Colombian psychologists provide a wide variety of services in an equally wide variety of settings:

- In hospitals and clinics, psychologists carry out assessment, diagnosis, evaluation, psychotherapy, prevention, and research. The relevance of health psychology is increasingly recognized in these settings.
- In the armed forces, psychologists have clinical, educational, and organizational duties. Due to the Colombian conflict (with the guerrillas) and state of war that exists in parts of the nation, the psychological work of the armed forces has emphasized rehabilitation. Many psychologists offer counseling to soldiers who have been wounded in combat or have become disabled in normal life.
- In business and industry, psychologists participate in selection, motivation, training, evaluating job performance, and enhancing the lifestyle of

employees, among other things. An ever-increasing number of psychologists in Colombia are working in business and industrial settings.

- Psychologists also provide services in schools and institutions of higher education. The psychological tasks important in these settings include aptitude testing, guidance and counseling, professional orientation, research on the teaching–learning process, and training in pedagogical competences.
- Psychologists conduct research in a variety of settings, most often in specialized centers or in universities. The work is most often done in multidisciplinary groups that focus on specific problems or issues.
- Psychologists working in academic settings are devoted to teaching, research, and administration. In the larger, urban universities, academic life is much more intense than in small institutions.
- Colombian psychologists also engage in traditional clinical practice. An increasing number of people feel comfortable consulting a psychologist for counseling and psychotherapy without fear of being stigmatized.

In spite of the legal recognition of psychology in Colombia, there are still nonpsychologists who provide psychological services. Shamans, witch doctors, and even Catholic priests act as psychologists without having had training in pastoral psychology. In addition, some general physicians, social workers, speech therapists, and teachers often provide psychological services without having appropriate training.

In various work settings described above, the relationship between

psychologists and nonpsychologists varies, but it is generally congenial. Clashes, friction, and power struggles occur, but these were more pronounced in the past. In general, psychologists in Colombia work well with teams that include other professionals.

10.4 FUTURE CHALLENGES AND PROSPECTS

Colombian psychologists frequently complain that too many psychology-training programs exist (there were 77 in 2003), and that instruction in these settings is not always adequate as current graduates are not meeting the scientific standards that have been traditional in Colombian psychology. The challenge of how best to train psychologists for the new century, for Colombia, and for the entire world, is a difficult and important challenge.

A related problem is the number of psychological professionals in Colombia. It's not that "too many" psychologists exist, but, due to the enormous popularity of psychology at the undergraduate level, it is probable that the unemployment rate for psychologists will increase. Currently, about 12% of Colombian psychologists are unemployed; this rate is similar to the unemployment rate in other professions.

Psychology has been traditionally a "female profession" in Colombia, and approximately 60–70% of Colombian psychologists are women. The contribution of men and women has been equally important, but women tend to devote themselves chiefly to applied activities. Managerial and research posts are generally taken by men (e.g., presidents of the Colombian

Society of Psychology, deans of colleges of psychology, researchers and authors in the science of psychology, conference organizers, and spokesmen for the discipline).

The future of psychology in Colombia seems to be promising. However, for future progress to occur, it will be necessary to develop new areas of work, organize doctoral programs, overcome the isolation and provincialism of the majority of Colombians, and improve the economic standards in all professions (this applies not only to psychologists, but also to economists, engineers, physicians, etc.).

It is likely that the profession of psychology will continue to be viewed as a high-status profession, and the social image of psychologists will remain positive. However, the profession is still identified with the clinic, and psychology is considered as merely a helping profession. It is seldom that an ordinary person knows that psychologists also work with animals, investigate chromatic perception, carry out studies on the localization of brain functions, are experts in computer applications, and evaluate governmental programs for illness prevention and health promotion. On the contrary, people think that psychologists only work in clinical settings, helping adults to resolve problems of living and guiding children who encounter school-related difficulties.

Psychologists are expanding the sphere of their contributions, particularly by becoming more engaged in nontraditional settings and tasks. Rural psychology is an area of growing importance in Colombia, as is the psychology of peace, reconciliation, and problem solving, especially in the context of war.

In the past, psychologists were very involved in political issues, in social change, in the search for social justice, and similar matters. Today, they are not as involved. Critical psychology, "engaged compromise psychology," and "liberation psychology" were very important in the decade of 1980s. These terms refer to enormous social issues related to social justice. Many psychologists think that politics is too important to leave only to politicians, but the majority of psychologists prefer to do their job well and not to involve themselves directly with Colombian politics.

Opportunities for international partnerships are abundant, yet are not fully realized. Few Colombian psychologists participate in international congresses (with the exception of the Interamerican Congresses of Psychology), attend conventions of the American Psychological Association, or publish in international journals.

It is obvious that Colombian psychologists can learn much from international psychology, as all psychologists stand to benefit from international partnership. However, communication needs to be bi-directional—south-to-north, as well as north-to-south. For psychologists in the United States, it is always surprising to find that there are relatively well-developed psychological communities in the developing countries. In the globalized world of the 21st century, international cooperation and the exchange of ideas, products, and people will increase dramatically. As Colombia becomes more involved in international psychology, it will succeed in understanding its local problems in global terms and contributing even more to the understanding of human behavior.

REFERENCES

Alarcón, R. (1997). *Orientaciones teóricas de la psicología en América Latina* [Theoretical orientations of psychology in Latin America]. Lima: Universidad Femenina.

Alarcón, R. (2002). *Estudios sobre psicología latinoamericana* [Studies about Latin American psychology]. Lima: University Ricardo Palma.

Ardila, R. (1973). *La psicología en Colombia, desarrollo histórico* [Psychology in Colombia, historical development]. Mexico City: Editorial Trillas.

Ardila, R. (Ed.). (1993). *Psicología en Colombia, contexto social e histórico* [Psychology in Colombia, social and historical development]. Bogota: Editorial Tercer Mundo.

Federación Colombiana de Psicología. (1974). *Funciones, responsabilidades y código ético del Psicólogo* [Functions, responsibilities, and ethical code for psychologists]. *Revista Latinoamericana de Psicología, 6,* 265–278.

Population Reference Bureau. (2002). *Cuadro de la población mundial* [Table of the world population]. Washington, DC: Author.

Sociedad Colombiana de Psicología. (2000). *Codigo ético del psicólogo* [Ethical code of the psychologist]. Bogota: Editorial ABC.

Wartenberg, L. (Ed.). (2003). *La cátedra abierta en población 2000–2003.* [Open chair on population, 2000–2003]. Bogota: Universidad Externado de Colombia.

IMPORTANT PUBLICATIONS

Amar Amar, J., & Abello, R. (1998). *El niño y su comprensión del sentido de la realidad.* [The child and his comprehension of the sense of reality]. Barranquilla, Colombia: Ediciones Uninorte.

Ardila, R. (1986). *Psicología del hombre Colombiano* [Psychology of the Colombian people]. Bogota: Editorial Planeta.

Carrillo, S., Gutierrez, G., & Carrillo, M. (1999). Calidad de vida en la vejez [Quality of life in old age]. *Avances en Psicología Clínica Latinoamericana, 17,* 77–93.

Dulcey-Ruiz, E. (1985). *Imagen de la vejez en los medios de comunicación social en Colombia* [Image of old age in mass media in Colombia]. Bogota: Center for Gerontological Psychology.

Gómez, V. (2000). Relación entre estrés e inmunidad una visión crítica a la investigación [Relationship between stress and immunity: A critical vision of research]. *Revista Latinoamericana de Psicología, 32,* 31–45.

González, J. M., Bernal, M. P., Rosado, M. C., Vásquez, R. (2001). *Investigaciones sobre salud sexual y familiar en el Caribe colombiano* (Research about sexual and family health in the Colombian Caribbean). Barranquilla, Colombia: Editorial Antillas.

Puche, R. (2000). *Formación de herramientas científicas en el niño pequeño* [Formation of scientific tools in small children]. Bogota: Arango Editores.

Riso, W. (1998). *Intimidades masculinas* [Masculine identities]. Bogota: Editorial Norma.

Toro, F. (2001). *El clima organizacional. Perfil de empresas colombianas* [Organizational climate. A profile of Colombian enterprises]. Medellin, Colombia: Cincel.

Zimmermann, M. (1995). *Psicología ambiental y calidad de vida* [Environmental psychology and quality of life]. Bogota: Ecoe Ediciones.

CHAPTER 11

Advances in Psychology in China

YUFANG YANG

Yufang Yang graduated with a B.S. degree in physics from Shandong University in 1977 and received her M.S. and Ph.D. degrees from the Institute of Psychology, Chinese Academy of Sciences, in 1982 and 1995, respectively. Since 1982, she has worked at the Institute of Psychology, studying language cognition, particularly spoken-language processing and its application in speech engineering. Yufang Yang is currently professor and director of the Institute of Psychology, Chinese Academy of Sciences, and secretary-general of the Chinese Psychological Society, editor-in-chief of Advances in Psychological Science *(a Chinese journal), and member of the editorial boards of* Acta Psychologica Sinica, Pattern Recognition and Artificial Intelligence, *and* Language Sciences *(Chinese journals).*

11.1 OVERVIEW

Basic ways of thinking about the human mind within Chinese civilization can be found in the writings of Confucius

(551–479 B.C.E.), and books about Western philosophical views of psychology appeared in China before the 16th century. However, modern Chinese psychology was established in the early years of the 20th century (Yang & Zhao, 2000).

Cai Yuanpei, a famous Chinese educational reformer who studied in Wundt's Institute of Psychology in 1908, published a book on parapsychology in 1912 after his return to China. In 1917, Cai became the president of Peking University and with his support Chen Daqi established the first psychological laboratory in China. In the early years of the 1920s, a group of scholars who had studied psychology in Western countries brought back ideas fundamental to modern psychology, and started teaching psychology at Chinese universities. Departments of psychology were established later in Peking University, Tsinghua University, Yenching University, and other universities. The Chinese Psychological Society (CPS) was founded in 1921 and the first psychology journal, *Psychology,* was published in

179

1922. The Institute of Psychology, Academia Sinica, was established in 1929. The outbreak of the Sino–Japanese war in 1937 caused a setback to the progress of Chinese psychology that lasted until the end of World War II.

After the founding of the People's Republic of China in 1949, scientific and educational institutions of psychology were restructured using the Soviet Union as a model. A new Institute of Psychology under the Chinese Academy of Sciences was established in 1951. The status of psychology within the university as a department was diminished when it became a mere section under the department of philosophy or in the school of education. Following the Soviet Union, Chinese psychologists viewed conditioned reflexes as the basis of human behavior and the mind as a reflection of the material and social world in which one lives. In addition, they stressed that psychologists should adopt a practical stance and work for socialist construction of the country. Educational reform and economic production gave impetus to the progress of developmental psychology, educational psychology, and ergonomics. From the late 1950s to mid-1960s, though still isolated from the outside world, Chinese psychologists adopted ideas from cybernetics, information theory, and computer science in their study of mental processes and in industrial and military applications. In some of these fields, the quality of Chinese psychologists' basic and applied research met international standards and a large number of psychologists trained in China became leading figures in various psychological fields. In the 1960s, the CPS had 1,056 members, with 24 provincial associations. Regrettably, the Cultural Revolution, which began in 1966 and lasted until 1976, delayed the development of Chinese psychology for almost a decade. During that period, psychology was denounced as a pseudoscience, and teaching and research were suspended throughout the country.

With the end of the Cultural Revolution, China adopted the policy of modernization and opening-up to the outside world, and psychology was rehabilitated and recognized as a scientific discipline. The past 25 years have seen vigorous and steady development of scientific research and the practice of psychology. In China, since the founding of the first department of psychology in Peking University in 1978, departments of psychology have been established at 38 universities across the country, which are mainly distributed in the eastern part of China. The first school of psychology was founded in Beijing Normal University in 2001. According to various presentations at national congresses of the CPS, there are at present about 10,000 psychologists in China. Of these, 40% are developmental and educational psychologists, 15% experimental and cognitive psychologist, 13% clinical, physiological, and neuro psychologists, 6% industrial and organizational psychologists, and 12% social psychologists.

In the fields of cognitive psychology and cognitive neuroscience, Chinese psychologists have made advancements in the study of perceptual organization and the understanding of Chinese language. Developmental and educational psychologists investigate the development of cognition, language, and social behavior, not only in normal children but also in retarded and gifted children. Biopsychology research is concentrated on the neurochemical basis of learning and memory, psychoimmunology, and drug addiction. Industrial and organizational psychologists investigate problems stemming from China's ongoing economic transition and social reform (Yang, 2003).

The progress and achievements of Chinese psychology have gained recognition in the international community. The CPS became a member of the International Union of Psychological Science (IUPsyS) in 1980, and Chinese psychologists have taken leading positions in IUPsyS and other international psychological organizations. Professors Qicheng Jing and Houcan Zhang were elected as vice presidents of the Union in 1992 and 2000 respectively. The 28th International Congress of Psychology was held in Beijing in 2004.

The CPS is a nongovernmental organization of Chinese psychologists. It is a member organization under the Chinese Association of Science and Technology. The CPS currently has 4,000 members. Qualified for membership are (a) psychologists who have positions as assistant research fellows or higher, (b) psychologists with an academic rank at or above assistant professor, (c) psychologists holding at least a master's degree, and (d) university graduates in psychology or related fields with more than 3 years of work experience in psychology. The CPS currently publishes two journals, *Acta Psychologica Sinica* and *Psychological Science*. The CPS has 4 working committees and 15 academic committees. The working body is its secretariat, affiliated with the Institute of Psychology at the Chinese Academy of Sciences.

All provinces and autonomous regions in China, including Tibet, have their own regional psychological societies. These societies operate under the regional associations of science and technology, and

receive academic guidance from the CPS. In addition to the CPS, there are three other independent psychological organizations: the Chinese Mental Health Association with 3,000 members, the Chinese Society of Social Psychology with 2,000 members, and the Chinese Ergonomic Society with 500 members.

The CPS and its academic committees, sometimes together with regional societies and other psychological organizations, organize various academic events to promote scientific research, professional practice, education and training, and the dissemination of information about psychology throughout China. The CPS organizes a national congress of psychology every 4 years.

11.2 EDUCATION AND TRAINING

In China, the education and training of psychology students are carried out in universities, research institutions, correspondence schools, vocational schools, and continuing education programs. Departments of psychology in comprehensive, medical, and teacher training universities, and at some military institutions, are the main settings where most undergraduate and graduate students are trained. Among them, the departments of psychology of Peking University and Beijing Normal University are most prominent because of their long history, quality of education, academic prestige, and the large number of students who have graduated from these institutions. Special research institutes of psychology, such as the Institute of Psychology of the Chinese Academy of Sciences, only train graduate students. In China, about 1,000 students graduate annually with bachelor's degrees and 500 students with master's or Ph.D. degrees. Correspondence schools and continuing education programs usually offer psychological courses to those who want to update their knowledge or obtain higher-education certificates such as a master's in business administration. Vocational schools train young students and adults, and confer licenses or certificates. As the importance of psychology is increasingly being recognized by society, China's comprehensive universities are planning to establish new departments of psychology. The government and educational institutions are also establishing vocational schools and continuing education programs for the training of psychologists. All of these measures have accelerated the training of psychologists and psychological practitioners to meet the needs of society.

11.2.1 Education and Training for the Bachelor's Degree

High-school students who prepare to study psychology in a university must take the National Entrance Examination. The examination subjects include Chinese, English, mathematics, and science (i.e., biology, chemistry, and physics). As psychology is one of the most popular majors at universities, the exam scores required for admission are higher than those of other majors at most universities.

The bachelor's curriculum consists of general courses and major courses. General courses include human anatomy, neuroanatomy, advanced mathematics, computer science, and a foreign language. Major courses include general psychology, cognitive psychology, developmental psychology, educational psychology, experimental psychology, physiological psychology, statistics, and psychological measurement. The psychological curriculum may be quite different in different university departments, depending on the nature and special requirements of the universities. For example, in the department of psychology of Beijing Normal University, the curriculum covers a wide range of psychology courses. Apart from general courses, it offers history of psychology, personality, psychopathology, social psychology, current issues in psychology, and other courses. The department of psychology of Peking University also offers psychopathology and psychotherapy.

To meet the demands of society, departments of applied psychology were founded in many universities where practical courses are offered. For instance, the department of psychology of Southwest Normal University offers courses in school counseling and sports psychology. The department of psychology of Shanghai Normal University offers courses in human resource management, advertising and market research, and school psychology. Currently, there are about 10 specialty tracks in applied psychology in Chinese universities; of these, human resource management and school counseling are the most popular.

The department of psychology in a university usually consists of teaching and research sections, experimental laboratories, and, occasionally, research centers or institutes. Internet systems and information resources are available to faculty members and students alike. Students have many opportunities to participate in scientific research and to join various academic and social activities.

11.2.2 Education and Training for Graduate Students

Applicants seeking admission to master's-degree programs take part in the National Entrance Examination. There are five subjects covered in the examination—the two general subjects of foreign language and politics, as prescribed by the National Examination Committee, and three major subjects prescribed by the university or institute recruiting the students. Competition among applicants is intense. The admission ratio is set nationally, with only one from every five applicants admitted; this ratio is even more stringent at China's leading universities.

It usually takes 3 years for a student to accumulate the required credits and complete the thesis required for the master's degree. The master's curriculum includes compulsory and selective courses. Compulsory courses are divided into two parts: general courses and major courses. Lectures are typically delivered in general courses, whereas class discussion is the primary mode of teaching in major courses. After accumulating sufficient credits, a master's student takes another year or two to complete the thesis under a professor's supervision and pass the oral defense. A successful thesis must demonstrate sound knowledge of the relevant field of psychology and appropriate research competency.

Applicants for the doctorate degree are required to have a master's degree and take part in the examination for admission mandated by the university. The exam typically includes a foreign language and two or three major subjects such as general psychology and experimental psychology. After passing the admission examination, first-year doctoral students complete their degree courses, including philosophy, a foreign language (usually English, German, or Japanese), and advanced courses related to their research interests. During the same year, they must also decide on the topic of their doctoral dissertations. Ability to conduct independent research is required for doctoral candidates, although they usually first work in a research team led by a professor, and participate as team members in lab meetings and academic activities (e.g., international collaboration and exchanges). Students may apply for funding from grant foundations with the permission of their mentor. There are also special programs established by the government for doctoral students to study abroad for short periods, from 3 months to 1 year. A successful dissertation should make an original contribution to scientific psychology and be worthy of publication in a reputable international journal.

Graduate study in psychology has been reformed in recent years. More and more students enter into doctoral programs directly after completing the required credits before obtaining a master's degree. It takes 4 or 5 years for these students to obtain their Ph.D. degrees.

In present-day China, students with education and training in psychology are able to find positions easily in government agencies, research and educational institutions, privately owned firms, and other applied settings. Psychology is becoming one of the most attractive fields for young people to choose as a career.

11.2.3 Financial Aid for Students

There are many kinds of financial aid for students in Chinese universities. Some financial aid comes from the government; other support comes from grants funded by individual and corporate donations. As bachelor's-degree candidates they must pay tuition and living expenses, and may face financial difficulties—especially, students from poor families. When they come to the university, they can apply for a loan, subsidy, or scholarship. Every university has an office dedicated to responding to and managing the financial needs of students.

Graduate students have fewer financial problems because their tuition and living expenses are included in the assistantship granted by universities. Furthermore, there are many kinds of financial awards available to graduate students. Graduate students are encouraged to work as administrative, research, or teaching assistants at the university, and allowed to work off-campus on a part-time basis.

11.2.4 Continuing Education

There is no official requirement that psychologists participate in continuing education activities during their careers. However, Chinese researchers and practitioners are eager to update their knowledge in various ways to better adapt to the rapid changes now taking place in China, and to cope with the new scientific advancements of the information age. The educational channels available to them include taking courses at continuing education institutions, passing the Adult National Foreign Language Examination and Comprehensive Major Course Examination to obtain higher degrees or certificates, studying or working as visiting scholars in other institutions at home or abroad, and participating in various kinds of training classes, correspondence and vocational schools, and workshops. The CPS also organizes some short training programs.

11.3 SCOPE OF PRACTICE

In the late 1970s, China adopted a market economy and implemented sweeping reforms in the transition from a planned economy as it began opening up to the outside world. Immense social changes and intense competition have caused a marked increase in the number of mental disorders. Improving people's mental health and their capacity to adjust to the social changes taking place in the country are of great importance to China's economic and social development. Under these circumstances, psychotherapy and psychological counseling developed rapidly in China, and recruitment and training of professional psychologists and the formulation of codes of conduct for practicing psychologists became an urgent concern. In 1993, the Regulations for Workers of Psychological Counseling and Psychotherapy in Health Systems was issued jointly by the CPS and the CMHA (Chinese Mental Health Association) (Chinese Psychological Society & Chinese Mental Health Association, 1993). The regulations laid out guidelines for the qualifications and responsibilities of a practitioner of psychotherapy and psychological counseling (Jing & Hu, 1998). Later, in 1999, the CPS and the CMHA developed documents that provided legal bases for psychotherapy and psychological counseling practices, and imposed a higher standard for workers in these fields.

With the development of psychology in China, new Chinese psychological tests were constructed. Many Western tests were also introduced to China, translated into Chinese, and normed on the Chinese population. In 1993, the CPS published the Regulations of Psychological Testing. This document included regulations for the appropriate use and management of psychological tests. The regulations pointed out that every member and organization under the aegis of the CPS has the responsibility to promote the correct and ethical practice of psychological assessment; this includes the sale of psychological tests as well as their use in research and clinical work. Simultaneously, the CPS also issued the Ethical Guidelines for Workers of Psychological Testing (Chinese Psychological Society, 1993a, 1993b) which embodied three principles. First, anyone who uses psychological tests in diagnosis, counseling, or personnel selection should meet the minimum qualifications approved by the Committee of Psychological Testing of the CPS. Second, the user should obey the principles of scientific objectivity in interpreting test results. Finally, the administration of the tests must not harm subjects in any way (Jing & Hu, 1998). These regulations have played a very important role in guiding the practice of psychological testing in China.

With the progress of economic globalization and China's entry into the World Trade Organization, China's economic and social development has prompted the Chinese government to pay more attention to professional psychology. In 2001, the Ministry of Labor and Social Security established regulations for the professional practice of psychological counseling. This was the first action by the government to regulate the professional conduct of psychological practitioners, and a special department within the Ministry was established to oversee the professional practice of psychology (Ministry of Labor and Social Security, PRC, 2001).

11.3.1 Work of Psychologists in Various Settings

Psychotherapy and psychological counseling. Chinese psychotherapy and psychological counseling began in the1960s. A seminal work on the synthetic treatment of neurasthenia had great influence throughout China; this treatment then developed into the more comprehensive, holistic psychotherapy (Li, 2001). In the 1980s, during China's reform period, psychotherapy and psychological counseling work developed steadily. In 1985, the CMHA was inaugurated and held its first national congress; subsequently psychological counseling centers were set up in Beijing and Shanghai, and in Hubei, Shandong and Shanxi provinces (Jing & Hu, 1998). In the beginning of the 1990s, the Committee of Psychological Counseling and Psychotherapy and the Committee of Student Psychological Counseling were established under the CPS. Psychotherapy and psychological counseling were no longer confined to hospitals but were made available through schools and local communities. Generally, the field can be divided into four parts: psychotherapy and psychological counseling in general hospitals, psychiatry in mental hospitals, psychological counseling in universities and schools, and community clinics for psychotherapy and psychological counseling.

There are outpatient departments of psychological counseling and psychotherapy in Chinese general hospitals. Some general hospitals have inpatient departments of psychosomatic diseases. Most medical psychologists are trained in medicine and receive additional training in psychology; they have prescription rights in hospitals. Other medical psychologists are trained in psychology, but they do not have prescription rights; and this has greatly restricted their performance.

In Chinese mental hospitals, psychiatrists treat patients with medicine and psychotherapy. They also work in psychological counseling centers and practice psychotherapy outside the hospital.

The mental health of students has become one of the most important problems in Chinese education. Psychological counseling centers have been set up in several universities and schools. Originally, most workers in these centers were part-time staff. Now, with the advancement of psychological counseling, the educational administrators have realized its importance and recruited more full-time staff. As for the professional background of the staff members in these counseling centers, some have been trained in psychology or medicine, but most come from other fields. It was suggested that psychological counseling in universities and schools should not only resolve students' mental problems, but should also help to establish new and constructive interpersonal relationships on campus to ensure a better adaptation to society upon graduation. In this regard, Chinese psychologists are working toward modernizing education.

Often, medical psychologists, psychiatrists, and applied psychologists work together in clinics that provide services to the public. Most psychotherapy or counseling clinics are supported by local governments; a few are supported by private institutions. Some NGOs, such as the Jinglun Family Science Center, offer free psychological counseling to the public and have a good reputation in society. Additionally, more and more psychological counseling hotlines have appeared on radio and TV. Special features on psychological counseling are often published in magazines and newspapers.

The development of Chinese psychotherapy and psychological counseling was influenced by Western theories and techniques as well as Chinese traditional medicine. Behavior therapy, client-centered therapy, cognitive therapy, supportive psychotherapy, Morita therapy, and psychoanalysis have all been integrated with traditional Chinese medicine. Cognitive-apprehension therapy, developed by Zhong Youbin (1998), is a good example of the synthesis of psychodynamic therapy and Chinese culture. In cognitive-apprehension therapy, the therapist encourages spontaneity in the clients in order for them to gain a more complete understanding of their disorder. A cure may come about when the patient apprehends the nature of the problem and brings into awareness that which had been unconscious. This therapy is also called *Chinese psychoanalysis*.

Some other prominent Chinese orientations in therapeutic practice are:

1. The directive orientation in which the therapist uses didactic and instructional methods to effect change.
2. The integrative orientation, influenced by traditional Chinese philosophy, in which the therapist analyzes the causes

of mental problems and disorders from a holistic point of view.

3. The natural orientation, based on the naturalism of Chinese Taoism, in which therapists attempt to follow "natural laws" in their practice.

Because most theories and techniques of psychotherapy and psychological counseling in China were imported from Western countries, the adaptation of these approaches to suit Chinese culture has become crucial to the profession. Recently, Chinese clinical psychologists conducted research to determine the effectiveness of indigenous theories and techniques rather than trying to adapt exclusively Western approaches to the sociocultural context of contemporary China.

Managerial psychology and industrial psychology. During the past two decades, Chinese managerial and industrial psychologists have focused on the development of a theoretical foundation for their field. Adopting a holistic approach derived from Chinese traditional culture, Chinese managerial and industrial psychologists have moved away from a laboratory-oriented theoretical model to a multidisciplinary, problem-oriented model. This development was facilitated by the process of reform in management under way in China (Wang, 2001).

The main features of recent developments in managerial and industrial psychology in China include the development of indigenous theories, the implementation of reforms to management, and the advancement of advertising and consumer psychology.

Chinese psychologists have put forth several innovated theories and models related to managerial and industrial psychology (Yu, 2001), including (a) synchronization motivation theory, which holds that high motivation for power can occur when both natural human needs and social needs are considered (i.e., an integrative index of material and spiritual motivations); (b) equity difference threshold theory, which emphasizes the perceptions of fairness in different conditions; (c) motivator and de-motivator continuum theory; (d) integration-assimilation theory, based on studies of cross-cultural management in multinational corporations, which provides a new avenue for solving problems caused by cultural conflict; and (e) the CPM leadership behavior model (the C factor is character and morale; the P factor is performance; the M factor is maintenance), constructed on documented differences between Chinese and Western models of leadership, in which Chinese leadership is based more on moral values than on the maintenance or improvement of performance.

Chinese psychologists have been intensely involved in efforts to resolve problems arising from the reformation of managerial practices. The influence of economic globalization has made it necessary to restructure the organization of state enterprises. In the process of the restructuring of state enterprises, research on changes in the decision-making styles of managers and psychosocial adjustment of workers promises a smooth organizational transformation. Organizational psychologists in China are currently investigating the influences of cultural development, organizational commitment and errors, psychological interactions among employees, and social norms in organizations. Recently, the focus of personnel assessment has changed from the assessment of employees to that of managers (Shi, 2001). The competence model plays a key role in the assessment and selection of senior managers at larger state enterprises such as China Telecom and China Mobile.

The psychological assessment of aircraft pilots and astronauts for recruitment is another important application of organizational psychology in China. Industrial psychologists have set assessment standards and selection methods appropriate to this task, which include activity observation, expert interviews, and task assessment. These researches have led to the formulation of national standards for the recruitment of pilots and astronauts.

To meet the social needs of displaced workers, Fang (2001) devised and implemented "Successful Job Search," a program designed to heighten workers' self-esteem in order to enhance their ability to learn new skills and to increase the likelihood of reemployment. Displaced workers who participated in this program had a significantly higher rate of reemployment than those who did not participate.

Since the 1980s, advertising in China has boomed, becoming an industry in its own right. For example, the Institute of Psychology of the Chinese Academy of Sciences developed a factorial system of trademark evaluation (Ma, 2001). At present, the systematic manipulation of the features of brand products to improve their visibility and prestige, and the cognitive effect of Web site advertising are the latest directions in advertising and research in Chinese consumer psychology.

Although engineering psychology in China has a short history, it has great relevance and vitality. Engineering psychology laboratories with advanced equipment were established in the Institute of Psychology of the Chinese Academy of Sciences and at Zhejiang University. Chinese psychologists have conducted ergonomic studies on illumination, visual display, and mental workload. With the development of industrial psychology and the popularization of computers, human–computer interaction has become the main focus of engineering psychology in China.

Forensic psychology. By becoming familiar with research in forensic psychology conducted in other countries and by investigating criminal behavior and anti-crime practices in China, Chinese psychologists established their own specialty of forensic psychology. The classification of crimes, causes for criminal acts, and comprehensive theories of criminal behavior are some of the issues that Chinese forensic psychologists study. In addition, forensic psychologists have investigated influences on eyewitness testimony and delineated basic standards for collecting evidence. Other research has centered on the application of psychological principles to judicial review and rehabilitation programs in prisons. Studies have also revealed the variables that influence eyewitness testimony and criminal confession. After more than 10 years' effort, the domain of forensic psychology is well established in China.

China has about 700 correctional facilities in 28 cities and provinces where thousands of psychotherapists, social workers, and trained psychological assistants are employed. Over 60% of the country's prisons have adopted some program geared toward the psychological rehabilitation of inmates. To meet the demand for the psychological rehabilitation and diagnosis of criminals, to assess treatment results, and to predict the rate of second offences, the

Criminal Personality Inventory was developed. This assessment tool, which has national norms and is available in a software version, is currently administered in many of the prisons in China. Work on the Criminal Personality Inventory has contributed to the effective treatment of inmates' psychological problems and to the reform of China's prison system (He, 2001).

Sports psychology. In the late 1970s, the establishment of the Committee of Sports Psychology within the CPS and the Committee of Sports Psychology in China's Sport Science Society marked the beginning of Chinese sports psychology. The main tasks of Chinese sports psychologists are the appraisal of psychological characteristics of outstanding athletes, selection of child and teen athletes, and implementation of psychological training and counseling for athletes and coaches. The psychological problems associated with intense competition are also studied. In the future, Chinese sports psychology will likely absorb pertinent advances in other fields of psychology such as cognitive psychology and psychology of learning, focus on the refinement of assessment devices, extend its domain of inquiry to include physical education, and upgrade the quality of training necessary for successful competition (Zhang & Ding, 1994).

11.4 FUTURE CHALLENGES AND PROSPECTS

The development of psychology in China over the past 80 years, especially during the last two decades, has laid the foundation for its promising development in the future,

both as a scientific discipline and as an applied profession. However, many obstacles and problems must be resolved before that promise can be fully realized.

Compared to other scientific disciplines and applied professions in China today, psychology is lagging behind. The reasons for this may be found in China's traditional culture and socioeconomic environment, and in the nature of psychology itself. For a long period in history, the government, the public, and even the scientific community did not view psychology as an important scientific discipline or as a potential contributor to social development. As of today, the number of Chinese psychologists relative to China's 1.3 billion population is far from adequate; hence, psychology has yet to realize its potential influence on Chinese government and society (Jing & Fu, 2001). The status of the psychological health of the Chinese people throughout the nation needs to be investigated in order to provide better service. We believe that education and the popularization of mental health will eventually help to promote the material and spiritual well-being of the people.

China is now undergoing a process of economic and social transformation. The rapid changes associated with this transformation have presented both problems and challenges in the areas of education, mental health, population growth, and social stability. These changes have also resulted in the tension between globalization and China's traditional values. The realities facing China today provide psychology, as a discipline and a profession, with a panoply of opportunities to utilize its scientific and practical capabilities as well as to stimulate its further development (Jing & Zhang, 1996). Some psychologists have shifted from a laboratory-oriented, pure theoretical model to a problem-oriented, multidisciplinary applied research model as social needs are always the most powerful driving force for the development of science and technology. The coming generation will see a rapid growth in the number of Chinese psychologists, as well as many noticeable achievements in Chinese psychology. Chinese psychologists—with their scientific research and applied practice deeply rooted in traditional culture yet intimately tied to economic and social modernization—will undoubtedly make distinctive contributions to world psychology as the 21st century unfolds.

REFERENCES

Chinese Psychological Society. (1993a). Ethical guidelines for workers of psychological testing. *Acta Psychologica Sinica, 25,* 222.

Chinese Psychological Society. (1993b). The regulations for psychological testing. *Acta Psychologica Sinica, 25,* 221–222.

Chinese Psychological Society & Chinese Mental Health Association. (1993). The regulations for workers of psychological counseling and psychotherapy in health systems. *Acta Psychologica Sinica, 25,* 223–224.

Fang, L. L. (2001). Psychology research in human resources. In Chinese Psychological Society (Ed.), *Contemporary Chinese psychology* (pp. 503–506). Beijing: People's Education Press.

He, W. M. (2001). The application of psychological correction in Chinese prisons. In Chinese Psychological Society (Ed.), *Contemporary Chinese psychology* (pp. 465–469). Beijing: People's Education Press.

Jing, Q. C., & Fu, X. L. (2001). Modern Chinese psychology: Its indigenous roots and international influences. *International Journal of Psychology, 36,* 408–418.

Jing, Q. C., & Hu, P. C. (1998). The development of standards and the regulation of the practice of clinical psychology in China. In A. N. Wiens (Ed.), *Comprehensive clinical psychology: Vol. 2. Professional issues* (pp. 73–82). New York: Pergamon.

Jing, Q. C., & Zhang, H. C. (1996). China's reform and challenges for psychology. In J. G. Adair, D. Belanger, & K. L. Dion (Eds.), *Advances in psychological science: Vol. 1. Social, personal, and cultural aspects* (pp. 271–291). Hove, UK: Psychology Press.

Li, X. T. (2001). Studies of Psycho-somatic relation on medical psychology: Wu-Jian therapy. In Chinese Psychological Society (Ed.), *Contemporary Chinese psychology* (pp. 159–163). Beijing: People's Education Press.

Ma, M. C. (2001). Some studies in advertising and consumer psychology research. In Chinese Psychological Society (Ed.), *Contemporary Chinese psychology* (pp. 476–480). Beijing: People's Education Press.

Ministry of Labor and Social Security, People's Republic of China. (2001). *The National Professional Regulation for Psychological Counselors.* Beijing, People's Republic of China: Central Radio and TV University Press.

Qian, M. Y. (2001). The development of psychotherapy and counseling in China. In Chinese Psychological Society (Ed.), *Contemporary Chinese psychology* (pp. 174–179). Beijing: People's Education Press.

Wang, Z. M. (2001). The development of managerial psychology and approaches to strategic human resource management. In Chinese Psychological Society (Ed.), *Contemporary Chinese psychology* (pp. 496–502). Beijing: People's Education Press.

Yang, X. H., & Zhao L. R. (2000). *The history of Chinese modern psychology.* Jinan, People's Republic of China: Shandong Education Press.

Yang, Y. F. (2003). Chinese psychology: Its current status and future prospect. *Bulletin of National Natural Science Foundation of China, 37,* 141–145.

Yu, W. Z. (2001). The development of managerial and economic psychology in China. In Chinese Psychological Society (Ed.), *Contemporary Chinese psychology* (pp. 486–491). Beijing: People's Education Press.

Zhang, L. W., & Ding, X. Q. (1994). Development of sport psychology in China: History, present status, and prospects. *Acta Psychologica Sinica, 26,* 324–330.

Zhong, Y. B. (1998). *Chinese psychonomic: Cognitive apprehension therapy.* Shenyang, People's Republic of China: Liaoning People's Press.

IMPORTANT PUBLICATIONS

Chen, Y. M. (2001). *Contemporary Chinese psychology.* Beijing: People's Education Press.

Jing, Q. C., & Fu, X. L. (2001). Modern Chinese psychology: Its indigenous roots and international influences. *International Journal of Psychology, 36,* 408–418.

Jing, Q. C., & Hu, P. C. (1998). The development of standards and the regulation of the practice of clinical psychology in China. In A. N. Wiens (Ed.), *Comprehensive clinical psychology:* Vol. 2. *Professional issues* (pp. 73–82). New York: Pergamon.

Jing, Q. C., & Zhang, H. C. (1996). China's reform and challenges for psychology. In J. G. Adair, D. Belanger, & K. L. Dion (Eds.), *Advances in psychological science: Vol. 1. Social, personal, and cultural aspects* (pp. 271–291). Hove, UK: Psychology Press.

Lin, W. J., & Sui, N. (2003). Research on biopsychology in China. *International Journal of Psychology, 38,* 138–149.

Ling, W. Q., Rosina, C., & Li, L. F. (2000). Chinese implicit leadership theory. *Journal of Social Psychology, 140,* 729–739.

Wang, S., Lin, Z. X., & Jing, Q. C. (1997). *Psychological science in China.* Changchun, People's Republic of China: Jinlin Education Press.

Wang, Z. M. (1992). Culture, economic reform, and the role of industrial/organizational psychology in China. In M. D. Dunnette & L. M. Hough (Eds.), *Handbook of industrial and organizational psychology* (2nd ed., pp. 689–726). Palo Alto, CA: Consulting Psychologists Press.

Wu, N. N., Zhou, X. L., & Shu, H. (1999). Sublexical processing in reading Chinese: A developmental study. *Language and Cognitive Processes, 14,* 503–524.

Yang, X. H. (2000). *General history of psychology.* Jinan, People's Republic of China: Shandong Education Press.

CHAPTER 12

Psychology in Japan

JUNKO TANAKA-MATSUMI AND KANAKO OTSUI

Junko Tanaka-Matsumi is a professor in the Department of Integrated Psychological Science, Kwansei Gakuin University, Nishinomiya City, Japan, and is also a professor emeritus of psychology at Hofstra University in New York, where she taught clinical psychology for 20 years until 2000. She received her Ph.D. in clinical psychology from the University of Hawaii at Manoa on an East–West Center graduate scholarship. A Fellow of the American Psychological Association and an associate editor of the Journal of Cross-Cultural Psychology, *she also serves on the editorial boards of* Psychological Assessment: A Journal of Consulting and Clinical Psychology, Asian Journal of Social Psychology, *and the* Multicultural Aspects in Counseling *series of Sage Publications.*

Kanako Otsui, M.A., is a doctoral candidate in the Department of Psychology, Kwansei Gakuin University. She obtained her bachelor's and master's in psychology from Kwansei Gakuin University, and also studied psychology as a special exchange

student at the University of North Carolina in the United States. She specializes in developmental clinical psychology and conducts research on social skills training of Japanese children and participates in Kobe city's educational intervention project to assist children with learning and behavioral problems in the classroom.

12.1 OVERVIEW

The English word *psychology* is routinely translated today as *shinrigaku* (心理学) in Japanese. This translation settled in the Japanese literature around 1877 when Amane Nishi translated the Western literature on "mental philosophy" into Japanese (Sato & Mizoguchi, 1997). Today, *shinrigaku* is an established discipline of psychology in Japanese academia as well as a popular word among the general public.

The history of modern psychology in Japan reflects the zeitgeist of Japan's sweeping societal reform called the Meiji

Restoration, which started in 1868 when Japan reopened its doors to Western countries after nearly 250 years of international isolation. Japan had shut down communication with the world at a critical time—just when Western countries were developing science and undergoing industrialization. Japanese citizens were not allowed to leave Japan, and overseas Japanese were not permitted to return to Japan during the legally enforced period of isolation. After the prolonged isolation, to catch up with the technological progress of the Western industrial world, the new Meiji government launched a series of reform programs in administrative, economic, social, legal, educational, and military domains. In addition, the Japanese government sent students to study modern science and technology in Europe and the United States. The early developmental history of psychology in Japan was distinguished by modeling and adapting Western psychological science as taught and researched in Europe and the United States.

The development of psychological science in Japan owes much to two great scholars of tremendous vitality and creativity: Yujiro Motora (1858–1912) and his student, Matataro Matsumoto (1865–1943). Both obtained their Ph.D.s in the United States In 1888, Motora gave Japan's first formal lecture on scientific psychology at the Imperial University of Tokyo. He studied experimental psychology under G. Stanley Hall at Johns Hopkins University and obtained his Ph.D. from Johns Hopkins only 9 years after Wundt had founded the world's first psychological laboratory in Leipzig in 1879. Motora's doctoral dissertation was entitled "Exchange: Considered as the Principle of Social Life." Hall and Motora (1887) published a manuscript in the first volume of the *American Journal of Psychology* on Weber's law and dermal sensitivity to gradual pressure changes. Motora also published a series of research papers entitled "Psychophysics," focusing on such topics as attention span and its relationship to children's learning (Hidano, 1998; Osaka, 1998, Oyama & Sato, 1999).

Matataro Matsumoto established Japan's first psychological laboratory at the Imperial University of Tokyo in 1903, and a second one at the Imperial University of Kyoto in 1906 (Osaka, 1999; Oyama, Sato, & Suzuki, 2001). Matsumoto's doctoral dissertation at Yale University in 1899 was entitled "Research in Acoustic Space," and was sponsored by E. W. Scripture. Edward Tichener (1901) quoted Matsumoto's experiment on acoustic space in his text *Experimental Psychology* (Hidano, 1998). Matsumoto also studied psychology under Wilhelm Wundt at the University of Leipzig, and played a major role in the development of both experimental and applied psychology in Japan. Matsumoto trained a number of able graduate students who later became influential psychologists establishing psychology departments and laboratories in other parts of Japan.

Between 1923 and 1931, additional psychological laboratories were established in major Japanese universities including Kwansei Gakuin University (1923), Nihon University (1923), Tohoku University (1923), Keio University (1926), Doshisha University (1927), Kyushu University (1927), Hiroshima Bunrika University (1929), Tokyo Bunrika University (1929; now, the University of Tsukuba), and Waseda University (1931). There were a total of 15 university-based psychological laboratories prior to World War II (Japanese Psychological Association [JPA], 2002).

In the 1930s and 1940s, the predominant research activities of Japanese psychologists focused on experimental psychology, specifically the areas of perception and sensation. Kanae Sakuma (1888–1970) of Kyushu Imperial University was sent to the University of Berlin in 1923 to study Gestalt psychology under Wolfgang Köhler. By the 1950s, Japanese psychologists had adopted the conceptual and empirical foundations of German Gestalt psychology represented by Köhler, Kurt Lewin, Max Wertheimer, and Kurt Koffka (Sakuma, 1999). Topics such as apparent movements, memory trace, optical illusions, perceptual constancies, and perceptual organization are still very strong areas of interest among Japanese research psychologists (e.g., Oyama, 1997). Tanaka and England (1972) gave an excellent overview of experimental psychological work conducted in Japan during the maturing years of experimental work and formative years of applied psychology prior to the 1970s.

Japanese psychologists also actively adopted the specialty of tests and measures, and published standardized intelligence tests and personality inventories (Oyama, Sato, & Suzuki, 2001; Sukemune, 1992). By the 1930s, Japanese translations of Sigmund Freud's collected works were available to the Japanese public. The psychiatrist Kiyoyasu Marui (1886–1953) conducted Japan's first lecture series on psychoanalysis at Tohoku University in 1923. Marui studied psychoanalysis under Adolf Meyer at Johns Hopkins University. Psychologist Megumi Imada (1894–1970) introduced J. B. Watson's behaviorism and William James' functionalism to Japanese psychology, and opened an experimental psychology lab at Kwansei Gakuin University in 1923 (Imada, 2001) where, in 1939, Yasho Kotake launched Japan's first conditioning research with human participants (Kotake & Miyata, 1958). Japanese psychologists adapted the works of various learning theorists including Ivan Pavlov, Clark Hull, Edward C. Tolman, and B. F. Skinner, and conducted laboratory experiments on classical and operant conditioning (Imada & Nakajima, 2003; Kotake & Miyata, 1973; Oyama et al., 2001). Following this tradition, the Japanese psychologist Masaya Sato of Keio University was elected president of the International Association of Behavior Analysis in 1997.

Organizationally, as scientific psychology began spreading across the Japanese university system, Matsumoto founded the Japanese Psychological Association (JPA) in 1927. The JPA is the oldest professional psychological organization in Japan. A total of 190 psychologists participated in the 1st annual meeting of the JPA, held at the University of Tokyo, and gave 66 presentations. In contrast, 75 years later in 2001, the 65th annual meeting of the JPA hosted 2,731 participants and accommodated 1,083 presentations (Japanese Psychological Association, 2002). The JPA's membership reached 6,522 by 2002.

The purpose of the JPA is to advance scientific psychology through the collaborative efforts of all members (JPA, n.d.). To this end, the JPA holds an annual convention, organizes a liaison committee to promote research collaboration among members, disseminates information concerning the scientific activities of members, makes contacts with national and international organizations in psychology and allied disciplines, and publishes periodicals as outlets of new knowledge. The JPA has five major divisions: (a) perception, physiology, thinking, and learning; (b) development and education; (c) clinical psychology, personality, forensics, and rehabilitation; (d) social, industrial, and cultural; and (e) methodology, principles, history, and general psychology (JPA, 2002). The JPA publishes three periodicals: the *Japanese Journal of Psychology* in Japanese on a bimonthly basis, a quarterly journal of the *Japanese Psychological Research* in English, and a more popular quarterly magazine, *Psychology World,* in Japanese.

Prior to World War II, there were only three psychological associations in Japan: the JPA (established in 1927), the Japanese Association of Applied Psychology (established in 1931), and the Japanese Society for Animal Psychology (established in 1933). The development of other psychological associations was both steady and diversified. In 1999, the leadership of the JPA established the Japanese Union of Psychological Associations (JUPA) in order to coordinate the diverse activities of a rapidly growing number of psychological associations. The JUPA includes 38 national psychological associations (see Table 12.1). The Science Council of Japan (SCJ) oversees the activities of all major academic organizations. The SCJ is affiliated with the Japanese government via the Ministry of Public Management, Home Affairs, Posts, and Telecommunications. The SCJ is affiliated with various international academic institutions.

The JPA is a national member of the International Union of Psychological Science (IUPsyS). The IUPsyS was founded in 1951 as an umbrella international organization supporting the development of basic and applied psychological science. Although the JPA is the oldest and most

comprehensive psychological organization in Japan, the Association of Japanese Clinical Psychology (AJCP), established in 1982, has emerged as the largest professional psychological organization with over 14,000 full or associate members. The Japanese Association of Educational Psychology is similarly large with its membership exceeding 7000.

Scientists and practitioners in Japanese psychology have tended to coexist as separate professional groups until recent years. Less than 10 years ago, Imada (1996a) introduced the integrative scientist–practitioner training model in psychology (the so-called Boulder model) to Japanese psychologists. The Boulder scientist–practitioner model has been successfully practiced in the United States for more than 50 years. Although there is a growing tendency to advocate evidence-based clinical psychology in Japan, its academic and professional status is yet to be firmly established.

Japanese psychologists hosted the 20th International Congress of Psychology in 1972 at Tokyo, which was attended by 2,562 participants from 52 countries (Sato & Mizoguchi, 1997). The 22nd International Congress of Applied Psychology was held in 1990 at Kyoto with 1,727 participants from 48 countries. These two major international conventions promoted international perspectives on the professional activities of Japanese psychologists. In addition, Japanese psychologists hosted the 1st International Congress of Family Psychology (Tokyo, 1990), the International Congress of Health Psychology (Tokyo, 1993), the 3rd International Congress of Behaviorism and Applied Behavioral Sciences (Yokohama, 1996), and the 2nd meet-

TABLE 12.1

The Member Organizations of the Japanese Union of Psychological Associations

Name of Association	Founded
The Japanese Psychological Association	*1927*
The Japan Association of Applied Psychology	*1931*
The Japanese Society for Animal Psychology	*1933*
The Japanese Group Dynamics Association	*1949*
The Japanese Society of Theoretical Psychology	*1956*
Japanese Society of Hypnosis	*1956*
The Japanese Association of Educational Psychology	*1959*
The Japanese Society of Social Psychology	*1960*
The Japanese Association of Criminal Psychology	*1963*
The Japanese Association of Special Education	*1963*
The Japanese Association of Clinical Psychology	*1964*
The Japanese Association of Counseling Science	*1967*
The Japanese Society of Youth and Adolescent Psychology	*1968*
Japanese Society of Biofeedback Research	*1973*
The Behavior Metric Society of Japan	*1973*
The Japanese Association for Behavior Therapy	*1976*
The Japanese Society for Study of Career Guidance	*1977*
The Japanese Society of Autogenic Therapy	*1978*
The Japanese Association for Behavior Analysis	*1979*
The Japanese Psychonomic Society	*1981*
The Japanese Association of Traffic Psychology	*1982*
The Association of Japanese Clinical Psychology	*1982*
The Japanese Association for Humanistic Psychology	*1982*
The Japanese Association for Rehabilitation Psychology	*1983*
Japanese Society for Physiological Psychology and Psychophysiology	*1983*
Japanese Association of Family Psychology	*1984*
The Japanese Association for Industrial and Organizational Psychology	*1985*
The Japanese Association for Sand Play Therapy	*1987*

TABLE 12.1
Continued

The Japanese Association for Student Counseling	*1987*
The Japanese Association of School Counseling and Guidance	*1987*
The Japanese Association of Health Psychology	*1988*
Japan Society of Developmental Psychology	*1989*
The Japanese Association for Brief Therapy	*1991*
The Japanese Association for Dohsa-hoa (Psychological Rehabilitation)	*1991*
Japan Society for Research on Emotions	*1992*
The Japanese Association for Personality Psychology	*1992*
The Japanese Association for Behavioral Science Research	*1994*
The Japanese Association of Industrial Counseling	*1996*

ing of the Asian Society of Social Psychology (Kyoto, 1997). The World Congress of Cognitive and Behavioral Therapies will be held in 2004 at Kobe under the sponsorships of the Japanese Association for Behavior Therapy, the Japanese Association for Behavior Analysis, and the Japanese Association for Cognitive Therapy. The number for Japanese psychologists attending international meetings has also increased steadily.

12.2 EDUCATION AND TRAINING

By 2002, Japan's population reached 127,435,000. Japan is a rapidly aging society; more than 18.5% of the current population is over 65 years of age, and the country has a dramatically reduced birth rate. Japan's population increased by only 0.11% in the past year, which is the lowest growth rate in the 50 years since World War II. It is estimated that there are approximately 20,000 psychologists in Japan

across different academic areas of specialty. This would give us a ratio of about 8 psychologists per 100,000. However, this is an overestimation if we wanted to find the ratio of professional psychologists in practice. This ratio would most likely go down to less than 5 per 100,000 if we counted only those who are certified by different organizations such as the Japanese Certification Board for Clinical Psychology, which has certified a cumulative total of 10,083 psychologists. There are other agencies issuing other certifications. Therefore, our conservative estimate is around 5 per 100,000.

Psychology is expected to play an important role in enhancing the quality of life in Japan. In 2002, a total of 48.6% of high school graduates (48.8% of males and 48.5% of females) advanced to universities (Ministry of Education, Culture, Sports, Science, and Technology, 2002). There are 686 universities in Japan. Of these, 14.4% are national, 10.9% are public, and 74.7% are private universities. Psychology is one of the most popular undergraduate and graduate majors in Japan. Within psychology, clinical psychology is the most popular specialty area.

In Japan, nearly 200 universities offer undergraduate and graduate training in psychology in either psychology departments or in departments of related disciplines such as education, sociology, and social welfare (Takuma & Yamamoto, 1996). University entrance examinations are national preoccupations in Japan. They are very competitive because university ranks and reputations have much to do with a student's future employment opportunities and advancement within Japanese society. Admission criteria for undergraduate programs in psychology include competitive entrance examinations on several academic subjects from both required (Japanese and English) and elective domains (e.g., biology, chemistry, geography, history, mathematics, and physics). Each university gives its own entrance examination. In addition, national universities practice the Center Examination System, administering a national exam to all students in order to rank their standardized test scores to qualify for specific schools.

Undergraduate psychology majors are trained in both basic and applied psychology, research methodology, and statistics. Students also participate in practica that involve experiments and surveys. Table 12.2 presents a list of possible course offerings in an undergraduate psychology program developed by the Japanese Psychological Association (2002) as part of certification system for psychologists. In applied psychology, students can be trained in clinically relevant supervised activities such as assisting children in schools or helping patients in hospitals. Furthermore, undergraduate practica also include more specialized activities such as case studies, counseling, and psychological testing (Ogawa & Nagai, 1997). Senior theses are required in the majority of undergraduate psychology programs, and many emphasize empirical research.

As for pedagogical methods, Japanese professors use textbooks, articles, and audiovisual material in the classroom. A number of psychology textbooks published in the United States and the United Kingdom have been translated into Japanese. For example, Zimbardo's (1980) popular introductory psychology textbook *Essentials of Psychology and Life* was translated into Japanese in 1983. The Japanese translation of Atkinson, Atkinson, and Fredrickson's (2002) *Hilgard's Introduction to Psychology* was published following the original publication in the United States. Japanese psychologists have developed their own basic psychology texts and experimental psychology manuals, as well as texts of specific domains within psychology. At more advanced levels, some influential Western volumes in psychology are available as Japanese translations. Major university libraries subscribe to a rich collection of psychology periodicals published in English.

Internet psychological resources are also available, and all the major Japanese psychological organizations have home pages on the Internet. Japanese psychologists and students use the Internet for literature searches, communication among colleagues and students, and electronic journal subscriptions. Universities are promoting the use of electronic bulletin boards, although this feature is not widely used. Major Japanese universities subscribe to PsycINFO, which is the American Psychological Association's database of psy-

TABLE 12.2

Undergraduate Courses in Psychology to needed Apply for Certification as a Psychologist by the Japanese Psychological Association (2002)

I. Basic Courses (more than 12 credits)

A. *Psychology*

      Fundamentals of Psychology

      History, Behavioral Science

      Fundamentals of Educational Psychology

B. *Research Methods in Psychology, Psychological Measurements*

      Research Design, Statistics, Survey Methods, Observation Methods,

      Interview Methods, Scales and Measurement, Personality Assessment,

      Psychological Testing

C. *Psychological Experiments, Psychology Practicum*

      Basic Experiments in Behavioral Science, Educational Psychology,

      Social Psychology, etc.

      Practicum in Educational Psychology, Behavioral Science,

      Clinical Psychology, Social Psychology, etc.

II. Elective Courses (more than 26 credits)

D. *Learning*

      Conditioning, Cognitive Learning, Language Learning, Memory,

      Reasoning

E. *Perception*

      Sensation, Perception, Cognition, Information Processing, etc.

F. *Educational Psychology*

      Educational Measurement, Educational Evaluation, Psychology in the

      Classroom, Psychology of Teachers, Academically Difficult Students,

      Caring for Special Children, Parent–Child Relationship, etc.

G. *Developmental Psychology*

      Infants, Toddlers, Children, Adolescents, the Elderly, Infant Development,

      Cognition, Personality, Learning, Culture and Development, Disability and Development

H. *Comparative Psychology*

      Animal Psychology, Comparative Behavioral Science, etc.

      Physiological Psychology, Neurological Psychology, Brain Physiology,

      Neurophysiology, Psychophysiology, etc.

I. *Clinical Psychology*

      Clinical Psychology, Mental Health, Psychiatry, Psychotherapy,

TABLE 12.2

Continued

Psychosomatic Medicine, Behavioral Medicine, Counseling,

Childhood Disorders, Behavioral Disorders, Psychological Assessment,

Adjustment Disorders, Forensic Psychology, Personality

Educational Counseling, Ego Psychology

J. Social Psychology, Group Dynamics

Disaster Psychology, Human Relationship, Group Behavior,

Interpersonal Cognition, Communication, Mass Communication,

Industrial, Organizational Psychology,

Labor Science, Human Engineering, Consumer Behavior,

Occupational Psychology

Environmental Psychology

Culture and Psychology

Family Psychology, Community Psychology

K. Other Allied Disciplines, Senior Graduation Thesis

---

chological literature from around the world. Computer labs are routinely used to present visual and auditory stimuli, run experiments, and perform data storage and analyses. Students have access to major statistical software packages such as the popular SPSS and SAS in computer labs. Academic and professional workshops are offered at all major psychology conventions for continuing education of professional psychologists and students.

In an age of sociocultural diversity, the University of the Air was established in 1982 as an innovative way to meet the needs for higher education of the Japanese people of all ages and walks of life. Courses are taught via television, cable television, radio, or at learning centers using videotaped lectures. Students can earn a bachelor's degree in a variety of academic disciplines including psychology. Over 100,000 students have enrolled in the University of the Air in the 22 years since its inception.

Admission to graduate programs is based on entrance examinations and interviews. In Japan, the majority of graduate students seek admission to the same university where they received their undergraduate education. This educational practice seems to reinforce Japan's hierarchical social structure and to create familiar coteries where members spend a great deal of time together. Traditionally, students and trainees are apprenticed into specific professors' seminars and research groups and are thus trained in specialized areas of psychology. Outstanding advanced graduate students may be funded competitively for their training and research with fellowships provided by the Japan Society for the Promotion of Science and other limited funding sources. However, graduate schools in Japan do not routinely provide full tuition waivers for teaching and research assistants, who are relatively few in number.

Japanese graduate programs have begun reorganizing graduate curricula to enable qualified doctoral candidates to earn their Ph.D.s after 5 years of training. Traditionally, graduate students completed all course requirements and left graduate school without completing their doctoral dissertation, particularly in the fields of humanities and social sciences. Doctoral dissertations have been considered a major career accomplishment rather than a demarcation point for the completion of graduate training or the beginning of an independent career.

Within the JPA membership, in the 20 years between 1982 and 2002, the number of doctoral degrees in psychology increased sixfold (Japanese Psychological Association, 2002). In 1982, only 10% of the members of the JPA held the doctorate. In 2002, the ratio increased to 24%. According to another survey (Takuma & Yamamoto, 1996), the number of graduate psychology majors has increased steadily between 1986 and 1995 at both master's and doctoral levels. A total of 473 doctorates were awarded in psychology between 1986 and 1995. Men earned 80.3% and women earned 19.7% of the doctoral degrees in psychology. The number of doctoral degrees granted in psychology accounted for 7.4% of the entire number of doctorates ($N = 6,398$) granted during the same 10-year period throughout Japan. Clearly, in line with Japan's increased emphasis on structural reforms in graduate education and the societal need for more trained professionals, the number of graduate students has risen substantially. Those successfully obtaining doctoral degrees have increased accordingly.

According to Imada's (1996a) analysis of the JPA membership data, 30.1% of university faculty members in psychology across ranks had doctoral degrees. In Japan, psychology graduate programs are housed mostly within the university schools of humanities or social sciences. Within these schools, the ratio of doctoral degrees to the number of graduate students completing the course requirements was only 22.9% for the humanities and 29.2% for the social sciences in 1998. The ratio was 88.3% for the natural sciences and 89.8% for engineering (Ministry of Education, Culture, Sports, Science, and Technology, n.d.). Because psychologists in Japan are working more frequently on multidisciplinary research projects with natural scientists, it is imperative that psychology graduate programs develop structured curricula to ensure that qualified candidates will complete and successfully defend their doctoral dissertations during their tenure as graduate students (Takahashi & Hatano, 1996).

12.3 SCOPE OF PSYCHOLOGICAL PRACTICE

Historically, Japanese society has valued on-the-job training of basically bachelor's-level employees. Prospective graduates with bachelor's degrees can sit for civil service examinations for jobs in psychology. Japanese psychologists typically work in four settings: educational, medical and social welfare, forensic, and labor and industry. More specifically, they work in educational institutions providing counseling, national and regional civil service facilities such as child guidance clinics and juvenile evaluation centers, research institutes, medical facilities, social welfare agencies, police and correctional facilities, or business and industrial settings. In recent years, business and industry have employed an increased number of psychologists. Their main role is to counsel employees who might complain of symptoms of anxiety, depression, and other adjustment difficulties due in part to the prolonged economic recession and consequent organizational restructuring throughout Japan.

Psychologists' salaries in Japan are commensurate with those of other specialized civil service workers if they work in relevant civil service settings. Very few full-time jobs for professional, practicing psychologists exist in Japan with benefits and compensations. Thus, independent practice is not a prevalent practice in Japan.

Aside from universities, national and private research centers employ research psychologists. The JPA (1990, 1995) has published *Psychological Institutions in Japan,* which shows a range of work sites that employ research psychologists. Major examples include the ATR (Advanced Telecommunications Research), Human Information Processing Research Laboratories, the Brain Science Institute, the Institute of Statistical Mathematics, Metropolitan Institute of Gerontology, National Center for Neurology and Psychiatry, National Institute of Industrial Health, the National Institute of Special Education, the National Research Institute of Police Science, and the Research Institute of the National Rehabilitation Center for the Disabled (JPA, 2002). These institutions hire psychologists to conduct scientific research.

The steep increase in the number of applicants to graduate psychology programs during the past decade can be attributed to the tremendous popularity of clinical psychology and to the recent establishment of a system to certify clinical psychologists. In 1988, the AJCP established a legal entity called the Japanese Certification Board for Clinical Psychologists (JCBCP), Inc. The JCBCP has dramatically altered the status of psychology in Japan. The criteria that must be met before earning certification as a clinical psychologist are a master's degree in psychology, supervised clinical practice for a minimum of 1 year, and passing a written examination and an interview, all administered by the JCBCP. The total cumulative number of certified clinical psychologists reached 10,083 in April 2003 (Japanese Certification Board for Clinical Psychology [JCBCP], n.d.) One major activity of the JCBCP is approving graduate programs in clinical psychology. As of July 2003, the JCBCP had approved a total of 95 master's programs in clinical psychology.

The JPA developed a separate system in 1989 to certify those who have taken the required undergraduate credits in psychology at a college or university. By 2000, nearly 6,500 qualified for certificates (JPA, 2002). About half of the JPA certified psychologists reside in Tokyo (20%) and its surrounding areas called the Kanto district (31%).

The Japanese Society of Certified Psychologists was established in 2001. This society was developed in the hope that, in the future, holding the certificate would become a minimum requirement for all psychologists intending to obtain certificates in more specialized areas of psychology, including clinical psychology. In addition to the JPA's certification system, a number of other psychological associations have developed their own certification systems. Examples include certifications for developmental clinical psychologists, health psychologists, industrial counselors, and school psychologists. Clearly, establishing a national system to examine credentials in various professional specialties has become one of the most pressing concerns confronting Japanese psychology.

Despite more than 100 years of experience with psychology, Japan has yet to develop a national licensing system for psychology. Neither the JCBCP nor the JPA certificate is a legal license to practice the profession of psychology. Currently, therefore, there are active movements to develop a national licensing system for professional psychology, legalized through an appropriate government agency so that professional psychologists will have an increased economic stronghold in Japan and rank equally with other nationally licensed professions.

Applied psychology develops in response to societal needs. In Japan, one such example is the establishment of the school-counselor system. In recent years, increased incidences of school-refusal behaviors and peer bullying have posed major challenges to the Japanese educational system. Reportedly, over 130,000 Japanese children have not attended school for more than one month. School problems such as these have alerted the Japanese educational system to place counselors in schools. The Japanese Ministry of Education, Culture, Sports, Science, and Technology started the school counselor system in 1995. In its first year, clinical psychologists certified by the JCBCP worked part-time as school counselors in 154 schools. By 2002, the school counselor system placed counselors in 5,500 schools throughout Japan (Murayama, n.d.). Most of these schools with part-time school counselors are middle schools covering 7th, 8th, and 9th grades. Elementary schools are yet to

be covered adequately by school counselors. The primary services offered by these psychologists include counseling students, consulting with teachers and parents, and disseminating information about counseling (Ishikuma, 1999).

A rich variety of assessment tools are available in Japan (Agari, 2001). Japanese psychologists have validated major Western personality inventories and adapted them for use with Japanese respondents. These tests include the Japanese versions of the Yatabe–Guilford Personality Test, the Maudsley Personality Inventory, the Minnesota Multiphasic Personality Inventory–II, and the NEO Personality Inventory, among others. Japanese translations and adaptations of major standardized intelligence tests are also available. Kannichi Tanaka (1882–1962) played a pioneering role in the development of the field of educational measurement in Japan. Intelligence tests adapted in Japan include the Tanaka–Binet Intelligence Scale, Kaufman Assessment Battery for Children, and Wechsler Intelligence Scale for Children-III, and its preschool and adult versions. Projective tests are also very popular in Japan. The Rorschach test, sentence completion test, thematic apperception test, the Baum test (known as Koch's Tree Test), and the house-tree-person test are some of the most frequently used projective tests.

In regard to psychological interventions, members of the AJCP responded that their theoretical orientations are psychodynamic (26.8%), nondirective or Rogerian (17.1%), psychoanalytic (15.7%), Jungian (13.1%), cognitive–behavioral (4.1%), existential–humanistic (2.9%), and behavioral (1.5%) (Ogawa, 2001). Naikan therapy and Morita therapy are the two indigenous Japanese psychotherapies developed in the first half of the 20th century (Tanaka-Matsumi, 2004). These therapies derive their epistemological origins from Buddhism and Zen Buddhism, respectively. Both deliberately minimize the use of verbal interactions between the therapist and the client, and both value self-observation and the acceptance of anxiety. As such, Reynolds (1980) called them "silent therapies." Morita therapy was developed specifically to help Japanese clients who had social anxieties and who were diagnosed with *Taijin Kyofusho* (interpersonal fears). Reviews of recent cultural and cross-cultural research on the relationship between psychological disorders and culture illuminate the prominence of specific presenting problems and suitable indigenous interventions (Tanaka-Matsumi, 2001).

In recent years, a group of Japanese clinical psychologists has embarked on promoting empirically supported or evidence-based interventions derived from the scientist–practitioner model of clinical psychology in Japan. Japanese publications on clinical psychology that promote the scientist–practitioner model have increased in the past few years as the nation seeks effective interventions in educational and clinical settings (e.g., Tanno, 2001; Uchiyama & Sakano, 2003).

Research projects that are noteworthy can be found in all areas of Japanese psychology. One distinctive project is longitudinal research on the intelligence of chimpanzees both in the laboratory and in the wild. At the Primate Research Institute of Kyoto University, established in 1948, Matsuzawa and his colleagues have studied language-like skills and the concept of numbers in chimpanzees. The research program was started in 1978 and has continued productively to the present, resulting in numerous international publications and conference papers (e.g., Kawai & Matsuzawa, 2000; Matsuzawa, 1985, 2001). With more than 50 years of continuous data collection on primates in the laboratory and field, the Japanese researchers have made major contributions to comparative science, the origins of human cognition and behavior, and the cultural transmission of knowledge.

In all domains of psychology, psychologists must follow codes of ethics developed by appropriate psychological organizations. The JPA has one in place as do other major associations and organizations. The ethical codes are essentially modeled after the APA's *Ethical Principles of Psychologists and Code of Conduct* (American Psychological Association [APA], 2002). The AJCP has the most elaborate ethical guidelines for clinical practitioners in Japan.

12.4 FUTURE CHALLENGES AND PROSPECTS

The development of modern scientific psychology in Japan has been both academically fruitful and professionally challenging. The legacies of early experimental psychology (from the beginning of the 20th century) are reflected in continued scientific psychological investigations of major topics in both basic and applied areas (Misumi & Oyama, 1989; Misumi & Peterson, 1990; Tanaka & England, 1972). In recent years, Japanese psychologists have vigorously investigated the history of psychology in Japan (e.g., Sato & Mizoguchi, 1997). Oizumi (2003) has published a directory of over 700 Japanese psychologists. These and other Japanese publications document the interest of Japanese psychologists in examining Japan's accomplishments in psychology, using appropriate historical and cultural perspectives (Azuma & Imada, 1994; Oyama et al., 2001).

More recently, Japanese psychologists have published culturally informed works in important areas of psychology. Selected research examples published in English include cross-cultural developmental research: patterns of mother–child interaction between Japanese and American mothers (e.g., Kashiwagi, 1984; Stevenson, Azuma, & Hakuta, 1986); culture, self-orientation, and attention (e.g., Kitayama, Duffy, & Kawamura, 2003; Markus & Kitayama, 1991); language development (Masataka, 2003); conceptual development (Hatano, Amaiwa, & Shimizu, 1987; Hatano & Inagaki, 2000); the performance-maintenance (PM) theory of leadership (Misumi, 1995); primary versus secondary controls of interpersonal relations (e.g., Yamaguchi, 2001); trust and commitment in Japan and the United States (Yamagishi & Yamagishi, 1994); and primate developmental research (Matsuzawa, 2001). Additional examples of Japanese research include investigations of conceptual frameworks and learned helplessness and irrelevance (Imada & Kitaguchi, 2002), and the development of engineering psychophysiology (Yagi, 2000), among others. These are just a few examples of many diverse contributions made by Japanese psychologists to the worldwide literature on psychology. Imada (1996b) has compiled a selected bibliography of psychology publications in English, with a specific focus on Japan, as part of an IUPsyS project.

The academic basis of psychology in Japan is strong. One major future challenge is the further development of structured graduate training programs in psychology to increase the number of Ph.D. holders in Japan. The number of graduate students completing their degrees is still relatively small as compared to other sciences. The recent emphasis on reforming the graduate curriculum in all academic disciplines in Japan will accelerate the number of doctoral-level psychologists employed at universities, research institutes, hospitals, and forensic sites. Furthermore, as major funding sources (such as the Japan Society for the Promotion of Science) now require postdoctoral fellowship applicants to relocate to another institution from the one where they trained as graduate students, the beneficial effects of the mobility of young scholars is anticipated. Such changes should foster more diversity within traditionally homogeneous academic departments.

Future professional opportunities for psychologists depend on both public acceptance and the availability of qualified psychologists. As Japan's population shows clear signs of rapidly aging, there will be a much greater need for gerontology research on the psychological well-being of the elderly and on the psychological effects of aging. Psychologists at the Metropolitan Institute of Gerontology in Tokyo, for example, conduct research on longevity and successful aging among Tokyo's centenarians (e.g., Shimonaka, Nakazato, & Honma, 1996). Similarly, for younger Japanese, as Japan undergoes a reformation in special education services to promote the UNESCO's doctrine of inclusion and individualized educational plans, we predict a definite need for an empirically validated assessment system to meet the educational needs of school-age children with developmental and learning disorders. We also predict the rapid growth of health psychology in Japan. The Japanese Association of Health Psychology has promoted basic and applied research on the relationship of mind–body interactions to health and illness. Furthermore, future research into psychological factors associated with human engineering, virtual reality, or, more generally, information technology and media diversity should offer or create advanced professional and scientific opportunities for psychologists and other scientists in Japan. Japanese psychologists are probing for alternative forms of psychology with an emphasis on methodology (Shimoyama & Koyasu, 2002).

The training needs of professional psychologists, including clinical psychologists, will continue to generate heated debates among diverse groups of experts with regard to content and qualifications. A major goal is to legalize a national licensure system for the professional practice of psychology. In this chapter, we reviewed the certification systems regulated by the JCBCP and the JPA. A number of other psychological associations have developed their own credentialing and certification systems including developmental psychology, educational psychology, health psychology, and industrial counseling, to name a few. Until more solid societal status is established for professional psychologists in practice, it is difficult to reliably estimate the nature of working relationships between psychology and other disciplines, such as medicine, in Japan.

Information technology has expanded the scope of psychologists' activities in Japan, and the Internet is used routinely at universities. Distance-learning programs have been initiated by a number of universities. Likewise, electronic bulletin boards are increasingly being used for instructional purposes at universities. Japanese psychologists can now communicate globally with their colleagues and have virtually unlimited accesses to information. Graduate students can easily search for educational programs in other countries and examine specific courses offered by experts. Enormous amounts of valuable information are routinely available to all psychologists, students, and the public. The equal opportunities provided by the Internet will most definitely stimulate competition among undergraduate and graduate programs in psychology and related disciplines.

In conclusion, scientific psychology in Japan has a rich history of about 100 years. Psychology is one of the most popular majors for undergraduate students, and it is an equally popular choice as a graduate specialty. The number of newly established graduate programs offering training in clinical psychology has increased remarkably. As reviewed in this chapter, the applied specialties will continue to generate new information and new systems of credentialing and certification by various associations, and, hopefully, the Japanese government will implement a licensing system to meet the needs of professional psychologists and the public. With globalization in information sharing, Japanese psychologists will have rich and challenging opportunities to ensure culturally appropriate services to those who need them most.

ACKNOWLEDGMENT

We express our gratitude to Sadahiko Nakajima and Hiroshi Imada for their helpful information during the preparation stage of this chapter.

REFERENCES

Agari, I. (Ed.). (2001). Shinri assessment handbook. *Handbook of psychological assessment* (2nd ed.). Niigata-city, Japan: Nishimura shoten.

American Psychological Association. (2002). Ethical principles of psychologists and code of conduct. *American Psychologist, 57,* 1060–1073.

Atkinson, R. L., Atkinson, R. C., & Fredrickson, B. (2002). *Hilgard's introduction to psychology* (14th ed.). New York: HBJ College and School Division.

Azuma, H., & Imada, H. (1994). Origins and development of psychology in Japan: The interaction between western science and the Japanese cultural heritage. *International Journal of Psychology, 29,* 707–715.

Hall, G. S., & Motora, Y. (1887). Dermal sensitivity to gradual pressure changes. *American Journal of Psychology, 1,* 72–98.

Hatano, G., Amaiwa, S., & Shimizu, K. (1987). Formation of a mental abacus and its use as a memory device for digits: A developmental study. *Developmental Psychology, 23,* 832–838.

Hatano, G., & Inagaki, K. (2000). Domain-specific constraints of conceptual development. *Journal of Behavioral Development, 24,* 267–275.

Hidano, T. (1998). Waga kuni no shinrigaku jikkennshitsu to jikken enshu [Japanese psychological laboratories in the early days]. *Shinrigaku Hyoron* [Japanese Psychological Review], *41,* 307–332.

Imada, H. (1996a). Shinrigaku senmonka no yousei nit suite: Kisoshinrigaku no tachibakara [On the training of professional psychologists: viewpoints of basic psychology]. *Shinrigaku Hyoron* [Japanese Psychological Review], *39,* 5–20.

Imada, H. (1996b). Psychology throughout the world: A selected bibliography of materials on psychology published in English 1974–1995. *International Journal of Psychology, 31,* 307–368.

Imada, H. (2001). Wagakuni no shinrigakkai eno koudoushugi no jyuyou: Imada Megumi to Kwansei Gakuin Daigaku shinrigaku kenkyushitsu o chushinni [Influence and acceptance of behaviorism in Japan: With special reference to Megumi Imada and the Psychology Department of Kwansei Gakuin University]. *Shinrigaku Hyoron* [Japanese Psychological Review], *44,* 433–440.

Imada, H., & Kitaguchi, K. (2002). Recent learned helplessness/irrelevance research in Japan: Conceptual framework and some experiments on learned irrelevance. *Integrative Physiological and Behavioral Science, 37,* 9–21.

Imada, H., & Nakajima, S. (Eds.). (2003). *Gakushu Shinrigaku ni okeru kotenteki jyokenzuke no riron: Pavlov kara rengou gakushu kenkyu no saisentan made* [Classical conditioning theories in psychology of learning: From Pavlov to the most recent research on associative learning]. Tokyo: Baifukan.

Ishikuma, T. (1999). *Gakkou shinrigaku* [School psychology]. Tokyo: Seishin Shobo.

Japanese Certification Board for Clinical Psychologists (JCBCP). (n.d.). *Japanese Certification Board for Clinical Psychologists.* Retrieved September 20, 2003, from http://www.4.ocn.ne.jp/jcbcp/what.html

Japanese Psychological Association. (1990, 1995). *Psychological institutions in Japan.* Tokyo: Japanese Psychological Association.

Japanese Psychological Association. (2002). *Nippon Shinrigakkai 75 nenshi* [A 75-year history of the Japanese Psychological Association]. Tokyo: Japanese Psychological Association.

Japanese Psychological Association. (n.d.). *Japanese Psychological Association.* Retrieved September 20, 2003, from http://www.soc.nii.ac.jp/jpa/index-e.html

Kashiwagi, K. (1984). Japan-U.S. comparative study on early maternal influences upon cognitive development: A follow-up study. *Japanese Psychological Research, 26,* 82–92.

Kawai, N., & Matsuzawa, T. (2000). Numerical memory span in a chimpanzee. *Nature, 403,* 39–40.

Kitayama, S., Duffy, S., & Kawamura, T. (2003). Perceiving an object and its context in different cultures: A cultural look at new look. *Psychological Science, 14,* 201–206.

Kotake, Y., & Miyata, Y. (1958). Our seventeen years of research on conditioned responses in man. *Psychologia, 1,* 158–166.

Kotake, Y., & Miyata, Y. (1973). Ningen no jyoken hansha [Human conditioning]. *Shinrigaku Monograph* [Psychology Monograph], *13.*

Markus, H., & Kitayama, S. (1991). Culture and the self: Implications for cognition, emotion, and motivation. *Psychological Review, 98,* 224–253.

Masataka, N. (2003). *The onset of language.* New York: Cambridge University Press.

Matsuzawa, T. (1985). Use of numbers by a chimpanzee. *Nature, 315,* 57–59.

Matsuzawa, T. (2001). *Primate origins of human cognition and behavior.* New York: Springer.

Ministry of Education, Culture, Sports, Science, and Technology. (n.d.). *Shiryo 4-2. Hakase Jyuyo Jyoukyo (Heisei 10 nendo)* [Document 4-2. Doctoral degrees granted in 1998]. Retrieved September 20, 2003, from http://www.mext.go.jp/b_menu/

Ministry of Education, Culture, Sports, Science, and Technology. (2002). *School policy survey.* Retrieved September 20, 2003, from http://www.jinjapan.org/stat/stats/16EDY29.html

Misumi, J. (1995). The development in Japan of the Performance-Maintenance (PM) Theory of Leadership. *Journal of Social Issues, 51,* 213–223.

Misumi, J., & Oyama, T. (Eds.). (1989). Special issue: Applied psychology in Japan. *Applied Psychology: An International Review, 38,* 307–451.

Misumi, J., & Peterson, M. F. (1990). Psychology in Japan. *Annual Review of Psychology, 41,* 213–241.

Murayama, M. (n.d.). *School counselor no genjo to kadai* [The current status and issues of the school counselor]. Retrieved September 20, 2003, from http://www.netty.ne.jp/csl/CSLJNL_37SCGK1.html

Ogawa, T. (2001). Assessment to giho kenkyu, 1: Toueiho [Assessment and therapy techniques: Projective tests]. In H. Shimoyama & Y. Tannno (Eds.), *Rinsho shinrigaku kenkyu* [Clinical Psychology Research] (pp. 143–162). Tokyo: Tokyo University Press.

Ogawa, T., & Nagai, T. (1997). Rinsho shinrigaku ni okeru senmon kyoiku ni tsuite [On the professional training of clinical psychology]. *Shinrigaku Hyoron* [Japanese Psychological Review], *40,* 163–168.

Oizumi, H. (2003). *Nippon shinrigakusha jiten* [Directory of Japanese psychologists]. Tokyo: Kuresu Shuppan.

Osaka, N. (1999). Jikken shinri shashincho ni miru meijiki no shinrgaku jikken to kotenteki Jikkenn kiki [Classical experimental apparatuses and instrumentation in the birth period of psychology in Japan as viewed from the Illustrated Picture Book of Instrumentation in Experimental Psychology]. *Shinrigaku Hyoron* [Japanese Psychological Review], *41,* 333–358.

Osaka, R. (1998). Meiji kara Showa shoki ni itaru jikken shinrigaku no keisei katei—Motora Yujiro to Matsumoto Yataro o chushin toshite [Retrospection of Japanese experimental psychology in the Meiji and Taisho era: With special reference to the achievements of Professor Y. Motora and Professor M. Matsumoto]. *Shinrigaku Hyoron* [Japanese Psychological Review], *41,* 333–358.

Oyama, T. (1997). Apparent motion as an example of perceptual stability. *Perception, 26,* 547–551.

Oyama, T., & Sato, T. (1999). Tokyo daigaku ni okeru shinrigaku koten jikken kiki nitsuite-bihin daicho o tegakari to shite [Historical instruments in the Department of Psychology, University of Tokyo: An analysis of the old instrument registry book]. *Shinrigaku Hyoron* [Japanese Psychological Review], *42,* 289–312.

Oyama, T., Sato, T., & Suzuki, Y. (2001). Shaping of scientific psychology in Japan. *International Journal of Psychology, 36,* 396–406.

Reynolds, D. (1980). *The quiet therapies: Japanese pathways to personal growth.* Honolulu: University Press of Hawaii.

Sakuma, A. (1999). Waga kuni ni okeru Gestalt shinrigaku-Sakuma Kanae no gyoseki wo chushin toshite [Gestalt psychology in Japan]. *Shinrigaku Hyoron* [Japanese Psychological Review], *42,* 326–345.

Sato, T., & Mizoguchi, H. (1997). *Tsushi Nihon no shinrigaku* [A history of Japanese psychology]. Kyoto, Japan: Kitaoji Shobo.

Shimonaka, Y., Nakazato, K., & Honma, A. (1996). Personality, longevity, and successful aging among Tokyo metropolitan centenarians. *International Journal of Aging and Human Development, 42,* 173–187.

Shimoyama, H., & Koyasu, M. (Eds.). (2002). *Shinrigaku no atarashii katachi: Houho eno ishiki* [New forms of psychology: Attention to methodology]. Tokyo: Seishin Shobo.

Stevenson, H., Azuma, H., & Hakuta, K. (Eds.). (1986). *Child development and education in Japan.* New York: Freeman.

Sukemune, S. (1992). Japan. In V. S. Sexton & J. D. Hogan (Eds.), *International psychology: Views from around the world* (pp. 259–272). Lincoln, NE: University of Nebraska Press.

Takahashi, K., & Hatano, G. (1996). Hattatsu shinrigaku ni okeru senmon kyouiku. [Professional training of developmental psychology]. *Shinrigaku Hyoron* [Japanese Psychological Review], *39,* 21–30.

Takuma, T., & Yamamoto, K. (1996). Shinrigakukei no hakase gakui jyuyo no chosa-1986 nendo yori 1995 nendo made [A survey of the status of awarding the doctorate degrees in psychology].

Shinrigaku Hyoron [Japanese Psychological Review], *39,* 81–136.

Tanaka, Y., & England, G. W. (1972). Psychology in Japan. *Annual Review of Psychology, 23,* 695–732.

Tanaka-Matsumi, J. (2001). Abnormal psychology and culture. In D. Matsumoto (Ed.), *The handbook of culture and psychology* (pp. 265–286). New York: Oxford University Press.

Tanaka-Matsumi, J. (2004). Japanese forms of psychotherapy: Naikan therapy and Morita therapy. In U. P Gielen, J. M Fish, & J. G. Draguns (Eds.), *The handbook of culture, therapy, and healing* (pp. 359–393). Boston: Allyn & Bacon.

Tanno, Y. (2001). *Evidence rinsho shinrigaku* [Evidence-based clinical psychology]. Tokyo: Nippon Hyoronsha.

Tichener, E. B. (1901). *Experimental psychology: A manual of laboratory practice.* New York: Macmillan.

Uchiyama, K., & Sakano, Y. (Eds.). (2003). *Evidence-based counseling: EBC. Special issue of Gendai no Esprit* [Esprit of today]. Tokyo: Shibundo.

Yagi, A. (2000). Engineering psychophysiology in Japan. In R. Backs & W. Boucsein (Eds.), *Engineering psychophysiology* (pp. 361–368). Mahwah, NJ: Earlbaum.

Yamaguchi, S. (2001). Culture and control orientations. In D. Matsumoto (Ed.), *The handbook of culture and psychology* (pp. 223–244). New York: Oxford University Press.

Yamagishi, T., & Yamagishi, M. (1994). Trust and commitment in the United States and Japan. *Motivation and Emotion, 18,* 129–166.

Zimbardo, P. G. (1980). *Essentials of psychology and life* (10th ed.). Glenview, IL: Scott Foresman.

IMPORTANT PUBLICATIONS

Azuma, H., Kashiwagi, K., & Hess, R.D. (1981). *Hahaoya no taido koudo to kodomo no chiteki hattatsu* [The effect of a mother's attitude and behavior on the cognitive development of the child: A U.S.-Japan comparison]. Tokyo: University of Tokyo Press.

Imada, H., & Nageishi, Y. (1982). The concept of uncertainty in animal experiments using aversive stimulation. *Psychological Bulletin, 91,* 573–588.

Markus, H., & Kitayama, S. (1991). Culture and the self: Implications for cognition, emotion, and motivation. *Psychological Review, 98,* 224–253.

Matsuzawa, T. (1985). Use of numbers by a chimpanzee. *Nature, 315,* 57–59.

Misumi, J. (1985). *The behavioral science of leadership.* Ann Arbor, MI: University of Michigan Press.

Morita, S. (1998). *Morita therapy and the true nature of anxiety-based disorders* [Shinkeishitsu]. (A. Kondo, Trans.). Albany, NY: State University of New York Press. (Original work published 1928)

Tanaka, K. (1926). *Kyoikuteki sokuteigaku* [Educational measurement]. Tokyo: Matsumura Sanshodo.

CHAPTER 13

Psychology in Singapore

ELIZABETH NAIR

A first-generation Singapore citizen by birth, Elizabeth Nair nee Chacko graduated with a bachelor's in psychology from the University of Western Australia (1972) under the Colombo Plan Scholarship. In the civil service, she was the last head of the Personnel Research Department, Singapore Ministry of Defense. After completing a Ph.D. in psychology at the University of Nottingham, U.K, in 1989 she was appointed lecturer at the National University of Singapore.

Elizabeth Nair was organizing chair and scientific committee co-chair of the XXV International Congress of Applied Psychology held in Singapore in July 2002. Her awards include the Efficiency Medal (1984), Singapore; Sir Ratan Tata Visiting Fellowship (1997), Calcutta; Distinguished International Psychologist (2001), Division 52, American Psychological Association; and the inaugural Award for Outstanding Service to Psychology in Singapore (2003), Singapore Psychological Society. She is an executive committee member, International Union of Psychological Science (2000–2004) and board member, International Association of Applied Psychology (1998–2006).

13.1 OVERVIEW

Singapore is an island city-state, about 650 km^2, with a 193-km coastline. The climate is tropical with no pronounced rainy or dry seasons. The terrain is lowland with a gently undulating central plateau. Located between Malaysia and Indonesia, it is a focal point for Southeast Asian sea routes.

The Singapore workforce has traditionally been engaged mainly in sea-going trade and financial activities, and in supporting the trading activities of the hinterlands of its neighboring countries. More recently, manufacturing, especially in the electronics industry, has assumed greater importance. Over the last decade, Singapore has been actively engaged in establishing itself as a regional and international education hub.

In this socio-geographical historical setting, psychology was first offered as a subject within the context of tertiary programs such as teacher training, business and management, social work, sociology, and nursing. Graduates in psychology were all trained overseas, mainly in the United Kingdom, Australia, and the United States In 1979, a group of 40 psychologists formed the Singapore Psychological Society (SPS). This is the sole national association for the profession; as of March 2003, there were 250 members, excluding student members. With a population of over 4 million, this works out to 6.2 psychologists per 100,000. This compares with 140 Singapore physicians per 100,000 (Statistics Singapore, 2002).

Singapore psychologists in the civil service enjoy Division I status on job entry, compared to Division 2 status for social workers and physiotherapists. Their salary is commensurate with the Division 1 pay scale, though less than that for medical and legal officers. Entry requirements, especially for clinical psychologists, now stipulate postgraduate qualifications. Salaries for academics are similar across disciplines for all members of the same college and are largely determined by academic rank.

As of 2003, 21.6% of members of the SPS have a Ph.D.; 41.2% have a master's; 35.2% have a bachelor's degree; and .8% have a postgraduate diploma in psychology as their highest qualification. In effect, two out of three SPS members have postgraduate training in psychology.

Members of the SPS received their highest tertiary-level psychology training from over 14 countries. These include, predominantly, Australia (28%), the United Kingdom (19.6%), Singapore (17.6%), the United States (13.6%), New Zealand (6%), Canada (4.8%), and India (3.6%). Other countries where a few Singapore psychologists were trained include Germany, South Africa, Philippines, Brazil, Netherlands, ROC Taiwan, and Italy.

The 54 Singaporean Ph.D. holders graduated from universities in the United States (22), Australia (12), the United Kingdom (11), New Zealand (2), Canada (2), Germany (2), Singapore (1), India (1), and Italy (1). Graduate training for psychologists with a master's in psychology was taken in Singapore (25), the United Kingdom (23), Australia (22), the United States (9), Canada (9), India (7), Netherlands (2), and in Germany, Brazil, South Africa, and the Philippines (1 each).

Singapore psychologists had postgraduate training in the following specialized areas: clinical (37), counseling (35), education (26), social (10), occupational (7), cognitive (7), industrial–organizational (6), experimental (5), developmental (4), ergonomics (4), school (4), forensic (2), and sport psychology (2). Specialization areas of the 54 members with a Ph.D. were predominantly in clinical (14), counseling (6), social (7), education (5), cognitive (5), ergonomics (4), occupational (2), experimental (2), developmental (2), and sports psychology (2). Specialized areas for the 103 with a master's degree in psychology were predominantly in counseling (28), clinical (24), and education (21), with lesser numbers in occupational (5), industrial–organizational (4), social (3), school (3), experimental (3), cognitive (2), and developmental psychology (2).

A comprehensive psychology program leading to a major in psychology was first initiated at the National University of Singapore (NUS) in 1986. The number of academic psychologists has now overtaken that of practitioners (Nair, 2002). The next largest group of Singapore psychologists is in teacher training and education. Council members of the SPS in recent times have been drawn largely from the clinical, counseling, and educational settings.

Academics from NUS feature predominantly in the organization and the scientific program for the XXV International Congress of Applied Psychology was co-organized jointly by the SPS and NUS. There were more than 1,600 international registrants at this congress, held in July 2002 in Singapore (Nair, 2003). The editors of the SPS flagship journal, the *Asian Psychologist*, have until now been NUS academics. There are some indications of a recent disengagement between NUS academics and the SPS council, marked in 2003 by a discontinuation of the award of a prize for the top psychology student at NUS, for many years conferred by the SPS.

The SPS maintains a register of psychologists, and a Web site that displays profession-related documents, including the Society's code of ethical practice, supervision guidelines, and the membership directory (Lim, 2002). While the critical number of practitioners is still too small to press for legislation for registration, the SPS is effectively serving the role of a watchdog for maintaining standards of professional practice within the country. The SPS is affiliated with two umbrella organizations, namely the National Council of Social Service and the Singapore Professional Center. It has played an active part over the years in both these organizations, working with social service agencies as well as other professional bodies, respectively.

13.2 EDUCATION AND TRAINING

In *Asiaweek*'s (n.d.) "Best Universities 2000: Overall Ranking for Multidisciplinary Schools," NUS ranked 5th on a list of 77 universities from all over Asia, Australia, and New Zealand. Kyoto University (83.17%) received the highest score. Universities were ranked on a composite scale that included academic reputation, student selectivity, faculty resources, research, and financial resources. Details of the ranking criteria and procedure are found at the Web address in the reference list. Comparing universities in developed countries in the same list, the ranks for the top universities in Australia and New Zealand were as follows: Australian National University: 8; University of Melbourne: 9; University of New South Wales: 10; University of Sydney: 13; and University of Auckland: 21.

In 1986, the NUS commenced an undergraduate program leading to a major in psychology in the department of social work and psychology. The first cohort graduated with a pass degree in 1989, and the first batch with an honors degree in psychology graduated in 1990. The initial cohorts underwent an aptitude test, which influenced selection for the program. The aptitude test was subsequently eliminated.

Master's and Ph.D. candidates have enrolled at NUS in increasing numbers over the years. In 2002, there were 26 master's candidates and 10 Ph.D. candidates in various stages of progress toward their degrees (Singh & Kaur, 2002). A part-time master's of social sciences (applied psychology) course was offered commencing in 1998; 27 students were participating in this program as of 2001. The program has since been discontinued in favor of focusing on full-time postgraduate courses as a priority. Scholarships, tuition waivers, and student loans are available for full-time students on a competitive basis.

NUS was the first among Southeast Asian institutions to have 100% of its psychology faculty trained at the doctoral level (Singh, 2000). Local and expatriate academic staff qualified from reputable universities in the United States (11), the United Kingdom (6), and Canada (1). Singh and Kaur (2002) have provided a detailed and comprehensive account of the program, academic staff, and research publications, and international contributions for the first 15 years of the psychology program at NUS. Research grants are available for academic staff, applications are peer-reviewed, and for grants above $150,000, six external reviews of the grant application are required.

The NUS psychology program has the benefit of an excellent infrastructure in terms of computer-assisted instructional capabilities. An integrated virtual-learning environment enables the mounting of lectures and discussion groups on the Web, in addition to depositing handouts and student submissions of assignments into the virtual work bins in the individual course Web pages. Students can access lectures online for all courses in which lecturers opt to webcast their course. In the first quarter of 2003, the staff was allocated cordless laptops as part of the regular update of hardware at NUS. Individual laser printers were allocated in early 2002, though after the first university-funded cartridge, the payment for subsequent ink cartridges is provided by the departmental fund, research grants, or individual initiatives.

The NUS library has an excellent current collection of psychology books and journals, including electronic publications. Library staff is responsive to requests to purchase relevant texts, references, and ancillary materials. The multimedia resource library functions smoothly in tandem with requests from staff for instructional support (i.e., online, Web-based, and archival).

The psychology program has research laboratories for cognition and biopsychology and stress, and shares the use of an observation room. An animal laboratory is a notable exception. The department maintains a collection of testing materials. Individual staff members purchase specialized assessment tools and classified psychological tests from their research grants, and are personally responsible for maintaining the security and proper use of these items. The department maintains under its purview two computer clusters for teaching purposes as well as for use by students for their research projects. The NUS computer library continually updates publications, statistical software, and accompanying manuals and guides; these are available for borrowing by staff and students (apart from limited license use for software).

The NUS academic staff teach a set of core psychology modules and electives in the undergraduate program that leads to a bachelor of arts (3 years) or a bachelor of social science with honors (4 years). They are also engaged in individual and group supervision of undergraduate students' research projects.

An exhaustive digital library search of the complete PsycINFO and Sociological Abstracts databases was conducted employing Ovid Technologies on April 30, 2003, using the key words "Singapore psychology" and "Singapore psychological studies." This search identified 77 publications originating from two tertiary institutions in Singapore. Of these, 72 were from NUS, and 5 from Nanyang Technological University (NTU).

The five NTU publications dated from 1997 (1) to 2001 (2) and 2002 (2). Each of the following journals carried one article each: *Journal of Mathematical Psychology, International Journal of Psycholinguistics, Applied Psychology: An International Review, Educational Research*, and the *Korean Journal of Thinking and Problem Solving*.

There were 72 publications in psychology originating from NUS. These dated from 1990 to 2003, with peaks in 2000 (14), 1999 (12), 1998 (10), 2002 (8), 1997 (7), 1994 (6), and 2001 (5). Of these, 26 were single-authored publications and 46 were collaborative. Counting only first authorship, the most prolific Singapore psychologists were R. Singh (12), D. Chan (10), G. Bishop (7), R. Howard (6), E. Nair (5), C. W. Chu (4), C. Ward (4), F. K. Chua (3), and V. Bernhard-Opitz (3).

The work of NUS academics was published in 42 journals. These included *Personality and Individual Differences* (6), *Applied Psychology: An International Review* (5), *British Journal of Social Psychology* (5), *Psychologia: An International Journal of Psychology in the Orient* (4), *Psychology and Health* (3), *Journal of Experimental Psychology: Learning, Memory and Cognition* (2), *Substance Use and Misuse* (2), *Organizational Behavior and Human Decision Processes* (2*), Criminal Behavior and Mental Health* (2), *Journal of Psychology in Chinese Societies* (2), *Multivariate Behavioral Research* (2), and *Counseling Psychology Quarterly* (2). The

publication list also included four book chapters and a book.

The following journals published one article each out of the 72 NUS publications that emerged from the digital library search: *Journal of Occupational Health Psychology, Psychology, Crime and Law, Journal of Research in Personality, Journal of Autism and Developmental Disorders, Human Performance, Child Development, Journal of Applied Psychology, Journal of Research on Adolescence, Journal of Adult Development, Praxis de Kinderpsychologie und Kinderpsychiatrie, Psychosomatic Medicine, Journal of Business and Psychology, Journal of Health Psychology*, and *Autism*. The list also included the *Journal of Cross-Cultural Psychology, Journal of Applied Social Psychology, Organizational Research Methods, Asian Journal of Social Psychology, International Journal of Selection and Assessment, Applied Psycholinguistics, Evolution and Human Behavior, Personality and Social Psychology Bulletin, Child Abuse and Neglect, Journal of Social Issues*, and *Cognition*.

Additionally, the publication list included *Cognitive Development, Biological Psychology, International Journal of Intercultural Relations, Australian Journal of Psychology*, and *Journal of Social Psychology*. On the whole, the publications consisted of the work of tenured and non-tenured NUS staff, students in collaboration with staff, and visiting academics on sabbatical. This publication list does not include technical reports, working papers, research monographs, or conference proceedings. It is an encapsulated depiction of the research output of a relatively new psychology program with 16 academic staff carrying a workload that includes teaching, research, and supervision.

The Singapore Management University (SMU), officially incorporated in January 2000, is the first government-funded, privately managed university in Singapore. It offers degrees in management, economics, and information-systems management. Students at SMU can opt to do psychology, listed under sciences, as an optional general-education module.

The Singapore Institute of Management (SIM) has been providing continuing education for more than three decades, mostly to meet the needs of the workforce to upgrade their educational qualifications while holding a full-time job. In 1992, SIM launched the Open University Center in Singapore. It currently offers a B.A. or B.Sc. in psychology, with the caveat that the availability of honors in psychology is under negotiation with the U.K. Open University. There are options to pursue a single major in psychology or a double major with economics or management. The SIM Open University Center also offers introductory psychology modules in its certificate of social sciences course.

The National Institute of Education (NIE), a teacher-training establishment, was incorporated in 2000 as part of the Nanyang Technological University (NTU). The academic grouping titled Psychological Studies at NIE represents the second largest group of academic psychologists in Singapore. Apart from teaching psychology modules as part of the teacher-training courses, a postgraduate course, titled Master of Arts in applied psychology is offered by Psychological Studies, with the option of majoring in educational psychology or counseling psychology.

No financial aid is provided to students for the postgraduate course. The target group includes teachers, psychologists, and counselors. Modules are taught in the evenings to facilitate participation from students who hold full-time day jobs. Students in the postgraduate course have to complete a 15,000-word thesis and fulfill a practicum as part of the course requirements. Formal teaching methods include lectures and small group discussions.

Almost all psychological studies faculty, including teaching staff for the postgraduate course (10) and additional NIE-based dissertation supervisors (15), have doctorates. The countries where they obtained their doctoral qualifications are the United States (11), Singapore (6), Australia (6), and Germany (1). Their instructional program is augmented by a team of 9 adjunct faculty and a varying number of site supervisors each year, totaling 17 since 1998.

13.3 SCOPE OF PSYCHOLOGICAL PRACTICE

The code of ethics of the Singapore Psychological Society was formulated in 1989 and was specifically designed to be congruent with that of the American Psychological Association. At present, some parts need to be revised to respond to the changing technology and applications of the discipline.

All research conducted at NUS by staff and students must first be cleared by a department-based ethics committee. A full multidisciplinary faculty ethics committee of four to five persons scrutinizes research projects that indicate the use of deception or stress, or use a sample of children aged 14 years or younger. Otherwise, the chair of the ethics committee expedites approval. In uncertain cases, the Ethical Principles of

Psychologists and Code of Conduct of the American Psychological Association (1992) is used as reference and guideline, with the updated 2002 revision increasingly being consulted.

Research methodologies and professional practices have been governed largely by the tertiary training that psychologists receive. The training profile of psychologists in Singapore is international and largely influenced by research and practices in the United States, United Kingdom, and Australia. There is a need to deliberately realign applications, particularly in service delivery, to better accommodate the differing cultural, social, religious, and ethnic backgrounds of the population. Training in a cultural and philosophical milieu that is vastly different from that of the local population has sometimes translated into rejection of the newly returned and newly qualified practitioners and researchers. They are fired with the enthusiasm of early idealism and the belief that they have ready answers for society's problems. In actuality, arrival in Singapore, after immersion in a different cultural context, requires a relearning of social cues, innuendos, nonverbal language, and the local patois in order to enlist acceptance by both clients and fellow workers. This is often not understood by the newly returned or recently arrived psychologist.

Because nearly everyone speaks English in Singapore, a foreign visitor may be misled into believing that Singapore's citizens also share similarities in religious beliefs, philosophy of life, general responses to assertive behavior, or public displays of emotion. However, there are vast differences in how various ethnic groups think, feel, behave, and interact. These cultural scripts need to be understood and differentiated before practitioners can effectively provide service, whether in a clinical or organizational context. It becomes especially important when psychological assessments and interpretations contribute to important decision-making by the individual, his or her family, the courts, organizations, or the government.

It is only after a period of some years that the practitioner becomes sufficiently socialized to be able to contribute in a manner that is sensitive and relevant to the cultural context. One example of Singaporean cultural practice would be the operation of a general principle that one does not contradict an elder in the presence of others, even if the latter makes statements that are factually incorrect. This has to do with social expectations for younger people to "show respect" and not to force a senior to have to "save face." Thus, a wife generally would not contradict her husband in front of others, and a junior executive would not point out any errors on the part of his or her senior manager. The younger generation today operates on slightly different premises, and this also contributes to intergenerational misunderstandings at home, in school, and in the workplace.

The needed adaptations have more to do with effective communication rather than with changing core concepts of ethical practice or experimental rigor. This differentiation is not often clearly understood. An orientation or reorientation program for newly returned or arrived practitioners and academics would help reduce frustrations and misunderstandings on the part of the international psychologist and his or her clients, students, and coworkers.

The SPS is currently reviewing guidelines to implement the accumulation of continuing-education credits for psychologists who have registered their qualifications with the society. An introductory module for new entrants to the country can be a part of such a program.

The following paragraphs will bear upon the work of psychologists in different work settings in Singapore. The Ministry of Defense, prior to 1986, had the single largest group of psychology practitioners in Singapore (Nair, 2002). Ministry of Defense psychologists engage in psychological assessment, selection testing for specific key vocations, survey research on the morale and motivation of the troops and of public perceptions of military service, ergonomics, and field psychology. Psychologists work with different sections in the army, navy, and air force, as well as with the military's medical services.

Both civilian and military psychologists employed by the Ministry of Defense work in teams together with other social and behavioral scientists, especially in organizational research and in the development and delivery of leadership and management programs. The early mistrust of the intentions and motives of the psychology researcher has evolved into a relationship of trust and cooperation. This battle was won partly by initiating psychology scholarships for soldiers, who were then appointed on a dual-career track of soldier–psychologist, and followed a planned career path of command and professional appointments. The mix of military and civilian, male and female, psychologists and other social and behavioral scientists is a good formula for balance and equanimity, which is particularly valuable in a team often working under volatile and tense situations. The present professional leadership climate is reportedly somewhat

insular, and Ministry of Defense psychologists have been notably absent for more than a decade within the wider professional community.

The largest group of practicing psychologists in Singapore is now in the area of educational and instructional psychology. They are mainly affiliated with the Ministry of Education and the National Institute of Education. Chang (2002) wrote a cogent account of the development of the importance of psychology in teacher education in Singapore. Educational psychologists have become visibly active in the national professional society and have been well represented on the SPS council over the last decade. Their work involves curriculum development for teacher training, providing school-based psychological services for teachers and students, and training counselors.

The services of the educational psychologists are valued greatly by consumers. Stress-related illness is common in the Singapore school context, both among teachers and students (Nair, 1995). The former eventually suffer from burnout, with many choosing to leave the profession, resulting in a chronic teacher shortage. Students are often beset with worries about performance in the continual stream of assessments and examinations. Many are distressed by their inability to match their own expectations for academic achievement. There is a need for the services of many more school-based educational psychologists.

Woodbridge Mental Hospital has long been associated in Singapore with mental illness, and the name was greeted with dread and derision. Over the years, the physical facilities and therapeutic interventions within the hospital have undergone radical transformations. It is now closely associated with the Institute of Mental Health, which is physically co-located, and the image has changed to one of enlightened and positive therapy that maintains the self-esteem of the patient.

Woodbridge Mental Hospital was converted from a government-subsidized hospital to a restructured private hospital in 2000. This change led to several of the longer-serving psychologists leaving the hospital to take up positions in other government ministries. However, the team that is now in place at Woodbridge and the Institute of Mental Health continues to play an active supportive role within the national professional community. Led by the incumbent head of psychological services, Lyn Chua, the team of psychologists at Woodbridge assumed responsibility for the precongress psychology workshops conducted in conjunction with the XXV International Congress of Applied Psychology in Singapore.

There is a good working relationship at Woodbridge with a multidisciplinary team that includes psychiatrists, medical social workers, occupational therapists, and nurses. The work of the clinical psychologists was described as psychometric assessment, including that of intellectual capacity, personality, and neuropsychological functioning. Therapies were undertaken for the treatment of emotional, interpersonal, psychiatric, and behavioral problems that may be associated with physical or mental illness, or which reflect difficulties in adjusting to the challenges of daily living. The spectrum of psychological disorders treated ranges from anxiety, obsessive–compulsive behavior, and depression to addiction. Toward this end, behavior therapy, cognitive–behavior therapy, psychotherapy, and group therapy are employed.

At various times, the psychologists at the Institute of Mental Health have also been involved in providing corporate services such as personnel selection and the assessment of government scholarship applicants. They also assumed leadership in the National Emergency Behavior Management System that provides psychological support in times of civil and national emergencies. This comprised a multi-ministry system, requiring coordination across the civil service.

The clinical, health, and research psychologists at the Institute of Mental Health have also been involved in the teaching of medical students, advanced psychiatric nurses, and trainee psychologists, as well as in the postgraduate psychotherapy course. They have also undertaken health education for the general public and corporations. Activities included stress management workshops, mental health education talks, and smoking cessation clinics and workshops.

The multidisciplinary Early Psychosis Intervention Program, which includes psychologists, has initiated dialogue with physicians trained in Chinese medicine to create better awareness between traditional and nontraditional mental health professionals. This represents a radical departure from previous practices, and bodes well for better integration and acceptance of mental health promotion activities in the Singapore context. With increasing awareness of psychological problems, there has been a concomitant increase in demand for clinical psychological services and a shortfall of clinical psychologists to meet this demand. Nonpsychologists do not provide clinical psychology services within the hospital and clinic settings.

The primary role of the psychologists in the psychological service branch of the Prisons Department is to conduct assessment interviews for corrective training and preventive detention reports for the courts. Psychologists in correctional and rehabilitation settings may be uniformed or civilian. Their duties also include assessment and classification of inmates and conduct of specialized treatment programs for sex offenders. Additionally, they conduct special training lessons on a core-skills program for uniformed staff, who, in turn, conduct it for inmates; modules include topics such as anger and stress management.

Civilian prison psychologists are also charged with the responsibility for the mental welfare of prison staff. This involves staffing a hotline for stressed employees. Counseling duties are shared with social workers, whereas classification duties are shared with counselors. Research is undertaken in working groups as the need arises. Psychologists also provide expertise in relation to staff selection, training, and development.

Prison psychologists often proactively initiate continuing education and upgrading of skills, and these activities are well funded. Psychology staff strength is reportedly low compared to correctional agencies in more developed countries, and high compared to less developed countries. There is a need for more exposure and specific training to deliver clinical psychology services within the correctional settings.

Ozawa (2002) presented a detailed and cogent account of how psychological services contribute to the dispensation of transformative justice within the criminal, family, and juvenile justice centers of Singapore. His account illustrates how the specialized input of psychologists is valued

and plays an integral part in the determination of magisterial court orders. The psychologist's input is particularly significant for decisions pertaining to the maintenance of a balance between deterrent sentencing necessary for societal protection, and the law and court becoming the driving force behind restoration of individuals, families, and even communities.

The Singapore police force houses a team of psychologists in their psychology unit. Their main role is to support the effective functioning of the police in the execution of their duties. It is a comparatively young team, largely staffed by individuals with only undergraduate qualifications, the minimum being an honors degree from NUS or its equivalent. Police psychologists are given an opportunity to pursue postgraduate psychology training overseas on a competitive basis after some years of work experience. They have in recent years engaged in collaborative organizational and rehabilitation research initiatives with consultation from NUS academics.

Psychologists in private practice have arguably reached equilibrium with academic psychologists in terms of numbers. They engage in cognitive, neuropsychological and personality assessments, with referrals from psychiatrists and counselors. Many other professions also provide counseling services in the private sector, though they do not generally attempt psychological assessment.

Increasing numbers of psychologists are now engaged in business and industrial establishments. Their work includes recruitment, assessment, selection, training, human resource development, and organizational development. Psychology graduates are also engaged in market research, advertising, and selling. As in the case of clinical psychologists in private practice and in business and industry, recent years have seen an influx of expatriate psychologists from Europe, Australia, and New Zealand, providing therapy and consulting services in Singapore.

13.4 FUTURE CHALLENGES AND PROSPECTS

It is envisaged that the next 20 years will see an accelerated growth in the provision of psychological services in Singapore, especially in the private sector, in response to a growing and seemingly bottomless demand for educational assessment and stress management services. Second, there is a local, regional, and international quest for the assessment of managerial potential, and for the selection and placement of high performers from various industries in the global marketplace. As a long-standing trade, financial, and, more recently, an information technology hub, modern and urban Singapore is well placed to be a focal point of convergence where psychological selection activities are headquartered for the region.

The influx of psychologists from developed countries to Singapore, many of whom are seeking to provide services in clinical, counseling, and educational settings, and for job placement, is likely to accelerate. This is expected for two reasons: first, because the demand will be there and, second, because the physical and social living environment, quality of life, and remuneration are all highly attractive to foreign expatriates from the developed world.

The political climate in Singapore is welcoming and encourages skilled and gifted expatriates to take up residence in Singapore. Though Singaporeans may initially view the influx with concern and experience some anxiety because of the competition, there will be a realization before the end of this decade that immigration has multiple benefits for all concerned.

It is also expected that the next 25 years will see a better capability to fulfill the need for the services of many more educational and school psychologists. This need can only be met with a combination of local and expatriate psychologists.

The XXV International Congress of Applied Psychology, held in Singapore in July 2002, was a huge success mainly because of the successful harnessing of electronic global communication technology (Nair, 2003). The leadership of the scientific committee was comprised of divisional committee chairs and their members from all over the world. Communication and dialogue were effectively maintained through the Internet and Web pages. This exercise illustrates the vast potential for international undertakings and collaborations by psychologists, unfettered by geographical distance, travel time, and fatigue. Singapore had the infrastructure necessary to fully support this international conference.

Research endeavors have also been greatly facilitated by advances in information technology, and the storage of psychology publications in electronic databases easily accessed even from a home-based computer. This bodes well for international collaborations and a higher quality of research output.

The general public's perception of psychologists falls into two categories. First, many members of the public still do not know the difference between a psychologist and a psychiatrist, and assume that, like psychiatrists, all psychologists work with the mentally ill. A second group is aware of the research that psychologists conduct, and holds the view that a psychologist can provide the answer to all the mysteries of human behavior. There is, therefore, an often naive and plaintive request to "please explain this strange behavior." Sometimes we have the research to provide the answer; at other times, the request falls into the "mind-reading" category, and a satisfactory answer cannot be given.

There is a need, therefore, for a continuing process of public education with regard to the various specializations within psychology, and to how psychologists derive their knowledge, the skills they possess, and the kind of questions that they are equipped to answer. Few psychologists in Singapore are prepared to take a position and present their perspectives and insights in the media. This is due partly to modesty and partly to a fear of making mistakes and being accused of misrepresenting the profession in some way. This fear and reticence needs to be overcome if the task of public education with regard to the profession is to succeed.

One controversial issue is a determination of the extent to which an expatriate or a returning local Singaporean can contribute in a professional capacity on arrival in the country after many years away. Because successful interpersonal behavior is determined largely by one's understanding of culture, there should be provisions for the learning and socialization process before practicing in Singapore, so that the new arrival can make an effective contribution. The content and duration of such a program could be deliberated on and guidelines determined by the national professional association. Incorporation of such a program would enhance the standard of professional services rendered and contribute to the credibility of the profession within the country, regionally, and internationally. The delivery of the program could be formalized within a tertiary institution and run by certified trainers and consultants.

Because the global marketplace has become a reality and the virtual world is now so important in our daily lives, geography has lost its capacity to separate the people of the world. The existence of economical air travel means that we can easily go to sleep in one country and wake up in another, sometimes on the opposite side of the world. Effective delivery of psychological services in another country requires more than physical appearance in that country, or even writing electronic letters and entering designated chat-rooms at predetermined times. To be fully effective, psychologists need to engage in a deliberate and conscious plan of action to understand the psyche of the country's inhabitants.

One effective way to prepare American psychologists for active engagement in international psychology is to institutionalize opportunities in the teaching of psychology programs, and for undergraduates and postgraduates to spend a semester learning about psychology in another country. Living and studying abroad provides many experiential learning opportunities that will equip them well when they enter the world of work as psychologists.

REFERENCES

American Psychological Association. (1992). Ethical principles of psychologists and code of conduct. *American Psychologist, 47,* 1597–1611.

Asiaweek. (n.d.). *Asia's best universities 2000: Special report.* Retrieved May 2, 2003, from http://www.asiaweek.com/asiaweek/features/universities2000/schools/multi.overall.html.

Chang, A. C. S. (2002). Psychology in Singapore education. *Applied Psychology: An International Review, 51,* 204–217.

Lim, K. M. (2002). Singapore Psychological Society: Membership and activities (1999–2002). *Asian Psychologist, 3,* 74–77.

Nair, E. (1995). *Action research on stress management in Singapore schools.* Singapore: Singapore Teachers' Union.

Nair, E. (1997). An introduction to Singapore and psychology in Singapore. *International Psychology Reporter, 1,* 1–9.

Nair, E. (2002). Dichotomous issues in psychology: Intransigency or developmental phase? *Applied Psychology: An International Review, 51,* 236–250.

Nair, E. (2003). Hindsight lessons aka experiential wisdom: A review of the XXV ICAP. *Applied Psychology: An International Review, 52,* 165–174.

Ozawa, J. P. (2002). Transformative justice: Psychological services in the criminal, family, and juvenile justice centers of the subordinate courts of Singapore. *Applied Psychology: An International Review, 51,* 218–235.

Singh, R. (2000). [Psychology in] Southeast Asia. In A. E. Kazdin (Ed.), *Encyclopedia of psychology* (Vol. 7, pp. 403–411). New York: American Psychological Association and Oxford University Press.

Singh, R., & Kaur, S. (2002). Psychology at the National University of Singapore: The first 15 years. *Applied Psychology: An International Review, 51,* 181–203.

Statistics Singapore, 2002. (2003, April 4). *Social indicators 2002.* Retrieved May 1, 2003, from http://www.singstat.gov.sg/keystats/annual/indicators.html

IMPORTANT PUBLICATIONS*

Chan, D. (1998). Functional relations amongst constructs in the same content domain at different levels of analysis: A typology of composition models. *Journal of Applied Psychology, 83,* 234–246.

Chan, D., Schmitt, N., Sacco, J. M., & DeShon, R. P. (1998). Understanding pretest and posttest reactions to cognitive ability and personality tests. *Journal of Applied Psychology, 83,* 471–485.

Chua, F. K. (1999). Phonological recoding in Chinese logograph recognition. *Journal of Experimental Psychology: Learning, Memory, and Cognition, 25,* 876–891.

Nair, E. (1995). *Action research on stress management in Singapore schools.* Singapore: Singapore Teachers' Union.

Nair, E. (1997). *Work ethic: A cross-cultural study of India and Singapore.* (IHV Research Monograph No. 5). Kolkata, India: Indian Institute of Management.

Singh, R., Choo, W. M., & Poh, L. L. (1998). In-group bias and fair-mindedness as strategies of self-presentation and intergroup perception. *Personality and Social Psychology Bulletin, 24,* 147–162.

Singh, R., & Tan, L. S. C. (1992). Attitudes and attraction: A test of the similarity attraction dissimilarity repulsion hypotheses. *British Journal of Social Psychology, 31,* 227–238.

Ward, C., & Chang, W. C. (1997). "Cultural fit:" A new perspective on personality and sojourner adjustment. *International Journal of Intercultural Relations, 21*(4), 525–533.

Ward, C., & Kennedy, A. (1993). Where's the culture in cross-cultural transition: Comparative studies of sojourner adjustment. *Journal of Cross-Cultural Psychology, 24,* 221–249.

Ward, C., & Rana-Deuba, A. (1999). Acculturation and adaptation revisited. *Journal of Cross-Cultural Psychology, 30*(4), 422–442.

---

* Determined by national and international impact and by journal citations from the Web of Knowledge.

CHAPTER 14

Psychology in India

BLANCHE BARNES

Blanche Barnes, who is from India, is an academician and clinical psychologist. A master's-degree holder from Bombay University (1965), she specialized in clinical psychology at the National Institute of Mental Health and Neurosciences (1968) and, thereafter, obtained her Ph.D. from Bombay University (1982). She was a Visiting Academician at Seafarers' International Research Center, University of Wales, Cardiff (1995), and conducted research for the International Transport Workers' Federation, United Kingdom. She brought innovative changes in the post-graduate curriculum in clinical psychology during her tenure as a professor of clinical psychology and chair of the department of psychology, SNDT Women's University, Mumbai, a position she held from 1987 to 2002. (SNDT university was named in honor of its founder, Shrimati Nathibai Damodar Thackersey.) Blanche Barnes also served as dean of the faculty of social sciences, director of the department of post-graduate studies and research, and director

of the College and University Development Council at SNDT Women's University. She was the president of the Bombay Psychological Association (1994–2002), and hosted the Southeast Asia Regional Conference on Psychology in December 2001.

14.1 OVERVIEW

From the wisdom of ancient sages to the present behavioral scientists, psychology in India has benefited from different dimensions, visions, and perspectives. The innermost fabric of the Indian psyche is much influenced by ancient culture, wisdom, and insights, and Indian psychology cannot be divorced from Indian philosophy and belief systems. Indian behavior also is influenced by a multitude of individual and cultural factors, and, in addition, other cultures have influenced and shaped Indian behavioral norms during colonial rule. Often, naive psychologists, in the name of modernity and progress, have adopted behavioral parameters and constructs from the West entirely, missing out on the deep insights embedded in the Indian scriptures. No Indian should ever overlook the *Vedas* and *Upanishads* (approximately 1000 B.C.E.), which contain mystical treatises on the nature of God and the relation of soul and matter that have described the mind as part of greater consciousness, confined to the sensory processes (Kapur, 2001a). Even the *Atharva Veda* (800 B.C.E.) enumerated a list of 20 types of mental illnesses along with appropriate therapeutic processes such as *atharvani* (psychotherapy), *daivya* (naturopathy), and *anushyaja* (herbal medicines and amulets). Patanjali's *Yoga Sutras* is also a respected treatise on total health, addressing the physical, mental, and transcendental phenomena in our lives (Balhodhi, 1991). As for the *Bhagavad Gita,* it laid down the code of conduct and ideal conditions necessary to maintain good mental health.

Indians have come a long way from this rich cultural heritage. Psychology, known as *manashastra,* now has emerged as a distinct and popular specialization, covering various fields such as clinical, industrial, counseling, social, and educational psychology, as well as clinical neuropsychology, parapsychology, psychology of women, comparative psychology, Indian psychology, experimental psychology, and cognitive science.

The development of psychology in India initially began with clinical psychology. The interpretation of the dynamics of behavior was not unfamiliar to Indian philosophers and seers, and dream interpretation, hypnosis, health and well-being, relaxation, and yoga were familiar subjects in Indian thought. Against this backdrop, psychoanalysis fit in well and influenced the field of psychology for many years.

Four especially significant personalities who left their mark on Indian psychology were G. Bose (1886–1953), M. V. Gopalaswamy (1896–1957), M. V. Govindasamy (1904–1961), and H. Narayan Murthy (1927, still living in 2003). Bose, a qualified medical professional, was familiar with Patanjali's (the founder of Yoga, 300 B.C.E.)*Yoga Sutras* and the application of yoga for therapeutic purposes. He used hypnotism for the treatment of the mentally ill and attempted to understand the dynamic principles of the human mind, independent of Freud's work. He introduced psychoanalysis as an important component at the postgraduation degree course at Calcutta University, which was, incidentally, the first university in the world to introduce psychoanalysis at the master's level (Prabhu, 2001). Bose did his Ph.D. dissertation on the "Concept of Repression," and in 1921 he founded the Indian Psychoanalytical Society. Renowned as India's "doctor of the mind," and very much a "son of the soil," he made a systematic study of the *Puranas* (scriptures that contain the essence of Vedas), and attempted to link Indian culture and philosophy to analytical theory. He advocated a *guru–shishya* (teacher–student) relationship as a desirable paradigm for psychotherapy. Bose believed in psychophysical parallelism and rejected the mechanistic behavioral approach in psychology from the very beginning. He called his ideas the "theory of mental life." He also propagated a complicated theory as to how *gunas* (attributes) can control knowledge and ignorance. According to Bose, knowledge in turn can end up with introversive or extroversive facets that give rise to *sattva* (equanimity), *rajas* (dynamic action), and *tamas* (dull inaction). Bose's work influenced not only psychoanalysis and psychology, but also other social sciences and philosophy.

The second prominent figure in the initial stages of development of psychology was M. V. Gopalaswamy, who studied with Charles Spearman. After returning to India, Gopalaswamy established the department of psychology at Mysore University in 1924. This is the second oldest department in the country. In 1955 he moved on to the All-India Institute of Mental Health (AIIMH) to establish an independent department of clinical psychology. Unfortunately, his tenure at AIIMH was cut short by his untimely death in 1957.

M. V. Govindaswamy, the third major figure in the history of Indian psychology, was a brilliant scholar. Enriched by psychiatric training from Johns Hopkins University in the United States and additional training at the Maudsley Hospital in London, he instituted the same high standards of teaching and learning at the AIIMH (now called the National Institute of Mental Health and Neurosciences [NIMHANS]) when he was appointed as its first director in 1954. He was considered to be an able physician, competent psychiatrist, and discerning psychologist. He had innovative ideas, and was convinced of the validity of indigenous methods of treatment, especially those that were practiced in India. He established an *ayurvedic* research unit at NIMHANS (ayurvedic medicine, also known as the "science of life," is an Indian system of healing and health promotion that dates back to approximately 6,000 B.C.E.). In addition, he studied various practices depicted in Indian scriptures, Buddhist philosophy, and many other disciplines in order to research and disseminate information on Indian philosophy, thought, action, and behavior.

Based on his insight and scholarly study of the Indian scriptures, he introduced Indian psychology into the curriculum for both medical and nonmedical students for the first time in India. In addition, Professor Govindaswamy, trained both as a psychologist and psychiatrist, was uniquely qualified to meld the two professions, and he introduced clinical psychology as a profession.

H. Narayan Murthy obtained his D.Sc. in clinical psychology in France and subsequently carried on the tradition of Indian psychology and ayurvedic medicine. He also introduced clinical neuropsychology and behavioral medicine to India.

NIMHANS established clinical psychology as a profession when it awarded the first diploma in medical psychology in 1957, which is now the M.Phil. degree in medical and social psychology. This intensive course of study required completion of a 2-year internship in a mental health setting. Many other universities introduced psychology programs in the late 1950s and early 1960s in different regions of India. The eminent psychologists who developed specialization programs are listed in Table 14.1.

Many psychologists who were trained in the West incorporated western constructs into their school's curriculum, unmindful of the consequences and forthcoming backlash against the development of psychology in India. The practice of imitating western ideas and adapting their tests was later intensely criticized by the same psychologists who imported psychology from the West. As Asthana (1988) bemoaned, "The concerns of western psychology of yesteryears are the current interests of the Indian psychologists" (pp. 155–156). Likewise, Pandey (2001) noted, "Indian research in psychology is 'largely imitative' relying

TABLE 14.1
Major Psychology Programs, Specializations, and Founders

University	Specialization	Name of the Psychologist
Mysore University	Social Psychology	B. Kuppuswamy
University of Madras	Personality/Clinical Psychology	T. N. Shanmugam
Pune University	Experimental Psychology	V. K. Kothurkar
Patna University	Experimental Psychology	S.M. Moshin
University of Mumbai	Applied Psychology	N. Mukerjie
Allahabad University	Applied Social Psychology	D. Sinha
Andhra University	Parapsychology	Rama Rao
Utkal University	Indigenous Psychology	R. Rath
Gorakhpur University	Social Deprivation	L. B. Tripathi
Sagar University	Personality	H. S Asthana
Bharathiar University	Counseling Psychology	N. Rao
University of Kerala	Personality	E. I. George
Aligarh Muslim University	Social Psychology	N. Ansari
Calicut University	Social Psychology	M. A. Faroqi
Sri Venkateswara University	Counseling Psychology	N. Rao
Osmania University	Educational Psychology	E. G. Parameshwaran
Panjab University	Psychometrics Methods	P. S. Hundal
Delhi University	Industrial Psychology	G. C. Gupta
Banaras Hindu University	Experimental Psychology	M. M. Sinha
Nagpur University	Psychometrics Methods	B. N. Mukerjie
NIMHANS	Clinical and Social Psychology	M. V. Govindswamy
IIM, Ahmedabad	Organizational Behavior	U. Pareek
SNDT Women's University	Clinical Psychology	B. L. Barnes

heavily on Western models and concepts" (p. 20).

Indian psychologists began to standardize tests in the 1960s without any regard to indigenous needs and the development of behavioral constructs that were unique to the Indian worldview. Further, there was nothing but a mechanical and cursory attitude towards psychometric validation. These tests were superficial, both in content and application. This large and uncritical adaptation of Western psychometric instruments in India was derisively referred to as "adaptology." Pareek and Rao (1974) and Pestonjee (1988) published detailed compilations of these Indian standardized tests.

Today, we are at a crossroads, where "the East meets the West" in understanding and articulating these behavioral constructs that are unique or parallel in each culture. Cross-cultural psychology has gained center stage, be it in India or elsewhere, because understanding and responding to cultural diversity is perhaps the foremost challenge for psychologists worldwide. Even presuming there are common behavioral markers across cultures, the differences one notes in the expression of these behaviors are so dramatic that it is difficult to generalize and draw universal conclusions about any existing behavioral parameters. Hence, norms established for one subcultural group in India are often not appropriate for application to other subcultures. The issue of standardization within the cultural context has become a matter of great concern to Indian psychologists.

India is a vast country. Its current population is slightly greater than one billion, with a literacy rate of 65%. India has 29 states and six union territories. There are 18 official languages, 325 recognized Indian languages, and numerous dialects. Understanding and providing services for this diverse multicultural and multilingual population, in which each group possesses its own customs, traditions, and values, is a challenging task for Indian behavioral scientists. Hence, psychologists have taken up region-specific issues for test construction and standardization that are related to specific ethnic differences.

Many attempts have been made to formalize the various organizations and associations representing psychology in India, and most such attempts have failed miserably. These associations, started by few dynamic visionaries, have all been unable to sustain their activities. However, a few well-established organizations have stood the test of time. One of them is the Indian Association of Clinical Psychologists (IACP), founded in 1968, which publishes the refereed biannual *Indian Journal of Clinical Psychology*. The Indian Psychological Association also publishes the refereed *Journal of Indian Psychology*. Another journal in circulation with a strong academic reputation is the *Journal of Psychological Studies*. Other popular journals are the *Bombay Psychologist*, *Journal of Creativity and Intelligence*, *Journal of Personality and Clinical Psychology*, and *Journal of Community Psychology*. Qualified clinical psychologists who are certified by the IACP have greater employment opportunities in mental hospitals and psychiatry departments of general hospitals, children's mental health clinics and child guidance centers, and other government and nongovernment organizations (NGOs). At present, there is no government regulatory body that prescribes the minimum qualifications, wages, and standards for employment as a psychologist. Psychologists are considered paramedical personnel in medical settings, welfare officers in industrial organizations, and counselors in schools, whether working alone or as a member of an interdisciplinary team.

As in many parts of the world, in India too females monopolize the psychology major. Of these, only a select few make psychology a career. In addition, their occupational history is often checkered due to marriage and migration from one place to another, depending on the needs of their families. Hence, it is very difficult to keep track of qualified professional psychologists across India. In general, the students who major in psychology do not intend to make it a profession. Their lack of commitment to the profession has delayed the development of Indian psychology as a discipline and profession.

14.2 EDUCATION
AND TRAINING

India is a land of many controversies, and education is one of them. The country has great traditions of learning that date back centuries; for example, Nalanda and Takshashila were famous ancient centers of learning which attracted thousands of students across the globe. Nalanda, the first residential international university in the world, was one of the early Buddhist universities in which the famous Chinese scholar Huan Tsang studied, whereas Takshashila, once known as the world's best university, was situated about 2000 years ago in what we now call Afghanistan. Later the *gurukul* concept (in which one's teacher also serves as one's spiritual guide) was adopted throughout India as a mode of education. This model had great appeal to Indian academicians; given this tradition, it is not surprising to find esteemed scholars and intellectuals throughout India. Education has always been a high priority across many segments of India's population.

The *University Institutions in India* (Association of Indian Universities, 2001) lists 306 recognized universities in India. Most universities include psychology as one of the subjects offered at the undergraduate level. The introduction to psychology course is very popular among arts and humanities students. There are also about 106 universities that offer psychology degrees at the master's level with various specializations.

Each university stipulates its admissions criteria depending on the needs of departments. Psychology is more popular in the cities. In metropolitan areas, the selection criterion for the major in psychology is officially a grade of B+ or better,

which invariably moves up to A+ as the cutoff point for admission. Psychology attracts the best students from the arts and humanities, and even some natural science majors. However, in a semirural setting, applicants admitted to graduate courses in psychology need a minimum grade C+ in the subject. There are some concessions for admission for those castes and tribes identified by the Indian constitution that are culturally and economically disadvantaged. At present, highly specialized psychology courses are offered in some universities that lead to greater opportunities for fieldwork and practical training, and eventually to lucrative job opportunities. At the undergraduate level, courses in general, social, experimental–cognitive, abnormal, developmental, applied psychology, and statistical methods are offered. Other courses include counseling, consumer behavior, organizational psychology, and child guidance. The duration of undergraduate education is 3 years, requiring a total of 96 credits.

The number of students enrolled in psychology at graduate, postgraduate, and doctoral levels is insignificant in proportion to the literate population of the country. A 2-year master's program with a minimum of 64 credits will require rigorous admission criteria such as an entrance test and also an interview in some universities. However, the master's-degree programs that offer applied specializations usually have a heavier practicum workload. Applied professional courses currently offered in India include clinical, organizational behavioral, educational, counseling, applied social, indigenous, health, and animal psychology, as well as cognitive neuroscience and psychotherapy. The graduate psychology curriculum has built-in modules or papers on experimental psychology. This restricts enrollment to a maximum of 20 students per class, both at the master's and at the more advanced levels.

Some universities encourage research at the master's level. Students are free to conduct research projects or theses on any research topic, and are allowed to gain expertise in any specialization by way of practica. Universities are accredited and ranked by the National Assessment and Accreditation Council (NAAC), and the best schools use innovative methods of learning and teaching. They also engage in field-based training programs that provide psychological services for the community. In addition, students participate actively in seminars, workshops, and guided reading.

Those students who have the acumen necessary for research are encouraged to earn the M.Phil. degree in psychology. This course of study varies in duration at different universities. The minimum duration is three semesters of theoretical coursework, fieldwork, and a research project. A typical program requires 40 credits. At some universities, such as NIMHANS, coursework is 2 years in duration, including intensive internship training. Similar training is given at Central Institute of Psychiatry at Ranchi and Chandigarh, and at Kasturba Medical College at Manipal. To qualify as a clinical psychologist, candidates must undergo a 2-year supervised internship.

A Ph.D. program, stressing either theory or empirical research, is offered at almost all the universities after completion of a master's degree program. Students are admitted to a Ph.D. program only after intense scrutiny. The University Grants Commission (UGC) currently mandates a pre-Ph.D. course requirement before allowing formal enrollment in a doctoral program. The most common duration for the Ph.D. program is 3 years. However, some universities have not set any time limits for completion of the doctorate.

Psychology in India at the undergraduate and graduate levels places great emphasis on experimental–cognitive psychology, both theoretical and practical, and other core subjects. The experimental–cognitive psychology practical course is eight credits. Teaching is a combination of lecture and discussion. The maximum enrollment for each class is 25 students at the undergraduate level and 20 at the graduate level.

The UGC approves various degree programs as well as all curricula. As of 2002, modular courses are mandated by the semester system in the UGC's 10th Plan program. This paradigm shift in teaching has been welcomed by departments of psychology. There is yet another body that has been introduced recently to ensure quality in education. The NAAC assesses each department and university and grades the performance of each accordingly. Under the World Trade Organization's General Agreement on Trade in Services (GATS), even education has been considered to be a service-oriented industry that is accountable to the stakeholders.

Despite the emphasis on education, large numbers of Indians often have no prospects for employment even after graduation, and this dismal reality has produced unrest among the youth. The NAAC has attempted to address this problem by ensuring better standards in education that are internationally comparable. This will facilitate inter-university and international mobility.

There are a few distinct universities that have been accorded special status by UGC and designated as Centers of Advanced

Studies. These departments are noted for their exceptional research and innovative curricula. One example is the Indigenous Psychology program at Utkal University in Bhuvaneshwar. The second center that enjoys this status is Allahabad University's Department of Applied Social and Cross-Cultural Psychology. The third department accorded this status is the program in Issues Related to Aging at Sri Venkateswara University.

Each of the following universities has also made distinct contributions to the developments in the field of psychology:

Allahabad University: Applied Social, Clinical, and Cross-Cultural Psychology
Andhra University: Parapsychology
Bangalore University: Clinical Psychology, Psychology of Women
Calcutta University: Clinical, Industrial Psychology
Delhi University: Industrial Psychology, Cognitive Science
University of Kerala: Yoga and Well-Being
University of Mumbai: Industrial, Social, Clinical, Counseling Psychology
Mysore University: Animal Psychology, Psycho-Ecology
NIMHANS: Clinical Psychology, Clinical Neuropsychology
University of Pune: Experimental, Cognitive Science, Industrial Psychology
Punjab University: Personality, Psychometrics
SNDT Women's University: Clinical Psychology, Psychology of Women
Sri Venkateswara University: Psychology of Aging
Utkal University: Indigenous Psychology, Animal Psychology

Psychology is also a popular subject and an integral part of the curriculum of engineering, management, and medicine. Each of these schools has a department of humanities that monitors psychology courses. Even the armed forces and police have modules on psychology in their training curricula.

Psychometric evaluation is popular in India. Many of the doctoral dissertations of the 1960s and 1970s focused on the adaptation of tests that had been standardized abroad. Though some revisions were made from the original tests, the constructs were the same as those used in the West, and hence, their reliability and validity are questionable for the Indian population. Jnana Prabhodini, a Pune-based organization, is actively involved in standardizing educational and cognitive tests for school children. Recently they produced a CD-ROM on intelligence and aptitude measurement called "I AM," which is computerized and easy to operate. However, the questions of reliability, validity, and item analysis for the test are still not resolved. Until now, psychology has been considered as a subject only to be taught in the classroom. However, there have been a few attempts to promote distance education for psychology in India. For example, the University of Madras has recently developed a distance-education course in psychology with a required practicum. Other universities are likely to adopt this model of distance learning for psychology because the subject is very much in demand.

The contributions an eminent psychologist can make by publishing books are illustrated by the popular works of J. Pandey (2000, 2001). These edited books provide a good overview of psychology in India and illustrate many culturally relevant issues pertaining to psychology. Even the indigenous thought process and the Indian world view are covered comprehensively in these volumes.

D. Sinha's contribution to applied social issues in India is also well documented (1986). M. Kapur's (1995) *Child Mental Health* provides a cultural perspective on child development and describes the pathological conditions confronting many Indian children. U. Pareek and T. V. Rao (1974) published a compilation of tests and instruments in India that is very popular among psychologists. A subsequent edition was published by D. M. Pestonjee (1988) as the *Second Handbook of Psychological and Social Instruments.*

Many Indian psychologists have assimilated western ideas and believe that "West is best." They are eager to go to the United Kingdom and the United States for further specialization. However, very few are actually able to realize this. Indian psychologists who study abroad are generally the recipients of Indian or foreign scholarships, such as a Commonwealth Fellowship or the Fulbright scholarship.

There are a number of psychologists who have successfully sought jobs abroad and are professionally successful in other countries. A psychologist usually is considered qualified for employment after a master's degree. However, in the case of clinical psychology, an M.Phil. or Ph.D. degree with a supervised internship, as stipulated by the NIMHANS curriculum, is required. The Rehabilitation Council of India, a statutory government body that was formed in 1992, also recognizes this qualification. So far, no regulatory body has been empowered to license psychologists in India. After completing their master's degree, the majority of psychologists seek employment with the Indian government, NGOs, private companies, or universities.

Occasionally, psychologists and professors of psychology at universities and colleges update themselves with UGC-approved refresher courses conducted by the academic staff colleges of various universities. These continuing education programs provide a platform for additional knowledge and familiarization with changing trends in psychology.

14.3 SCOPE OF PSYCHOLOGICAL PRACTICE

Many people, irrespective of their academic qualifications, practice psychology in India. These pseudo-professionals often mislead the ill-informed and ignorant public. Those who are trained in psychology do adhere to the ethical code and conduct stipulated by the American Psychological Association, standards that are widely accepted internationally for the practice of psychology. However, in India, there are no stringent rules and regulations that govern the practice of psychology. There are no consumer laws applicable to this profession, and as long as psychologists provide services and satisfy the public, their work is accepted. The only body that is even informally recognized for setting standards is the IACP. This organization recommends the M.Phil. in medical psychology with internship as the minimum requirement to practice clinical psychology. In addition, those who do not have this qualification but who have worked at least for 7 years in a mental health setting under supervision can register as members of the IACP.

Psychoanalysis has long dominated Indian psychology. To a certain extent, this model fits the Indian worldview and thought process. Writing from an Indian philosophical perspective, K. Ramakrishna Rao (2001) has contrasted consciousness in Indian and Western perspectives. In the Indian tradition, (a) consciousness and mind are viewed as different; (b) consciousness is believed to be nonintentional, whereas mind is perceived to be intentional; and (c) one's goal is to develop practical methods for transforming the human condition via the realization of consciousness. In the Western tradition, (a) consciousness is equated with the mind; (b) intentionality is regarded as its defining characteristic; and (c) one's goal is to attain rational understanding of consciousness/mind (Pandey, 2001).

One can sense the inherent differences in perception of the constructs of consciousness and mind that exist between East and West. Rao (2001) believes that, despite the historical head start that Indian psychologists have in the study of consciousness, they have confined themselves to, and are preoccupied with, the most mundane issues of psychology. Rao believes that empirical research in phenomenological consciousness and information processing, extrasensory perception, psychokinesis, implicit memory, subliminal perception, yoga theory and practice, transcendence, meditation, near-death experiences, and reincarnation should be the focus of Indian psychologists.

Indian researchers have made some preliminary contributions to parapsychology as it relates to extrasensory perception and personality factors, neuroticism, meditation, and reincarnation (Stevenson & Pasricha, 1980). As J. Prasad (1973) wrote,

"Parapsychology in India has a long past but a brief history" (p. 43). Parapsychology did get support from the UGC and a Department of Parapsychology was started at Andhra University under the leadership of Rama Rao, who received national and international acclaim for his pioneering research in this area.

India has historically attracted many scholars from the West who came to study and understand the Indian philosophy of life and living. Many of these scholars were interested in psychological issues, and in fact there is a blend of theoretical constructs and psychological practices of East and West found in the discipline of psychology in India. One of these Western visitors was C. G. Jung, who subsequently incorporated many Indian constructs into his analytical theory. Impressed with the Indian tradition of a phenomenological approach to consciousness, Jung explored cultural consciousness, archetypes, symbolisms, and dream analysis, all of which were easily accepted by Indian psychologists. Later, Indian psychologists, impressed with Carl Rogers's nondirective phenomenological approach, once again used his client-centered therapeutic constructs to bring out the restrained, inhibited people of India, a people burdened by an authoritarian and patriarchal society. The behaviorist orientation also was easily adopted in India, and in the 1970s many Indian psychologists became behavior therapists. NIMHANS started an independent unit to train psychologists in behavioral and cognitive therapies. Today, with a steep rise in depression and a high incidence of suicide, especially among adolescents, psychologists have increasingly adopted cognitive–behavioral therapies to respond to the needs of this population.

For any therapeutic program to be successful, clients should be relaxed. In the West, N. Jacobson's progressive muscle relaxation has been the most popular technique. In contrast, the Indian psychologist has preferred *pranayama*, a deep-breathing exercise derived from an age-old indigenous meditation technique designed to produce harmony between mind and body. Currently, yoga is becoming more and more popular as a therapeutic technique for all types of mental and psychosomatic disorders. It facilitates concentration and establishes awareness of the mind and body. Another effective technique is *shavasana* or *yoga nidra*, a method to relax the whole body and enter into a deliberate state of sleep. Yoga can bring about harmony and balance between mind, body, and spirit. It is a holistic treatment program with many prophylactic advantages. Many departments of psychology have incorporated yoga into their curriculum.

NIMHANS developed an independent unit in neuropsychology, the first in India, under its Department of Clinical Psychology. Many Indian psychologists have adapted Western neuropsychological test batteries that have been standardized for the Indian population. These adaptations include the NIMHANS Neuropsychological Test Battery, the PGI Battery for Brain Dysfunction, and the AIIMS Comprehensive Neuropsychological Test Battery in Hindi, the national language.

Many Indian psychologists deplore their colleagues' tendency to ape the West and uncritically adopt its tests, and insist that Indian psychologists must appreciate their own cultural and social heritage. Hence, there is a marked trend towards indigenization, both in medicine and the behavioral sciences. Kapur (2001b) has conducted extensive research in child psychology and child pathology, and has confirmed the beneficial effects of an Indian system of childcaring and rearing.

Indian psychologists also want to understand the country's indigenous population, which previously was neglected and marginalized. Utkal University has taken a lead in understanding tribal cultures and what they have to offer to other Indians. However, no effort to understand indigenization can be complete unless a region's dialects are understood, and this poses a great challenge to behavioral scientists. The research done on these tribal populations has provided insight into inherent intellectual and cognitive abilities, and has also suggested new treatment and therapeutic interventions. Teaching coping skills, such as assertiveness training and problem solving, has helped indigenous people cope with the modernization of society. The pharmacological effects of plants (Mandal, 2000) such as *bramhi*, *neem*, *aswagandha*, *shankapushpi*, *haldi*, and *tulasi*, have been shown to reduce stress and to improve cognitive functions.

Recently, Canada-based A. Paranjpe (2001) provided *vedantic* views on human behavior, the structure of human personality, the spiritual nature of humankind, the method of realizing the spiritual self, and the cognitive processes necessary to render the ego powerless and selfless in order to attain mental peace. Hence, it is necessary to improve human conditions before one can attain *samabhava* or mental tranquility with detachment. Such an attitude tremendously enhances and improves cognitive abilities (Paranjpe, 1984).

Indian psychologists have been especially interested in studying intelligence and memory. Intelligence operates through all the motor and sensory organs, which are considered to be various gates to the environment that enrich experience. In addition, there are internal functions, which are subtle, like mind (*manas*), ego awareness (*ahamkara*), and intelligence (*buddhi*). All of these functions operate holistically under different mental faculties (Pandey, 2000). However, Indian psychologists have not translated indigenous constructs of intelligence into indigenous measures of intelligence. Rather Western tests and their modifications are used. For example, Indian psychologists still use adaptations of the Stanford–Binet test of intelligence. Even in the West, these tests have undergone periodic drastic revisions. Tests that are standardized in India are redundant and obsolete by contemporary standards but are still widely used in clinical, educational, and counseling practice.

S. Pal did pioneering work in test standardization in 1925 for the population of Bengal. Later, psychologists also took up the task of standardization, but V. V. Kamath's (1935) efforts are especially laudable. Kamath developed a test that he named the Binet–Kamath Test of Intelligence and which he made available in three different languages: Marathi, Kannada, and English for the population of Western India. Meanwhile, performance tests of intelligence also became popular, such as the Bhatia's Test of Intelligence, a modified version of Alexander's Test of Intelligence. Indian psychologists attempted to standardize other intelligence scales, too, the most popular being Ramalingaswamy's Wechsler's Adult Performance Intelligence Scale, Malin's Vineland Social Maturity Scale, and Phatak's Draw-a-Man Test.

Srivastava, Tripathi, and Misra (1996) prepared a comprehensive status report on intelligence testing in India. The National Library and Educational Psychological Tests (NLEPT) at the National Council of Educational Research and Training has catalogued Indian tests, and the NLEPT has published an *Indian Mental Measurement Yearbook on Intelligence and Aptitude Tests*. According to Srivatava et al., "Intelligence in the Indian philosophical treatises has been treated as a state, a process and an entity, the realization of which depends upon one's effort, persistence and motivation" (p. 23).

Many Western constructs have been adapted to study personality, using both projective and objective tests. Notable among Indian adaptations of personality tests are the Thematic Apperception Test and Children's Apperception Test; the Minnesota Multiphasic Personality Inventory (MMPI), with Indian norms and cutoffs for diagnoses; the 16PF; the State-Trait Anxiety Inventory (STAI); the Bem's Sex-Role Inventory; the Beck Depression Inventory and Anxiety Inventory; and the Hamilton Rating Scale for Depression.

Industrial–organizational psychology has made great inroads in India's metropolitan areas where psychologists tend to be well paid, often working as team members with managerial staff. In the current environment, in which there is massive downsizing and reduced staffing due to technological developments, the trend is to retain only those employees who are outstanding performers. Psychologists are trained to identify star performers in terms of their organizational effectiveness. U. Pareek (1981), the doyen of organizational psychology in India, has introduced innovative ideas for psychological interventions and research in Indian organizations, developing scales to measure organizational-role stress, leadership styles, and many other constructs. With the standards developed by the International Organization for Standardization (ISO 9002) being implemented earnestly in India, emphasis is being placed on minimum standards of working for Indian organizations. In the process, human factors, previously neglected, have received increasing attention. With this shift in the focus, the need for industrial–organizational psychologists is especially felt. Psychologists in organizations facilitate human relations, improve leadership skills, promote innovation, enhance communication, and facilitate teamwork. In addition, psychologists are often called on for crisis management and stress management. Downsizing with high-tech innovations has brought in high accountability and responsibility in employees. The inability on the part of employees to cope with these organizational changes and the failure of organizations to change the mind-set of employees has led to serious repercussions in job efficiency and mental health. To overcome this stress, employee counseling and employee assistance programs have been rendered in most of the organizations.

The problems connected with psychology that affect the transportation industry has not received sufficient attention. The hijacking of planes, disruption of railway tracks, and bombing of buses are all politico-psychologically based events. There are other issues that need attention, too, such as heat, noise, vibration, climatic variation, pollution, workload, and conditions that result in high stress as well as accidents. The quality of life of India's workforce also is adversely affected by erratic working hours, poor eating habits, boredom, and monotony. In addition to concerns about absenteeism and alcoholism,

industries are troubled by high rates of death due to various diseases and accidents, which are mainly attributed to "human elements" (Barnes, 1992). In order to reduce the number of errors made by workers, industry has introduced special courses in human relations and the communication process; these often accompany additional training in the use of scientific and technological equipment and tools.

India has been devastated by disasters from time to time, both natural and man-made, including famine, flood, earthquakes, and industrial disasters such as the Bhopal tragedy. Added to these problems is terrorism due to political, religious, and linguistic fanaticism. Being subjected to any form of trauma leaves unforgettable memories and, sometimes, a hate-inspired desire for revenge. These experiences also produce a need for humanitarian assistance programs to mitigate the trauma. Psychologists have responded to these needs, working with earthquake victims at Kutch Bhuj, for example. In this situation, psychologists worked under the aegis of UNICEF and used Eye Movement Desensitization and Reprocessing (EMDR) to help 16,000 victims (Mehrotra, 2000).

Psychologists in India have also been concerned about the well-being of women. This is a national concern because women are an underutilized resource in India, and discrimination and systematic social injustice on the basis of gender is commonplace (Miranda, 1995). There is a great need to understand women in their totality (including their quality of life, health and mental health, traumatic life events, equality status, and pathology), and comprehensive evaluations have to replace simplistic studies that treat gender as only a demographic variable. These changes are necessary to understand sex differences in psychological research (Barnes, 1996). The other areas in the psychology of women that need to be studied in India are violence against women, abuse and neglect of the girl child, women's health, single-women-headed households, morbidity in women, aging and delayed life span, dowry deaths, prenatal sex determination, rape, abortion, and related topics. Comprehensive assessments that address these issues will be important in understanding sex differences in attitudes, attributes, and behavior in India. Most of the research in this area has centered on political and economic issues related to women. In India, for example, motherhood has been deified and few women are allowed to deviate from this role. Indian women often accept traditional values and perpetuate stereotypic gender roles. Among career and noncareer women, domestic duties have historically been considered more important than the provider role (Bharat, 1995). Indian women often fear success, and positive life changes such as a job promotion may trigger clinical depression. Conversely, a low need for achievement in professional women in India has been noted (Khanna, 1992). Indian women need to be taught assertion skills and cognitive behavior therapeutic techniques to "break the glass ceiling" and surge forward to self-actualization.

It is estimated that there will be 117 million elderly women in India by the year 2025. With the increasing feminization of poverty, aging will increasingly come to be seen as a women's issue (Prakash, 1993). Psychologists can help Indian women identify psychosocial support systems that lead to empowerment not only economically but also psychologically. Women who experience trauma also need crisis intervention and 24-hr help through tele-counseling and, in the future, Web-based counseling.

The incidence of adolescent suicide is on the rise in India, where students encounter great pressure to excel in academics. Often unable to cope with familial demands for academic excellence, adolescents may exhibit intense fear, anxiety, addiction, depression, and, ironically, poor academic performance. In addition, many children in India need special attention and psychological interventions; these children are socially, economically, and culturally deprived and have no opportunities to self actualize or to realize the full potential of their lives.

HIV/AIDS is another domain where psychologists can make a difference in India. Currently, the government's National AIDS Control Organization (NACO) uses psychologists to provide family interventions, behavior modification, and group therapy, and these psychologists train counselors to provide HIV/AIDS counseling. Indian citizens living with HIV and AIDS are overwhelmed by emotional and social problems unique to the country's traditional society, and these concerns are compounded by the challenges they must confront in coping with a debilitating illness. Social support groups for these patients, in addition to active policy decisions by the Indian government to improve their quality of life, are essential. Similar services are needed for patients with cancer, leprosy, and Alzheimer's disease.

Culture-specific mental health problems, such as mass hysteria and possession by spirits, are not uncommon in India. In addition, there are three unique syndromes that are commonly reported in psychiatric practice, namely, *dhat, koro*, and *jhijhini*. *Dhat* (semen loss) is a common concern among men who present with depression and anxiety. Patients experiencing *koro* develop a dysmorphic perception of their penis (Chakraborty, 1983). Chakraborty's study revealed anxiety to be the root cause of this disorder. *Jhinjhini* results in complaints of tingling, numbness, muteness, paralysis, helplessness, and collapsing, with fear of impending death, and is attributed to evil spirits. It is characterized by a rapid onset and cessation within few hours (Nandi, Banerjee, Saha, Sen, & Bhatacharjee, 1992). Another culturally specific tradition found in India is the treatment of sexual minorities like transsexuals and hermaphrodites, called *hijras*. There was always a third sexual identity in the Indian scriptures, called *napumsaka,* indicating an impotent or nonfunctioning male. The *Atharvaveda* (a sacred text of the Indo-Aryans) refers to *pandaka,* effeminate males who dress and behave like females. Indian tradition and culture has traditionally accepted this form of gender variance; however, homosexual or transgendered individuals often confront discrimination in India as elsewhere in the world. The Humsafar Trust, an advocacy group of predominately gay men devoted to healthy living, is fighting for the rights of transgendered people who are marginalized in Indian society. The Humsafar Trust estimates there are around 2.5 to 3 million transgendered males in India who need the society's support to attain a better quality of life and freedom from sexual stigma.

14.4 FUTURE CHALLENGES AND PROSPECTS

India is a vast country with immense human resources. Since professional psychologists constitute a miniscule proportion of the total population, their visibility at the government level is negligible. However, it is time for psychologists to make their presence felt at the government level and take part in policy making. Achieving professional visibility and gaining creditability are the biggest challenges for psychologists in India.

D. Sinha (1993) has observed that there is a growing maturity in Indian psychology, both in its theoretical constructs and its application. However, J. B. P. Sinha claimed, "most of the work [of Indian psychologists] is imitative and hence mediocre; it perhaps is a motivational problem, a lack of that kind of commitment that is needed for creatively blazing our own trails" (1993, p. 135).

A second issue with profound implications for the profession is the almost exclusive enrollment of women in psychology programs. Currently, less than 5% of male students elect psychology as a major. Because of scarce job opportunities and sex stereotyping, psychology has failed to attract males. To overcome this bias, it may be necessary to reserve some percentage of seats in psychology programs for men. However, the unfortunate fact is that many women, saddled with multiple roles, are unable to give their total commitment to the profession. The growing female monopoly in psychology is viewed with considerable apprehension by academic psychologists.

A third issue is that, for many students, psychology is just an idle academic pursuit, and there is little genuine commitment to research. Dissertations often address routine topics, studying variables and constructs that have already been well established. Simply applying these relationships to different linguistic samples or a new population is sufficient to earn a Ph.D. degree in psychology in India. This imitative work fails to contribute to the discipline or profession.

Psychologists in India have too long ignored rural areas and marginalized populations. They have a responsibility to Indian society and therefore must develop innovative programs to reach out to the populations previously considered unreachable. The adoption of socially responsible attitudes and practices will enhance the image of psychology. However, this will require a paradigm shift in our existing attitudes and work culture. The passivity and inertia that characterizes most Indian psychologists cannot sustain a caring profession. However, over the years, this attitude is slowly changing as psychologists become more involved in community programs that provide HIV/AIDS counseling, rehabilitation of street children, and services for the destitute.

The Internet is another tool psychologists can use to deliver counseling services. Currently, there are popular Indian Websites addressing violence toward women, the legal rights of women, HIV/AIDS awareness, professional counseling, health and medicine, and sexual-orientation issues. This avenue of communication is invaluable for clients experiencing distress, anxiety, or trauma, and for those who are unable to communicate directly with a psychologist. The Internet also has been a boon to Indian researchers. The paucity of literature available in Indian libraries has been replaced by unparalleled access to information on the Internet.

Indian psychologists frequently have neglected their rich scriptures that actually provide splendid examples of behavioral management and coping. However, recently, Indian psychology has begun to move toward its own culturally familiar intellectual landscape. Hence, training in and knowledge of Indian philosophy and anthropology are necessary to understand the Indian ethos. The nuances of ethnic diversity and multiculturalism in India are also critical to an understanding of Indian psychology.

In conclusion, the status of psychology in India reflects positive trends. Indian psychologists have come to realize that indigenization is imperative to the evolution of the profession and necessary to understand the Indian psyche and the complexity of India's diverse culture. Varied specializations will develop different professional targets in the future. Clinical psychology will widen its sphere to include behavioral medicine and health psychology. Industrial–organizational psychology looks forward to expanded involvement in human-resource management. Community psychology will address various problems such as HIV/AIDS, aging, and the mistreatment of women who are a culturally, socially, and economically marginalized population. However, it is clear that along with these opportunities, there are many challenges and much unfinished business waiting for Indian psychologists.

ACKNOWLEDGMENTS

I appreciate the valuable suggestions given by Professor S. W. Deshpande, Shri Ashok Rao Kavi, Professor Mewa Singh, Dr. Anuradha Sovani, and Jennie Mendes in preparing this manuscript.

REFERENCES

Association of Indian Universities. (2001). *University institutions in India.* New Delhi: AIU House.

Asthana, H. S. (1988). Personality. In J. Pandey (Ed.), *Psychology in India: The state-of-the-art: Vol. 1. Personality and mental processes* (pp. 155–156). New Delhi: Sage.

Balhodhi, J. P. (1991). Holistic approach to psychiatry: Indian view. *NIMHANS Journal, 9,* 101–104.

Barnes, B. L. (1992). Stress in transport workers. *Indian Journal of Clinical Psychology, 19,* 14–17.

Barnes, B. L. (1996). Quality of life and mental health of Indian urban women. *Bombay Psychologist, 13*(1 & 2), 45–52.

Bharat, S. (1995). Attitudes and sex-role perceptions among working couples. *Indian Journal of Comparative Family Studies, 26,* 371–388.

Chakraborty, A. (1983). An epidemic of Koro in West Bengal (India). *Indian Journal of Psychiatry, 25,* 138–139.

Kamat, V. V. (1935). *Measuring intelligence of Indian children.* Mumbai: Oxford University Press.

Kapur, M. (1995). *Mental health of Indian children.* New Delhi: Sage.

Kapur, M. (2001a). Mental health, illness, and therapy. In J. Pandey (Ed.), *Psychology in India revisited: Developments in the discipline: Vol. 2. Personality and health psychology* (pp. 412–472). New Delhi: Sage.

Kapur, M. (2001b, December). *Childcare in ancient India and developmental psychology.* Invited address at the Southeast Asia Regional Conference on Scientific and Applied Psychology, Mumbai, India.

Khanna, S. (1992). Life stress among working women in relation to anxiety and depression. *Psychologia, 35,* 111–116.

Mandal, M. K. (2000). Physiological foundation of behavior. In J. Pandey (Ed.), *Psychology in India revisited: Developments in the discipline: Vol. 1. Physiological foundation and human cognition* (pp. 58–93). New Delhi: Sage.

Mehrotra, S. (2001, December). *EMDR in action for Kutch-Bhuj earthquake victims.* Symposium conducted at the Southeast Asia Regional Conference on Scientific and Applied Psychology, Mumbai, India.

Miranda, J. (1995). *Feminism in psychology: Accelerating paradigmatic shifts.* Mumbai: Research Center for Women's Studies, SNDT Women's University.

Nandi, D. N., Banerjee, G., Saha, H., Sen, B., & Bhatacharjee, A. (1992). An epidemic of "Jhinjhini:" A strange contagious psychogenic disorder in village in West Bengal. *Indian Journal of Psychiatry, 34,* 366–369.

Pandey, J. (Ed.). (1988). *Psychology in India: The state-of-the-art: Vol. 2. Basic and applied psychology.* New Delhi: Sage.

Pandey, J. (Ed.). (2000). *Psychology in India revisited: Developments in the discipline: Vol. 1. Physiological foundation and human cognition.* New Delhi: Sage.

Pandey, J. (Ed.). (2001). *Psychology in India revisited: Developments in the discipline: Vol. 2. Personality and health psychology.* New Delhi: Sage.

Paranjpe, A. C. (1984). *Theoretical psychology: Meeting of the East and West (paths in psychology).* New York: Plenum.

Paranjpe, A. C. (2001, December). *Traditional indigenous versus modern models in psychology and medicine.* Invited address at Southeast Asia Regional Conference on Scientific and Applied Psychology, Mumbai, India.

Pareek, U. (1981). *Role stress scales: Research report.* Ahmedabad, India: Indian Institute of Management.

Pareek, U., & Rao, T. V. (1974). *Handbook of psychological and social instruments.* Baroda, India: Samasthi.

Pestonjee, D. M. (1988). *Second handbook of psychological and social instruments.* New Delhi: Concept Publishing.

Prabhu, G. G. (2001). Indian clinical psychologist of the millennium: The 3G phenomena. *Indian Journal of Clinical Psychologist, 28,* 149–154.

Prakash, I. J. (1993). Gender aging: Psychosocial Issues. *Indian Journal of Gerontology, 7,* 24–29.

Prasad, J. (1973). Parapsychology in India. In A. Angoff & B. Shapin (Eds.), *Parapsychology today: A geographical view* (pp. 43–52). New York: Parapsychology Foundation.

Rao, K. R. (2001). Consciousness studies: A survey of perspectives of research. In J. Pandey (Ed.), *Psychology in India revisited: Developments in the discipline: Vol. 2. Personality and health psychology* (pp. 19–62). New Delhi: Sage.

Sinha, D. (1986). *Psychology in a third world country: The Indian experience.* New Delhi: Sage.

Sinha, D. (1993). Sinha's anxiety test three decades after. *Indian Journal of Personality and Clinical Studies, 8*(1-2), 1–6.

Sinha, J. B. P. (1993). The bulk and the front of psychology in India. *Psychology and Developing Sciences, 5,* 135–150.

Srivastava, A. K., Tripathi, A. M., & Misra, G. (1995). Western and Indian perspectives on intelligence: Some reflections. *Indian Educational Review, 30,* 30–45.

Srivastava, A. K., Tripathi, A. M., & Misra, G. (1996). The status of intelligence testing in India: A preliminary analysis. *Indian Educational Review, 31,* 1–11.

Stevenson, I., & Pasricha, S. K. (1980). A preliminary report on an unusual case of the reincarnation type with xenoglossy. *Journal of the Society for Psychical Research, 74,* 331–348.

IMPORTANT PUBLICATIONS

Abhedananda, Swami. (1983). *Yoga psychology.* Kolkata, India: Ramakrishna Vedanta Math.

Agarwal, A., & Saxena, A. K. (Eds.). (2003). *Psychological perspectives in environmental and developmental issues.* New Delhi: Concept Publishing.

Henry, S. R. K., & Sinha, D. (1997). *Asian perspectives in psychology: Cross-cultural and methodological series.* New Delhi: Sage.

Kapur, M. (1995). *Mental health of Indian children.* New Delhi: Sage.

Pandey, J. (Ed.). (2000). *Psychology in India revisited: Developments in the discipline: Vol. 1. Physiological foundation and human cognition.* New Delhi: Sage.

Pandey, J. (Ed.). (2001). *Psychology in India revisited: Developments in the discipline: Vol. 2. Personality and health psychology.* New Delhi: Sage.

Paranjpe, A. C. (1984). *Theoretical psychology: Meeting of the East and West (paths in psychology).* New York: Plenum.

Pareek, U., & Rao, T. V. (1974). *Handbook of psychological and social instruments.* Baroda, India: Samasthi.

Pareek, U., & Sisodia, V. (Eds.). (1999). *HRD in the new millennium.* New Delhi: Tata McGraw-Hill.

Pestonjee, D. M. (1988). *Second handbook of psychological and social instruments.* New Delhi: Concept Publishing.

Sayeed, O. B., & Pareek, U. (2000). *Actualizing managerial roles.* New Delhi: Tata McGraw-Hill.

Sen, A., & Sen, A. K. (Eds.). (1998). *Challenges of contemporary realities: A psychological perspective on the future of human society.* New Delhi: New Age International.

Sinha, D. (1986). *Psychology in a third world country: The Indian experience.* New Delhi: Sage.

Sinha, J. B. P. (2000). *Patterns of work culture: Cases and strategies for culture building.* New Delhi: Sage.

CHAPTER 15

Psychology in Pakistan

NOSHEEN KHAN RAHMAN

Nosheen Khan Rahman received her M.A. in psychology from Government College, Lahore, and her Ph.D. in educational psychology from Fordham University, New York City. She completed a fellowship in rational emotive behavior therapy at the Albert Ellis Institute in New York City. She was trained in both individual and group psychotherapy under the personal supervision of Dr. Albert Ellis.

Nosheen Khan Rahman joined the department of psychology at Lahore College for Women in 1982 as an assistant professor. In 1985, she joined the Center for Clinical Psychology, a post-master's professional training program in clinical psychology at Punjab University in Lahore. She is currently professor and director in the same department, as well as president of the Pakistan Association of Clinical Psychologists and member of the Advisory Board of Amin Maktab, a nonprofit institution in Lahore for the education of slow learners.

Norsheen Khan Rahman has published over 17 articles and presented many papers

at several national conferences. Her research interests include the rehabilitation of schizophrenics, development of indigenous psychological tests, and adaptation of psychological tests into the Urdu language for use with the Pakistani population. Currently, she is engaged in cowriting a self-help book, Overcoming Depression, *in Urdu.*

15.1 OVERVIEW

Although Pakistan gained independence in August 1947, the history of psychology in the region marking Pakistan's boundaries dates back to the 1920s. Psychology in Pakistan initially grew out of philosophy. In the beginning, there were only three departments of philosophy in Lahore—at Forman Christian College, Government College, and Islamia College—where master's programs were offered in both philosophy and psychology. After World War II, there was particular interest in the development of intelligence testing. For example, Professor Charles Herbert Rice, who at that time was principal at Forman Christian College, developed the Hindustani (Indian) Binet Scales. The college, however, was forced to close down its psychology classes in 1952 due to lack of qualified faculty. At Government College, Professor Gyanesh Chander Chatterji, who was trained in the United Kingdom, became chairperson of the twin departments of philosophy and psychology and created laboratories for clinical and experimental psychology. A group intelligence test based on the work of Terman, Burt, and Ballard was also developed to assess the intellectual level of 1st-year students who were newly admitted to the college. Later, other group intelligence tests used in the United Kingdom were culturally adapted for use with students at the college—the junior series to assess the intellectual level of 1st-year students and the senior series to assess the intellectual level of senior students (Aslam, 1975). A clinical division in was created in the department to cope with increased stress among the population caused mainly by the harsh realities of World War II. At the same time, a children's clinic was also established. The Indian subcontinent was ruled by the British at this time, and the Indian Army, represented by a large Muslim infantry, fought alongside Allied Forces against the Germans in the West and the Japanese in the East. There were many cases of soldiers suffering from shell shock and the deprivations of war, which were attended to by psychologists. In addition, psychologists of the subcontinent played an important role in organizing propaganda. During the period immediately following independence in 1947, Government College became the center for psychological testing in both East and West Pakistan.

Syed Mohammad Hafeez Zaidi and Furrukh Zahooruddin Ahmad in Karachi; Shahab-ud-din Mohammad Moghni in Peshawar; and Ghulam Jilani, Mohammad Ajmal, Qazi Mohammad Aslam, and Rafia Hasan in Lahore carried out pioneering work in the development of psychology in Pakistan and went on to establish independent departments of psychology at various government universities. All had received their degrees in the United Kingdom except for Ahmad who was trained in the United States.

In 1962, Ajmal, though trained in Western intellectual traditions and a great proponent of Jung's analytical psychology, laid the foundation for an indigenous psychotherapy in Pakistan based on Sufi doctrines (i.e., divinely inspired humanism) in the quest of establishing a scientific approach to healing (Haque, 2000).

The psychology department at Karachi University was established in 1955. Here, the focus of training was more empirical and less philosophical. In the early years, regular visits from American psychologists and sociologists helped students become acquainted with the latest developments and trends in Western psychology. Many cross-cultural studies were conducted, and the first professional journal of psychology in the country, the *Pakistan Journal of Psychology*, was published in June 1965.

In 1957, a master's program in psychology was inaugurated at Islamia College in Lahore but was closed down in 1971 due to lack of funds. It was restarted in 1999 but again closed down in 2002 due to functional problems caused by the cancellation of its affiliation with Punjab University (formerly known as the University of the Punjab).

At Sind University in Jamshoro, the department of psychology emerged as an independent unit in 1958. In 1962, the University of the Punjab in Lahore established a department of applied psychology where two American psychologists, along with local faculty members worked as teachers and researchers. The department offered both bachelor's honors and master's programs, though later only the master's program continued. It was at this time that psychology became a part of the faculty of science.

The department of psychology at Peshawar University was established in 1964. It had a well-equipped laboratory for experimental psychology. In 1969, the department also started a journal, *Pakistan Psychological Studies*, and in 1973 a doctoral program was begun.

In East Pakistan, there were two psychology departments, one at Dacca University and the other at Rajshahi University; both offered a master's in psychology. M. Phil. and Ph.D. programs were also functional but lacked a formal curriculum. The focus was mainly on research. Psychologists in East Pakistan were employed mainly by the Ministry of Education, with only a few working in the selection centers of the armed forces, civil service, and NGOs. Later, in 1971, East Pakistan broke away from Pakistan to become Bangladesh.

In 1979, a master's program in psychology was introduced at the Lahore College for Women. In 2002, it was awarded the status of a university and now offers a master's in applied psychology instead of the previous degree. In the same year, Government College in Lahore also gained the status of a university.

After the establishment of independent departments of psychology at various universities in Pakistan's four provinces, the Center for Excellence in Psychology was founded, which led to the creation of the National Institute of Psychology in 1976. The main focus of the institute has been to conduct advanced research on psychosocial issues and to organize national seminars and workshops designed to update psychologists on the latest developments in the field both in Pakistan and abroad. The department also offers master's, M.Phil., and doctoral programs.

In the early 1980s, there was a mushrooming of graduate departments of psychology in the Punjab colleges, offering master's programs in Bahawalpur, Gujranwala, Islamabad, Jhang, Mianwali, Multan, Rawalpindi, and Sialkot. The psychology department at Balochistan University in Quetta, which offered psychology only at the bachelor's level, started its master's program in psychology in 1989. Graduate classes at Mohammaden Anglo Oriental College, Lahore, started in 1998. Recently, Fatima Jinnah Women's University in Rawalpindi, a government university for women established in 1999, initiated a master's program in the behavioral sciences. In 2001, Bahawalpur University began its master's program in applied psychology. At present, a few colleges are introducing a 4-year program in psychology at the undergraduate level, which is replacing the 2-year and 3-year honors programs.

Earlier, clinical psychologists had to leave the country to acquire the necessary specialized training, but with an increase in the incidence of psychological disorders in the country, there was a strong need to set up a post-master's professional training program in Pakistan. This suggestion was first made in 1982 by psychologists at a conference in Kohat organized by psychologists in the armed forces. Consequently, two institutes of clinical psychology were established under the directive of General Muhammad Zia-μl-Haq, then president of the Islamic Republic of Pakistan, who was also the guest of honor at the conference. As a result of this conference, the Karachi Institute was created in 1983 at Karachi University with Farrukh Zahooruddin Ahmad as its director, and the Lahore Institute was established in 1984 at Punjab University with Rafia Hasan as director. Today, the Lahore and Karachi institutes provide supervised clinical training and post-master's research in clinical psychology. In 2000, another post-master's training institute in clinical psychology was established at Bahria University in Karachi.

According to the 1998 census (Population Census Organization, Statistics Division, 2001), the population of Pakistan was estimated to be 132,352,279, of which 68,873,686 were male and 63,478,593 female. The total number of master's graduates in psychology at the end of 2002 is estimated to be 8,168, according to data provided by all Pakistani universities offering master's programs. Consequently, the ratio of psychologists with a master's in psychology per 100,000 people is approximately 6:100,000; this ratio underscores the dearth of psychologists in Pakistan. The ratio for trained clinical psychologists with a minimum of a 12-month post-master's diploma is approximately 1:400,000, whereas the ratio of psychiatrists is 1:600,000 (Gadit & Khalid, 2002). The ratio of physicians, represented by the Pakistan Medical and Dental Council in April 2003, to the Pakistani population is 74:100,000. Psychological services are primarily avail-

able at the urban centers of larger cities: Faisalabad, Hyderabad, Islamabad, Karachi, Lahore, Multan, Peshawar, Quetta, Rawalpindi, and Sialkot.

The lack of psychological services is clearly problematic as Pakistan is a developing country with limited resources. Only 44% of the population is literate, and 67% of the population lives in the rural areas where psychological services are not available (Population Census Organization, Statistics Division, 2001). Even among the educated, there remains very little awareness about nonmedical approaches to the treatment of psychological disorders. For example, there are few referrals from psychiatrists to clinical psychologists. In fact, the majority of patients who do approach clinical psychologists are those who have taken psychotropic medication for several years without relief. Although their symptoms may be managed with medication, there is a strong possibility that these patients will present with secondary problems, including addiction and long-term side effects. Furthermore, most clinical psychologists are not sufficiently confident to start independent practice, preferring to work as subordinates to psychiatrists who already have their own private clinics. However, a few enterprising psychologists have established private practices in major cities.

The starting salary, with allowances, for a clinical psychologist working in government health services is approximately $2100. Although the salary structure for government psychologists and psychiatrists is the same (i.e., the Basic Pay Scale, or BPS), the maximum salary level for a clinical psychologist is BPS-19, whereas for a psychiatrist it is BPS-20. There is no separate department of psychology within the health department; psychology is sub-sumed by a department of psychiatry. Though clinical psychologists work along-side psychiatrists, the department is always headed by a psychiatrist. The social work department, however, enjoys independent status and provides consultative services to different departments within hospitals. In departments of education, psychologists are also paid the same salary as other pro-fessionals. However, in the private sector, salaries vary among different professionals depending upon the demand for their ser-vices.

Due to a lack of awareness about the beneficial services psychologists can offer to business and industry, community cen-ters, prisons, and schools, there are not enough positions for psychologists as compared to other professionals. However, there are positions for clinical psycholo-gists in the psychiatry departments of all teaching hospitals where the medical model of treatment prevails.

Different national organizations have been set up to represent the discipline and profession of psychology in Pakistan. The largest of these is the Pakistan Psycholog-ical Association (PPA), formed in 1968 at Dacca in the former East Pakistan. The basic membership criterion for the Associ-ation is a master's in psychology. Most members are teachers at colleges and uni-versities, whereas others work in clinics and hospitals, for NGOs, in marketing, and in selection centers for the civil services and armed forces.

The Pakistan Association of Clinical Psychologists came into being in 1988. It was formed because of the perception that the PPA was not sufficiently invested in representing the professional concerns of clinical psychologists. The association promotes the role of clinical psychologists in mental health in Pakistan, develops ethics in the practice of clinical psychol-ogy, and works for the licensed practice of clinical psychology. It has partially achieved its mission; for example, in government health departments, it is now necessary to complete a 12-month post-master's diploma in clinical psychology in order to gain employment as a clinical psychologist.

The Society for the Advancement of Muslim Psychology was also established in 1988 through the efforts of Farrouk Ajmal and Azhar Ali Rizvi. The goal was to create an indigenous model of psychology and psychotherapy based on the traditional Islamic theories of personality and behavior developed by renowned Muslim scholars.

The main objectives of these national organizations include promoting the status of psychology in Pakistan by heightening awareness among the public, providing guidance and training to students, facili-tating research, as well as convening con-ferences, seminars, symposiums, and workshops. Although these organizations work independently, they collectively facilitate one another by working for the further development of psychology in Pakistan. They also seek to raise awareness among government agencies and NGOs of the role of psychologists in assessment and counseling, particularly in stress manage-ment. Moreover, they encourage communi-ties to adopt the concept and practice of prevention with respect to psychiatric dis-orders. At present, four journals of psychol-ogy are published in Pakistan, three under the auspices of post-master's departments of psychology in different universities and one by a psychological association.

15.2 EDUCATION
AND TRAINING

The role of psychology in the study of human behavior is still new to Pakistan, and the profession continues to be viewed with suspicion. Despite this lack of awareness, psychology has made some inroads into Pakistani society. Currently 1% of psychologists in Pakistan have received their training outside the country, and independent departments for both psychology and applied psychology exist. Most universities offer master's programs in the subject, with some offering M.Phil. and doctoral programs as well. At the moment, there are 22 independent departments of psychology at different state universities and colleges across Pakistan; five are in Lahore; four in Islamabad, three in Karachi; and one each in Bahawalpur, Gujranwala, Jamshoro, Jhang, Mianwali, Multan, Peshawar, Quetta, Rawalpindi, Sialkot, and Sind. With the proliferation of master's programs over the last two decades in the various colleges of the Punjab province, there has been a remarkable increase in the number of psychologists. However, the quality of education has fallen as most of these colleges do not have the infrastructure to launch a graduate program. Most new departments do not have qualified faculty or access to well-equipped laboratories and libraries.

However, the University of the Punjab in Lahore (aka Punjab University) is a renowned university in Pakistan. Established in 1882, it is the oldest and largest university in the country. There are 45 departments on campus, supported by 608 faculty members of whom 166 hold doctorates. The university has 16,861 students, more than 1,000 of whom are graduate students. The university has two independent departments of psychology: the Department of Applied Psychology, with 203 students and over 8,000 books and journals in its library, and the Center for Clinical Psychology, with 44 students and over 3,500 books and journals in its library. Another prominent university is Quaid-i-Azam University in Islamabad, known especially for its advanced research at the post-master's level.

For the past few years, a master's in psychology has been offered at private universities such as Hamdard University in Karachi and Al-Khair University in Lahore. An undergraduate program is currently being offered at the Lahore University of Management Sciences. The Institute of Behavioral Sciences in Karachi offers short courses in community mental health for training facilitators like nurses and social workers. Aga Khan University in Karachi trains counselors through a 2-year training program.

Education departments also offer psychology courses as a part of their curriculum. The Institute of Educational Research at Punjab University offers a master's and doctorate in educational psychology. Military academies do not have formal educational programs at the post-master's level; their focus is on the development of indigenous ability, aptitude, and personality tests for screening and selection purposes. Nevertheless, some psychologists in the armed forces pursue post-master's specialization at the departments where such programs are offered.

At the undergraduate level, the primary criterion for admission to most universities in Pakistan is academic performance. It includes 10 years of high school, which culminates in the secondary school certificate (matriculation), and 2 years of college, after which the intermediate certificate is awarded. Students obtain bachelor's degree in the arts or sciences on completion of 2 years of undergraduate study following the intermediate certificate. Quotas are set mainly at national institutes that are funded by the government.

For admission at the graduate level, most universities require an entrance examination based on the undergraduate psychology curriculum. Admission is offered based on the average of the score obtained in the admission test, grades accumulated in psychology at the bachelor's level, and a rating of the interview. There is one seat reserved for a student athlete and one reserved for a disabled student in each department. According to the Punjab Province Director of Public Instruction, only 10% of students pursue their education at the graduate level. Among these, the majority of the students in psychology are female.

Universities in Pakistan have a uniform undergraduate curriculum in which five subjects are taught. Two are compulsory: English and Islamic studies, or ethics and Pakistani studies. Two are elective from the major field of study, and one is chosen from an optional minor area. The examination system is annual and in essay form. However, Karachi University also offers a 3-years honors baccalaureate. The aims and objectives of the bachelor's in psychology are to assist students in developing a comprehensive familiarity with the discipline and to motivate them to continue their studies.

In the past, separate programs in psychology and applied psychology were offered for the bachelor's, each with separate course outlines. What follows is the course outline for the bachelor's

curriculum in psychology at government universities according to the Higher Education Commission in Islamabad as of 2002. Areas covered by the two theory examinations and one practicum include:

1. Biological bases of behavior, learning, attention, cognition, emotion, memory, motivation, perception, sensation, personality, and research methods.
2. Other areas of psychology including abnormal, clinical, developmental, educational, organizational, and social psychology along with psychometrics.
3. Practicum that covers fundamental statistics (e.g., measures of central tendency and variability, and correlational analysis) and requires that students conduct 10 classic experiments (e.g., mapping cutaneous sensation, meaningful versus nonsense learning, trial position effect under massed versus distributed practice, memory as a function of recitation, method of serial reproduction, negative after-image, perceptual grouping, reaction time, retention for complete versus interrupted tasks, retroactive inhibition, and transfer of training).

Core courses in the revised 2002 master's curricula in psychology and applied psychology were developed by the University Grants Commission, a government entity that approves the curricula at all government institutions. These core courses are identical for all universities in Pakistan, but optional specialized courses may vary depending upon the resources available to each department. The core curriculum is as follows: cognitive and affective processes, experimental psychology and behavioral neuroscience, history and systems, psychopathology and mental health, psychological measurement, social psychology, research methods, and statistics. Optional specialized courses include child, clinical and counseling, educational, health, industrial–organizational, and military psychology as well as human resource management and the psychology of mass communications. The most popular specialization is clinical psychology. All government universities subsidize undergraduate and graduate studies. Financial aid is available only to a few needy students.

Post-master's programs in psychology (both M.Phil. and Ph.D.) are offered at Karachi University, Peshawar University, Punjab University, and Quaid-i-Azam University, and at the Institute of Clinical Psychology in Karachi and Lahore. The minimum duration for a master's in philosophy program is 2 years, which includes 1 year of coursework and another of research. All doctoral programs include 1 year's course work followed by at least 2 years of research. The common coursework for M.Phil. and Ph.D. programs at all universities includes advanced research methods and statistical computer analysis. Areas of specialization include counseling and guidance, community psychology, consumer behavior and marketing, cross-cultural psychology, industrial–organizational psychology, military psychology, psychological assessment, psychobiology and psychopharmacology, psychopathology, school psychology, and special education. In addition, the Institute of Clinical Psychology at Karachi University offers specializations in hypnotherapy, occupational therapy and rehabilitation, psychoanalysis, substance abuse, therapy and practice (including cognitive–behavior therapy and crisis intervention), and vocational counseling. Meanwhile, the Center for Clinical Psychology at Lahore offers

specializations in adult clinical psychology and psychiatry, psychology and psychiatry of childhood and adolescence, developmental disabilities, neuropsychology, psychodiagnosis, and rehabilitation for substance abusers. Each student chooses one area of specialization for each of the two terms of coursework covered in the 1st year. In the second term, two additional compulsory courses in abnormal and clinical psychology are also taught. Furthermore, each student is expected to complete a research proposal by the end of the 1st year. Doctoral students are also expected to pass a comprehensive examination in clinical psychology.

Besides the M.Phil. and the Ph.D. programs, the two institutes in Karachi and Lahore also offer a post-master's diploma in clinical psychology. The coursework for both diplomas is similar. It includes clinical psychological assessment, professional ethics and legal issues in clinical psychology, neuropsychology, psychopharmacology, and therapeutic interventions. At the Lahore Institute, trainees receive clinical supervision at the Institute's clinic and at the psychiatric departments of teaching hospitals. Furthermore, students are provided with supervised training at both adult and child settings, although at the Karachi Institute clinical training is provided at the institute's clinic only. In addition, students at the Lahore Institute receive training in speech therapy and in the rehabilitation of substance abusers and schizophrenics. Personal growth groups for students are an integral part of the training throughout the program. Finally, during their last term, students must complete a research project.

The method of instruction at the undergraduate and graduate level is primarily lecture based; seminars and group discussions are adjunctive methods often used in graduate instruction. In post-master's programs, practical application is emphasized more than theory. Undergraduate and graduate classes vary in size from 40 to 60 students. However, the maximum class size at the graduate level is approximately 20. The majority of state and private universities have access to the Internet; a few departments also have indigenous and translated psychometric tests, libraries with the contemporary literature on psychology, and computer labs.

In Pakistan, no license is required in order to practice as a psychologist. However, the Pakistan Association of Clinical Psychologists only offers membership to individuals who hold a post-master's diploma in clinical psychology. Promotion of faculty members at government and private universities depends on their record of full-time teaching, success in publishing in national and international journals, and participation in national and international conferences, practica, symposiums, and workshops.

15.3 SCOPE OF PSYCHOLOGICAL PRACTICE

With the increase in urbanization, there has been a corresponding rise in social problems in Pakistan. For example, drug abuse has become a difficult problem since the late 1970s, with heroin addiction on the rise. Furthermore, there is an increase in the suicide rate among young people due to unemployment. Consequently, there is an urgent need to expand the role of psychologists in the health sector.

Despite the increasing number of practicing psychologists in Pakistan, no ethical guidelines have been established by any of the existing professional associations. However, students pursuing the advanced diploma in clinical psychology are exposed to ethical guidelines formulated by the American Psychological Association and the British Psychological Society as a part of their coursework. Furthermore, since there is no existing legal framework to regulate the practice of psychology, many people with only a master's degree can advertise and engage in private practice (Zaman, 1991). On a more promising note, the Pakistan Association of Clinical Psychology has made the 12-month diploma in clinical psychology mandatory for employment by the health department. However, there is a need for legal statutes to be formulated and enforced in order to curb malpractice.

There is also an urgent need to improve the curriculum of the master's programs in psychology. The programs currently offered at government and private universities are primarily theory based, allowing few opportunities for supervised practical training. There must be a change in emphasis in the application of psychological principles to the study and modification of human behavior.

In post-master's programs in clinical psychology, the treatment modalities that are taught are mainly borrowed from the West. Most psychodiagnostic tests are Urdu adaptations of psychological instruments developed either in the United Kingdom or the United States. Research conducted with Pakistani clients shows the effectiveness of most Western treatment modalities in remediating various forms of psychopathology (Ahmad & Jaleel, 1983). However, the process of intervention must be adapted to the cultural context and values of clients. Ahmad and Jaleel suggested that psychoanalysis can be practiced, but only with a select group of the Pakistani elite who have the financial and psychological resources that the majority lack. It is clear that long-term psychodynamic treatment is neither convenient nor affordable.

Like psychotherapy, the investigative methodologies and approaches to data analysis taught in the master's and doctoral programs are also borrowed from the West. Although the main focus remains on quantitative research, mixed design research, which includes both qualitative and quantitative approaches, is also conducted. Very little research is carried out nationwide; for example, there is a paucity of epidemiological data on the prevalence of different psychological disorders in Pakistan. Government agencies and private organizations conduct national surveys, but only on problems that have socioeconomic or sociopolitical significance. Ansari (2001) examined the studies that were recently published in Pakistani journals. He found that the theoretical and philosophical treatment of psychological issues, which had previously commanded a central place, declined sharply while topics in developmental and educational psychology showed a marked increase.

In the area of test construction, there is great demand for tests of achievement, aptitude, intelligence, personality, and vocational interests. Educational and psychological measurement has long been a fundamental part of master's programs in psychology. Furthermore, many federal educational policies have supported vocational counseling programs that incorporate the administration of ability, interest, and personality measures. During the 1970s, a well-funded section in the curriculum wing

of the Ministry of Education was created to oversee counseling and testing. Ambitious test construction programs for counseling were initiated, in which psychologists, educators, and educational administrators were involved. Ultimately, the projects succeeded merely in adapting and translating imported English tests of ability, aptitude, personality, and psychopathology into Urdu or, at most, in developing local norms (Dar, 1982). Due to a lack of coordination or cooperation or both, psychologists at different institutions have been working in parallel to adapt and translate the same imported tests. Given limited financial resources and personnel, a more systematic, perhaps national, approach is recommended in order to consolidate these fragmented efforts.

There are very few indigenous psychological tests in Pakistan. Rahman and Sitwat (1997) pioneered the development of an indigenous symptom checklist, written in Urdu, as a screening device for psychopathology (i.e., for anxiety, depression, somatization, and schizophrenia). It was revised in 1999 by Rahman, Dawood, Jagir, Mansoor, and Rehman; norms for psychiatric and nonpsychiatric populations were also established. Siddiqui (1992) developed an indigenous test for the diagnosis of depression; norms for clinical and nonclinical groups were developed from data gathered across the four provinces of Pakistan. Hussain (2001) developed an indigenous group intelligence scale; norms were developed for male respondents from personnel sampled at seven Pakistani Army Selection Centers.

Most of the available literature on psychology has been imported from the West. Consequently, the undergraduate and graduate programs in psychology depend heavily on books and journals written in English. However, recently, an indigenous psychology based on Islamic principles has been introduced. In the 1970s, the master's program in psychology in the Punjab province developed a course in Muslim psychology based on the work of Ibn-e-Sina, Ghazali, Razi, and Ibn-e-Miskewayah (Jamal, 1996). In spite of these efforts, the evolution of a Muslim psychology is limited mainly to the work of Ajmal (1986) and Rizvi (2000). Rizvi developed the Ghazali inventory in 1984 to measure personality, based on the work of the Muslim scholar Ghazali, and promoted the use of bibliotherapy, developed by another renowned Muslim scholar, Ashraf Ali Thanvi, for the treatment of psychological disorders (Rizvi, 2000).

Another indigenous model of therapy is known as *Zikr Allah*, which means "Remembering God" (Awan, 2003). It is based on meditation techniques practiced by early Islamic Sufis (mystics). The focus is on gaining nearness to Allah, as Allah is peace and all peace emanates from Allah. According to Islam, there is a spiritual heart or center, called the Qalb, found within the physical heart. The Qalb must be cleansed to attain nearness to Allah and peace. Purifying the Qalb requires invoking and chanting certain of Allah's 99 names, which represent His essence, such as mercy and compassion, accompanied by rapid and deep breathing. For example, when inhaling, one imagines the word *Allah* penetrating deeply into one's Qalb; when exhaling, one imagines the word *Hu* (Him Alone) striking one's Qalb. This exercise is performed repeatedly for a minimum of 15 minutes, at least twice daily. By sincerely remembering God in this manner, the Qalb is cleansed, and psychological equilibrium

is restored. There is no scientific evidence to support the effectiveness of this therapy, but clinical psychologists in practice report success with clients suffering from various psychological disorders.

Spiritual healers are also very popular for the treatment of psychological disorders. These healers treat their patients by performing *damm* (prayers), giving *taweezes* (amulets), and blowing religious verses on drinking water. There is no direct interaction between spiritual healers and psychologists. However, a majority of people with emotional problems seek the counsel of spiritual healers as they are more numerous and probably more trusted.

At present, the primary occupations available to Pakistani psychologists include teaching at the undergraduate (60%) and graduate (15%) level, conducting psychological assessment for personnel selection (7%) in the civil service and armed forces, delivering psychotherapy services in various clinical settings (7%), working in research centers and special education institutions (4%), and the "other" category (7%), which includes working in NGOs (Ansari, 2001).

In a study of 786 patients diagnosed with various psychological disorders, it was found that 670 came to psychotherapy after receiving the services of a series of psychiatrists from whom they received psychotropic medication and electroconvulsive therapy. The results showed that all benefited from psychotherapy and were medication free at the conclusion of treatment (Ahmad, 1979). Such findings led to collaboration with the World Health Organization in the 1980s. One outgrowth of this collaboration is the community mental health program at Rawalpindi General Hospital, which aims to educate people about mental health and provide psychological services to people in the communities where they live (Mubbashar & Saeed, 2002).

Selection centers in both the civil service and armed forces are staffed by psychologists, expert in constructing and administering psychological tests. The selection center of the federal Public Service Commission has eight full-time psychologists. In the selection process for the identification of suitable candidates, the psychological report, based on tests of ability, personality, and psychopathology, plays an important role. It has been observed by the chief psychologist at the selection center that approximately 990 candidates are tested each year, of whom about 374 are recommended for employment.

The armed forces recruit psychologists with a master's degree in psychology to serve on a selection panel in military induction centers. The main task of these psychologists is to assess the ability, aptitude, and personality of candidates who are recruited as officers, using psychological test batteries developed at their own selection centers. The psychological report is given top priority in the final selection of the candidates. At General Headquarters in Rawalpindi, there is a psychological center headed by a chief psychologist who constructs tests and materials related to the military's needs. In the 33 combined military hospitals across the country, there are 25 separate departments of psychiatry headed by a psychiatrist. However, there are no positions for clinical psychologists in these psychiatry departments and, currently, only two clinical psychologists work on contract for military personnel and their families, one in Lahore and the other in Rawalpindi. Although their primary function is to administer psychodi-

agnostic tests that have been adapted or translated into Urdu, they also provide counseling and psychotherapy when needed.

Finally, psychologists in business and industry are increasingly involved in conducting surveys on consumer preferences and in the marketing of products, in addition to their more traditional activities of personnel selection and the delivery of communication skills and stress management training in the workplace.

Since the two post-master's programs in clinical psychology were inaugurated in the early 1980s, 331 individuals have completed the diploma, one has earned an M.Phil., and 17 have been awarded doctorates in clinical psychology. However, there remains a critical shortage of clinical psychologists, especially in view of the sharp increase in psychological disorders in Pakistan (World Health Report, 2001). For example, substance abuse is a major problem in Pakistan, with the number of chronic heroin users as high as 500,000 (U.N. Drug Control Program, 2002). Although there are many substance abuse treatment facilities across the country, most only provide detoxification, which ensures a high relapse rate. It has been observed that few centers integrate the psychological, spiritual, and social aspects of rehabilitation with more successful outcomes. The most popular program currently underway was started in 1992 by the Dost (Friend) Foundation, an NGO based in Peshawar. The Foundation, whose staff includes psychologists, psychiatrists, physicians, and social workers, provides treatment for substance abusers, outreach harm-reduction services for street users, and prevention programs targeted at different groups in the community. It also seeks to protect human rights and facilitate the social integration of vulnerable prisoners such as juvenile offenders, substance abusers, and women and children.

Psychologists in Pakistan must also address the pressing issues brought about by the country's rapid social change. These issues center on the effects of industrialization and the migration from villages to cities. Psychosocial maladjustment is tied to conflict between rural and urban ways of life, tensions within various ethnic and religious groups, and challenges to traditional attitudes and values. An example is the transformation of towns into sprawling cities and the relative neglect of villages, which has widened the gap between the urban (of the population) areas in Pakistan. This widening gap has created adjustment difficulties for rural youth who often choose to migrate to the cities. Although the national language is Urdu and the official language is still English, there are communication problems owing to the different languages used in each of Pakistan's four provinces: Balochi in Balochistan, Pushto in the North West Frontier, Punjabi in the Punjab, and Sindhi in Sind.

There is growing awareness in the country of the important contributions that clinical psychologists can make in university teaching, basic and applied research, and professional practice. However, one factor that has affected the relationship between psychologists and psychiatrists is the lack of a clear distinction in the Urdu language between the two occupations. Psychiatrists go by many names, such as Mahir-e-Imraze Damaghi (expert in psychiatric medicine), Mahir-e-Nafsiyat (expert in psychology), and Mahir-e-Manshiyat (expert in drug addiction), which confuses the public as to the competencies and role of psychologists. However, while differences exist in interests and expertise, clinical psychologists have generally maintained congenial relationships with the psychiatrists, physicians, social workers, and other allied health professionals with whom they work.

15.4 FUTURE CHALLENGES AND PROSPECTS

Pakistan is a developing country, with more than 50% of the population below 18 years of age (Population Census Organization, Statistics Division, 2001). As a developing country, Pakistan is at a crossroads. This reality places great responsibility on Pakistani psychologists. At present, there are manifold psychosocial problems in Pakistan, as sampled in the following list:

1. After September 11, 2001, the Muslim Ummah (i.e., those who follow the principles of Islam throughout the world) is in a quandry. Muslims perceive themselves as being stereotyped as terrorists and oppressed, resulting in widespread anxiety and a feeling of helplessness at not being able to defend themselves against anti-Islamic bias in the media. This is especially true in Pakistan.

2. The incidence of HIV/AIDS is also on the rise in East and South Asian countries, especially in the Indian subcontinent. In Pakistan, as of December 2002, there were 1,765 reported cases of HIV, of which 233 had AIDS (Razaque, 2002). However, these figures are considerably lower than the 80,000 to 100,000 forecast by the World Health Organization for Pakistan alone (Razaque).

3. According to the latest data, there are 500,000 heroin addicts in Pakistan, of whom 75,000 are needle users (U.N. Drug Control Program, 2002). This high level of mainlining the drug has shown a marked increase since 1993 (Narcotics Control Division, 1993).

4. The incidence of suicide among the young has multiplied in recent years in Pakistan. Patterns of suicide over 2 years were analyzed in a report published by a major Pakistani newspaper (Khan & Reza, 2000). This report documented 306 suicides in 35 cities. Men outnumbered women by 2:1; there were more single than married men who committed suicide, with an opposite trend among women. Domestic problems were cited as the most common reason. The majority of victims were under 30 years of age.

5. The incidence of depression is rising not only among females but also among young males who are frustrated and depressed due to high levels of unemployment.

6. Child labor is very common. Due to the large size of many families, lack of education, and high unemployment, children of poor families are often forced to work at a very young age.

7. Runaway children have become a growing problem. Since there are very few social services available, children are forced onto the streets.

8. Juvenile prisoners in Pakistani jails are at the mercy of the police. Due to the harsh conditions in the jails and absence of counseling services and rehabilitation programs, these juveniles tend to become hardened criminals over time.

9. Although almost half of the Pakistani population is female (Population Census Organization, Statistics Division, 2001) and women all over the world are joining the workforce in increasing numbers, women in Pakistan continue to be marginalized, and most are forced to remain at home where they assume sole responsibility for all domestic tasks.

10. With a very dense population of 140 million, Pakistan has a population growth rate of 3.1%, the highest in all of Asia (Khan & Reza, 2000).

11. After almost 56 years of independence, Pakistan has only a 44% literacy rate (Population Census Organization, Statistics Division, 2001).

Zaidi (1975), a social scientist, emphasized that economic development is possible when policymakers consider the human aspect of change and become more sensitive to the needs of people. If the circumstances listed above are to be addressed, local, regional, and national government must reevaluate their priorities. Policymakers need to give mental health its due by adopting a multidisciplinary approach that involves psychologists, psychiatrists, and social workers instead of maintaining a myopic view by focusing solely on psychiatrists.

These pressing issues also highlight the pivotal role that psychologists can play. Not only can they aid communities to assert themselves in an increasingly chaotic world but they can also help people overcome personal conflicts. Well-planned public campaigns can also reduce the stigma and discrimination attached to psychiatric disorders and aid those seeking professional help. Because of the demographics of the population, preventative programs should receive as much support as efforts at remediation.

Transforming clients from their status as hospitalized patients into productive members of society is also cost effective. Mental health services should, therefore, be provided at the local level, using all available resources. To best meet the needs of the mentally ill, large custodial institutions should be replaced by community-care facilities and home support, with hospitalization available only when necessary. A shift toward community care will require an infrastructure of health workers and services at the community level, along with affordable housing and sheltered employment.

Human resource development is necessary because of Pakistan's status as a developing country. Although primary-care settings are the most useful for the initial delivery of health services, specialists are needed to provide more focused treatment. Specialists on mental health care teams ideally should include psychologists, psychiatrists, nurses, social workers, and occupational therapists who, working together, can offer patients comprehensive care and facilitate their reintegration into the community.

It is extremely important that master's and doctoral programs in clinical psychology be formed at all the universities and postgraduate institutions in Pakistan in order to correct the dismal ratio of one clinical psychologist per 400,000 people. Although the goal of bringing mental health services to the local community within the next generation is an enormous challenge, it may be achievable if graduate-training programs in psychology are implemented at major universities in all four provinces of Pakistan. Regardless of spe-cialization, training in these programs must center on meaningful application of knowledge and skills.

More research into the biological and social aspects of mental health is needed in order to increase the understanding of factors that influence the cause, course, and outcome of mental disorders and to develop more effective interventions. Such research should be collaborative and international so as to identify cross-cultural variations in psychological dysfunction. Clearly, building Pakistan's research capacity is another urgent priority.

Because of the emphasis placed on the medical model of treatment, healthcare jobs continue to be filled by psychiatrists. This is partly due to a lack of awareness among the policy makers of the important role psychologists can play in the delivery of healthcare. As a result of ignorance, psychologists are often not hired, or they work as junior professionals. In order to provide optimal mental health services, positions for clinical psychologists must be created in the health departments of all provinces. Moreover, the fact that behavioral sciences are currently taught by psychiatrists in a majority of Pakistani medical colleges demonstrates that employment opportunities for psychologists are also available and needed in medical education.

The outdated Lunacy Act of 1912 was repealed in 2001 and replaced with a Mental Health Ordinance proposed by the president of Pakistan. The Ordinance recognizes psychiatric patients as individuals and guarantees their basic human rights. The federal government also established the Mental Health Authority (MHA), which has the responsibility of advising the government on all matters related to the promotion of mental health and prevention of mental disorders. Though these are positive steps, nonmedical professionals in mental health, including clinical psychologists, unfortunately were not included in the process or outcome. The emphasis was once again on the medical model. For example, the MHA plans to form boards at the provincial level that will include a chairperson, a health services director general, two psychiatrists, two expert medical practitioners, and a prominent citizen, but no representation is given to clinical psychologists ("Clinical Psychologists," 2001). In 2001, the governor of Punjab Province formed a task force on substance abuse. Although this was also a commendable decision, the team that was formed had a psychiatrist but again did not include a single clinical psychologist.

It is most unfortunate that a large part of the Pakistani population seeks psychological help from a variety of nonprofessionals; including psychic healers and *aamils*, who exorcise spirits and offer talismans for every ailment and desire. Measures must be taken to educate the public on the advantages and disadvantages of such treatments.

Pakistani psychologists are encouraged to study the philosophical treatises of Muslim scholars in order to devise and refine indigenous models of therapy that fit the needs of the Pakistani people and link Eastern and Western traditions. One such example is the use of rational emotive behavior therapy with Muslim clients. There are many commonalities between the values of Islam and the philosophy of rational emotive behavior therapy, such as the fallibility of human beings in a worldly environment, condemnation of the sin rather than the sinner, the superficiality of material wealth,

unconditional self-acceptance and unconditional acceptance of others, and the quest for long-term versus short-term hedonistic goals.

American psychologists can learn much about Islamic values and their implications for professional practice from Pakistani psychologists. Islamic law articulates the relationships among human beings. Rights of kith and kin are defined (e.g., deference to parents and responsibilities toward children), as are those pertaining to neighbors, orphans, strangers, teachers, and travelers. Islamic law, then, is a charter of human rights, which leads to a traditional and "settled" society. Since the parameters of social exchanges are clearly delineated by Islamic law, the work of Pakistani psychologists is shaped by religious and cultural values.

With the world becoming a global village in which information from one end reaches the other in seconds, there is a great need for cooperation among psychologists from all countries. Pakistani values are highly integrated with those of Islam, whereas Western values tend toward the secular. Seizing opportunities to collaborate on research, especially cross-cultural projects, will foster communication and understanding of different cultural values and views.

Although the field of psychology in Pakistan remains marginalized, the growing importance given to mental health offers a promising future for psychologists and for the nonmedical treatment of psychiatric disorders. This future is slowly being realized. Since March 2000, the Center for Clinical Psychology, in consort with the Government Hospital for Psychiatric Diseases in Lahore (now, the Punjab Institute of Mental Health), established a self-supporting treatment program for women based on personal hygiene, social competencies, and vocational skills

(Rahman, 2001). The Center and Government Hospital then were able to respond to the needs of their 190 female patients who had not been receiving rehabilitation services because they represented only 16% of the patient population.

Well-known psychologists and heads of psychology departments were interviewed in the course of writing this chapter. The majority of them were optimistic about the future of psychology in Pakistan over the next 25 years, provided a concerted effort is made to carry out the recommendations mentioned earlier. Pakistan must produce professionals in all specialties of psychology, and the PPA must educate the government, the private sector, and the general public to appreciate the potential contribution of psychology to the individual and communal life in Pakistan.

ACKNOWLEDGMENT

I would like to thank Saima Dawood and Aisha Sitwat for their assistance in compiling information and data from the four provinces of Pakistan that are included in this chapter.

REFERENCES

Ahmad, F. Z. (1979). Clinical psychology in Pakistan. *Pakistan Journal of Psychology, 10,* 3–18.

Ahmad, F. Z., & Jaleel, S. S. (1983). The scope of psychoanalytical therapy in Pakistan. *Pakistan Journal of Psychology, 14,* 3–22.

Ajmal, M. (1986). Muslim contributions to psychotherapy and other essays. *Psychological Research Monograph, 5*(1).

Ansari, Z. A. (2001). Development of psychology in Pakistan. In S. H. Hashmi (Ed.), *The state of social sciences in Pakistan* (97–108). Islamabad: Allama Iqbal Open University.

Aslam, Q. M. (1975). Fifty years of psychology: An autobiographical narration. *Pakistan Journal of Psychology, 8,* 3–40.

Awan, M.A.(2003, April). Treatment of mental illnesses through Zikr Allah. *Al-Murshad* [The Spiritual Teacher], *24,* 4–6.

Clinical psychologists must for MHA. (2001, February 24). *The News,* p. 3.

Dar, I. S. (1982). Test development for vocational counseling in Pakistan: Problems and issues. *Pakistan Journal of Psychology, 13,* 25–31.

Gadit, A. A., & Khalid, N. (2002). *State of mental health in Pakistan.* Karachi: Hamdard University Hospital Press.

Haque, A. (2000). Pakistan. In A. E. Kazdin (Ed.), *Encyclopedia of psychology* (Vol. 6, pp. 27–31). New York: Oxford University Press.

Hussain, S. S. (2001). *Development, validation and standardization of group verbal intelligence test in Urdu for adolescents.* Unpublished doctoral dissertation, Quaid-i-Azam University, Islamabad, Pakistan.

Jamal, Y. (1996). Society for advancement of Muslim psychology. In Z. Yousaf & Y. Jamal (Eds.), *Proceeding: Second Muslim psychological conference: Role of Muslim psychologists in present crisis of Ummah* (pp. 5–6). Lahore: Institute of Muslim Psychology.

Khan, M. M., & Reza, H. (2000). The patterns of suicide in Pakistan. *Crisis, 21,* 1–6.

Mubbashar, M. H., & Saeed, K. (2002). *Community psychiatry: A Pakistani perspective.* Islamabad: Pakistan Psychiatric Society.

Narcotics Control Division. (1993). *National survey on drug abuse in Pakistan.* Islamabad: Author.

Population Census Organization, Statistics Division. (2001). *1998 census report of Pakistan* (Census Publication No. 160). Islamabad: Pakistan Government Office.

Rahman, N. K. (2001). Community mental health program at Government hospital for psychiatric diseases, Lahore. In M. H. Mubbashar & A. Humayun (Eds.), *Proceedings of 13th International Psychiatric Conference: Vol. 2. Mental health in the new millennium: Freud, freedom and future* (pp. 55–163). Islamabad: Pakistan Psychiatric Society.

Rahman, N. K., Dawood, S., Jagir, S., Mansoor, W., & Rehman, N. (1999). *Standardization and validation of Symptom Checklist - R on psychiatric and nonpsychiatric populations.* Unpublished manuscript, University of the Punjab at Lahore, Center for Clinical Psychology.

Rahman, N. K., & Sitwat, A. (1997, February). *Factor analysis of Symptom Checklist developed at the Center for Clinical Psychology, Punjab University, Lahore.* Paper presented in 11th International Psychiatric Conference, Karachi, Pakistan.

Razaque, A. (2002). *Epidemiological situation of HIV/AIDS in Pakistan: Punjab area.* Lahore: Government of Pakistan.

Rizvi, S. A. A. (2000). Pakistan organization promotes development of Muslim psychology. *Psychology International, 11,* 6.

Siddiqui, S. (1992). *The assessment of attributional styles of depressives and nondepressives through an indigenously developed depression scale.* Unpublished doctoral dissertation, Quiad-i-Azam University, Islamabad, Pakistan.

U.N. Drug Control Program. (2002). *Drug abuse in Pakistan: Results from the year 2000 national assessment.* New York: Author.

World Health Organization. (2002). *AIDS epidemic update.* Geneva: Author.

World Health Report. (2001). *Mental health: New understanding, new hope.* Rawalpindi, Pakistan: WHO Collaborating Center for Mental Health Research and Training and the Institute of Psychiatry, Rawalpindi General Hospital.

Zaidi, S. M. H. (1975). Psychology in the service of nation. *Pakistan Journal of Psychology, 8,* 3–24.

Zaman, R. M. (1991). Clinical psychology in Pakistan. *Psychology and developing societies, 3,* 221–234.

IMPORTANT PUBLICATIONS

Ajmal, M. (1986). Muslim contributions to psychotherapy and other essays. *Psychological Research Monograph, 5*(1).

Bano, M., & Shah, A. A. (2000). Emotional problems in physically handicapped children In the North West Frontier Province (NWFP), Pakistan. *Saudi Journal of Disability and Rehabilitation, 8,* 178–180.

Ghaznavi, S. S. (1998). *Nabi akarm: Bator mahir-e-naphsiyat* [The Holy Prophet: As a psychologist]. Lahore: Alfaisal Publishers.

Hassan, I. N. (Ed.). (1996). *Psychology of women.* Islamabad: Allam Iqbal Open University.

Paal, S. A. (1998). *Ghair tabaee naphsiyat* [Para-psychology]. Lahore: A-One Publishers.

Rahman, N. K. (2001). Community mental health program at Government hospital for psychiatric diseases, Lahore. In M. H. Mubbashar & A. Humayun (Eds.), *Proceedings of 13th International Psychiatric Conference: Vol. 2. Mental health in the new millennium: Freud, freedom and future* (pp. 55–163). Islamabad: Pakistan Psychiatric Society.

Rahman, N. K. (1991). Rational Emotive Therapy and its application in Pakistan. *Proceedings of 8th International Conference of the Pakistan Psychological Association: Vol. 4* (pp. 110–118). Islamabad: Pakistan Psychological Association.

Rehman, G., & Aziz, S. (1996). Index of religiosity: The development of an indigenous measure. *Journal of Indian Academy of Applied Psychology, 22,* 79–85.

Rizvi, S. A. A. (1994). *Muslim traditions in psychotherapy and modern trends.* Lahore: Institute of Islamic Culture.

Zaman, R. M. (1997). The adaptation of Western psychotherapeutic methods to Muslim societies: The case of Pakistan. *World Psychology, 3,* 65–87.

CHAPTER 16

Psychology in Thailand

SOMBAT TAPANYA

Sombat Tapanya received a B.Sc. in psychology at Chiang Mai University in Thailand, an M.S. in special education and an M.S. in counseling education from Southern Connecticut State University, and a Ph.D. in psychology from the University of New Brunswick, Canada. He worked as psychologist at Somdet Chaopraya Psychiatric Hospital from 1973 to 1985, and then moved to the Department of Psychiatry, Faculty of Medicine, Chiang Mai University where he is now an assistant professor.

Tapanya's main interests are in the areas of stress reduction, violence and abuse prevention, peace education, and adherence counseling; he has conducted training workshops in Thailand, Laos, and China. Currently, he is one of the principal investigators in a project to maintain adherence to highly active antiretroviral therapy (HAART) with over 700 AIDS patients in Northern Thailand.

16.1 OVERVIEW

With Buddhism as its major religion for the past millennium, Thailand found the Western interest in the science of the mind as nothing new. Meditation has long been the main vehicle for inner exploration in the East, and it has been common knowledge and commonly practiced among the Thais, not unlike the early methods of introspection in the field of psychology.

Western "scientific" psychology, however, is another matter entirely. When the first mental health clinic was established in Bangkok in 1953, with support from the World Health Organization (WHO) and the Thai Ministry of Public Health, early groups of Thai psychologists were mostly those who graduated from arts, language, and education programs (Thai Psychiatric Association, 1977), and they were ill-equipped to adapt and derive optimal benefit from this scientific method to which modern Thai psychology aspires.

Although psychology was introduced to Thailand over 50 years ago, it is still in its infancy as a profession. While the number of psychologists in the United States and some other Western countries has increased exponentially, the number of Thai psychologists is growing at a much slower rate. A comparison with our colleagues in other mental health fields is instructive. At the Department of Mental Health in the Ministry of Public Health, for each of the past 3 years the average number of psychologists employed by the Department has been around 90, whereas there were around 80 social workers, 150 psychiatrists, and 1000 nurses within the same organization. The figure for psychologists does not represent the total number of psychologists in Thailand, as there are many more of them in other settings and organizations. However, because the jobs most psychologists hold require them to be in large institutes such as hospitals and universities, over 80% of Thai psychologists are based in urban areas.

The term *psychologist* itself may even be confusing or misleading in the Thai context. As in the United States and other Western countries, this term could mean only those with a license to practice psychology or those with graduate degrees in psychology. However, there is tremendous variability in the levels of education and training for psychologists in Thailand. The author personally estimates (as there are no surveys conducted in this area) that over 80% of Thai "psychologists" only have a bachelor's degree, about 15% have earned a master's degree, and about 5% have a doctorate degree (all from overseas and most likely none have completed an internship or postdoctoral training).

There are a few psychology specialties in Thailand (e.g., experimental, social,

educational, counseling), but they are far fewer in number than in the United States A large number of Thai psychologists are found in clinical or educational settings.

If it is acceptable to regard those who hold degrees in psychology and teach or conduct research as psychologists, there are far more psychologists in academic settings than in clinical settings. Since psychology as a subject is most often first introduced to those who study education first, academicians in Thailand were more familiar with the subject in the context of education or teaching rather than in the clinical context.

The term *psychologist* did not exist in the Thai language until in the early 1950s when the first group of Thai clinical psychologists was recruited from candidates with bachelor's degrees in language arts and education from universities in Bangkok. As there were no formal programs of study in psychology in Thailand at the time, these early Thai psychologists were trained on the job by senior psychiatrists who had received some rudimentary training in psychological assessment in the United States as a part of their training in psychiatry. Thus, the first generation of Thai psychologists functioned as psychological technicians working primarily with children. The job title "psychologist" was first officially recognized by the Thai government in 1959 (*100 Years,* 1989), but most of the professional time of the individuals identified with this rubric was devoted to administering intelligence tests and projective tests. Referrals came exclusively from psychiatrists who used psychological test results to aid in diagnosing and planning treatment. Over the years, some attempts were made to develop Thai versions of intelligence and projective tests.

However, these early attempts proved futile, and at present, Thai psychologists are still using American or European tests such as WAIS, WISC, Bender Gestalt, TAT, Sentence Completion Blank, and Rorschach. Individual test items have been translated and adapted for use with the Thai population, but there have been no serious efforts to develop Thai norms.

Many objective tests, mainly questionnaires, have been translated into Thai, modified and field-tested with pilot subjects until they acquired satisfactory psychometric properties. The latest substantial work in this area is the Thai text *Manual of Psychological Assessment* (Patrayutawat, 2002) which is a collection of almost all of the paper-and-pencil tests and questionnaires available in the Thai language, along with descriptions of their psychometric properties. Judging from the scarcity of available Thai texts on the subject, this text stands a good chance of being widely used among Thai psychologists in the future. A text on clinical psychology, *Clinical Psychology: From Theory to Practice* (Sukatungka, 2002) is another recent publication that is a required reading for graduate students in clinical psychology at Mahidol University in Bangkok.

Two other important texts on psychodynamic psychotherapy that have been used widely by mental health professionals in Thailand over the years were written by a senior psychiatrist, Dr. Pramote Chaosilp, who devoted most of his professional life to this area of work: *Manual for Psychoanalytic Theories* (Chaosilp, 1983) and *Group Psychotherapy for Inpatients* (Chaosilp & Kongsakol, 1999), which is actually a translation of Irving D. Yalom's *The Theory and Practice of Group Psychotherapy* (Yalom, 1975).

There are also two well-known books by Thai psychologists that have been regarded as classics in their related fields: *Theories and Techniques of Behavior Modification* by Sompote Iamsupasit (Iamsupasit, 2000), now in its fourth edition, and *Developmental Psychology* by Pramual Dickinson (Dickinson, 1984).

Although educational psychology has enjoyed the advantage of having an early start through its affiliation with the field of education all through the years, the field has a somewhat negative image as an academic discipline because the majority of those who have entered this field have not met high academic standards. The large and ever-increasing number of graduates from numerous teachers' colleges throughout the country provides evidence in support of this claim. Although a master's degree program in educational psychology and guidance was first established at Chulalongkorn University in 1961 (Kowtrakul, 2001) and such program can now be found in almost all of the universities in Thailand, there is only one textbook that has received wide acclaims from professionals in this field, *Educational Psychology* by Surang Kowtrakul, now in its fifth edition (Kowtrakul, 2001).

16.2 EDUCATION AND TRAINING

The first bachelor's degree program in psychology with a clearly identified clinical psychology track was established at Chiang Mai University in 1964. The first Thai university to offer a master's degree program in clinical psychology was Mahidol University in Bangkok in 1979. Few developments have occurred since then and there is still only one master's degree program in clinical psychology in Thailand. After three decades, a few other universities have established graduate tracks in psychology; these include master's degree programs in various subfields of psychology such as industrial psychology, counseling psychology, developmental psychology, and social psychology. Chulalongkorn University is the oldest and most prestigious university of the country, and its Department of Psychology, which at first was one of many departments within the College of Education, elevated its status in 1996 to become the College of Psychology. In 2001, this program started offering Thailand's first doctoral programs in counseling psychology, social psychology, and developmental psychology.

Admission requirements for candidates of undergraduate programs in psychology have been debated over the years. There has been considerable ambivalence between choosing students from their high school language arts track or those from the science track. There are advantages and disadvantages for each group. Although those from the science track may be talented at science subjects and statistics or research methods, they tend to lack the sensitivity often found among psychologically minded individuals from the language arts track; conversely, language arts students tend not to be inclined toward mathematics and science. Thus, the requirements for admission into the program vary both among university programs and from year to year. There are no national standards or policies regarding this matter.

As for graduate programs, Thamasart University's requirements may serve as a good example. Admission requirements typically include having graduated from a bachelor's degree program in psychology with a GPA of at least 2.5 or some work experience in fields related to psychology, or both. In some cases, students who are provisionally admitted with insufficient background knowledge may be required to take additional psychology courses before being fully accepted as a student in the program. An internship of one semester (approximately 14 weeks of full-time work) at a relevant agency or institution is required for students to graduate from the program.

The most recent development in graduate level education in psychology is at Ramkamhang University (RU) in Bangkok. In 2003, RU started offering doctorates in counseling psychology and industrial and organizational psychology. RU is an "open university" where students from any part of the country can take courses in a long-distance learning program without having to attend classes on a regular basis. However, judging from the low number of faculty in the Department of Psychology and their academic and clinical backgrounds, its new doctorate programs do not inspire confidence in their quality.

With the current government's efforts to encourage universities to be more financially independent through privatization, many universities come up with their own plans to attract students who can pay tuition. Creating new programs appears to be an easy answer to this challenge. Thus, more and more universities now offer various programs to generate additional income. Some of the more common programs are those that offer classes to working adult students who can attend classes during weekends or at the university's branches in various provinces so students do not have to miss work or leave their home communities to go to Bangkok. Similar to other educational institutions,

RU may be following this trend since new graduate programs can substantially increase revenue for the university.

Another new trend that has emerged in graduate schools in various Thai universities is establishing affiliations with universities in North America, Europe, and Australia. Students who are in graduate programs at such universities are required to spend at least 1 year studying at the affiliated university overseas. In the near future, it is likely that such an arrangement will take place in the field of psychology. A similar program has recently been proposed for the Department of Psychology at Chiang Mai University.

16.3 SCOPE OF PSYCHOLOGICAL PRACTICE

There are currently three governing organizations for Thai psychologists: the Thai Clinical Psychologist Association, the Thai Psychological Association, and the Thai Guidance Counselor Association. Many years ago, a suggestion was made to merge the Thai Clinical Psychologist Association and the Thai Psychological Association. Most clinical psychologists were opposed to the idea because of their concern that academicians who had no clinical experience would dominate the new association. The issue recently emerged in a discussion between members of the two associations, with a suggestion that there should be one umbrella organization with various divisions, much like the structure of the American Psychological Association with its 55 divisions.

The Thai Psychologist Association has an official Thai name that translates as the "Thai *Clinical* Psychologist Association," but the word "clinical" was omitted from the English title, reflecting some reluctance to use the word. This organization was established in 1983, and currently has about 250 members. Rounding that figure up to 300 by including those who are not members of the association yields a ratio of 0.5 psychologists per 100,000 of the Thai population (currently 60 million). The Psychiatric Association of Thailand was established in 1953 and has 392 members; the Thai Psychiatric Nurse Association was established in 1986 and has 968 members. These Thai mental health associations developed around the same time but the psychiatric association is clearly the most well-established among them; the psychiatric nursing association is the largest in size, and the psychology association is the smallest. This situation is easy to comprehend since psychiatrists traditionally hold higher positions in mental health organizations, and have greater political clout and easier access to resources.

Within the medical community, physicians (mostly psychiatrists) have referred to Thai psychologists as "paramedical professionals." Until recently, most psychiatrists preferred to limit the role of psychologists who work in psychiatric hospitals to that of technicians who take orders from psychiatrists, administer tests, and write reports. During the past two decades, as more psychologists have had the opportunity either to train in Western countries or receive training from those returning from overseas or from visiting foreign experts, the role of psychologists has been expanded to include treatment, the promotion of mental health, and research. The fact that there are only about 400 psychiatrists in the country, with 80% of these practicing in urban areas, also made it necessary for psychologists to take up other functions such as individual and group psychotherapy, the promotion of community mental health, counseling for drug addicts and HIV positive individuals, and research.

A similar situation exists for psychiatric social workers and nurses; relatively few of these professionals are found in Thailand. There is a certain irony in this interplay of demand and supply. While there are too few psychologists to serve the Thai population, relatively few jobs are available for the existing pool of psychologists. Those jobs that are available usually require only a bachelor's degree, the pay is minimal, and the potential for career advancement is limited vis-à-vis other health professions. Most Thai psychologists perform professional services without sufficient supervision from experienced psychologists with more extensive training.

Similar contradictions are also reflected in the recent trend among medical schools and government hospitals. Although buzz words and phrases such as "holistic approaches to medicine" and "multidisciplinary teams" have become widespread, there have been no serious attempts to increase the number of Thai psychologists. In fact, Thai medical schools now tend to recruit only new faculty with medical training.

The dominance of the medical model in Thailand is illustrated by recent curricular changes at a major Thai medical school. While the "biopsychosocial" model of health care has been highly praised by academic leaders in Thai medical schools, the proposed new curriculum reduced the behavioral science content to about 5% of the total curriculum. Insofar as medical students in Thailand start their 6-year medical education right after high school, they have

no opportunity to take other courses such as introduction to psychology or sociology to provide them with a broader perspective on health and illness. This reduction in the behavioral component of health and illness produces physicians who are ill-equipped to cope with the daunting public health problems that currently confront Thailand. Similar to the American situation, Thailand is experiencing budgetary limitations on health care spending and an epidemic of diseases such as heart disease, stroke, cancer, addictions, and sexually transmitted diseases, all of which are rooted in human behavior.

The primacy of medicine and the selection of physicians for top managerial and administrative positions mean there is not much room for other professionals such as nurses, social workers, or psychologists to be promoted in medical schools. In addition, there is no precedent for free-standing or autonomous departments of psychology or behavioral science in medical schools. Almost all psychologists in medical settings work in departments of psychiatry, although a few can be found in other departments such as pediatrics, family medicine, and neurology.

Relationships with psychiatry are usually courteous, albeit somewhat strained. On a professional level, psychiatrists, with a few exceptions, regard psychologists as either second-class members of the mental health team or subordinates to be given orders and dismissed after their duties have been performed. A few senior Thai psychologists with extensive overseas training and experience have been treated with a curious ambivalence that reflects both respect and disdain.

Psychologists working in hospitals have no admitting privileges and cannot write notes in patients' charts. Prescription privileges are unheard of, and the training available in Thailand would not be sufficient to support prescriptive authority. A positive trend, however, has occurred in recent years with a small but increasing number of psychologists assuming major administrative duties and becoming involved in shaping national health policy. Some psychologists who work in the Ministry of Public Health also are active in designing and implementing training programs and developing educational materials such as those for AIDS counseling, telephone counseling, suicide prevention, and stress management. However, because of their limited training and education, the quality of their products still has much room for improvement.

A few innovative attempts to use Buddhist monks and community members to provide mental health services have been made over the years. In particular, Buddhist monks have been seen as a potential source for recruiting community mental health workers. Sporadic efforts have been made over the years to train monks in basic counseling skills, although there have been no systematic and well-coordinated countrywide projects to date. Similar projects were attempted with teachers and community leaders, with no clear-cut results reported. Although they are commonplace in rural provinces, indigenous healers have been largely ignored in Thailand, and only a few hospitals have attempted to integrate folk healers into their system of care. With the current surge of interest in alternative approaches to medicine, an increasing number of rural, provincial hospitals have begun to set up traditional Thai medicine clinics within the hospital compounds where patients can receive services from massage therapists and herbalists.

Counseling those with HIV/AIDS is another area in which psychologists have been active with multidisciplinary teams. Psychologists working in this area have made important contributions and are widely respected by their Thai physician colleagues who appreciate and understand the critical role of behavioral change in addressing this serious and recalcitrant problem.

An interesting recent development in the field of AIDS care has also taken place. As the use of highly active antiretroviral therapy has become better known among Thai health workers, it soon became clear that there was a serious problem due to noncompliance among patients. Specifically, failure to take the drugs as prescribed in order to lower the virus load has raised the possibility of producing new strains of the AIDS virus that are resistant to the treatment. Hence, a new project involving over 700 patients from 37 hospitals in the northern region of Thailand has been proposed with collaboration between the Thai government and the Bangkok Office of Population Council. As a part of this project, two Thai psychologists, who have done extensive work in the area of enhancing treatment compliance, were invited to head the team charged with designing an adherence-counseling program. Through this program, AIDS workers are trained to help patients increase and maintain their level of adherence. This is another indication that Thai psychologists are enjoying increasing acceptance and appreciation from other professions in the health-care field outside of psychiatry.

In terms of professional status and privileges, psychologists are still somewhat undervalued relative to other health-care professionals such as nurses and physical therapists. In part, this is due to the fact that training standards for those professions are more rigorous and extensive than those for psychologists.

Over the past few years, there have been proposals to establish standards for training and licensing for psychologists in Thailand, and these efforts eventually paid off. In 2003, a Royal Decree announced that henceforth clinical psychologists would be required to have a license in order to practice psychology (Royal Gazette, 2003). This new Thai law establishes a professional committee to prepare a licensing examination. According to the Royal Decree, clinical psychology is defined as "conduct performed for human beings relating to the examination, diagnosis, and treatment of psychological disorders resulting from conditions of the mind, personality, intelligence level, emotion, behavior, adaptation, stress, or neurological pathology; including research, promotion and assessment of mental health through methods or instruments specific to clinical psychology that have been approved of their status by the Ministry." Individuals who will be qualified to take the license examination include those with a degree in clinical psychology or the equivalent from an educational institute approved by the professional committee, and they must have undergone at least 6 months of internship at an approved hospital or organization. Those who are not Thai citizens and are graduated from overseas institutes must have a clinical psychology license from an approved institution in their own country. Admittedly, the current requirements are rather minimal compared to those in other countries, but they are a starting point from which we can build on and develop higher standards in the future.

In recent years, nurses have become more interested in the behavioral aspects of health and illness, and more master's theses are focused on behavioral issues. There is a strong likelihood that, if Thai psychologists are not active in the development of their skills in health psychology and behavioral medicine, Thai nurses will become recognized as the experts in behavioral science in the near future.

Because of the limited opportunity for career advancement within hospitals and medical settings, some psychologists expanded their professional roles and have formed affiliations with nontraditional agencies and organizations. A few of these alliances have been quite successful, and the psychologists involved have become well-known among governmental, nongovernmental, and private organizations. These psychologists often initially became involved by conducting workshops for health promotion and the prevention of mental or behavioral problems. Some have led working groups that created practice manuals for child-abuse prevention; others have developed intervention and training programs for health volunteers who work with AIDS and HIV positive individuals with support from international organizations such as the WHO and UNICEF. Some Thai psychologists have also begun to provide psychological services such as AIDS counseling and crisis intervention in surrounding countries, including Laos and China.

The Thai public often still confuses psychology with psychiatry and psychologists with psychiatrists, and every Thai psychologist has been asked numerous times to explain the differences between the two professions. Public education and the stronger presence of psychologists in Thai society are required to resolve this confusion.

The early influences on clinical psychology came from a pioneer group of psychiatrists who were developing their own profession in the early 1950s. For this reason, psychoanalytical theories were the main approaches that were initially accepted and widely used. However, with the rapid progress made in the field of pharmacology and the availability of psychotropic drugs, the majority of those involved with Thai psychiatry now seem to be more likely to pay only lip service to psychoanalytical approaches, while in practice the use of medication proves to be much more convenient and cost-effective (and more lucrative for those in private practice). Only a handful of Thai psychiatrists are now practicing psychotherapy, and not all of these are strong advocates of psychodynamic approaches. A few have been trained in cognitive–behavior therapy and some in family therapy.

In the early 1970s, in response to the "human potential movement" and the widespread popularity of the Roge0rian approach, Gestalt therapy, encounter groups, transactional analysis, transcendental meditation, and a host of "new age" methods of personal growth in Western countries, some Thai psychologists who had been trained overseas began to import these ideas and techniques to Thailand. As some of the methods such as self-awareness training seemed to fit in well with the background of many Thais (who were Buddhists and were familiar with the practice of mindfulness training and meditation), the personal growth movement was well received by the young adult population at the time, especially within the university communities and later on among private business organizations.

The movement, however, seemed to fade away within two decades when in the 1990s the increasing ease of international travel and exchange along with the greater accessibility to the Internet, and improved computer literacy helped to make some Thai psychologists become more interested in translating and adapting Western psychological assessment tools for use with the Thai population. Many paper and pencil assessment tools are now available in Thailand. Through the Internet, many Thai psychologists now are up-to-date with current development in their various fields of interest, although this does not mean they have better opportunity for training since this could not possibly be accomplished through long-distance education.

Within the current decade, Thailand has experienced a reemergence of Rogerian client-centered approaches in psychology, education, and medicine. This is reflected in the growth of counseling psychology through a rapid increase in the number of graduate programs in the field, in the advocacy of student-centered approaches in education, and in patient-centered approaches in medicine. Continuing efforts in human rights and children rights by international agencies such as UNICEF and various nongovernmental organizations have also helped eliminate corporal punishment from Thai schools, and these efforts have been supported by the introduction of a new child protection law (the Child Protection Act of 2003). Thai psychologists have also been active in this development, participating in national and provincial committees for the development of "Guidelines for Minimal Standards of Child Care" and "Guidelines for the Assessment of Risk Factors in Child Rearing." These guidelines will be used by government officials and child protection workers in the effort to ensure that Thai children are well cared for and that risk factors for abuse and neglect are reduced.

Similar to the situation in the U.S. and some parts of Europe where the presence of psychological casualties of war (World War II, in particular) and the Veteran Hospitals' helped created clinical psychology, social situations in Thailand shape the functions and responsibilities of Thai psychologists. We are now faced with rapid socioeconomic changes and urbanization, the weakening of social ties and family unity, and the constant bombardment of consumerism where instant gratification, sometimes through violent means, has become the norm. The political instability and economic hardships among neighboring countries such as Myanmar, Laos, Cambodia, and various ethnic minority groups also create a situation where hundreds of thousands of migrant workers (including a large number of children and women) spilled across the border. Thousands of these individuals were placed in camps for displaced persons and many remained there for years. Such social conditions result in a loss of the sense of community, increased alienation, the use of drugs and alcohol, the ever-increasing prevalence of chronic, behaviorally related illnesses and diseases (AIDS, heart diseases, diabetes, obesity, eating disorders, accidents and suicide), and interpersonal violence (e.g., child abuse, domestic violence, sexual violence, and youth violence). These are a few of the challenges that Thai psychologists and other mental health professionals with limited training and education have to tackle and treat.

16.4 FUTURE CHALLENGES AND PROSPECTS

Most Thai clinical psychologists working in medical settings, especially those in traditional psychiatric hospitals, see little room for professional growth; the future seems quite bleak. Indeed, over the past two decades it has been common for psychologists with the strongest academic and clinical backgrounds to leave hospital settings for more professionally rewarding opportunities such as universities or medical schools. The majority of those who remained in the psychiatric hospitals were either very dedicated to the patients they served or else found that their limited educational background and training made it difficult to find employment elsewhere.

As the "founding fathers" of Thai psychology reach retirement age, it is necessary for a younger generation of psychologists to work hard to improve the status of the profession. With a growing appreciation for the relevance of behavioral science to public health, the time seems ripe for psychologists in medical settings to rise to the occasion and prove that they are important members of the health care system. However, if this goal is to be attained, it is critical for Thai psychologists to improve the education and training opportunities available in Thailand. As this may not be possible in the near future, due to the current economic crisis affecting the Thai economy and that of surrounding Asian countries, the only other option appears to be to have more young Thai psychologists receive training overseas. Unfortunately, the recent economic crisis resulted in the elimination of many scholarships for Thai graduate students; those scholarships that remain tend to concentrate on the natural sciences and technology rather than on the social sciences and psychology.

In summary, Thai psychologists face multiple challenges. There is a tremendous need to standardize training requirements and upgrade the educational requirements for the profession so that at least some graduate training is the norm rather than the exception. The power and influence of the profession also is limited by the relatively small number of psychologists in Thailand and by the profession's history as a handmaiden of psychiatry. However, Thai psychologists are actively investigating new professional roles and creating new opportunities for the application of psychological skills in diverse health care settings.

REFERENCES

100 years of mental health and psychiatry. (1989). Bangkok: Tanawich.

Chaosilp, P. (1983). *Manual for psychoanalytic theories.* Bangkok: Sahaprachapanich.

Chaosilp, P., & Kongsakol, R. (1999). *Group psychotherapy for inpatients.* Bangkok: The Thai Psychiatrist Association.

Dickinson, P. (1984). *Developmental psychology* (2nd ed.). Bangkok: Praepitaya.

Iamsupasit, S. (2000). *Theories and techniques of behavior modification* (4th ed.). Bangkok: Chulalongkorn.

Kowtrakul, S. (2001). *Educational psychology* (5th ed.). Bangkok: Chulalongkorn.

Patrayutawat, S. (2002). *Manual of psychological assessment.* Bangkok: Medical Media.

Royal Gazette. (2003, July 23). *120* (Section 72 a), 1–4.

Sukatungka, K. (2002). *Clinical psychology: From theory to practice.* Bangkok: Medical Media.

Thai Psychiatric Association. (1977). *Textbook of psychiatry.* Bangkok: AksornThai.

Yalom, I. D. (1975). *The theory and practice of group psychotherapy* (2nd ed.). New York: Basic Books.

IMPORTANT PUBLICATIONS

Chaosilp, P. (1983). *Manual for psychoanalytic theories.* Bangkok: Sahaprachapanich.

Chaosilp, P., & Kongsakol, R. (1999). *Group psychotherapy for inpatients.* Bangkok: The Thai Psychiatrist Association.

Dickinson, P. (1984). *Developmental psychology* (2nd ed.). Bangkok: Praepitaya.

Iamsupasit, S. (2000). *Theories and techniques of behavior modification* (4th ed.). Bangkok: Chulalongkorn.

Kowtrakul, S. (2001). *Educational psychology* (5th ed.). Bangkok: Chulalongkorn.

CHAPTER 17

Psychology in Poland: A Country in Transition

IRENA HESZEN-NIEJODEK

Irena Heszen-Niejodek graduated from the University of Warsaw, receiving an M.A. in psychology in 1965 and a Ph.D. in 1970. In 1978, she received a habilitation *(a post-doctoral degree) in psychology, and in 1993, the title of professor in the humanities.*

In 1965, Irena Heszen-Niejodek joined the Warsaw Medical Academy and in 1980 moved to the Silesian University in Katowice. Since 1993, she has been senior professor and chair of the Department of Health and Developmental Psychology at the Silesian University. Since 2003, she has been employed at the Warsaw School of Social Psychology as chair of the Department of Health Psychology.

Irena Heszen-Niejodek is the author or editor of 11 books and more than 100 articles. She has supervised over 20 doctoral dissertations and more than 150 master's theses. She is a member of the Committee of Psychological Sciences of the Polish *Academy of Sciences and a delegate from Poland to the International Union of Psychological Science. She holds memberships in the Polish Psychological Society, International Association of Applied Psychology, Society for Stress and Anxiety Research, European Association of Personality Psychology, and European Health Psychology Society. Her interests include stress management, health promotion, and spirituality as a dimension of health.*

17.1 OVERVIEW

The history of psychology as a distinct discipline is relatively recent. It is widely accepted that scientific psychology originated when Wilhelm Wundt founded the first laboratory in experimental psychology in Germany in 1879 (Hilgard, 1987). But interest in psychology has a much longer history and in Poland can be dated as early as the second half of the 13th century. This is when Enazmus Witelo, a philosopher of nature, published his theory of optic perception (Burchardt, 1991). Psychological descriptions and psychological reasoning have also been appearing in Polish belles lettres since the 16th century.

The history of scientific psychology in Poland reflects to some degree the history of the country, with its long and dramatic struggles for independence (Davies, 1981). From 1795 to 1918, Poland did not exist as an independent country, having been partitioned among Austria, Germany, and Russia. However, two Polish universities were allowed to function. Laboratories in experimental psychology were established at both: in Cracow by Wladyslaw Heinrich in 1903 and in Lvov (now in the Ukraine) by Kazimierz Twardowski in 1907. The first practical applications of scientific psychology in the world occurred in Poland at the end of the 19th century (Stachowski, 2000). The work of Jan Dawid (1896) on the learning of a native language is an example, also illustrating how Polish psychologists struggled to preserve Polish culture in the time of partition.

In 1918, after World War I, Poland regained her independence. Several university centers of psychology in Cracow, Lvov, Poznan, Warsaw, and Vilnius (now in Lithuania) were very active in both research and teaching until the beginning of World War II in 1939.

The short period in the history of Polish psychology after World War II, from 1948 to 1956, deserves special attention. Formally, Poland regained her sovereignty, but in reality Poland was governed according to Soviet ideology. Traditional psychology was generally devalued and criticized as a "bourgeois" discipline. Instead, a new Marxist psychology, based on the principles of dialectical materialism, was proposed. In fact, such a Marxist psychology never came into existence, although obligatory courses devoted to politico–ideological topics had an important place in the curriculum, and a sort of "Pavlovization" of psychology did occur. The admission of new students was halted for a few years, and in some fields, psychologists were treated as subordinates to other specialists (e.g., psychiatrists). Of the foreign psychological literature that was available in Poland, translations of Russian books predominated.

After 1956, when the Soviet Union relinquished some control over Poland, master's-degree programs in psychology were renewed at three universities: Cracow, Poznan, and Warsaw. Institutions of higher education obtained some autonomy and independence. But, during the years of communist domination, Polish psychologists were still rather isolated from those in Western Europe and the United States, and it was very difficult to arrange any form of scientific exchange. Literature on psychology from other countries was seldom available, and financial resources for going abroad were limited. Some scholars were refused passports; others were allowed to go abroad under the condition that they fulfill certain political requirements, which usually meant gathering information for the security services. Of course, very few took advantage of such offers. However, as the years passed, an increasing number of academic psychologists managed to leave Poland for several months of study, mainly in the United States These psychologists brought back to Poland not only theoretical and empirical literature but also measurement tools. American psychology is highly valued among Polish psychologists and has helped shape Polish psychology.

When the communist era ended in 1989, and with the economic and political reconstruction of the country underway, Poland became a fully independent country. No political restrictions were applied to people going abroad, and international exchange increased dramatically. Today, many Polish psychologists are members of prestigious international scientific societies, with some serving as members of boards or even as presidents. They participate in international research programs and arrange and attend international conferences, and many serve as members of the editorial boards of prestigious international journals. (It is worth noting that the initial proposal for an international congress of psychology was made in 1881 by a visionary young Polish psychologist, Julian Ochorowicz, who also called for an international organization of psychologists [Rosenzweig, Holtzman, Sabourin, & Belanger, 2000]). The only limit to international participation is financial, but it is hoped that matters will improve after Poland joins the European Union in 2004.

At present, there are about 10,000 psychologists in Poland, and this number is rapidly increasing. Poland has a population of close to 38,000,000, and there are about 26 psychologists per 100,000 citizens. By comparison, there are 2,000 psychiatrists, which means there are about 5 psychiatrists per 100,000 citizens. Almost all psychologists live in urban areas, with the majority residing not far from university centers and about half are members of the Polish Psychological Association.

Several psychological organizations, both professional and academic, are registered in Poland; two of the most influential are the Polish Psychological Association (*Polskie Towarzystwo Psychologiczne* [PTP]) and the Committee of the Psychological Sciences of the Polish Academy of Sciences (*Komitet Nauk Psychologicznych Polskiej Akademii Nauk* [KNP PAN]). The PTP (http://www.ptp.psychologia.pl), renewed after World War II, has continued the work of its predecessor of the same name, which was founded in 1907 in Warsaw (Polish Psychological Association, 1992a). The KNP PAN is one of the committees affiliated with the Polish Academy of Sciences and emerged in 1972 as a separate unit from the Joint Committee of Pedagogical and Psychological Sciences (Marszal-Wisniewska, 2002).

The revised charter of the PTP specifies the purpose of this psychological organization as the "development and dissemination of psychology as a science and as a profession, [with special focus on] serving people in solving life problems and maintaining health" (Polish Psychological Association, 1988, p. 5). Activities directed toward these goals include, among others, overseeing education and training in psychology at the postgraduate level outside the universities, constructing and refining diagnostic tools, ensuring the maintenance of high standards in the practice of psychology, encouraging and organizing scientific meetings, publishing books and journals, and representing the profession to government agencies and NGOs. The PTP is also a national member of the International Union of Psychological Sciences.

The structure of the PTP is rather complicated but has been adapted to the purposes described above. Apart from the central board in Warsaw, there are more than 20 boards of local divisions, located in the largest Polish cities. These divisions integrate psychologists living in an area and focus on local interests and needs. There are also 12 national sections of the PTP that serve to gather together psychologists with similar research interests. Some of the sections are quite active and have international links (e.g., the sections on developmental psychology, forensic psychology, health psychology, and psychotherapy). In addition, the PTP has its own agencies, eight altogether, which are relatively independent units that offer psychological services. The most important are the Institute of Health and Sobriety Psychology, the Laboratory of Psychoeducation, and the Laboratory of Psychological Tests.

Some important psychological events are organized under the auspices of the PTP. The convention of the PTP, which is held every third year, is the biggest assembly of Polish psychologists and brings together more than 1,200 participants. The convention is a mostly scientific program but also includes an important administrative component, the general assembly of local representatives, which makes decisions crucial to the future of the PTP. Another event that takes place at the PTP convention is the granting of two prestigious awards. One award, in memory of Stefan Blachowski, is given in recognition of the scholarly achievements of a young academic, and the Bogdan Zawadzki Memorial Award honors outstanding professional achievements in the field of psychology.

For many years, the PTP was the only Polish organization to unify and represent psychologists. That situation has changed with the foundation of the KNP PAN, which oversees the status of psychology as a discipline. The KNP PAN articulates standards for university education and training

in psychology, publishes scientific books and several journals on psychology, and organizes annual colloquia that focus on recent advances in psychological research. Membership in the KNP PAN is highly selective. Members are elected by ballot from among psychologists with the degree of "habilitated Ph.D." (i.e., a research degree following the doctorate, whose holders are independent scientists not under the supervision of a professor). Elections take place every third year. In the last election, 24 new members were selected from more than 200 candidates holding the habilitated Ph.D.

Clearly, the PTP and the KNP PAN are complementary organizations. Since the establishment of the KNP PAN, the PTP has focused its activities on the problems facing applied professional psychology and its practice. However, both organizations share two compelling interests: education and training in psychology, and the legal aspects of psychology as a profession. The president of the PTP is a permanent member of the KNP PAN, which ensures cooperation and coordination between the two groups.

Psychological organizations in Poland cooperate and are unified in their stance toward government agendas that influence the science and practice of psychology. They share a common outlook on academic plans that are proposed by the Ministry of National Education and Sport, and work hard to get legislation enacted to regulate the profession of psychology. However, there are key differences between those who pursue careers in academic psychology versus professional psychology. In psychology, tracks for careers in research and in practice are rather separate. Only in the specialty of clinical psychology are found psychologists who combine the roles of scientist and practitioner. However, this has resulted in a situation in which the academic careers of clinical psychologists suffer. In general, the academic and professional communities are isolated without a sense of tension existing between them.

In Poland, psychology is highly respected, both as a science and as a profession. Psychologists are often invited to present their opinions in the media or to participate in interdisciplinary discussions. Psychological knowledge is disseminated in popular magazines. Other specialists cite the work of psychologists and also refer patients to them. But, the role that psychologists can play as expert consultants to the government on important policies that impact the psychosocial lives of Poles has been underestimated. The positions that psychologists hold in the workplace are quite diverse. In psychiatric hospitals, psychologists have a long tradition of working cooperatively with psychiatrists; at the moment, there are 494 psychologists compared to 1,066 psychiatrists in psychiatric facilities. Although the professional status of psychologists is lower than that of physicians, it has been improving.

Paradoxically, there is no legal act in Poland that formally recognizes the profession of psychology. As a result, psychologists are usually employed in positions where they are given designations such as "physicians," social workers, and teachers, and earn comparable salaries to those occupations. For example, after 14 years of practice, a clinical psychologist in a hospital holds a position called *physician* and earns 400 euros per month. A psychologist in a school holds the position of *teacher* and earns 350 euros per month after the same number of years in practice. A junior psychologist with one year of practice may be employed as a school social worker, earning 300 euros per month. Sometimes, a local board decides the position and salary for a psychologist (e.g., a psychologist working in local administration earns 400 euros whereas a psychologist at an outpatient clinic earns 215 euros). Junior faculty with Ph.D.s earn 475–755 euros per month, a recent improvement. All figures quoted above are gross salaries, from which at least 25% is deducted for taxes and health insurance. The incomes of psychologists, although modest, are actually somewhat higher because many have secondary jobs or private practice.

17.2 EDUCATION AND TRAINING

There are two types of psychological studies in Poland: full-time and part-time. Psychological faculty and institutes are free to devise their own admissions criteria, with more flexible criteria used to admit part-time students. Candidates for full-time studies usually have to take a highly competitive entrance examination. There are more than 10 applicants for each seat in most universities, and there are as many as 20 candidates for each position at prestigious universities. Part-time studies are not very popular, in part because such students have to pay for their education. Not more than five applications for a place are submitted, so it is easier to qualify as a part-time student. The number of places for freshmen is specified by each university, although the Ministry of National Education and Sport recommends that the number of full-time and part-time students be equal.

Several forms of financial support are available, but only for full-time students. Students coming from families with a very low income (i.e., less than 100 euros per person per month) may receive a modest monthly scholarship. The percentage of students qualifying for this assistance is low; the data for the whole student population are not available, but for example, at Silesian University, less than 8% of the student population qualifies. Students ranked in the top quarter of their academic class are awarded a special scholarship in recognition of their achievements. A very limited number of top students may compete for a scholarship established by the Ministry of National Education and Sport. A special scholarship is available for students with disabilities. On rare occasions, a part-time student facing a difficult personal situation is partly exempted from paying tuition. In addition, various student activities in areas such as art, science, and sports, are funded by university sources. In cafeterias, students can eat inexpensive meals that are partly prepaid by the Ministry of National Education and Sport; the cost of students' accommodation in hostels is also partly reimbursed.

These financial conditions are unfair to part-time students, who have to pay for their tuition without financial assistance, because the Polish constitution guarantees the right of all citizens to receive an education. However, since 1989, a market economy has been gradually introduced into Poland, and one consequence of the subsequent adjustment is that state universities are not being adequately subsidized in the national budget. In fact, the financial situation in higher education seems to worsen every year. University administrators and faculty make great efforts to raise extra funds just to survive because the finances allocated in the state budget are insufficient to cover even basic expenses. The only university "products" eligible for sale and reimbursement according to the rules of the free market are educational services. In the beginning, this "educational business" was objected to by the academic community; now it is regarded as a necessity. The commercialization of higher education, resulting from the introduction of tuition fees and the shifting of responsibility for financing education from the state to the individual, challenges the integrity of academe.

In Poland, the basic autonomous unit within a university is the college. There are 14 institutions that offer a 5-year master's degree in psychology, but their positions in the organizational structure of the university differ. Only the University of Warsaw employs a sufficient number of professors, and so is entitled to establish a separate college of psychology. Elsewhere, institutes of psychology take responsibility for psychological education, but not as separate units. They are attached to other institutes that teach related disciplines such as pedagogy, philosophy, or sociology; in these cases, multidisciplinary colleges can be established (e.g., a college of education and psychology).

Two private institutions of higher education offer master's degrees in psychology: Catholic University in Lublin, under the auspices of the Catholic Church, and the Warsaw School of Social Psychology. Catholic University was established in 1918 and has awarded master's degrees in psychology since 1981. Psychology was present in the curriculum much earlier, but students who selected psychology as their major graduated with a master's in

Christian philosophy, and few possibilities for work were available to them. This reflected the antagonistic stance of the communist government towards the Catholic Church; the government also refused to subsidize the University. Catholic University was financed by the Catholic Church and by parishioners' donations. Since 1993, the government has been partially subsidizing the university's expenses, and as in state universities, full-time students do not have to pay tuition.

The Warsaw School of Social Psychology was founded in 1996 by a group of professors employed by the Institute of Psychology at the Polish Academy of Sciences. The school is financially self-sufficient and tuition is moderately expensive. However, the school's modern educational methods and high teaching standards attract many applicants, particularly because students with outstanding records may be exempted from tuition or awarded scholarships. The school accepts 1,000 new students of psychology every year and has developed rapidly, graduating several hundred students each year, which is much higher than the graduation rate of 80–120 students per year at state universities.

Both Catholic University in Lublin and the Warsaw School of Social Psychology have received the certificate of quality assurance from the University Accreditation Commission. The commission is a prestigious non-governmental entity appointed by representatives of the best Polish universities to preserve high teaching standards threatened by the increasing commercialization of higher education in Poland. State universities that have been awarded the certificate of quality assurance in the field of psychology are Jagiellonian University in Cracow, Gdansk University, Adam Mickiewicz University in Poznan, and the University of Warsaw. Before the political transformation of 1989, the number of students admitted into universities each year was limited by the Ministry of National Education and Sport. Under the government's new Act of Higher Education, each university has now been granted the authority to specify its own admission policy and the limits on student intake. The number of students in psychology has increased rapidly, and about 2,000 new psychologists graduate from Polish universities every year, with several hundred graduating from the Warsaw School of Social Psychology alone.

All institutions of higher education that train psychologists apply the European Credit Transfer System, which has enhanced students' mobility both within the country and abroad. In a sense, it is regrettable that Polish students of psychology have not fully exploited opportunities for travel abroad. During the 2001–2002 academic year, only 3,691 students participated in Poland's largest exchange program, Socrates–Erasmus; this represents less than 0.5% of the full-time student population.

In Poland, a bachelor's degree is usually awarded after 3 years of study, but psychology is one of the few exceptions. According to the widely held opinion of scientists in the field, 5 years of study and the preparation of a master's thesis are necessary to qualify as a psychologist. Basic standards for instruction have been delineated by the Ministry of National Education and Sport. They specify the total number of required teaching hours and the number of hours to be devoted to each of the obligatory subjects. The obligatory courses for full-time students require 1,185 hr, but the number of hours over 5 years of study must total at least 2,600. Elective coursework can include extensions of obligatory courses as well as optional courses offered by a university, depending on local possibilities (e.g., applied psychology and a "master's seminar"). In the part-time system, the number of required hours is set at a minimum of 80% of that required of the full-time students.

The obligatory courses are:

- General courses (405 hr): philosophy with logic (45 hr), biological mechanisms of behavior (90 hr), foreign languages (180 hr, English is mandatory), physical education (60 hr), and other (30 hr, e.g., computer science)
- Basic courses (330 hr): introduction to psychology (60 hr), history of psychological thought (30 hr), research methodology and statistics (120 hr), and psychometrics and psychological diagnosis (120 hr)
- "Disciplinary" courses (450 hr): cognitive processes (90 hr), development over the lifespan (60 hr), emotions and motivation (60 hr), individual differences (60 hr), personality (60 hr), and social psychology (120 hr)

The 5-year master's degree program in psychology at the Silesian University, the academic home of the author, will be presented as an example of a postgraduate program. The curriculum consists of obligatory courses plus another 60 hr devoted to development across the lifespan. Five branches of applied psychology are included: clinical, educational, forensic, health, and the psychology of work and management. They are taught during obligatory introductory courses, each of which is 30 hr in length. After completing this coursework, students select one branch as a main specialty and another branch as a secondary specialty. The main specialty requires 510 credit hours and

the secondary specialty, 90 hr. Various modes of instruction are used: lectures, seminars, and laboratory work. In addition, two extra 75-hr practica are offered at institutions that employ experienced psychologists, who serve as supervisors.

Besides this form of specialization, students have to select several so-called faculty courses from among the few dozen offered by professors. This system works according to the rule of the market; if enrollment is low, the course is canceled. The topics of faculty courses reflect the professional skills or scientific interests of the professor, such as autism, negotiation skills, smoking cessation, and sexuality, among others.

The choice of a master's seminar is a singularly important decision. The seminar starts at the beginning of the seventh semester, after the first 3 years of study have been completed; it is four semesters long and earns 180 hr of credit. The expected outcome is a master's thesis in which theoretical arguments and the results of the student's own original empirical study are presented. The thesis typically receives two independent evaluations, one from the professor who led the seminar group and the other from an independent reviewer.

In Poland, a 4-year doctoral degree is offered. However, there is a provision to apply for the degree without attending courses, by contracting individually with a professor. There is no uniform curriculum, but usually lectures are delivered on general psychology, methodology, computer science and statistics, and related subjects such as economics, history, and philosophy. Regardless of whether candidates attend lectures or not, they are required to pass examinations and prepare doctoral dissertations under the supervision of a professor. The dissertation must be reviewed and accepted by two other professors. Although the percentage of graduate students applying for the Ph.D. was low several years ago, it has recently increased to about 20%. As a professional group, psychologists strive to improve their qualifications in the face of rising unemployment and strong competition. Poland has about 1,000 psychologists with doctorates (Brzezinski & Strelau, in press).

Education and training in psychology involve a variety of pedagogical methods, although the lecture has become the dominant form due to economic reasons. Lectures are delivered to large groups of students of up to 100. A seminar typically has about 25 students; master's seminars are smaller, with about 10 students. Laboratory groups that focus on the acquisition of professional skills may be limited to six students. The number of students concurrently enrolled in practica depends on the situation at the site of the field placement (e.g., some teaching hospitals only accept two students). Usually, classes meet weekly for two "teaching hours" (i.e., 1.5 "clock hours"). At the end of the semester, students are required to complete a paper, or pass an oral examination or a written test to obtain course credit.

After the political changes in 1989, Poland has become more open to international influences. All kinds of teaching resources have become available, such as foreign books, journals, and tools for psychological measurement. All state and most private universities theoretically have access to the Internet. However, in reality, only the leading universities are able to afford these resources. Elsewhere, the number of books and journals, especially foreign literature, as well as the size and quality of computer laboratories are found wanting. For example, *PsycINFO*, the basic source of bibliographic data in psychology, is available at only two or three universities.

Owning to the initiative of Jan Strelau, an outstanding scholar at the University of Warsaw, students of psychology have a unique source of psychological knowledge that meets the highest academic standards, his three-volume *Psychology: An Academic Handbook*, published in 2000 (Strelau, 2000). About 50 leading academic psychologists, representing all fields of psychology as a science and most branches of applied psychology, contributed to the handbook. It is available throughout Poland and is recommended at all universities that offer a master's degree in psychology. The handbook has made it possible to meet, if not exceed, the minimum standards for instruction in psychology.

According to Polish academic tradition and modern policies on university teaching, the master's degree in psychology is aimed at imparting general theoretical knowledge rather than practical skills. The knowledge base is broad, not limited to psychology as a discipline; students also become familiar with different investigative methodologies. Master's programs take into consideration the fact that today's graduates will probably change jobs and professional roles about five times during their working lives. Hence, it is more critical to equip graduates with a relatively comprehensive theoretical foundation as opposed to practical techniques that may become irrelevant or obsolete. No licenses or certificates that attest to the mastery of professional skills are required for graduation. It is expected that such skills will be acquired during postgraduate training.

Unfortunately, the system of postgraduate professional training is still in its developmental stage. Clinical psychology is the only branch of applied psychology in which postgraduate training is consistently available. The curriculum follows the standards adopted in postgraduate medical training and applies only to psychologists employed by the healthcare system. All costs are covered by the Ministry of Health and Welfare. Psychologists employed in educational settings are eligible to apply for promotion within a step system available to all teachers, but they are not offered regular ongoing professional training to augment these applications. Promotions in the educational sector are based on seniority only, and postgraduate courses are taken at the applicants' own initiative.

A new curriculum of postgraduate training in clinical psychology has recently been adopted to conform to the new medical training schema. Admission is possible after a year of clinical practice. Training lasts for 5 years, including 2 years of basic instruction and 3 of advanced coursework. The first part, 410 hr in all, encompasses 3 months of clinical experience in each of the four branches of medicine in which many psychologists are employed: psychiatry, neurology, pediatrics, and cardiology. Several courses on clinical psychology and ethics are also included.

After completing the first part of training, the student chooses one of the four medical branches mentioned above for advanced training. Advanced training includes 13–15 months of clinical experience and 440 hr of coursework.

The basic level of training (the first 2 years) includes:

- General topics, such as the biological bases of human behavior, cognition, and emotion, theories of personality and human development, stress and conflict
- Clinical topics, such as behavioral medicine, psychopathology, psychosomatics, and selected neurological topics relevant to health psychology
- Professional performance, which centers on the ethical practice of professional psychology and the role and functions of a psychologist on the therapeutic team
- Professional skills, incorporating mastery of psychological diagnosis, communicating the diagnosis to the therapeutic team and to members of a patient's family, and developing a treatment plan that is matched to a diagnosis and that respects the patient's individual needs

The detailed curriculum of advanced training (the next 3 years) depends on the chosen specialty within clinical psychology. It aims to prepare students to function competently, ethically, and independently in identifying and resolving diagnostic and therapeutic dilemmas, developing and delivering health promotion and prophylactic programs, and making a variety of professional decisions based on sound clinical judgment and expertise. "Specialization" is conferred after passing a three-part oral, written, and practical exam. This program is affiliated with the Ministry of Health and Welfare and housed in authorized healthcare institutions (Heszen-Niejodek, 1988; Puzynski, Brzezinska, Czabala, Kadzielawa, & Tylka, 2002).

Besides this system of postgraduate training in clinical psychology, some additional options are available. The PTP offers paid courses on different psychotherapies at its own teaching laboratories, directs trainees to centers that offer continuing education classes, issues licenses in psychotherapy, and recommends psychologists who are experts in forensics. In addition, universities also arrange some form of postgraduate training in different fields of applied psychology according to local needs and available resources. Registrants pay for courses and receive a certificate on completion of training.

17.3 SCOPE OF PSYCHOLOGICAL PRACTICE

In 2001, after many years of effort on the part of both the PTP and the KNP PAN, the Polish parliament passed an act that formally recognized the profession of psychology and established a council of psychologists. The act reflects the high status of psychology as a profession, ensures its legal protection, and constitutes the basis for its development in the decades ahead. Unfortunately, after stormy debates, the parliament adopted a 5-year *vacatio legis*, which means that implementation of the act will be postponed till 2006 (Toeplitz-Winiewska, 2001)!

The author was fortunate to serve as a chair of the team that prepared the Ethical and Professional Code of Psychologists. The general assembly of the PTP approved the code in 1988. It was updated in 1991 to reflect the changing needs of society after the transformation of the political system by including safeguards against the abuse of psychological knowledge and of psychologists who engage in political activity.

The code includes a preamble, general principles, and three detailed sections that cover psychological practice, research, and the teaching and dissemination of psychological knowledge. The code emphasizes that the good of humanity should be the highest guiding value in all areas of psychological activity. For example, this value is acknowledged in the part of the code which asserts that the application of a special set of interpersonal skills to influence others implies responsibility for the outcomes of such activity and warrants adherence to the highest ethical standards of practice. The 50 articles contained in the code specify how psychologists should conduct themselves in different professional scenarios. Difficult and ambiguous situations are given special consideration (e.g., working with a court-referred client, and the influence of a psychologist's personal views on disseminating psychological information) (Polish Psychological Association, 1992b).

The code is used in specialty courses on professional ethics that are included in the curricula of most universities offering the master's degree in psychology, and in postgraduate training programs in clinical psychology. Alleged infractions of the code are reviewed and adjudicated by the Fellow Court of the Board of Directors of the PTP. Violators are punished according to the regulations of the court.

What of the current status of Polish psychology as a science and profession? To understand the essential characteristics of contemporary psychological research, it is necessary to examine its sources. The standards for contemporary research methodology in Poland were laid down by Kazimierz Twardowski (1866–1938) of Lvov University. He is regarded as a cofounder of the Lvov–Warsaw School of Philosophy, which is among the most important schools of philosophy today (Brzezinski & Strelau, in press). The most influential theoretical achievement of Twardowski was the theory of purposeful action and its offshoots. Twardowski's line of theoretical thinking and his methodological standards were further developed by his disciples (who chaired almost all of the psychological departments after Poland regained her independence in 1918), and by their disciples in turn.

The most appreciated and influential among Twardowski's students was Tadeusz Tomaszewski (1910–2000) of the University of Warsaw, who is regarded as author of the mature theory of purposeful action (Tomaszewski, 1963), rooted in Twardowski's ideas. The essential thesis of the theory is that the specific form of any human activity is purposeful behavior. The most general goal of this activity may be formulated as regulation of the relationship between the person and the environment. The course of human activity is constantly adapting to a continually changing environment in order to maximize the probability of fulfilling the original purpose of action. According to Tomaszewski, the subject matter of psychology as a discipline is purposeful action, with the person as its agent.

Tomaszewski's theory of purposeful action was used as a theoretical framework by his disciples in the University of Warsaw, which currently employs psychology professors who are internationally renowned. The theory exerted a significant influence on psychological research all over Poland, providing a conceptual foundation for more detailed theorizing and empirical inquiry into specific kinds of human activity, such as decision-making and learning. It has also proved to be useful in several branches of applied psychology, in the analysis, description, and explanation of different human occupations, including Marek Wosinski's studies of teaching and the author's work on the practice of medicine.

Although the books mentioned previously did draw the attention and interest of the addressed specialists (teachers and physicians), the theory of purposeful action as elaborated within general psychology has not exerted any distinct influence on the economic, political, and social transition that has taken place in Poland since the late 1980s. Polish social psychology has proved to be more responsive to the new challenges. An important psychological project, executed in cooperation with sociologists, is the yearly Polish General Social Survey, providing material for a systematic analysis of Polish society. Social psychologists participate in monitoring the social effects of political reforms. Also, new branches of applied social psychology have developed, such as organizational psychology, economic psychology, and the psychology of advertising (Lewicka, 2001).

One of Tomaszewski's disciples who is very active in the international arena is Jan Strelau of the University of Warsaw, who is now at the Warsaw School of Social Psychology. Strelau is well-known and highly regarded as the author of the regulatory theory of temperament. His recent book on temperament (Strelau, 1998), which was published in Poland and in the United States, received a prize from the Foundation in Aid of Polish Science in 2000. This award is so prestigious that it is sometimes called "the Polish Nobel." Tomaszewski's theory of purposeful action has clearly influenced Strelau's work, focused on temperament from the perspective of mutual relationships between a person and the environment in which human activity plays a decisive part (Strelau, 1998).

Janusz Reykowski, another distinguished psychologist of the so-called Warsaw School of Psychology, is the author of an original theory on the regulatory role of emotions. The theory is now well-supported empirically, although Reykowski's original intention was only to articulate the theoretical ideas of Tomaszewski (Reykowski, 1974). Józef Kozielecki, also from the University of Warsaw, developed the psychological theory of decision making, referring to Tomaszewski's notion that tasks direct purposeful action toward specific final results (Kozielecki, 1977).

At least one more person from the scientific community in psychology should be mentioned, namely Kazimierz Obuchowski. Obuchowski developed his own line of interdisciplinary thinking based on a synthesis of the literature in many areas of psychology as well as his own empirical work. Obuchowski's aim is to formulate the most general principles about human functioning in the context of the immediate environment. Obuchowski (2004) applies basic concepts, some drawn from the natural sciences and philosophy, to explain how people defend themselves against entropy and even manage to develop in the process.

A host of Polish scholars are involved in empirical research rather than theoretical work as a way to advance psychology. Their research is conducted according to the methodological standards promulgated by Jerzy Brzezinski (1997), who also adheres to Tomaszewski's view of psychology. According to Brzezinski, because psychology is an empirical science, laboratory experiments are recommended as the best method of expanding and deepening psychological knowledge. In Poland, the experimental approach is common to psychophysiology and social psychology, with the latter field well known for interesting studies with inventive designs. At the moment, some of these ingenious experiments have been questioned from an ethical standpoint, with the result that social psychologists are reluctant to investigate areas such as stress and stress management.

In most branches of applied psychology, empirical studies are conducted in natural settings. Research designs tend to be ex post facto. Self-report questionnaires, both adapted and indigenous, are usually employed as measurement tools. Psychologists are paying more attention to the psychometric properties of these instruments. Clinicians are probably the only group of Polish psychologists who conduct qualitative case studies in evaluating the effectiveness of their interventions; however, relatively few such studies are carried out.

A variety of intervention strategies are used in Poland and their use depends not only on the purpose to which they are applied, but also on the competencies of the psychologists who apply them. Classical psychoanalysis and psychodynamic psychotherapy based on object-relations theory are applied by clinical psychologists to patients suffering from neuroses and personality disturbances. Erickson's short-term strategic therapy has become very popular and is widely used in different areas of psychological practice.

Behavioral and cognitive–behavioral therapies are widely employed to help psychiatric and medical patients. Cognitive–behavioral therapies, in particular, constitute the basis for stress-management programs that are gaining in popularity among psychologists who work with vulnerable groups such as managers and police officers. Gestalt therapy, aimed at personal development, is the strategy of choice in the field of education. Family problems are dealt with through some form of systems therapy, including communication, structural, and strategic therapies. In business and industry, not only are stress-management interventions used, but also special group approaches to promote integration and cohesiveness among workers.

The number of psychologists who are qualified to implement these interventions and who possess the necessary licenses or certificates is dramatically low. A host of persons offer and deliver different forms of psychotherapy without sufficient training; this situation cannot be changed because of the lack of regulatory legislation. To give one example, the technique of neurolinguistic programming (NLP) is applied to the development of interpersonal skills rather than as psychotherapy, and this training is highly valued by business professionals. Unfortunately, it attracts laypeople without any psychological preparation who, after limited personal experience, feel ready to take on the role of a trainer.

Psychological interventions applied in Poland are most often of foreign origin, although in practice they have been adjusted to the sociocultural context. With reference to theory and research methodology, it is not easy to separate foreign influences from indigenous ones. In the current era of global access to information and its rapid dissemination, a complex array of influences from multiple sources determine the final form of one's thinking and activity. However, many Polish scientists in psychology who graduated from the University of Warsaw continue to be influenced by Tomaszewski's original theory of purposeful action. Even this theory, though developed relatively independently within

Poland, is related to the ideas of interactional psychology on the one hand and to the theory of goal-directed behavior on the other. These relationships provide fascinating evidence that psychological ideas tend to cross continue to evolve after crossing national borders as they evolve.

Psychometric instruments usually have an inventor or group of inventors, thus making it simple to specify whether they are adapted or indigenous. In Poland, many adapted techniques are applied in diagnosis and research. When applied to diagnosis, measures that have been adapted tend not to respect the sociocultural values of the patient, and this is an obvious weakness. In research, adapted measures make possible transnational comparisons and the accumulation of data on the psychometric properties of such measures.

Of Poland's 10,000 psychologists, about 20% are employed as clinicians in healthcare, up to 20% work in business and industry, and another 20% have jobs in education. A large group of about 15% consists of researchers, many of whom are employed by the Polish Academy of Sciences, by universities and other institutions of higher education, and by research centers in health, industry and other areas. Those employed in higher education are responsible not only for research but also for teaching. The remaining 25% of psychologists practice privately, or have jobs in the police force and other divisions of the judicial system, and in churches, where they conduct assessments, deliver psychotherapy services, and consult. Psychologists who work outside the profession do so as civil servants, journalists, managers, or as unqualified workers. A growing number of new graduates are initially unable to find employment. However, they usually find jobs within a year, with about half taking up positions that are unrelated to their expertise. On the other hand, veteran psychologists are sometimes dismissed and replaced by younger, better-qualified colleagues.

The majority of psychologists in health-care are employed in medical settings; most of these are in psychiatry, with smaller numbers in neurology, pediatrics, and internal medicine and surgery, especially cardiology, oncology, and physiology. Psychologists are likely to work in general medical–surgical hospitals, teaching hospitals, and rehabilitation–prophylactic centers; smaller hospitals and polyclinics usually have no psychologists on staff. For the most part, psychologists work directly with patients. They are involved in diagnostic and therapeutic processes, although a physician is ultimately responsible for each patient's care. In many medical units, psychologists are also expected to disseminate psychological information by giving lectures for physicians and medical staff. Psychologists employed in research–teaching clinics are often invited to participate in interdisciplinary research. In response to contemporary challenges, crisis-intervention centers have recently been established. Their initial purpose was to help victims of a flood that ravaged southern Poland in 1997; now they provide services for people affected by different life crises (e.g., domestic abuse or depression caused by unemployment).

Psychologists working in business and industry have been most affected by the consequences of the economic and political transformation in Poland. The model of professional activity has changed from the traditional role of a vocational psychologist (i.e., matching people to job requirements) to confronting new challenges that have arisen as a result of the bankruptcy and restructuring of state industries, growing unemployment, and the emergence of new companies governed by principles of the free market. To solve the problem of unemployment, work clubs affiliated with regional offices of employment have been established. The psychologists who work with these clubs help displaced workers to adjust to being unemployed and coach clients in how to locate new jobs. In the rapidly growing private sector, psychologists are hired by new companies to administer human resource departments where they engage in personnel selection and evaluation, facilitate the integration and cohesiveness of employees, and assist in the advertising and marketing of commercial products.

The role of psychologists within the educational system has not changed much during Poland's transformation. Psychologists continue to work in schools at different levels, in kindergartens, in centers for educational and vocational counseling, and in institutions for neglected, orphaned, and retarded children. These psychologists carry out fairly typical diagnostic and therapeutic activities, and are also employed as teachers.

The role of psychology as a profession and the benefits of employing psychologists are appreciated in Poland. Unfortunately, economic difficulties have led to a slowdown in employment and so there are limited opportunities for psychologists, at least for the time being. However, it is a commonly held view that the number of psychologists is not adequate to meet the needs of Polish society and that their services are sorely needed. Regrettably, the current economic situation is such that many recently trained psychologists either remain unemployed for months or are compelled to accept jobs for which they are overqualified.

17.4 FUTURE CHALLENGES AND PROSPECTS

The Polish experience with recent economic and political transformations leaves one hesitant to draw conclusions when looking to the future. For many years, it seemed impossible that the Communist regime would ever fall. When it did, a new and uncertain reality was welcomed with enthusiasm and a shared hope for happiness and prosperity. Unfortunately, it soon turned out that the transformation would be a long and sometimes painful process, with painful sequelae, such as the 18% unemployment rate. However, in many ways, the future of psychology in Poland looks very positive. A clear line of theoretical development exists in Polish psychology, derived from the work of Twardowski in the 19th century, through to the theoretical achievements of Tomaszewski, and resting now on contemporary psychologists such as Strelau, Reykowski, and others. Human action is postulated as purposeful, aimed at regulating psychological processes within the person and the relationship between the individual and the environment. An example of the directions that theoretical development is taking is provided by Reykowski's theory of political behavior.

Reykowski's research has focused on the psychological preconditions of democratic functioning. He has found systematic differences in the cognitive construction of the concept of democracy based on the level of political thinking. Differences in how people construe democracy and think politically are linked to education and political experience, and have implications for Polish attitudes toward democratic transformation and approaches to political conflicts. Reykowski's research sheds light on the massive disappointment with democratic transformation that at present can be observed in Polish society, and has been presented in scholarly journals, in the popular press, and to government leaders.

The economic and political transformation of Poland has involved dramatic changes that have been perceived as challenges by some people and as threats by others. The consequences of coping effectively or ineffectively with such changes have led to a kind of polarization of the population. Some have gained from the transformation, while others have suffered. Thus, current social needs call for two forms of psychological help, such as counseling during life-changing transitions on the one hand, and providing support during life-changing crises on the other. Relevant intervention strategies will inevitably appear, along with a comprehensive theory of change that incorporates the dynamics of macrosocial change with psychosocial adjustment.

U.S. achievements in psychology have exerted the strongest influence over Polish psychology to date, shaping its normative, cognitive–behavioral view of the human being. However, another approach rooted in existentialism and centered on each human being as a unique entity has also emerged. These two trends are complementary, rather than exclusive. Both are applicable to many psychological issues, such as coping with stress or understanding the spiritual dimension of human experience.

Given the threats and challenges of the contemporary world, it is likely that psychology will be expected to provide continuing insights into uncharted aspects of human behavior and experience. As a consequence, the relationship between American and Polish psychology will surely become more reciprocal.

Poland elected to join the European Union in 2004, which will probably intensify contacts with Western Europe, especially in terms of faculty and student exchanges. As a consequence, the influence of Western Europe on Polish psychology may increase after some years, perhaps surpassing that of the United States. An important factor that will shape the future of Polish psychology is the Internet and the World Wide Web. Access to the Internet has only recently become widely available to Polish scientists, facilitating the exchange of information, international cooperation, and mutually beneficial professional development. However, in Poland, the Internet is generally available to only 40% of 15- to 19-year-olds and 1% of those over the age of 60. Undoubtedly, these numbers will rapidly rise in a united Europe, resulting in, among other benefits, the increased dissemination and influence of psychological knowledge on the lay public.

It is even more difficult to make predictions about the profession of psychology than about psychology as a science. Two factors make prediction difficult. The first is the expected rapid increase in the number of psychologists in the near future and the second is the dynamic growth of the Warsaw School of Social Psychology.

In 2002, about, 2000 psychologists graduated from Polish universities; this is a higher number of graduates than in the past, and represents about 20% of the entire workforce of employed psychologists. The popularity of psychology among the young remains very high and so the number of psychologists is anticipated to grow significantly. However, the author objects to the opinion that departments of psychology and other university departments contribute to the country's jobless rate by training students in a field with limited employment oppurtunities. On the contrary, attending a university delays entry into the workforce. Moreover, graduates in psychology are well-equipped to compete for jobs. However, the number of traditional positions available to psychologists will be insufficient and new graduates will have to seek employment outside psychology or attempt self-employment.

At present, almost half of all recently graduated psychologists attended the Warsaw School of Psychology. This proportion will rise in the future because the school has just opened a new campus in Sopot and other campuses will soon be established. The successful development of a financially self-sufficient institution of higher education in a rather poor country is an interesting phenomenon in itself. In the foreseeable future, will the majority of psychologists in Poland have graduated from the same institution? It may well be that the Warsaw School of Psychology will determine the standards of education and training in psychology that will come to define the profession of psychology in Poland in the future.

ACKNOWLEDGMENTS

I am indebted to Zofia Ratajczak, head of the Institute of Psychology at the Silesian

University, and Malgorzata Toeplitz-Winiewska, president of the Polish Psychological Association, for reviewing the first version of this paper and for their valuable comments. I wish to thank Janusz Reykowski for sending me specially prepared written information about his recent research, Sonia Kedziora for the information about psychological interventions, and Jerzy Brzezinski, Jan Strelau, and Kazimierz Obuchowski for providing me with manuscripts that were in press. I also wish to acknowledge the contributions of Anita Galuszka of the Institute of Psychology at Silesian University and Jolanta Zycinska of the Warsaw School of Social Psychology.

REFERENCES

Brzezinski, J. (1997). *Methodology of psychological research*. Warsaw: Panstwowe Wydawnictwo Naukowe.

Brzezinski, J., & Strelau, J. (in press). Psychology in Poland during a period of transformation of the political system (1990–2002). *European Psychologist*.

Burchardt, J. (1991). *Cosmology and psychology of Witelon. Studia Copernicana, 30*. Wroclaw, Poland: Ossolineum.

Davies, N. (1981). *God's playground: A history of Poland*. New York: Columbia University Press.

Dawid, J. W. (1896). *Child mental resources: A contribution to empirical psychology*. Warsaw: Wydawnictwo Przegladu Powszechnego.

Heszen-Niejodek, I. (1988). Clinical psychology: The Polish view. *Clinical Psychology Forum, 18,* 15–21.

Heszen-Niejodek, I. (1992). *Doctor and patient: Psychological studies*. Cracow Universitas.

Hilgard, E. R. (1987). *Psychology in America. A historical survey*. New York: Harcourt Brace Jovanovich.

Kozielecki, J. (1977). *Psychological theory of decision* (2nd ed.). Warsaw: Panstwowe Wydawnictwo Naukowe.

Lewicka, M. (2001). Social psychology in Poland. *European Bulletin of Social Psychology, 13,* 4–18.

Marszal-Wisniewska, M. (2002). *Committee of Psychological Sciences of the Polish Academy of Sciences: Report*. Unpublished manuscript.

Obuchowski, K. (2004). *Codes of mind and emotions*. Lodz, Poland: Wyzsza Szkola Humanistyczno-Ekonomiczna.

Polish Psychological Association. (1988). Charter of the Polish Psychological Association. *Psychological News, 6,* 4–21.

Polish Psychological Association. (1992a). *Directory of Polish psychologists*. Warsaw: Author.

Polish Psychological Association. (1992b). *Ethical and professional code of psychologists*. Warsaw: Author.

Puzynski, S., Brzezinska, A., Czabala, Cz., Kadzielawa, D., & Tylka J. (2002). *Program of specialization in clinical psychology*. Unpublished manuscript.

Reykowski, J. (1974). *Experimental psychology of emotions*. (2nd ed.). Warsaw: Ksiazka i Wiedza.

Rosenzweig, M. R., Holtzman, W. N., Sabourin, M., & Belanger, D. (2000). *History of the International Union of Psychological Science (IUPsyS)*. Hove, UK: Psychology Press.

Stachowski, R. (2000). The history of psychology: From Wundt to the latest times. In J. Strelau (Ed.), *Psychology: An academic handbook* (Vol. 1, pp. 25–66). Gdansk, Poland: Gdanskie Wydawnictwo Psychologiczne.

Strelau, J. (1998). *Temperament: A psychological perspective*. New York: Plenum.

Strelau, J. (2000). *Psychology: An academic handbook*. Gdansk, Poland: Gdanskie Wydawnictwo Psychologiczne.

Toeplitz-Winiewska, M. (2001). Why will we not have an act to regulate the profession of psychology? *Psychological News, 4,* 99–102.

Tomaszewski, T. (1963). *Introduction to psychology*. Warsaw: Panstwowe Wydawnictwo Naukowe.

Wosinski, M. (1978). *Cooperation between teacher and students*. Katowice, Poland: Uniwersytet Slaski.

IMPORTANT PUBLICATIONS

Brzezinski, J. (1997). *Methodology of psychological research*. Warsaw: Panstwowe Wydawnictwo Naukowe.

Kozielecki, J. (1987). *Transgressive conception of man: Psychological analysis*. Warsaw: Panstwowe Wydawnictwo Naukowe.

Obuchowski, K. (1982). *Codes of orientation and structure of emotional processes*. Warsaw: Panstwowe Wydawnictwo Naukowe. (Original work published 1970)

Reykowski, J. (1974). *Experimental psychology of emotions*. Warsaw: Ksiazka i Wiedza. (Original work published 1968)

Strealu, J. (1998). *Temperament: A psychological perspective*. New York: Plenum.

Strelau, J. (Ed.). (2000). *Psychology: An academic handbook* (Vols. 1–3). Gdansk, Poland: Gdanskie Wydawnictwo Psychologiczne.

Tomaszewski, T. (1979). *Introduction to psychology*. Warsaw: Panstwowe Wydawnictwo Naukowe. (Original work published 1963)

Tomaszewski, T. (Ed.). (1982). *Psychology*. Warsaw: Panstwowe Wydawnictwo Naukowe. (Original work published 1975)

Twardowski, K. (1913). *About psychology, its subject matter, tasks, method, relation to other disciplines, and development*. Warsaw and Cracow: Ksiegarnia Gubrynowicza i Syna.

Witwicki, W. (1962/1963). *Psychology for students of higher education* (Vols. 1–2). Warsaw: Panstwowe Wydawnictwo Naukowe. (Original work published in 1925/1927)

CHAPTER 18

Psychology in Russia

Tatiana Balachova, Galina Isurina, Sheldon Levy, Larissa Tsvetkova, and Ludvig I. Wasserman

Tatiana Balachova graduated from Leningrad State University, now St. Petersburg State University (SPSU), and received her Ph.D. in clinical psychology from Bekhterev Psychoneurological Research Institute/SPSU. She completed a postdoctoral fellowship in pediatric psychology and child abuse and neglect at the University of Oklahoma Health Science Center, and is currently on its faculty.

Galina Isurina graduated from SPSU. She received her Ph.D. in clinical psychology from the Bekhterev Institute/SPSU. Isurina is an associate professor of clinical psychology at the College (Faculty) of Psychology, SPSU.

Sheldon Levy received his B.A and M.A. from U.C.L.A., an M.P.H. from Yale, and a Ph.D. in clinical psychology from the University of California, Davis. He is clinical associate professor of family medicine and adjunct associate professor of community health at Brown University Medical School. Between 1995 and 1997 he served as a member of an advisory committee that provided consultation on primary care to the U.S. Department of Health and Human Services for the summit meetings between Vice-President Gore and then Prime Minister of Russia, Victor Chernomyrdin.

Larissa Tsvetkova received her Ph.D. in social psychology from SPSU. Currently she is the dean of the College (Faculty) of Psychology at SPSU. She is also chair of the Academic Council on Psychology at SPSU and of the Scientific and Methodological Council on Psychology and Pedagogy at the Russian Ministry of Education, Moscow.

Ludvig I. Wasserman received his M.D. from the First Leningrad School Medicine (now St. Petersburg State Medical University) and his Dr. Sc. Med. and Ph.D. in clinical psychology from the Bekhterev Institute. He is professor of clinical psychology and director of the Laboratory of Clinical Psychology at the Bekhterev Institute. He is also a professor of clinical psychology at SPSU.

18.1 OVERVIEW

Two important traditions of clinical and experimental research, associated with I. P. Pavlov, N. N. Lange, V. M. Bekhterev, and others, played a decisive role in the development of psychology in Russia. Most of the early psychological laboratories were established by psychiatrists to serve the needs of psychiatric patients and to facilitate clinical research. For example, the first psychology laboratory was inaugurated by Bekhterev at the Kazan University psychiatric clinic in 1886. In 1894, he opened a laboratory at the Military-Medical Academy in St. Petersburg. This was the second psychology laboratory in Russia. Professor V. F. Chiz founded a similar laboratory at Urievsky University and Professor A. A. Tokarskiy established another at a psychiatric clinic in Moscow (Botsmanova, Guseva, & Ravich-Scherbo, 1994).

By the beginning of the 20th century, there were eight psychological laboratories in Russia. There, the tradition persisted of considering psychology as a natural science, and psychiatrists were recognized as the professionals most skilled in study of psychological phenomena. Bekhterev founded the St. Petersburg Research Psychoneurological Institute in 1907 (renamed Psychoneurological Institute in his honor). The Bekhterev Institute has become the leading center for clinical psychology in Russia. Bekhterev formed an interdisciplinary group of specialists in psychiatry, biology, pedagogy, and other disciplines to provide psychoneurological research and education. The institute had clinics and provided medical education for doctors with a broad social–psychological orientation. The institute also established the first Russian laboratory for the study of personality.

The other research tradition emphasized the role of psychology as a fundamentally experimental science. Lange, who believed that psychology laboratories should be established in departments of psychology, founded such a laboratory at Odessa University (Botsmanova et al., 1994). The creation of the Russian Society of Experimental Psychology in 1891 was the next important event in history of Russian psychology. The first Institute of Psychology (currently the Psychological Institute of the Russian Academy of Education) was founded by G. I. Chelpanov in Moscow in 1914 (Botsmanova et al.).

After the Russian Revolution and the Civil War, and beginning in the 1920s, the sociopolitical perspective of communist ideology and government regulation interrupted the development of psychology as a science. The empirical approach and freedom of scientific debate were replaced by a political–ideological approach that made compliance with Marxism–Leninism ideology a key component in the evaluation of any psychological research. If a person, a university department, or an entire field of psychology were considered not to be fully compliant with mainstream communist ideology, the department might be closed, the theory prohibited, and, perhaps, the scholar fired or even imprisoned. During this time, psychoanalysis was prohibited. (This prohibition continued until the period of *perestroika* during the late 1980s; for more information see Etkind, 1997a.) Psychological testing was called a "pedological perversion" (i.e., it was deemed to be perverse and unacceptable) and was prohibited in accordance with a decree of the Central Committee of the Communist Party. In addition, during the 1920s and 1930s, university departments and research laboratories of psychology were closed by Stalin's government. The only officially accepted "scientific" psychology was Pavlov's theory (Windholz, 1999). Marxist–Leninist philosophy and psychology were developed as substitutes. Because of this, as well as the political and social isolation of the Soviet Union during the "cold war," the evolution of Russian psychology was delayed, so it has been called an "interrupted science" (Etkind, 1997b; Grigorenko, Ruzgis, & Sternberg, 1997). After Nikita Khrushev came to power and denounced many of the abuses of Stalin during the 20th Party Congress in 1956, there were democratic changes in society in the areas of art, education, and science. This led to the establishment of psychology departments in the mid-1960s.

The first departments or "faculties" of psychology were opened at Moscow State University and Leningrad (now St. Petersburg) State University in 1966. Before this time, philosophy departments at these universities had offered a degree in psychology. The Moscow school of psychology maintained the philosophical traditions in its method of analyzing psychological phenomena. In contrast, the Leningrad school of psychology developed a natural sciences view of humans and their individuality. There have been a growing number of students since 1996 who have been accepted into psychology programs at these universities, and currently 115 full-time psychology students each year enter as majors in the psychology departments at Moscow State University and St. Petersburg State University.

During the Soviet period, the interests of psychologists were represented by the Psychological Society of the Soviet Union, which was established during the 1960s. In 1992, after the demise of the Soviet Union, the Russian Psychological Society became the successor organization. The Society is the major professional association of Russian psychologists and has chapters in all regions of Russia. The most recent convention of the Russian Psychological Society was held in St. Petersburg in June 2003 and focused on "Psychology and Culture."

In the late 1980s, during the period of *perestroika*, new regional professional psychological associations were established. This was possible because of new opportunities for decentralization and the freedom to develop nongovernmental organizations and societies without Communist Party control. Among the associations that developed during this period was the Society of Practical Psychologists in Moscow and the Association of Training and Psychotherapy in St. Petersburg. The practical orientation of these new associations reflected the growing interest of psychologists in applied psychology, such as organizational consulting and psychotherapy, as well as the development of new forms of service delivery, including private practice. The associations have worked in collaboration with governmental organizations, and they played an important role in promotion of private psychological services and nongovernmental organizations.

There are no data on the number of psychologists in Russia. It is estimated that the Russian Psychological Society has 5,000 to 6,000 members.

The salary of psychologists is dependent on what settings they are in (e.g., business, education, medical) and in what sector (i.e., public or private) they work. The average income of a psychologist in business is much higher than that in other settings such as universities. Salaries of psychologists who work in public institutions depend on how many years the psychologist has worked in the field, his or her degree, and factors associated with the institution. Given the current economic situation in Russia, psychologists have some advantages relative to professionals in other fields. Because of the demand for psychological services, the need for psychologists is greater than the number of psychologists who are available. As a result, there are many job vacancies, and most qualified psychologists are able to find suitable employment and advance professionally.

18.2 EDUCATION AND TRAINING

Psychology "faculties" or colleges, offer degrees in psychology at several universities. In addition, there are departments of psychology in other colleges, such as biology, history, or philosophy, and at pedagogical institutes of higher education. To be admitted to a university program, prospective students must take admission exams. A department or college decides on a list of subjects covered by the admission exams. This list must be approved by a central admissions committee of the university. The leading psychology colleges in Russia (e.g., Moscow State University and St. Petersburg State University) have admission exams on the same subjects: biology, math, Russian language, and literature and composition. Based on a 2003 government regulation, all admission tests to public institutions of higher education in Russia must be in written form. Students who have passed the tests then compete for

"budgeted vacancies" in which they are exempt from paying fees. Such students receive a monthly stipend from their university based on academic achievement and financial need. Currently, this stipend is 200 rubles, which is equivalent to about $7 USD per month.

The Ministry of Education determines the number of budgeted vacancies for each academic major in the country. The following are budgeted vacancies in psychology allocated at the major Russian universities: Moscow State University and St. Petersburg State University have 65 vacancies in "specialist" psychology programs (5 years of study), and 25 vacancies in clinical–psychology programs (5 years of study). Additionally, a new training curriculum has been developed recently which separates the traditional course (5 years) into two separate programs: bachelor and MAGISTR (a degree like a master's that is awarded after 2 years of graduate school and completion of other academic requirements). Currently there are 25 vacancies in bachelor's programs in psychology (4 years of study), and 25 vacancies in *magistr* (1–2 years for students who have completed bachelor or specialist programs) budgeted by the Ministry of Education at the each of the major universities.

There is strong competition for admission to a psychology major at Russian universities. For example, there are about 600 candidates for the 115 budgeted vacancies at the Moscow State University and St. Petersburg State University each year. Candidates who passed exams successfully, but have not been awarded positions may participate in a "contest" (a competition that includes written exams and interviews) for paid vacancies, and, if admitted, will have to pay for their own education.

A total of 200 full-time students, both budgeted and paying, enter the Faculty of Psychology at Moscow State University and at St. Petersburg State University every year. Additionally, there are 75 budgeted part-time students entering the evening program (these students have classes every night), and 50 budgeted students participate in correspondence courses ("*zaochnaya*" education) at the faculties of psychology. In addition, there are some vacancies for paid education. Requirements for the number of subjects and hours students must take are standardized across universities. Study plans for majors at state universities are approved by Ministry of Education. All students have to meet course and hour requirements, and usually take the same classes. Students may be required to take more or fewer hours of coursework and longer or shorter programs depending on whether the form of education is full-time, part-time, or correspondence. Full-time (day) students take 36 h of coursework each week (6 days of class weekly), whereas part-time (evening) students have 20 h of coursework (5–6 days of class). Students who study by correspondence must participate in two full-time study sessions per year at their universities, each lasting 24 working days. In addition, part-time (evening) students and, in particular, correspondence students must devote a significant number of hours to independent study.

After students receive the specialist's or bachelor's diploma, they may continue their education in a *magistr*'s degree program. These programs usually take 1 year for specialists and 2 years for bachelors. Students have to take exams and compete to be admitted to a *magistr*'s program. Colleges determine the procedures for these competitions. Typically,

students are required to take exams in general psychology and in their specialization (e.g., industrial or social psychology). Faculties of psychology, as well as some medical universities, have a separate major in clinical psychology.

In describing the system of education in psychology in Russia, it is necessary to point out a problem that has arisen during the past decade that may be affecting the quality of training of psychologists. The need for psychologists has grown beyond the supply of trained individuals. Because of this need, as well as the necessity of finding employment for people in other fields, such as engineering, who have been displaced because of the economic transition in Russia, some universities have begun to train people with minimal qualifications in psychology. These students usually take psychology classes on various subjects for 7 to 9 months. Afterwards, these students receive a diploma attesting to their completion of an applied psychology major, such as "practical psychologist" or "consultant–psychologist." However, employers recognize that the quality of this "retraining" is not comparable to traditional preparation in psychology at most universities. Currently, employers usually inquire about the kind of diploma that was awarded, from what university, and how much educational participation was required.

Many private institutes for higher education have opened recently and offer education and training in psychology. There are about 50 such institutes in Moscow and about 30 in St. Petersburg. Many of these private institutes seek to become accredited by the state. To be accredited, an institute must meet certain criteria. Their curriculum, personnel, and methodological base must meet national standards for education in psychology, developed by the Educational-Methodical Union of Psychology in Moscow. The Union has a Presidium that is formed by leading psychologists throughout the country, mostly from Moscow and St. Petersburg. The Presidium reviews the curricula of psychology programs and other issues pertaining to professional standards in psychology education. National standards for education in psychology are approved by the Ministry of Education.

The curriculum in psychology consists of four main parts:

1. *General social–economic and philosophical education*, which includes economics, foreign languages, history, philosophy, physical education, and sociology. Students at higher educational institutes study these subjects regardless of their major.
2. *Coursework in the natural sciences* are required for all students with natural science majors. Psychologists study informatics, mathematics, and current concepts in natural sciences.
3. *General psychology subjects* are required for all psychology programs at state institutes of higher education. These include general psychology, experimental psychology, psychological assessment, practicum in psychology, psychophysiology, anatomy of the central neural system, the physiology of higher neural activity, genetics, anthropology, social psychology, engineering or industrial psychology, developmental psychology, clinical psychology, sport psychology, political psychology, pedagogical psychology, rehabilitation psychology, economic psychology, forensic psychology, comparative psychology, history of psychology, and statistical methods.
4. *Areas of specialization* are of importance for students in "specialist" programs. A list of cognate areas required for a specialist degree has been developed by the chairs of departments that offer specialization within the psychology major. There are about 15 specializations. The curriculum for a specialization is based on the tradition as well as the research interests and professional experiences of instructors.

In addition to listed subjects, the curriculum includes practica in which students rotate into different institutions or organizations in order to obtain supervised practice in psychology; "production" practice, in which students perform some psychological work such as psychological assessments and interviews under supervision; pedagogical practice, in which students teach psychology at schools and universities; and research practice. In addition, students write a several literature reviews on different subjects. During their first 3–4 years, students take general education and general psychology courses. In their last 2 years, they take courses in an area of specialization of their choice. After completing all required courses, students must defend their diploma project and pass the state exams to receive a "specialist" diploma with the qualification of "psychologist."

Students who earn a bachelor's degree in psychology receive a general education in psychology. The curriculum for the bachelor's degree does not include training in a specialization. However, students who have earned a bachelor's degree may specialize in a *magistr*'s program. After receiving the bachelor's degree, students complete their coursework and defend their diploma project; they then receive a bachelor's diploma in psychology.

The curriculum for the *magistr*'s degree includes general–philosophic courses including problems in theoretical psychology, teaching psychology at institutions of higher education, computer technology in science and education, methods of mathematical modeling in psychology, and problems of general psychology. In addition, students take courses in their specialization. As in the specialist curriculum, the list of specialty courses depends on the traditions and research interests of the chair and instructors who staff the *magistr*'s program. After completing their coursework, students must defend their *magistr*'s thesis. Students who complete this program receive a diploma of *magistr* of psychology.

Upon graduating from a university with a *magistr*'s degree or "specialist in psychology" (requiring 5–6 years of full time university study), a graduate may practice as a psychologist. There are additional requirements and a licensure exam for practice as a clinical psychologist. In addition, graduates may continue on to doctoral studies. To be admitted to a doctoral program, students take entrance exams in psychology, philosophy, and a foreign language, as well as participate in a competition for a vacancy. The Ministry of Education determines the number of vacancies at the doctoral level. Typically, there are more applicants than vacancies. Similar to other budgeted students, Ph.D. students receive a monthly stipend. Graduate study includes coursework and passing examinations in foreign language, philosophy, and psychology. The psychology exams have two parts. The first part covers the student's

specialization (e.g., social psychology) while the second part is based on content area of the student's thesis. After passing their Ph.D. exams, students have to complete and defend a research thesis. After all requirements are completed, the student will receive a doctorate in psychological science. This process takes 3 years full-time study or 4 years part-time study (e.g., correspondence). A doctorate is required before one can attain the rank of assistant or associate professor in Russia.

Beyond the Ph.D., there is yet a higher scientific degree in Russia called "Doctor of Sciences." In order to earn this title, a person must complete additional research that makes a significant contribution to science, and usually write and defend another thesis. This degree is required for some academic positions, and is required for promotion to the rank of full professor.

A variety of methods have been used in teaching psychology: lectures, seminars, practica, and active forms of teaching such as training sessions for small groups of 6–16 students. Students learn didactic material as well as practical skills, such as psychological assessment, that include familiarization with original Russian tests and adapted tests first developed in other countries (Anastasi, 1982; Balachova, Levy, Isurina, & Wasserman, 2001).

Universities and most faculties have their own libraries. For example, there are about 100,000 items including research monographs and books for students in Russian, English, German, and French in the library of the Faculty of Psychology at St. Petersburg State University. Psychology textbooks are not required because each faculty of psychology has its own traditions and specific emphases. In preparing this chapter, a survey was conducted of publishing companies to determine which psychology books were most in demand. Based on the survey data, textbooks on general psychology, experimental procedures in psychology, and consulting with organizations are most popular. Books on these topics are in great demand since relatively few are available to students.

Less than 0.5% of Russian psychologists have been able to study in other countries. However, most universities have collaborative agreements for research and training with foreign universities that may include opportunities for student and faculty exchanges.

Continuing education is required for psychologists who teach at universities or at institutes of higher education or work in clinical settings. The contract between the administration of a university and a professor states that he or she must deliver certain courses, prepare materials for students, and continue his or her education. Sponsoring scientific conferences is also a tradition at Russian universities. Information about conferences is disseminated to virtually all psychologists, who may submit abstracts to the organizational committee. For example, St. Petersburg State University has a long history of hosting an annual conference, *Ananievskie Chtenia*, named for Ananyiev, founder of the Leningrad school of psychology.

18.3 SCOPE OF PSYCHOLOGICAL PRACTICE

Over the last several years, increased attention has been paid to psychological practice in Russia. The new psychological institutes and organizations established in Russia during the last 10 years illustrate the current orientation, major concepts, research methodologies, and strategies for intervention that characterize contemporary Russian psychology. For example, such institutes as the Institute of Psychotherapy and Consulting, Institute of Psychoanalysis, Institute of Gestalt Therapy, and Institute of Training have been opened since 1990. The names of the institutes reflect the interests of participating psychologists, as well as the requests for psychological services that have been received.

New departments have also been established at numerous universities. The following departments have been inaugurated in the College of Psychology at St. Petersburg State University: Psychology of Behavior and Prevention of Behavioral Abnormalities; Social Adaptation, Psychological Correction of Personality, and Social Work; Psychological Aspects of Professional Activities and Management; and Political Psychology. These departments characterize the new trends in Russian psychology and reflect the interests of Russian psychologists, the needs of Russian society, and significant events that have affected the nation and the world; all are based on an implicit understanding that the mission of psychology is to help people and support their development, and to further progressive, humanistic ideas.

There are no specific laws regulating the practice of psychology in Russia. However, two criminal acts regulate forensic evaluations and psychological practice under the auspices of the Ministry of Internal Affairs. A license is required for psychologists to provide clinical services, such as psychological assessments and consultations, by order of the Ministry of Health.

University graduates with a degree in psychology (with a "specialist" or *magistr* diploma) may work in a variety of settings, and the number of psychologists working in various settings has been growing rapidly since 1960s. In addition to psychologists who work at academic and higher educational institutions, psychologists work at clinics, schools, and other organizations such as military, crisis centers for women, asylums, and displaced persons, consultation centers for children and families, hotlines, and businesses. For example, for a population of approximately 140 million, there are approximately 5,000 psychologists with a specialization in medical (clinical) psychology working in hospitals and outpatient clinics. Also about 8,500 psychologists work for the institutions of the Ministry of Internal Affairs in such settings as the court system, prisons, and medical centers. Psychology in education has been most rapidly growing field of psychological practice since 1980s. Currently, there are approximately 64,000 psychologists working in educational settings, including day-care centers, preschools, schools, institutes of higher education, centers for professional orientation, and 850 medico–psychological–pedagogical centers for assessment and consultations for children and families that have been established around the country by the Ministry of Education.

In education, psychologists may work in public and private schools and in schools for advanced studies (for gifted students). In addition, they work at boarding institutions for orphans and children with disabilities. There are no budgeted positions for psychologists in public schools and institutions; however, a director may designate funds from a school's budget to hire a psychologist. School psychologists have varying responsibilities. Most often, these entail the psychological assessment of children and consultation with parents. Psychologists may also work with students who have difficulties in peer relationships or they may teach a course in psychology, perhaps as an after-school activity. Unfortunately, school psychologists earn a very low salary (currently, a university graduate earns approximately 500 rubles or about $17 USD per month). At the 2003 Congress of Practical Psychologists in Education held in Moscow, an analysis of the last 13 years of Russian school psychology was presented. Because of this analysis, new directions were targeted. A resolution at this meeting stated that the training of psychologists to work in education should include not only knowledge of school issues, but also information about the quality of life, health, and social well-being of children.

The main functions of psychologists working in business and industry are recruiting and working with personnel (i.e., selection, testing, training), public relations, job analysis, and optimization of work processes, psychological aspects of organizational development, and re-engineering and organizational consulting. Approximately 80% of these activities are performed by external consultants; the remaining 20% are carried out by psychologists employed by the organizations.

Medical/clinical psychologists in Russia work primarily in mental health settings such as psychiatric hospitals, day-treatment programs, and outpatient clinics. There is a trend to expand psychological services to other settings such as multispecialty primary health-care polyclinics, clinics for internal medicine, and rehabilitation centers. A few psychologists work in cardiology, oncology, or pediatrics settings. In addition, psychologists may work in specialized health facilities such as health centers of the union of artists, police (*militsia*) recruitment and treatment clinics, rehabilitation centers, centers for evaluation of disabilities, and others. Psychologists work at consultation and rehabilitation centers such as crisis centers (e.g., telephone hotlines), offices that deliver psychological support to HIV AIDS patients, rehabilitation centers for people who return from war zones, etc.

Although the development of psychoanalysis in Russia was interrupted, reconstructive psychodynamic individual and group therapy were developed during the Soviet period (Karvasarsky, 1985). Therapy in humanistic and behavioral traditions has been also practiced in Russia.

In response to emerging substance abuse problems and the need for services for this population, intensive efforts have been taken to develop psychotherapies for substance abuse. Many psychology positions were opened in alcoholism treatment clinics in 1970s–1980s to improve quality of services. Alcoholism is considered a disease and treatment is provided by both physicians and clinical psychologists. Psychotherapy, with a mostly cognitive-behavioral orientation and an emphasis on motivational interventions, group therapy, and family therapy has been developed (Balachova, Erishev & Ribakova, 1996; Bratus, 1997).

In 1975, the first Russian manual on family therapy was published (Myager, 1978; Mishina, 1999). It includes family-oriented individual and group therapy, as well as family sessions. The next step in development of family therapy in Russia

has moved the focus from individual and dyad relationships to family systems, including children and other family generations (Eidemiller, 1996). Despite a popular expression used during the Soviet period, "Children are our future," mental health services for children have been underdeveloped in Russia. The lack of psychological services for children and families in clinical settings recently has been partially offset by services provided by psychologists at educational settings, such as schools and pedagogical–psychological centers.

When opportunities for communication and exchange with Western colleagues were restored after *perestroika*, many Western psychologists visited Russia, starting with Carl Rogers and Virginia Satir. There have been increased opportunities to learn more about developments in Western psychotherapies. Russian psychologists have been aware of, and some have practiced, therapies that have been prominent in the West, such psychodynamic therapy, person-centered therapy, cognitive–behavioral therapy, and various approaches to family therapy. In the last decade, psychotherapies that are more avant-garde have been imported from the West such as neurolinguistic programming. Some Western therapies, however, have been marketed in Russia and adopted by some psychologists and alternative practitioners without any attempt to assess their scientific validity. Currently, virtually all of the different approaches to psychotherapy are practiced in Russia.

About 70% of clinical psychologists work in psychiatric clinics, where they generally conduct psychological evaluations and neuropsychological testing (Tonkonogy, 1973; Kabanov, Lichko, & Smirnov, 1983; Dorofeeva, Meerson, &

Wasserman 1997; Balachova & Handler, 1998; Churvinskaya & Schelkova, 2002). Russian psychologists use many tests developed by American psychologists, such as the Wechsler Intelligence Scales for Adults and Children, Minnesota Multiphasic Personality Inventory (MMPI), the Rorschach test, and the Thematic Apperception Test (TAT). Unlike American psychology, psychological evaluation in Russia includes the use of both tests and "pathopsychological investigations." Pathopsychological investigations include experimental tasks, interviews, observations, analyses of the history of the illness, and comparison of experimental data with data on the patient's life (Zeigarnik, Nikolaeva, & Lebedinsky, 1987). In contrast to the test approach, the pathopsychological approach uses a more flexible, qualitative, hypothesis-testing strategy. A few core principles of pathopsychology form the foundation of clinical psychological assessment in Russia. These principles are:

1. Psychological assessment is a systemic, qualitative analysis of the whole person.
2. Results must provide qualitative and quantitative characteristics of both disturbed and intact parts of the psyche.
3. Experimental tasks must involve the patient's mental processes and personality aspects (Zeigarnik, 1976).

With this approach, experimental tasks provide qualitative information regarding a patient's cognitive and personality functioning. Psychologists choose the tasks and tests, and the program of the investigation may be changed in the process of assessment in accordance with the unfolding results and new hypotheses which the psychologist wants to evaluate.

The traditions of pathopsychological evaluations are strengths of Russian clinical psychology that have helped to overcome the weakness associated with having few reliable tests. Most psychological tests have not been fully standardized in Russia, and it was impossible to purchase psychological tests in Russia for a long time. Copyright laws have only been observed in Russia for the last few decades, and it was once routine for psychologists to develop their own test materials. However, private psychological testing companies have risen since the end of 1980s, usually marketing old versions of foreign tests. For example, the Wechsler Intelligence Scale for Children of 1949 is still being used in Russia. A Russian version of the scale was prepared in 1973 by A. Panasuk. The sample used was not representative for children of the Soviet Union at that time, and these scales are certainly not appropriate for Russian children of the beginning of the 21st century. Data on fluctuation IQ scores over time are not available, and the Flynn effect (the tendency of IQ scores to increase across generations; see Kanaya, Scullin, & Ceci, 2003) has not been recognized in Russia. However, psychologists are aware of a discrepancy in diagnostic labels and IQ ranges, and use about a 10-point correction on WISC interpretations (Balachova & Handler, 1998).

In Russia, the diagnosis of mental retardation and school placement decisions are made by medico–pedagogical commissions that include physicians, psychiatrists, special education experts, and psychologists. The commissions may use psychological assessments and tests data, but do not rely on IQ scores in the same way these data are used in the United States and other countries. The subjectivity of such diagnostics has raised some concerns; however, adequate tests are simply not available in Russia at the present time. Standardized tests need to be developed in order to improve mental health diagnostics and special education policies.

The psychotherapy psychologists provide in clinics and other settings is called "psychological correction" (Isurina, 1990). Despite their significant contributions to the development of psychotherapy since the 1960s and their solid training in and experience applying psychotherapy, Russian psychologists may not offer psychotherapy because it is considered a medical treatment. Under Russian law, only physicians who received training in psychotherapy, such as psychiatrists and "narcologists" (medical doctors who provide substance abuse treatment), may provide psychotherapy. Psychologists may provide psychotherapy in medical settings only under the supervision of physicians, and any therapeutic practice by a psychologist who is not working under supervision would be called consultation or correction rather than psychotherapy.

Although psychologists cannot admit patients to a hospital or write case notes, they can write psychological reports based on their assessments and evaluations. In psychiatric clinics, psychologists are considered staff members who work under the supervision of the medical director. Psychologists may not assume leadership positions in psychiatric departments. Even the chairpersons of clinical psychology departments at medical faculties and institutions are often physicians who have received some training and conducted some research in clinical psychology. The salary of psychologists in medical institutions depends on how many years the psychologist has

worked in the field, and his or her degree, and the average income of psychologists is similar to those of other health professionals. Psychologists, including clinical psychologists, are prohibited by law from prescribing medications. Only physicians may prescribe medication in Russia, and Russian psychologists have no real interest in expanding their scope of practice in this area.

There have been discussions between psychologists and physicians about pursuing the legal right for psychologists to provide therapy, most recently at the 2003 Convention of the Russian Psychological Society in St. Petersburg. Several organizations, such as the Russian Association of Psychotherapy, the Federal Center on Psychotherapy at the Bekhterev Institute, and the Russian Psychological Society have developed a draft of a new law on psychotherapy that will allow psychologists to provide psychotherapy. The draft was discussed at the convention and submitted to a legislature for debate. Another important document, an ethical code for Russian psychologists, was discussed at the convention. A draft has been developed and is currently under consideration.

Since the end of the Soviet period, many psychologists have opened private practices. Private practices offer psychological assessment and educational/vocational course for children, high school graduates, and young adults. Psychologists work at private institutes for enhancement of children's learning skills, academic knowledge, and creativity; at business consulting and management institutes; couple and sexual problems therapy centers; and private educational institutes that provide training in psychology, psychotherapy, and other specialities. Many practices offer treatment for substance abuse and "psychological correction" for children and families because of the lack of public services for children and the stigmatization and low quality of treatment associated with public substance abuse clinics. Although there are few private institutions, the numbers of institutions oriented toward business and organizational psychology and training (including advanced training seminars for psychologists) are growing.

The growth of private clinical practice to date has been limited because there has not been a tradition of private practice in Russia and much of the public is either unaware of these services or does not believe in them. It is estimated that 10%-15% of clinical psychological services are provided through private practitioners (Balachova et al., 2001). Limitations also result from the fact that most people cannot afford these services. During the Soviet period, there were no private services, and public medical and psychological services public were provided free of charge. The medical insurance concept has been introduced recently in Russia. Public medical insurance only covers psychological services provided by assigned (depending on place of residence) public services such as clinics or educational centers. Psychological services may not be available at all public clinics and centers. In addition, the quality of services is not always sufficient because of high caseload and limited training of providers. People who have private medical insurance may choose an alternative or private treatment provider; however, only few businesses provide private medical insurances, and most people cannot afford purchasing private insurance. Because of the economic situation in Russia, very few people can afford to pay out of pocket for private psychological services. In addition, reports have appeared in the Russian press of charlatans who practice without appropriate qualifications and licenses, and this may dissuade people from obtaining private services.

Only during the last 30 years have there been graduates in psychology from Russian universities. Because of the consequent lack of psychologists, ministers have tended to provide many traditional psychological services. A recent survey revealed that young people do not have clear idea about the work of psychologists (Osipov, 2000). Another study indicated that university students with personal problems prefer to ask friends for advice and do not want to seek professional help (Mama, 1997).

There has been a tradition of alternative medicine that offers the psychotherapeutic services of healers or "shamans." This tradition has been particularly strong mostly in rural areas such as Siberia and in the far east of Russia. However, there has been growing interest in alternative medicine in Russia and a growing number of such services providers in urban areas since 1980s. Some of the new folk beliefs and treatments involve "healing water" and the treatment of "the evil eye." These treatments may use some elements of traditional folk medicine, but they also provide more contemporary ways of presenting "cures." This may include filling concert halls was patients or using television to reach mass audiences. Professionals have warned the public about possible negative effects of these treatments, such as those that can be caused by a delay in search for medical attention, but they are still popular among the public.

18.4 FUTURE CHALLENGES AND PROSPECTS

Psychology in Russia has changed dramatically over the last 10 years, and there has been a renaissance of traditions in Russian science based on the work of Pavlov, Bekhterev, Vigotsky, and other Russian scientists. Psychological practice has grown tremendously in such areas as psychotherapy and organizational consulting, and it will continue to develop. There has been an increased demand for basic and applied research to serve the needs of psychological practice. For example, there have been recent calls for more epidemiological research, psychotherapy outcome studies, and investigations of preventative interventions.

Many psychological approaches exist in Russia now. There is no longer a government monopoly on training in psychology, funding for research, or the delivery of services. This has resulted in a tremendous change from the ideological control that the government exerted on scientific and applied psychology during the Soviet era. It is now important to protect psychology as a canonical discipline and to ensure the integrity of education, research, and services provided by the country's psychologists. This goal places considerable responsibility on Russian academic psychology and the professional community. Since the period of *perestroika* and the dissolution of the Soviet Union, many new psychological procedures have been developed or refined, and, hence, there is some urgency to license psychologists who will provide professional services. In addition, there is a need to evaluate and accredit of those institutes that provide training in psychology.

An ethics code for Russian psychologists has not yet been developed. Likewise, policies and procedures for the protection of human subjects in research and clinical practice have not been promulgated. The time is ripe to develop an ethics code and procedures for its implementation, as well as establish an institutionally based process that would review psychological research proposals and adjudicate complaints at the "local" level. Only a few Russian universities have institutional review boards, and these typically limit their scope to the review of international research projects. Currently, there are no human subject protection laws or regulations that require review of research conducted by Russian scientists. It is expected that policies and procedures for the regulation of professional practice and the conduct of research will appear soon.

New opportunities for interdisciplinary collaboration in such areas as neuroscience, politics, and natural sciences, and child development have recently emerged. Psychologists are actively working with other professionals in preventing juvenile delinquency, consulting with politicians, and countering terrorism. We believe that an interdisciplinary team approach, coupled with timely responses to emerging psychosocial and sociocultural issues will characterize Russian psychology in future.

The Internet has opened new paths for professional correspondence, conferences, publications, and training. However, a very small proportion of the Russian population has access to computers and the Internet. Psychologists in business usually have access to the Internet, along with a few who work for government institutions. However, we anticipate that such services will be more available to psychologists and that the

Internet will become an increasingly important professional resource.

After decades of isolation and distrust, Russian psychologists welcome opportunities to communicate with colleagues from abroad and to join the worldwide psychological community. Many psychologists from other countries visit Russia to share their knowledge and experience. Russian psychologists also have opportunities to meet their foreign colleagues personally and to establish collaborative relationships. Courses in such contemporary topics as child abuse and neglect, family therapy, and substance abuse prevention have been developed and directed jointly by Russian and foreign psychologists. Russian psychologists have appreciated the role that psychologists from other countries have played in democratizing and humanizing Russian society during *perestroika*, as well as their assistance in improving the quality of psychology education and services throughout the country. The influence of the international psychological community can be seen in ongoing efforts to form a licensing law, to create ties with the Orthodox Church, to prevent delinquency and substance abuse, to stimulate entrepreneurial talent, to promote tolerance for cultural and religious differences, to build service-delivery systems for children and families, and to modernize education and training.

Although the current economic situation in Russia limits international collaboration, there are no political or social barriers limiting collaborative efforts. American psychologists and colleagues from other countries work together with Russian psychologists on various educational, research, and clinical projects, and Russian psychologists continue to express strong interest in international projects,

collaboration with colleagues from other countries, and opportunities to study abroad.

The main obstacle to the development of psychology is the lack of resources for research and services, and the extremely low salaries of psychologists compared to those in the business sector. Because of the high demand for psychologists, the field will continue to grow. However, because current salaries for psychologists are so poor, many psychologists have positioned themselves in higher paying but nonpsychological jobs, and will continue to do so until the Russian economy improves.

REFERENCES

Anastasi, A. (1982). *Ïcuxoëosu×ecêoe mecmupoßaнue* [Psychological testing]. Moscow: Progress.

Balashova, T. N., Eryshev, O. F., & Rybakova, T. G. (1996). *ÏcÈxoTepaÏÈÿ B cÈcTeMe ÏpoôÈëaêTÈêÈ peÖÈÄÈBOB aëêoÃOëÈç Ma* [Psychotherapy in the complex of relapse-preventive treatment of alcoholism]. In O. F. Eryshev & T. G. Rybakova (Eds.), *ÄuHaMuêa peMuccuÙ u npoôuëaêmuêa pe¯ouoßoß ß ëe×eHuu aëêosoëuçMa* (pp. 140–156). St. Petersburg: Bekhterev Institute Press.

Balachova T. N., & Handler, L. (1998, February). *Teaching and learning personality assessment in Russia.* Paper presented at the meeting of the Society for Personality Assessment, Midwinter Meeting, Boston, MA.

Balachova, T. N., Levy, S., Isurina, G. L., & Wasserman L. I. (2001). Medical psychology in Russia. *Journal of Clinical Psychology in Medical Settings, 8,* 61–68.

Botsmanova, M. E., Guseva, E. P., & Ravich-Scherbo I. V. (1994). *Ïcuxoëosu×ecêuй ÈHmcumym Ha Moxoßoй: ucmopu×ecêuй oðçop* [Psychological Institute on Mohovoi: Historical overview]. Moscow: Psychological Institute of the Russian Academy of Education.

Bratus, B. S. (1997). Alcoholism in Russia. In D. Halpern & A. Voiskounsky (Eds.), *States of mind: American and post-Soviet perspectives on contemporary issues in psychology* (pp.198–214). New York: Oxford University Press.

Churvinskaya, K. R., & Schelkova, O.Y. (2002). *Медиципсêаÿ психодиаsНостиêа и иНжеНериÿ çНаНиü* [Medical psychodiagnostics and engineering of knowledge]. St. Petersburg and Moscow: Academia.

Eidemiller, E. G., (1996). *Memoдbl сеМеùНо ù диаsНостиêu u психотерапии* [Methods of family assessment and therapy]. St. Petersburg: Piter.

Etkind, A. (1997a). *Eros of the impossible: The history of psychoanalysis in Russia.* Boulder, CO: Westview Press.

Etkind, A. M. (1997b). There are no naked thoughts: Psychoanalysis, psychotherapy, and medical psychology in Russia. In E. L. Grigorenko, P. Ruzgis, & R. J. Sternberg (Eds.), *Psychology in Russia: Past, present, future* (pp. 59–82). Commack, NY: Nova Science.

Grigorenko, E. L., Ruzgis, P., & Sternberg, R. J. (Eds.) (1997). *Psychology in Russia: Past, present, future.* Commack, NY: Nova Science.

Isurina, G. L. (1990). Механèçmû ïсêх-оëоÄè×есêоé êоppeêÖÖè ëè×НостÈ в ïроöecce Ãруïïовоé ïсêхотераïèè в свете êоНöеïÖèè отНоøеНèé [Mechanisms of psychological correction of personality during group therapy in light of the concept of relationships]. In B. D. Karvasarsky & S. Leder (Eds.), *ÃруппоВаÿ психотерапиÿ* (pp. 89–120). Moscow: Medicine.

Kabanov, M. M., Lichko, A. E., & Smirnov, V. M. (1983). *Memoobl психоëosu×есêоù ouasНостиêu u êoppeê÷uu В êëuHêêe* [Methods of psychological diagnostics and correction in clinic]. Leningrad: Medicine.

Kanaya, T., Swillin, M. H., & Ceci, S. J. (2003). The Flynn Effect and U.S. policies: The impact of rising IQ scores on American Society via mental retardation diagnoses. *American Psychologist, 58;* 778–790.

Karvasarsky, B. D. (1985). [Psychotherapy]. Leningrad: Medicine.

Mama, K. B. (1997). *АНаëuç психоëosu×есêuх проöëеМ стуоеНтоВ* [The analysis of psychological difficulties of students]. Unpublished magister thesis, St. Petersburg State University, St. Petersburg, Russia.

Mishina, T. M. (1999). Russian group therapies mirror culture. *Psychology International, 10,* 1–5.

Myager, V. K. (Ed.). (1978). *СеМеùНаÿ психотерапиÿ при НереВblх u психи×есêuxçаöoëеВаНuÿx* [Family psychotherapy with the mentally ill]. Leningrad: Bekhterev Institute Press.

Osipov, A. (2000). *Bblöop спе÷uaëbНости у ÞНоøеù bblпусêНuêoв cpeoНeu øêoëbl* [Choice of a profession by men, high school graduates]. Unpublished magister thesis, St. Petersburg State University, St. Petersburg, Russia.

Tonkonogy, J. M. (1973). *ВВеоеНue В êëuHu×есêуÞ НеùропсихоëosuÞ* [Introduction to clinical neuropsychology]. Leningrad: Medicine.

Wasserman, L. I., Dorofeeva, C. A., & Meerson, Y. A. (1997). *Memoobl Неùропсихоëosu×есêoù ouasНостиêu: Ïраêmu×есêoe pyêoВoocmВo* [Methods of neuropsychological diagnostics: Practical manual]. St. Petersburg: Stroilespechat.

Windholz, G. (1999). Soviet psychiatrists under Stalinist duress: The design for a "new Soviet psychiatry" and its demise. *History of Psychiatry, 10* (39, Pt. 3), 329–347.

Zeigarnik, B. V. (1976). *Ïатопсихоëosuÿ* [Psychopathology]. Moscow: Moscow State University Press.

Zeigarnik, B. V., Nikolaeva V. V., & Lebedinsky V. V. (Eds.). (1987). *ÏраêmuêéуМ no natonсихоëosuu* [Practicum in pathopsychology]. Moscow: Moscow State University Press.

IMPORTANT PUBLICATIONS

Ananiev, B. G. (1968). *×еëоВеê êaê преоМет поçНаНuÿ* [A human as an object of study]. Leningrad: Leningrad State University Press.

Bozovitch, L. I. (1968). *ëu×Hocmb u ee ôop-МupoBaHue e oemcêoM Boçpacme* [Personality and its development in childhood]. Moscow: Prosveschenie.

Brushlinskii, A. V. (Ed.). (1997). ĬcÈXoëoÃÈ×ecêaÿ Hayêa B PoccÈÈ XX CToëeTÈÿ: ĬpoõëeMbI TeopÈÈ È ÈcTopÈÈ [Psychological science in Russia in 20th century: Problems of theory and history]. MocêBa: ÈçÄaTeëbcTBo ÈHcTÈTyTa ĬcÏXoëoÃÈÈ PoccÈécêoé AêaÄeMÈÈ Hayê. Moscow: Institute Psychology Russian Academy of Science Press.

Elkonin, D. B. (1960). *Child psychology.* Moscow: Moscow State University Press.

Karvasarsky, B. D. (Ed.). (2000). ĬcÈXoTepaÏeBTÈ×ecêaÿ çHÖÈêëoÏeÄÈÿ [Encyclopedia of psychotherapy]. St. Petersburg: Piter.

Leontiev, A. N. (1975). *ÄeÿmeëbHocmb CoçHaHue ëu×Hocmb* [Activity. Consciousness. Personality]. Moscow: Politisdat.

Lomov, B. F. (1984). *Memoдoëos×ecêue u meopemu×ecêue npoõëeMbI ncuxoëosuu* [Methodological and theoretical problems of psychology]. Moscow: Nauka.

Luria, A. R. (1973). *OcHoßbl Heũponcuxoëosuu* [The fundamentals of neuro psychology]. Moscow: Moscow State University Press.

Merlin, V. S. (1964) *O×epê TeopÈÈ TeMëepaMeHTa* [Essay on development of temperament]. Moscow: Prosveschenie.

Muasischev, V. N. (1995). *Ĭcuxoëosuÿ omHoøeHuῐ* [Psychology of relationships]. Moscow: Pedagogy.

Pavlov, I. P. (1951). *ĬoëHoe coõpaHue mpyдoB* [Full collection of papers]. Moscow and Leningrad: Publishing of Academy of Sciences USSR.

Rubinshtein S. L. (1959) *ĬpÈHÖÈÏbI È ĬyTÈ paçBÈTÈÿ ĬcÈXoëoÃÈÈ* [Principles and ways of development of psychology]. Moscow: Publishing of Academy of Sciences USSR.

Teplov, B. M. (1961). *ĬpoõëeMbl uHдuBuдyaëbHblx paçëu×u÷.* [Problems of individual differences]. Moscow: Academy of Pedagogical Sciences RSFSR.

Vygotsky, L. S. (1983). *Ècmopuÿ paçßumuÿ ßblcøux ôyHêцuῐ CoõpaHue co×uHeHuῐ ToM 3.* [Genesis of the higher mental functions. The collected works (Vol. 3)]. Moscow: Pedagogy.

Zeigarnik, B. V. (1976). *Ĭamoncuxoëosuÿ* [Psychopathology]. Moscow: Moscow State University Press.

CHAPTER 19

Psychology at the Cross-Roads: The View from Turkey

HALE BOLAK BORATAV

Hale Bolak Boratav is a social psychologist who studied and worked in academia in Turkey and the United States. She received her B.A in psychology from Boğaziçi University and her Ph.D. from the University of California at Santa Cruz. Boratav has held a postdoctoral position as a scholar in feminist studies at the University of California and a teaching appointment in the psychology and women's studies departments at the same university. In 1998, she joined the Psychology Department at Istanbul Bilgi University.

Hale Bolak's research interests include family dynamics, identity processes among urban youth, cultural perspectives on emotions and love, gender and sexuality, and sexual harassment. Her research has been funded by grants from the Social Science Research Council and the Population Council. She is a member of many professional organizations, and is the international liaison to the Division of International Psychology, American Psychological Association. Her publications have appeared in Gender and Society, Qualitative Sociology, and Feminism and Psychology, and as chapters in edited books.

19.1 OVERVIEW

Culturally as well as geographically a bridge between the East and the West, Turkey provides a unique vantage point for a discussion of the state of psychology. Scientific psychology had an early start in Turkey, but its maturation as an academic and a professional field extends over many years. In 1915, a German professor, Georg Anschütz, was invited to teach an experimental psychology course at İstanbul University, and later held the first psychology chair in the philosophy department. Upon his departure in 1919, a Swiss-trained

Turkish psychologist, Şekip Tunç, took over the psychology chair and was quite instrumental in helping popularize psychology through his translation of several classics by authors such as William James and Sigmund Freud (McKinney, 1960). The first experimental psychology program, library, and laboratory were started in 1937 at the same department by another invited German professor, Wilhelm Peters, who was joined by Mümtaz Turhan, a German-trained Turkish Ph.D. In 1939, Muzafer Sherif, the famous Turkish psychologist and one of the founders of social psychology (Sherif, 1935; Sherif, Harvey, White, Hood, & Sherif, 1961), came back with a Ph.D. from the United States, and was the first chair of psychology established within the philosophy department of Ankara University, which he held until 1945.

Overviews of the history of psychology in Turkey (Acar & Şahin, 1990; Başaran & Şahin, 1990; Kağıtçıbaşı, 1994) point to its European origins, and address the curious question of why the rich cultural heritage of Turkish society, bearing the legacies of great civilizations in Anatolia (one of the oldest continually inhabited regions in the world), did not produce an indigenous psychology. The fall of the Ottoman Empire after World War I and the founding of the Turkish Republic in 1923, accompanied by the introduction of secular reforms of Kemal Atatürk, provided a context within which Western scientific ideas emerged as an alternative to, and challenged, traditional systems of knowledge and belief. Previously, issues of psychological relevance were largely relegated to the mystic and religious realms. The great thinkers of the Islamic world like Ibn Sina (Avicenna) dwelled on the questions of the

soul and the mind. Likewise, there was a fairly articulated approach to mental illness and healing within the Islamic tradition that was secular and positive. In fact, the teachings of certain unorthodox mystic religious sects, such as those of Mevlana Rumi, have been compared to contemporary ideas within humanistic psychology (Başaran & şahin). These philosophical and religious answers to questions of psychological relevance may have served to suppress the development of psychology as an independent discipline.

The recognition of the need for psychology is traced to the late Ottoman period of Westernization when, frustrated with the social, economic, and military situation of the empire, and calling for social reforms, the civilian–military intellectuals began to look to the West for answers. Within their overarching project of social change and westernization, they saw a role for psychology as part of the education of the "modern individual." At this time, psychology's role was confined to the cultivation of intellectuals and educators. In fact, the introduction of psychology courses in teacher training institutes as early as 1915 coincided with the first psychology course offered in İstanbul University.

An important outcome of this early interest in social and psychological issues was the translation of many Western psychology books and articles into Turkish. But the development of a scientific orientation to psychology is associated with the republican period, and, more specifically, with the establishment of the first psychology programs at İstanbul and Ankara universities in the late 1930s.

Psychological research developed against the backdrop of World War II in Europe, with at times paradoxical implications. While German professors like Wilhelm Peters who fled the Nazi regime found refuge in Turkey and made important contributions to the development of this new discipline, the increasing political conservatism in the 1940s made for a very inhospitable climate for progressive social scientists and intellectuals like Muzafer Sherif. Sherif's ultimate decision to leave Turkey and emigrate to the United States was a major benefit to the development of American social psychology, and an equally great loss for psychology in Turkey. During his tenure in Turkey, between 1936 and 1945, Sherif produced an impressive amount of research marked by topical as well as methodological diversity. His work ranged from laboratory experiments in psychophysics, to translation and standardization of the Terman-Merrill and Army Beta tests, and to the study of the role of technological change on the perceptions and judgments of rural peasants.

Social change is another aspect of the cultural context within which psychology developed in Turkey. In the relatively short span of 80 years since the founding of the Turkish republic, Turkey experienced significant social, political, economic, and cultural transformation. The early work of Sherif and Turhan helped launch a tradition of social, psychological field research on social change, carried on, most notably, by two of Sherif's students (Başaran, 1969; Kray, 1964). Wide-scale social change starting in the late 1950s became a focus of researchers with an interdisciplinary orientation (e.g., Kandiyoti, 1974), and would become the first area of interdisciplinary collaboration between psychologists and other social scientists (e.g., Kağıtçıbaış, 1973). Changing family structure and dynamics, attitudes and values,

and socialization and gender roles were studied in relation to both internal migration fostered by urbanization and industrialization, and emigration of Turkish workers to European countries, particularly Germany, starting in the 1960s (Gitmez, 1983).

For almost 50 years, psychology education was confined to İstanbul and Ankara universities (the latter program remaining attached to the philosophy department until 1982). It was supported by foreign scholars and mostly served to train high school teachers. Starting in the mid 1950s, there was an increased impact of American psychology in Turkey, with American psychology texts being translated into Turkish, and Fulbright scholars lecturing and doing research in the field (McKinney, 1960).

With a growing number of Anglo–Saxon and U.S.-trained Turkish psychologists, new undergraduate psychology departments began to open up in large cities, starting at Middle East Technical University and Hacettepe University in Ankara in the 1960s and followed by Boğaziçi University in İstanbul and Ege University in İzmir in the 1970s. In the late 1970s there was also a gradual increase in graduate programs. The 1980s and 1990s witnessed a proliferation in psychological research, accompanied by another growth spurt in programs. A perusal of the curricula of the current 13 psychology programs reflects a wide spectrum of psychology courses and theoretical perspectives, a concern with methodological sophistication, and a largely North American approach.

This increase in the number of psychology programs corresponded to a growing recognition of the need in Turkey for psychological services. The wide-scale urbanization process of the 1960s provided an impetus for the expansion of educational and health services in urban centers. With the state continuing to be the major employer, psychologists now work in a broad range of public and private settings that provide health, educational, and social services for children, adults, and the elderly, including hospitals, schools, the military, prisons, the police, labor unions, research institutes, NGOs, the media, advertising firms, industries and other business, traffic administration, and private practice or consultancy. Although exact figures are hard to obtain, the number of professionals currently working with the title *psychologist* is estimated to be around 3,000, with close to 300 graduates joining the field each year, and approximately 5% working in private practice. Given that Turkey's population is roughly 65 million, this number corresponds to approximately 4–5 psychologists per 100,000 people, with the overwhelming majority working in urban centers.

Psychology in Turkey is still commonly perceived primarily as clinical psychology, and even then, the difference between a psychologist and a psychiatrist is not well understood. Although the stigma associated with receiving psychological services has diminished, those who benefit from these services are mostly urban. The majority of the people in Turkey still tend to rely on their strong family, kinship, and friendship networks to confide in and for social support, and, especially in rural areas, may consult indigenous healers. Most of those who interface with the mental health system are seen by psychiatrists, and tend to receive drug treatment rather than psychotherapy. Psychologists are in the minority compared to physicians and psychiatrists, and sometimes report to social workers who are in administrative positions.

With the proliferation of the need for psychological services in the period of 1970–1980, the professional needs of people working in the field also demanded more attention. Although efforts to form a national organization of Turkish psychologists date back to 1956 when an association was established in İstanbul, it later merged with a more functional Turkish Psychological Association (*Türk Psikologlar Derneği*) or TPA, founded in 1976 in Ankara. The TPA is the scientific and professional organization of psychologists in Turkey. It has been a member of IUPsyS since 1992 and of the European Federation of Psychologists Association (EFPA) since 1991. The planning and execution of many professional activities in the areas of research, application, education, and publication are carried out by the TPA. In the absence of a professional board, the TPA also monitors the observance of professional ethics and of the rights of people working with the title *psychologist.* Currently, the TPA has branches in four major cities and representatives in 22 of the 81 provinces of Turkey, with a current total of 1,771 regular and 677 affiliate members around the country (Turkish Psychological Association, 2003).

One of the major goals of the TPA is to be a bridge between academic and professional psychologists, and between psychologists and the general public. In collaboration with university psychology departments, it has organized biannual psychology conferences since 1982. A very important venue for the presentation of the latest research and a meeting ground for scholars and professionals, these conferences also feature several world-renowned keynote speakers. Psychology students also organize their own annual conferences. Since 1998, TPA has hosted an active Website (www.psikolog.org.tr) visited by approximately 1,000 people per month. The Website functions primarily to facilitate communication among the members, but is also becoming a source of psychoeducational services to laypeople. In response to pleas from psychology graduates for more academic guidance in their professional work, the TPA also has been offering continuing education courses.

The TPA promotes the advancement of scientific psychology in Turkey through the publication of scholarly periodicals and books. The most notable peer-reviewed journal is *Türk Psikoloji Dergisi* (*Turkish Psychology Journal*), which has been indexed in the Social Science Citation Index since 1994. In its 26th year, this journal is published quarterly, and is the primary outlet for high quality research of international standards. Aiming to build a resource base of psychological literature in Turkish, the biannual *Türk Psikoloji Yazıları* (*Turkish Psychological Review*) is another peer-reviewed journal that publishes comprehensive review articles and research articles based on scale and test development in Turkey.

With the inclusion of Turkey on the candidate list for full membership in the European Union (EU), and with enhanced efforts to get a professional code passed in the parliament, dynamic discussions are taking place in the psychological community about the directions that need to be taken. On the occasion of the 25th year of TPA, a psychology summit was held in December 2001 to identify the priorities and corresponding action plans that need to be implemented.

19.2 EDUCATION AND TRAINING

In Turkey, psychology undergraduate education is a 4-year program. High school graduates take a competitive university entrance examination and are placed in an undergraduate program by the Student Selection and Placement Center (ÖSYM). In 2003, approximately 1.5 million candidates took the examination, of which one third expected to be placed in a university program. The process that leads to this placement starts in the last 2 years of high school, when students are divided into different tracks depending on the score on the examination that each discipline requires. The selection into psychology programs is based on performance on the mathematics and verbal portions of the test. After the scores are announced, candidates make a short list of choices and rank their preferences. Placement in a psychology program is jointly determined by the candidate's score on the examination, his or her preference list, the minimum score requirements of the various psychology programs, and the admission quotas set by programs. Once a student is placed in a program, opportunities for transfer to other programs or universities are very limited. Psychology has historically been one of the most popular choices made in social sciences, its preference rating being within the upper 15th percentile (compared with 31st for sociology) (Başaran & Şahin, 1990).

As of the 2002–2003 academic year, there were 13 undergraduate psychology programs in Turkey, offered in psychology departments within the faculty of science and letters at both state and private universities. State universities require a nominal educational fee, and a small group of students may qualify for the need-based tuition waiver from the government. Each private university has a quota for successful students who are awarded scholarships. Of these 13 universities, all but 3 (Dicle, Mersin, and Uludağ) are in the three major cities of Turkey, with 6 (Boğaziçi, Haliç, İstanbul, İstanbul Bilgi, Koç, and Maltepe) in İstanbul, 3 in Ankara (Ankara, Hacettepe, and METU), and 1 in İzmir (Ege). The Haliç and Maltepe programs are the most recent and have no graduates yet. The program in Boğaziçi has consistently required the highest minimum entrance examination score, followed closely by METU. With the growing popularity of the psychology major, the scholarship quotas of private universities for successful candidates with high scores have been going up as well, making them increasingly more attractive to strong students.

The total number of students enrolled in undergraduate psychology programs during the academic year 2001–2002 was 1,945, with 475 of these being new students (Er & Duman, 2001). During the year 1986–1987, when there were only six psychology departments in the country, the number of newly accepted students was 305 (Başaran & Şahin, 1990). Since the mid-1990s, with new departments emerging on the scene, the total quota for psychology has been going up 4–5% a year.

As the ultimate authority in matters concerning universities since 1982, YÖK (Higher Education Council of Turkey) identifies the subfields of psychology and loosely regulates the common requirements of the psychology curricula. The core areas that are expected to be represented in the curricula include social, developmental, experimental, psychometrics, and the

broadly defined applied psychology that includes clinical and industrial–organizational (I–O) psychology. A recent report on undergraduate programs provides an informative overview of the commonalities and differences between the different undergraduate psychology programs in Turkey (Er & Duman, 2001).

The undergraduate curricula also vary on a number of dimensions. There are differences in the number and variety of departmental electives offered, and the minimum number of credits and other requirements for graduation, such as a senior thesis and internship. Nine of the 13 programs have some kind of training in English proficiency, but the language of instruction is Turkish with the exception of Bilgi, Boğaziçi, Koç, and METU where it is English. Given the insufficiency of Turkish scientific publications in psychology, original or translated, a good command of English gives students a major advantage in terms of staying current with the most recent developments in psychology.

Overall, the undergraduate psychology programs are quite rigorous. Curricula are based largely on the North American model with its emphasis on a general education in psychology that weighs more heavily on the academic than on the applied side. In a few departments, a continental European influence can also be detected.

All candidates for graduate work in Turkey are required to take a centralized graduate-education examination called LES (which tests general mathematics and verbal competency) and get a satisfactory pass score. Several other criteria are used in admissions decisions, depending on the programs. Almost every graduate psychology program requires a GPA of at least 2.00, a statement of purpose, and recommendation letters, and screens the candidates further through a written examination in the specific field of study, as well as an interview. Programs in which the language of instruction is English also require a minimum TOEFL score or they may conduct their own English proficiency examination. One of the requirements for the conferring of the graduate degree is getting a succesful pass score on a centrally administered foreign language examination.

As of 2003–2004, eight of the universities with a BA program in psychology are offering graduate programs. For the master's programs, six accepted students in social psychology, three in developmental, two in experimental, two in clinical, and three in I–O psychology. The quota for graduate admissions varies from program to program, and from year to year. Generally, the quota for a master's program tends to be 5–10, and that of a doctoral program, 3–5. The demand for graduate education is highest in the areas of clinical, social, and developmental psychology, with clinical psychology programs being the most popular and, hence, the most selective. On the other hand, there being more MA programs in social psychology than in any other area of psychology may be one of the legacies of the late Turkish social psychologist Muzafer Sherif.

Those who successfully complete a master's program and want to continue their academic career are encouraged to seek scholarships and to explore the possibilities of graduate work abroad. Although exact numbers are not known, a rough estimate is that about half of those who finish a graduate program in Turkey are appointed to an academic position in a university and the other half may split their time between private practice and work in institutional settings (Şahin, 1997). Most of those with graduate degrees work in urban areas.

A typical curriculum of a master's in clinical psychology includes core courses in research methods and statistics, child and adult psychopathology, approaches to individual and group psychotherapy, and diagnostic evaluation, as well as elective courses such as play therapy, mental retardation, clinical psychopharmacology, and professional ethics, depending on the program. The curriculum is based on the scientist–practitioner model, blending theory, research, and application into an integrated whole. In addition to lecture and seminar courses, there are internships that are intended to provide supervised clinical experience in diverse clinical settings such as mental hospitals, psychiatry units, or the outpatient clinics attached to the psychology departments, as in Boğaziçi University and METU.

I–O psychology is a relatively new but burgeoning specialty of psychology in Turkey. Although there are master's level and certificate programs in human resource management and organizational behavior, the number of master's level programs in I–O psychology is currently very limited, and most graduates of master's level programs in I–O are able to find lucrative jobs soon after graduation. A recent report (Ergin & Sümer, 2001) suggests there are about 20 I–O psychologists with doctoral degrees in Turkey.

Psychometrics is another area where the lack of qualified people is particularly keenly felt. There is currently only one graduate program, and more are sorely needed, given the urgency of developing culturally valid assessment tools. Graduate training in forensic psychology, an area of psychology that is gaining increasing recognition, is only offered through two institutes—one connected with Ankara University and the other with İstanbul University.

In any given year, only about 10–15% of graduates have the chance to get admitted to graduate program in psychology. Many students with a bachelor's in psychology turn to other alternatives such as the graduate programs in guidance and psychological services whose mission is to train individuals who will provide psychological services in educational settings. These programs are housed in the schools of education spread throughout the country, and confer many more undergraduate as well as graduate degrees each year than is possible through Turkish departments of psychology.

Currently, a person needs to have at least a master's in psychology to qualify as an expert psychologist in Turkey. In reality, though, the majority of the people practicing psychology have only a bachelor's degree. Given the scarcity of graduate programs in the country, continuing education is the only option available to bridge the gap between psychology education and the training needs of the profession. In the absence of licensing requirements for the professional practice of psychology, the TPA has assumed some of the functions of a professional board, and has been playing an increasingly active role in meeting the continuing education needs of psychologists. Continuing education workshops are also offered at the biannual conferences cohosted by the TPA and various psychology departments. At this time, the TPA does not have any power to require participation in these courses, but those who enroll in them hope to be able to use their accrued continuing education credits towards getting certified if and when the desired changes are made in the legislation.

Several bibliographies provide an overview of the work done by Turkish psychologists. Some of these bibliographies address the field as a whole (Bilgin, 1988), while others are area specific (Kağıtçıbaşı, 1976, Şahin, Şahin, Yasak-Gültekim, et al., 1994; Şahin, Şahin, Oral, et al., 1995).

Many textbooks in psychology have been published in Turkey, but the majority are translations. In a relatively recent overview of the field (Şahin, 1997), the number of textbooks published in Turkey had reached 65, and many more have been added since then, with at least 17 books to date published by the TPA alone. The social psychology text *The Individual and People* (Kağıtçıbaşı, 1976), now in its 10th edition (2000), is an important original contribution. The increase in the number of original textbooks and edited books in the recent years in areas as diverse as I–O psychology (Tevruz, 1996, 1998), cognitive behavioral therapy (Savaşır, Boyacıoğlu, & Kabakçı, 1998), and health psychology (Okyayüz, 1999) may gradually reduce the current dependence on translations. Relatively few books by Turkish psychologists have received international attention; a noteworthy exception is *Family and Human Development across Cultures: A View from the Other Side* (Kağıtçıbaşı, 1996a), which was subsequently translated into Turkish as *Kültürel Psikoloji* (*Cultural Psychology*).

Türk Psikoloji Dergisi (*Turkish Psychology Journal*) is the most noteworthy research journal. *Türk Psikoloji Yazlar* (*Turkish Psychological Review*) publishes translations of review articles and research articles based on scale and test development in Turkey. *Türk Psikoloji Bülteni* (*Turkish Psychological Bulletin*) contains translations from international journals. Another peer reviewed journal that has a mostly clinical audience is *3P: Psikiyatri, Psikoloji, Psikofarmakoloji (3P: Psychiatry, Psychology, Psychopharmacology)*.

In Turkey, psychological testing instruments are widely used. Some popular tests have been standardized, including the MMPI (Minnesota Multiphasic Personality Inventory) (Savaşır, 1981), State-Trait Anxiety Inventory (Öner & Le Compte, 1985), the WISC-R (Wechsler Intelligence Scale for Children-Revised) (Savaşır & Şahin, 1988), and NEO-PI-R (Neuroticism, Extraversion, Openness to Experience Agreeableness, and Conscientiousness-Personality Inventory-Revised) (Gülgöz, 2002), and a developmental screening inventory for children up to age 6 has been devised (Savaşır, Sezgin, & Erol, 1992). The total number of psychological assessment tools in use was estimated to be around 400 not too long ago (Şahin, 1997). In the last decade, the most informative reference in this regard has been a book that reviewed 179 of the psychological tests used in Turkey (Öner, 1994). Only 27% of the tests reviewed in this book were originals, with the rest being either translations or adaptations of foreign instruments; however, in the recent years, the numbers of original tests have increased.

Variations exist among universities in terms of the state of art with regards to instructional facilities. Access to high-speed computers and the Internet is available in all departments, which serves to compensate for the lack of a wide selection of periodicals and books in some libraries. Private universities have an advantage in terms of continuing to buy books, and newer universities such as Bilgi have opted to expand their electronic data bases so that many psychology journals including those issued by The American Psychological Association (APA) can be reached as full-text documents.

The TPA is considering the possibility of offering continuing education courses over the Web in the future. There is also interest in offering online assessment techniques and virtual clinics; however, without a law regulating practice, the TPA is wary of adding to the already existing difficulties regarding professional standards and ethics, and apprehensive about the extra problems to be expected when such services are offered in cyberspace.

19.3 SCOPE OF PSYCHOLOGICAL PRACTICE

The majority of psychologists employed by the state in psychologist positions work in such ministries as labor and social security, health, education, and justice, in police departments under the Ministry of the Interior, and in the armed forces. Psychologists are also increasingly employed by private educational institutions and rehabilitation centers for various groups with special needs, NGOs, research centers, the media, and in business and industry. According to 1990 TPA records (Başaran & Şahin, 1990), most psychologists in Turkey worked in the health sector (46%), academia (16%), early child care and education (15%), and guidance and psychological services (8%), or provided rehabilitation services for special groups (8%). Those working in industry (1%) and in some other sectors (administrator, private practice, media, and research center) (6%) were in the minority. Although the percentage of psychologists in private practice as providers of mental health and consulting services is still very small, it is growing.

Currently, the title *psychologist* can be used by anyone who has an undergraduate degree in psychology; thus, having a bachelor's in psychology is the minimum requirement to be appointed to a position of psychologist. Standard definitions of the profession and of the different areas of specialization are still lacking. This situation is a matter of concern for many in the psychological community who would like to see further educational requirements for work that requires specialization. An equally serious problem is that Turkish law subsumes psychological services under the general category of health services, and only physicians are authorized to provide psychological supervision, with the work of psychologists being conducted mostly under the supervision of psychiatrists or other medical personnel. Furthermore, as the laws regulating the licensing of professionals in the health services were legislated at a time when psychology was not yet represented outside the university, they do not allow the private practice of people holding this title (Başaran & Şahin, 1990). To do this, psychologists need to join with a psychiatrist in private practice or ask for permission from the Ministry of Education to declare their office a "guidance center." With psychology not yet considered a profession entitled to private practice, professional associations such as the TPA cannot function as boards and, hence, can neither grant permission for private practice nor bring a charge against someone in private practice.

The myriad problems caused by the current legislation are by no means specific to private practice. Among these are ambiguities and inevitable conflicts between expectations of those who are hired for the psychologist positions and various state and private-sector employers, the underutilization of the information and skills of many who fill those positions, and potential abuses of power by those who are authorized to supervise psychologists. The TPA is often called on to help with role definitions for people who provide psychological services in different settings, and the organization works with the government to coordinate the efforts to establish psychology as a profession and to clarify and protect the status of psychologists under Turkish law. There is an urgent need for a professional code that recognizes psychology as an independent science and profession that is not limited to health services (i.e., one requiring medical supervision), brings clarity to the professional title, and mandates the regulation of the ethical practice of psychology by a professional board.

Beyond terminating their memberships in the association, the TPA has limited professional control over the activities of members who violate professional ethics. Not waiting until that time when the association becomes a board, the TPA has attempted since the 1980s to establish ethical principles for the profession of psychology in Turkey. The following three APA publications have been translated into Turkish to guide the practice of professional psychology in Turkey: *General Guidelines for Provision of Psychological Services*, *Specialty Guidelines for the Delivery of Services—Clinical Psychologists*, and *Ethical Principles of Psychologists and Code of Conduct*. The current project of the ethics commission within the TPA is to empirically validate some general principles derived from the APA and EFPA (European Federation of

Psychologists Associations) against the realities and needs of the Turkish situation, with the hope of generating a culturally appropriate set of ethical guidlines (Korkut, 2001; Sezgin & Yılmaz, 2001).

Role definitions and range of activities expected of psychologists vary depending on the institution and the supervising personnel, and may include psychological assessment and evaluation through interviews and testing, psychotherapy, research, and educational work. The best known and the most widespread area of psychological practice is clinical psychology. Since the number of qualified clinical psychologists with advanced degrees is inadequate to meet the needs of people in Turkey, psychology graduates are recruited for positions that require them to function as professional psychologists.

A small number of clinical psychologists work in clinics, including those in universities. There are few clinical psychologists in private practice, and these individuals are concentrated in the major metropolitan centers. The majority of psychologist positions are in hospitals—primarily in psychiatric units, but also in other departments, including neurology, pediatry, oncology, surgery, and cardiology. University hospitals have historically been the most selective, hiring almost exclusively psychologists with advanced degrees. Clinical psychologists' strong background in research methodology and statistics makes them particularly desirable as supervisors of medical student research and as research collaborators with psychiatrists (Başaran & Şahin, 1990).

Psychologists working in institutional settings (including those with professional clinical training) are faced with the vexing problem of a professional hierarchy in which they are expected to work under the supervision of psychiatrists and other physicians. Some practitioners argue for interim solutions, such as recognizing the work of psychologists as psychological health services rather than as supplementary health services, attaining more privileges, lobbying for differentiation of ranks based on educational qualification, and education of medical personnel regarding the knowledge, skills, and role definitions of a psychologist. Problem areas in clinical practice and the difficulties experienced by practitioners are closely intertwined, and point to the need for more graduate programs, and, at the very least, a consensus on standards of practical training.

Psychologists in Turkey are recognized increasingly for the contributions they make to the different settings in which they work. The first time the general public became acquainted with the work of psychologists was after the two devastating earthquakes in 1999. Under the auspices of the TPA, hundreds of psychologists and psychology students were trained, and they participated as volunteers in the earthquake-stricken areas. In addition to emergency psychological relief work, the affected population was screened for chronic psychiatric problems like PTSD (posttraumatic stress disorder), and intervention plans were implemented. For many psychologists, this was their first large-scale encounter with PTSD. The increased public respect in the recent years for psychology and psychologists, and the somewhat diminished stigma associated with receiving psychological services, especially in large cities, is partly an outgrowth of these efforts.

In Turkey, psychologists are employed in large numbers by institutions that provide social services, especially for children. Psychologists also are hired for administrative and counseling positions in orphanages, nurseries, and school settings. For example, Guidance and Research Centers (RAMs) of the Ministry of Education that provide free services to children and young people up to age 17 are a major employer of psychologists. Nursing homes for the elderly, boarding houses for university students, and the growing numbers of rehabilitation centers are some other institutional settings where psychologists work.

Another promising field of applied work is I–O psychology. A range of factors, including the rigor of psychology education, particularly in research methodology, and the growing recognition of the role of human factors in determining output quality, has made psychology graduates increasingly more popular hires in industry. Job satisfaction of people who work in this field tends to be high both because of higher levels of compensation and because, through their international contacts, private businesses are more open to innovation and more information about what is expected of psychologists (Şahin, N. H., personal communication, 2003). Psychologists may work in different capacities within such departments as public relations or human resources, or provide their services as consultants. With very few academics specializing in I–O psychology and with the scarcity of experts in applied work, the consulting needs of the public and private sectors are mostly met by consultants with dubious qualifications (Aycan, 2001).

An exciting development since the late 1990s has been the establishment of traffic psychology as a legally recognized area of specialization. In a country in which the majority of traffic accidents are known to involve human error, and traffic accidents are among the leading causes of fatalities, the potential for the contribution of traffic psychology and psychologists to traffic safety is obvious. Since the passage of a traffic bill in 1997, drivers with licenses temporarily suspended due to traffic violations are required to undergo computer-assisted psychotechnical assessment and psychiatric evaluation in the approximately 20 centers in Turkey before they can retrieve their license at the end of the suspension period. Psychologists are pushing to make a niche for themselves in this area, working on the development of comprehensive assessment procedures that address the real causes of traffic violations, such as traffic safety skills, as well as attitudes, behaviors, and personality characteristics relevant to traffic or transportation (Sümer, 2001).

Although health psychology does not formally exist in Turkey, and so far little research has been conducted in this area (e.g., Özark-Fourreau & Sunar, 1999), hundreds of psychologists work in what is still a clinical field in Turkey. There are few professionally trained health psychologists; therefore, psychologists with or without a graduate degree, as well as psychiatric nurses, attempt to meet the needs that exist in health services. Many areas of health psychology such as risk perception, health maintenance, coping, and doctor–patient communication call for a culturally informed understanding of how individuals make sense of health and illness; investigations of these meaning systems may need to start with qualitative studies that can then form the basis for large-scale quantitative research.

Academic psychologists can be found in psychology departments as well as in university hospitals and other university departments, including education and business administration. By 2001, the number of academic staff in psychology departments alone had reached 162. Currently, more than half of the Ph.D.s in these departments are from overseas, and the majority of these are psychologists from the United States.

Academic research is done in almost all areas of psychology. Although still limited, the mostly laboratory-based "pure" scientific research of the experimental type is growing, and shows a notable progress in such areas as learning (Aydn & Pearce, 1997; Köksal, Domjan, & Weisman, 1994), neuropsychology (Karakaş, 2002; Schulz & Canbeyli, 2000), memory (Tekcan & Aktürk, 2001), cognitive–experimental (Ayçiçeği & Harris, 2002), and psycholinguistics (Aksu-Koç, 1994; Nelson, Aksu-Koç, & Johnson, 2001). Some of this research is carried out collaboratively with international colleagues, and finds publication outlets in prestigious journals.

On the other hand, social psychological research has always been well represented, with psychological implications of social change being an important focus. A comprehensive review done in the 1970s and 1980s (Acar & Şahin, 1990) included most of the relevant research on migration, family dynamics, gender, and socialization. Since then, this strand of social-psychological research has been continued in studies situating attitudes, values, and family practices in the context of social change (Bolak, 1997; Hortaçsu, Baştuğ, & Muhametberdiev, 2001; İmamoğlu & Karakitapoğlu, 1999; Sunar, 2002). In a country in which sharp differences based on social class, gender, and, particularly, rural–urban distinctions

remain high, the use of simple dichotomies like individualism–collectivism does not seem appropriate to characterize the sociocultural environment (Göregenli, 1997; Kağıtçıbaşı, 1997); instead, strong family and kinship bonds and interdependence seem to continue to predominate (Kağıtçıbaşı, 1996a; Sunar & Okman-Fişek, in press).

The uneasy fit between Western psychological knowledge and skills, and the needs of the local context, has been a long-standing concern of researchers in Turkey. Psychologists are generally well aware of the role of culture on psychological phenomena (Kağıtçıbaşı, 2000), even if most of the work that gets done is not necessarily culturally grounded, and often, at best, reflects cultural adaptation. My informal survey of psychologists, as well as my review of the contents of the *Turkish Psychology Journal* from its inception to date, suggested a very low level of indigenization—an observation that fits with an earlier study of the same journal for the period 1978–1992 (Öngel & Smith, 1999). In this comparative study, Soviet psychology came out quite highly indigenized, while Turkish psychology seemed strongly invested in integrating within mainstream psychology. The contrast was particularly striking with regard to the attempts to relate results to local conditions and the use of local tests.

While the existence of some standards to be followed, particularly in methodology, may have proved to be an advantage, the importation of psychological concepts and methods has impeded the development of indigenous paradigms. Psychologists in Turkey have acknowledged the need for a more local or indigenous knowledge base to guide the development of theory, methodology, and effective practices. Culturally informed theory development also exists, particularly in the areas of family and human development (Fişek, 1991; İmamoğlu, 1987; Kağıtçıbaşı, 1990, 1996a), with research often addressing issues of dependence–independence–interdependence (Kağıtçıbaşı, 1994). In I–O psychology, the case has been made for the importance of balancing current global trends against the realities of the Turkish organizational culture including paternalism (Aycan, 2001). These conceptualizations make important contributions to cross-cultural theory building.

The area of assessment seems to have been particularly slow to respond to cultural concerns. The widely studied area of family and couple dynamics is an example (Fişek, 2002). Construct validation research (e.g., Alp & Diri, 2003; Sümer, Sümer, Çiftçi, & Demirutku, 2000) is relatively new to Turkey, and attempts to construct indigenous tests have lagged behind the translation of tools imported from the West, which often are not evaluated for their cultural appropriateness (Kağıtçıbaşı, 1994). A recently developed model explains the lower level of cognitive skills in disadvantaged groups in terms of the adaptive difficulties of the rural and immigrant communities relative to the urban middle class (Gülgöz, cited in Gülgöz & Kağıtçıbaşı, 2004). Accordingly, an intervention program based on a multidimensional and plastic conceptualization of intelligence was designed and is currently being used to support the cognitive

development of 11–13-year-old children from disadvantaged backgrounds.

Advocating the compatibility of indigenous and universalistic conceptualizations, Çiğdem Kağıtçıbaşı, a leading scholar in the cross-cultural field, has made a strong plea for the use of integrative approaches by psychologists in the "majority world" (developing countries). A particularly well-received example of integrating indigenous psychological knowledge and culture-sensitive theorizing is her conceptualization of the construct of the *autonomous-related self* (Kağıtçıbaşı, 1996b), which refers to the development of the self in a family context where urban lifestyles coexist with collectivistic cultural values. This new synthesis informed the theoretical work and intervention in the 10-year longitudinal Turkish Early Enrichment Project (TEPP) by Kağıtçıbaşı and her colleagues (Bekman, 1998; Kağıtçıbaşı, 1995; Kağıtçıbaşı, 2002; Kağıtçıbaşı, Sunar, & Bekman, 2001).

A quick glance at the 25-year index of the *Turkish Psychology Journal* (Er et al., 2002) shows that, over time, the areas of psychology represented have increasingly diversified. Starting in the 1990s, the numbers of articles in clinical psychology have gone down, while articles representing other areas of psychology have increased. Particularly noteworthy is the growth of publications in experimental and developmental psychology and, in the last 5 years, in psychometrics. Some of the current research programs in assessment promise to result in indigenous assessment tools (e.g., Somer, Korkmaz, & Tatar, 2002) and to contribute to the cross-cultural literature (e.g., Gülgöz, 2002).

19.4 FUTURE CHALLENGES AND PROSPECTS

Psychology in Turkey seems to be on its way to maturity with a promising future. The fact that the field has continued to grow since the 1980s despite the lack of legal and public recognition and sufficient economic resources is quite impressive and a cause for optimism. The sustained and successful work towards getting the *Turkish Psychology Journal* into the Social Science Citation Index is one example of the industry within the psychological community. Currently, the same energy is being invested in getting a professional code passed in parliament. The notable progress in both the discipline and the profession in the last 25 years will likely continue. However, the road ahead may be bumpy.

The development of more favorable science policies and legal structures, more relevant and more appropriate research (Kağıtçıbaşı, 2000), as well as a closer interface and better collaboration between academics and professional communities are among the priorities for the near future. Senior scholars in the field (Kağıtçıbaşı, 1994; Şahin, 1997) have argued that the application potential of psychological knowledge to the solution of a wide range of social problems has yet to be exploited fully in Turkey. In fact, recognition of the potential contributions of social sciences within the larger scientific community is relatively recent. The fact that the Turkish Scientific and Technical Research Council (TÜBTAK) still does not support psychological research, unless it is in the area of psychophysiology, reveals the relative low esteem given to the social sciences. A major challenge for Turkish psychologists is to promote their work and to create a niche for themselves among the socially relevant sciences (Kağıtçıbaşı, 2000).

Both basic and applied psychological research will continue to expand in the future in Turkey, coming to include previously underrepresented areas of psychology such as positive psychology (Değirmencioğlu & Özdemir, 2003), feminist psychology (Bolak-Boratav, 2001, 2002), sexism (Sakall, 2001), and ethnic prejudice (Bikmen & Sunar, 2003). Relatively new applied areas such as I–O psychology, health psychology, traffic psychology, and forensic psychology will continue to develop; however, if this is to be achieved, more graduate programs are necessary.

The public recognition and appreciation of psychology and psychologists will continue to grow in the near future. Notwithstanding the aforementioned reticence about going to psychologists, the rapid process of social change, along with the radical and sometimes misguided policy decisions taken in political, economic, and social arenas in the last 25 years has presented major life stressors and adjustment problems for people in Turkey, making psychology increasingly relevant to the public. The slowly growing public demand for psychological services is expected to continue, especially in urban areas.

The number of psychology undergraduate programs will also increase in the next 25 years. So far, academic programs have been a major strength of Turkish psychology, with fairly uniform curricula and rigorous standards. If the new programs can continue to attract strong faculty and maintain high standards, and if new graduate programs become a reality, the field will be served well. In the context of the legal vacuum, the recent growth in the numbers of graduates has been increasingly problematic, raising the urgency of a clear direction for psychology education in Turkey. There is broad consensus that a 4-year program in psychology as a basic science does not prepare someone to become a specialist in any area of psychology, and that at least 1 year of graduate work beyond the undergraduate degree is necessary for specialization. However, there is no consensus on what the educational requirements should be for a practicing psychologist, or what the model and criteria should be for restructuring the psychology curricula. Currently, there is consideration of whether or not the European system based on the scientist–practitioner model may be more relevant to Turkey's needs, especially given the scarcity of graduate programs. What the undergraduate education should be like, who should be able to use the title *psychologist,* and the specifics of the pending licensing code are controversial issues that psychologists in Turkey are debating. At the same time that this discussion is taking place, there are hopes that Turkey may be given a negotiation date in 2004 for entry into the EU. With Turkey's entry into the EU, the free circulation of psychologists in Europe would become possible for those who hold a European diploma.

Hence, psychology in Turkey is at a crossroad. An ever-growing community of academics and professionals, Turkish psychologists need to coordinate their efforts towards better research and practice, as well as better solutions to the problem of professional training. For example, the historically rich and unique cultural legacy and traditions of Turkey are not formally integrated into the education and training of psychologists. A new course in the clinical program at Ankara University that addresses the relevant contributions of some aspects of indigenous culture, such as Sufism, toward understanding individual psychology is a salient exception.

There are many reasons to be optimistic. The passage of the professional code would be a major turning point. The insufficiency of material resources is still a major problem, although the situation looks a little better compared to that of even 10 years ago. The number of international research partnerships, international publications, and international psychology conferences being held in Turkey is on the increase. The ability of psychologists in Turkey to maintain contact both with international developments in their discipline and with the local issues of their country has been noted as a particular strength (Başaran & Şahin, 1990) and will continue to serve the field well. There is an active interest within the psychological community in moving forward with a cohesive agenda. The TPA is likely to remain as an important bridge between the discipline and the profession.

Sixty-five years after Muzafer Sherif became the first Turk to chair a psychology program in Turkey, he will be honored with a special tribute before the 2004 psychology conference to be hosted by the Psychology Department at İstanbul Bilgi University. This exciting event will, hopefully, provide an occasion to reflect on how far psychology in Turkey has progressed since its modest beginnings.

REFERENCES

Acar, G., & Şahin, D. (1990). Psychology in Turkey. *Psychology and Developing Societies, 2,* 241–256.

Aksu-Koç, A. (1994). Development of linguistic forms. In R. Berman & D. Slobin (Eds.), *Relating events in narrative: Cross-linguistic development study.* (pp. 329–385). Hillsdale, NJ: Earlbaum.

Alp, E., & Diri, A. (2003). Bilişsel Yetenekler Testi'nin (CogAT®) Ana Sınıfı ve Birinci Sınıf Öğrencileri için Kurultu Geçerliği Çalışması. (A validation study of CogAT for Turkish kindergarden and first grade students). *Türk Psikoloji Dergisi, 18,* 19–31.

Aycan, Z. (2001). Human resource management in Turkey: Current challenges and future trends. *International Journal of Manpower, 22,* 252–261.

Ayçiçeği, A., & Harris, (2002). How are letters containing diacriticals represented? Repetition blindness for Turkish words. *European Journal of Cognitive Psychology, 14,* 371–382.

Aydn A., & Pearce, J. M. (1997). Some determinants of response summation. *Animal Learning & Behavior, 25,* 108–121.

Başaran, F. (1969). *Attitudes about towns.* Araştırma, V. Ankara: Üniversitesi Basmevi.

Başaran, F., & Şahin, N. (1990). Psychology in Turkey: Country status report. *Social and human sciences in Asia and the Pacific.* (RUSHAP Series, 34). Bangkok: UNESCO.

Bekman, S. (1998). Long-term effects of the Turkish home-based early intervention program. In U. Gielen, & A. L. Comunian (Eds.), *The family and family therapy in international perspective* (pp. 401–417). Trieste, Italy: Edzioni Lint.

Bikmen, N., & Sunar, D. (2003) The relationship of national and religious identities in Turkey. Manuscript under review.

Bilgin, N. (1988). *Başlangcndan günümüze Türk Psikoloji Bibliyografyas* [Psychology in Turkey from its beginnings to the present]. İzmir, Turkey: Ege Üniversitesi Edebiyat Fakültesi Yayn.

Bolak, H. (1997). When wives are major providers: Culture, gender and family work. *Gender and Society, 11,* 409–443.

Bolak-Boratav, H. (2001). Feminist Psikoloji: Nedir, nasıl gelişti, psikolojiye katkıları (Feminist psychology: The field, its development, and contributions to psychology). *Türk Psikoloji Yazıları, 4,* 1–19.

Bolak-Boratav, H. (2002). Social psychology of power and empowering possibilities. *Feminism & Psychology, 11,* 311–318.

Değirmencioðlu, S. M., & Özdemir, M. (2003, Aug). *The positive impact of relief work on young people.* Paper presented in a symposium titled "Engagement, enjoyment, and intrinsically-motivated goals: Positive psychology and individual development" at the European Conference on Developmental Psychology, Milan, Italy.

Er, N., & Duman, T. (2001). Türkiye'de ve dünyada psikoloji lisans eğitiminin kısa bir panoraması [A short panorama of the psychology undergraduate education in Turkey and the world]. *Türk Psikoloji Bülteni, 7,* 17–42.

Er, N., Solmuş, T., & Uçar, F. (2002). 1978 "den 2002" ye (50. Sayya) Türk Psikoloji Dergisi Serüveni [The adventure of the *Turkish Psychology Journal* from 1978 to 2002 (50th issue)]. *Türk Psikoloji Dergisi, 17,* 103–127.

Ergin, C., & Sümer, C. (2001). Türkiye'de endüstri ve örgüt psikolojisi eğitimi [Industrial/Organizational psychology education in Turkey]. *Türk Psikoloji Bülteni, 7,* 113–115.

Fişek, G. O. (1991). A cross-cultural examination of proximity and hieararchy as dimensions of family structure. *Family Process, 30,* 121–133.

Fişek, G. O. (2002, April). Türkiye'de aile araştırmalarında değerlendirme [Assessment in family studies in Turkey]. Prof. Dr. Işık Savaşır Klinik Psikoloji Sempozyumu. Bilkent Üniversitesi, Ankara, Turkey.

Gitmez, A. (1983). *Yurt dışına işçi göçü ve geri dönüşler.* [Out migration of workers and the return home]. İstanbul: Alan Yayıncılık.

Göregenli, M. (1997). Individualist-collectivist tendencies in a Turkish sample. *Journal of Cross-Cultural Psychology, 28,* 787–794.

Gülgöz, S. (2002). Five factor theory and NEO-PI-R in Turkey. In R. R. McCrae & J. Allik (Eds.), *The five-factor model of personality across cultures* (pp. 1–23). New York: Kluwer.

Gülgöz, S, & Kağıtçıbaşı, Ç. (2004). Intelligence and intelligence testing in Turkey. In R. J. Sternberg (Ed.), *International handbook of the psychology of human intelligence* (pp. 248–269). Cambridge, UK: Cambridge University Press.

Hortaçsu, N., Baştuğ, S., & Muhametberdiev, O. (2001). Change and stability with respect to attitudes and practices related to marriage in Ashkabat, Baku, and Ankara: Three Turkic cultures. *International Journal of Psychology, 36,* 108–120.

İmamoğlu, E. O. (1987). An interdependence model of human development. In Ç. Kağıtçıbaşı (Ed.), *Growth and progress in cross-cultural psychology* (pp. 138–145). Lisse, Netherlands: Swetz & Zeitlinger.

İmamoğlu, O., & Karakitapoğlu, A. Z. (1999). 1970 "lerden 1990" lara değerler: Üniversite düzeyinde gözlenen zaman, kuak ve cinsiyet farkllklar [Values from the 1970s to the 1990s: Differences observed as a function of time, generation, and gender]. *Turkish Psychology Journal, 14,* 1–18.

Kağıtçıbaşı, Ç. (1973). Psychological aspects of modernization in Turkey. *Journal of Cross-cultural Psychology, 4,* 157–174.

Kağıtçıbaşı, Ç. (1976). *İnsan ve insanlar* [The individual and the people]. Ankara: Türk Sosyal Bilimler Derneği.

Kağıtçıbaşı, Ç. (1990). Family and socialization in cross-cultural perspective: A model of change. In J. Berman (Ed.), *Nebraska symposium on motivation, 1989* (Vol. 37, pp. 135–200). Lincoln, NE: University of Nebraska Press.

Kağıtçıbaşı, Ç. (1994). Psychology in Turkey: The origins and development of psychology. Some national and regional perspectives. *International Journal of Psychology, 29,* 729–738.

Kağıtçıbaşı, Ç. (1995). Is psychology relevant to global human development issues? Experience from Turkey. *American Psychologist, 50,* 293–300.

Kağıtçıbaşı, Ç. (1996a). *Family and human development across cultures: A view from the other side.* Hillsdale, NJ: Erlbaum.

Kağıtçıbaşı, Ç. (1996b). The autonomous relational self: A new synthesis. *European Psychologist, 1,* 180–186.

Kağıtçıbaşı, Ç. (1997). Individualism and collectivism. In J. W. Berry, M. H. Segall, & Ç. Kağıtçıbaşı, (Eds.), *Handbook of cross-cultural psychology* (Vol. 3, pp. 1–49). Boston: Allyn & Bacon.

Kağıtçıbaşı, Ç. (2000). Turkey. In A. E. Kazdin (Ed.), *Encyclopedia of psychology* (pp. 125–127). New York: Oxford University Press.

Kağıtçıbaşı, Ç. (2002). Psychology and human competence development. *Applied Psychology: An International Review, 51,* 5–22.

Kağıtçıbaşı, Ç., Sunar, D., & Bekman, S. (2001). Long term effects of early intervention: Turkish low-income mothers and children. *Applied Developmental Psychology, 22,* 333–361.

Kandiyoti, D. (1974). Some social psychological dimensions of social change in a Turkish village. *British Journal of Social Psychology, 25,* 47–62.

Karakaş, S. (2002). From time-domain waveforms to oscillation dynamics: An evolving approach to brain's electrical activity. *International Journal of Psychophysiology, 45,* 35–40.

Kıray, M. (1964). *Ereğli: Ağır sanayiden önce bir sahil kasabası* [Ereğli: A coastal town before heavy industry]. Ankara: DPT Yaynlar.

Korkut, Y. (2001). Bir an önce harekete geçme zaman: Türkiye'de etik ilke ve kurallara duyulan büyükgereksinim karşısında neler yapılabilir? [It is time to act: What can be done about the major need for ethical principles and regulations in Turkey?]. *Türk Psikoloji Bülteni, 7,* 220–224.

Köksal, F., Domjan, M., & Weisman, G. (1994). Blocking of the sexual conditioning of differentially effective conditioned-stimulus objects. *Animal Learning & Behavior, 22,* 103–111.

McKinney, F. (1960). Psychology in Turkey: Speculation concerning psychology's growth and area culture. *American Psychologist, 15,* 717–723.

Nelson, K. E., Aksu-Koç, A., & Johnson, C. E. (Eds.). (2001). *Children's language, Vol. 10.* Hillsdale, NJ: Erlbaum.

Okyayüz, Ü. H. (1999). *Sağlık psikolojisi* [Health psychology]. Ankara: Türk Psikologlar Derneği Yayınları.

Öner, N. (1994). *Türkiye'de kullanılan psikolojik testler: Bir başvuru kaynağı* [The psychological tests used in Turkey: A resource book]. İstanbul: Boğaziçi University.

Öner, N., & LeCompte, A. (1985). *Durumluluk-Sürekli Kaygı Envanteri El Kitabı* [State Anxiety Inventory-Manual for the Trait]. İstanbul: Boğaziçi University.

Öngel, Ü., & Smith, P. B. (1999). The search for indigenous psychologies: Data from Turkey and the former USSR. *Applied Psychology: An International Review, 48,* 465–479.

Özarık-Fourreau, P., & Sunar, D. (1999). Cultural and psychological factors predicting condom use in Turkish young men [Special Issue]. *Boğaziçi Journal, 13* (1–2), 157–179.

Şahin, N. (1997). Psychology. In TÜBA *Cumhuriyet döneminde Türkiye'de bilim: Sosyal Bilimler* [Science in Turkey during the Republican period: Social sciences] (pp. 203–226). Ankara: Author.

Şahin, N., Şahin, N. H., Yasak-Gültekin, Y., Durak, A., Oral, A., & Ungan, Ü. (1994). *Türkiye'de ergenlik dönemi araştırmaları bibliyografyası 1980–1994.* (cilt 1) [The bibliography of research on adolescence in Turkey 1980–1994 (Vol. 1)]. Ankara: Türk Psikologlar Derneği Yayınları.

Şahin, N., Şahin, N. H., Oral, A., Ungan, Ü., Yasak, Y., Durak, A., et al. (1995). *Türkiye'de ergenlik dönemi araştırmaları bibliyografyası 1980–1994* (cilt 2) [The bibliography of research on adolescence in Turkey 1980–1994 (Vol. 2)]. Ankara: Türk Psikologlar Derneği Yayınları.

Sakallı, N. (2001). Beliefs about wife beating among Turkish college students: The effects of patriarchy, sexism, and sex differences. *Sex Roles, 44,* 599–610.

Savaşır, I. (1981). *Minnesota Çok Yönlü Kişilik Envanteri El Kitabı: Türk standardizasyonu* [Manual for Minnesota Multiphasic Personality Inventory: Turkish standardization]. Ankara: Sevinç Matbaası.

Savaşır, I., Boyacıoğlu, G., & Kabakçı, E. (Eds.). (1998). *Bilişsel davranışçı terapiler* [Cognitive behavioral therapies]. Ankara: Türk Psikologlar Derneği Yayınları.

Savaşır, I., & Şahin, N. (1988). *Wechsler çocuk zeka ölçeği (WISC-R)* [Wechsler Intelligence Scale for Children]. Ankara: Milli Eğitim Basımevi.

Savaşır, I., Sezgin, N., & Erol, N. (1992). 0-6 ya çocuklar için gelişim tarama envanteri geliştirilmesi. [Devising a developmental screening inventory for 0-6 year old children]. *Türk Psikiyatri Dergisi, 3,* 33–38.

Schulz, D. & Canbeyli, R. (2000). Lesions of the bed nucleus of the stria terminalis enhances learned despair. *Brain Research Bulletin, 52,* 83–87.

Sezgin, N., & Yılmaz, (2001). Psikoloji mesleiğnin etik ilkeleri: Türkiye'deki duruma bakış ve öneriler [The ethical principles of the profession of psychology: A look at the situation in Turkey and suggestions]. *Türk Psikoloji Bülteni, 7,* 218–219.

Sherif, M. (1935). A study of some social factors in perception. *Archives of Psychology, 27,* 1–60.

Sherif, M., Harvey, O. J., White, B. J, Hood, W. R., & Sherif, C. W. (1961). *Intergroup conflict and cooperation: The Robber's cave experiment.* Norman, OK: University of Oklohoma Book Exchange.

Somer, O., Korkmaz, M., & Tatar, A. (2002). Beş Faktör kişilik envanteri'nin geliştirilmesi-1: Ölçek ve alt ölçeklerin oluşturulması [Development of Five Factor Personality Inventory-1: The construction of the scale and subscales]. *Türk Psikoloji Dergisi, 17,* 21–33.

Sümer, H. C., Sümer, N., Çiftçi, D. S., & Demirutku, K. (2000). Subay kişilik özelliklerinin ölçülmesi ve yapı geçerliği çalımşası [Measurement of officer personality attributes: A construct validity study]. *Türk Psikoloji Dergisi, 15,* 15–26.

Sümer, N. (2001). Trafik psikolojisi uygulamalar: Görev alanları, beceriler ve standartlar. [Applications of traffic psychology: Areas of practice, skills, and standards]. *Türk Psikoloji Bülteni, 7,* 72–76.

Sunar, D. (2002). Change and continuity in the Turkish middle class family. In R. Liljeström & E. Özdalga, E. (Eds.), *Transactions: Vol. 11. Autonomy and dependence in the family* (pp. 217–237). İstanbul: Swedish Research Institute.

Sunar, D., & Okman-Fişek, G. (in press). Contemporary Turkish families. In U. Gielen & J. Roopnarine (Eds.), *Families in global perspective.* Boston: Allyn & Bacon.

Tekcan, A. İ., & Aktürk. M. (2001). Are you sure you forgot? Feeling of knowing in directed forgetting. *Journal of Experimental Psychology: Learning, Memory and Cognition, 27,* 1487–1491.

Tevruz, S. (Ed.). (1996). *Endüstri ve örgüt psikolojisi* [Industrial and organizational psychology]. Ankara:Türk Psikoglar Derneği Yayınları.

Tevruz, S. (Ed.). (1998). *Endüstri ve örgüt psikolojisi II* (Industrial and organizational psychology II). Ankara: Türk Psikologlar Derneği Yayınları.

Turkish Psychological Association. (2003). *Archives of the Turkish Psychological Association.* Ankara: Author.

IMPORTANT PUBLICATIONS

Aksu-Koç, A. (1988). *The acquisition of aspect and modality: The case of past reference in Turkish.* New York: Cambridge University Press.

Alp, İ. E. (1994). Measuring the size of working memory in very young children: The mitation sorting task. *International Journal of Behavioral Development, 17,* 125–141.

Berger, J., Conner, T. L., & Fişek, M. H. (Eds.). (1974). *Expectation states theory: A theoretical research program.* Cambridge, MA: Winthrop.

Canbeyli, R. S., Lehman, M., & Silver, R. (1991). Tracing SCN graft efferents with DiI. *Brain Research, 554,* 15–21.

Fişek, G. (1991). A cross-cultural examination of proximity and hierarchy as dimensions of family structure. *Family Process, 30,* 121–133.

İmamoğlu, E. O. (1987). An interdependence model of human development. In Ç. Kağıtçıbaşı (Ed.), *Growth and progress in cross-cultural psychology* (pp. 138–145). Lisse, Netherlands: Swetz & Zeitlinger.

Kağıtçıbaşı, Ç. (1990). Family and socialization in cross-cultural perspective: A model of change. In J. Berman (Ed.), *Nebraska symposium on motivation, 1989* (Vol. 37, pp. 135–200). Lincoln, NE: University of Nebraska Press.

Kağıtçıbaşı, Ç. (1996). *Family and human development across cultures: A view from the other side.* Hillsdale, NJ: Erlbaum.

Kağıtçıbaşı, Ç., Sunar, D., & Bekman, S. (2001). Long term efects of early intervention: Turkish low-income mothers and children. *Applied Developmental Psychology, 22,* 333–361.

Karakaş, S., & Başar, E. (1998). Early gamma response is sensory in origin: A conclusion based on cross-comparison of results from multiple experimental paradigms. *International Journal of Psychophysiology, 31,* 13–31.

Köksal, F., Domjan, M., & Weisman, G. (1994). Blocking of the sexual conditioning of differentially effective conditioned-stimulus objects. *Animal Learning & Behavior, 22,* 103–111.

Savaşır, I., Sezgin, N., & Erol, N. (1992). 0-6 yaş çocukları için gelişim tarama envanteri geliştirilmesi. [Devising a developmental screening inventory for 0-6 year old children]. *Türk Psikiyatri Dergisi, 3,* 33–38.

CHAPTER 20

Psychology in Germany

INGRID PLATH AND LUTZ H. ECKENSBERGER

Ingrid Plath received a B.A. (Hons.) degree from the University of Stellenbosch in South Africa, a Diplom *in psychology from the University of Frankfurt am Main, and her doctorate in psychology from the University of Tübingen. She joined the research staff of the German Institute for International Educational Research (Deutsches Institut für Internationale Pädagogische Forschung [DIPF], a member of the Leibniz Association of nonuniversity research institutes in 1989. Her interests include research integration, meta-analysis, the handling of knowledge, social psychology of science, and problems regarding the transmission of theoretical knowledge into practice, as well as issues of cultural contexts and education. Recently, she has been involved in scientific management and evaluation. She is the author and co-author of several articles and books including* Understanding Meta-Analyses: A Consumer's Guide to Aims, Problems, Evaluation, and Developments.

Lutz H. Eckensberger obtained his Diplom *in psychology in 1964 and his doctorate in 1970. After receiving his habilitation in 1972, he became a professor at the University of the Saarland (Saarbrücken) in the same year and was awarded the chair in developmental psychology in 1976. In 1996 he moved to Frankfurt am Main where he currently is the director of the German Institute for International Educational Research and head of its section on education and culture; he is also professor in the psychology department at the University of Frankfurt. From 1985 to 1986 he was a fellow at the Center for Advanced Studies in Berlin. Apart from his focus on methodology, his main interests are in the field of moral development from a cultural and action theory perspective, and the contextualization of morality in issues of health and environment, which implies the analysis of relations between facts and norms, cognition and affect, and control and risk-taking. He has published over 90 articles in books and journals and edited 15 books.*

20.1 OVERVIEW

The history of psychology in Germany should be recounted as the history of psychology in German-speaking countries in general (in particular Germany, Austria, and Switzerland). Traditionally, there has been and still is much mobility across the German-speaking region. The historical aspects can only be outlined here (for more details see Goebel, 1992; Lück, 2002; Wertheimer, 1970).

Germany has played a central role in establishing psychology as an institutionalized science. Mutually supportive trends in natural science (i.e., demystification of the body, foundation of institutes) and philosophy (i.e., elementism, materialism) paved the way for Wilhelm Wundt to found the first psychological institute in Leipzig in 1879. Wundt was one of the first scholars to regard himself as a psychologist, defining psychology as the study of the perception of the inner world in his 1873 treatise, *Fundamentals of Physiological Psychology*, which called for introspection under experimental conditions. Wundt founded the *Journal of Psychology and Physiology of the Sense Organs* in 1890 with Ebbinghaus, and *Philosophical Studies* in 1883, renamed *Psychological Studies* in 1905. The Society for Experimental Psychology was established in 1904 and renamed the German Psychological Society (Deutsche Gesellschaft für Psychologie [DGPs]) in 1929. Wundt's institute affected the development of psychology in other countries both because it led to the foundation of similar laboratories (e.g., at Harvard, the Sorbonne, and Graz) and because some of Wundt's students introduced his approach elsewhere, transforming it along the way (e.g., James McKeen Cattell, G. Stanley

Hall, William James, Hugo Münsterberg, Edward Wheeler Scripture, and Edward B. Tichener in the United States). Wundt also laid the foundation for both traditional experimental psychology and modern cultural psychology. Karl Bühler's *Crisis of Psychology* (1927) shows that Wundt followed a particular paradigm in that he made certain assumptions about humans (e.g., atomism, sensualism, mechanism, subjectivism). These were challenged later, leading to a variety of schools which followed different paradigms based on different assumptions about human functioning. Some of these paradigms were explicit countermovements; others emerged independently. Four of the eight schools or paradigms that emerged after Wundt were conceptualized in German-speaking contexts: Gestalt psychology, act psychology, psychoanalysis, and *geisteswissenschaftliche* psychology based on an understanding approach that involves interpreting and describing human behavior and experiences, rather than seeking explanations as in the natural sciences (its main proponents being Wilhelm Dilthey and Eduard Spranger). Some of these schools are still very much alive or have been revived, although they have undergone tremendous transformations.

World War II was a decisive event in the historical development of German psychology. The period before and during the war was characterized by the exodus of a large number of scientists who were pioneers in many fields of psychology (e.g., Charlotte and Karl Bühler, Wolfgang Köhler, Kurt Lewin, Fritz Heider, Max Wertheimer, and William Stern). About 35% of the psychology professors and 15% of the members of the DGPs emigrated. Some were dismissed, such as William

Stern and Max Wertheimer, some were imprisoned in concentration camps, like Heinrich Düker, and some were murdered, including Kurt Huber and Otto Selz. During this time, psychology underwent an ideological shift toward the racism of the Nazi regime. Some approaches, including Gestalt psychology and the psychology of expressive behavior, were adapted to fit this ideology. The development of psychometric tests, particularly for selection purposes in the armed forces, led to the upsurge of psychology as a profession. Diploma courses for psychology were established in 1941 in an attempt to standardize education and infuse teaching and research with Nazi ideology. The structure of academic education in psychology took on the basic form that it still has today.

The period after World War II was characterized by different trends in the two Germanies: the Federal Republic of Germany in the West and the German Democratic Republic in the East (for details on psychology in East Germany see Kossakowski, 1992). Although the importance of psychology as a science and profession gradually increased in both countries, it was more pronounced in the West. There, the DGPs was reestablished in 1947 after having been disbanded in 1945. The Association of German Professional Psychologists (Bundesverband Deutscher Psychologinnen und Psychologen [BDP]) had already been founded in 1946.

In the East, the Society for Psychology (Gesellschaft für Psychologie [GP]) was only established in 1962, with academics and practitioners as members. After reunification in 1990, the GP was abolished, its members having the option of joining the DGPs if they fulfilled its membership requirements or, alternatively, the BDP if they did not.

From a scientific standpoint, the international stature of postwar German psychology clearly decreased. West Germany basically followed the American mainstream, like psychology in most other parts of the world. A few research programs continued to follow the more uniquely German traditions, which varied in their international impact. In Heidelberg, Graumann cultivated phenomenology. In Cologne, Groeben based his work on a psychology of subjectivity and intersubjectivity, working on dialogical models and using discourse analysis; various psychological theories were developed, taking up *geisteswissenschaftliche* concepts of intentionality (vs. causality) and understanding (vs. explanation) from a more restricted perspective. In Munich, Heckhausen developed his Rubicon model of motivation. Kaminski in Tübingen advanced ecological psychology. Boesch and Eckensberger at Saarbrücken and Werbik at Erlangen promoted cultural psychology, which ultimately led to the foundation of the Society for Cultural Psychology in 1986 in Salzburg.

In the late 1960s, in the throes of the student revolt, Holzkamp in Berlin called for a critical and emancipatory psychology, which was highly politicized at first, but then incorporated aspects of cultural psychology and Russian activity theory. Interestingly, these approaches were later taken up by the Society for Sociocultural Studies and the International Society for Cultural Research and Activity Theory, which merged to form the International Society for Cultural and Activity Research in 2002. Following a totally different tradition, Bischof developed a biologically based motivational model, which is also rather distinctive. The lifespan program which Baltes developed at the Max Planck

Institute in Berlin has had an international impact.

The DGPs (http://www.dgps.de) is the main organization for psychologists working in the academic sector. At present, it has 2,212 members. Membership prerequisites are a doctorate in psychology, two sponsors who are members, and at least two publications other than the dissertation. Associate membership is possible for persons who have a diploma in psychology or an equivalent degree in a related discipline and are involved in research projects or in practice relevant to psychological research. The DGPs has 15 divisions representing various specialties of psychology; divisional membership ranges from 31 to 348. The DGPs' quarterly journal, *Psychologische Rundschau* (*Psychological Review*), publishes information about the latest developments in academia as well as theoretical and empirical articles.

The largest and most influential organization for professional psychologists is the BDP (http://www.bdp-verband.org). It has 12 divisions focusing on different academic and professional matters. The Psychological Psychotherapists' Association is also under the auspices of the BDP. In addition, there are 16 regional groups (representing *Länder*, equivalent to states in the United States). Membership requires a diploma in psychology earned at a German university or an equivalent degree from abroad. After the structural reform of the BDP in April 2002, membership was extended to include, for example, persons who graduate with a diploma in an applied branch of psychology. Students can become extraordinary members and are organized under the Federal Association of German Psychology Students of the BDP. At present, the BDP has about 14,500 members, the number having declined noticeably from 17,000 at the turn of the century. This is partly due to the financial cost of having to become a member of the state chambers of psychological psychotherapists, which was mandated with the passage of the 1999 law regulating professional practice.

The BDP lobbies government authorities as well as social groups and seeks to increase public awareness about what psychology as scientific discipline and professional practice can contribute to society. It also cooperates with NGOs such as the Association of Free Professions in Germany and the Trade Union of Employed Workers. The BDP's monthly journal, *Report Psychologie*, reports on current developments regarding professional issues and relevant policies.

The DGPs and BDP cooperate at the level of the Federation of German Psychologists' Associations, a body in which these two organizations debate and decide on scientific and professional matters in a complementary manner. For example, in the domain of education and training, a joint commission was established. However, there is some tension between the two organizations as a result of the difference in social prestige accorded to academics versus practitioners. There is, however, some overlap in membership between these two organizations (327 of the DGPs' members also have membership in the BDP).

Various other organizations for psychologists exist that represent either specific fields of work (e.g., school psychologists, school teachers of psychology, and various therapeutic traditions) or different approaches to psychology (e.g., *Neue Gesellschaft für Psychologie* [*New Society for Psychology*], which espouses a critical–emancipatory approach to psychology).

Statistics on the number of psychologists in Germany tend to be fairly unreliable because they are not systematically and comprehensively collected. It is generally estimated that there are 40,000 and 45,000 psychologists in a population of about 82 million. Though not all students who graduate in psychology work in the field, the number of students awarded a diploma can serve as a rough guide to the growing number of psychologists in Germany. Based on data published by the Federal Office for Statistics, the number of students studying psychology has more than doubled in less than 30 years, rising from 13,333 in 1975 to 34,684 in 2001 (compared to about 80,000 medical students). Well over 2,000 students per year have been awarded a diploma in psychology from 1993 onward, the maximum being 2,798 in 1999.

In the civil service, a federal salaried-employee tariff prescribes and regulates what persons earn regardless of their specialization. The salary depends on factors such as age, marital status, and level of education, as well as job responsibilities. There are some legal disputes about the level at which psychological psychotherapists are to be paid; however, legal opinions generally are that they ought to receive the same salary as medical specialists if they are licensed, or that of medical doctors without specialization if they are not licensed. Salaries range from approximately 30,000 to 45,000 Euros per year. In the private sector, matters are not as clear because salaries depend on the specific tariff agreements effective in a particular field of work; in smaller agencies or institutes, these are not applicable. A therapeutic session costs about 80 Euros. Much higher salaries are possible in the private sector for consulting and self-employed psychologists, especially in coaching, personnel development, and counseling, a field of work in which many nonpsychologists are also active.

20.2 EDUCATION AND TRAINING

Most psychologists receive their education and training in Germany. However, it is no longer unusual for students to study abroad for a semester or two. Especially for those aspiring to careers in research and teaching at German universities, studying or working abroad, particularly in the United States, has become increasingly important. Interestingly, it is also becoming more attractive for foreign students to study in Germany, a trend that is expected to increase. Study in other European countries has also been supported by student exchange programs of Erasmus and Sokrates, a subgroup of EU research programs which fund projects that promote European cooperation and mobility in the educational sector.

The German educational system is tiered, under state (*Länder*) rather than federal jurisdiction, with admission to three types of secondary schools based on academic achievement. This tiered system extends into tertiary education, with universities being more prestigious than so-called "applied" universities (*Fachhochschulen*), where criteria for admission are less strict. Psychologists are predominantly educated at universities, which means that students must pass an exit examination (*Abitur*) at the academically most demanding type of secondary school (*Gymnasium*). This examination is not uniform and is administered after 12 to 13 years of schooling.

Since 1969, a central office for the allocation of places to study (*Zentralstelle für die Vergabe von Studienplätzen* [ZVS]) regulates admission to the psychology major at universities in order to cope with the large number of applicants. Admission is based largely on the average grade obtained on the *Abitur*. To major in psychology, top grades are required, equivalent to "A"s in the United States, and are as high as those for medicine, veterinary medicine, and pharmacy, disciplines that also restrict admission. Students can choose their universities; however, their final placement is in the hands of the ZVS. Only four universities select their own students on the basis of interviews. The popularity of psychology and difficulty in obtaining admission to the major are evident from the fact that fewer than 30% of those who apply are accepted.

Many different types of psychology departments exist. So-called *A* institutes at universities are responsible for teaching psychology as a major. *B* institutes teach psychology as subsidiary subject in other courses of study offered at these universities. *C* institutes are located within teacher-training institutes. *D* institutes are oriented toward medical psychology and were founded in the 1970s to teach medical psychology, which had become a compulsory subsidiary subject for medical students. Finally *E* institutes are departments of psychology that have no teaching obligations (e.g., Max Planck Institutes [MPIs]). The establishment of MPIs outside of universities increased the prestige of psychology in academic circles. At present, there are two MPIs for psychology in Munich (one for psychiatry, clinical psychology, and epidemiology and the second for psychological research), one in Leipzig (for neuropsycho-

logical research), and one in Berlin (for educational research).

The structure and organization of the institutes vary considerably. A few of the *A* institutes are separate departments. For the most part, psychology departments are units within larger umbrella departments that typically include philosophy or education; to a lesser extent they are linked to departments of social or natural sciences. This alignment is visible in the doctorates awarded in psychology at these departments as they differ with respect to the abbreviation added to the doctorate (i.e., *Dr.phil.*, *Dr.rer.soc.*, or *Dr.rer.nat.*—with *rerum sociologicae* and *rerum naturalium* signifying an umbrella department of either social or natural sciences).

Psychology as major can be studied at 45 universities (Lindner, 2003). Students qualify with the *Diplom*, a diploma equivalent to a master's degree, though most professors consider the diploma to be a slightly better qualification. Most of these universities offer psychology as a subsidiary subject in other courses of study as well, most often teacher training or educational science. The diploma is necessary to gain access to additional courses required for licensure in psychological psychotherapy or to pursue a doctorate. A doctoral recipient can continue his or her studies in order to obtain a habilitation, the qualification needed for an academic career in research and teaching.

Only one of the 15 private universities in Germany offers coursework in psychology. This is a B.A. program restricted to cognitive psychology. As an aside, few B.A. and M.A. programs exist in Germany today; these innovations are still being tested in terms of their marketability. The two military universities at Munich and Hamburg also offer courses in psychology, but only as subsidiary subjects. There is only one university specializing in distance learning (*Fernuniversität Hagen*). It provides a variety of possibilities for obtaining a degree; however, psychology is offered only as a subsidiary subject (i.e., ecological and business–organizational psychology, the psychology of social processes, and methodology) within courses leading to a master's degree (the *Magister*, not the M.A.).

Nine semesters are required to complete the full course of education in psychology. In reality, the average time taken to complete the major is longer, ranging from 10.9 to 14.9 semesters, according to the Center for Higher Education Development (2003). The major is divided into two phases: basic studies (four semesters, ending with a prediploma examination) and advanced studies (five semesters, usually prescribing an empirical rather than a theory-based thesis, and ending with the main diploma oral and written examinations). Basic studies have until now included general psychology, developmental psychology, differential–personality psychology, social psychology, and methodology (i.e., statistics and research design), as well as subsidiary subjects such as biology, physiology, and philosophy. Advanced studies include psychological diagnostics and intervention; evaluation and research methodology; clinical psychology and psychopathology, depth psychology and psychotherapy, education and school psychology, forensic psychology, industrial–organizational and work psychology, and social psychology, with a practicum added at an institution of one's choice. The breadth of subjects is a defining feature of the curriculum. Within this framework, students have few opportunities to specialize

(e.g., in environmental, ecological, or traffic psychology). By attending courses and either presenting papers, completing written assignments, or passing tests, students obtain credits which certify that they have completed the requirements in prescribed fields.

A general framework examination in psychology regulates the course of study offered by universities. The latest adaptation of these regulations was passed in November 2002 and will soon be implemented. The new framework gives greater opportunity for specialization by extending the range of applied subjects, rearranges some subjects from advanced to basic status, and assigns credit to courses so that international comparisons according to the European Credit Transfer System are possible. The framework examination is intended to promote comparability between degrees awarded throughout Europe and to encourage students to study and gain experience in different European countries.

A distinction between undergraduates and graduates is not customary in German universities. Until recently, there has not been a degree like the B.A. that distinguishes undergraduate from graduate students. Although there is a prediploma examination in psychology that allows one to distinguish between students in basic or advanced studies, this is not a degree and has no official standing in the marketplace.

Systematic courses leading to the doctorate are rare. Since awarding the title of doctor is left to the authority of the faculty, there are variations in the requirements across universities. Generally, an independent scientific investigation must be conducted and examinations in major and subsidiary subjects must be passed. As a rule, it takes 4–5 years to complete the doctorate.

The degrees awarded in 2001 provide a rough impression of the proportion of diploma graduates who continue their university education. According to the Federal Office of Statistics (2002; further information may be obtained by contacting the authors), the number of doctorates was 351 and the number of habilitations 45, compared to 2,691 diplomas in psychology overall. The ratio of doctorates to diplomas is fairly low (Scientific Council, 2002): In 2000, about 12% of psychology graduates continued their studies toward the doctorate. In comparison, 21% of all university graduates went on to earn a doctorate; in medicine, for example, about 80% received doctorates. Differences in the proportion of graduates from psychology versus those in other fields who earn doctorates reflect the fact that the doctorate is the qualifying degree in some disciplines and professions.

A variety of locally developed resources are available to support teaching. There are German textbooks, journals, handbooks, and encyclopedias covering the entire range of psychological specialties, as well as many psychometric tests. Publishers such as Hogrefe, Hans Huber, Beltz, and Deutscher Psychologen Verlag, which is affiliated with the BDP, publish psychological books and journals. Hogrefe, in particular, is internationally known. It has established a test center and publishes most of the psychological tests constructed and used in Germany. It has also developed a computer-based testing service containing over 250 psychodiagnostic tools. Translations of outstanding English textbooks were common in the 1960s and 1970s, but students are now expected to have a facility in English.

The Center for Psychology Information and Documentation (ZPID) assembles the German equivalent to PsycINFO (http://www.zpid.de). It compiles databases on psychological literature published in German-speaking countries, tests, audiovisual media, and Internet resources to meet the needs of scientists and practitioners.

All universities have homepages, but the extent to which the teaching staff post their material there or offer courses in this way varies; the number who do so is increasing rapidly, however (Batinic, 2000). Students have free Internet access from their universities' computer centers, and can apply for free email. They have begun creating their own homepages to publicize matters of interest to students.

The size of psychology departments varies considerably. Statistics differ depending on whether they, for example, include students taking psychology as a subsidiary course or only psychology majors. Judging from the number of applicants accepted as first-year students between 2000 and 2003 (ZVS, 2003), the largest psychology departments are in Hamburg, Berlin (Free University), Trier, and Bremen, with between 160 and 170 new students each year. These universities are followed closely by Bielefeld, Marburg, Bochum, Dresden, Giessen, Munich, and Münster, with between 120 and 130 new students annually. All of these universities have 11 or more professorships and a scientific staff of 15 to 44. The university in Leipzig and the Humboldt University in Berlin, both located in the former East Germany, can also be included among the departments with the largest number of professors. The ratio of students to teaching staff differs across departments, however. The number of tenured professors is also indicative; there are a total of 441 in all *A* institutes, ranging from 4 to 19 per department, with a median of 9 (Lindner, 2003).

Psychology departments at German universities have informal reputations as being outstanding in certain specialties. Whether this reputation is accurate is difficult to establish. There is no tradition of ranking universities or departments. One reason for this is the recent introduction of procedures to assess the quality of research and teaching. Apart from that, students, as noted, have few options in their choice of universities. In the 1990s, *Spiegel*, a well-known weekly magazine, began publishing university rankings based on a questionable methodology. Recently, the Center for Higher Education Development (CHE) undertook to put these rankings on a methodologically sound footing (http://www.dashochschul-ranking.de). They do not publish overall ranks, but rather indicate the quartile in which a university department falls on indicators such as facilities, third-party funding, number of publications, average time required to complete coursework, and students' and professors' assessment of the department. Depending on the criteria used, departments in the outstanding group differ. With regard to research indicators (i.e., publications, funding, and dissertations), the top 11 psychology departments in 2001 are, in alphabetical order: Berlin (Humboldt University), Bochum, Bremen, Dresden, Jena, Konstanz, Leipzig, Marburg, Regensburg, Trier, and Tübingen. It is worth noting that old and new psychology departments in the former East Germany are in the top group.

Studying in Germany is still free except for an administrative fee payable each semester for the official time stipulated to complete the course of study. Less affluent students can apply for state assistance under terms prescribed by federal law. This support is primarily available to persons with German passports who pursue higher education before the age of 30. In some cases, grants are given to foreigners, for example, to those applicants who have lived in Germany for several years, are refugees, or have been granted asylum. The amount depends on the income of the applicant's parents and their own household income; to date, the maximum monthly allocation is 585 Euros. Financial aid is awarded for 1 year, with support available throughout the period of study if eligibility criteria continue to be met and progress is made toward the completion of coursework. Half of the support is granted in the form of an interest-free state loan, repayable in about 4½ years after graduation. If studies are completed within the stipulated time and the examination results are excellent, the amount to be repaid is reduced. However, only about 15% of students obtain state support and most of them receive less than the full amount.

Grants and bursaries are also available from various foundations and organizations, especially for highly gifted students (e.g., *Studienstiftung des Deutschen Volkes* [German National Academic Foundation]). It is also possible to apply for special loans at education credit programs.

Due to limited public funding, debates about whether tuition fees should be introduced are increasing. The introduction of fees is also viewed as a way to reduce the time spent studying, a topic of growing concern because, in comparison to other countries, the average German student is about 28 years old when graduating. However, this fact may reflect in part socio-demographic factors; some students are already qualified in a different field before they pursue psychology, and many have a family, which forces them into part-time study.

In Germany, one differentiates between continuing education (*Fortbildung*) and further education (*Weiterbildung*). While *Fortbildung* serves to actualize and extend one's expert knowledge in a field, *Weiterbildung* implies acquiring knowledge and skills in a new field to obtain a special qualification. Although continuing education (*Fortbildung*) for psychologists is not generally regulated by law, some informal standards exist. The Academy for German Psychologists (DPA), affiliated with the BDP, offers many opportunities for continuing education. Credits for continuing education can be obtained by attending conferences or workshops. Several further-education curricula have been established in various specialties, particularly to assist psychologists in competing with other professional groups by publicizing their competencies through the certificates awarded. Other further-education programs have been instituted because of legal requirements (e.g., psychotherapy, traffic psychology) and these usually also stipulate the conditions for continuing education. Private institutions and associations also provide further-education courses.

In the former East Germany, further education, particularly in clinical psychology, tended to be more advanced than that in West Germany; for example, psychotherapists in the east had already achieved parity with physicians. Thus, the regulations instituted after reunification in 1990 from their point of view seemed like a step back.

Since the 1999 law on psychotherapy, licensure is mandatory for psychological psychotherapists who want to open a practice that is accredited within the health insurance industry. Consequently, further education courses qualify persons who have a diploma in psychology to become licensed psychological psychotherapists or child and youth psychotherapists, who are only allowed to work with clients up to 21 years of age (persons with degrees in educational science or special education can also obtain the latter license). These courses are available at several universities and accredited academies. The regulations specify a total of at least another 4,200 hr of training either full-time over 3 years or part-time over 5 years. Courses consist of theoretical and practical training (a 1-year clinical–psychiatric practicum and a 6-month psychosomatic or psychotherapeutic practicum in a physician's or psychotherapist's practice or at an institution funded by an insurance carrier). The status and training conditions vary in different states and clinics. There are few openings for practical training at psychiatric institutions and salaries are minimal or nonexistent during training, with no support provided by federal authorities. The law, however, recognizes psychological psychotherapy as a healing profession and gives psychotherapists insurance parity with physicians, provided they use approved therapeutic methods. At present, behavior therapy, psychoanalysis, and depth psychotherapy are the only interventions accepted by insurance companies, although client-centered approaches are likely to be added to this list. At the end of 1999, about 10,500 psychological psychotherapists and 1,500 child and youth psychotherapists as well as 9,000 medical psychotherapists were accredited (Bundesanstalt für Arbeit, 2001).

The modification of the German road traffic law in 1998 and the road traffic license act contain provisions that specify requirements for the qualifications and certification of psychologists working as consultants in this area. This has made further education programs necessary in this specialty. In fact, the law specifically mentions the traffic psychology division of the BDP and its responsibility to provide further education. Traffic psychology is a specialty that deals with a wide range of topics concerning road traffic ranging from issues of road and car safety, driving behavior, and accident patterns to interventions and counseling for traffic offenders. The BDP must determine that traffic psychologists are qualified and recertify them every 2 years if they can document having earned at least 16 hr of continuing-education credit. The minimum qualifications are a diploma in psychology and education and training in traffic psychology either at a university or through a further-education program sponsored by the BDP.

Regulations pertaining to certification and further education in forensic psychology were passed in 1995 by the Federation of German Psychological Associations. The purpose of this certification is to document the competencies of psychologists who offer their services to the legal system. Similarly, the Federation developed further-education curricula and certification for both organizational and clinical psychology. A further-education program for neuropsychology has also been developed in cooperation with the Society for Neuropsychology and the German Association for Neurology. At present, a further-education program is being designed for emergency psychology.

20.3 SCOPE OF PSYCHOLOGICAL PRACTICE

Apart from the laws and regulations governing psychotherapists and traffic psychologists, the titles of *Diplom-Psychologe* (psychologist with diploma), *Psychologischer Psychotherapeut* (psychological psychotherapist), and *Kinder-und Jugendpsychotherapeut* (child and youth psychotherapist) are protected by the German penal code. Furthermore, the law on nonmedical practitioners, dating back to 1939, regulates therapeutic activities by nonlicensed psychologists. In general, however, the statutes regulating the work of psychologists can vary depending on the specialty and state in which one is employed. The DGPs and BDP have jointly passed ethical guidelines that also constitute the rules of professional conduct for the BDP. They were agreed upon in 1999 and replace the previously separate guidelines of the two organizations. In 2002, largely initiated by the BDP, a DIN standard (the German equivalent of the International Organization for Standardization [ISO]) was passed, which stipulates the standards for aptitude testing. These ethical codes and laws do not address the context of culture or history within which psychology is practiced (e.g., assessment and therapy), although it is acknowledged that they should.

As mentioned, after World War II, mainstream German psychology began to follow mainstream Anglo-American psychology, adopting supposedly international standards without extensive critical debate concerning their validity and value. An indigenous psychology, such as those that emerged in Asia during the last decade, does not exist in Germany. Hence, the dominant conceptual perspectives, research methodologies, and intervention strategies in Germany tend to follow in the Western tradition. Numerous foreign tests have been imported and adapted to German norms, although there are many German psychometric instruments that meet international standards.

In a recent BDP survey of its members (Report Psychologie, 2002), 52% indicated that they were self-employed or consultants, 35% were salaried employees, 4% were civil servants, 3% were students, and 2% were pensioners. The remaining were either unemployed or enrolled in further-education programs. The main field of work is psychotherapy (37%), followed by counseling (19%), supervision and coaching (14%), industrial–organizational, market, and work psychology (10%), and training, health promotion, and environmental psychology as well as forensic psychology (between 3% and 4%). As staff members of universities and research institutes are usually not in the BDP, academic work was not sampled by this survey.

About 66% of respondents are licensed as psychological psychotherapists. This does not imply, however, that they work as psychological psychotherapists: 80% of the psychologists with supervision and coaching as their main field of work are licensed, 52% of the traffic psychologists, 34% of the school psychologists, and 15% of industrial–organizational and work psychologists. Conversely, only 86% of the 1,573 respondents who identified psychological psychotherapy as their main occupation possess a license. Behavior therapy is the most frequently used technique (43%), followed by depth psychotherapy (28%), client-centered counseling (12%), and systems approaches (12%). The remaining psychologists apply psychoanalytic or other techniques.

Psychologists in hospitals and clinics work mainly in departments of neurology, psychotherapy, and psychiatry. Increasingly, however, they work with chronically ill persons (e.g., cancer patients). Work conditions depend on the structure and organization of the institution. Apart from treating patients, their work entails cooperating with physicians, social workers, and other allied health professionals. Usually, they are given some autonomy to determine their job duties. In large clinics, psychologists are involved in diverse activities, mainly diagnostic assessment and psychotherapy, but also in training nursing staff, organizational management, and public relations. Their legal status has improved considerably since the enactment of the psychotherapy law; as noted, psychologists have parity with physicians if licensed.

There are various types of private practices in psychotherapy. These include practices that are licensed, registered, and accredited by the health insurance industry; those that are licensed, but not accredited (e.g., client-centered psychotherapists); and those with limited permission to perform psychotherapy under the law on non-medical practitioners (see above). Only those mentioned first have the possibility of being reimbursed by insurance companies.

In business and industry, psychologists perform a variety of tasks ranging from personnel selection and evaluation, ergonomics, and the prevention of accidents to consulting on organizational development and management. Psychologists employed by the federal railway's psychological service fulfill similar tasks, as do psychologists working for airlines. In addition, psychologists are involved in marketing and opinion surveys, but face competition from economists, education scientists, and graduates of media and communication fields. The Federal Employment Agency employs over 450 psychologists in its psychological services, primarily to carry out psychological assessment.

School psychologists are usually employed by the state, as part of the state supervisory school authority, which, among other things, is responsible for school inspections. This close connection can have an unfavorable influence on their working relations with schools. The statutes regulating their work vary, depending on the specific state. There are no precise statistics about the number of school psychologists per pupil.

According to information provided by the school psychology division of the BDP, the standing conference of state education ministers recommended in 1974 a ratio of one school psychologist for every 5,000 pupils; however, this is far from being the case. According to a 2001 survey by the education ministry of Saxony, the ratio was approximately one psychologist per 15,000 pupils for the country as a whole, ranging from about 1:8,000 to 1:20,000 per state. This situation is unacceptable to the BDP's division of school psychology. School psychologists provide individual counseling to parents, teachers, and pupils. They deal with issues such as learning disorders, achievement motivation, personal and relationship problems, and the special concerns of highly gifted pupils. They collaborate with teachers in pedagogical matters, mediate conflicts, coordinate services with other institutions, provide information on career planning, conduct psychological testing, and serve as official evaluators of school programs. They also provide group supervision for teachers and offer continuing education courses.

The psychological services of the armed forces employ approximately 170 psychologists and 300 technical assistants. Their work primarily involves applying aspects of clinical psychology, industrial–organizational and work psychology, and ergonomics, and encompasses diagnosis, counseling and therapy, teaching and training, and the development of methods for evaluating job performance. Apart from supporting the military leadership in management tasks, psychologists accompany the armed forces on foreign assignments. They are involved in preparatory training and provide support for soldiers in critical situations during and after their mission. In many units, psychologists provide services to soldiers' families.

Psychologists also work in the police force and penal system. These positions are usually under state jurisdiction. At present, about 140 psychologists are employed by state or federal police; their number per state varies from 1 to 28 (Schmalzl, 2003). Since the 1960s, the activities of police psychologists began to expand beyond education, which had been their main area since the 1920s. Education remains one of their main duties because training for certain positions within the police force demands a completion of selected courses in psychology. Another activity involves providing psychological services, such as personnel selection and development, counseling and casework, and support for police operations. The situation of police psychologists is not without problems; as members of an independent profession, officers are somewhat reluctant to concede that they need assistance from others outside of their profession and tend to distrust such advice. Psychology is usually housed in an administrative unit and, thus, lacks authority to give directives. Since the 1980s, the number of psychologists in the police has increased considerably and future prospects in this sector appear favorable.

Data on the work of psychologists in prisons are difficult to obtain. Often, psychologists are categorized with sociologists, educational scientists, or teachers. On an average, there are 0.71 such professionals per 100 inmates throughout Germany. Job duties include therapeutic interventions and the provision of expert testimony.

It is estimated that about 15% of all psychologists engage in research and teaching (Bundesanstalt für Arbeit, 2001). These are professorships and a few positions for scientific staff. Most scientific staff are untenured and work part-time. Most of these positions are at universities, which usually allocate a portion of their scientific staff positions for the purpose of qualifying young scientists. Of course, such jobs also become available through research projects funded by third parties, such as various private foundations, or the German Research Foundation which has a very rigorous reviewing process and is the most prestigious funding source. Various ministries also set aside money for applied research projects. The positions available at research centers outside of universities are even more limited (e.g., MPIs; Leibniz Institutes for basic and applied research). At both universities and research institutes, untenured staff are usually busy with dissertation or habilitation projects, while simultaneously teaching courses, supervising students' theses, and collaborating on research projects. The framework law on higher education stipulates that these staff can be employed on limited contracts for 6 years prior to receiving their doctorates and for another 6 years after that to qualify with a habilitation, which enables them to apply for tenured-track professorships at universities. The possibility of obtaining a professorship is small though, between 20 and 60 applications per opening are typical, depending on the specialty.

Universities and research institutes are governed by international standards. This pertains especially to publication standards. At times, one has the impression that the only valued contributions made by these psychologists are those published in English rather than German. For better or worse, the lingua franca of science is English. This puts speakers of languages other than English at a decided disadvantage: Not only must they write in a second language or pay for translations, but they also must publish in journals dominated by editors from a different country. This reality has led to heated debates in the DGPs. Nevertheless, the proportion of English publications by German-speaking psychologists has grown from about 6% in 1980 to 17% in 2000 (Krampen, Montada, & Shui, 2002). Publishing in English does not necessarily mean that the work is recognized by the international community. In addition to language, international networking is important. For instance, the *German Journal of Psychology* was founded in 1977 and published in English by the German Psychological Society under the auspices of the IUPsyS in order to infuse the Anglo-American market with German psychology, but was discontinued in 1994 because of low demand.

Statistics on shortage and surplus of psychologists in various work settings are hard to come by. Even when they exist, the categories used often mix psychologists with related occupational groups. However, compared to all those with academic degrees, the situation is relatively favorable for psychologists (Bundesanstalt für Arbeit, 2001). The number of unemployed psychologists (approximately 2,500) has decreased by about 23% from 1993 to 2001, as compared to 13% for persons with other academic degrees. However, the rate of unemployment for psychologists is slightly higher (5%) than that for other persons with a degree (3%). The number of job openings for psychologists has remained fairly stable in 2002 despite the recession, and can be viewed positively considering a decline of almost 22% in the number of job openings for persons with academic degrees (Unimagazin, 2003).

In psychology, most job openings are in the health sector, followed by those in social services, universities, research institutes, and to a lesser extent public agencies and consulting firms. Nearly half of these entail medical or therapeutic work, about 30% social work and support services, 10% education and training, 8% research, and 5% administration.

Since the 1999 law on psychotherapy, the number of health-sector jobs that require a license to practice has increased steadily, but so has the number of self-employed practitioners registering as unemployed. Within the health insurance industry, the possibility of establishing a practice is very limited. At present, this is mainly possible in rural areas or in the former East Germany.

Based on the responses of 1,630 West and 154 former East German psychologists to surveys conducted in 1990–1991 and 1991–1992, Schorr (1995) compared various parameters of their respective work settings. The results provide insight into how psychologists relate to nonpsychologists. Disregarding the specific differences between West and East, social workers, physicians, and nursing staff were the professionals with whom psychologists predominantly collaborated; they had relatively little contact with psychiatrists and academics from related disciplines. Respondents noted the greatest overlap in their job duties with physicians and social workers. The results also indicated that conflict with coworkers is relatively rare: only about 11% to 17% of respondents reported frequent conflict. Additional information on psychology as a profession will become available in 2003 (Schorr, in press), including chapters on education and training (Krampen, 2003; Krampen & Schorr, 2003).

20.4 FUTURE CHALLENGES AND PROSPECTS

Some of the ongoing and anticipated local developments in psychology have already been mentioned. For example, reforms in tertiary education, such as the creation of B.A. and M.A. programs, were initiated both to make the degrees awarded in Germany comparable to those awarded internationally and to respond to the challenges posed by the unification of Europe. At present, five psychology departments offer courses leading to a B.A., usually without an option to pursue an M.A. Another recent reform centers on the possible attainment of a diploma in psychology at four "applied" universities (*Fachhochschule*); however, this is limited for the moment to business–economic psychology, communication psychology, and rehabilitation psychology. It is unclear how B.A., M.A., or diploma holders will fare in the German marketplace.

There is no doubt that the importance and reputation of psychology as a science and profession in Germany have increased tremendously since its foundation. This is certainly due to its orientation as a natural science. In a recent survey (Pawlik, 2000) of 30 European psychologists, no one answered "yes" when asked whether it is possible to identify a specifically European psychology versus the dominant American psychology, and whether this would be desirable. It seems that within Europe, psychology as a science is regarded as universal and identified with the American approach, which rests on measurement, experimentation, prediction, and causality (i.e., the physical ideal), or on functionality and systems and their transformation (i.e., the biological ideal). It is highly likely that this situation will remain for the foreseeable future.

Future trends in psychology cannot be viewed in isolation. International developments in science and social changes brought about by globalization will have to be taken into account. These circumstances will surely lead to an intensification of international cooperation and exchange as well as an increase in contextually sensitive and multidisciplinary approaches to theory, research, and practice.

Through the Federation of German Psychological Associations, the DGPs and BDP have been long-standing members of the IUPsyS. Within the German-speaking area, international partnerships will continue to develop; they are already being fostered, for example, via the Association of German-speaking Professional Psychologists' Associations (ADP) established in 1998, whose member organizations include BDP as well as the Austrian, Liechtensteiner, and Swiss equivalents. The BDP is a member of the European Federation of Psychologists Associations (EFPA) and, in this capacity, participates in international partnerships. One of the EFPA's main activities of late has been the development of a European framework that stipulates minimum standards for training psychologists, with the possibility of introducing a European diploma in psychology. These European activities will not only increase but also lead to an enrichment of mainstream psychology. German psychology is regaining some influence in the international arena as an increasing number of psychologists are taking up positions in the United Kingdom and United States.

Many German academic psychologists are members of international or foreign psychological associations. It is worth mentioning some who are particularly active. Kurt Pawlik was president of the IUPsyS until recently. Rainer Silbereisen was president of the International Society for the Study of Behavioral Development (ISSBD). Michael Frese is currently president of the International Association of Applied Psychology (IAAP). Although these presidencies do not necessarily mean that there is a German influence on these associations, it may in fact be so. Frese, for example, follows an action–theory framework that might influence IAAP at a substantive level.

The growing integration of Europe will also influence the teaching, research, and practice of psychology in the workplace. The influence of sociopolitical forces on the kind of research questions posed in psychology is growing and thus increasing the significance of applied psychology. Sociopolitical issues such as family structures, aging populations, environmental problems, multicultural societies, mobility and multilingualism as well as increasing fundamentalism of all kinds are challenges that practitioners and policy makers are increasingly having to deal with. This decidedly influences the kind of questions that need answers and thus has consequences with respect to funding policies. How this will affect theory, research, and practice in detail and in the long run is difficult to predict, however.

Internationally, psychology has been diagnosed as a fragmented discipline. Not only is psychology fragmented, but attempts to address this phenomenon also are fragmented (see Fragmentation of Pyschology, 2000). The retreat into the laboratory, which went hand in hand with the experimental ideal of operationalizing and manipulating isolated variables, is, perhaps, the main reason for disciplinary fragmentation. This becomes especially evident when trying to apply psychology in different life contexts, such as in cultural psychology, ecological, or environmental psychology. Contextualization does not merely concern the application of psychological theories and methods *in vivo*, but calls for a comprehensive reorganization of the discipline. Some psychologists recommend establishing strong disciplinary coherence as well as a clear demarcation from other disciplines in terms of concepts, methods, and applications. Others advocate theoretical and methodical pluralism. Still others propose splitting psychology into independent branches like behavioral versus humanistic psychologies. Finally, there are proposals in Germany and other Western countries to abandon psychology altogether in favor of cognitive science and other biologically orientated paradigms, such as sociobiology, that would unify the diverse and segregated perspectives in psychology.

Contextualization leads to the issue of a multidisciplinary perspective in psychology, a perspective that probably will gain momentum. This may prompt a new, integrative human science that would include physiological (i.e., proximate) and phylogenetic (i.e., ultimate) causes as well as subjective and cultural meaning systems in its epistemological repertoire. This would not only provide the means for contextualization, but would also generate new questions and encourage a reorientation towards older, neglected issues. For example, the role of religion will become more prominent than is the case now, particularly as indigenous psychologies emerged in the 1990s that advocate culture-specific psychologies rooted in different theologies (e.g., Islam, tribal religions). This multidisciplinary process is likely to be supported by the forces that underlie globalization. Issues of application will trigger questions about the relation between facts and norms and between ethics and responsibilities. The subtle infusion of culturally based ideas may have a variety of effects, some positive and others negative, on both psychology and the general public. For certain, the impact of transforming psychology into a contextually sensitive and multidisciplinary science and profession will require monitoring changes to existing theory, research, and practice, and in public opinion.

In the course of these developments, psychology will have to take note of what has and is happening in other disciplines such as biology, philosophy, physics, and physiology, all of which have an impact both on substantive and methodological trends. This applies especially to developments in the philosophy of science because of their influential role in how psychology defines itself.

ACKNOWLEDGMENTS

We would like to thank our colleagues for providing us with information on various aspects of psychology in Germany: Günter Krampen and Inge Lindner, both on matters of education and training; Bernd Jötten, chair of the BDP division of school psychology; and Hans Schmalzl of the central psychological services of the Bavarian police; as well as colleagues in the offices of the DGPs and BDP.

REFERENCES

Batinic, B. (Ed.). (2000). *Internet für Psychologen* [Internet for psychologists]. Göttingen: Hogrefe & Huber.

Bühler, K. (1927). *Die Krise der Psychologie* [Crisis of psychology]. Jena, Germany: Fischer.

Bundesanstalt für Arbeit. (2001). *Arbeitsmark-Information für qualifizierte Fach- und führungskräfte: Psychologinnen und Psychologen* (compiled by Manfred Bausch) [Employment market information for qualified personnel: Psychologists]. Bonn: Zentralstelle für Arbeitsvermittlung der Bundesanstalt für Arbeit, Arbeitsmarktinformation.

Center for Higher Education Development. (2003). *Fächer, Einzelranking, Studiendauer* [Subjects, individual ranking, length of studies]. Retrieved October 30, 2003, from http://www.stern.de/CHE 4/CHE4?module=Hitliste&esb=32&idk_left=4&id k_right=

Fragmentation of psychology. (2000). [Special issue]. *Journal of Mind and Behavior, 21*(3).

Goebel, J. (1992). Germany. In V. S. Sexton & J. D. Hogan (Eds.), *International psychology: Views from around the world* (pp. 159–181). Lincoln, NE: University of Nebraska Press.

Kossakowski, A. (1992). German Democratic Republic. In V. S. Sexton & J. D. Hogan (Eds.), *International Psychology: Views from around the world* (pp. 149–158). Lincoln, NE: University of Nebraska Press.

Krampen, G. (2003). Forschung und Lehre in der psychologischen Nebenfachausbildung [Research and teaching in psychology as a subsidiary subject]. In A. Schorr (Ed.), *Psychologie als Profession: Das Handbuch*. Bern: Huber.

Krampen, G., Montada, L., & Shui, G. (2002). ZPID-Monitor 1999–2000 zur Internationalität der Psychologie aus dem deutschsprachigen Bereich: Ein Kurzbericht [Short report on ZPID-monitoring of the internationality of psychology in the German-speaking region]. *Psychologische Rundschau, 53,* 205–211.

Krampen, G., & Schorr, A. (2003). Forschung und Lehre in der psychologischen Hauptfachausbildung [Research and teaching in psychology as a major]. In A. Schorr (Ed.), *Psychologie als Profession: Das Handbuch*. Bern: Huber.

Lindner, I. (2003). *Studienführer Psychologie* [Study guide for psychology]. Würzburg: Lexika Verlag.

Lück, H. E. (2002). *Geschichte der Psychologie. Strömungen, Schulen, Entwicklungen* [History of psychology. Directions, schools, developments] (3rd ed.). Stuttgart: Kohlhammer.

Pawlik, K. (Ed.). (2000). Thirty tele-interviews on psychology in Europe [Special issue]. *European Psychologist, 5,* 90–161.

Report Psychologie (2002). Mitgliederbefragung 2001 [Survey of members]. *Report Psychologie, 27*(5–6), 310–313. [Compiled by Armin Traute.]

Schmalzl H. P. (2003, March). *Polizeipsychologie in Deutschland: Entwicklungslinien, Schwerpunkte, Perspektiven* [Police psychology: Developmental trends, priorities, perspectives]. Paper presented at the Conference Polizei and Psychologie, Frankfurt/am Main.

Schorr, A. (1995). German psychology after reunification. In A. Schorr & S. Saari (Eds.), *Psychology in Europe: Facts, figures, realities* (pp. 35–58). Göttingen: Hogrefe and Huber.

Schorr, A. (Ed.). (in press). *Psychologie als Profession: Das Handbuch* [Psychology as profession: A handbook]. Bern: Verlag Hans Huber.

Scientific Council. (2002). *Empfehlungen zur Doktorandenausbildung* [Recommendations on education and training of doctoral candidates]. Retrieved October 30, 2003, from http://www.wissenschaftsrat.de/texte/5459 -02.pdf

Statistisches Bundesamt. (Ed.). (2002). Bildung und Kultur: Studierende an Hochschulen [Culture and education: Students at universities]. Wintersemester 2000/2001, Fachserie 11, Reihe 4.1. Wiesbaden: Statistisches Bundesamt.

Unimagazin. (2003). Arbeitsmarkt Psychologen: Viele Möglichkeiten [Job situation for psychologists: Many opportunities]. *Unimagazin Perspektiven für Beruf und Arbeitsmarkt, 2,* 8–12.

Wertheimer, M. (1970). *A brief history of psychology.* New York: Holt, Rinehart, & Winston.

Wundt, W. (1873). *Grundzüge der physiologischen Psychologie* [Fundamentals of physiological psychology]. Leipzig: Engelmann.

Zentralle für die Verga be von Studienplätzen. (2003). *Studienangebot für den Studiengang Psychologie* [Courses on offer for the subject psychology]. Retrieved October 30, 2003, from http://www.zvs.de/Studienangebot/02_2/001/Psych.htm

IMPORTANT PUBLICATIONS*

Aebli, H. (1981). *Denken: Das Ordnen des Tuns* [Thinking: The organizing of doing] (Vols. 1 and 2). Stuttgart: Klett-Cotta.

Baltes, M. M., & Baltes, P. B. (Eds.). (1986). *The psychology of control and aging.* Hillsdale, NJ: Erlbaum.

Bischof, N. (1985). *Das Rätsel Ödipus: Die biologischen Wurzeln des Urkonflikts von Intimität und Autonomie* [The Oedipus mystery: The biological roots of the primal conflict of intimacy and autonomy]. Munich: Piper Verlag

Boesch, E. E. (1976). *Psychopathologie des Alltags: Zur Ökopsychologie des Handelns und seiner Störungen* [Psychopathology of everyday life: On the eco-psychology of action and its disruption]. Bern: Huber.

Dörner, D., Kreuzig, H., Reither, F., & Stäudel, T. (1983). *Lohausen: Vom Umgang mit Unbestimmtheit und Komplexität* [Lohausen: On handling indeterminacy and complexity]. Bern: Huber.

Graumann, C. F. (Ed.). (1978). *Ökologische Perspektiven in der Psychologie* [Ecological perspectives in psychology]. Bern: Huber.

Grawe, K., Donati, R., & Bernauer, F. (1994). *Psychotherapie im Wandel: Von der Konfession zur Profession* [Psychotherapy in transformation: From creed to profession] (4th ed.). Göttingen, Germany: Hogrefe & Huber.

Heckhausen, H. (1989). *Motivation und Handeln* [Motivation and action] (2nd ed.). Berlin: Springer-Verlag.

Herrmann, T. (1976). *Die Psychologie und ihre Forschungsprogramme* [Psychology and its research programs]. Göttingen: Hogrefe & Huber.

Hofstätter, P. R. (1972). *Psychologie: Das Fischer Lexikon* [Psychology: The Fischer dictionary] (rev. ed.). Frankfurt am Main: Fischer Taschenbuch Verlag.

Holzkamp, K. (1972). *Kritische Psychologie: Vorbereitende Arbeiten* [Critical psychology: Preparatory work]. Frankfurt am Main: Fischer Taschenbuch Verlag.

Kaminski, G. (Ed.). (1976). *Umweltpsychologie* [Environmental psychology]. Stuttgart: Klett.

Lienert, G. A. (1978). *Verteilungsfreie Methoden in der Biostatistik* [Distribution-free methods in biostatistics] (Vols. 1 and 2). Meisenheim am Glan, Germany: Verlag Anton Hain.

Pawlik, K. (1971). *Dimensionen des Verhaltens* [Dimensions of behavior] (2nd ed.). Bern: Huber.

Thomae, H. (1988). *Das Individuum und seine Welt: Eine Persönlichkeitstheorie* [The individual and its world: A personality theory] (2nd ed., rev.). Göttingen: Hogrefe & Huber.

---

* The task of compiling a list of the 15 most influential German publications on German psychology is impossible to fulfill without resorting to certain restrictions based in large measure on subjective choice. We decided to exclude all classical works by renowned German scholars such as Ebbinghaus, Freud, Wundt, and so forth, as well as journal articles or textbooks intended primarily for teaching. Proceeding from a list of influential German-speaking psychologists, one of the main criteria for inclusion was our assessment of the impact of their books on later theory development and research.

CHAPTER 21

Strengthening Psychology in Spain

José M. Prieto and Yolanda García-Rodríguez

José M. Prieto is a professor of personnel psychology at the Complutense University of Madrid. His interests include personnel assessment and training, as well as knowledge management within the context of new information technologies. He has been a member of the executive board of the Spanish Psychological Association (1980–1994) and the Spanish Federation of Psychological Associations (since 1995), secretary general of the International Association of Applied Psychology (1998–2006), and member of the European Network of Organizational Psychologists (since 1984). He served as president of the 23rd International Congress of Applied Psychology held in Madrid in 1994. He was also the Spanish delegate to the assembly of the International Union of Psychological Science and the European Federation of Psychologists Associations (EFPA), serving as secretary of the EFPA's committee on scientific affairs. José Prieto has also served as a member of the editorial board of 13 Spanish, European, and international psychology journals, and founded Revista de Psicología del Trabajo y de las Organizaciones.

Yolanda García-Rodríguez is a professor of work psychology with interests in occupational health and ergonomics. She supervises the doctoral program in intelligence, personality, and work psychology in the Department of Individual Differences and Work Psychology at the Complutense University of Madrid. García-Rodríguez has researched the links between unemployment and psychosocial disorders among unemployed people. Her current research focuses on the nexus between risk perception and accidents in the workplace. In 1993 she published a book on the psychological impact of unemployment. She also has published on learned helplessness and expectancy values.

21.1 OVERVIEW

Six historic events stand out as important in the advancement of scientific psychology in Spain during the 20th century. These turning points have precise dates: 1902, 1921, 1957, 1980, 1988, and 1998; each occurrence is summarized in Carpintero (1982, 1992, 1994), Prieto, Fernández Ballesteros, and Carpintero (1994), and Prieto and Berdullas (2003).

The first chair of experimental psychology was established in 1902 in the Faculty of Sciences at the University of Madrid. The incumbent was Luis Simarro (1851–1921), disciple of Jean Charcot. He combined associationism with histological experimentalism. In 1887, Simarro trained Santiago Ramon y Cajal (1852–1934) to produce Golgi preparations of the cerebral cortex; careful study of the functioning of neurons and synapses would earn Ramon y Cajal the Nobel Prize in Medicine in 1906. Ivan Pavlov obtained the Nobel Prize in Medicine in 1904, shortly after lecturing in Madrid on conditioned reflexes. These researchers and these dates mark a change of direction from rational psychology toward scientific psychology in Spain (Carpintero, 1994). This period may be considered the first milestone; Spanish psychology grew out of what is now known as neuroscience.

Leading figures in applied psychology included Gonzalo Rodríguez-Lafora (1886–1971) in Madrid and Emilio Mira-López (1896–1964) in Barcelona; both were psychiatrists. Rodríguez-Lafora studied in Germany under Emil Kraepelin and Alois Alzheimer, and his research focused on the assessment and treatment of mentally impaired children as well as senile age dementia. Mira-Lopez studied vocational guidance and personnel assessment methods and developed psychological tests using electromechanical apparatus and drawings of patterns.

The 2nd International Congress of Psychotechnics was held in Barcelona in 1921, and the traffic safety research presented at this conference established traffic regulations and standards for Barcelona. This congress was the second milestone in the history of Spanish psychology. The focal point for this period was "psychotechnics," a classic expression in European psychology introduced in 1903 by William Stern to distinguish between psychotherapy (the assessment and treatment of abnormal behavior) and psychotechnics (the assessment and treatment of normal behavior). Edouard Claparède highlighted this expression by creating the International Association of Psychotechnics in 1920, known since the 1950s as the International Association of Applied Psychology.

The Spanish Civil War (1936–1939) interrupted these developments and the large majority of psychologists went into exile. Francisco Franco's regime (1939–1975) considered psychological research and intervention too progressive. Many Spanish psychologists moved to Latin America; in Spain, this resulted in (a) reintroduction of rational psychology under scholasticism as a section in Faculties of Philosophy, and (b) a gap between cohorts of psychologists trained before 1930s and those trained after 1970. In the United States, Clark Hull chaired a subcommittee of Psychologists to Aid Spanish Democracy that included, among others, Gordon Allport, Kurt Lewin, and Edward Tolman (Finison, 1977). José Germain (1897–1986) studied with Edward Claparède at the Rousseau Institute in Geneva and with Wolfgang Köhler at the Institute of Psychology in Berlin's Humboldt University. He became the contact person in Spain sometime after the Spanish Civil War for leading scholars from abroad.

In 1946 he created the *Revista de Psicología General y Aplicada* (*Journal of General and Applied Psychology*); in 1948, he was appointed director of the Department of Experimental Psychology at the National Council of Scientific Research, and in 1952, he forged the Spanish Psychological Society (http://fs-morente.filos.ucm.es/publicaciones/Iberpsicologia/index.htm). He was a founding member of the International Union of Psychological Sciences. Germain is considered the patriarch of contemporary psychology in Spain and his work linked the interests of psychiatrists and psychologists during the 1950s to 1970s.

Mariano Yela (1921–1994) studied psychology at the University of Chicago under Louis Thurstone and Carl Rogers. In 1957, he attained a chair in psychology at the University of Madrid, and for several years was part-time visiting professor in the Department of Psychology at the University of Louvain. He introduced multivariate psychology in the study of intelligence and verbal behavior. José Luis Pinillos (1919–) completed his training at the University of Bonn and at Maudsley Hospital in London with Hans J. Eysenck, and became chair of psychology at the University of Valencia in 1961. His research focused on personality and social psychology as well as the psychology of consciousness, and his book *Principles of Psychology* (1976) has influenced thousands of students. Miguel Siguán (1918–) furthered his studies at the Tavistock Institute in London and researched the psychological aspects of human relations in work settings. In 1962, he obtained the chair of psychology at the University of Barcelona and proceeded to study industrial relations as well as education and language, specializing in bilingualism and the role of multilingualism in Spanish culture. Yela, Pinillos, and Siguan are considered the masterminds behind the evolution of scientific psychology in Spain during the 1970s. This third milestone is extremely significant because the discipline then became the academic home for psychologists trained in different European and American universities.

The fourth milestone occurred in 1980. Two terms capture the essence of this period: *facultad* and *colegio*. In Spain (and in many European universities) the term *facultad* means an organizational and policy-making cluster of academic departments with a similar knowledge–expertise base that forms a unit within a university's administrative structure. The first faculty of psychology was created in 1980 at the Complutense University of Madrid; it meant that, in formal terms, the dean of psychology was first among equals in the governing body of the university. Gradually, in each university one or several departments of psychology lobbied to achieve the status of a faculty, and by 2002, there were 17. During the 1990s, a national Conference of Psychology Deans started to meet, at least twice yearly, to share information and deal with administrative and policy-making issues; this group also served as a think tank for Spanish psychology.

Also in 1980, the Spanish Psychological Association (SPA), known as Colegio Oficial de Psicólogos (http://www.cop.es/), was founded. In Spain, the term *colegio* means a self-governing body of a profession in which higher education is a prerequisite. Psychology obtained the status of *colegio* through a law passed by the Spanish Parliament and backed by the Spanish king in 1979. The status of *colegio* means that national or regional governments must contact the Council of *Colegios* (national level) or the regional *colegio* regarding subjects related to the profession. A *colegio* is not a trade union and does not deal with salary issues. Enrollment is obligatory and a university degree, in this case in psychology, is a requisite. The main purpose of a *colegio* is to prevent unqualified people from joining the profession.

Thus, 1980 was the fourth milestone because it led to important consequences for psychology since (a) as a scientific discipline, the status of *facultad* secured the highest recognition within the university system, and (b), as an applied discipline, the status of *colegio* warranted the highest recognition within the profession for university graduates. A climate of conviviality and cooperation prevails among principals of both institutions.

In 1988, the National Council of Universities created a task force to evaluate existing programs that train students in each of the 10 faculties of psychology already established. The purpose was to design an obligatory curriculum to be used by each faculty. The members included five full professors and a delegate appointed by the SPA. They were requested to focus on (a) models of psychology training in European and American universities, (b) contemporary topics covered in psychology textbooks, and (c) goals, needs, and interests shared by skilled researchers and practitioners actively engaged in traditional specialties of psychology. They generated (a) a new and unique predoctoral degree, known as *Licenciado en Psicología*, requiring a minimum of 300 credits (1 credit = 10 hr), and (b) a set of 13 mandatory subjects required in any curriculum acceptable for a university degree in psychology and for registered professional

practice. This was the fifth milestone because it resolved a long controversy within the international arena about the adequacy of a distinctive and unique degree in psychology (for instance, the master's in psychology) versus as many degrees as there are specialties (for instance, a master's in clinical psychology, industrial psychology, and so on).

The sixth milestone has a precise date: November 20, 1998. The Spanish Ministry of Health enacted a law creating the academic qualifications for a psychologist specializing in clinical psychology. This law provided psychologists with the right to conduct psychological diagnosis, assessment, and treatment. Only university graduates with an academic qualification in psychology are entitled to participate in clinical psychology training programs. A national committee of this specialty was created, and leading figures in departments of clinical psychology and the SPA were appointed. This committee produces syllabi for training and professional examinations, establishes vacancies available each year in the public health system, regulates the qualification and credential system, and audits centers and units regarding quality of services and facilities when necessary. In 2002, after 4 years of legal wrangling, the Spanish Supreme Court ruled on four separate appeals from the Spanish Council of Medicine and several national psychiatric associations against the government's decision to give clinical psychology the same status as psychiatry in the catalogue of specialties within the public health system. This decree and the Supreme Court ruling constitute the sixth milestone because it marked the establishment of clinical psychology in public and private settings.

During the 1950s to 1970s, the number of psychologists in Spain was small because psychology was organized as a postgraduate program exclusively for university graduates. The Graduate School of Psychology and Psychotechnics was created in 1953 at the University of Madrid, and in 1964 at the University of Barcelona. These programs had tremendous influence because many of their graduate students attained management and decision-making posts in a large number of public and private organizations around the country. These senior graduates recruited a younger cohort of graduates in psychology who took the baton from them during the 1970s and 1980s.

During the 1980s and 1990s, the status of *facultad* and *colegio* made it possible to estimate accurately the number of psychologists in Spain, differentiating university graduates in psychology (*facultad*) and registered psychologists (*colegio*). Based on data from the National Institute of Statistics and the Ministry of Education and Culture, the average number of graduates was 2,500 in 1982–1983; 5,100 in 1992–1993; and 6,200 in 2001–2002. After 1999–2000 there seems to be a significant difference between the number of students enrolled in psychology (25% males, 75% females) and the number of students who obtained the university degree in psychology (20% males, 80% females). Thus, males are underrepresented and females overrepresented when they complete their studies.

The number of registered psychologists in the SPA increased very rapidly: about 2,300 in 1980s when the registry was first established; 19,700 in 1989; 28,600 in 1998; and 32,100 in 2002. About three out of four registered psychologists are female;

however, this ratio becomes evenly balanced among scholars, work and organizational psychologists, and sport psychologists. By 2000, the geographic dispersion of registered psychologists reflected the following percentages in cities: where the population was one million or more (19%), between half a million and a million (14%), between 100,000 and 500,000 (28%), between 50,000 and 100,000 (7%), and below 50,000 (32%) (Santolaya, Berdullas, & Fernández, 2001).

Quintanilla and Diaz (1994) reported that the unemployment rate among registered psychologists was 11%, a level below the unemployment rate for the general population (17%) and for university graduates (14%). About 43% of this sample worked full-time as psychologists and 20% part-time; the rest carried out activities indirectly related to their university degree—for instance, working as teachers or civil servants. About 30% of members had a monthly salary more than twice the living wage. About 57% of males obtained wages over 2.8 times the living wage, whereas 34% of females earned less than 1.5 times the living wage. Males worked more hours per week than females. Work and organizational psychologists spent more time on the job and traveling, and they earned the highest average salary: 3.3 times the living wage. The analysis of income taxes showed significant differences in tax liabilities according to gender. Female psychologists charged lower fees per hour and carried out more part-time activities as psychologists than males. About 6% of males and 14% of females had a part-time employment contract, whereas 88% of males and 84% of females had full-time employment.

21.2 EDUCATION
AND TRAINING

An indepth reform of the university system was launched by the Spanish Parliament in 1983; it lasted until 2001 when the governing party enacted a new law. In 2001, the parliament passed a law to improve the quality of the general education system.

At the national level, psychology as a discipline remains structured around six common core areas of scientific knowledge and expertise: (a) developmental and educational psychology, (b) the methodology of behavioral science, (c) personality, psychological assessment, and treatment, (d) psychobiology, (e) psychology of basic and cognitive processes, and (f) social psychology.

Table 21.1 lists the number of tenured posts among professors and lecturers in each common core area of psychology as of 2003. The largest area is developmental and educational psychology, and the smallest is psychobiology. The largest categories are, in order, professor and full professor or chair, with the ratio between these two categories at 3:1 for all academics in Spain. However, the ratio in psychology ranges from 3:1 for developmental psychology to 13:1 for psychobiology, with a modal ratio of 4:1. The ratio of 13:1 in psychobiology is the consequence of strong internal conflicts between scholars devoting themselves to animal research in laboratories versus neuropsychological studies of humans in hospitals, with a consequent deadlock in promotions.

In Spain, there is a distinction between faculties and schools. A Ph.D. degree is obligatory for chairs and professors because they work mainly with students enrolled in master's and doctoral programs. The Ph.D. is not obligatory for chair lecturers or assistant lecturers in schools that grant only the bachelor's degree, which is not the case in faculties. Among lecturers, a Ph.D. is highly recommended but not obligatory. The largest number of chair and associate lecturer positions is in the area of developmental and educational psychology; this is because they teach psychology in the school for teachers, nurses, occupational therapists, speech therapists, or social workers. There has been an increase of 87% in total number of tenured scholars in 1990 (896) as compared to 2003 (1,679) (Prieto, 1992). This is an unobtrusive measure of the evolution of stable employment for academic psychologists.

During the mid-1980s, the national council that regulates university affairs included psychology in the catalogue of social and legal sciences; however, in some universities, psychology is part of the health sciences. Historically, psychology was associated with the humanities and, for years, its inclusion in the catalogue of experimental sciences remained an unfulfilled aspiration.

From 1983–2002, the following procedure was used in promoting candidates to tenured posts in the university. Each university announced vacancies as they became available, and candidates with a Ph.D. had the right to submit their applications and obtain the support of the department. An ad hoc committee of five members, two of them members of the local university, evaluated (a) the credentials and publications of each candidate, (b) a written report on the state of the specialty and a profile of the vacant post, and (c) a lecture on an unpublished study. A minimum of three positive votes out of five was required for a faculty member to become tenured in each category.

TABLE 21.1

Academic Structure of Spanish Psychology Organized by Areas of Expertise

| | Categories among Tenured Professors | | | | |
| | Faculty | | School | | |
Area of Expertise	Chair	Professor	Chair	Lecturer	Total
Developmental and educational psychology	57	198	73	168	496
Methodology of behavioral sciences	22	164	0	1	187
Personality, psychological assessment, and treatment	44	255	8	22	329
Psychobiology	10	125	0	0	135
Psychology of basic and cognitive processes	51	220	3	13	287
Social psychology	45	166	16	24	251
Total	229	1,128	100	228	1,679

Note. Faculty: Ph.D. obligatory, mostly higher education for the master's degree in psychology; faculty chair: catedrático de Universidad; faculty professor: profesor titular; school: Ph.D. non-obligatory, mostly schools for bachelor's degree in many disciplines; school chair: catedrático escuela universitaria; school lecturer: profesor escuela universitaria.

Each phase of the evaluation was open to professors and graduate students so as to generate favorable publicity and enhance the transparency of the process; however, the outcome has been endogamy, a pervasive tendency not to fill tenured posts from outside an institution. Soler (2001) examined European data regarding the percentage of university professors and lecturers in ecology and zoology employed and trained at the same university: Spain ranked second (88%) after Portugal (91%). Navarro and Rivero (2001) examined whether the address of a scientist's first publication coincided with his or her current address as a faculty member in science departments: Only 5% of scholars in Spain had published their first paper while working in another institution (vs. 93% in the United States). The situation is somewhat different for Spanish psychology as a consequence of the fact that in the 1960s and early 1970s, master's or doctoral programs existed only at the Universities of Madrid or Barcelona. Thus, the large majority of scholars who obtained a tenured post at other Spanish universities during the late 1970s and 1980s had to move to another campus to forge new departments or research units.

A new procedure was launched after the 2001 legal reforms, but its implementation began in mid-2003. The evaluating committee includes seven members, all allocated randomly at the national level. So, the number of candidates is rather large and allows robust comparisons vis-à-vis publications as well as teaching and research activities in definite fields of expertise. The evaluation procedure goes on for several weeks.

The National Council of Universities announces vacancies and sets the total number of openings countrywide. Potential candidates, either Spanish or European Union (EU) citizens, submit applications. A national committee of seven members, all appointed by drawing lots, evaluates the expertise and scholarship of each candidate. Those who succeed receive a credential of capability (*habilitación*) to lecture and conduct research in higher education. Only those who receive the credential may apply for the vacant post, and the university may accept or reject the appointment.

As for nontenured posts, 1,265 Fellows applied for renewal of their nonpermanent employment in Spanish universities in 2003, with 31% considered unsuitable by the Quality and Certification National Agency after an analysis of their teaching and research records. This means that two out of three obtained a new contract because their contribution was considered of high quality.

The fifth milestone identified in the previous section affected not only the university degree, but also the curricula for any university program, including psychology. Table 21.2 presents the mandatory subject matter in any core curriculum for a university degree in psychology.

After the 1983 legislation, between 300 and 390 credit hours (i.e., between 4 and 5 years) represented the academic load required to obtain a master's degree in psychology. Normally, this training occurs after high school when students are about 18 years old. The contents and credits of

Table 21.2 depict about 40–45% of the range of academic activities carried out at each university. Each faculty of psychology has been quite autonomous in defining specific courses during the first cycle and in setting the number of remaining credits required for specialization during the second cycle. Each cycle involves at least a 2-year academic period. During the second cycle, students have autonomy in individualizing compulsory and optional courses. By 1999, the National Council of Universities recommended fixing the number of credits for a program at around 300 and reappraising academic demands to make it possible to attain a university degree in 4 years. By 2002, psychology programs required from 300–330 credits before a degree was awarded.

New settings were targeted for 2003 by the Spanish government as a consequence of the Sorbonne Declaration in May 1998 and the Bologna Declaration in June 1999 on the European opportunities for Higher Education. These key documents are supported by European Ministers of Education from 29 signatory countries and seek to reform higher education in each country so as to arrive at an overall European convergence. The first outcome has been the European Credits Transfer System (ECTS) to facilitate free movement of university students. There is a long tradition in Europe of "wandering" students. The ECTS has activated the European Credit as the basic appraisal unit for any full-time university student. Each European Credit is defined as a minimum of 25 hr and a maximum of 30 hr of in-class and out-of-class activities under the supervision of a professor, as well as time devoted to study. The ECTS prescribes 30 credits per semester as a standard workload. Discussions and deliberations,

TABLE 21.2

Mandatory Subjects for a University Degree in Psychology in Spain

Subject Domain in the 1st Cycle	Credit	Subject Domain in the 2nd Cycle	Credit
Psychological assessment Basic principles, data-collection techniques, psychological tests	6	*Practicum* An integrated set of psychological practices and activities that must be completed in university centers or other organizations where students are placed. Students should become acquainted with problems and applications in psychological practice. Practicum might be partially or totally related to research programs by those promoted by their university. Tutors will supervise and evaluate practicum	9
History of psychology Psychological theories and systems, institutional and deontological aspects	5	*Psychopathology and psychological treatment* Pathological and psychological processes, abnormal psychology, and intervention techniques	9
Research methods Observation methods, experiments, surveys, descriptive and inferential statistics, psychological measures, qualitative approaches	16	*Educational psychology* School learning and instruction, contents and variables in school learning, the educational relationship, school and educational psychology	9
Basic psychological processes Learning and conditioning, attention, memory, motivation and emotion	19	*Psychology of groups and organizations* Group structures, processes and relationships; psychological approaches to organizations, including types of organizations and strategic action in groups and organizations	9
Psychobiology Genetics and evolutionary principles, fundamentals of neuroscience, physiological psychology, ethology	16	*Psychology of thought and language* Reasoning mechanisms and problem solving, productive thinking, verbal expression and comprehension, thought and language	9

TABLE 21.2 Continued

Developmental psychology	11	*Observations*
Developmental mechanisms, features, and stages; development of differentiated psychological processes		The overall ratio of practical exercises to theories will be at least 2:5 of the total academic load. For each core subject, the ratio between training in skills and theory should be 1:3 of noted credits. For instance, 3 credits of practical exercises and 6 credits of theory make a core subject of 9 credits
Personality	8	
Personality and individual differences, theoretical approaches, empirical dimensions, contemporary issues in personality research		
Social psychology	9	
Psychosociological theories, basic psychosocial processes, social attitudes, collective behavior, environment and behavior		

Note. 1 credit = 10 hr of class.

held from 2000 to 2003 under the umbrella of EFPA, anchored the standard European Credit in psychology at 25 hr, which entails 750 hr per semester. Further details regarding higher education standards for undergraduates in psychology at the European level can be explored at http://www.europsych.org/.

In 2003, taking into consideration new standards in higher education within the EU, the Spanish Conference of Psychology Deans pressed for 240 credits to obtain a university degree in psychology plus 120 credits to obtain a master's degree in psychology. There was a consensus supporting clinical psychology, educational psychology, and work and organizational psychology as cardinal master's programs at the national level while allowing for additional master's degrees at the local level.

Military psychology follows a similar scheme: A predoctoral degree in psychology obtained at a university is a requisite plus a diploma in military psychology

obtained through supervised training. In 1999, the Spanish Parliament enacted a law regulating staff arrangements and occupational profiles, and psychologists were included as members of the military health brigade with the same status and promotion opportunities available to other health staff.

Regarding doctoral programs, the Spanish government enacted a reform in 1998 that established standardized criteria, procedures, and certificates for all universities (García-Rodriguez, 2003). There are three types of programs: those backed by only one department, by several departments in the same university, or by several departments in different universities. A fourth modality is now in progress: programs backed by different departments in different states of the EU. Each program includes a didactic and a research component. The didactic period requires 20 credits (i.e., 200 hr of attendance at seminars) and 12 credits of participation in a research project; both periods are under the instruction or supervision of a professor. A few seminars focus on methodological issues, but the majority hinge on theoretical issues. These two periods last a minimum of 2 years, and afterwards doctoral students undertake their dissertation project that takes about 2–3 years to complete. A committee of five professors evaluates doctoral dissertations which are almost always written in the Spanish, Catalan, or Basque languages. Because the language of dissertations is not English, the research appears in a somewhat provincial rather than EU framework. The department, from the outset, appoints a tutor with a doctoral degree; often the tutor and dissertation director are the same.

Until the summer of 2002, entrance to a university in Spain was based on an essay examination passed by 80% of high-school students. This national procedure was supervised by an ad hoc committee that built a unique set of exercises and grading system for every student in the country, as well as a list of students passing the test. It permitted the free movement of students in search of openings at Spanish universities. However, by the summer of 2003, following the 2001 law, each university had complete autonomy in fixing procedures and admission quotas.

Entrance to Ph.D. programs is not especially competitive; about 80% of applicants are accepted, and top marks are not a requisite. By contrast, dropouts among undergraduates are above 50%, and about 30% require an extra year to complete their coursework and obtain a university degree. For instance, data from the academic year 1999–2000 show that the total number of registered students in psychology was 60,654, but only 6,248 obtained their degree (10%).

In a similar vein, only 10% of doctoral students complete their dissertation within 4–5 years after their enrollment, or 2 years after seminars and research projects end. About 70% never submit a final version of their dissertation. Under former guidelines, there was a deadline for completion of the dissertation, but this no longer exists.

In the academic year 2000–2001, psychology ranked third in total number of students (with 58,719 students enrolled throughout Spain) after law (155,359) and economics and business administration (145,854). There are 48 state universities and 18 private universities, but only 10% of psychology students matriculate into private universities. Two thirds of higher education costs at state universities are subsidized by national or regional budgets. Furthermore, about two out of three university students reside at their parents' home while completing a degree. Higher education is considered a social right for students residing in any city where a university is located.

The following is a list of the top 10 state universities that train most of the psychology students in Spain, ordered by the number of new openings in the 2002–2003 academic year and the cut-off admission mark (ranging from a minimum of 1 to a maximum of 10 points). The Open University, known as National University for Distance Education, has no limits to the number of annual openings.

1. Complutense University of Madrid: 740 openings and 5.9 as cut-off
2. University of Barcelona: 575 openings and 5.96 as cut-off
3. University of Valencia: 500 openings and 6.06 as cut-off
4. Autonomous University of Madrid: 445 openings and 5.88 as cut-off

5. Autonomous University of Barcelona: 400 openings and 5.98 as cut-off
6. University of Sevilla: 310 openings and 6.13 as cut-off
7. University of Granada: 300 openings and 5.64 as cut-off
8. University of the Basque Country: 300 openings and 5.00 as cut-off
9. Santiago de Compostela University: 300 openings and 5.7 as cut-off
10. University of Malaga: 285 openings and 5.38 as cut-off

The percentage of multidisciplinary research projects supported by state universities between 2000 and 2002 included 33% under health sciences, 51% under technology, and 78% under humanities and social sciences. In the same period, private universities supported only 1% under humanities and social sciences, 1% under health sciences, and 0% under technology. These data suggest that private universities in Spain do not support research.

Psychology is not included as a specific research discipline in the catalogue endorsed by the Council of Advanced Scientific Research in Spain that supports 40% of research done under technology, 32% under health sciences, and 18% under humanities and social sciences. It means that researchers in psychology are conspicuously absent from this community of advanced researchers. This is the consequence of the fourth milestone, mentioned earlier: Jobs ensuring stability increased for professors in the 1970s and 1980s in new departments of psychology. By 2003, this path was closed for advanced researchers in psychology.

Teaching techniques are related to the number of students and longevity of a given faculty of psychology. Three methods prevail: expository, directive, and discovery based.

- Expository methods such as lectures and talks, with or without group participation, as well as demonstrations prevail in large classes.
- Directive methods such as buzz groups, debates, field trips, group tasks, questions-and-answer sessions, and role-playing are customary when classes are small.
- Discovery methods, such as case studies, games, simulations, and Web-based training are used when the focal point is self-directed or experiential learning, mainly in applied psychology specialties and Ph.D. programs.

Some faculties of psychology that date from the 1970s accumulated old equipment used in the past in laboratory research and years later for classroom demonstrations. Audiovisual aids were standard in classrooms during the 1990s, but LCD projectors connected to online computers in the classroom are the norm in 2003. Spanish and English books and journals on psychology are more common than those published in other languages such as French or German. Russian books on some subjects are also available as a consequence of translations made in Cuba or Moscow. For instance, several books of Alexander Luria were translated first into Spanish and only later into English; this was also the case with books written in French by Jean Piaget and in German by Sigmund Freud.

The Complutense University in Madrid hosts the largest library on psychology and has stockpiled books and journals on psychology since the early 1900s. These are mainly in English, French, German, and

Spanish. In a similar vein, the SPA publishes a CD-ROM every year known as *Psicodoc* that includes bibliographic references since 1975 on psychological literature produced in Spanish, both in Latin American countries, the United States, and Spain. The entire database is available online at http://psicodoc.idbaratz.com/. The Website interface is in Spanish.

21.3 SCOPE OF PSYCHOLOGICAL PRACTICE

The fourth milestone described earlier sets the background for understanding how applied psychology gained prominence in Spain during the 1980s and 1990s. The SPA grew as the institutional nucleus. It is organized at the national level and ruled by the National Council in which each regional branch has a seat. Only registered members of the SPA may legally use the term "psychologist." It is a professional title protected by a law of the Spanish Parliament enacted in 1979. Those who are not registered members of the SPA but have a university degree in psychology may have sanctions brought against them by the SPA if they use the term *psychologist* professionally.

The four main aims of SPA are (a) organizing professional practice in each specialty, (b) maintaining a code of ethics and deontological rules, (c) protecting professional interests, and (d) representing the profession in various institutional settings. The basic requisite to become registered is the predoctoral degree in psychology known as *Licenciado in Psicologia*, and application to the executive board. Holders of a doctorate in psychology may become registered as

practitioners only if they have this degree; if not, they may apply to be registered as nonpractitioner members. Registration is obligatory except for public servants when they act on behalf of the administration. Professional practice is based on independent service to the customer and community, and maintaining patient confidentiality is obligatory. Continuous training is required and emphasizes, for example, how to distinguish working hypotheses from decisive judgments in psychological report writing. Based on scientific standards, psychologists must make public their expertise within the community of practitioners and contribute to congresses and publications.

A few versions of the SPA ethics code were drafted between 1987 and 1993. An online version of the current code is available in English at http://www.cop.es/English/docs/code.htm and in Spanish at http://www.cop.es/vernumero.asp?id=7. The principal authors of the Spanish code contributed as coauthors to the 1995 ethics code of the EFPA, also available online at http://www.efpa.be/Ethics/ethicspagina.htm. It addresses classical issues such as (a) professional competence and qualifications, (b) relationships with other professions, (c) relationships with clients, (d) restrictions in psychological research, (e) privacy rights regarding information gathering and reporting, (f) restrictions to advertising psychological services, (g) fees and honoraria, (h) adjudication of complaints, and (i) guidelines for forming regional national ethics commissions. Some articles express psychology's reaction to the dreadful events that occurred during the Spanish Civil War and the Franco dictatorship. For instance, Article 7 rejects the involvement of psychologists in torture or degrading practices during armed conflicts, civil wars, revolutionary movements, and terrorism. Article 8 states unambiguously that every psychologist must inform the SPA about any violation of human rights, maltreatment, or degrading conditions of imprisonment of any person that they discover during the exercise of their profession.

A National Deontological Committee was created in 1994, and soon afterwards each regional branch of the SPA created a committee committed to analyze deontological complaints. Members are appointed to 4-year terms.

Three different studies have addressed the professional activities of SPA members. In 1990, Diaz and Quintanilla (1992) supervised a series of face-to-face interviews based on a survey administered to a randomized sample of 606 members of the SPA; error estimate was 4%. In 1998, a survey designed to analyze professional activities was mailed to a nonrandom sample of SPA members: 6,765 or 25% responded (Santolaya et al., 2001). The executive board of the SPA also instigated an exchange of views among leaders of each division and the outcome was a book that summarizes the main findings and trends for each professional specialty (Colegio Oficial de Psicologos, 1998).

The distributions of psychologists by area of expertise, by gender, and by private versus public sector are reported in Table 21.3. Clinical psychology is the only field that has doubled its members from 1990 through 1998. All other fields have declined in number. These differences may reflect the different responses to random (1990) versus nonrandom (1998) surveys, or there may be a genuine decline in membership in some fields. The distribution by gender highlights a systematic increase in the per-

centage of women in almost every field except academics. Males prevail among military and police psychologists, sport psychologists, and university professors. About 97% of psychologists employed in traffic safety programs are in the private sector, as is the case among clinical psychologists (80%), sports' psychologists (75%), organizational psychologists (73%), and educational psychologists (58%). By contrast, 94% of military and police psychologists are in the public sector, as is true for university professors and research psychologists (67%), forensic psychologists (58%) and community psychologists (57%).

Without exception, the cognitive and behavioral perspective was identified as the preferred treatment orientation for every field in the 1998 survey (Santolaya et al., 2001), ranging from 44% among forensic psychologists to 71% among sport psychologists. The second most popular category was eclectic, ranging from 10% among clinical psychologists to 29% among traffic safety psychologists. About 12% of psychologists indicated they identify behavior modification as their primary theoretical perspective; close to 10% stated that they followed a psychodynamic approach whereas 4% specified that they followed orthodox psychoanalysis.

The 1998 survey (Santolaya et al., 2001) also focused on work settings. About 48% were self-employed and the rest employed by consulting firms (7%), schools (7%), city councils (5%), hospitals (5%), or mental health centers (4%).

In 1993, a national opinion poll was carried out to assess the image of psychology and psychologists in Spain. This survey identified the features of psychologists as compared to other professional groups and the dimensions underly-

TABLE 21.3
Distribution of Spanish Psychologists by Area of Expertise

	Percentage				
Field	1990	Females	1998	Females	Private Sector
Clinical psychology	29.9	67.8	68.4	70	80
Community psychology	9.2	53.2	4.4	68	43
Educational psychology	38.5	63.2	15.3	73	58
Forensic psychology	—	—	1.1	68	42
Military and police	—	—	0.2	38	6
Organizational psychology	16.3	39.3	8.0	56	73
Scholars/researchers	6.3	55.1	0.5	42	33
Sport psychology	—	—	0.3	48	75
Traffic safety	4.8	84.3	1.6	82	97

Note. Adapted from Díaz & Quintanilla (1992), pp. 42, 43, and 66, and from Santolaya, Berdullas, & Fernández (2001), pp. 242, 245.

ing professional practice in psychology (Berenguer & Quintanilla, 1994). A random sample of 1,523 subjects, stratified by region and municipality, was surveyed using structured interviews. In this sample 21% of respondents had had professional contact with a psychologist. About 80% of respondents ranked psychology as an advanced knowledge-based profession. Clinical psychology, educational psychology, and work psychology were the main professional profiles that respondents identified. The major work activities attributed to psychologists were the diagnosis of emotional problems (87%), administration of psychological tests (86%), vocational guidance (73%), psychotherapy (72%), personnel selection (68%), relaxation training (66%), consulting with businesses (56%), and training and development programs (50%). Activities not attributed to psychologists included palmistry (91%), fortune-telling (80%), hypnosis (73%), and prescribing medication (54%).

A Likert scale ranging from 1 (low) to 5 (high) was used to classify economists, educators, physicians, priests, psychiatrists, social workers, teachers, and psychologists in nine categories (Berenguer & Quintanilla, 1994). The highest rated feature for psychologists was "socially useful profession" in which they were ranked 3.96, below physicians (4.59) and teachers (4.47), but in the same range as economists (4.05) and psychiatrists (3.93). The lowest rated dimension was "professional practice entails personal sources of trouble," in the same range of social workers, psychiatrists or physicians, and above teachers, priests, educators, and economists. Regarding the label "profit-making profession," psychologists ranked 3.6, below physicians, economists, psychiatrists, and educators.

The number of new books on psychology published in Spain ranged from 525 in 1991 to 1,145 in 2001. About 5% were softcover books. The number of books on psychology that were translated into Spanish was 238 in 1991, 316 in 1996, and 534 in 2001. This suggests not just an open mind toward foreign approaches to psychology but also a reliance on translators who often may not know the intricacies of psychological terminology.

21.4 FUTURE CHALLENGES AND PROSPECTS

In Latin American countries, the majority of publishing companies in psychology went into bankruptcy during the 1980s and 1990s because of the slow market for Spanish books. Although there is a market of 400 million Spanish-speaking people, this market may actually be below 100 million in terms of people capable of purchasing books for higher education and training.

Bilingualism is an unresolved matter in faculties of psychology, where only one of five professors and one of eight students speak English fluently. Many can read texts in English, but they cannot interact when they participate in international congresses or meet visiting scholars. For instance, lectures in English are rare in psychology classes and direct translation is necessary to reach most of the audience. This is also the case among Ph.D. students because only 40% spend time at foreign, mainly European, universities, where English is not the indigenous language. The language issue

also has consequences for promotion within universities because recruitment and selection procedures require expertise in the local Spanish dialect. At some universities, demonstrated competence in Basque, Catalan, or Galician is required, whereas, by contrast, advanced European universities require English as the official language of scholarship. Within the scientific community worldwide, Spanish, Catalan, or Basque languages are regional and do not have value for scholars in an increasingly cosmopolitan discipline and profession. A related consequence is that many professors write papers in Spanish, with only 5% capable of writing in English without the assistance of a translator. Quite often, Spanish researchers base hypotheses and predictions on translations made into Spanish, rather than on the original text, which causes frequent misunderstanding as evidenced by independent translations. Moreover, nuances are frequently lost because ideas are not captured in their original wording.

Bilingualism is an important requisite among university graduates and scholars in the large majority of European universities. However, as a direct consequence of the current use of Spanish in most Latin American countries, many scholars in Spain identify with a community of non-English-speaking scholars. In other words, Spanish seems to be a cantonal language within the European scientific and technological community. It often is a language used to disperse expert knowledge written in English by authors from diverse countries. In a similar way, Hispanic psychologists in the United States or Latin America resort to English as the authoritative language; they use Spanish as a peripheral language to reach non-English-speaking students or graduates. The rejection rates for Spanish journals are often below 30%, whereas the rejection rates for English journals are typically above 70%. Therefore, Spanish becomes the communal language for internal consumption within a regional and vernacular area separate from the worldwide scientific community. The national committee in charge of evaluating research, backed by the Spanish Council of Universities and the Ministry of Education, has enacted eight criteria to evaluate the scholarly production of Spanish researchers. The second criterion states that research will be evaluated as strong if published in prestigious journals that are included in the Social Science Citation Index. This criterion implies that research written in Spanish is "low profile" and has generated antagonism between bilingual and monolingual psychologists in Spain.

Two Spanish journals are published entirely in English. *Psychology in Spain* was founded in 1997 and is published annually by the SPA. Its purpose is to disseminate in English a selection of the best articles published annually in SPA-sponsored journals under the supervision of an editorial board that combines leading figures in universities and in professional fields. Publication in this journal gives recognition for high-quality research written in Spanish. *The Spanish Journal of Psychology* was founded in 1998 and is published annually by the Complutense University of Madrid. The editorial board is composed of professors of the University, who are committed to promoting sound empirical research and innovative methodologies. The large majority of articles have been written in Spanish and translated into English.

There are two journals that combine English and Spanish articles: *Psicologica*

(launched in 1980 and sponsored by the University of Valencia) and *Psicothema* (co-sponsored by the SPA and University of Oviedo). In 2001, two new journals in English and Spanish were launched: *Revista Internacional de Psicología Clínica y de la Salud* (*International Journal of Clinical and Health Psychology*) and *Revista Internacional de Psicología y Terapia Psicológica* (*International Journal of Psychology and Psychological Therapy*).

In 1995, the SPA inaugurated a new service for its members: free access to the Internet. The main beneficiaries were psychologists from rural areas because it allowed them to access information as easily as scholars with free online connections on campus or at their work sites. The homepage of the SPA (http://www.cop.es/) is the starting point for all kind of searches related to psychology in Spain. In addition, departments of psychology have started to produce specific homepages, mainly in Spanish, but in a few instances in English. The pioneering homepage was launched in 1993 to support the International Congress of Applied Psychology held in Madrid in 1994. Also, the Complutense University of Madrid has developed an online test bed at http://forteza.sis.ucm.es/apto/ to facilitate e-learning for students in work and organizational psychology; students are requested to produce term papers in hypertext in a multimedia framework, combining text, images, sound, and animation. Virtual-reality technologies are also being used, for example, to treat phobias and generate psychological tests. Since 1994, CD-ROMs have been created that contain abstracts and full-text papers presented at congresses of psychology in Spain. However, the majority of scholars, practitioners, and students are only users, not producers of multimedia documents. They remain loyal to the print media. Again, lack of fluency in English is a barrier because English is the metalanguage of the Internet. For example, newsgroups in Spanish on psychological subjects exist, but they are not as active as similar groups constructed in English because oral communication in English prevails in the electronic exchange of information.

Finally, there is a 3-year European project, known as EuroPsy, funded under the EU's Leonardo da Vinci Program. It started in 2001 and is nearing completion. The overall aim has been to develop a basic framework for a European diploma in psychology. This project opens the way for the free movement of Spanish psychologists within the EU. The European diploma will be a far-ranging, but tailored certificate of competence for professional activity in specific fields of expertise.

In Spain, left-wing governments are prone to support socially minded and progressive professions, whereas right-wing governments favor dominant, conservative professions and the status quo. Whichever party is in power, the main challenge in the near future is the inclusion of psychologists as health staff in the national catalogue of health-related professions. This will have important consequences; for instance, it will allow psychological services to be covered by insurance policies and treated as tax deductions. Spanish psychologists have discussed the need for this change with leading members of the Spanish parliament as well as the government's Minister of Health (a physician). In a similar vein, new regulations are being developed regarding accreditation and credentialing for private and public health centers. In this context, terms such as "psychological assessment" or "psychodiagnosis" are critically impor-

tant and have to be carefully defined in government regulations and policies. These regulations will also affect Ph.D. programs of excellence in psychology at both the national and European level.

REFERENCES

Berenguer G., & Quintanilla, I. (1994). La imagen de la psicología y los psicólogos en el Estado Español [Image of psychology and psychologists within the Spanish State]. *Papeles del Psicólogo, 58,* 41–68.

Carpintero, H. (1982). The introduction of scientific psychology in Spain. In W. Woodward & M. G. Ash (Eds.), *The problematic science: Psychology in nineteenth century thought* (pp. 255–275). New York: Praeger.

Carpintero, H. (1992). Spain. In V. S. Sexton & J. D. Hogan (Eds.), *International psychology: Views from around the world* (pp. 364–372). Lincoln, NE: University of Nebraska Press.

Carpintero, H. (1994). *Historia de la psicología en España* [History of psychology in Spain]. Madrid: Eudema.

Colegio Oficial de Psicólogos. (1998). *Perfiles profesionales del psicólogo* [Professional profile of psychologists]. Madrid: Colegio Oficial de Psicólogos de España. Online version: http://www.cop.es/perfiles/

Díaz, R., & Quintanilla, I. (1992). La identidad profesional del psicólogo en el Estado Español [The professional identity of psychologist in the Spanish state]. *Papeles del Psicólogo, 52,* 22–74.

Finison, L. (1977). Psychologists and Spain: A historical note. *American Psychologist, 32,* 1080–1084.

García Rodríguez, Y. (2003). Doctoral studies in psychology in Spain. *European Psychologist, 8,* 28–33.

Navarro, A., & Rivero A. (2001). High rate of Inbreeding in Spanish universities. *Nature, 410,* 14.

Prieto, J. M. (1992). Studying psychology in Spain. *International Journal of Psychology, 27,* 350–363.

Prieto, J. M., & Berdullas, M. (2003). Clinical psychology in Spain is as sound as a bell. *European Psychologist, 8,* 54–57.

Prieto, J. M., Fernández Ballesteros R., & Carpintero, H. (1994). Contemporary psychology in Spain. *Annual Review of Psychology, 45,* 51–78

Quintanilla, I., & Díaz, R. (1994). Some demographic and economic characteristics of practitioners. *Applied Psychology: An International Review, 43,* 151–155.

Santolaya, O. F., Berdullas, T. M., & Fernández, H. J. R. (2001). The decade 1989–1998 in Spanish psychology: An analysis of development of professional psychology in Spain. *Spanish Journal of Psychology, 4,* 237–252.

Soler, M. (2001). How inbreeding affects productivity in Europe. *Nature, 411,* 132.

IMPORTANT PUBLICATIONS

Amón, J. (1976). *Estadística para psicólogos,* [Statistics for psychologists] (Vols. 1 and 2). Madrid: Pirámide.

Anguera, M. T. (1982). *Metodología de la observación en las ciencias humanas* [Observation methodology in human sciences]. Madrid: Cátedra.

Bermúdez, J. (1985). *Psicología de la Personalidad* [Personality psychology]. Madrid: Universidad Nacional Educación a Distancia.

Carpintero, H. (1987). *Historia de la psicología* [History of psychology] (Vols. 1 and 2). Valencia, Spain: Nau llibres.

Fernández-Ballesteros, R., & Carrobles, I. (1981). *Evaluación conductual: Metodología y aplicaciones* [Behavioral assessment: Methodology and applications]. Madrid: Pirámide.

Hernández Hernández, P. (1991). *Psicología y enseñanza del estudio: Teoría y técnicas para potenciar las habilidades intelectuales* [Psychology and teaching how to study: Theory and techniques to improve intellectual skills]. Madrid: Pirámide.

Jiménez Burillo, F. (1981). *Psicología social* [Social psychology]. Madrid: Universidad Nacional Educación a Distancia.

Peiró, J. M. (1983). *Psicología de la organización* [Organizational psychology] (Vols. 1 and 2). Madrid: Universidad Nacional Educación a Distancia.

Pinillos, J. L. (1975) *Principios de psicología* [Principles of psychology]. Madrid: Alianza.

Sánchez Canovas, J. (1986). *El nuevo paradigma de la inteligencia humana* [The new paradigm of human intelligence]. Valencia, Spain: Tirant lo Blanc.

Tous, J. M. (1986). *Psicología de la personalidad: Diferencias individuales, biológicas y cognitivas en el procesamiento de la información* [Personality psychology: Individual, biological and cognitive differences in information processing]. Barcelona: Promociones Publicaciones Universitarias.

CHAPTER 22

Psychology in the United Kingdom

INGRID C. LUNT

Ingrid C. Lunt is professor of educational psychology and dean of research degrees at the Institute of Education, University of London. She was president of the British Psychological Society from 1998 through 1999 and president of the European Federation of Psychologists Associations from 1993 through 1999. Her research interests are professional psychology, ethics and professional practice, higher professional development and learning, and inclusive education.

22.1 OVERVIEW

This chapter focuses on the United Kingdom, that is, England, Scotland, Wales, and Northern Ireland. Although these four countries constitute the kingdom of Great Britain and Northern Ireland, increasing regionalization and devolution is leading to growing differences in political and legal systems, which, to an extent, influence educational and professional systems. This

increasing political devolution has led the main psychology organization of the United Kingdom, the British Psychological Society (BPS; www.bps.org.uk/index.cfm), in 2000 to set up offices in the national regional centers of Belfast (Northern Ireland), Cardiff (Wales), and Glasgow (Scotland), while retaining one organization that represents psychology across the nation. In addition, the BPS collaborates extensively with the Psychological Society for Ireland (PSI); many PSI members belong to the BPS, while the PSI has tended in the past to adopt procedures of the BPS (e.g., accreditation policies, code of conduct). Thus, much of this chapter describes arrangements that are uniform across the islands.

22.1.1 Early History

Psychology in the United Kingdom is about 100 years old (Bunn, Lovie, & Richards, 2001), coinciding to a large extent with the age of the BPS. The BPS was formed in October 1901, when 10 scholars—9 men and 1 woman—met at the University College–London to form the Psychological Society (renamed the BPS in 1906). According to the minutes recorded in 1901, the aims of the BPS were "to advance scientific psychological research, and to further the cooperation of investigators in the different branches of psychology" (as cited in Bunn et al.). These scholars came from various backgrounds: education, law, medicine, philosophy, and physiology. Membership was restricted to recognized instructors in some field of psychology and to scholars whose publications were deemed influential. At the time, a very small number of universities offered psychology degrees: Cambridge and University College–London founded their laboratories in 1897; Aberdeen, Edinburgh, and Glasgow in the early 20th century; and Oxford not until 1936. Now, there are over 100 institutions of higher education in the United Kingdom offering psychology degrees.

As in many other countries, psychology originally established itself as a scientific discipline, and, indeed, the BPS was from the start dominated by physiologists and experimental psychologists, who met to discuss their research. Psychology as a science was the major orientation for at least the first 50 years of the BPS, and it is only in the past 50 years that the balance has begun to shift toward a more professional orientation for psychology. Although there have been predictable tensions within the BPS, the organization succeeds in holding together both the scientific and applied dimensions of psychology and represents both aspects of the field. Following the scientific beginnings of the discipline, social and clinical psychology received a signifi-

cant boost from World War I, after which the new branch of military psychology emerged as a separate applied specialty. Around this time, in 1913, the first educational psychologist, Cyril Burt, was appointed by the London County Council to evaluate school pupils for their suitability for mainstream education. In 1916, the first consulting psychologist was appointed to accompany the consulting neurologist assigned to the British Expeditionary Force. Between the two world wars, military and selection activities provided a growing context for psychologists' work, though it was not until after the World War II that psychology in the United Kingdom, as in many other countries, formally established itself and began to flourish as an applied profession. This was the period when the National Health Service (NHS) was established in 1948, and it is still the case that the majority of clinical and educational psychologists in the conntry work for public services including the NHS and educational institutions.

Clinical psychology provides the largest group of applied psychologists. Although there were a few psychologists working in clinical settings before 1948, clinical psychology was not formally recognized until after World War II, and it was not until 1966 that a separate division, the Division of Clinical Psychology, was formed within the BPS (Bunn et al., 2001). Similarly, although Cyril Burt was appointed as the first educational psychologist in London in 1913, educational psychology really blossomed when the Summerfield report appeared in 1968. This government-sponsored report established the role and training of educational psychologists (Summerfield, 1968). The timing of this report coincided with a period in which both clinical and educational psychology were to see major expansions in numbers. There are now about 6,000 clinical psychologists in the United Kingdom and about 3,000 educational psychologists (figures will always be estimates until there is a requirement for a national registry or licensing system). More recently, both counseling psychology and health psychology have emerged as rapidly growing branches of applied professional psychology.

22.1.2 Organizations

Although the BPS is the oldest, largest, and most representative organization for the discipline and profession in the United Kingdom, two other organizations must be mentioned: the Experimental Psychology Society (EPS) and the Association of Educational Psychologists (AEP). The EPS was formed in 1946 as the Experimental Psychology Group in order to facilitate research in experimental psychology and scientific communication among experimental psychologists and those working in cognate fields. It became the EPS in 1958. Membership, currently about 600, is open to doctoral-level researchers in experimental psychology, broadly defined, who have delivered a paper at a meeting of the EPS and have published in psychological or cognate journals (Experimental Psychology Society, 2003).

The AEP was formed in 1962 as a trade union and professional body for professional educational psychologists. At the time, a group of educational psychologists believed that the BPS did not adequately meet the professional and employment needs of educational psychologists and had too scientific a focus. Currently, AEP mem-

bership is about 3000 and includes about 95% of those working as educational psychologists in the public sector. The AEP publishes a journal and provides member services such as weekly mailings of position vacancies, negotiation over pay and work conditions, and representation of members in litigation.

The most recent organization of psychologists is the Association of Business Psychologists (ABP), which was formed in 2001 by a group who believed that the BPS did not adequately meet their needs, in particular through its Division of Occupational Psychology.

There are also a large number of psychotherapy associations in the United Kingdom that are aligned with different schools or traditions of psychotherapy. Two major "umbrella" or federal organizations bring together these psychotherapy associations: the United Kingdom Council for Psychotherapists (UKCP; www.ukcp.org.uk) and the British Confederation of Psychotherapists (BCP; www.bcp.org.uk). The UKCP is a national organization of nearly 80 different psychotherapy organizations representing different traditions of psychotherapy, which are clustered within the UKCP as autonomous sections. The UKCP maintains a voluntary registry of psychotherapists and exists "to promote and maintain the profession of psychotherapy and high standards in the practice of psychotherapy for the benefit of the public throughout the U.K." (United Kingdom Council for Psychotherapy, 2003).

The BCP, established in 1993, is a national body that convenes 12 training and professional organizations in the field of psychoanalysis, analytical psychology, psychodynamic psychotherapy, and child psychotherapy. Its purpose is to maintain appropriate standards in the selection, training, and professional practice of psychodynamically oriented psychotherapists (British Confederation of Psychotherapists, 2003). The BCP also maintains a voluntary registry of appropriately qualified psychotherapists because at the present time there is no legal requirement for their registration. The British Association of Counseling and Psychotherapy (BACP) is the other major organization to which psychotherapists may belong, depending on their orientation.

Within the BPS, there are a large number of clinical psychologists who are also psychotherapists; and over the past 20 years, the BPS has maintained a strong interest in the training and regulation of psychotherapists and holds a special position, along with the Royal College of Psychiatrists, in the UKCP. A number of psychologists choose to have their names both on the Register of Chartered Psychologists and on one of the registries of psychotherapists mentioned above.

22.1.3 The British Psychological Society

The BPS is the main organization for psychologists in the United Kingdom and represents the interests of both scientists and practitioners. It was founded in 1901 and incorporated by Royal charter in 1965. It has one overarching objective:

> To promote the advancement and diffusion of a knowledge of psychology pure and applied and especially to promote the usefulness of members of the Society by setting up a high standard of professional education and knowledge (British Psychological Society, 2002, p. 2).

The activities of the BPS include the following:

1. Publication of a monthly in-house magazine, *The Psychologist,* and 10 scientific journals (most named the *British Journal of* [e.g., Educational] *Psychology,* including the *British Journal of Psychology* per se).
2. Publication of newsletters for its constituent scientific sections and professional divisions.
3. Publication of books under the imprint BPS Blackwell.
4. Conferences, including an annual conference, as well as over 10 specialist conferences each year.
5. Support for nine professional divisions (clinical, counseling, educational, forensic, health, neuropsychology, occupational, teaching, and research psychology), 13 scientific sections (cognitive, consciousness and experiential, developmental, educational, history and philosophy, lesbian and gay psychology, mathematical, psychobiology, psychology of women, psychotherapy, social, sport and exercise, and statistics and computing), seven regional branches (Northern Ireland, Scotland, Wales, Northwest England, Southwest England, West Midlands, and Wessex and Wright), and one specialty group (Psychologists Working in Social Services).
6. Maintenance of the Register of Chartered Psychologists for professionally qualified psychologists, a guideline of ethical principles and code of conduct, and a mechanism for investigating and adjudicating ethical infractions.
7. Accreditation of nearly 700 undergraduate degrees and over 100 postgraduate

professional training courses in psychology.

8. Status as the representative authority for the European Community's Directive, which has been delegated the task of evaluating the equivalence of psychologists' qualifications across countries.

The BPS had 36,477 members at the end of 2002; these included 10,611 chartered psychologists (i.e., those fully qualified and entitled to practice as psychologists and whose names appear on the Register of Chartered Psychologists), a large number of graduate members (those with a psychology degree), 5,688 student subscribers, and a number of other grades of membership including associate fellows, ordinary members, affiliates, and international affiliates. At the present time, membership in the BPS is open to a wide range of individuals, not only to those who are qualified to work as psychologists.

It is very difficult to estimate the total number of psychologists working in the United Kingdom, in part because the title is not yet protected, thus allowing anyone to use the title *psychologist*. However, as stated above, there are well over 10,000 chartered psychologists whose names appear on the BPS registry and who work as professional psychologists. It is likely, however, that there are a substantial number of psychologists who practice without being registered, for example, those in private practice or those who do not wish to belong to the BPS. In addition, the estimated 3376 psychologists working as academic faculty at over 135 universities that offer psychology degrees (Higher Education Statistics Agency, 2003) are not required to be chartered and, therefore, may not be on the register or belong to the BPS.

The BPS is organized in part by the 9 professional divisions, 7 geographical branches, and 13 scientific sections. The divisions represent areas of professional psychology in which there are educational and training routes recognized by the BPS. The branches cover most regions of the United Kingdom, including Northern Ireland, Scotland, and Wales, which have increasing political autonomy, with significant omissions of London and the Southeast. The scientific sections represent areas of academic psychology in which members have a special interest; a new section may be formed following a proposal by a certain minimum number of members, which is then voted on by the membership and the council. Most divisions, branches, and sections hold meetings and conferences, and publish newsletters. The professional divisions represent professional psychologists whose names appear on the Register of Chartered Psychologists. They are properly qualified and have agreed to abide by the ethical principles and code of conduct of the BPS; they are also subject to the disciplinary procedures that are administered by the BPS and intended to protect the public from incompetent or irresponsible practice.

The BPS is the body with delegated responsibility for accrediting university programs and for determining professional qualifications. The existence of BPS's professional divisions is an important element of this responsibility because it is through eligibility for membership in these divisions that professional qualifications are awarded. According to the divisional membership rosters in 2002, there were 10,611 chartered psychologists, as noted earlier. These constitute professionally qualified psychologists working as clinical (45.0%), educational (13.5%), counseling (12.8%), forensic (9.5%), health (9.6%), neuro (5.9%), and occupational (29.4%) psychologists. However, this is a likely underestimate of total number of chartered psychologists since there is currently no requirement for psychologists to be registered with the BPS or any other body. There will also be a small degree of overlap in divisional membership as it is possible to qualify as a member of more than one division.

Psychologists, like other professional groups, tend to cluster in large urban areas, and in the United Kingdom, the vast majority work in London and in the southeast region of the country. One estimate of regional dispersion is the spread of BPS members by regional branch. Branches consist of BPS members who live in the defined region. The branch with most members is Wessex and Wright, with almost 4,000 members, and Northwest England and the West Midlands each has over 3,000 members; these areas represent major conurbations. However, the figures are considerably skewed by the fact that there is no BPS branch in the southeast part of the country that covers London and which is where a substantial number of psychologists work, as well as where there is the greatest concentration of private practitioners. Thus, it must be assumed that a substantial number of psychologists are not members of the BPS.

It has never been straightforward to estimate the proportion of psychologists to the population. The Summerfield Report of 1968 recommended that there should be one educational psychologist per 5,000 school children (Summerfield, 1968), and there have been a number of formulae used in determining National Health Service (NHS) employment planning. The recom-

mendations of the Summerfield Report were never fully implemented, although legislation in the field of special education and the requirement that requests for additional resources to support students with disabilities be evaluated by educational psychologists led to significant expansion in the 1980s. Since that time, local government and public sector employment have given more focus to quasi-market arrangements that have produced great variation across the country in the number of employed psychologists and, therefore, in the ratio of psychologists to population.

As a learned society and a professional body, the BPS is asked to consult on governmental policy and is responsible for coordinating between 50 and 60 responses each year to governmental requests for scientific and professional input. Since the majority of psychologists work for governmental departments, in particular the Department of Health, Department of Education, Department of Employment, and the Prison Service, there is close involvement by government in such matters as human-resource planning. This is especially true for clinical psychologists and the Department of Health, where for many years there has been at least one clinical psychologist employed to promote productive relationships and information exchange on relevant issues.

22.2 EDUCATION AND TRAINING

The university system in the United Kingdom consists mainly of the bachelor's degree (3–4 years), which may be the B.A. or B.Sc., the master's degree (usually 1–2 years leading to M.A., M.Sc., or M.Phil.), and the doctoral degree (usually 3–4 years of full-time study) leading to the traditional Ph.D. or, increasingly, to professional doctorates such as the D.Clin.Psy., D.Ed.Psy., and Psy.D. Doctoral level qualification (D.Clin.Psy.) or its equivalent is required for the practice of clinical psychology in the United Kingdom; doctoral level qualifications will likely be required in the future for other areas of professional psychology such as counseling psychology and educational psychology (Donn, Routh, & Lunt, 2000; Scott, Brown, Lunt, & Thorne, in 2004). Following the Bologna Agreement signed in 1999, efforts were begun to create a European Higher Education Area (see Lunt, 2002a), which will probably entail a two-cycle system similar to that in place in the country. At the present time, psychology degrees are offered by universities, by higher education colleges, and through higher education courses in a small number of other colleges. The British government's White Paper of 2003 made radical proposals for the development of higher education, which include the possibility of at least 40 additional institutions of higher education that would have the title and powers of a university.

Although in the past students received a means-tested grant from the government to support their university studies, all students are now required to pay for their university education. Typically, they secure reduced interest loans, which means that many students complete their university education in considerable debt. Whereas previously students in the United Kingdom tended to apply to universities away from their home town, the reduction in financial support has resulted in more students applying to their local university and in some young people being dissuaded from pursuing a university education. The question of university funding, including the level at which universities may charge fees, is currently a subject of great debate in the country. Up until now, fees for different degrees were set by the Higher Education Funding Council, which also allocates funds to universities according to enrollment figures. There are current proposals that would permit universities to set their own fees, charging as much as the market (i.e., students in certain disciplines) can bear.

Universities within the United Kingdom are usually organized through colleges called *faculties*. Psychology departments are housed in colleges of social science, medicine, or natural or biological sciences, and, occasionally, in a college of arts. To an extent, these differences determine the orientation and content of the curriculum as well as the amount of government funding awarded to the department. Thus, if psychology is a laboratory-based field in a biological science college, the funding it receives will be greater than if it is a humanities-based field in an arts college. Each psychology department is headed by a professor of psychology, and most departments are staffed by several professors. Tenured academics begin their career as lecturers and may be promoted to senior lecturers, to readers, and finally to professors; thus, the title and position of professor indicates seniority, status, and usually permanent tenure.

Psychology is one of the most popular undergraduate degrees. For example, in 2001, there were 65,736 applicants for undergraduate degrees in psychology, of whom 10,655 were accepted; this figure increased to 13,615 in 2002. This means that there is a cohort of over 10,500 students entering psychology each year (Higher Education Statistics Agency, 2003). In 2001–2002, there were about 10,600 graduate students in psychology across all year groups, including part-time students (Higher Education Statistics Agency); these include research students studying for the Ph.D. and graduates studying for professional qualifications such as those in clinical, counseling, educational, and occupational psychology. There has been a considerable increase in the number of postgraduate students engaged in part-time study; the figures for 2001–2002 show that over 50% of postgraduate students are part-time. Because of psychology's popularity, universities can set high entrance requirements. Students are normally required to achieve A levels, which is the end-of-school graduation qualification, usually at age 18, needed to enter a university. The most popular subjects require the highest grades or point totals; psychology is one such subject and, therefore, it is relatively difficult to gain a place to study psychology, particularly at a prestigious university. Each university has a fixed number of places in each discipline, and popular subjects such as psychology, may have as many as 20 applicants for each place. However, the government has made an explicit commitment to improve access and increase university enrollment; this has led to universities admitting more students from nontraditional backgrounds (e.g., without traditional academic qualifications) and more mature students, who may also work part-time through university study to support themselves.

About 80% of those who earn a bachelor's degree in psychology in the United Kingdom do not go on to become profes-sional psychologists. Many enter the labor market at this level whereas others seek professional qualifications in another profession. This is mainly so because the number of places in professional graduate training programs is very limited and is usually determined by the availability of jobs within government departments. For clinical and educational psychology training, the majority of places in the graduate programs are funded by the government through the Department of Health or Department of Education, with the number of places set by employment needs and forecasts.

22.2.1 Undergraduate Curriculum

The Higher Education Statistics Agency, which is the central source for higher education statistics, lists 174 institutions of higher education in Great Britain and Northern Ireland, with the vast majority of these offering psychology degrees. Thus, there are over 130 higher education institutions that offer psychology degrees and about 700 different undergraduate degree programs in psychology accredited by the BPS. In addition, there are a substantial number of undergraduate psychology degrees that have not been accredited by the BPS. Accreditation by the BPS is frequently sought by university departments because such accreditation is a requirement for postgraduate professional training; students who wish to continue as professional psychologists must have completed an accredited program, and this has created a demand for such programs.

The BPS sets a qualifying examination that provides the yardstick against which psychology degrees are evaluated and accredited, and which enables them to confer the Graduate Basis for Registration (GBR). This means that degree programs provide the BPS-recognized foundation for professional training. In order to advance to professional training, which will lead to the title of chartered psychologist (C. Psychol.), graduates must have obtained the GBR (i.e., a bachelor's degree in psychology that meets all the requirements set by the qualifying examination). The BPS monitors all undergraduate programs in psychology and organizes visits to universities in order to accredit the particular program as meeting the standard set by the qualifying examination. These mechanisms that are in place ensure that all graduates who progress to postgraduate professional training have an adequate grounding in psychology.

The qualifying examination is sometimes taken by those who have graduated from a non-BPS-accredited program and who wish to obtain the GBR. The examination consists of five papers and a portfolio of reports of practical work, including laboratory work. The papers are (a) cognitive psychology and psychobiology, (b) developmental and social psychology, (c) individual differences and conceptual and historical issues, (d) an advanced option from clinical, cognitive, cultural, developmental, educational, health, occupational, or social psychology, and (e) research design and quantitative methods in psychology.

Most university departments combine different pedagogical approaches to teaching, using large lectures, small seminars, and even tutorials; a few psychology departments have introduced problem-based learning, and some also require an internship year away from the university as part of the bachelor's degree. All psychol-

ogy departments offering a degree that confers the GBR have substantial laboratory-based teaching. The popularity of the subject means that undergraduate classes are full, although there are usually not more than 30 students per instructor.

22.2.2 Professional Training

To a large extent, professional training in psychology is regulated by the BPS. This is because, since 1988, the BPS has maintained a voluntary Register of Chartered Psychologists who meet BPS qualifications and are, therefore, deemed properly qualified. As noted earlier, the BPS achieves this through its qualifying examination that provides the yardstick against which university degrees are evaluated and by determining the level and content of the undergraduate degree in psychology (i.e., the GBR).

At the graduate or professional training level, universities offer programs in clinical, counseling, educational, forensic, health, and occupational (organizational) psychology, which are also evaluated and reaccredited by the BPS every 5 years. The BPS provides criteria that must be met by the universities and against which programs are evaluated. At present, the BPS has accredited 396 joint honors undergraduate programs at 96 institutions of higher education and 108 graduate training programs (31 in clinical psychology, 1 in clinical neuropsychology, 9 in counseling, 12 in forensic, 17 in educational, 20 in health, and 18 in occupational psychology) at 47 institutions of higher education. Graduation from these institutions culminates in chartered psychologist status. Chartered psychologist status is defined by the acquisition of the GBR plus at least 3 years of education and supervised practice in a recognized branch of professional psychology (i.e., a 3 + 3 or a 6-year model of graduate education and training).

Professional training in psychology is specialized in the United Kingdom. This means that a graduate in psychology must choose which professional branch of psychology to pursue. All build on the foundation of the GBR and all are completely separate qualifications. At the present time, professional qualification in clinical psychology is at the doctoral level, usually through the 3-year D.Clin.Psy. or equivalent (see Donn et al., 2000), whereas qualification for other professional psychology specialties is normally through a 1- or 2-year master's degree, although there are moves to extend doctoral level training to counseling and educational psychology. The BPS has made a commitment to 3-year postgraduate and doctoral level training in educational psychology by the year 2006 and in that year will cease to accredit other forms of professional training in this specialty.

Psychology degrees offered by British universities vary considerably in their coverage. Although many follow a curriculum that provides the GBR, thus making their graduates eligible to apply for professional training, there are also psychology departments that specialize, for example, in cultural, developmental, experimental, or social psychology. In these departments, graduates may progress toward a career in research via the Ph.D., but they cannot be professionally trained as future chartered psychologists. There are also many combined honors degrees that link psychology with other subjects such as linguistics, philosophy, and sociology. Since psychology is such a popular subject, there is great demand for it both as a single honors subject and as part of a combined honors degree.

At the postgraduate level, different specialties follow separate programs whose curriculum is determined by the BPS. The qualification for clinical psychology, for example, involves four internship placements that cover work in adult mental health, child and adolescent psychology, and learning disabilities. All clinical psychology programs require a research project. Although the dominant approach within clinical psychology in the United Kingdom is cognitive–behavioral, programs are usually eclectic in orientation and students must study different approaches within the field. Similarly in educational psychology, in which postgraduate training is currently a 1-year master's followed by 1 year of supervised practice, half of the training year is spent on internship, and an empirical study is required for the dissertation. The curriculum in educational psychology is heavily influenced by the role that educational psychologists play in the public sector and, therefore, includes assessment and educational interventions, legislation related to special education, and courses on child psychopathology. All postgraduate professional training programs cover ethics, laws, and professional issues related to applied practice.

Professional training in psychology is undertaken in small groups, usually about 12–15 students, and involves intensive teaching and learning methods. Lectures are rare, whereas seminars and interactive learning are more typical. Most professional training programs integrate learning on internship with learning at the university and have developed pedagogies to enhance this. There is considerable one-to-one supervision and small instructor–student ratios.

22.2.3 U.K. Universities

As mentioned earlier, over 100 universities in the United Kingdom offer undergraduate programs in psychology. Universities are evaluated for their scholarly productivity through the national Research Assessment Exercise and for the quality of their teaching through the Quality Assurance Agency. It is, therefore, possible for the public to see "league tables" that rank universities according to the research output of faculty by discipline; in this way, it is possible to identify which psychology departments gained the top Research Assessment Exercise scores. Similarly, it is possible to see which departments gained the top teaching scores in the last Quality Assurance Agency's evaluation. Almost all British universities are state funded, and the only private university does not currently offer programs in psychology.

22.2.4 Qualifications Obtained in Other Countries

The BPS is the designated authority for evaluating the equivalence of qualifications obtained by those trained outside the United Kingdom and has been authorized by the government to carry out this function. There is a committee and staff within the BPS whose task is to evaluate the equivalence of qualifications of those educated and trained in other countries. Individuals who wish to move to the country must complete forms detailing their qualifications; these forms are then compared with the requirements of a particular specialty. Outcomes are communicated through a Statement of Equivalence or, more usually, through the requirement to

undertake further training, research, or internship. The majority of psychologists seeking to move to the United Kingdom are in the clinical field, and the majority of those originate from Anglophone countries such as Australia, New Zealand, and South Africa. For psychologists qualified within the European Union (EU), mobility is influenced by EU Directives that aim to facilitate the free movement of professionals across EU member states (Lunt, 2002a, 2002b). At present, there is limited free movement, partly because of different languages used across the EU and because the directive permits each member state to demand compensatory requirements. These requirements bring the qualifications of an applicant trained in another country to the same standard as the host country, thus placing considerable obstacles to individual mobility (Hall, Lunt, & Ritchie, 2003). However, there are moves within the EU and other European countries to develop a common qualification that will facilitate mobility between different European countries (Lunt et al., 2001; Peiro & Lunt, 2002). This is partly due to proposals within the EU as well as projects funded by the EU that call for a new directive on professional mobility that will replace the previous directives. For example, a research and development project funded by the EU's Leonardo da Vinci program and coordinated by the author is intended to develop a European framework for educating and training psychologists. This framework is currently being formulated as a European diploma in psychology, which provides a European standard for the education and training of professional psychologists at the level of independent practice (see www.europsych.org).

22.3 SCOPE OF PSYCHOLOGICAL PRACTICE

At the present time, psychologists in the United Kingdom are not regulated by law. The title *psychologist* is not protected or regulated, and there is no restriction on the use of the title. However, the title *chartered psychologist* is one that is issued by the BPS under the terms of its Royal charter, by which the BPS is authorized to grant suitably qualified members the right to refer to themselves as chartered psychologists. This right is protected by the courts and serves as a proxy for regulation. A voluntary Register of Chartered Psychologists is maintained that guarantees certain qualifications of title holders as well as their commitment to abide by the ethical principles and code of conduct.

Members of the BPS have voted three times to move toward statutory regulation and have spent years trying to achieve this by working with the government, by drafting potential legislation, and by public campaigns, initially for a freestanding registration council for psychologists. Finally, there is the political will necessary to move toward the statutory regulation of psychologists; the government has decided to regulate psychologists under the Health Professions Council, which was established by the Health Act of 1999 to regulate professions that are wholly or in part concerned with health and which currently regulates 12 professions allied to medicine (though not dentists, medical doctors, or nurses, who have their own legislation).

The BPS currently maintains a set of ethical principles and code of conduct as well as a mechanism to adjudicate and sanction ethical infractions. Chartered psychologists are bound by the ethical principles and code of conduct, and are disciplined if they commit misdemeanors. The ethical principles and code of conduct are reviewed regularly both by the Ethics Committee of the BPS and by the Investigatory and Disciplinary Committees that constitute the mechanism for disciplinary procedures. Recently, the ethical principles and code of conduct were reviewed to ensure that they are in line with those of the European Federation of Psychologists Associations' (EFPA) metacode of ethics (European Federation of Psychologists Associations, 1995) that provides an overarching framework for European psychologists. The EFPA has an active Standing Committee on Ethics that is convened and chaired by a British psychologist and which has regular academic and professional contacts with events taking place outside Europe, particularly in North America, mainly through joint conference presentations.

As mentioned, the main areas of professional practice are reflected in the professional divisions of the BPS, with the health area providing the major context for psychologists' work in the United Kingdom, followed by the areas of education and of work and organizations. The large majority of psychologists in the country are employed in the public sector, with a small minority working in private practice; there may be a slight shift toward more private practice, but the public sector health and education departments continue to be major employers of psychologists. This means that the NHS is closely involved in determining pay and work conditions for clinical, counseling, and health psychologists, whereas the Department for Education and Schools (DfES) determines to a large extent the pay and work conditions of educational psychologists. The emphasis on public sector employment means that psychologists in the United Kingdom may appear to have less independence than in some countries, although in both NHS and DfES psychologists have relatively high status.

Within the NHS, clinical psychologists are involved in assessment and interventions with different client groups and increasingly have training and consulting functions. Clinical psychologists in the mental health field use a wide range of assessment tools and typically administer brief behavioral or cognitive–behavioral therapies. There has been a growing trend for psychologists to work in teams both in the NHS and DfES. Educational psychologists play a major role in special education evaluation and, to some extent, still function as gatekeepers in the placement of children within the school system. This has led to tensions among educational psychologists, many of whom are required to evaluate pupils for special education placement, although they prefer to train and consult with school personnel.

At present there is a shortage of clinical and educational psychologists. This is due in part to the limitations in the number of training places and partly because of the demographic profile of the profession (i.e., a large cadre of psychologists, who entered the field when it was expanding dramatically, are nearing retirement). Within the health service, there has been a growing trend for other health professionals, often nurses, to acquire psychological skills such as counseling and behavior therapy and to use these in hospitals. Psychotherapy in the United Kingdom has been long practiced by psychiatrists, social workers, clergy, and lay people, and is by no means exclusive to the field of psychology. However, clinical psychology has also long sought statutory regulation in order to protect the public from unqualified practitioners.

22.4 FUTURE CHALLENGES AND PROSPECTS

Psychology continues to be one of the most popular subjects of university study; in 2003–2004, there was an increase of 20% in the number of students applying to study psychology over the previous year. University departments of psychology are clearly thriving. Psychologists continue to enjoy relatively high status and pay, and there are many opportunities for employment given the overall shortage of psychologists. As in most countries, at least in the Western world, female students outnumber male students by a factor of over 7 to 1; this imbalance persists through graduate school and into the profession with the result that psychology is likely to become almost completely dominated by women. This has led to some concern that the profession may lose status in the same way that other female-dominated professions have in the past (e.g., nursing). Within professional bodies, the tension between the science and practice of psychology continues to be powerful, and the BPS struggles to ensure that it represents the interests of both effectively.

The success and expansion of psychology has meant that the discipline itself has expanded, leading to questions concerning the unity and diversity of psychology. As in other countries, psychology is developing more and more specializations, mainly scientific, but also professional, as psychologists establish new areas of work and new patterns of education and training. This means that psychology itself is becoming increasingly diverse; some consider it as a cognitive science or neuroscience, whereas others classify it within the domain of cultural studies. Traditional positivist approaches have tended to give way to more constructionist epistemologies, and psychology is increasingly multi-disciplinary with contributions by anthropologists and sociologists and by neuroscientists and physiologists.

Traditionally, psychologists in the United Kingdom have tended to look to the United States for international exchange and collaboration. More recently, there have been increased contacts with other European countries, and the BPS is an active member of both the EFPA and International Union of Psychological Sciences (IUPsyS). The increased contact with European countries is strengthened both by initiatives of the EU and by projects such as those mentioned earlier (Lunt et al., 2001), which aim to develop a common framework for psychological training across Europe. Nevertheless, Anglo-Saxon and Anglophone traditions remain a powerful pull across the Atlantic. Psychology in the United Kingdom appears to have a healthy future in terms of its student enrollment, its contributions to research and to policy, the success of many university departments, and a favorable media presence.

REFERENCES

British Confederation of Psychotherapists. (2003). Retrieved November 17, 2003, from http://www.bcp.org.uk

British Psychological Society. (amended 2002, November). *The Royal charter, statutes and rules.* Leicester, UK: Author.

Bunn, G. C., Lovie, A. D., & Richards, G. D. (2001). *Psychology in Britain.* Leicester, UK: British Psychological Society.

Donn, J., Routh, D., & Lunt, I. (2000). From Leipzig to Luxembourg (via Boulder and Vail): History of clinical psychology training in Europe and the United States. *Professional Psychology: Research and Practice, 31,* 423–428.

European Federation of Psychologists' Associations. (1995). *European metacode of ethics.* Brussels: Author.

Experimental Psychology Society. (2003). Retrieved June 30, 2003, from http://www.eps.ac.uk

Hall, J., Lunt, I., & Ritchie, P. (2003, July). *Mobility for professional psychologists: Europe, Canada, USA.* Paper presented at the meeting of the European Congress of Psychology, Vienna.

Higher Education Statistics Agency. (2003). Retrieved November 20, 2003, from http://www.hesa.ac.uk

Lunt, I. (2002a). Editorial. *European Psychologist, 7,* 167–168.

Lunt, I. (2002b). A common framework for the training of psychologists in Europe. *European Psychologist, 7,* 180–191.

Lunt, I., Bartram, D., Georgas, J., Jern, S., Job, R., Lecuyer, R., et al. (2001). *A European framework for psychologists' training: Final report of a project funded by the EU Leonardo da Vinci program.* London: Institute of Education.

Peiro, J. M., & Lunt, I. (2002). The context for a European framework for psychologists' training. *European Psychologist 7,* 169–179.

Scott, D., Brown, A., Lunt, I., & Thorne, L. (2004). Milton Keynes, UK: Open University Press Professional doctorates: *Integrating Professional and academic knowledge.*

Summerfield, A. (1968). *The Summerfield report.* London: HMSO.

United Kingdom Council for Psychotherapy. (2003). Retrieved June 30, 2003, from http://www.ukcp.org.uk.

IMPORTANT PUBLICATIONS

Argyle, M. (1992). *The social psychology of everyday life.* London: Routledge.

Baddeley, A. (1990). *Human memory: Theory and practice.* Boston: Allyn & Bacon.

Broadbent, D. E. (1958). *Perception and communication.* Oxford: Pergamon.

Bryant, P. E. (1974). *Perception and understanding in young children: An experimental approach.* New York: Basic Books.

Burt, C. (1940). *The factors of the mind.* London: University of London Press.

Eysenck, H. J. (1979). *The structure and measurement of intelligence.* Berlin: Springer.

Galton, F. (1883). *Human faculty and its development.* London: Macmillan.

Goswami, U. (1992). *Analogical reasoning in children.* Hove, UK: Erlbaum.

Gray, J. A. (1975). *Elements of the two-process theory of learning.* New York: Academic Press.

Harré, R. (1979). *Social being.* Oxford: Blackwell.

Jahoda, G. (1992). *Crossroads between culture and mind.* London: Harvester.

Spearman, C. (1927). *The abilities of man.* London: Macmillan.

CHAPTER 23

Psychology in Egypt

RAMADAN A. AHMED

Ramadan A. Ahmed is a professor of psychology in the Department of Psychology at Menoufia University in Egypt. He obtained his B.A. in psychology and LL.B. in law from Cairo University, and M.A. in psychology from Alexandria University. He received his Ph.D. in cognitive psychology from the University of Leipzig, Germany, in 1981. His research interests include concept development and the development of moral judgment cross-culturally, social perception, attitudes toward family members, women's psychology, and the history of psychology, especially in Egypt and other Arab countries. Since obtaining his doctorate, Ahmed has taught psychology in Egypt, the Sudan, and Kuwait. Ramadan Ahmed is a member of several international and national psychology associations and has presented his works at several international psychology conferences. He has published 3 books, 26 book chapters, and more than 40 scientific articles. With Uwe P. Gielen, he edited the first review of Arab psychology, Psychology in the Arab Coun-*tries. At present, he is on leave from Kuwait University where he is a professor of psychology. He was awarded Egypt's Incentive Award in Social Sciences in psychology in 1994.*

23.1 OVERVIEW

The field of psychology has not been alien to the Muslim and Arab world. The statement of H. Ebbinghaus, "Psychology has a long past, but only a short history" (Caudle, 1994, p. 135) is very much applicable to this part of the world. In ancient times, the Egyptians had already formed many psychological–philosophical ideas about phenomena such as delusions, dreams, epilepsy, hysteria, and how to treat some mental–physical abnormalities (Girges, 1967). Caudle (1994, p. 135) wrote, "One of the earliest known documents dealing, in part, with psychological issues is the Edwin Smith Surgical Papyrus, named for the first Westerner who owned it. This Egyptian document, which dates back to perhaps 3000 B.C., describes behavioral effects of head injuries, and the brain and its convolutions. Its author, a surgeon, may have recognized in a primitive way that the brain controls behavior, a notion that became lost for thousands of years." In the middle ages, Muslim scholars (e.g., Al-Kindi [Abou-Yousef Yaqoub, 796–873]; Al-Farabi [Abou-Nasr Mohammed Ibn-Tarkhan, 870–950]; Ibn-Al-Heitham (Al-Hassan Ibn-Al-Hussein, 965–1039); Ibn Sina or Avicenna [Abou-Ali Al-Hussein, 980–1037], Al-Ghazzali [Abou-Hamed, 1058–1111]; Al-Damiri [Kamal el-Din Mohammed Ibn Moussa, 1341–1405]; and Ibn Khaldoun [Abdel-Rahman Ibn Mohammed Al-Hadrami, 1332–1406]) developed more or less scientific ideas concerning a wide variety of topics that mostly belong to psychology as it is known today (Ahmed, 1992, 2002). Moreover, the first hospital established in Cairo in the 9th century (similar to those built in Damascus and Baghdad at the same time) included a separate section for mentally ill patients who were provided medication and care by the state. The first mental hospital in the Arab world and Africa was established in Cairo in 1880.

Psychology as a coherent and separate scientific discipline appeared in Egypt, and the entire Arab world, at the turn of the 20th century. Among some early writings published was *The Doctor's Approach to Insanity* by the Egyptian physician Soliman Nagaty in 1891 (Ahmed, 1992). Psychology was taught for the first time in 1908 in Egypt at Cairo University, the oldest secular university in the Arab world. Since the discipline's establishment as a minor subject included philosophy and sociology, some books on psychology were published

from 1908 through the early 1930s (Farag, 1987).

In 1929, the Egyptian government invited a Swiss educator, E. Claparéde, to visit Egypt in order to review the national system of preuniversity education, and to submit recommendations for its improvement. Claparéde administered the Stanford–Binet Test of intelligence and some other tests to a large sample of Egyptian schoolboys. The tests had been translated into Arabic and administered by an Egyptian team led by Ismail M. Al-Qubbani and Abdel-Aziz H. El-Koussy. (A very early attempt to adopt a scale for intelligence in Egypt was made by the Egyptian physician Hassan Omar in 1928, who translated and adopted the Binet Scale for Intelligence into the Arabic language.) The report, submitted by Claparéde upon completion, stated that his mission was of educational value, permitting Egyptian scholars to gain exposure to modern psychological concepts (Soueif & Ahmed, 2001). Claparéde's report emphasized the importance of improving the educational system by implementing psychological and educational sciences in Egypt. Most significantly, Claparéde recommended that an advanced institute of higher education be established to train candidates for secondary school teaching. This institute was soon founded as the College of Education at Ain Shams University, which had three important impacts on psychology and education in Egypt and other Arab countries:

1. Development of a curriculum pertinent to educational psychology and to mental health
2. Creation of a clinic for remedial teaching
3. Academics at a level that produced distinguished graduates who were sent

abroad (to the United Kingdom, especially) to obtain Ph.D.s in educational psychology (Meleika, 1997; Soueif & Ahmed, 2001)

Psychology as a science started in Egypt in the mid-1930s when the first Egyptian pioneers in psychology returned home after they earned their degrees in England (e.g., Abdel-Aziz H. El-Koussy in 1934) and in France (e.g., Ahmed E. Rageh in 1938, Yousef Mourad in 1940, and Mustapha Zewar in 1942). Rageh was the first Egyptian and Arab psychologist to obtain a Ph.D. in industrial psychology, El-Koussy discovered the "K" factor (i.e., the spatial factor, named after El-Koussy) in 1934, and M. Zewar was the first Arabic psychoanalyst with a medical and psychological background. These pioneers had a great impact on the development of psychology and education, not only in Egypt but throughout the Arab world (Abou-Hatab, 1992; El-Koussy, 1935; Farag, 1987). As a result of their efforts

1. Many Egyptian graduate students were sent abroad to France, Britain, and, later, the United States, whereas others obtained their degrees locally.
2. Psychology programs were increased and expanded to cover a variety of topics and approaches.
3. Programs for graduate studies (the diploma, M.A., and Ph.D. degrees in psychology) were formed.
4. Psychological laboratories were established.
5. Some psychological clinics were opened (the first in Cairo in 1934).
6. Many psychology books were published in Arabic in Egypt, and a number of research studies were conducted by Egyptian psychologists.
7. Several psychological tests were translated into Arabic (e.g., the 1916 Stanford–Binet Test, in the 1930s). Moreover, some indigenous intelligent scales were devised by Al-Qubbani in the early 1930s (Ahmed, 1999).
8. The Egyptian Association for Psychological Studies was founded in 1948.
9. The first Egyptian journal of psychology, the *Journal of Psychology*, was published quarterly between 1945 and 1953 under the editorship of Y. Mourad and M. Zewar. The Journal of Psychology attracted well-known Western psychologists such as Sir Cyril Burt from Britain and J. Casneuve from France, who wrote articles originally for the *Egyptian Journal of Psychology* in English or French. At the same time, the Association of Integrative Psychology was founded, mainly by the psychology staff working at Cairo University (Soueif & Ahmed, 2001; Taha, Kandeel, Mohammed, & Abdel-Fattah, 2003). Close to that time the Association of Nonmedical Psychotherapists headed by a university professor of law, the late Chancellor Mohammed Fathy, was formed. The association launched a strong campaign to call for legalization of the practice of psychotherapy by qualified nonmedical psychologists, and the association's efforts, along with the support of some physicians, psychiatrists, and political figures, had led finally in 1956 to issuing the required law (Ahmed, 1999).

The 12 state universities and their branch campuses are distributed throughout the country, and thus psychology students can be found in every Egyptian county. However, most psychological services and doctoral-level psychologists, as well as the two Egyptian psychology associations are in larger cities. Psychological services include clinics and psychiatric hospitals, psychological centers in industry, prisons, rehabilitation institutions, and schools, and facilities for the handicapped. These services are predominantly found in Cairo and to a lesser extent in Alexandria and in the Delta and upper Egyptian counties (Ahmed, 1992, 2002; Ahmed & Gielen, 1998; Ibrahim, 1989; Ministry of Defense, 2000; Zahran & Elias, 1989).

Due to the expansion of psychology departments during the last three decades and students' increased exposure to the field, graduate enrollments in master's and doctoral programs have grown steadily. Abou-Hatab (1992) estimated the number of psychology graduates from 1958–1986 to be 15,000, with the number of highly qualified M.A. or Ph.D. holders to be 100. By now, an estimated 20,000 psychology graduates and 2000–2200 M.A.s and Ph. D.s are active in Egypt (Ahmed & Gielen, 1998). The ratio of active psychologists is about 3 psychologists per 100,000 people, which, though still markedly inadequate, is the highest of any Arab country.

There are two associations in Egypt. The Egyptian Association for Psychological Studies (EAPS), founded in 1948 in Cairo, is one of the 20 national psychological associations that formed the International Union of Psychological Sciences (IUPsyS) in 1951, and represented Egypt at the IUPsyS until 1964. Eventually, EAPS withdrew from the IUPsyS due to administrative and financial reasons, then in 1987, rejoined IUPsyS. In 2002, membership in the EAPS was around 1200 psychologists who held mostly master's degrees or doctorates, or both. Most EAPS members are Egyptians, although some members are from other Arab countries. The EAPS is run by a council that consists of nine members elected at the annual meeting. Among the functions of the council are preparing the internal rules and regulations, forming the committees necessary to fulfill the aims of the association, calling ordinary or extraordinary meetings according to rules, and putting into effect the resolutions of the general meeting. The council is elected to a 3-year term by a secret ballot at the annual meeting. Election of one third of the members of the council is held every year.

The EAPS has three categories of membership. Members must be psychology graduates able to contribute to the objectives and resolutions of the association. Fellows must be members of the association for at least 7 years and must make outstanding scientific contributions to psychology or have rendered outstanding services to psychology. Affiliated members must have a university degree and should be interested in psychology and be willing to benefit from the activities of the association.

The second professional association is the Egyptian Psychologists Association (EPA). It was established in the early 1980s and now has more than 1650 academic and nonacademic members. Whereas the EAPS is academically oriented, the EPA tends to be more "practitioner oriented," and was designed to be a contact point for clinicians (King, 1984). As a result, the relationship between the EAPS and the EPA could be considered complementary rather than competitive.

At present, each of the Egyptian associations has its own psychology journal. The EAPS has published the *Egyptian*

Journal of Psychological Studies since September 1991, and its English journal, *Arab Psychologist,* since 2000, the latter in collaboration with the Arab Association of Psychology (AAP). The EPA has issued its own journal, *Psychological Studies,* since January 1991. Although the EAPS and the EPA are professional associations, they receive some governmental support and are subject to government inspection and control, especially regarding their financial transactions.

Since 1985, the EAPS has held its annual conferences at an Egyptian university. Such conferences provide an opportunity for Egyptian and Arab psychologists to make contact and present their research. The EAPS' annual meetings could have a positive effect on the image of psychology among the public and the government. Since 1993, the Arab Conference of Psychology has convened yearly in conjunction with the annual meetings of the EAPS (Ahmed & Gielen, 1998). No tension exists in Egypt between scientists and practitioners in psychology, as most practitioners are basically scientists and it is rare for someone to engage in only psychotheraphy. Besides the annual conference of the EAPS, the major activities of both the EAPS and the EPA are lectures and symposia held at least once a month on topics related to psychology or allied disciplines. The EPA is especially interested in offering training programs, particularly on psychological testing, for young psychologists. Moreover, the EPA has established recently an online service to help Egyptian and Arab psychologists locate and use previously published Arab psychology research. At the 6th annual conference of the EAPS in 1990, it was suggested that the AAP be established.

During the EAPS' 9th annual conference in 1993, the General Secretariat of the suggested AAP was formed (Taha et al., 2003), but no further steps have been taken. In Egypt, as in the other Arab countries, psychology faces a lack of recognition by the public. As Melikian (1984, p. 74) has noticed, "Psychology has not left a noticeable impact on industry or government. It has not been recognized as a potential contributor to development planning. Whatever consulting role psychologists have played has been primarily restricted to ministries of education and occasionally ministries of health (and/or social affairs, industry, and interior). However, special education and human services are the areas in which [Egyptian and Arab] psychologists have made a significant impact."

Studies have also shown that the image of psychology is weak among the general population and government officials, even among psychology students themselves (see Ahmed, 1992; Ahmed & Gielen, 1998; and Soueif, 1978). As a result, the status and role of psychology in relation to other disciplines and professionals (e.g., physicians, psychiatrists, social workers, psychiatric nurses) are not clearly identified. In most cases, psychologists' status and roles are limited and controlled by other professionals, such as physicians and psychiatrists. Although salaries for psychologists are consistent with those of social workers and teachers, psychologists' salaries are usually not as high as physicians, psychiatrists, or even psychiatric nurses. It is worth noting that in various work settings, especially in the Ministry of Health, there is a generally congenial relationship between psychologists and psychiatrists, physicians, social workers, and nurses.

23.2 EDUCATION
AND TRAINING

The first department in which psychology was taught was the Department of Philosophy at Cairo University; later, it was taught at the Department of Philosophy and Sociology at Alexandria University, and then at the Department of Psychological and Sociological Studies at Ain Shams University. Separate psychology departments were established in 1974 at Cairo, Alexandria, and Ain Shams Universities (Soueif, 1991).

Soon after they began to teach psychology at Cairo University, the faculty felt the need for students to obtain further training in psychology, especially in research methodology. Consequently, master's and doctoral programs were initiated in the 1940s. Graduate studies were expanded to include a diploma of clinial psychology at Ain Shams University in 1956 and an applied psychology diploma at Cairo University in 1958. More recently, diplomas for mental health and educational psychology have been established at the College of Education at Ain Shams University that were emulated by colleges of education at other Egyptian universities.

Today Egypt has 12 state universities that offer bachelor's, master's, and doctoral degrees in psychology: Cairo University, Alexandria University, Ain Shams University, Assuit University, Tanta University, Mansoura University, Zagazig University, Helwan University, Suez Canal University, Menoufia University, Minia University, and the South Valley University. Departments of psychology are housed in different administrative units of universities, and all universities have branch campuses around the country. Al-Azhar University in Cairo,

the oldest continuously operating institution of higher religious learning in the world, is not considered a state university though it is public. Al-Azhar University was established in 970 C.E. as a school of Islamic studies and witnessed major changes in the 1960s that permitted modern scientific subjects like psychology to be included in the curriculum. Al-Azhar University currently has psychology and educational psychology departments. Also, the American University in Cairo, established in 1920, has offered courses in psychology for many years, which made it possible for students to minor in psychology while obtaining degrees in other departments in the social sciences (e.g., sociology).

Egypt also has six private universities, one of which—the Sixth of October University—recently established a psychology department in its College of Social Sciences. In addition to bachelor's, master's, and doctoral programs, there are a diverse array of diploma programs in psychology (e.g., educational psychology and mental hygiene) (Abou-Hatab, 1992; Farag, 1987). Diplomas are considered to be professional rather than academic degrees. Besides the graduate diploma in educational psychology that is granted by all Egyptian colleges of education, a graduate diploma in applied psychology is offered by the colleges of arts at Cairo and Menoufia universities. The emphasis of this training program, which is the only one of its kind, is clinical application, and students are qualified primarily to perform limited assessment techniques at the request of a physician (King, 1984). The College of Arts at Ain Shams University also offers a graduate diploma in clinical psychology.

Some research centers and institutes offer psychology programs at the master's and doctoral levels and provide psychological services and facilities to conduct psychological research. Among the centers and institutes that offer graduate programs in psychology is the Institute for Higher Studies on Childhood at Ain Shams University and the Institute for Educational Research and Studies at Cairo University. Other centers that provide research facilities and psychological services are the Center for Childhood, Center for Psychiatric Medicine, and a counseling center at Ain Shams University, the Center for Childhood Handicapped at Al-Azhar University, and the Center for Psychological Research and Studies at Cairo University (Abdel-Fattah, 1998, 1999). The National Center for Social and Criminological Research in Cairo has several research units, including ones that study criminal behavior and public opinion. The National Center has produced important psychological research since its inception in 1956 (e.g., a cannabis consumption longitudinal study and a study investigating the changing role of Egyptian women).

Scores on the secondary school certificate are the only criterion for admission to undergraduate study in psychology at Egyptian universities. It should be mentioned, however, that psychology in Egypt and in other Arab countries is still taught in the colleges of arts or education that generally accept students with lower scores on the secondary school certificate than is typical for colleges of engineering, medicine, and pharmacology. Psychology in Egypt has not been able to attract high-scoring students, especially males. Top-quality secondary school graduates tend to select more lucrative and prestigious fields of study. Although women form about two thirds or more of the undergraduate student body in psychology at the Egyptian (and Arab) universities, only a few pursue graduate studies. Abou-Hatab (1992) reported that 35% of the psychologists in Egypt are women and that psychology staff are predominantly male. Another possible reason is that psychology is primarily identified with colleges of arts or education where the enrollment of men has declined over the last 30 years.

The full-time undergraduate program in psychology requires 4 years to complete. Undergraduate and graduate curricula in psychology in Egypt are very similar to the American curricula. All courses offered at the undergraduate level and the qualifying years for the master's and doctoral degrees are compulsory. Undergraduate psychology programs cover areas such as Arabic and English languages, introduction to philosophy, and introduction to sociology as well as psychology courses in biological, cognitive, developmental, history and systems, learning, physiological, social, group dynamics, personality, pathology, assessment, clinical and counseling, criminal, industrial–organizational, educational psychology, research methods and design, and statistics. Most of the psychological texts are in Arabic and very few are in English.

Admission for graduate study in psychology (e.g., diploma, M.A., and Ph.D. programs) in colleges of arts or education require a bachelor's in psychology with not less than "good" grades and one qualification year in which advanced courses in measurement, research design and statistics, psychology theories, and clinical or counseling psychology are taken. Master's students must also score above 350 on the Test of English as a Foreign Language (TOEFL) examination before defending their theses. As for the doctorate, some

Egyptian universities such as Cairo University require 1 or 2 years of qualification, usually with a clinical orientation, before granting M.A. holders with good grades to enter a doctoral program.

Graduate degrees typically include the special diploma (at some universities 1 year of advanced coursework in psychology is required instead) that requires 1 or 2 years beyond a B.A.; M.A.s and Ph.D.s require, aside from the qualification year(s), a minimum of 1 and 2 years, respectively. Both master's and doctorates require a thesis in psychology (Abou-Hatab, 1992; Ahmed, 1992, Ahmed & Gielen, 1998; Farag, 1987). The percentage of Egyptian psychologists who have graduate degrees (i.e., the special diploma, M.A., or Ph.D.) is estimated to be 10%.

Limited financial aid is only available to master's and doctoral students in psychology. However, Cairo University has a reciprocal program with the Ministry of Health, whereby B.A. students are hired to work in Ministry hospitals if they are concurrently enrolled at the university in a 1-year Diploma of Applied Psychology program. During and after this diploma, students are eligible for scholarships through the Ministry that allow them to continue their studies (King, 1984). No more than 10 students are enrolled in this program each year; however, to date, nearly 400 students have completed this special diploma.

Since 1974, most psychology departments at Egyptian state universities have been distinct and separate units located in either colleges of arts or education, with the exception of the Institute for Higher Studies on Childhood at Ain Shams University, where graduate programs in psychology and sociology are offered in a merged department.

The following state universities train most Egyptian psychologists: Cairo University, Ain Shams University, and, to a lesser extent, Alexandria University. The universities at Cairo and Ain Shams could be considered as the most outstanding due to the number of the faculty and staff, quality of teaching, number of published studies, equipment, and training and research facilities.

Lecturing is the most frequent pedagogical method used to teach psychology at Egyptian universities. Class size reflects the increasing number of students enrolled and the ever-worsening ratio of the number of students to the number of instructors (Soueif & Ahmed, 2001). Psychology taught at the Egyptian universities, as in most of Arab universities, tends to emphasize theory rather than research and practice. Moreover, some advanced fields, such as animal behavior, mathematical psychology, neuropsychology, psycholinguistics, and psychopharmacology are not included in the curriculum. Psychological education and training in Egypt, especially at the undergraduate level is relatively general. Specialization at the graduate level depends on the nature of the thesis.

Books are the most preferred resource in teaching psychology at Egyptian universities, with journals taking a secondary role. Computer hardware and software, along with Web and distance-learning capabilities, are used very rarely at the undergraduate level, and these resources are not widely available; therefore, they have little impact at the graduate level. Translated psychometric tests predominate (Ahmed, 1997, 1999). However, several attempts have been made to construct indigenous tests, particularly of personality.

Several textbooks that cover almost all traditional domains of psychology have been published during the last 60 years. At Cairo and Ain Shams Universities, Egypt's finest institutions of higher education, some standard and influential texts in psychology have been authored in clinical, industrial, and social psychology, as well as in psychological measurement and statistics. Examples are Mustapha I. Soueif's (1985) edited book, *A Source Book in Clinical Psychology*, and the 7-volume book, *Readings in Social Psychology in the Arab Countries*, edited by Lewis, K., Meleika (1965–2002). In addition, some psychology journals are published in Egypt, such as the *Egyptian Journal of Psychological Studies* (published by the EAPS), *Psychological Studies* (published by the EAP), and the *Arab Psychologist* (published by the EAPS and the AAP). All three journals publish articles in both Arabic and English. The *Journal of Psychology*, published by the General Egyptian Book Organization since 1987, features articles in Arabic only. The Counseling Center at Ain Shams University publishes the *Journal of Psychological Counseling*. Most colleges of arts and education in Egypt have local outlets publishing scientific research in psychology. Recently, the preparation of dictionaries and encyclopedias in psychology and psychoanalysis has received attention (Taha et al., 2003). A bachelor's degree in psychology is considered to be sufficient by all government departments for the degree holder to work as a psychologist. The Ministry of Health, however, encourages psychologists to obtain the graduate diploma at Cairo University after they have been appointed; as previously noted, this degree is very clinically oriented.

To engage in the professional practice of psychology in Egypt, a doctorate in any field of psychology is required in addition to a license. If the individual has a Ph.D. and is a faculty member at an Egyptian university, the license is automatic. A Ph.D. without a faculty appointment may apply to take a licensing examination, after which the application would be reviewed by a committee of nine persons from the Ministry of Health (including a legal advisor, a professor of neurology, and a professor of psychiatry from Cairo University), and a license may then be granted. However, to date, no one has ever been granted a license in this way. There is no provision for master's-level practice except under the auspices of the Ministry of Health program (King, 1984). After an aggressive and widespread campaign that called for legalization of the practice of psychotherapy by qualified nonmedical psychologists, the 1956 law that governed private practice was issued. It should be noted that despite the efforts already mentioned, the number of licensed and qualified nonmedical Egyptian psychologists who currently practice psychotherapy remains insignificant (Ahmed, 1999).

The number of psychologists who have been educated and trained outside of Egypt is generally small and represents approximately 5–10% of all psychologists working at Egyptian universities. This figure has gradually decreased over the last two decades for several reasons. First, according to Egyptian law, only master's-degree holders who are working at a state university can be sent abroad to earn their doctorate. Second, there is greater opportunity today than ever before to obtain advanced degrees from Egyptian universities. Third, economic hardships have led to a reduced number of psychology students (and other students in the humanities and social sciences) who would be able to study abroad.

Continuing education, including attending conferences and participating in workshops, is important to Egyptian psychologists working at universities; however, due to the limited budget and funding for such activities, as well as language barriers, the number of Egyptian psychologists who attend international and regional conferences and workshops is quite small.

23.3 SCOPE OF PSYCHOLOGICAL PRACTICE

In the early 1990s, the EAPS and the EPA joined forces to design a code of ethics to govern and regulate the activities of Egyptian psychologists. Efforts were undertaken to ensure that the code, derived from that of the American Psychological Association, would be suitable for Egyptian culture and balance the needs of Egyptian society with the growing internationalization of psychology. In 1995, and on the occasion of the 11th annual meeting of the EAPS, the first Egyptian, and Arab, code of ethics for psychologists was approved (Taha et al., 2003); however, no further steps have been taken to implement this code or to establish a mechanism for the adjudication of ethical violations.

Of the many contributions of Egyptian psychologists to theory, the most prominent are Abdel-Aziz H. El-Koussy's three-dimensional model of intellect, Yousef Mourad's theory of development, Ahmed Z. Saleh's theory of learning, Fouad E. El-Sayed's hierarchical model of intelligence, Ramzia El-Ghrib's dimensional model of practical ability, Mustapha I. Soueif's theories on creative thinking and personality, and Fouad A. Abou-Hatab's four-dimensional model of cognitive processing. Unfortunately, with the exception of Soueif's and Abou-Hatab's work, these theoretical formulations have received little attention outside of the Arab world (Abou-Hatab, 1984, 1992).

Egyptian and Arab psychologists have published widely over the last 60 years, including articles in the following areas: social, personality, cognition, educational, psychopathology, women's issues, substance abuse, children's drawings, aging, delinquency and criminal behavior, cross-cultural comparisons, measurement, developmental, religion, history of psychology, counseling, reading, psycholinguistics, experimental, physiological, and physiological psychology (Ahmed, 1992, 1998; Ahmed & Gielen, 1998).

Although it is not possible to review all of the psychological studies conducted in various domains of the discipline in the past six decades, several avenues of research deserve mention:

1. The standardization of psychometric instruments, adapted from the West, has been an important research interest of Egyptian psychologists since the early 1930s. At that time, Al-Qubbani and El-Koussy were active in the translation, validation, and standardization of many tests, mainly of intelligence, and compiled Egyptian norms for the appropriate interpretations of test scores. Their work, as well as the construction of indigenous psychometric instruments, is being continued today (Abou-Hatab, 1992, 1993, 1996; Ahmed, 1992, 1997, 1999, 2002; Ahmed & Gielen, 1998; Meleika, 1997).

2. From the early 1960s to the present, Egyptian psychologists have attempted to replicate studies cross-culturally.

These studies include investigations of attitudes, childhood development, creativity, moral development, personality, and psychopathology (Ahmed, 1992, 2002; Ahmed & Gielen, 1998; Soueif & Ahmed, 2001). Soueif (1998b, p. 581) concluded, "By and large, cross-cultural research seems to be one of the few truly promising areas of research among Arab (and Egyptian) psychologists."

3. Finally, there are programs of research that address the changes taking place in Egyptian culture and society. For example, many interdisciplinary studies have been undertaken in response to the recent rise in cannabis consumption. One of these was a 35-year project at Cairo University on variables that have lead to and maintained cannabis use in recent years, and many interdisciplinary studies have been conducted to explore the various aspects of the problem (Ahmed, 1992, 1997, 2002; Ahmed & Gielen, 1998; *British Journal of Addiction*, 1988; Soueif, 1998a, 1998b, 2001; Soueif & Ahmed, 2001). The project has inspired other Egyptian and Arab psychologists to investigate and respond to the problem of substance abuse. Modernization and women's issues have also received wide attention from Egyptian researchers (Abou-Hatab, 1992; Farag, 1987).

The last three decades have witnessed a growing trend in Arab psychology, especially in Egyptian psychology, to relate the discipline to Islam. Some psychologists have focused on the contributions of the early Arab and Muslim scholars to psychology, whereas others have tried to recast psychology in a distinctly Islamic framework (Abou-Hatab, 1988; Ahmed, 1992). Such efforts are taking place in other Islamic countries like Pakistan (Ahmed & Gielen, 1998). However, it is too early to evaluate the impact of these changes (Ahmed, 2002).

Several attempts have been made to identify and define the services offered by psychologists in Egypt. Soueif (1958) pioneered this effort by delineating the role of clinical psychologists in psychiatric clinics. Abdel-Rahman, Abdella, and Mesieha (2002), Al-Sabwah (1996), and Zahran and Elias (1989) conceptualized the role of school psychologists in preuniversity educational settings. Soliman and Ibrahim (1998) discussed the academic qualifications necessary for psychological counselors in Egypt in light of the 21st century's challenges, present and future. Finally, Hamza (1987) and Ibrahim (1989) have shed some light on the role of psychologists in the Ministry of Industry, specifically in the Authority for Productivity and Vocational Training, and in the Ministry of Labor, respectively.

Psychology graduates in Egypt and in many Arab countries have difficulties finding employment because of their lack of qualifications and the lack of awareness in the public and private sectors of psychology's importance. Only in the oil-producing Arab states do psychology graduates have a relatively good opportunity to work in the field (Ahmed, 1992; Ahmed & Gielen, 1998).

Psychology graduates in Egypt join the profession by either providing psychological services to meet the needs of the public or by teaching. Students who graduate with an advanced degree in psychology have essentially two career choices: an academic position at a university or hospital work, in which case they may be hired as psychologists by the Ministries of Defense,

Education, Health, Industry, Interior, or Social Affairs. Here, psychologists work in inpatient or outpatient clinics of public hospitals, in institutions serving the aged, juvenile delinquents, or the physically and mentally handicapped, and also in prisons, schools, industry, or the armed forces. Students who graduate from colleges of education are almost certain to move directly into teaching jobs at public intermediate or secondary schools, or, if they obtain a master's or doctorate, a post at one of the national universities.

The Ministry of Health operates several mental hospitals in Cairo, Alexandria, and Tanta. Some of these are for men only and include separate units for substance-abuse and criminal patients. Psychosis is the main criterion for admission to inpatient care. Private mental hospitals are beginning to appear in Cairo and Alexandria. Finally, most Egyptian universities with colleges of medicine offer some outpatient psychiatric care.

Psychology graduates in Egypt can work in different settings such as hospitals and clinics that belong to the Ministry of Health, provided they obtain higher qualifications after they are appointed, especially the Diploma of Applied Psychology. A number of psychology graduates have joined the Ministry of Education to work as school psychologists; during the last 10 years, the Ministry of Education has hired over 5000 school psychologists to work in intermediate and secondary schools (Soueif & Ahmed, 2001). It is hoped that more psychology graduates will be hired in order to fulfill the Ministry's plan to assign a psychologist to every intermediate and secondary school in the county. The armed forces in Egypt have benefited from psychological services since the early 1950s (Taha et al., 2003). A significant step in this direction occurred when the Ministry of Defense opened its Psychological Affairs Center in 2000. The center has several units with different tasks and assignments and has recruited a group of highly qualified and well-trained psychologists. Several studies and applied tasks have been carried out since the center was established, including the development of specific job descriptions (Ministry of Defense, 2000). Although few psychology graduates join the ministries of communication and transportation, industry, and interior (where they work as psychologists in the prisons and other rehabilitation institutions), more psychology graduates are hired yearly by the Ministry of Social Affairs to work as psychologists in several units, departments, and institutions that serve especially juvenile delinquents, the elderly, and the physically impaired.

Psychology graduates with excellent grades can join research centers, such as the National Center for Social and Criminological Research. They can also take academic jobs, teaching in departments of psychology, educational psychology, and mental health, where they work as teaching assistants and increase their chances to pursue advanced degrees.

Although the number of psychology graduates working in the aforementioned settings has increased markedly during the last two decades, this number is still not sufficient to meet the needs of the Egyptian population. There is hope that more psychology graduates will be hired in the future. However, psychologists in some work settings have made outstanding contributions. Examples include the Unified Arab Classification of Professions and Jobs that was completed under the auspice of the Ministry of Labor and which represents the first Arab descriptive index of occupations in Egypt (Ibrahim, 1989; Taha et al., 2003). Psychologists have also played a key role over the last 40 years in constructing and validating psychological tests used in the General Authority for Productivity and Vocational Training, Ministry of Industry; these tests guide the selection of applicants for various occupations (Hamza, 1987).

As in other developing countries, some psychological activities are performed by nonpsychologists. Such activities include psychotherapy, which some physicians, clerics, and indigenous healers practice. Fortunately, such practices are on the decline. Another example can be found in some work settings, such as in the Ministries of Social Affairs and Interior, in which some psychological job functions and services are occasionally carried out by social workers and sociologists.

Since the early 1960s, universities in other Arab countries, especially in the oil-producing states, have hired Egyptian psychologists to work in their psychology departments or in their psychiatric hospitals and mental health clinics. For example, the number of Egyptian psychologists with Ph.D.s who are permanently or temporarily employed by psychology departments in the oil-producing Arab countries may be as high as 50–60% of the total number of the staff at these universities. In addition, some Egyptian psychologists have immigrated to Australia, Canada, France, and the United States.

23.4 FUTURE CHALLENGES AND PROSPECTS

Several attempts have been made to trace the progress of psychology in Egypt (Abou-Hatab, 1992, 1993, 1996, 1997; Ahmed, 1992, 1997, 1999, 2002; Ahmed & Gielen, 1998; Eissoy, 1989; Farag, 1987; King, 1984; Safwat, 1996; Soueif, 1988, 1991; Soueif & Ahmed, 2001). All of these conclude that psychology in Egypt and other Arab countries (Al-Nabolsey, 1999; Khaleefa, 1997) has grown stronger, yet suffers from several shortcomings, much like psychology in other parts of the developing world.

The following points highlight Egyptian psychology's strengths:

1. Psychological literature, written mostly in Arabic by Egyptian authors, has been growing rapidly since the early 1940s, mainly because the subject is taught in Arabic. As a result, many psychological texts have been translated into Arabic. Moreover, many Western psychometric tools have either been translated into Arabic or adapted to suit Egyptian culture. These accomplishments have propagated psychological knowledge throughout the Arab world.

2. Based on a combination of economic, political, and cultural factors, Egypt began in the early 1960s to supply newly established Arab universities with trained professors who fit into the cultural context of other Arab countries with relative ease. Egyptian psychologists are estimated to represent about 70% of the total number of psychologists in the Arab world.

3. Egypt has 60 psychology departments that constitute about 56% of all psychology departments in the Arab world. As a result, many Arab psychologists have received their education at Egyptian universities, especially at Cairo and Ain Shams Universities.

4. Egyptian psychological research is estimated to constitute more than 70% of the total investigations in psychology in the Arab world. Nearly, 60% of all psychological scales in use in Arab countries were constructed or translated, and standardized, by Egyptian psychologists working in Egypt or employed by Arab universities (Ahmed, 1992; Ahmed & Gielen, 1998; Soueif & Ahmed, 2001).

5. Egypt has two very active psychology associations that seek opportunities for collaboration.

The following are the shortcomings that characterize psychology in Egypt and in other Arab countries:

1. Egyptian psychologists continue to import Western psychology in typically unsystematic ways. Much of Egyptian psychology, both scientific and professional, reflects the assumptions, theories, methods, instruments, and research results of the West. This epistemological dependence inhibits the creativity in Egyptian psychologists and stifles the emergence of an indigenous psychology. It may also weaken the professional identity of Egyptian psychologists.

2. Egyptian psychologists are relatively unaware of the cultural nature of the discipline and have therefore neglected to integrate their national heritage with modern developments in psychology. Much Egyptian and Arab research and practice neglects contemporary cultural and social realities of the region. This has led, among other things, to a psychology lacking in relevance. Moreover, there is a lack of interdisciplinary cooperation that would synthesize the efforts of psychologists with other social scientists.

For example, anthropologists tend to have a solid grasp of indigenous realities and often use the participatory research methods in their research. Such contextually sensitive investigatory approaches have been underutilized by Egyptian and Arab psychologists who still favor artificial paper-and-pencil tests.

3. Egyptian and Arab psychology is not well-presented in the international arena for several reasons, the most obvious of which is that almost all psychological research here is published in Arabic. In addition, few Egyptian psychologists attend international or regional psychology conferences.

4. The healthy development of the discipline is constrained because psychology departments housed in colleges of arts suffer from an inflexible bureaucracy with respect to budgeting and administration. For example, there is no "reliable and well-structured policy for research funding, and the scholarly worth of most ongoing research must remain questionable" (Soueif & Ahmed, 2001, p. 225).

5. There is little specialization in Egyptian and Arab psychology (Safwat, 1996). Because most are regulated by the state, psychology departments offer only general psychology programs that produce general psychologists. There are no special tracks or departments for child, clinical, or industrial psychology. Due to the lack of specialization, Egyptian psychologists have experienced serious difficulties in developing and sustaining research and training programs in specific areas of psychology. Once developed, however, these specialty areas could lead to a greater international impact and produce much-needed

experts to advance the status of psychology in Egypt.

6. Egyptian psychologists have an ambiguous professional identity rooted in the artificially created dichotomy between educational psychologists belonging to institutes or colleges of education and their counterparts working at the colleges of arts.

There is a growing need to establish a psychology that fits more closely with the cultural and social realities of human experience in this area of the world (Khaleefa, 1997). Three factors will help Egyptian and Arab psychology move in this direction (Ahmed & Gielen, 1998):

1. The recognition and development of indigenous psychologies. These have been developed in countries such as China, Japan, India, and Mexico.
2. The establishment of regional associations and journals for psychology in the Arab world, as in Asia, Europe, Latin America, and Oceania. In this context, an "Arab Union of Psychology" would be of great value.
3. The gradual decline, via advancements in communications technology, of the dominance of American psychology over psychologies in other regions of the world, coupled with renewed interest in research on issues pertinent to an evolving Egyptian culture and society.

At present, the main challenge for Egyptian psychology is to provide high-quality degree programs in traditional areas of psychology while creating new programs, particularly interdisciplinary ones, that will attract the finest students and faculty members. To do so, it is nec-essary to evaluate current and potential resources, and build on these assets in order to develop areas of strength that will enhance the visibility of psychology in Egyptian higher education and better serve the nation (Ahmed, 1997, 1999). In addition, Ahmed and Gielen (1998) suggested the foundation of an institute of Arab psychology in Cairo in order to develop effective networks of communication and cooperation between different disciplines across national and cultural borders. The ultimate goal of such an institute would be to establish a culture of creative theorizing, cumulative research, and informed criticism.

REFERENCES

Abdel-Fattah, K. I. (1998). Research centers in some Egyptian universities, I. *Journal of Psychology (Egypt), 12,* 158–163. [In Arabic]

Abdel-Fattah, K. I. (1999). Research centers in some Egyptian universities, II. *Journal of Psychology (Egypt), 13,* 134–139. [In Arabic]

Abdel-Rahman, M. E., Abdella, H. I., & Mesieha, J. I. (2002, December). *A work's guide for school psychologists in intermediate and secondary schools in the Arab Republic of Egypt.* Paper presented at the Convention for Psychological Counseling, Ain Shams University, Cairo, Egypt. [In Arabic]

Abou-Hatab, F. A. (1984, September). *Research on a four-dimensional informational model for cognitive processes.* Paper presented at the meeting of the International Congress of Psychology, Acapaleo, Mexico.

Abou-Hatab, F. A. (1988, August). *Islamic paradigm for psychology.* Paper presented at the meeting of the International Council of Psychologists, Singapore.

Abou-Hatab, F. A. (1992). Psychology in Egypt. In V. S. Sexton and J. D. Hogan (Eds.), *International psychology: Views from around the world* (pp. 111–128). Lincoln, NE: University of Nebraska Press.

Abou-Hatab, F. A. (1993). Psychology in the Arab world: Case study from developing nations. *Egyptian Journal of Psychological Studies (Egypt), 2,* 1–27. [In Arabic]

Abou-Hatab, F. A. (1996). Psychology as seen from Arabic, African, and Islamic perspectives: Unfulfilled hopes and hopeful fulfillment. *Egyptian Journal of Psychological Studies (Egypt), 6,* 3–23. [In Arabic]

Abou-Hatab, F. A. (1997). The march of psychology in the Arab world and its horizons of development. *Egyptian Journal of Psychological Studies (Egypt), 6,* 9–56. [In Arabic]

Ahmed, R. A. (1992). Psychology in the Arab countries. In U. P. Gielen, L. L. Adler, & N. Milgram (Eds.), *Psychology in international perspective: 50 years of the International Council of Psychologists* (pp. 127–150). Amsterdam: Swets & Zeitlinger.

Ahmed, R. A. (1997). An interview with Mustapha Soueif. *World Psychology, 3,* 1–15.

Ahmed, R. A. (1998). *Bibliography of psychological studies in the Arab world.* Unpublished manuscript, Menoufia University at Cairo, Egypt.

Ahmed R. A. (1999). An interview with L. K. Meleika. *International Journal of Group Tensions, 28*(1–2), 155–170.

Ahmed, R. A. (2002, March). *Psychology in the Arab world: Present status and future estimations.* Paper presented at the meeting of the International Conference on Social Sciences, Kuwait University, Kuwait City, Kuwait. [In Arabic]

Ahmed, R. A., & Gielen, U. P. (1998). Introduction. In R. A. Ahmed & U. P. Gielen (Eds.), *Psychology in the Arab countries* (pp. 3–48). Cairo: Menoufia University Press.

Al-Nabolsey, M. A. (1999). Toward the future of psychological sciences. *Psychological Studies (Egypt), 9,* 225–233. [In Arabic]

Al-Sabwah, M. N. (1996, December). *A scientific conception of the roles of the school psychologist.* Paper presented at the Professional Conference on Modernizing the Role of Social Worker and Psychologist in the Context of Developing the Educational Process, Cairo, Egypt. [In Arabic]

British Journal of Addiction. (1988). Conversation with Mustapha Soueif. *British Journal of Addiction, 18,* 131–139.

Caudle, F. M. (1994). History of psychology. In R. J. Corsini (Ed.), *Encyclopedia of psychology* (2nd ed., Vol. 2, pp. 135–142). New York: Wiley.

Eissoy, A. M. (1989). Psychological research in Egypt: Methodology and topics. *Journal of Psychology (Egypt), 3,* 7–9. [In Arabic]

El Koussy, A. A. H. (1935). Space perception. *Monographs of the British Journal of Psychology, 89*(1, Serial No. 20).

Farag, S. E. (1987). Egypt. In A. R. Gilgen & C. K. Gilgen (Eds.), *International handbook of psychology* (pp. 174–183). New York: Greenwood Press.

Girges, S. (1967). *From pharaohs to the nuclear age: The story of mental health in Egypt.* Cairo: Ministry of Cultural Affairs. [In Arabic]

Hamza, G. M. (1987). The role of psychologists in the Authority for Productivity and Vocational Training. *Journal of Psychology, 1,* 31–54. [In Arabic]

Ibrahim, M. F. (1989). The role of psychologist in the Ministry of Labor. In F. A. Abou-Hatab (Ed.), *The yearbook in psychology* (Vol. 6, pp. 439–444). Cairo: Anglo-Egyptian Bookshop. [In Arabic]

Khaleefa, O. H. (1997). The predicaments of Euro-American psychology in a non-Western culture: A response from Sudan. *World Psychology, 3*(1–2), 29–64.

King, D. W. (1984). Psychology in the Arab Republic of Egypt. *International Psychologist, 25,* 7–8.

Meleika, L. K. (Ed.). (1965, 1970, 1979, 1985, 1990, 1994, 2002). *Readings in social psychology in the Arab countries* (Vols. 1–7). Cairo: General Egyptian Book Organization. [In Arabic]

Meleika, L. K. (1997). *Clinical psychology: Part 1. Evaluation of abilities.* Cairo: V. Kerelos Press. [In Arabic]

Melikian, L. H. (1984). The transfer of psychological knowledge to the third world countries and its impact on development: The case of five Gulf oil-producing states. *International Journal of Psychology, 19,* 65–77.

Ministry of Defense. (2000). *Psychological Affairs Center.* Cairo: Ministry of Defense Press for Journalism and Publishing. [In Arabic]

Omar, H. (1928). *Intelligence measurement.* Cairo: Al-Aaseri Bookshop. [In Arabic]

Safwat, A. (1996). Psychology in the Arab nation and its challenges in the future century. *Psychological Studies, 6,* 1–4. [In Arabic]

Soliman, A. S., & Ibrahim, H. (1998, December). *The qualification of psychological counselors and the 21st century's challenges: Reality and the future estimations.* Paper presented at the International Conference on Psychological Counseling, Cairo, Egypt. [In Arabic]

Soueif, M. I. (1958). The role of the clinical psychologist in the psychiatric clinic. *Journal of Mental Health (Egypt), 1,* 10–32. [In Arabic]

Soueif, M. I. (1978). *Modern psychology.* Cairo: Anglo-Egyptian Bookshop. [In Arabic]

Soueif, M. I. (Ed.). (1985). *A source book of clinical psychology.* Cairo: Dar el-Maaref. [In Arabic]

Soueif, M. I. (1988). National scientists' mission in the Arab world, or toward an Arab national school in the behavioral sciences. *National Review of Social Sciences (Egypt), 25,* 103–141. [In Arabic]

Soueif, M. I. (1991). Psychology in Egypt throughout half a century: A dialogue between science and society. *Egyptian Journal of Psychological Studies (Egypt), 1,* 17–30. [In Arabic]

Soueif, M. I. (1998a). Drug use, abuse, and dependence. In R. A. Ahmed & U. P. Gielen (Eds.), *Psychology in the Arab countries* (pp. 495–516). Cairo: Menoufia University Press.

Soueif, M. I. (1998b). Conclusion. In R. A. Ahmed & U. P. Gielen (Eds.), *Psychology in the Arab countries* (pp. 569–582). Cairo: Menoufia University Press.

Soueif, M. I. (2001). Practical clinical psychology in the Egyptian cultural context: Some personnel experiences. *International Journal of Group Tensions, 30,* 241–266.

Soueif, M. I., & Ahmed, R. A. (2001). Psychology in the Arab countries: Past, present, and future. *International Journal of Group Tensions, 30,* 211–240.

Taha, F. A., Kandeel, S. A., Mohammed, H. A., & Abdel-Fattah, M. K. (2003). *Encyclopedia of psychology and psychoanalysis* (2nd ed.). Cairo: Gharib Press.

Zahran, H. A., & Elias, F. G. (1989). Psychologists in the Ministry of Education. In F. A. Abou-Hatab (Ed.), *The yearbook in psychology* (Vol. 6, pp. 433–438). Cairo: Anglo-Egyptian Bookshop. [In Arabic]

IMPORTANT PUBLICATIONS

Abou-Hatab, F. A. (1973). *Mental abilities.* Cairo: Anglo-Egyptian Bookshop. [In Arabic]

Ahmed, M. A. (1962). *Psychological and educational measurement.* Cairo: Mektabt Nahada al-Mesria. [In Arabic]

Ahmed, R. A., & Gielen, U. P. (Eds.). (1998). *Psychology in the Arab countries.* Cairo: Menoufia University Press.

Fathy, M. (1950–1965). *Criminal psychology: Science and practice* (Vols. 1–4). Cairo: Maktabt el-Nahada el-Mesria. [In Arabic]

Ghoneim, S. M. (1975). *Psychology of personality: Determinants, measurements, and theories.* Cairo: Dar el-Nahada al-Arabia. [In Arabic]

Hana, A. M. (1959). *Educational and vocational guidance.* Cairo: Maktabt el-Nahada el-Mesria. [In Arabic]

Khairy, E. M. (1957). *Statistics in education and psychology.* Cairo: Dar el-Nahada al-Arabia. [In Arabic]

Mourad, Y. (1954). *Principles of general psychology.* Cairo: Dar el-Maaref. [In Arabic]

Rageh, A. E. (1961). *Industrial psychology.* Cairo: Modern Printing Establishment. [In Arabic]

Soueif, M. I. (1958). Extreme response sets as a measure of intolerance of ambiguity. *British Journal of Psychology, 49,* 329–334.

Soueif, M. I. (1963). *Introduction to social psychology.* Cairo: Anglo-Egyptian Bookshop. [In Arabic]

Soueif, M. I. (1967). Hashish consumption in Egypt: With special reference to psychosocial aspects. *Bulletin on Narcotics, 1,* 1–12.

CHAPTER 24

Psychology in Iran

BEHROOZ BIRASHK

Behrooz Birashk completed his M.A. and Ph.D. in counseling psychology at the University of Illinois at Urbana–Champaign. He joined the Ministry of Health and Medical Education in 1980. In 1985, he joined the Iran Medical University School of Medicine and the Tehran Psychiatric Institute as a faculty member. He is an associate professor of psychology and dean of the Department of Clinical Psychology and Behavioral Sciences. His research interests include mental illness, psychotherapy interventions, personality-related disorders, counseling, AIDS, and addictions.

Behrooz Birashk also acted as member of an international scientific committee for an international congress on cognitive–behavioral psychology. He is a member of American Psychological Association (APA), International Cognitive–Behavioral Association, Iranian Academy of Medical Sciences, Iranian Counseling Association, and the Iranian Association of Clinical Psychology. He is

also the ex-president of the Iranian Psychological Association (IPA), the current president of Iran Music Therapy Association, and a member of the Scientific Board of Clinical Psychology at the Ministry of Health and Medical Education. He is on the editorial board of three journals of psychology and psychiatry, and has written 7 books and edited 12 others.

24.1 OVERVIEW

Psychology has existed as a specialized and independent subject in Iran for about 100 years; however, its history is mingled with the history of the development of psychotherapy in Iran. Early in Iran's history, people with mental illness were believed to be entrapped by wicked ghosts. Treatments included trepanation (making a hole in the skull in order to release the ghosts), seclusion and restraint, physical punishment, burning, and all kinds of torture (Shamloo, 2000).

The treatment of people with mental illness in ancient Iran, as in other parts of the world, was tremendously influenced by superstition. There are references to mental illnesses and their treatment, both with and without drugs, in ancient Iranian texts, particularly in the *Avesta* (the most ancient scriptures of Zoroastrianism). Some of the oldest Iranian scripts divide the human body into four parts: the physical body, spirit, psyche, and mind. Treatments were based on this fourfold typology, and included the application of syrups, plants, concoctions, as well as the whispering of spells, a practice believed to eradicate wicked ghosts.

According to the Assyrians, Ahoora Mazda created all the good things in life while Ahriman created pain and illness. Fighting illness was believed to be the duty of clergy, who were the representations of Ahoora Mazda.

Islamic physicians helped preserve and transmit the Greco–Roman heritage during the dark age of Western civilization (Mehryar, Muharreri, & Khajavi, 1992). The Jondi Shapoor Hospital and Medical School were founded in the last years of the Sassanid period, and both soon became internationally famous. Jondi Shapoor Hospital was important to psychology and psychiatry because the physicians employed there understood and emphasized the brain's influence on the body and believed that the brain regulated physical symptoms. At the peak of Islamic civilization, there were physicians like A.M. Zakariya-e-Razi, A.A. Ahvazi Arjani, Avicenna (Ibn Sina), and Seyed Esmaeel Jorgani who shaped the future of medical practices in Iran (Mehrabi et al., 2000).

Avicenna (Ibn Sina) was a pioneer in neurology and psychology who emphasized the reciprocal interaction of body and mind. In the book *Al-Qanun*, in a chapter related to brain illnesses, Avicenna discusses 12 symptoms that he calls *reflexes of the brain's condition*. This chapter also describes paralysis, tremulousness, memory, thought, and hallucinations. His explanation of delirium parallels 20th century concepts and is both detailed and precise (Mehryar et al., 1992).

Avicenna also writes about the importance of the body and its influence on the mind, and he believed that the mind was constantly aware of the body and especially designed to take care of it. Just as the body is influenced by the mind, the mind is influenced by the body. Avicenna also discusses memory disorders, mental disorders, and delirium. He believed that many disorders resulted from a lack of harmony between the brain and the body.

Muhammad Zakariya-e-Razi was an ancient Islamic physician who wrote books and pamphlets on disease and mental health. His unique treatments are recorded in Islamic history and highly respected. *Teb Al Fonoon*, one of his oldest books, explains disordered human emotions and their treatment (Mehrabi et al., 2000). Some of his books also discuss medical ethics and physician–patient relationships. "Razi" used conditioned reflexes in treating patients, and he was enthusiastic about this approach to treatment. Therefore, it is appropriate to regard him as the first physician in the Islamic period who practiced behavior therapy. Movafagh Haravi was another physician who lived before Avicenna. He describes the use of plants as medicines in his book, and he frequently prescribed these medicines for obsessions, madness, and melancholy. In fact, the basic treatment for all mental disorders was with plants in the middle ages. Unfortunately, superstitious beliefs once again began to spread in European countries, and ancient concepts about demons and possession became prominent. Some of these ideas spread to Iran, and science and psychology lost their popularity. It is worth mentioning, however, that at the same time mental patients were being burned at the stake in Europe, there were centers in Iran that were providing compassionate and humane care for patients with mental illness. The most famous psychiatric hospital at this time was Dar al Shafa in Yazd Province.

24.1.1 The Current Status of Psychology in Iran

Psychology in Iran, as in other parts of the world, was profoundly influenced by the work of Wilhelm Wundt in Germany. However, modern psychology in Iran began in 1933 when the late Ali Akbar Siassi established the first laboratory of psychology by the order of the minister of culture in Dar Al Moalemin. Many of the basic instruments for this laboratory were donated from abroad. In 1935 and 1936, the first Iranian I.Q. tests were administered by Mohammad Bagher Hooshyar and Asad Ollah-e-Bijan.

Tehran University was established in 1934 and included traditional schools such as medicine, science, law, literature, and human sciences. However, Ali Akbar Siassi, president of the university, was interested in psychology and actually had written several books on psychological topics. Because of his interests, the first laboratory of psychology had been founded at the college of literature and human sciences at Tehran University in 1938.

The department of psychology eventually became independent of philosophy, and a psychology degree (B.A.) was offered. After some years, a graduate degree in general psychology (M.A.) was offered by the Institute of Psychological Research and Training Sciences. Other universities were established in Isfahan, Shiraz, Tabriz, and Mashhad, and these schools soon began issuing degrees in psychology.

Many clinical psychologists with M.A. degrees and a few with Ph.D. degrees have graduated from these centers, and these psychologists are busy workings in various institutes, university centers, or clinics throughout Iran.

24.1.2 Psychology Journals

There are certain popular journals that most Iranian psychologists read and in which most Iranian psychological research is published (Ghobari & Bolhari, 2001). These journals include *The Journal of Psychology* (Quarterly Journal of the Iranian Association of Psychology), *Quarterly Journal of Andeesheh Va Raftar* (mind and behavior; a journal of psychiatry and clinical psychology published by Tehran Psychiatric Institute), *The Journal of Psychology and Education* (published by the psychology faculty at Tehran University), *Journal of Pazhohesh ha ye Ravan Shenakhti* (published by an NGO), and *Quarterly Journal of Tazeha ye Olum e Shenakhti* (published by the Iranian Center for Cognitive Science Studies). The Iranian Counseling Association also has a quarterly called *Journal of Tazeha Va Pazhoheshhaye Moshavereh* (counseling, research, and development). The Iranian Psychological Association has plans to begin publication of a journal in the near future.

24.1.3 Psychological Associations

The first Iranian Psychology Society was established in 1968. After the Islamic Revolution in 1978, the association stopped its activity. Currently, there are four organized nongovernmental psychological bodies in Iran with different goals. In 1995, the Iranian Psychological Association was established with the permission of the Ministry of Science, Research, and Technology. It has 4,200 members and 7 divisions: (1) exceptional children, (2) counseling, (3) clinical, (4) research, (5) measurement, (6) theoretical, and (7) educational psychology. The Iranian Association of Psychology was formed in 1997. Also in 1997, with the permission of the Ministry of Science, Research, and Technology, the Iranian Counseling Association was established with 1,380 members. In 2002, with the permission of Ministry of Health and Medical Education, the Iranian Association of Clinical Psychology was formed. The goals of these associations are to improve the knowledge of psychology and to support psychologists in Iran. Each of these associations has its own publications.

24.2 EDUCATION AND TRAINING

24.2.1 Clinical Psychology

The first clinical psychology course was taught in 1965 in Tehran University. S. Shamloo wrote the first book in this field, titled *Clinical Psychology*. A year later, the first psychology clinic was founded. Clinical psychology was a known, recognized, and accepted field of study by the 1970s when the first clinical psychology master's degrees were awarded by Tehran University at the psychiatry department in Roozbeh Hospital. These 3-year courses consisted of 2 years of theoretical and practical work related to clinical psychology and 1 year devoted to clinical training and writing the thesis. This center stopped functioning after 5 years of training graduates, following the Islamic Revolution in 1978. After the revolution, the Tehran Psychiatric Institute, a branch of Iran University of Medical Sciences, began to offer an M.S. in clinical psychology in 1985. There have been 16 graduating classes and more than 196 M.A. graduates from this institute. In the 1990s the Ministry of Health and Medical Education agreed to permit the M.S. degree in clinical psychology to be offered at the Welfare and Rehabilitation Sciences University in Tehran.

The Ministry of Health and Medical Education established a center in 1977 for the purpose of teaching, managing, observing, and supporting psychiatrists, clinical psychologists, and psychiatric nurses. At the same time, with the support of a psychiatrist named Iraj Siassi, the Ministry of Health employed some psychology graduates with B.A. degrees. After completing a 6-month intensive course in psychology, these employees were permitted to work in hospitals, particularly Razi hospital, the largest psychiatric hospital in the Middle East. After the Islamic Revolution in 1978, the Welfare Organization and Rehabilitation Association was abolished and many of its functions were transferred to a new organization. The name of this new center was changed to Tehran Psychiatric Institute in 1979.

By decree of the Council of Cultural Revolution, the Ministry of Science, Research, and Technology in 1990 started a clinical psychology M.A. program at Mashhad Ferdowsi University. Since 2000, clinical coursework has been offered at Isfahan and Shiraz Universities, and today psychology is one of Iran's most attractive fields of study for students, researchers, and the general public (Kamarzarin, 2002).

At present, there are seven branches of psychology in Iran. The Ministry of Health and Medical Education is responsible for training in clinical psychology (M.A. and Ph.D.). The other branches of psychology, regulated by the Ministry of Science, Research, and Technology, are general (at 16 universities), educational at (8 universities), clinical (at 13 universities), exceptional (at 7 universities), industrial and measurement (at 3 universities), and health psychology (at 1 university). About 4500 students are accepted in Iran universities as psychology majors each academic year, and currently, 17,650 students are studying psychology. This number includes those students taking correspondence courses through Payame-Nour University.

The M.S. degree in psychology, awarded in general, clinical, exceptional children, and educational approaches, is available through 27 universities in Iran. About 183 graduate students are accepted each academic year in these centers, and at present 534 graduate students are working towards psychology degrees in these programs.

Finally, 111 students are studying general and educational psychology at the Ph.D. level at 10 universities in Iran, and 135 students are studying other psychology specialties at the Ph.D. level. These statistics have been released by the Ministry of Science, Research, and Technology. The Ministry of Health and Medical Education also has two centers for training clinical psychologists at the M.A. and Ph.D. levels. At present, there are 32 Ph.D. students studying clinical psychology in Iran. In addition, thousands of other students receive B.A. and M.A. degrees from the Islamic Azad University, but unfortunately, no precise statistics are available on those opting for psychology. According to the report of the Ministry of Science, Research, and Technology in 2002, approximately 17,000 students were studying psychology in Iran at different levels.

There are four female students at the B.A. level for every male student; however, there are no significant differences in the number of female and male students at the M.A. and Ph.D. levels (Ministry of Science, Research, and Technology, 2003).

The Tehran Psychiatric Institute, a part of Iran University of Medical Sciences, is the leading center for training clinical psychologists and a World Health Organization Collaborating Centre for Mental Health. Since 2000, this Institute has been recognized as a National Scientific Center for Education and Research. The Institute has 101 psychiatrists, 57 psychiatric nurses, and 196 clinical psychologists trained at the M.A. level. In 1997, the Tehran Psychiatric Institute established the first Ph.D. course in clinical psychology; to date, two Ph.D. students in clinical psychology have graduated from the Institute. The University of Welfare and Rehabilitation Sciences and the Tehran Psychiatric Institute had accepted 30 Ph.D. candidates as of 2003.

There are three levels for psychology education in Iran. The first level is the bachelors, which requires 4 years of study and passing 146 units. The M.A. degree requires 2 years of study and passing 32 units specific to clinical psychology. Some private or semiprivate universities train psychologists and offer the B.A., M.A., and Ph.D. degrees. There are 281 psychology faculty teaching in 52 centers under the Ministry of Science, Research, and Technology, and 70 psychologists working in 34 centers of the Ministry of Health and Medical Education. Psychology is taught to almost all students getting a bachelor's degree, and it is taught in medical schools as well. The Council of Cultural Revolution designs both schedules and syllabi, and so colleges have little latitude in making changes. However, access to the Internet, satellite systems, and books in the English language are producing dramatic changes at many universities.

24.2.2 Undergraduate Admission Requirements

The Iranian Ministry of Science, Research, and Technology determines eligibility for admission to undergraduate programs. In general, admission is highly competitive, and there are many more qualified applicants than the institutions of higher education can accommodate. Candidates must meet the following requirements for studying psychology: (a) they must hold a high-school diploma with a major in experimental sciences, humanities, or mathematics and physics and (b) they must successfully pass the nationwide entrance examination administered annually (each summer) by the Iranian Ministry of Sciences, Research, and Technology. The duration of Bachelor of Science (B.S.) study is about 4 years or at

least 8 semesters, and 148 credits are required before the B.S. degree is awarded.

24.2.3 Graduate Admission Requirements

24.2.3.1 MASTER OF SCIENCE OR ARTS

To be admitted to the Master of Science or Arts programs, candidates must hold a bachelor's degree in psychology (or a related field), and successfully pass the nationwide entrance examination administered annually by the Ministry of Science, Research, and Technology and/or the Ministry of Health and Medical Education separately. For the M.S. in clinical psychology, candidates must successfully pass the nationwide entrance examination administered annually by the Ministry of Health and Medical Education, as well as an oral examination. In addition, Islamic Azad University has its own entrance examination.

The Master of Science requires 2 years or 4 semesters, and 32 credits hours, including 4 to 6 credits of thesis. For the M.S. in clinical psychology, students must pass the following courses: advanced developmental psychology, medical psychology and neuropsychology, theories of personality, research methods and statistics, cognitive tests in clinical psychology, advanced psychopathology, projective techniques in psychology, diagnostic interviewing techniques, theories of psychotherapy, and a practicum. In addition, students must pass a course titled "Muslim Scholars' Views on Psychology." This course reviews the theories of Islamic philosophers and scientists about the soul and psyche, and allows students an opportunity to discuss the relationships between psychological conditions and somatic disorders.

24.2.3.2 PH.D. IN PSYCHOLOGY

The graduation requirements for a Ph.D. program in Iran include 42–50 credit hours of coursework as well as a 1-year internship. Students in clinical psychology have to pass a comprehensive examination before starting their internship, as well as 20 credit hours of dissertation.

The courses required for clinical psychology students for a Ph.D. include the following: statistics and research methodology, advanced psychopathology, mental health and health psychology, advanced theories of psychotherapy, personality theories and psychopathology, child and developmental psychology, neuropsychology and neuropharmacology, cognitive–behavioral techniques, group therapy and family therapy, assessment and treatment, history and systems of psychology, and a practicum.

24.2.4 Grading System

In Iran, the grading system is usually numerical. Instructors may report grades from 20 as the highest passing grade to 0 as the lowest failing grade. Grade 10 is the lowest passing grade that may be reported for undergraduate work and grade 12 is the lowest passing grade assigned for graduate courses (grades of 15 are required for the Ph.D.).

Undergraduate and graduate students are required to achieve a grade point average of 12 and 14, respectively, each semester. If they fail to meet this standard, they are placed on academic probation.

Students on probation are permitted to take only a limited number of courses until they are off probation.

24.2.4.1 THE MASTER'S THESIS AND DOCTORAL DISSERTATION

A thesis or dissertation submitted in partial fulfillment of the requirements for a degree must be presented in its final form to the department concerned no later than the date specified in the university calendar. The candidates must present a thesis or a dissertation as evidence of his or her ability to perform original scholarly research and to interpret and present its results.

At the beginning of the thesis or dissertation phase, the following steps must be taken:

1. Candidates may recommend to the department concerned a particular subject related to their field of study and a major field advisor as the chairperson of the thesis or dissertation committee. The major field advisor for a thesis or a dissertation must be at least a full-time assistant professor or a faculty member of a higher academic rank.
2. Once the topic has the approval of the department, candidates may recommend two faculty members as their minor field advisors with the approval of the major field advisor. A doctoral candidate may recommend only assistant professors and those with higher academic ranks as minor field advisors. Instructors may be recommended as minor advisors for master's candidates.
3. Candidates must submit a proposal to their thesis or dissertation committee (the major field advisor and the two minor field advisors) that determines its acceptability. The thesis or dissertation

is completed under the guidance of the members of the committee.

4. When the thesis or dissertation has the approval of the committee, the candidate is recommended for the final examination. This examination is open to the public and is conducted by the major field advisor, the minor field advisors, as well as a referee in the case of a masters' thesis, and at least three outside readers and a referee in the case of a doctoral dissertation.

5. Candidates who successfully pass the oral examination are recommended for the degree by the related school.

6. If the final examination is unsatisfactory, the thesis or dissertation committee may recommend a second examination after a period of additional study.

In 1990, the Ministry of Health and Medical Education established the Board of Clinical Psychology. Its members are selected from among highly competent faculty members of the institutions of medical sciences throughout the country by the Ministry. The Board is responsible for designing questions for the written section of the different examinations and conducting the oral examination, as well as planning and supervising all the activities of clinical psychology in the country.

24.3 SCOPE OF PSYCHOLOGICAL PRACTICE

The number of psychologists in Iran is growing rapidly, but the exact number in different specialties is hard to estimate. However, overall there are 9.3 psychologists for every 100,000 people in Iran (Ghobari & Bolhari, 2001). They work in public and private psychiatric hospitals and in psychiatric wards in general hospitals, as well as in counseling centers (Mehrabi et al., 2000). In addition, many psychologists are working in the private sector and are not included in the list of official organizations and ministries.

According to the report of the Ministry of Science, Research, and Technology, in 2002 there were 280 psychologists practicing or teaching in Iran. A number of additional unidentified psychologists—those who do not hold any professional position—need to be added to this figure. However, an association for psychologists was recently formed at the national level (the Iranian Psychological Association—IPA), which may help to identify some of latter groups and allow the calculation of the precise number of psychologists in Iran.

Because of the economic problems currently confronting Iran, there are numerous young psychologists searching for employment. However, with the improvement of economic conditions, there should be full employment for all psychologists with appropriate academic credentials (Ghobari & Bolhari, 2001).

In addition to government organizations, many psychologists work in the private sector in either mental health clinics or with psychiatrists and neurologists in private practice. Since the beginning of the 1990s, the Higher Counsel of Youth and Adolescents, under the direct supervision of the Iranian President, has established specific criteria for founding counseling centers, and many psychologists are now working as a counselors or therapists in these centers.

Most Iranian psychologists work in Tehran (the capital) or in big cities. Almost all rural areas in Iran have a shortage of psychologists, and few hospitals in small cities have the psychologists needed to provide counseling or psychotherapy (Ghobari & Bolhari, 2001).

In addition to psychologists, religious figures and traditional healers provide psychological help to people who show symptoms of stress, emptiness, or anxiety (Langsley, Barter, & Amirmoshiri, 1983; Shahmohammadi, Bayanzadeh, & Ehsanmanesh, 1998). In their attempts to help people cope with their problems, these healers try to combine psychological treatment with traditional approaches to healing, such as *Zaar* (a type of traditional psychodrama), prayer, and pilgrimage.

There is seldom conflict or tension between psychologists and theologians over the application of the methods and techniques of clinical psychology in treating clients. However, certain psychological theories (e.g., Freud's ideas on sexuality as the basis for most human behavior) are clearly not acceptable to Islamic religious leaders. The conflict is seldom a problem insofar as there is relatively little interaction between clinicians and theologians; when it occurs, both sides look for common ground and stress similarities rather than differences. Psychologists are generally well accepted in academic settings as well as in the community as a whole, and their contributions to public health are increasingly acknowledged.

Most psychologists in Iran work in traditional mental health settings, clinics, polyclinics, or private, public, or university counseling centers. In these settings, they provide diagnostic services, interviews, psychological testing, and psychological or psychotherapeutic interventions. There is a good relationship and collaboration between psychologists, psychiatrists, and neurologists. Most of the psychiatrists, neurologists, and other physicians recommend biological treatments in conjunction with psychological, behavioral, or cognitive treatments.

The Bachelor of Science (B.S.) degree in psychology is required for all individuals who are working in psychology or counseling, or any other helping profession. This is a minimum level of education required for all psychologists to be eligible to work in public and private settings; however, most hospitals, medical universities, clinics, or the private sector prefer to hire psychologists with more advanced training, such as M.S. or Ph.D. degrees in clinical psychology or related areas. Most of the psychologists with Ph.Ds. in clinical psychology or related areas are employed in the Ministry of Health and Medical Education. They work as therapists in treatment centers, or teach psychology or psychotherapy and other related subjects to medical or psychology students. Psychologists with degrees in other psychological specialties are hired as faculty members of the universities operated under the auspices of the Ministry of Science, Research, and Technology. Most psychologists with Ph.Ds. in Iran have graduated from universities in the United States, England, Canada, Australia, or India, and a few have been trained in France and Germany.

Psychologists are not permitted to admit patients to hospitals because this privilege is restricted to physicians (Ghobari & Bolhari, 2001). However, psychologists working in hospitals (mental or general) often help physicians by writing chart notes and monitoring the patients' mental and psychological reactions to treatment and hospitalization. They also apply standard interventions such as cognitive-behavioral counseling, or family therapy.

In Iran, psychology students are taught the most important theories in psychology, as well as the major approaches to personality, counseling, and psychotherapy. All psychologists are familiar with different schools of thought, but most clinical and counseling psychologists prefer rational–emotive behavior therapy (REBT), cognitive–behavioral, client-centered, or analytical approaches.

Over the last decade, psychologists have discovered effective ways to compete with other healthcare providers, such as integrating their services into the primary healthcare system, and they have carved out a specialized position defined by their education, knowledge, and expertise. For example, psychologists can open private offices or counseling centers, and there is now a systematic methodology for billing for these services. However, even psychologists in private clinics still have to be affiliated with a psychiatric clinic or have a psychiatrist available for consultation.

In Iran, psychologists and psychiatrists acknowledge each other's distinct areas of competence and value each other's opinions. Despite psychiatrists and psychologists being aware of each other's complementary roles in treatment of people with psychological problems, psychologists are often uncomfortable and dislike being dependent on psychiatrists in official and organizational systems (Ghobari & Bolhari, 2001), desiring to treat their patients independently. They hope to establish laws regulating the practice of psychology and counseling. In fact, such a plan has now been approved (and ratified) by the Iranian parliament. In the near future, laws will be in place that will allow the indepen-dent practice of psychology and counseling throughout Iran.

Currently, psychologists in Iran are confronting challenges and controversies such as the impact of religious beliefs and attitudes on mental health and psychological well-being. Preliminary findings support an association between religious beliefs and practice and positive mental health. For instance, Jalili (1998) discovered that there was a significant and meaningful correlation between religious beliefs and mental health. This study showed that there were negative correlations between psychopathology and religious beliefs and attitudes. Likewise, Qods (1998) showed that there was a negative correlation between praying and anxiety in university students in Tehran. In some studies, reliance on God has been shown to reduce stress and anxiety (Bolhari, Ehsanmanesh, & Karimi, 2000). These examples illustrate one of the most important areas of Iranian psychological research, the examination of the interface between psychology and religious beliefs or practices (Ghobari, Nasafat, & Khoda-yari, in press).

24.4 FUTURE CHALLENGES AND PROSPECTS

General health indicators have been improving in Iran. These achievements have been possible because of the primary healthcare (PHC) system (Shadpour, 2000; Statistical Center of Iran, 2000). Local staff run health networks, and this model has spread to most parts of the country and has brought about immense changes in the promotion and maintenance of community health. Medical care also has improved because of an increase in human resources and their optimal distribution (Yasamy et al., 2001). The number of physicians has increased (90,000 in 2003 compared to 47,373 in 1990). Likewise, the number of hospital beds almost doubled in the last 20 years. Outpatient services are also available in 65 public clinics and 328 private clinics (Shadpour, 1994). Presently, there are 735 psychiatrists in Iran, and about 50 new psychiatrists graduate every year (Mehrabi et al., 2000). There are also 25 clinical psychologists with doctorates, more than 389 clinical psychologists with master's degrees, and 5000 individuals with bachelor's degrees in psychology (World Health Report 2000, 2002).

There are four periods in the history of modern Iranian mental health services. The first period, which lasted until the 1940s, was when medical schools were established in the country. In the second period, in the 1960s, psychiatry and, later, psychology emerged as specialties. The third period spans the 1970s, when efforts were directed towards achieving comprehensive mental healthcare by the society for rehabilitation of the disabled and community mental healthcare (Yasamy et al., 2001). The Ministry of Health and Welfare (later changed to Ministry of Health and Medical Education) initiated a series of epidemiological studies, built a number of new psychiatric hospitals and mental health centers in different regions, and initiated training programs in psychiatry, psychiatric nursing, and clinical psychology. All these activities were integrated to form the Tehran Psychiatric Institute after the Islamic revolution in 1979 (Yasamy et al.). The fourth period started in October 1986, when a multidisciplinary team of professionals, including psychologists, drafted the National Program of Mental Health (NPMH) that was subsequently adopted by the government. The main strategy of this new program was to integrate new activities into the already efficient primary healthcare system (Ghobari & Bolhari, 2001).

Integration of mental health into the primary healthcare system occurred from 1988 to 1990, and successful pilot programs were developed in Shahr-e-Kord and Shahreza in the central Islamic Republic of Iran. Evaluation studies showed significantly increased knowledge of health workers and improved skills in patient screening in these regions compared to the control area (Hassanzadeh, 1992; Shahmohammadi, 1990). Following this, a number of developments occurred in the country that led to a more rapid expansion of this program. Several factors contributed to this acceleration (Bagheri Yazdi et al., 2001; Mohit, Shahmohammadi, & Bolhari, 1998), including the creation of a mental health unit within the Ministry of Health and Medical Education; declaration of mental health as a specific component of primary healthcare; formation of a national mental health advisory committee, members of which were mainly faculty members from medical schools; the preparation of educational manuals for all levels of healthcare delivery (1998); reviews and workshops on the national program (1991) and mental health research methodology (1993); annual celebration of mental health week in October, since 1985; improved mental health awareness on the part of other health staff through workshops, seminars, and conferences; and improved public awareness about mental health through the mass media (Yasamy et al., 2001).

24.4.1 Areas of Need

In a rapidly changing society as in the Islamic Republic of Iran, where even the basic demographic structure is not comparable to what it was 12 years ago, it would be inappropriate to adhere rigidly to the priorities and guidelines appropriate for an earlier period. Since 2001, psychologists have argued about whether the NPMH should be maintained or radically revised. A realistic view would be to keep the first NPMH intact as a manifesto but to add new articles to it to respond to emerging demands. Thus, instead of arranging formal and time-consuming meetings to improve the wording of a new NPMH, it would be more effective simply to appoint additional committees to deal with different mental health problems. Such task-oriented committees could solicit input from the community and from experts in particular fields, and use this information to develop new programs and projects. These smaller programs could be addendums to the NPMH. Using this approach, the continuity of the NPMH program will be ensured, while the country can efficiently respond to new demands and emerging needs. The emerging needs of Iran include continued integration of services, improving the quality of service delivery, addressing urban mental health needs, mental health promotion, child and adolescent mental health, substance abuse prevention, providing mental health services in response to natural disasters, primary prevention, better training for mental health professionals, cost-effectiveness studies for psychological services, and enhanced international cooperation.

Mental health services are provided for an increasing proportion of the public, and the number of rural and urban health centers that provide mental health services has increased dramatically (i.e., services are now available at 54% of health centers). These improvements extend to both urban and rural areas (Yasamy, et al., 2001).

The Iranian national mental healthcare system is found in all areas of the country, and each district has psychologists who consult with other providers. Psychologists provide psychological assessment as well as psychotherapeutic intervention in clinics and psychiatric hospitals (Ghobari & Bolhari, 2001). They also play an active role in providing primary mental healthcare in Iran, and it is widely acknowledged that the services of psychologists are essential to an effective primary healthcare system.

Currently, psychology in Iran is developing a new identity that respects and integrates three different themes in its history: its religious and philosophical roots, its Western intellectual and international grounding, and its orientation to meeting the present needs of Iranian society (Kamarzarin, 2002). This integration, when fully realized, will result in a renaissance of the profession of psychology in Iran.

ACKNOWLEDGMENTS

I want to express my gratitude first to my friend and colleague Susan Rahmatian, faculty member of English Department at Tarbiat Moalem University for her editorial suggestions and remarks, which proved to be very helpful. In addition, special thanks and appreciation go to Mojgan Salavati, a Ph.D. student in clinical psychology, for her assistance in gathering data and her follow-up efforts to accomplish this work.

REFERENCES

Bagheri Yazdi, S. A., Malekafzali, H., Shahmoham-madi, D., Naghavi, M., & Hakmat, S. (2001). Eval-uation of function of auxiliary health workers (*behvarz*) and health volunteers in mental health care delivery in the framework of PHC system in Brojen City, Chahamahal, and Bakhtiari province. *Hakim, 4*(2), 100–110.

Bolhari, J., Ehsanmanesh, M., & Karimi, K. I. (2000). Relationship between the stressors, stress symptoms, and reliance on God (*Tavakkol*) in medical students. *Andeesheh Va Raftar: Quarterly Journal of Psychi-atry and Clinical Psychology, 6*(1), 25–34.

Ghobari, B., & Bolhari, J. (2001). The current state of medical psychology in Islamic Republic of Iran. *Journal of Clinical Psychology in Medical Set-tings, 8*(9), 34–43.

Ghobari, B., Nasafat, M., & Khodayari, M. (in press). Reliance on God and its effect on reduction of anxiety, *Journal of Psychology.*

Hassanzadeh, M. (1992). Evaluation of the integra-tion of mental health into the Shahreza city health centers. *Daru Va Darman, 10*(110), 15–20.

Jalili, K. H. (1998). *Investigating the relationship between religious beliefs and mental health in the mothers of exceptional children.* Unpublished master's thesis, Azad University of Birjand, Mash-had, Iran.

Kamarzarin, H. (2002). Country profile: Iran. *Psy-chology International, 13*(4), 5–6.

Langsley, D. G., Barter, J. T., & Amirmoshiri, A. (1983). Psychiatry in Iran and China. *International Journal of Social Psychiatry, 29,* 39–47.

Mehrabi, F., Bayanzadeh, S. A., Atef-Vahid, M. K., Bolhari, J., Shahmohammadi, D., & Vaezi, S. A. (2000). Mental health in Iran. In I. Al. Issa (Ed.). *Al. Junun: Mental illness in the Islamic world* (pp. 139–161). Madison, CT: International Universities Press.

Mehryar, A. H., Muharreri, M. R., & Khajavi, F. (1992). Neuropsychiatric disorders in the oldest medical textbook in Persian written around 985 A. D. *Hamdard Medicus. Quarterly Journal of Bait al Hikmat, XXXV, 1,* 5–23.

Ministry of Health and Medical Education. (1987). *Draft of the National Programme of Mental Health in Iran.* Tehran: Ministry of Health Publication.

Ministry of Health and Medical Education. (2003). *Annual reports from the numbers of psychology students and universities.* Tehran: Ministry of Health and Medical Education.

Ministry of Science, Research, and Technology. (2003). *Annual reports from the numbers of psy-chology students and universities.* Tehran, Iran.

Mohit, A., Shahmohammadi, D., & Bolhari, J. (1998). Independent national evaluation of mental health. *Andeesheh Va Raftar: Quarterly Journal of Psychiatry and Clinical Psychology, 3*(3), 4–16.

Qods, S. (1998). *The impact of prayer on reeducation of anxiety in college students.* Unpublished master's thesis, Islamic Azad University, Tehran, Iran.

Shadpour, K. (1994). *Primary health care in the Islamic Republic of Iran* (pp. 68–69). New York: UNICEF.

Shadpour, K. (2000). Primary health care networks in the Islamic Republic of Iran. *Eastern Mediter-ranean Health Journal, 6*(4), 822–825.

Shahmohammadi, D. (1990). *Comprehensive report of research project on the integration of mental health in primary health care in Shahr-e-Kord vil-lages.* Tehran: Ministry of Health and Medical Education.

Shahmohammadi, D., Bayanzadeh, A., & Ehsan-manesh, J. (1998). Pathways to psychiatric care in Iran. *Andeesheh Va Raftar: A Journal of Psychia-try and Clinical Psychology, 3*(4), 4–14.

Shamloo, S. (2000). *Mental health* (7th Ed). Tehran: Roshd.

Statistical Center of Iran. (2000). *Iran statistical year book.* Tehran: Author.

World Health Report 2000. (2002). *Mental health: New understanding, new hope.* Geneva: World Health Organization.

Yasamy, M. T., Shahmohammadi, D., Bagheri Yazdi, S. A., Layeghi, H., Razzaghi, E. M., & Bina, M. (2001). Mental health in the Islamic Republic of Iran: Achievements and areas of need. *Eastern Mediterranean Health Journal, 7*(3), 381–391.

IMPORTANT PUBLICATIONS*

Arani, T. (1978). *Psychology.* Tehran: Aban.

Behzad, M. (1978). *Genetics for psychology students.* Tehran: Javidan.

Ghasemzadeh, H. (1982). Some points on the training of clinical psychologists. *Baztab: A Journal of Psychology and Psychiatry, 3*(4), 62–79.

Houshyar, M. B. (1938). *Practical psychology: Experiments of psychology in the laboratory.* Tehran: Matbouat.

Khajehnouri, E. (1975). *Wonder of the inner world.* Tehran: Smog.Mansour, M. (1971). *Genetic psychology: Psychological development from childhood to old age.* Tehran: Chehr.

Okhovat, V., & Barahani, M. N. (1973). The estimation of intelligence with Rorschach test indices. *Journal of Tazehaye Ravanpezeshki, 4.*

Saheb-al-Zamani, N. (1963). *Unsettled soul.* Tehran: Ataei.

Shamloo, S. (1982). Clinical psychology in the past and present. *Baztab: A Journal of Psychology and Psychiatry, 3*(4), 9–30.

Siassi, A. A. (1969). *Psychology or psychology of upbringings.* Tehran: Dehkhoda.

* All of these books and articles are written in Persian (Farsi).

CHAPTER 25

Psychology in Israel

REBECCA JACOBY

Rebecca Jacoby is currently head of the medical psychology graduate program at the Tel Aviv-Yaffo Academic College and chair of the Professional Committee of Medical Psychology, Israel Ministry of Health. Until 2002, she served as director of the postgraduate medical psychology program at the Department of Psychology, at Tel Aviv University, and as chair of the Division of Medical Psychology of the Israel Psychological Association. She is also editor of the medical psychology section of Dialogue: Israel Journal of Psychotherapy. *Her main research and clinical interests are the subjects of hope, coping with breast cancer, and doctor–patient communication.*

25.1 OVERVIEW

Israel is a young Middle East country on the Mediterranean coast with a population of about 6.5 million, composed mostly of Jews who immigrated from all over the world. Although immigration from Europe began before World War II, the largest waves of immigration arrived as survivors of the Holocaust, followed by immigrants from North and South Africa, South America, and recently from Ethiopia and the former Soviet Union. The non-Jewish population consists of about 1.5 million people. The result is a multifaceted population divided into numerous communities differing in religion, traditions, and values, and characterized by cultural, economic, and social gaps as well as continuous conflicts and tensions.

Since its establishment in 1948, Israel has been almost continuously in a state of war or military tension with some of its neighbors. Israelis' encounters with bereavement have been continuous throughout the country's existence, during which 19,100 soldiers and 1,344 civilians have been killed. Injured soldiers and civilians, widows, orphans, bereaved parents, and individuals suffering from posttraumatic stress disorder (PTSD) are additional victims of these tragic circumstances. The ongoing state of conflict and the compromised sense of security deepen the gulf between different political streams and escalate public debates. The most tragic expression of this escalation was the assassination of Prime Minister Yitzhak Rabin in November 1995. The combination of external threats and internal tensions exact a high price from individuals in both emotional and physical domains, transforming Israel into a "stress laboratory" (Breznitz, 1983, p. 269), which in turn has influenced the work and research of Israeli psychologists. Extensive research has been dedicated to the evaluation of the cognitive and emotional harm sustained by the holocaust survivors (Baider, Peretz, & Kaplan De-Nur, 1992; Nadler & Ben-Shusan, 1989; Shmotkin & Lomarantz, 1998), veterans and prisoners of war (Lieblich, 1994; Solomon & Shalev, 1995), and victims of terrorist attacks (Witztum & Kotler, 2000), as well as their impact on the second and third generations (Bar-On, 1995; Dasberg, 1987; Lev-Wiesel & Amir, 2000). The special needs of these populations have stimulated the development of unique therapeutic frameworks and crisis intervention models (e.g., Lahad, 1997, 1999).

Before the declaration of the Israeli state, when the Jewish population included only about 600,000 people, psychological activities were relatively limited. Attempts made during this period by intellectuals to disseminate psychoanalytic theory did not command much attention because the Jewish population was struggling for survival, and because the Zionist and socialist ideologies that prevailed at that time promoted the renunciation of personal aspirations for the common good. (Ben-Ari & Amir, 1986; Levinson, 1997).

Beginning in the 1930s, after the arrival of a group of psychoanalysts from Germany, psychoanalytic thought began slowly to permeate the Israeli awareness. This was manifested in the founding of the Psychoanalytic Society (1933) and the Psychoanalytic Institute (1936), both in Jerusalem, and later in the application of psychoanalytic principles to education and medicine. For example, the Youth Immigration and the Kibbutz movements, which absorbed children and adolescents from all over the world, especially from Nazi-occupied countries, applied these ideas when planning institutions for children and developing guidelines for their education. In parallel, there were developments in the fields of psychometrics and vocational psychology, and centers were founded to deal with educational and occupational counseling for adolescents and adults.

The rapid growth of the Jewish population in the years following the establishment of Israel required immediate solutions for its absorption, education, and employment. This led to a large-scale development of institutions and centers that provided medical, mental health, educational, and welfare services. Psychologists have come to play an increasingly integral role in these endeavors.

The Israel Psychological Association was founded in 1957. During the same year, the first psychology department was launched at the Hebrew University of Jerusalem. In 1958, a psychology department was opened in Bar-Ilan University and later in Tel Aviv University (1966), Haifa (1966), and Beer Sheba (a specialization in psychology in 1967 and a Department of Behavioral Sciences in 1969). In 1985, a graduate program in industrial psychology was opened as part of the industrial management studies of the Israel Institute of Technology (Technion) in Haifa. During the last decade, a number of colleges have been opened in Israel, offering programs in psychology and behavioral sciences.

During the 1960s, psychological services in the fields of health, education, and welfare began to be institutionalized. The Ministry of Health and the General Sick Fund established interdisciplinary teams that included psychiatrists, clinical psychologists, and social workers who worked in psychiatric hospitals and mental health clinics throughout the country. The psychologists were responsible for psychodiagnostics and for psychotherapy and counseling, a majority using a psychoanalytic approach. The Ministry of Education founded counseling centers that employed educational psychologists who dealt mainly with diagnosing learning disabilities and directing children with behavioral problems into special education programs. The Ministry of Labor founded a number of centers for career counseling, while the Ministry of Welfare employed psychologists in local welfare departments. During this period, Israeli psychologists could specialize in three areas: clinical, educational, and occupational psychology. Later, a rehabilitation psychology division was founded in order to meet the needs of a growing number of casualties of wars, terror attacks, and traffic accidents. Finally, developmental and medical divisions were founded during the 1980s.

In sum, the psychological profession has consistently grown since the establishment of the state of Israel and has been given an increasingly central role in facilitating the young, heterogenic, and stress-ridden society to cope with the threats that they continuously encounter.

Because life in a continually stressed country creates unique psychological needs, one would expect that psychologists in Israel constitute a strong and influential professional body; however, this is not the case. Although the profession is considered prestigious, its status in the social service sector is relatively low, both in terms of professional status and salary. In a country troubled by defense and economic problems, mental health services are not a national priority and do not receive sufficient financial support.

At the end of 2000, according to the Ministry of Health (2002), there were 5927 psychologists listed in the Israel Psychologists' Registration Book (0.93 per 1000 people) compared to 3,206 psychologists listed at the end of the 1990s (0.66 per 1000 people). Today there are around 7,000 listed psychologists (1.08 per 1000). Thus, the number of psychologists has grown. However, the growth in the number of psychologists in public services has not been rapid because of a constant shortage in financial resources and available positions.

At the end of 2000, there were 29,895 registered physicians (4.70 per 1000), of whom 931 specialized in psychiatry (0.11 per 1000) and 152 in child psychiatry (0.02 per 1000). By the end of 2000, there were 28,224 registered nurses (4.40 per 1000), of which 16,973 were practical nurses (2.70 per 1000). Most prominent has been the growth of art therapy and occupational therapy. There were 937 art therapy professionals at the end of 2000 (0.15 per 1000) as compared to 55 by the end of the 1990s (0.01 per 1,000) and 1,965 occupational therapy professionals at the end of 2000 (0.31 per 1000) when compared with 249 by the end of the 1990s (0.05 per 1000) (Ministry of Health, 2002).

According to these data, 70% of Israeli psychologists are women, 60% were born in Israel, 10% in East Europe, 7% in West Europe, 9% in North America, 10% in South America, and 4% in Africa and Asia. Of these psychologists, 72% were trained in Israel, reflecting the growing maturity of the profession.

The highest concentration of psychologists is found in cities, primarily in Tel Aviv, Petach Tikva (in the center of Israel), and Jerusalem. There are fewer psychologists at the periphery of the country, although this by no means lessens the importance or quality of their work. Indeed, unique intervention programs have been developed and implemented at the periphery to address the special needs of the local population, such as the Community Stress Prevention Center in the northern border town of Kiryat Shmona (Lahad & Cohen, 1998b) that was developed to aid the inhabitants in coping with the threats associated with living close to the border. The model developed in Kiryat Shmona has been widely used internationally (see Krkeljic & Pavlicic, 1998).

The salary of psychologists working in the public sector is low, particularly considering the fact that they invest many extra hours at home and often pay for their own supervision, workshops, and continuing education programs. In 1973, psychologists who were members of the Israel Psychological Association joined the Organization of Academics in Social Sciences and Humanities; since then their salary has been linked to professional wage agreements.

In 1997, the public service psychologists waged a struggle to improve their employment conditions, which included a strike that lasted for several months. However, employment conditions for these psychologists have not improved significantly. Consequently, most public sector psychologists supplement their income by maintaining a private practice.

Two professional bodies deal with the legal, ethical, and professional issues that pertain to the regulation of professional practice: the Israel Psychological Association (IPA) and the Council of Psychologists (COP). The IPA, of which most of the Israeli psychologists are members, was established in 1959 with the aim of promoting the professional status of Israeli psychologists. Its activities are primarily aimed at the encouragement of professional development, including the organization of professional meetings and workshops as well as the publication of *Psychologia: Israel Journal of Psychology*. The IPA is also responsible for the formulation and implementation of the ethics code. IPA committees are elected by democratic elections. The IPA includes six divisions: clinical, educational, rehabilitation, developmental, medical (health), and occupational psychology. IPA membership requires registration and annual dues. The COP was established in 1977. It includes 27 members who represent relevant government offices, departments of psychology at the universities, and the divisions of the IPA. The COP is responsible for implementing the Law of Psychologists (legislated in 1977) and serves as an advisory body to the Minister of Health on all the topics related to psychology. The COP nominates the professional committees that are responsible for internship programs, training institutions, examinations, and the qualifications of supervisors.

In Israel, there are several professional societies including the Israel Society for Neuroscience, Israeli Psychotherapy

Association, Family Therapy Association, Israeli Association of Group Psychotherapy, Israeli Association for Cognitive–Behavioral Therapy, and the Hypnosis Association. These societies also include physicians, social workers, art therapists, and counselors.

25.2 EDUCATION AND TRAINING

Psychology is one of the most popular fields of academic study in Israel, and the competition at the graduate level, particularly in the clinical field, is fierce. The five Israeli universities offer graduate programs in both experimental and applied areas of psychology. The Israel Institute of Technology (Technion) offers an M.A. degree in industrial psychology. A bachelor's degree in psychology or in behavioral sciences can also be obtained from several other colleges.

The entry requirements for a B.A. in psychology are threshold grades in the matriculation examination and a psychometric examination. Since 1998, it has been possible to be admitted solely on the basis of matriculation examinations. Every year, about 200 students are accepted to the psychology B.A. program in each of the institutions from about 1500 applicants.

Competition becomes more extreme at the graduate level, particularly in the clinical areas that are in high demand, because the number of openings for the M.A. degree is very low compared to the number of B.A. graduates. Several areas of specialization are offered at the graduate level, with the applied areas corresponding to those represented by the IPA divisions. The specializations include clinical psychology (adult and child), educational psychology, rehabilitation psychology, neuropsychology, social psychology, cognitive psychology, psychophysiology, developmental psychology, organizational–occupational psychology, industrial psychology, and, recently, medical (health) psychology. Between 1991 and 2001 there was also a counseling specialization at Tel Aviv University. Some of the above areas are represented at all Israeli universities, whereas others are unique. About 10–20 students are accepted to each of the programs every year.

Admissions criteria for the M.A. include a minimum average grade for the B.A. coursework (85 out of 100), a test for advanced studies in psychology, letters of recommendation, and personal or group interview.

A Ph.D. is awarded by all Israeli universities to students who fulfill the specific requirements of doctoral studies at a given university, which always includes a doctoral dissertation. In the last few years, there has been a rise in the number of students wishing to continue with their doctoral studies, and a number of universities accept students who have excelled in their B.A studies directly into doctoral programs. However, due to the limited vacancies in these programs, many students apply for advanced studies abroad. There is a special department in the Ministry of Health that approves academic programs from foreign universities. Sometimes the applicant is required to complete certain courses in order to be eligible for professional recognition in Israel. Degrees acquired via distance learning are not accepted by the Ministry of Health or by any of the universities. A Psy.D. is not offered in Israel and is not recognized as an academic degree.

University tuition is about $2500 per year, roughly equivalent to two mean monthly salaries. Scholarships are awarded at every level of academic training, based on achievement, with the number of available scholarships varying among the different institutions. There are also subsistence scholarships available for students coming from low-income families, as well as scholarships dedicated to certain student populations (e.g., those belonging to certain immigrant communities). Part of the assistance is given through employment of students as research and teaching assistants.

Psychology departments in the universities are housed in the faculties of social sciences or humanities, except for Ben-Gurion University in Beer Sheba and in the colleges in which psychology is taught as part of behavioral studies. Until recently, colleges awarded only B.A. degrees in psychology. However, in April 2003 the Academic College of Tel Aviv–Yaffo received final approval for an M.A. program in psychology. The program, inaugurated in October 2003, launched the first medical psychology specialization in Israel. This development represents an emerging view that universities should focus more on research, whereas colleges should focus on training the practitioners.

All Israeli universities maintain high academic standards, and many Israeli scientists have attained international standing. For example, the winner of the 2002 Nobel Prize in Economics was the Israeli psychologist Daniel Kahneman, whose prospect theory (1979) was developed jointly with the late Amos Tversky.

Most faculty members in universities are researchers; only a minority are clinicians. Therefore, senior practitioners working in this field are contracted to teach some clinical courses. These teachers do not have an academic position, do not receive recognition for their work, and are not involved in the decision-making concerning curricula. It seems likely that the growing trend to separate colleges, which train practitioners, and universities, which train researchers, will further widen the gap between the practitioners and researchers, and this may eventually compromise the level of training given to students.

Lecturing is the main method of teaching at the B.A. level due to the high number of students, with some courses having as many as 200 students. The majority of courses taken during the B.A are basic ones such as introduction to psychology, statistics and research methods, physiological psychology, cognitive psychology, psychology of learning, developmental psychology, personality theories, psychopathology, and social psychology. During their 3rd year, students participate in seminars, which are held in smaller groups and which allow them to gain experience in independent research while receiving personal supervision.

The restricted number of students in graduate programs and the structure of courses, which include seminars and training groups, permit learning and experimentation in small groups. This enables teachers to give personal attention to each student and to assess their individual abilities and difficulties. Students in the applied areas participate weekly in a 2-day practicum for a 10-month period. Each student is assigned to work with several clients, and the work done is closely monitored and supervised by a senior psychologist. Such fieldwork exposes the students to rich clinical experiences and affords opportunities to translate theoretical knowledge into practice.

In every academic institution and hospital there is a library that includes books, journals, psychometric examinations, and computer terminals. Most of the books and journals required for psychology studies are written in English and therefore require students to be proficient in English from the outset of their studies. There are a number of journals in Hebrew such as *Israel Psychoanalytic Journal, Psychologia*, and *Dialogue: Israel Journal of Psychotherapy*, but they cover a very limited part of the curriculum. The issue of the language of a publication creates a dilemma. On one hand, there is a desire to maintain the primacy of the Hebrew language, and senior psychologists are urged to disseminate their knowledge in Israel by publishing in Hebrew. On the other hand, in order to be promoted within academia and to be part of the international scientific community, Israeli psychologists must publish in English. Doctoral students and, often, master's students are required to take a course in scientific writing in English. This course is especially important for those students who intend to pursue an academic career.

In the past, when journals were sent via regular mail, they reached Israel a few months after their publication date. Today, both faculty members and students have immediate access to electronic databases and are able to keep up to date, as well as maintain connections and cooperation with colleagues from all over the world.

The practice of psychology is under the authority of the Ministry of Health and requires a master's degree in psychology as well as an internship that is supervised by the professional committees nominated by the Council of Psychologists.

The *Law of Psychologists*, passed in 1977, defines who can register as a psychologist and who is qualified to practice psychology and sets the limits of the profession and each of its specializations. The registration in the *Psychologists' Registration Book* is open to those who have completed a master's degree in psychology.

Today, there are about 7,000 registered psychologists in Israel. In order to register as a specialist in a specific area of psychology, the candidate must complete 2 years of internship and pass certain examinations. The internship consists of supervised experience in hospitals, outpatient clinics, university clinics, educational settings, and several other approved training sites depending on the area of specialization. There is a shortage of positions and fellowships available for interns in psychology, so that in reality the internship is typically spread over 4 years in the form of half-time positions. Psychology graduates can specialize only in the area of their academic studies. Specialization in a different area requires the approval of the professional committee, which usually mandates additional studies. Psychologists are not allowed to prescribe medication or administer electroconvulsive therapy. A license to practice hypnosis is given to psychologists who fulfill the requirements of the Ministry of Health, which include basic training, supervision, and examination in hypnosis.

Most practicing psychologists continue their education and training after graduation, either at the institutions where they work or in continuing education programs at the universities. The Ministry of Health and the professional divisions of the IPA hold annual workshops and conferences that serve both as professional and social meetings. Several universities offer continuing education programs in psychology and psychotherapy, but these programs have not received formal accreditation by professional organizations. The greatest demand is for psychotherapy training. In 1971, the first psychotherapy-training program was opened as part of the continuing education program through the Faculty of Medicine at Tel Aviv University. The program is intended for psychiatrists, clinical psychologists, social workers, and art therapists. Later, additional programs were opened, both in academic and private institutions. In 1995, a postgraduate program was launched at Tel Aviv University, granting a diploma in medical psychology. This program served as the foundation for the M.A. program in medical psychology that recently opened at the Academic College of Tel Aviv–Yaffo. Additional continuing education programs offer courses in hypnosis, psychodiagnosis, cognitive–behavioral therapy, and group therapy.

Many Israeli psychologists are members of international professional organizations and routinely participate in international conferences. Israel has hosted a number of international psychology conferences as well. Regrettably, security concerns in our region limit the ability of the Israeli psychologists to hold international conferences in the country and force them to cancel scheduled events due to the reluctance of some of our colleagues to visit Israel.

25.3 SCOPE OF PSYCHOLOGICAL PRACTICE

Israel is a pluralistic country that has absorbed immigrants from all over the globe during various periods; as a result, the field of psychology is characterized by a broad range of theoretical views and

therapeutic methods. While the psychoanalytic and dynamic approaches reigned until the 1970s, other theoretical and therapeutic approaches were subsequently imported and absorbed, including the cognitive–behavioral approach introduced by psychologists who studied abroad during the 1980s and the Lacanian approach introduced by South American immigrants. Some of the new approaches were adapted to suit the needs of the local population (e.g., Lahad & Cohen, 1998a; Lieblich, 1982). In addition, special techniques were developed to fit the unique needs of specific populations such as soldiers and civilians suffering from PTSD.

Today, there is no leading theoretical or paradigmatic approach in Israeli psychology. The diversity of accepted approaches is reflected in both academic curricula and professional practice. However, an inspection of the development of the psychological profession during the past 30 years reveals an intriguing difference between academia and public services. Although in academia psychology is studied as an independent major in the faculties of social sciences or humanities and not in the schools of medicine, in the public health sector, most psychologists are subordinated to psychiatrists and are very much affected by their superiors' professional perceptions.

Another important distinction exists between the professional approach to public service and to private practice. In the private sector, psychologists are at liberty to choose any theoretical approach and technique they deem appropriate; in the public sector, budgetary and personnel limitations dictate the approach to professional practice. For example, due to recent reforms in the mental health services, the Ministry of Health adopted a 30-min basic therapy unit. A committee composed of physicians will determine how many such basic therapy units should be allotted to different types of interventions, such as psychodiagnosis and psychotherapy. Hence, the work of psychologists in the public sector is affected by the norms that are accepted in the medical professions, in which the emphasis has gradually shifted from quality to quantity.

Psychologists wishing to practice psychology in Israel are required to specialize in one of the six recognized IPA specializations listed above. The requirements for these specializations are based on rules and regulations defined by the Council of Psychologists.

Clinical psychologists work in general and psychiatric hospitals, in public clinics, and in private clinics and institutes. Because clinical psychology is a mental health profession, clinical psychologists in public institutions work in units headed by physicians. The bulk of their work involves personality assessment and psychotherapy in its various forms. A variety of psychotherapeutic techniques, both short- and long-term, are commonly used, including psychoanalysis, dynamic therapy, cognitive–behavioral therapy, and psychophysiological techniques such as relaxation, biofeedback, EMDR, and hypnosis. The wave of terror attacks in the last few years has drawn many psychologists to specialize in stress management procedures.

Educational psychologists are usually employed by the Ministry of Education and work primarily in municipal psychological services. These services are based in, and function via, the existing educational system: preschools, primary and secondary schools, and special education institutions. Educational psychologists diagnose maturity level, learning disabilities, and cognitive, emotional, and behavioral disabilities. They assist students with special needs, advise the pedagogical staff, and provide assistance during acute stress situations. The work of educational psychologists requires coordination and cooperation with teachers and school administrators as well as with the child's family.

Developmental psychologists work mostly in child development centers, neonatal hospital wards, and family healthcare units. Developmental psychologists deal with identifying, diagnosing, and treating children with developmental delays, neurological disturbances, genetic syndromes and inborn deficiencies, early attachment difficulties, and behavioral problems. The work of developmental psychologists requires the cooperation of families, pediatricians, family physicians, family health nurses, social services, and preschool teachers.

Rehabilitation psychologists work in general hospitals, rehabilitation centers, and clinics. Their role is to diagnose and assist individuals with physical, mental, emotional, and social disabilities to attain their maximal level of functioning. The rehabilitation process requires a concentrated effort of professionals from many fields including physicians, occupational therapists, physiotherapists, social workers, and career counselors. The area of rehabilitation is highly developed in Israel because of the constant flow of victims of wars and terrorist attacks, as well as the high rate of traffic accidents. The field of neuropsychological assessment and treatment of head injuries is particularly advanced in Israel.

Medical psychology is a relatively new specialization in Israel and has received recognition from the Ministry of Health in 2001. Until then, clinical and rehabilitation psychologists as well as social workers filled some of the roles of health psychologists within the medical system. With the recognition of this field as a separate specialization and the opening of academic programs, it is likely that medical psychologists will gradually fill the positions in general hospitals and clinics. The field of medical psychology focuses on the interrelationships between mind and body, and subsumes the entire continuum from health to illness. The work of medical psychologists includes preventive interventions such as stress management, psychological preparation for medical procedures, support for patients undergoing medical treatments, and emotional assistance to patients with acute, chronic, and terminal diseases. Medical psychologists work in cooperation with the medical staff, take part in decision making, and often serve as mediators between doctor and patient.

Social–occupational–organizational psychology incorporates five subfields: career counseling, organizational counseling, employee evaluation, social psychology, and ergonomics. Common to all of them is the focus on the relationship between the individual's inner world and personal integration into different social groups including the world of work. Although social psychologists are primarily engaged in research, in academia or in research institutes, occupational and organizational psychologists work mainly in large corporations and in manpower companies, and deal with assessing and evaluating applicants and employees, organizational counseling, and consulting on work-related problems.

Psychological services in the Israeli Defense Force are provided by two bodies.

The first is responsible for providing mental health services and is part of the Medical Corps. Its functions include diagnosing and extending psychological assistance to soldiers and their families. The unit is headed by a psychiatrist and is staffed by psychiatrists, psychologists, and social workers. The second, established and headed by psychologists, is the Behavioral Sciences Unit, which focuses on diagnosis and organizational counseling in addition to conducting research relevant to these fields. In the past, psychological activities in the Israeli army were based on lessons learned from the U.S. military; however, through the years, unique tools and work methods have been developed or adapted to the needs of the Israeli army. Today, there is also a separate psychology unit in the Air Force, and there have been growing demands to establish similar units in the other services.

Psychologists in Israel also work in prisons, addiction treatment centers, geriatric institutions, rehabilitation centers, hostels, immigration–absorption centers, government offices, the Israel Cancer Association, and first-aid emotional assistance centers, among others. A few years ago, a new center (Natal) was founded to offer psychological support to individuals who have been physically and emotionally traumatized by terrorist attacks.

Volunteer work is common in Israel. Very often, teams of specially trained psychologists travel abroad to assist others in coping with severe stress situations such as war, earthquakes, or terrorist attacks.

Israeli NGOs are engaged in peace activities in three domains: grassroots extra parliamentary organizations; Arab–Jewish research centers; and human rights NGOs (Pappe, 1999). In recent years, groups of psychologists, as well as other academics who believe that professional collaboration can help to defuse Israeli–Palestinian tension have been engaged in establishing joint projects between Israel and Palestine. One of those projects, launched in 1993, involved psychologists from Tel Aviv and Gaza universities, whose major goal is to enable physicians and psychologists from Gaza to receive training and supervision from Tel Aviv faculty members. Additional joint research and educational projects as well as publications and conferences are aimed at finding the path from intractable conflict toward reconciliation between the two nations (see Bar-Tal, 2002).

The domain of ethics in psychology has not been of central importance for many years. Recently, however, there has been a growing interest in the ethical practice of scientific and professional psychology, particularly from senior psychologists. An ethics code was approved by the IPA in 1998, adopted by the COP, and recently added as an obligatory course to the M.A. curriculum.

The ethics code expresses the position of the IPA with regard to the professional value system, as well as the professional conduct by which psychologists are expected to perform their work. The code includes guiding principles and ethical standards. The guiding principles are values that have been defined as the aspirational goals of the profession and include expertise, integrity, professional responsibility, respect of human rights and human beings in general, care for the welfare of others, and social responsibility.

Specific ethical standards are derived from these guiding principles and define the rules and practice of professional behavior. These include general standards of behavior applicable to the scientific and professional activities of all psychologists, as well as specific standards of behavior applicable to specific psychological activities such as assessment, psychodiagnosis, psychotherapy, counseling, research, and publishing. During the past year the ethics committee of the IPA has offered a workshop for senior psychologists that included lectures and discussions aimed at the evaluation and improvement of the existing ethics code. Key problems raised in the workshop have centered on the definition of the profession, boundaries of the profession, confidentiality and privilege, and ethical dilemmas in psychotherapy.

25.4 FUTURE CHALLENGES AND PROSPECTS

The future of psychology as a profession and the status of Israeli psychologists will greatly depend on the efforts of psychologists, both in the academy and in the professional field, toward strengthening the profession. These should include the resolution of intra- and interprofessional conflicts, the strengthening of the professional organization, the development of continuing education programs, and the promotion of greater independence from the medical profession. Finally, the Israeli psychological community must situate itself in the international psychological arena. The latter task is getting more difficult in recent years since the last Intifada has broken out because there are voices emerging from the international scientific community that Israeli psychologists be barred from participating in the scientific and professional community worldwide. This situation is highly regrettable as the Israeli academia in general is the stronghold of liberalism and tolerance, and the Israeli psychologists in particular are continually engaged in efforts to promote cooperation and diffuse the Israeli–Palestinian tension.

Before describing how the future of Israeli psychology might appear 25 years from now, I will examine the status of psychology and psychologists in Israel today, with a focus on the major conflicts and challenges faced by the discipline. In this context, several distinctions are critical. The first concerns the difference in prestige between psychology as a profession and psychologists in the field. The second concerns the difference in status between psychologists in the public and private sectors. My discussion of psychology and psychologists requires consideration of the following parameters: society, the employer, coworkers (e.g., physicians and social workers), the profession of psychology, clients, and the psychologists themselves. Clearly, there are reciprocal relations between these parameters; they sometimes complement each other and sometimes conflict. However, an attempt to delineate the multidimensional context in which psychology exists and in which psychologists function will facilitate understanding of the processes that will determine the future influence status of psychology and psychologists in Israel.

25.4.1 Society

The status of a profession in society is determined by several factors such as supply versus demand (with regard to both university curricula and employment opportunities), the influence of professional organizations and unions, educa-

tion, and income. In Israel, there is a gap between the prestige that the profession enjoys in the general population and the acknowledgement and legitimacy granted to it by the establishment. The high public prestige is reflected in the extremely great demand for undergraduate and graduate studies, and long waiting lists for counseling and therapy in public clinics and in private practice where the cost of testing and therapy is high. In spite of this, psychologists are underrepresented in the decision-making bodies, government committees, and public positions. Given that Israel is in an almost continual state of turbulence, one would expect to hear the voice of Israeli psychologists, but this is not the case. Often, after a terrorist attack, the media interviews physicians, social workers, or counselors who sometimes offer advice on issues that are more within the scope of expertise of psychologists. When psychologists are mentioned, it is mostly via reports on breaches of an ethics code (e.g., sexual relations with a client). The media fails to report on socially responsible and productive activities in which psychologists are engaged (e.g., voluntary activities), perhaps because psychologists are not sufficiently represented in the media. Moreover, the general public does not always distinguish between a psychologist, social worker, or counselor.

25.4.2 The Employer

Employers' perception of psychologists working at their institutions can be deduced from objective and practical criteria such as salaries, the number of positions, and resource allocation (e.g., research laboratories) relative to other professionals. Despite the prestige of the profession, the number of positions and resources allocated to psychology departments in universities and hospitals are substantially lower than those allocated to medical schools. Because there are not enough positions available for psychologists in the Israeli health system, the employment of psychologists frequently depends on the goodwill of the department head who more often prefers to employ a social worker or use the allocated budget to purchase a new instrument. This situation persists because of the hierarchical structure of the health system whereby management positions most often are given to physicians. This structure situates psychology under psychiatry and restricts the options of the chief psychologist. Hence, psychological services in medical settings, in contrast to social work services, are not independent. Therefore, a major challenge for psychologists is to modify the obsolete medical hierarchy. For instance, medical psychology should be separated from mental health services, and efforts should be made to develop an independent psychological unit headed by a psychologist working directly under a hospital administrator. With the recognition of medical psychology as a new division in the IPA, there is hope that this specialty will achieve equal status with the medical professions including psychiatry. In fulfilling this aim, academic and applied psychologists are working together to develop a curriculum that will provide essential knowledge and skills for future medical psychologists to assume key roles in the medical system as specialists.

25.4.3 Coworkers

Another factor that affects the status of the psychologist is the perception of the profession by coworkers (e.g., physicians, nurses, social workers). Although many psychologists have successfully integrated into the medical system and have earned the respect of their coworkers, this is often because of their personality and experience rather than because of the coworker's awareness and understanding of the central contribution of psychology to therapy, rehabilitation, and prevention. In order to promote such awareness and understanding, psychologists must market themselves and what their profession has to offer. This requires adoption of a proactive stance and empirically demonstrating their effectiveness through outcome research. Psychologists who have been trained in psychodynamic psychology have more difficulties in making such a shift, and, hence, their contributions are less clear to their coworkers. Psychologists who use short-term interventions and therapeutic tools whose effectiveness can be assessed after a relatively short time (e.g., hypnosis, biofeedback) earn more appreciation and cooperation. However, it follows that the medical system becomes competitive and stressful given the extensive overlap in responsibilities among different professional groups. Indeed, in some institutions social workers or nurses are reluctant to include psychologists on the medical team. It is important to note that many psychologists work part-time and, therefore, are not always available to clients or to staff. Consequently, their services are often forfeited, and members of other professions are approached for assistance. Therefore, psychologists must act to define their profession clearly in order to ensure their unique contribution and rightful play on professional teams.

25.4.4 The Profession

Sociologists maintain that the aim of all professions is to control the relevant domain of knowledge, including the use of a unique technical language. The purpose of this control is to prevent the infiltration of the profession by members of other professions who may pose a threat to its authority and status. The strength of a professional group is derived from the fact that it reduces internal competition and stress between its members and acts as a cohesive unit when confronted by external forces threatening its uniqueness (Abbott, 1988). Over the years, psychologists in Israel have made several mistakes, some of which might be irreversible. Sometimes out of a desire to convey to the public the importance of the profession and sometimes out of sheer financial motives, psychologists have "sold" their knowledge. Public workshops, lowered thresholds for admission into professional training, and breaching of professional boundaries have cheapened the profession and transformed its knowledge into a commodity. This is compounded by the internal struggles among the various divisions that have further weakened and split the profession, and have enabled other professions to invade psychologists' purview. For instance, there is no law regulating psychotherapy in Israel and, thus, no prohibitions on practicing psychotherapy. However, the law covering psychologists restricts the use of psychotherapy to clinical psychologists. This has created a paradox in which members of var-

ious professions such as physicians, social workers, and art and occupational therapists are allowed by law to practice psychotherapy, while psychologists from nonclinical specializations (e.g., developmental, educational, and rehabilitation) are not permitted to do so. More alarmingly, in recent years a variety of so-called psychological interventions have been offered to the public by nonprofessionals. Newspapers are flooded with advertisements of workshops promising equilibrium and healing, and it is clear that some of those who offer these workshops are charlatans who exploit the vulnerability of the public. Problems stemming from the existing law regarding psychotherapy have occupied the COP for the past few years, but no solutions have been found that are unanimously acceptable.

25.4.5 Clients

The profession of psychology suffers from the stigma of mental illness that remains attached to the need for psychological treatment. Even when psychotherapy is sought because of physical illness, it is often construed as tacit admission of a mental problem. A study by Schoenberg and Shiloh (2002) examined the attitudes of patients in general hospitals toward receiving psychological help. Themes suggestive of approach–avoidance conflict were identified. Approach tendencies were associated with high emotional distress, awareness of freedom of access to care, and belief in the relationship between mind and body. Avoidance tendencies were linked to fears of embarrassment, social stigma, exposure to anxiety-evoking material, misconceptions and stereotypes about the nature of psychological treatment, a prior negative therapeutic experience, and threat to one's independence. The results showed that despite the relative openness of Israelis toward psychological treatment, stigma and fear are commonplace.

25.4.6 The Psychologist

The work of psychologists, like that of other helping professions, creates burnout. Even if during the early years of a career, a psychologist is rewarded by the satisfaction derived from work and by continued professional growth, psychology is a highly demanding occupation. Appropriate rewards, either in terms of financial incentives or status, are conspicuously lacking in the public sector. Psychologists learn to reward themselves by attending workshops and private training that require time and money. Therefore, many psychologists, particularly senior ones, are not motivated to remain in the public system and turn to private practice.

In summary, it appears that the major task which must be undertaken by Israeli psychologists is to reduce the paradoxical gap between the high prestige of the profession and its low status in the public sector. Psychologists must work to ensure that their voice is heard in the media and in the health system. Psychologists should undertake the task of educating the public about the wide range of activities that they carry out, encouraging the effective use of the available psychological services, and eliminating the stigma associated with psychological treatment. No less important is the necessity of broadening crucial psychological services such as those offered by oncology wards. Clearly, these activities require the allocation of substantial financial resources (e.g., the provision of positions, grants, and fellowships by universities and by the Ministry of Health).

Psychology in Israel faces another paradox in which, on one hand, life in its "stress laboratory" provides fertile ground for research and practice in psychology, yet, on the other hand, the constant threats to the country's security damages the economy. Therefore, even if psychologists manage to convince decision makers of the importance of their work, under the present circumstances, psychological research and services may continue to be viewed as a privilege.

If security in the Middle East improves and the economy recovers, the science and profession of psychology will gain a more central role and Israeli psychology will strengthen its ties to psychologies of other countries. For the past few years, international psychology has undergone a positive transformation in which the emphasis has shifted to themes of hope and optimism (see Jacoby & Keinan, 2003; Snyder & Lopez, 2002). We hope that this positive development will prevail in our country and that we will be able to focus more on the brighter side of human functioning and experience.

REFERENCES

Abbott, A. (1988). *The system of professions.* Chicago: University of Chicago Press.

Baider, L., Peretz, T., & Kaplan De-Nour, A. (1992). Effect of the Holocaust on coping with cancer. *Social Science and Medicine, 34,* 11–15.

Bar-On, D. (1995). *Fear and hope. Life stories of five Israeli families of Holocaust survivors: Three generations in a family.* Cambridge, MA: Harvard University Press.

Bar-Tal, D. (2002). From intractable conflict through conflict resolution to reconciliation: Psychological analysis. *Political Psychology, 21,* 351–365.

Ben-Ari, R., & Amir, Y. (1986). Psychology in a developing society: The case of Israel. *Annual Review of Psychology, 37,* 17–41.

Breznitz, S. (1983). *Stress in Israel.* New York: Van Nostrand Reinhold.

Dasberg, H. (1987). Psychological distress and Holocaust survivors and offspring in Israel, forty years later: A review. *Israel Journal of Psychiatry and Related Sciences, 24,* 243–256.

Jacoby, R., & Keinan, G. (2003). *Between stress and hope: From a disease-centered to a health-centered perspective.* Westport, CT: Praeger.

Kahneman, D., & Tversky, A. (1979). Prospect theory: An analysis of decision making under risk. *Econometrica, 47,* 263–291.

Krkeljic, L., & Pavlicic, N. (1998). School project in Montenegro. Stress and trauma among school children: A model of preventive psychological work in accordance with the BASIC-Ph approach. In M. Lahad & A. Cohen (Eds.), *Community stress prevention* (Vol. 3, pp. 51–61). Kiryat Shmona, Israel: Community Stress Prevention Center.

Lahad, M. (1997). BASIC Ph: The story of coping resources. In M. Lahad & A. Cohen (Eds.), *Community stress prevention* (Vols. 1–2, pp. 117–145). Kiryat Shmona, Israel: Community Stress Prevention Center.

Lahad, M. (1999). The use of drama therapy with crisis intervention groups, following mass evacuation. *The Arts in Psychotherapy, 26,* 27–33.

Lahad, M., & Cohen, A. (1998a). Critical incident stress debriefing, the Israeli experience. In M. Lahad & A. Cohen (Eds.), *Community stress prevention* (Vol. 3, pp. 10–13). Kiryat Shmona, Israel: Community Stress Prevention Center.

Lahad, M., & Cohen, A. (1998b). Eighteen years of community stress prevention. In M. Lahad & A. Cohen (Eds.), *Community stress prevention* (Vol. 3, pp. 1–9). Kiryat Shmona, Israel: Community Stress Prevention Center.

Lev-Wiesel, R., & Amir, M. (2000). Posttraumatic stress disorder symptoms, psychological distress, personal resources, and quality of life in four groups of Holocaust child survivors. *Family Process, 39,* 445–459.

Levinson S. (1997). Psychology in Israel. *Psychologia: Israel Journal of Psychology, 6*(1), 109–120.

Lieblich, A. (1982). Living with war in Israel: A summary of Gestalt therapy work. *Series in clinical and community psychology: Stress and anxiety, 18,* 103–115.

Lieblich, A. (1994). *Seasons of captivity: The inner world of POWs.* New York: New York University Press.

Ministry of Health, Department of Medical Professions, Health Information and Computer Services. (Copyright 2002). Retrieved November 29, 2003, from http://www.health.gov.il/

Nadler, A., & Ben-Shusan, D. (1989). Forty years later: Long-term consequences of massive traumatization as manifested by Holocaust survivors from the city and from the kibbutz. *Journal of Consulting and Clinical Psychology, 57,* 287–293.

Pappe, I. (1999). The peace-oriented NGOs in Israel. *Civil society: Democratization in the Arab world: A monthly publication of the Ibn Khaldun center for development studies, 8*(86). Retrieved November 29, 2003, from http://www.ibnkhaldun.org/newsletter/1999/feb/essay2.html/

Schoenberg, M., & Shiloh, S. (2002). Hospitalized patients' view on inward psychological counseling. *Patient Education and Counseling, 48,* 123–129.

Shmotkin, D., & Lomranz, J. (1998). Subjective well-being among Holocaust survivors: An examination of overlooked differentiations. *Journal of Personality and Social Psychology, 75,* 141–155.

Snyder, C. R., & Lopez, S. J. (2002). *Handbook of positive psychology.* New York: Oxford University Press.

Solomon, Z., & Shalev, A. Y. (1995). Helping victims of military trauma. In J. R. Freedy & S. E. Hobfoll (Eds.), *Traumatic stress: From theory to practice* (pp. 241–261). New York: Plenum.

Witztum, E., & Kotler, M. (2000). Historical and cultural construction of PTSD in Israel. In A. Shalev, R. Yehuda, & A. Mcfarlane (Eds.), *International handbook of human response to trauma* (pp.103–114). Dordrecht, The Netherlands: Kluwer.

IMPORTANT PUBLICATIONS

Antonovsky, A. (1987). *Unraveling the mystery of health: How people manage stress and stay well.* San Francisco: Jossey-Bass

Bar-Tal, D. (2000). *Shared beliefs in a society: Social psychological analysis.* Thousand Oaks, CA: Sage.

Ben-Eliyahu, S. (2003). The promotion of tumor metastasis by surgery and stress: Immunological basis and implications for psychoneuroimmunology. *Brain, Behavior, and Immunity, 17,* S27–S36.

Breznitz, S. (1983). *The denial of stress.* New York: International Universities Press.

Frenk, H., & Dar, R. (2000). *A critique of nicotine addiction.* Dordrecht, The Netherlands: Kluwer.

Koriat, A. (1993). How do we know that we know? The accessibility model of the feeling-of-knowing. *Psychological Review, 100,* 609–639.

Lieblich, A., Tuval-Mashiach, R., & Zilber, T. (1998). *Narrative research: Reading, analysis, and interpretation.* Thousand Oaks, CA: Sage.

Merari, A., & Friedland, N. (1985). Social psychological aspects of political terrorism. In S. Oskamp (Ed.), *International conflict and national public policy issues: Applied social psychology* (Vol. 6, pp. 185–205). Beverly Hills, CA: Sage.

Mikulincer, M., & Shaver, P. R. (2003). The attachment behavioral system in adulthood: Activation, psychodynamics, and interpersonal processes. In M. Zanna (Ed.), *Advances in experimental social psychology* (Vol. 35, pp. 53–152). New York: Academic Press.

Nadler, A., & Fisher, J. D. (1986). The role of threat to self-esteem and perceived control in recipient reactions to aid: Theory development and empirical validation. In L. Berkowitz (Ed.), *Advances in experimental social psychology* (Vol. 19, pp. 81–124). New York: Academic Press.

Shmotkin, D., Blumstein, Z., & Modan, B. (2003). Tracing long-term effects of early trauma: A broad-scope view of Holocaust survivors in late life. *Journal of Consulting and Clinical Psychology, 71,* 223–234.

CHAPTER 26

Psychology in Australia

ALISON F. GARTON

Alison Garton received an M.A. honors degree from St. Andrews University and a D.Phil. in experimental psychology from Oxford University. She is currently professor of psychology at Edith Cowan University in Perth, Western Australia, a position she has held since 2001.

Alison Garton's professional career, all in Australia, has included working in universities, working for state government, and serving as executive director of the Australian Psychological Society (1996–2001). She has taught developmental, educational, and health psychology at undergraduate and graduate levels, conducted research, developed mental health policy, and managed clinical psychologists. A member, then chair, of the Psychologists Board of Western Australia between 1990 and 1994, she has recently been reappointed as a member. She is currently president of the Australasian Human Development Association and has had a long involvement with the Australian Psychological Society, of which she is a Fellow, in a number of roles.

Alison Garton has published numerous books and articles on developmental psychology, mainly in relation to children's language and cognitive development. She also has research interests and publications in adolescent leisure, health and well-being, and ethical aspects of professional practice.

26.1 OVERVIEW

Australia is both an island and the sixth largest country in the world. It comprises six states (New South Wales, Queensland, Tasmania, Victoria, South Australia, and Western Australia) and two territories (Australian Capital Territory [ACT] and Northern Territory). Federation of the six states took place in 1901 with the territories joining later. The federal capital city of Australia is Canberra located in ACT, midway between the largest population centres of Melbourne and Sydney. The parliament of Australia first met in Canberra in 1927.

The total population is nudging 20 million, most of whom live in towns and cities on the eastern seaboard. Approximately 1% of the population is indigenous Australians. A sizeable percentage (nearly 25%) of the population is born overseas. The official language is English. Australians are characterized by their warmth and friendliness, their love of sports and outdoor activities including barbeques, and their fierce patriotism both at the local state level as well as nationally.

Psychology in Australia is but 60 years old, if the formation of a professional association is any recognition of the status of a profession. In October 1944, the first meeting of the Australian Branch of the British Psychological Society was held in Sydney, signaling the arrival of psychology as a discipline and a profession. An earlier history of psychology in Australia (Taft & Day, 1988) was published to coincide with two landmark events: the bicentenary of the country and the hosting of the International Congress of the International Union of Psychological Science (IUPsyS), both hallmarks of maturity.

Psychology had been taught in various universities around Australia prior to the 1940s. At the University of Tasmania in 1902, the first student was enrolled in the first introductory course in psychology. During the mid-1910s, Morris Miller, a lecturer in philosophy and economics, began dabbling in the use of psychological tests. As a consequence of his interest, he not only assisted with the drafting of mental deficiency legislation in 1920 but was also appointed director of the state psychological clinic. The chief secretary of Tasmania at the time saw the need for a link with the university, and in 1928, Morris Miller was appointed to the Chair of Psychology and Philosophy.

Earlier, at the University of Sydney, Tasman Lovell was appointed as lecturer in philosophy but by 1925 was teaching a 3-year course in psychology. His interests in psychoanalysis and experimental psychology were complemented by the applied, psychometric approach of his colleague Alfred Horatio "Piggy" Martin. Lovell was appointed as the first professor of psychology in 1929 and given his own department. Students completing the program rose from 5 in 1929 to 21 in 1938.

Some psychology had been taught since the inception of the University of Western Australia in 1913 (Richardson, 1995), and an independent department was established in 1930 under the leadership of Hugh Fowler, one of the original psychology students. The beginnings of the department were checkered as war and military service, in particular the army psychology service, consumed staff time. The main focus of the department was on teaching, and despite university attempts to reintegrate psychology with philosophy, the department remained and a Chair was appointed in 1946. The first professor, Ken Walker, was finally appointed in 1952, and from that time the department grew in size, strength, and stature. Clinical training was first offered in 1949 (Smith, 1999) as a full-year course named IIIC, the first such course in Australia. It was upgraded to a 2-year, full-time diploma in clinical psychology in 1956, and it finally achieved master's status in 1966.

The department of psychology at the University of Melbourne was established in 1946 (Buchanan, 1996), although psychology in one form or another had been taught since 1886, notably through philosophy and the teacher training college. In 1946, Oscar Oeser was appointed head and professor, recruiting staff from Western Australia where he had stopped over en route to Melbourne from Europe. There was considerable emphasis on social and industrial psychology. The first students graduated in 1948, and since then student numbers have increased dramatically. Major changes in staffing and areas of expertise in the 1970s helped lift the teaching and research profile of the department, and the later merger in 1991 with the psychology department of the then Melbourne College of Advanced Education represented further growth in depth and breadth. In 1991, the department moved to the Faculty of Medicine, received much-needed increased funding, changed its name to the School of Behavioral Science, and forged a link with the psychologists in the university Department of Psychiatry.

According to Cooke (2000), in the 1940s there were few practicing psychologists despite the popularity of the subject at universities and the apparent popular knowledge of the field. It took World War II to enable Australian psychologists to demonstrate their worth. Scientific studies of psychological weapons such as propaganda added to the international literature on warfare and the military. In addition, there was considerable popular interest in psychology in relation to such things as personality (some of the Freudian terminologies had made their way into the popular press), child development, love, sex, and marriage. Australian research in these domains supported the popular media and added to the international scientific study of psychological domains.

On the commencement of war, psychologists were quick to offer their services in areas such as recruitment for the armed forces. Such recruitment was seen as an extension of existing vocational guidance services. In 1942, a national psychological service was established within the army, but these psychologists were often undertrained and were greeted with skepticism by nonpsychologists. In 1943, a committee was formed to provide advice to the Directorate of Manpower regarding the use of civilians in the war effort and the return of members of the services to civilian life. One major handicap to the efficient functioning of the committee was a lack of knowledge of how many psychologists were available to assist and what qualifications they might have. By late 1943, after a survey, nearly 1500 people had registered as psychologists with the committee, but only 695 had 2 years or more of training (Cooke, 2000). There were other interesting facts that emerged from the survey: There was a disproportionately high number of females, but this may have reflected the fact that those on active service were excluded; more than half of the 695 were employed by education departments, but only 51 were estimated as working in psychology positions full-time and 75 parttime; and, outside education departments, slightly more than 30 individuals were working as psychologists. The result of the survey showed that around 150 people had at least 2 years of psychology training and were working as psychologists in 1943. The survey also demonstrated that groups of trained psychologists existed in Perth and Sydney as a consequence of the university courses.

After the establishment of the Australian Branch of the British Psychological Society in 1944 (a process fraught with internal bickering and politics), psychologists had a focal organization and identity that enabled them to move forward, propelled by the efforts during the war. There was an increase in the number of employment opportunities, and psychologists began to serve in many government agencies and in universities. The Branch encouraged and supported these developments, and it grew in size and influence. However, the perennial battles between academics and practitioners were already occurring as the Branch tried to cater both to the profession and to the discipline (see Cooke, 2000). Issues grappled with (which continue to exercise the minds of office bearers and members to this day) included educational standards, ethical standards, annual conferences and other discussion/publication ventures, and qualifications for membership. These conflicts not only served to make psychology (as defined by membership of the professional association) both inclusive and exclusive but also placed the branch at the forefront internationally in dealing with these matters.

An independent Australian Psychological Society (APS) was mooted as early as 1952, and a major impetus was the issue of membership qualifications. Wrangling over the constitution took place during the early 1960s, a draft finally being presented to the 1965 annual meeting. The new APS was "born" in January 1966 after a smooth transition. However, "the first 15 years of the new APS were years of rapid change and bitter dispute" (Cooke, 2000, p. 127). What were the areas of contention? There were internal matters such as membership qualifications (again!), the creation of specialty divisions within APS, and the creation of a new practitioners' journal; in addition, external problems included the matter of registration by the states, access to health fund rebates, and the need to attain a higher profile for psychologists in social and political arenas. Meeting the needs of an increasing number of psychologists in both the discipline and the profession in a geographically vast country was difficult, and the attempt of APS to respond to the needs of all Australian psychologists was sometimes construed as being expensive and unnecessary.

Maintaining a balance for a diverse membership is a challenge that continues for the APS into the 21st century. Although there are other smaller organizations (often having more importance at the state level), the APS remains the largest, most prestigious, and influential association in Australia. More recent foci for endeavors within the APS have been the accreditation of university training courses in psychology, the development and redevelopment of codes of ethics for professional behavior and standards of practice, and working with external partners such as governments, government agencies, heads of departments and schools of psychology (HODSPA), and Registration Boards as they became established (with the support of the APS, which lead to some criticism of the role and the motives of the professional association).

Legislation exists in each state and territory in Australia to regulate the practice of psychology and to protect the public. Registration is compulsory for practice, and registration in one state permits registration in another through mutual recognition legislation that enables movement of psychologists throughout Australia. (Western Australia also has a residency requirement.) Registration is renewable annually after payment of a fee. Recent review of the legislation as directed by National Competition Policy has resulted in some changes to the various Acts, removing the capacity of the APS to nominate board members and requiring a greater transparency about disciplinary procedures.

Currently (2003), there are more than 13,000 members of the APS nationally, with the majority (73%) being full members (or above, such as Fellows), having obtained 4 years of accredited study in psychology or, from 2000, 6 years of accredited study. Nearly 72% of the total membership is female, although males dominate in the Fellow grade. As with many of the countries discussed in this volume, the profession is also aging, with 60% of the membership being between 40 and 65 years of age. Geographically, the membership is concentrated in the eastern states, with 34% (4,433) residing in Victoria, 33.5% in New South Wales, and only 6.6% (859) in Western Australia (Australian Psychological Society [APS], 2003a). If we look, instead, at current registration figures, there are slightly more than 2,000 psychologists registered in Western Australia (more than double the number of APS members), whereas the number of registrants in Victoria (4300) is almost identical to the APS membership numbers. Although this still shows geographical concentration in the eastern states, it also shows that proportionately fewer psychologists in Western Australia are members of the professional association, perhaps reflecting geographical isolation and the less immediate relevance of the APS.

The relationship between psychologists and other professionals is one of uneasy tension. The usual confusion between psychiatrists and psychologists exists in the community, and professional status issues are manifest in the public sector where not only are psychiatrists paid more, but often, though by all means not always, they assume superior professional and managerial roles and responsibilities. In the private sector, the professional relationship between psychiatrists and psychologists is marked by the exclusion of services provided by psychologists (and other health professionals such as social workers, physiotherapists, and occupational therapists) from Medicare, the Australian universal healthcare system. Clients of psychiatrists and other medical professions can be rebated for any medical services they receive. This is further commented on later in the chapter. The nonmedical health professionals (sometimes referred to as allied health professionals) have an umbrella organization (Health Professions Council of Australia) that advocates and lobbies for all member groups in areas such as private health insurance (which, when taken out by individuals, does cover ancillary services such as dental, psychological, and physiotherapy) and federal government policy on payment for certain allied health services to specific groups such as war veterans.

26.2 EDUCATION AND TRAINING

Over the past 60 years, education and training requirements for psychologists have changed dramatically. Although the length of training has increased as the knowledge and skill base has increased, other changes have been recorded to the curriculum itself. Much of the debate about training has taken place in the context of determining minimum qualifications for membership of the professional association (the APS, as noted above), for registration, and for the purposes of recognition or accreditation by the APS.

Psychology is predominantly taught at the tertiary level, although two states have a school curriculum (used for study in the final 2 years) and other states are introducing psychology as a school subject. There are some private educators who teach psychology as a skill, mainly as counseling; although a few have state vocational recognition, none has professional recognition or accreditation.

The undergraduate university degree program in Australia is based on a Scottish model: a 3-year degree followed by an integrated honors year. Students can exit their third year with a bachelor's degree (typically a B.A., B.Sc., or B.Psych.) or complete the fourth year and receive an honors degree. With the growth of psychology and the reorganization of the higher education sector on various occasions over the 1970s and 1980s, there was a plethora of named degrees such as B.Comm. or B.Econ. that contained a major in psychology. A rationalization introduced with the new *Accreditation Guidelines* (APS, 1995/2000) has lead to a reduction in the variation in nomenclature of degrees offered, although there are still local idiosyncrasies and differences. Thus, if someone claims to have a major in psychology from an Australian university, it is sometimes necessary to check the content of the degree carefully. The APS maintains a database of currently accredited courses; however, obtaining information about superseded courses is more difficult. Study is government subsidized, to a greater or lesser extent, with students' contributions to their undergraduate education being part of a scheme whereby payment is deferred until a certain salary level is reached. Currently, changes are being proposed by government to this scheme although the fundamental model will be retained.

Recently, the postgraduate diploma, an honors equivalent, has been offered as a fee-paying course, and students enrolled in this program are currently eligible for a government loan scheme. Other new developments tend to be driven by the corporatization of universities and the need to generate income, and, increasingly, departments of psychology are opening up their courses to students wishing to take selected courses without earning a degree. Postgraduate study incorporating coursework is generally full fee-paying, except for Ph.D.s for which scholarships are available on a competitive basis. Some of the scholarships are federally funded, whereas others come from a variety of sources including the universities themselves, industry partners, and philanthropists.

Registration Boards are governed by their respective Acts and have the power to approve courses in their jurisdiction. In reality, the majority defers to the work of the APS and accepts accreditation as indicative of a suitable training program. However, the whole issue of responsibility is vexing and an issue that the Registration Boards attempt to deal with from time to time, discussing approval and accreditation with HODSPA and the APS. Accreditation is expensive, involving as it does a site visit every 5 years for the 38 universities in Australia with a psychology program. These costs are largely borne by the APS, whereas the cost of preparation of the materials for the accreditation team is met by the universities. Registration Boards benefit from this process but do not have an active role; however, they clearly regard this as an abdication of their responsibility. A parallel process would be redundant and expensive, and ways to involve the Boards have been examined and tested over the years, albeit none has proved satisfactory. At present, a Memorandum of Understanding between the Boards and the APS is poised to be signed, enabling the formation of a body to oversee the existing process at a more formal level.

Because all Australian universities participate in the APS accreditation scheme, each adheres to the *Accreditation Guidelines* (APS, 1995/2000) that set standards for the full 6 years of education and training. Standards include staffing and other resource levels, recommended content areas (for the undergraduate curriculum only), and recommendations about research. Because the guidelines are only that, they are interpreted in various ways; however, in general, it means that, across Australia, all accredited courses are meeting standards acceptable to all of the discipline and profession and every university program meets the same standards. Variation occurs through reputation (based on eminent staff and research income and output), geographical location, and size of department. It is easier to offer a range of topics in lectures and as potential areas for research supervision with a staff of 45 than with a staff of 20. The latter inevitably become polymaths, teaching and supervising outside their own area of expertise as well as within it.

For registration, psychologists need to have completed 4 years of university study. Although the legislation varies from state to state, at present all states have the same minimum educational requirement for conditional or provisional registration, but this is being actively debated. This education is of the traditional science of psychology and has no practical component (indeed, the APS *Accreditation Guidelines* prohibit any

skills training). Instead, there is education in basic psychological processes, statistics, and research. For registration, there is a further requirement of 2 years' supervision while "on the job." In reality, this option is declining as employers are not offering positions for 4-year trained psychologists, or at least the jobs are not earmarked specifically for psychology graduates. The alternative route to full registration and also for membership of the APS (since 2000) is to complete 2 years of additional postgraduate training at the master's level. Such training is available throughout Australia, with clinical training being the most prevalent and most popular. Other specialty positions offered mirror the areas of specialization noted in the APS professional Colleges (clinical neuropsychology, community, counseling, educational and developmental, forensic, health, organizational, and sport psychology) and are aligned with their membership requirements.

In recognition of the increased knowledge and skill base required of competent practitioners, there has been a national move towards the D.Psych. degree, a 3-year training in an area of specialization. Compared to the M.Psych., the D.Psych. includes additional practical placement hours, a longer thesis (based on a more significant research project), and advanced coursework in the specialization. Graduates are only now beginning to emerge in the workforce, and it will be interesting to see if these psychologists end up as practitioners or educators. A few universities also allow students to complete a combined master's and Ph.D. degree; students complete all the coursework and placement units required for the Master's and then fulfill the requirements for the Ph.D. (which is based on the U.K. model for a doctorate, namely, all research). This option is popular for students wishing to keep their practice or academic paths open, but is limited by the number of Ph.D. places available at university and by the competitive nature of obtaining a place and a scholarship.

In the past, students wishing to pursue doctoral studies went overseas (either to the United Kingdom or United States), returning on completion of their degrees, usually to an academic post. This is rare today; highly trained and competent doctoral supervisors and cutting-edge research opportunities are accessible in Australia, so students stay at home. Most Australian students study in the home state or city in which they went to school and frequently complete all their studies at the same institution. There is not the movement that is characteristic of students in the United Kingdom and United States. Applied training, commencing as was noted in 1949 at the University of Western Australia, has its own tradition. Clinical psychology owes its origins and directions to the American scientist–practitioner model, and adheres to this model by introducing the science of psychology at the undergraduate level and then adding practice and skills at a graduate level. Although there is a general acceptance of the training model in Australia, concerns are voiced from time to time about its suitability (e.g., Montgomery, 1993). Local developments within the profession took place at the state level in the 1950s (mainly in Queensland and Western Australia), culminating in the formation of the Division (later Board and now College) of Clinical Psychologists within the APS in 1963.

Psychology is taught at universities, and every public Australian university has a department or school of psychology. The heads of these departments meet biannually and are represented where necessary in professional working parties. In a few instances, specialist graduate training programs are offered in other university schools, such as education, but clear and close links with the department of psychology need to be demonstrated. Many institutions are now multi-campus, and due to the popularity of psychology, it is often taught on more than one campus, either by different staff through the use of digital and video technology or by traveling staff. It is essential that institutions provide funding to support the campuses other than the main one because these branch sites are often located in outer suburban or rural areas. Psychology is also taught externally using distance-learning technology; these courses have historically been complemented with an on-campus lab component, but, increasingly, units are taught online and the lab is simulated so there is no campus attendance. (Incidentally, psychology is being taught overseas, mainly in Southeast Asia, using a combination of teaching techniques but often including face-to-face lectures in the home country, with Australian staff traveling to conduct lectures and local tutors providing support.) Library resources are also important, and there is an increasing tendency to move away from print-based media to online journals. Journal articles are obtained from the home institution and from other libraries. Departments of psychology also typically have a test library, housed in the department and supervised by a properly qualified test user (a psychologist). Tests kept here reflect those used in teaching and psychological assessment, commonly used personality and intelligence tests such as the MMPI and WAIS, plus others bought for a particular purpose or project.

Professional development (PD) has long been regarded as an ethical requirement for practicing psychologists and is enshrined in the *Code of Ethics* (the *Code*) (APS, 1997/1999) and its predecessors. Since 1997, PD has been mandatory for members of APS Colleges. This move caused strong disagreement among many psychologists who resented the implication that they were not keeping up-to-date and consequently PD had to be compulsory. The APS went to considerable lengths to publicize its decision and to provide a reasoned and reasonable rationale (e.g., Garton, 1994), emphasizing the fact that most psychologists nevertheless engage in PD routinely. College members have to attend and participate in a range of activities over a 2-year period. The system has changed since inception, and now it is a self-regulated system with random audits. Activities that "count" include conference attendance and paper presentation, workshop participation, and journal reading. All of these activities must include an evaluative or reflective component and be in addition to normal duties.

Some of the registration Acts recently enacted include a section about compulsory PD for annual renewal of registration. Until now, this has not been fully implemented, so it is unclear how this requirement will be assessed and monitored. Ideally, any legal requirement will "piggyback" on the APS system and enable APS College members who are also registered (and they would have to be) to continue as College members and as registrants. In 2003, a proposal to introduce the current PD system for all APS members was floated, to be phased in on a voluntary basis from mid-2004. This will extend the ethical requirement to all those who are required to adhere to the *Code*.

26.3 SCOPE OF PSYCHOLOGICAL PRACTICE

As discussed previously, psychologists are regulated by state or territory legislation throughout Australia. These Acts contain common elements in (a) the educational requirements for registration and (b) recognition of disciplinary actions of one another. The need for basic common elements was brought about in the early 1990s with the introduction of federal and state Mutual Recognition legislation enabling free movement of trades and services across Australia. Thus, in the case of psychologists, if you are registered in one state and move to another, you can stay registered, under the auspices of mutual recognition, without having to reapply or resubmit your credentials.

Each state or territory Registration Board delineates offences or breaches of ethical and professional conduct in its legislation. Some have also developed their own codes of ethics; others rely on the *Code* (APS, 1997/1999). The *Code* is revised regularly, around every 10 years, to reflect contemporary professional and social expectations of practitioner conduct. It was most recently revised in a major way in 1997 with some minor modifications in 1999 and 2002. The *Code* is a mixture of prescription and proscription, generally using exhortations such as "must" and "must not." Like many other professional codes, it does not espouse any particular ethical theory; instead, it is written to be practical and to encourage the highest standard of professional behavior.

The *Code* is accompanied by a series of ethical guidelines (APS, 2003b) that are reviewed every 5 years to ensure that they are still topical and current and represent appropriate practice. They complement the *Code* insofar as they deal with particular areas of practice and are linked explicitly with the principles and subsequent sections in the code. Currently, there are, inter alia, *Guidelines for the Use of Aversive Procedures* (APS, 2000), *Guidelines for Managing Professional Boundaries and Multiple Relationships* (APS, 1999), and *Guidelines on Reporting Child Abuse and Neglect and Criminal Activity* (APS, 2001). The APS has an ethics committee, operationalized through a set of *Rules and Procedures* (APS, 1998), which reviews complaints. An informal arrangement exists whereby complaints are directed to the appropriate Registration Board in the first instance; on completion of the Board's investigation and inquiry, the complainants, if they wish, can then direct the complaint to the APS. Registration Boards' investigations take an adversarial approach, with legal representation being used by the Boards and legal counsel usually retained by the psychologist against whom the complaint is lodged. Hearings involve cross-examination of the complainant and the psychologist, and the calling of witnesses. This can take several days. Disciplinary measures include removal or suspension from the register, effectively denying the psychologist the right to practice and, perhaps, an income, as well as restrictions on the scope of practice. The Board can also mandate a requirement for supervision and financial penalties as well. Boards vary in the manner in which hearings are conducted; some are public, others are held in private. They also vary in the way they promulgate the decisions, ranging from the full decision being made available on the Website for the Victorian Registration Board to a notice in the government gazette in Western Australia. The numbers of hearings are very small per Board per annum, with many of the complaints being investigated without a case being established.

The APS adopts a more conciliatory approach and discourages its members from obtaining legal advice if they are subject to a complaint. Formal legal representation is disallowed. Most of the work is conducted through written submissions, and decisions are made on the basis of the evidence and the facts of the case. Options for discipline include expulsion or suspension from membership, as well as reprimands and educative letters. None of these prevents a psychologist from practicing. Again, the number of complaints received and the number actually investigated are very small, and are reported in the APS *Annual Report* (e.g., APS, 2003a) each year.

The APS regards itself as the body that sets the standards for professional practice; besides the *Code, Standards of Professional Practice* for psychologists have been developed (Working Party on Standards of Professional Practice for Psychologists, 1985), as well as *Standards for the Delivery of School Psychological Services* (APS, 2000). These represent attempts to arm psychologists, particularly those working in government departments, with "ammunition" regarding professional practice expectations. They attempt to educate employers by specifying standards for practice. Psychologists in Australia work in government departments (around 30%; APS, 2003a), mainly as clinicians. Clinical psychology training is regarded widely as the basic training required for practice, and it is recognized by designated clinical positions in (state and territory) government departments of health, welfare, and justice. The services are provided free, and practitioners are salaried government employees. Educational psychologists (or guidance officers as they are quaintly called), although not always recipients of postgraduate education, also work in government departments of education, mainly at the state level. Psychologists in independent private practice represent 22% of the psychology community, many providing clinical services or working in organizational practice. Clients of those psychologists providing clinical services are eligible, if they have private health insurance, for rebates for those services. Universal healthcare coverage (Medicare) does not include psychological services. This issue has caused, and continues to cause, great consternation among psychologists and has been the subject of a great number of (unsuccessful) proposals to successive federal governments over the decades.

At present, there is largely a balance between demand and supply for practicing psychologists, although many claim that there has been a reduction in designated psychology positions as employers seek more generic workers. This has led to a growth of practitioners in the private sector, causing alarm among experienced psychologists at the entry of inexperienced newcomers whose standards of practice are not well established and who tend to charge lower fees, thus undercutting standard fee schedules. There is a perennial problem attracting and retaining psychologists (and other professionals) to remote and rural areas of Australia, with professional isolation being a major deterrent. Demarcation between psychologists and other professionals, such as general practitioners and

psychiatrists as well as occupational therapists and speech therapists, causes professional difficulties as psychologists try to maintain their uniqueness and identity. Many activities for which psychologists believe they are best trained (such as cognitive–behavioral therapy) are adopted by other professionals (often after training from psychologists). The tension between maintaining a professional uniqueness and "giving psychology away" is entrenched and difficult to resolve. Current federal government initiatives are encouraging general practitioners to fund psychologists to work alongside them. This should help break down some of the professional barriers that separate medical professionals and psychologists.

Most practicing psychologists, when asked, will state that they adopt an eclectic approach to their therapies and treatments. In reality, as all who are Australian-trained will have been grounded in cognitive–behavioral therapy, any other treatment approaches will have been learned outside the formal education system. These options are many and varied; Gestalt therapy, psychodynamic approach, EMDR, and executive coaching are training programs currently advertised. Cognitive–behavioral therapy remains, however, the treatment of choice for most psychologists in practice.

Academics comprise about 10% of the APS membership, but in all likelihood are a larger group of psychologists because many of them are not APS members, and they view the Society as providing services relevant only to practitioners. They are also generally not registered (and possibly not eligible for registration) because most often they are not practicing. As there are departments or schools of psychology in every public university in Australia, there are opportunities (albeit limited) for employment at all academic levels. Each department has at least one professor, who may or may not be head of department, with other staff in lower positions. Academic positions are less attractive than they used to be as the university sector struggles with funding, soaring student numbers, and other issues such as corporatization and globalization.

Australian psychology does not have a unique identity. Many of its theories and practices are derived from Europe or the United States. This observation is true of psychology in the broad Pacific-rim area (Garton, 2003). In the early days of psychological research, there was an attempt to study indigenous Australians, sometimes to demonstrate Western superiority or to justify educational assimilation. Most of the scholars involved in setting up departments of psychology in the 1930s and 1940s were educated to doctoral level, with the Ph.D. being earned overseas. They were thus exposed to international theories, methods, and debates. Although most Ph.D. students now study at home in Australia, it is still the case that theoretical and empirical work is conducted in an international context, facilitated by speedy air travel and e-mail. Practice is likewise informed by developments overseas.

Recent psychological work with indigenous Australians has focused on community development, providing indigenous communities with the skills and capabilities to assess their own needs, and to develop, provide, and deliver their own services. There is a growing recognition that indigenous Australians should be respected and cultural differences acknowledged (Dudgeon, Garvey, & Pickett, 2000), and that there is a need for sensitivity when working in culturally sensitive and affirming ways. Most of the work with indigenous communities promotes social justice, inclusion, ethics, reconciliation, and respect for cultural differences (Dudgeon et al.). Particular foci for community initiatives include child sexual abuse, domestic violence, youth suicide, and dealing with removal of indigenous children from their families. A holistic model, emphasizing wellness, is recognized as being appropriate, focusing on the individual within the community and involving the community in treatment. Community empowerment is a powerful driver of change and service delivery. Finding culturally appropriate therapy is a challenge. Indigenous psychologists are rare (there is only one in Australia trained to Ph.D. level, although there are many trained to 4 years and thus able to practice, and there are more in training). There are, however, some nonindigenous psychologists who have gained sufficient respect to be permitted to enter indigenous communities and work with them. Indigenous people also come into contact with psychologists in mental health services and prison services; again, the cultural appropriateness and relevance of these services are questioned, and research efforts are being directed at developing suitable services.

26.4 FUTURE CHALLENGES AND PROSPECTS

Psychology in Australia has been dominated by the discipline versus practice debate and by internecine "battles" between academic scientists-researchers and practitioners (Sheehan, 1994). Because this fundamental tension has existed for the past 50 years or so, it is unrealistic to expect any major change. Practitioners will continue to lobby governments for patient access to health rebates, and academic psychologists will continue to seek greater recognition of the discipline by the scientific community and by national research funding programs. Until there is greater public recognition of the discipline and profession, both academic and practicing psychologists will work to promote such awareness.

The study of psychology at universities will continue to be popular, although the harsh reality is that large first-year classes translate to small fourth-year classes and even smaller graduate enrollments. Many students simply want an education; others are more altruistic and see their future in terms of helping others. Psychology courses are often focused on the scientific side of the discipline, and this tends to put students off. Until the prevailing scientist–practitioner view is changed, the prevailing models of education and training are not likely to be changed. The *Accreditation Guidelines* (APS, 1995/2000) reflect this model of training, which is also supported (implicitly) by the Australian education system. The only potential development could be the movement of the nonuniversity and private sector into higher education, with an opportunity to provide acceptable education and training, or the adoption of a different model of education and training.

Social issues are another area where Australian psychologists have been active (Cooke, 2000). Psychologists for the Promotion of World Peace (PPOWP) (formerly, Psychologists for the Prevention of War) have been an Interest Group of the APS since the mid-1980s, established originally as part of an international move-ment against nuclear proliferation. The name change reflects a broader concern with global peace. This group has been active since PPOWP's inauguration, and media releases are constantly circulated, expressing psychologists' concerns about war and war-related activities. An annual calendar is produced, and other conflict-resolution products have been developed. This Interest Group has a large membership (including non-APS members) and will maintain its high level of activity as long as world conflicts continue.

Psychologists see themselves as having a social role, and, although there are some politicians who are (or were) psychologists, they have not taken on a political role. The development of a more political role through lobbying has been discussed from time to time, and some psychologists have called for a greater APS presence in Canberra, the seat of the federal government. Some members have even suggested that the APS headquarters should be moved from Melbourne to the capital Canberra. Such a strategy might result in greater government recognition of psychologists; however, psychological societies are naturally conservative and generally financially strapped, so relocation would require courage and commitment.

The Internet plays an important role in Australian psychology. It is the predominant means whereby all psychologists can keep abreast of international developments in theory and practice. Although practitioners were slower to embrace technological changes than academics, in the past 3 years or so, increasing numbers are online. Access to information is thus as good as in any industrialized country, although communications (such as satellite telecommunications) are not 100% reliable in rural and remote areas (this is a major political issue currently). "Telehealth," the use of the Internet to deliver psychological services to remote areas, has been developed in Australia and is used in mental health services, mainly by psychiatrists for patient review in Queensland and Western Australia, where distance is a major barrier to service delivery. Furthermore, with improved telecommunications, universities are using the electronic medium for delivery of education at both the undergraduate and postgraduate levels. Delivering postgraduate programs online is also a challenge because, though materials for coursework can be made readily available and hyperlinks to specialized information included, issues regarding supervised practical placements and the conduct of high-level research are proving more difficult to resolve.

What have Australian psychologists given the rest of the world? What can the world learn from Australian psychology? As the list of publications at the end of the chapter attests, psychologists are contributing in a major way to science and knowledge, deepening understanding of psychological processes. Applications of psychology are developed within Australia but donated to the international arena for universal use. Australian psychologists will continue to contribute to the global community of scientists and practitioners, developing world-class research, particularly at the interface of science and practice. All Australian psychologists have always balanced research and practice and, in the foreseeable future, will continue this tradition of applying science at the individual, community, and societal levels—a model of working that should be emulated and adopted internationally.

Despite some of the misgivings expressed previously, when balanced with some of the positive developments, psychology is in a healthy state in Australia. It is a growing profession, although this is a mixed blessing. A greater number of psychologists and a stronger knowledge base have led to new areas of specialization, each competing for professional recognition and resources. But a greater mass means that the public will gradually become more aware of psychologists in all facets of their lives, and the stereotyping of psychologists as "shrinks" can be diminished. There are threats to the continuing existence of psychologists (such as the creation of generic health or counseling positions), but there are, on balance, enhanced opportunities for national recognition. Greater ease of access and communication internationally will assist the discipline and the profession as we join in global networks to support our areas of interest, expertise, and specialization.

ACKNOWLEDGMENTS

I am grateful to Ross Day for his assistance in compiling the list of influential publications by Australian psychologists.

REFERENCES

Australian Psychological Society. (1995/2000). *Accreditation guidelines*. Melbourne: Author.

Australian Psychological Society. (1997/1999). *Code of ethics*. Melbourne: Author.

Australian Psychological Society. (1998). *Rules and procedures of the Ethics Committee and the Ethics Appeals Committee*. Melbourne: Author.

Australian Psychological Society. (1999). *Guidelines for managing professional boundaries and multiple relationships.* Melbourne: Author.

Australian Psychological Society. (2000). *Guidelines for the use of aversive procedures.* Melbourne: Author.

Australian Psychological Society. (2000). *Standards for the delivery of school psychological services.* Melbourne: Author.

Australian Psychological Society. (2001). *Guidelines on reporting child abuse and neglect and criminal activity.* Melbourne: Author.

Australian Psychological Society. (2003a). *Annual report.* Melbourne: Author.

Australian Psychological Society. (2003b). *Ethical guidelines* (4th ed.). Melbourne: Author.

Buchanan, R. D. (1996). *A fiftieth anniversary history: The Department of Psychology, The University of Melbourne 1946–1996.* Melbourne: University of Melbourne, Department of Psychology.

Cooke, S. (2000). *A meeting of minds: The Australian Psychological Society and Australian psychologists 1944–1994.* Melbourne: Australian Psychological Society.

Dudgeon, P., Garvey, D., & Pickett, H. (2000). *Working with indigenous Australians: A handbook for psychologists.* Curtin Indigenous Research Centre, Perth: Gunada Press.

Garton, A. F. (1994). Continuing profession development: Five important questions. *Bulletin of the Australian Psychological Society, 16,* 5–8.

Garton, A. F. (2003). Cognitive development. In J. P. Keeves & R. Watanabe (Eds.), *The handbook on educational research in the Asian Pacific region* (pp. 363–375). Dordrecht, Netherlands: Kluwer.

Montgomery, R. (1993). The bias towards academic psychology in preservice training and the needs of the psychology profession. *Australian Psychologist, 28,* 39–41.

Richardson, A. (1995). Psychology at the University of Western Australia (1913–1988): A brief history. *Bulletin of the Australian Psychological Society, 17,* 13–18.

Sheehan, P. W. (1994). Psychology as a science and profession: An Australian perspective. *Australian Psychologist, 29,* 174–177.

Smith, R. L. (1999). *Reflections of a clinical psychologist.* Perth: Hesperian Press.

Taft, R., & Day, R. H. (1988). Psychology in Australia. *Annual Review of Psychology, 39,* 375–400.

Working Party on Standards of Professional Practice for Psychologists. (1985). Standards of professional practice for psychologists. *Bulletin of the Australian Psychological Society, 7,* 31–34.

IMPORTANT PUBLICATIONS

Bradshaw, J. L., & Nettleton, N. C. (1983). *Cerebral asymmetry.* Englewood Cliffs, NJ: Prentice Hall.

Coltheart, M., Rastle, K., Perry, C., & Langdon, R. (2001). DRC: A dual route cascaded model of visual word recognition and reading aloud. *Psychological Review, 108,* 204–256.

Day, R. H., & McKenzie, B. E. (1977). Constancies in the perceptual world of the infant. In W. Epstein (Ed.), *Stability and constancy in visual perception* (pp. 285–320). New York: Wiley.

Feather, N. (1959). Subjective probability and decision under uncertainty. *Psychological Review, 66,* 150–164.

Halford, G. S. (1993). *Children's understanding: The development of mental models.* Hillsdale, NJ: Erlbaum.

Macmillan, M. B. (1991). *Freud evaluated: The completed arc.* Amsterdam: Elsevier Science.

Maze, J. R. (1954). Do intervening variables intervene? *Psychological Review, 62,* 226–234.

O'Neil, W. M. (1953). Hypothetical terms and relations in psychological theorizing. *British Journal of Psychology, 44,* 211–220.

Sutcliffe, J. P. (1960). "Credulous" and "sceptical" views of hypnotic phenomena: A review of certain evidence and methodology. *International Journal of Clinical and Experimental Hypnosis, 8,* 73–101.

CHAPTER 27

Psychology in Indonesia

SARLITO W. SARWONO

Sarlito W. Sarwono graduated as a professional psychologist in 1968 and received a doctorate in psychology in 1978 from the University of Indonesia, Jakarta. He received a postgraduate diploma in community development from the University of Edinburgh and nondegree training in the methodology of social psychology at the University of Leiden, the Netherlands. He is currently dean of the Faculty of Psychology, University of Indonesia, and a professor at the National Institute of Police Sciences; he has been a visiting professor at Cornell University and the University of Nijmegen, the Netherlands. Sarlito Sarwono's fields of research and practice are social and clinical psychology. He is a member of the Indonesian Psychological Association, Indonesian Sexology Association, American Psychological Association, International Association of Applied Psychology, and International Council of Psychologists. He is the author of 20 books and hundreds of journal, magazine, and newspaper articles on various topics in psychology (history of psychology, adolescence, the family, sexuality, and social psychology).

27.1 OVERVIEW

Psychology was introduced to Indonesia in 1952 by a psychiatrist, Slamet Iman Santoso. When he was installed as a professor of psychiatry in the Faculty of Medicine at the University of Indonesia, Santoso spoke about his involvement in treating patients with various "maladjustment syndromes" including neurotic, psychotic, and psychosomatic disorders. Due to the sociopolitical transition that was occurring as the colonial Dutch government prepared to leave Indonesia following the country's recent independence, it was necessary to fill posts in the government, military, police, and healthcare system that had been occupied by the Dutch with inexperienced and sometimes poorly trained Indonesians. In an effort to prevent and remediate these syndromes, Santoso proposed that Indonesia train psychologists in psychological assessment so that they could identify and place qualified workers in various health-care settings.

In 1953, a year after Santoso's inaugural speech, a nondegree course for assistant psychologists was first offered by the Faculty (or School) of Medicine at the University of Indonesia. A few years later, a department of psychology was established as part of the same faculty that, in 1960, became the independent Faculty of Psychology at the university. In the beginning, there were only 10 faculty members, including some Dutch professors, and approximately 20 students; the first student graduated in 1958. As of 2003, there are 125 faculty members, including 12 professors and 22 lecturers, who work in six departments (clinical, developmental, educational, experimental, industrial–organizational, and social psychology). The Faculty has graduated over 2500 students since being formed, and has approximately 1200 students currently enrolled in bachelor's, master's, and doctoral programs. Nationwide, there are more than 40 faculties, departments, or programs in psychology at state and private universities (see Sarwono, 1996, 2000 for more details on the history and current status of Indonesian psychology).

The number of psychologists who are registered as members of the Indonesian Alliance of Psychologists (HIMPSI), as recorded at its eighth triennial congress in 2000, is 6816 (Ismail, 2003). There are at least that many psychologists who are not registered, yet who practice in some form (e.g., some university professors are not registered). Among those registered with the HIMPSI, only 10–15 have doctoral degrees. Most members are registered with the Jakarta chapter (2,236), with the remainder spread either throughout the other provinces of Java (approximately 3350) or outside Java (400).

Most faculties and graduates in psychology are located on the island of Java. It is the most developed and densely populated island in the Indonesian archipelago and has many of the larger cities, including Jakarta, the nation's capital. A small portion of psychology graduates work as civil servants in hospitals, the military, law enforcement, rehabilitation institutes, or educational institutions at all levels. However, most psychologists seek employment in more lucrative settings such as advertising, commerce, finance, marketing, the media, and in the mining industry. They function as personnel officers in human resource departments or as marketing researchers and journalists. Other psychologists establish their own companies, offering their services as consultants or psychotherapists.

Except in clinical settings, such as in hospitals or private practice, psychologists are addressed according to their respective jobs (e.g., managers, supervisors). Salaries vary according to occupation. In general, newly graduated psychologists may earn two million rupiah per month, approximately $238, which is relatively high by Indonesian standards. It is higher than the amount earned by newly graduated attorneys, economists, or teachers. In hospitals, clinics, and private practice, psychologists will charge each client individually. The charge for a psychological evaluation or psychotherapy session ranges from one to three million rupiah, which is between $119 to $356; these rates are similar to those charged by physicians and psychiatrists of high repute in Jakarta. In general, a senior psychologist in Jakarta with at least 20 years of experience might take home anywhere from 20 million to 50 million rupiah per month, which translates into $2,376 to $5,940. In smaller cities and towns, salaries are lower due to the weaker economy.

The demand for psychology has grown rapidly, not only in the business sector but also in public and social sectors. However, in those areas of the country affected by violent conflict—for example, Aceh, Ambon, West Kalimantan, North Maluku, Central Sulawesi, and previously East Timor—there are virtually no psychologists. Some faculties of psychology (i.e., the University of Indonesia, Jakarta; Airlangga University, Surabaya; Gadjah Mada University, Yogyakarta; and Muhamadiyah University, Malang) have responded to the lack of psychologists by establishing crisis centers in the aforementioned zones of conflict. They have either trained or sent lecturers and advanced students to these areas with the goal of treating posttraumatic stress disorders commonly found in refugees and providing alternative educational programs for refugee children. However, the difficulties and challenges encountered in the field far outstrip the support that universities can offer. As a result, the Faculty of Psychology at the University of Indonesia has developed a master's program in intervention psychology to enable persons working in the field (e.g., local administrators, personnel from NGOs) to obtain psychological training in order to improve their effectiveness. Other graduate programs offered by the faculty are open to nonpsychology degree holders (e.g., architects, educators, engineers, lawyers, managers, medical personnel) who wish to earn a master's degree in various special-izations such as environmental, forensic, health, industrial–organizational, human resource, knowledge management, social, and sport psychology.

However, the number of master's and even doctoral degree holders in psychology without a bachelor's in psychology has fermented controversy. Many senior professors, deans, and prominent psychologists have had difficulty viewing psychology, particularly clinical psychology, from any perspective other than the medical model. This is because psychology had been historically situated within the faculty of medicine. According to this view, the role of psychologists is limited to the conduct of psychodiagnostic assessment, counseling and psychotherapy, and writing psychological reports. Therefore, practicing psychologists (in Indonesian, *psikolog*, which is adopted from the Dutch) are differentiated from other degree holders in psychology who engage only in teaching, research, and consultation, and who go by the title of psychology scientists (in Indonesian, *sarjana psikologi*).

Scientific and professional psychology also differs in their curricula. There are separate programs for training professional psychologists that grant degrees called "professional master's," providing opportunities to specialize in adult clinical, child clinical, educational, and industrial-organizational psychology.

Yet, the controversy surrounding the qualifications of psychologists has not ended with the emergence of these separate training programs. In reality, there is an older generation of psychologists who were not trained as specialists because of the general curriculum of the time, who consider themselves competent enough to perform complex and demanding psychological functions such as assessment and psychotherapy. Likewise, there are nonclinical degree holders without a bachelor's in psychology who also believe they are adequately prepared to carry out highly sophisticated psychological tasks. Some of the latter even work at hospitals and schools, or have opened their own private clinics.

In 2002, after it became evident that the government had little authority to combat professional malpractice, HIMPSI threatened to withdraw its affiliation with the Ministry of Manpower and establish its own regulatory system. It encouraged deans from faculties of psychology and representatives from various specialty divisions within HIMPSI (currently, these divisions include clinical, developmental, educational, industrial–organizational, social, and sport psychology) to form an independent regulatory entity to oversee the preparation of psychologists and practice of psychology. Through this entity, HIMPSI has since succeeded in gaining access to the undergraduate and graduate curricula of departments and faculties of psychology and in appointing its members to serve on committees that review the quality of the education and training of psychologists. HIMPSI also now adjudicates ethical infractions in cooperation with representatives from allied disciplines and professions (e.g., educators, guidance counselors, human resource managers, health providers). Ethical charges are discussed and resolved, and appropriate sanctions are enforced.

27.2 EDUCATION AND TRAINING

Entrance examinations for state universities are organized nationally under the auspices of the Ministry of Education and Culture.

There are no admission quotas. However, over the last two decades, competition for admission has become very intense. In 2003, for example, the Faculty of Psychology at the University of Indonesia accepted only 140 of 3,435 applicants, or 4.1%. Thus, only the brightest of students can enroll in prestigious state universities. Because these students typically hail from the best high schools and from families that are financially well off, the majority of students at reputable state universities are from the country's major cities. The remaining students enroll in lower-quality state universities or private universities, with the latter being rather expensive. Applicants who fail to gain admittance to the primary state universities in Indonesia can study abroad, provided they have sufficient funds. Clearly, applicants from rural or remote areas and from poor families have much less opportunity to obtain a decent university education.

To overcome this sociodemographic problem, the Ministry of Education and Culture instituted an alternative admissions policy for disadvantaged students. The policy offers the best students from the best high schools in remote areas a chance to enroll directly in a top state university without taking the national entrance examination. Every state university is now mandated to reserve at least 10% of its seats for these deserving students. Once enrolled, these students are eligible for scholarships funded by the university.

Although the finest state universities attract many viable applicants who have the resources to attend, not all can be accepted for various reasons (e.g., reasons of space or accommodation). Most universities strive to meet the needs of these students by offering evening classes for working students, international classes that provide dual degrees, and graduate programs. Tuition and fees are based on actual costs, without any subsidy from the government.

Throughout the history of psychology in Indonesia, there have been four versions of national curricula for the education and training of psychologists: the package version (1953), the credit-system version (1982), the undergraduate version (1994), and the consortium version (2002). All versions consist of core subjects in psychology; supporting subjects, including anthropology, biology, English, philosophy, physiology, sociology, and statistics and research methods; and national compulsory subjects, such as *kewiraan* or national defense, *pancasila* or the state philosophy, and basic humanities including religion (see Sarwono, 2003, for more information about the curriculum and educational programs in psychology, particularly at the University of Indonesia).

The University of Indonesia initiated the package curriculum. As previously described, the nondegree course for assistant psychologists, first offered in 1953, evolved into a full-degree program under an independent faculty of psychology in 1960. The curriculum was predicated on the medical model. Students were required to pass all courses in order to advance to the next level within the curriculum. At the conclusion of their didactic preparation, students completed internships in child development, clinical, educational, industrial–organizational, or social psychology. They also wrote a thesis and defended their work in a comprehensive oral examination. After passing their oral examination, students were awarded a *doctorandus* (adopted from Dutch usage, meaning "a doctor to be")

degree and a professional title of psychologist, which enabled them to matriculate into a doctoral program (i.e., to pursue an academic career) and work as general psychologists (i.e., to pursue a professional career). In total, the package curriculum required 5.5–6 years to complete. Until the 1970s, additional preparation was not needed to become a specialist; however, some psychologists obtained this type of advanced training abroad, mostly in the Netherlands.

Three other faculties of psychology that were founded after the one at the University of Indonesia also adopted the package curriculum. These faculties were at Padjajaran University in Bandung, West Java University, and Gajah Mada University in Yogyakarta. However, the faculties differed in terms of the content of their curricular packages. For example, the Faculty of Psychology at Padjajaran University considers itself to this day to be a faculty of exact sciences and, therefore, is available only to high-school graduates majoring in the physical sciences; the other two view themselves as faculties of social science and are open to all high school graduates. The curriculum at Padjajaran University also had options for undergraduates to narrow their focus on such areas as child, clinical, and industrial–organizational psychology; however, Padjajaran University's graduates were still addressed as general psychologists. The University of Indonesia and Gajah Mada University offered broader curricula designed to prepare generalists in psychology. Furthermore, at Padjajaran University, the emphasis was on experimental psychology, whereas the focus was on psychodiagnostics at the University of Indonesia and on methodology at Gajah Mada University.

In 1970, another prominent state university, Airlangga University in Surabaya, East Java, founded its own faculties of psychology. Since then, the four faculties of psychology have become models for similar faculties at state as well as private universities throughout Indonesia.

As noted, the number of new faculties of psychology throughout Indonesia has grown rapidly since the 1970s. In a colloquium meeting of faculties of psychology in Makasar in October 2003, it was reported that there were more than 50 faculties. This number seems low for a country of more than two hundred million people in an archipelago the size of the continental United States. However, to prevent the uncontrolled growth of new faculties of psychology, the Ministry of Education and Culture founded a consortium of psychology, a relatively unstructured entity comprising the faculties of psychology at the University of Indonesia, Padjajaran University, and Gajah Mada University. Together, these three faculties coordinate the activities of all other faculties of psychology in Indonesia. An important product of this consortium was the revision of the curriculum for psychology in 1982.

The 1982 curriculum was based on a semester-credit system. It was initiated by the Ministry of Education and Culture and influenced by the American higher educational system, as most university scholarships at the time, including those in psychology, came from the United States. The content and structure of the curriculum were generally the same as that of the package curriculum; that is, students had to earn 164–170 semester credits to receive a *doctorandus* degree. However, under the new system, the *sarjana muda* degree was eliminated (in the package curriculum, this degree was the equivalent of a bachelor's), and every subject in the curriculum was assigned semester credit.

In 1994, after having gained experience with American universities, which generally considered the *doctorandus* degree as equivalent to the bachelor's degree, the Consortium of Psychology, appointed by the Ministry of Education and Culture, reevaluated the curriculum and set the number of credit hours required for graduation at 144 (or eight semesters of credit). Graduates were awarded the *sarjana psikologi* degree. A *sarjana psikologi* is a basic degree in psychology and such degree-holders were not directly eligible for a program of doctoral study. Eligibility for the doctorate required a master's (in Indonesian, *magister*). The credit system mandated a minimum of 24 semester hours (four semesters) of graduate study in psychology for the master's.

A *sarjana psikologi* was not qualified to practice psychology because the curriculum consisted of only theoretical psychology and exposure to the content and methodologies of related scientific disciplines. To become a practicing psychologist (e.g., clinical, developmental, educational, or industrial–organizational), a *sarjana psikologi* must have completed another 24 credit hours of training, after which the professional title of *psikolog* was awarded.

The 1994 undergraduate curriculum gave students who were interested only in scientific psychology and who planned to seek employment or pursue a master's in other fields an opportunity to terminate their studies without having to enroll in courses related to professional practice. The 1994 curriculum also gave students who were academically or economically unable to remain in a degree program the chance to terminate their studies without penalty and return to the university at a later time.

The 1994 undergraduate curriculum also opened the possibility for students without a bachelor's in psychology to enter master's programs in psychology, including ones in developmental, educational, experimental, industrial–organizational, and social psychology. The flexible stance of the 1994 curriculum was intended to infuse psychology into other disciplines and professions, ranging from technology to theology.

However, the 1994 undergraduate curriculum did not distinguish professional psychologists who registered for additional training from those who terminated their degree with the minimum number of credit hours earned. This was unfortunate because local psychologists (a *psikolog* with a bachelor's degree plus professional training) were forced to compete with master's- and doctoral-level foreign psychologists as well as Indonesian psychologists trained abroad. Because the consortium appointed by the Ministry of Education and Culture did not function well due to changes in the Ministry's policy, a national association of faculties of psychology was founded by the Faculty of Psychology at the University of Indonesia. In 2002, this association decided to modify the psychology curriculum one more time. This curriculum provides master's training for the practice of professional psychology and awards graduates with a distinct academic degree (i.e., *magister psikologi*); HIMPSI provides the license to practice psychology.

At the University of Indonesia, new master's programs in applied psychology have been developed to meet the needs of nonclinical psychologists. These graduates are granted the degree of *magister* of applied psychology with specialization in the following areas: forensic psychology, health psychology, personnel psychology, psychometrics, social intervention, and sport psychology. The admission requirement for these programs is simply a bachelor's degree.

At the doctoral level, there is only one type of program, the Ph.D. program, which at present is offered only by the three faculties of psychology (the University of Indonesia, Padjajaran University, and Gajah Mada University). However, there appears to be a growing need for Psy.D. programs to encourage the continued professional development and specialization of graduates with the *magister* degree in applied, professional psychology.

Clearly, the 2002 curriculum and its future evolution rest on the premise that Indonesian psychology will advance toward internationally recognized standards. This eventuality will demand high academic quality in terms of faculty members, facilities, and administrative policies and procedures. At the moment, only those few faculties of psychology in Indonesia that have been accredited by the Ministry of Education and Culture can meet these standards. The remaining faculties and departments are not qualified to offer master's programs; in fact, many continue to graduate psychologists with a bachelor's degree. This practice violates the policy of HIMPSI in which the entry-level degree for the professional practice of psychology is the master's.

The major constraints to improving the quality of faculties of psychology are the lack of available scientific and professional literature on psychology and proficiency in English. Most books and journals are written in English, and the language proficiency of students and even some faculty members is quite low. Some material has been translated into Indonesian, however. In addition, there is a growing number of books published by Indonesian psychologists, and there are Indonesian journals of psychology as well. Regrettably, there are too few outlets for publication to cope with the rapid development of the science and practice of psychology. Conversely, imported books and journals are very expensive by Indonesian standards. The Internet, which enables Indonesian psychologists to access international journals, is not very helpful at this point for these psychologists due to their limited facility in English and with computers. Hence, a large proportion of the community of psychologists in Indonesia, particularly at disadvantaged universities in remote areas, must rely on dated literature that has been translated and a limited number of Indonesian books and journals.

The dearth of psychological literature and poor facility in English, coupled with inadequate financial resources make it difficult for Indonesian psychologists to develop new psychometric tests. Although psychologists at more advanced universities are engaged in test construction and adaptation, in most areas of Indonesia psychologists still use old versions of psychological tests that have questionable applicability to Indonesian culture, such as the Army Alpha Test, Draw-a-Person Test, Edwards Personal Preference Schedule, Kuder Interest Inventory, Raven's Progressive Matrices, Rorschach Inkblots, and Wechsler–Bellevue Scales.

27.3 SCOPE OF PSYCHOLOGICAL PRACTICE

Lay people very frequently associate psychology with medical science and practice (e.g., psychiatry). It is not uncommon, even today, for a client to ask for a prescription after a counseling session with a psychologist. It is also not unusual for people to hesitate to see a psychologist because of the stigma associated with seeking professional help; many Indonesians believe that the clientele of psychologists is limited to psychotics or schizophrenics.

This public misperception is inseparable from the history of psychology in Indonesia, which, as stated, began as an offshoot of the Faculty of Medicine at the University of Indonesia. However, that image of psychology remains intact because some psychologists believe in the traditional model as the only suitable paradigm for psychology. Thus, psychodiagnosis is of singular importance to them. Compounding this problem is the reality that many psychiatrists view psychologists as mere psychometricians. Diagnosis remains the purview of physicians in Indonesia, and psychiatrists have their own tests (e.g., the MMPI) to diagnose mental illness.

Another profession that has a long history of overlapping with psychology is school counseling. School counselors receive their training at teaching and educational institutes, not in faculties of psychology. These institutes house departments of guidance and counseling and educational psychology. To the dismay of many psychologists, alumni of these departments claim that they are qualified to perform psychological testing in educational settings.

Although members of other professions argue about their competence to administer, score, and interpret psychological tests, hardly anyone is involved in ensuring the security of such tests. After decades of use and misuse, test items have been leaked to the lay public such that many tests can no longer be validly administered. It is interesting to note that one can purchase confidential test materials in commercial bookstores! Even HIMPSI, the national organization of psychology, has been unable to prevent the inappropriate disclosure of confidential and copyrighted test material.

Because of Indonesia's rapid economic growth, more and more people need psychological services, not only in clinical settings, but also in many other contexts. For example, the National Family Planning Coordinating Board could benefit from access to psychological research and consultation in its efforts to modify the negative attitudes of many couples toward the use of contraceptives, or in its attempt to engage the public in a productive dialogue about controversial issues such as abortion or sterilization. The Ministry of Transmigration needs psychologists to study interactions between immigrants and indigenous people. Housing and resettlement programs need to know about the possible psychological consequences associated with moving people from traditional to high-rise housing. And, during the last four years in particular, psychologists have been urgently needed to respond to the causes and effects of intergroup conflict, crime and general violence, the growing number of refugees and street children, poverty, social disintegration, and many other issues related to the national economic, political, and social crisis that was triggered in 1997.

At the individual, family, and community levels, Indonesian society could benefit from the services of psychologists in preventing or remediating the following: marital discord and parent–adolescent conflict, child abuse and neglect, drug abuse, school-related problems including the high dropout rate, crime, traffic congestion, and the pollution of the environment. In business and industry, psychologists could help to improve the recruitment, selection, placement, and evaluation of personnel, train supervisors and managers to improve organizational climate, and advertise and market products.

In general, psychology in Indonesia has begun to deal with a broad spectrum of social issues that have little to do with its traditional role in diagnostic testing. At the same time, Indonesian psychology has started to interface with allied disciplines and professions, including economics, environmental science, law, management, and social work. Consequently, an increasing number of Indonesian psychologists are engaged in nonpsychological jobs; conversely, more and more nonpsychologists are involved in jobs whose functions could be categorized as psychological. For example, the well-known center for Achievement Motivation Training is not located in a faculty of psychology but rather at the Bandung Institute of Technology. Likewise, the most advanced assessment center belongs to National Telecommunication Company, also in Bandung. It is becoming commonplace in Indonesia to hear on-air radio psychologists or to read columns in the print and electronic media by psychologists who offer psychological advice; of course, it is not uncommon for nonpsychologists to offer psychological information to the public via these media.

Some psychologists have anticipated the unavailability of professionals to meet the rising demands of Indonesian society by training lay people or paraprofessional service providers. For example, psychologists who worked for an NGO called *Sahabat Remaja* (Friends of Youth) in the 1980s trained university students to serve as peer counselors. Their role was to respond to the reproductive health concerns of youth in six cities across Indonesia. The Indonesian Planned Parenthood Association trained sterilized husbands in Central Java to motivate other husbands to have vasectomies. Midwives are also trained as family planning counselors, and former addicts are trained to counsel current substance abusers who have sought treatment. In areas of the country torn by violence, local leaders are trained to mediate between conflicting parties, and police officers are trained to negotiate the peaceful resolution of street demonstrations.

Nevertheless, there is a sizable minority of psychologists who are hesitant to share their expertise with other professionals and even more reluctant to share it with the nonprofessionals. Their rationale is always the same: The practice of psychology requires great skill and ethics, both of which can be delivered properly only by trained professional psychologists.

However, in practice there are no professional institutions or organizations powerful enough to enforce these rules. The sole professional organization for psychologists in Indonesia, HIMPSI, is responsible for formulating and enforcing the code of ethics and procedures for their implementation. Nevertheless, HIMPSI was, and still is, run by part-time volunteers who do not have enough time to adjudicate every case of malpractice that is brought to their atten-

tion. Knowing its weakness, HIMPSI sought affiliation with the Ministry of Health in the 1980s, because the Ministry has the authority and mechanisms to regulate the practice of medical personnel (i.e., physicians and paramedics) throughout the country. However, many psychologists chafed at being subsumed by the national medical system. Therefore, after searching for the proper ministry (including the Ministry of Education and Culture), HIMPSI elected to align itself with the Ministry of Manpower. Since then, the license for practicing psychologists has been issued by that Ministry, based on the recommendation of HIMPSI.

Unfortunately, in practice, the Ministry of Manpower cannot enforce many of the regulations due to the lack of expertise, articulated procedures, personnel, and, most importantly, legal precedent. Consequently, the function of the Ministry is essentially that of a registry, which falls far short of what HIMPSI had sought. Recently, HIMPSI decided to join the Association of Faculties of Psychology, in the hope of persuading the deans to establish their own registry for psychologists and draft legislation to regulate the profession of psychology. Once written, a bill will be submitted directly to the Indonesian government for consideration as a presidential or governmental regulation.

Some crucial topics to be addressed in the proposed bill on professional psychology are preparation and competency in conceptual models, research methodologies, and intervention strategies that are indigenous to the psychology of Indonesia. As reported in the literature, there are distinct differences between Western and Eastern psychology, including Indonesian psychology. Collectivism (Smith, 1993), motivational gravity (Carr, 1994; Carr & MacLachlan, 1997), external locus of control (Chia, 1996), the social self (Ho, 1995), spiritualism (Howee, 1980), and universalism (Veeneklaas, 1949) represent some of the key features of Eastern psychology. They are not only described in books and journals, but also are encountered by Indonesian psychologists in their daily practices; for example, they influence respondents' answers to questionnaires (i.e., response sets and styles). Consequently, anthropology, sociology, and cross cultural psychology are compulsory in the psychology curriculum in Indonesia.

In applied practice, Indonesian psychologists must often operate from alternative, culturally sensitive paradigms in order to be effective. Face-to-face interviews are usually more likely to elicit cooperation than written questionnaires, which are suitable mainly for better educated urban dwellers; likewise, group interviews or focused group discussions appear to be more successful in extracting reliable and valid information than individual interviews. In the author's clinical experience, directive yet supportive counseling methods have proven more efficient and effective than client-centered or psychodynamic approaches. There are also differences between Indonesian psychology and Western psychology with respect to a variety of ethical practices, including those of respecting confidentiality and obtaining informed consent. For example, although the ethics code (HIMPSI, 2003) states that confidentiality and informed consent are obligatory when delivering psychological services, in rural areas, women and teenagers will not participate in an interview unless it is conducted in the presence of their peers. Furthermore, in practice, husbands and parents believe that they have an abso-

lute right to know everything that their wives or children disclosed during psychotherapy.

Clearly, there is a need to educate and train Indonesian psychologists in indigenous theories, investigative methods, and interventions. Complicating matters, however, is the fact that Indonesia is rapidly changing as a consequence of the confluence of several sociocultural forces, most importantly the growing cultural, ethnic, and religious heterogeneity of the country. Unfortunately, research studies suggest that indigenous psychology cannot cope with the massive and unprecedented transformation that Indonesia is undergoing, a transformation that is having a significant impact on the identity and development of individuals and the nation as a whole (Sarwono, 2003).

On the other hand, the rising demand for psychology must be met, and psychological services must be maintained in various settings. Clinical psychologists work in clinics and hospitals, in private and group practices, and in rehabilitation centers for substance abusers, commercial sex workers, and HIV/AIDS patients. In the military and police forces, the primary role for psychologists is the assessment of new recruits and placement of officers. Broader functions, such as psychological warfare, counter-terrorism, and community defense and security are occasionally carried out by psychologists, who consult with the armed forces and law enforcement agencies, but do not hold rank. In business and industry, psychologists are mainly concerned with the development of human resources, including selection, training, placement, and evaluation. In marketing, they perform a variety of tasks ranging from designing promotional campaigns to conducting marketing research. Social psychologists engage in basic research, write columns in newspapers, and serve as consultants to various institutions, including the local and central governments, NGOs, the military and police, and multinational corporations; they offer advice on problems ranging from community development to national politics. In schools, psychologists perform guidance and counseling functions, whereas at the university they teach and conduct research. In the domain of crisis intervention, psychologists help victims to regulate and overcome posttraumatic stress and assist school teachers to develop alternative educational programs for at-risk children who have dropped out of school. In the print and electronic media, some psychologists work as consultants to their readers or listening audience, respectively, answering questions on topics of general interest (e.g., premarital sex, family dynamics); some even have regular columns and have become celebrities in their own right.

27.4 FUTURE CHALLENGES AND PROSPECTS

In March 2003, the Indonesian government, through the Minister of Manpower, asked the Faculty of Psychology at the University of Indonesia to develop a test battery with which to select thousands of unskilled and semiskilled workers to be employed in foreign countries (e.g., the Middle East and East Asia). In the past, in their effort to reduce the cost of recruitment, workers were supplied to foreign companies illegally, which violated the government's employment regulations and resulted in the sexual abuse of many female workers. There is hope that the introduction of psy-

chological screening for prospective employees will end the practice of sending unqualified persons abroad.

However, to compete with other labor-exporting countries like Thailand and the Philippines, the cost of psychological screening must remain low. Thus, the faculty's team of experts must work creatively to develop an efficient yet psychometrically sound test battery. This case is but one example of the challenges that face Indonesian psychologists due to rapid national development in the context of a relatively conservative cultural environment. There are many other examples of how psychology helps government institutions and private enterprise respond to the many diverse challenges brought about by development. Some of these collaborative efforts include the alternative-education programs in high-conflict zones, family planning, nutrition education programs, interventions for conflict resolution, personnel recruitment and selection, and marketing campaigns. Other relatively new challenges for Indonesian psychologists include HIV/AIDS and controversial issues such as premarital sex, interfaith marriages, and human rights. Even more rare cases include cannibalism, pedophilia, lynch mobs, and intergroup violence. Most of these challenges demand shifts in psychological paradigms, not always easy in the Indonesian context because of the limited number of psychologists and, more important, the conservative medically oriented perspective they tend to adopt.

The availability of the Internet and World Wide Web influence only a minority of Indonesian psychologists. Psychologists in Indonesia who use these resources are mostly interested in facilitating communication among themselves. Except at a few prestigious universities, the Internet and World Wide Web are rarely used to develop networks of international colleagues or to search databases that contain scientific literature relevant to ongoing research projects. The limited use of information technology is partly due to the low proficiency in English of most Indonesian psychologists. It is also related to the lack of interest among Indonesian psychologists in doing research and, generally, in reading or writing (this is also characteristic of the Indonesian population). The majority of psychologists who know about the availability of Internet facilities and services might not have access to a personal computer, money to subscribe to an Internet provider, or proper telephone lines, particularly if they reside in remote areas of the country; other psychologists simply do not care about the Internet and World Wide Web. As a result, there is a relatively wide gap in terms of opportunity for professional growth between psychologists at prominent versus ordinary universities, between psychologists who work at universities versus those who work outside academia, between those who work in urban (e.g., Java) versus rural areas, and between psychologists working in business and industry versus those in other fields.

The diverse quality of psychologists in Indonesia and the ineffectiveness of HIMPSI as a professional organization complicate the problem. Thus far, the organization has not been very successful at solving the problem of licensure, the control of test materials, and the standardization of various tests. They also face new controversies such as the emergence of Islamic psychology (a sensitive issue in Indonesia), the use of peer counselors in regions of the country that lack sufficient numbers of psychologists, or human rights issues in the context of terrorism (e.g., the rights of the captured Bali bombers, who had been sentenced to death under the new anti-terrorism act, versus the rights of the victims and their families). Indonesian psychologists clearly need strong leadership and a better organized psychological association if they are not to fall behind other professionals in the country (e.g., educators, human resource managers, psychiatrists, social workers) and the standards set by national psychological associations in other countries (e.g., the United States) and by international psychological associations.

REFERENCES

Carr, S. C. (1994). Generating the velocity to overcome the motivational gravity in LDC (Less Developed Countries) business organizations. *Journal of Transactional Management Development, 1,* 33–56.

Carr, S. C., & MacLachlan, M. (1997). Motivational gravity. In D. Munro, J. F. Schumaker, & S. C. Carr (Eds.), *Motivation and culture* (pp. 133–156). New York: Routledge.

Chia, R. C. (1996, August). *Locus of control: Single and multiple component theories.* Paper presented at the meeting of the in Annual Convention of International Council of Psychologists, Banf, Canada.

HIMPSI. (2003). *Anggaran dasar, anggaran rumah tangga, kode etik psikologi Indonesia* [By–laws and ethics code of Indonesian psychology]. Jakarta: Author.

Ho, D. V. F. (1995, July). *Asian contribution to psychotherapy: What the East has to offer to the West.* Paper presented at the meeting of the International Council of Psychologists, Taipei, Taiwan.

Howee, C. O. G. (1980). *Sumara: A study of the art of living.* Unpublished doctoral dissertation, University of North Carolina, Chapel Hill.

Ismail, R. (2003, September). *Rencana undang-undang psikologi* [Draft of law on psychology]. Paper presented at the Workshop on Law on Psychology, University of Tarumanegara, Jakarta.

Sarwono, S. W. (1996). Psychology in Indonesia. *World Psychology, 2*, 177–196.

Sarwono, S. W. (2000). *Berkenalan dengan tokoh-tokoh dan aliran-aliran psikologi* [Introducing authors and schools in psychology]. Jakarta: Bulan Bintang.

Sarwono, S. W. (Ed.). (2003). *Buku emas Fakultas Psikologi Universitas Indonesia: Dari yang pertama ke yang utama* [The golden book of the Faculty of Psychology, University of Indonesia: From the first to the top]. Jakarta: University of Indonesia, Faculty of Psychology.

Sarwono, S. W. (2003, August). *Motivational values of three conflicting ethnicties in West Kalimantan.* Paper presented at the International Convention of Asian Scholars, Singapore.

Smith, P. B. (1993). *Social psychology across cultures: Analysis and perspectives.* New York: Harvester Wheatsheaf.

Veneklaas, C. (1949). *Het rassenconflict in de opvoeding in Indonesia* [Racial conflict in the uprising of Indonesia]. Groningen, The Netherlands: J. B. Walters.

IMPORTANT PUBLICATIONS

Dirgagunarsa, S. (1996). *Psikologi olah raga* [Sport psychology]. Jakarta: Badan Pendidikan Kristen Gunung Mulya.

Dirgagunarsa, S. (1997). *Konseling dan psikoterapi* [Counseling and psychotherapy]. Jakarta: Badan Pendidikan Kristen Gunung Mulya.

Hassan, F. (2000). *Berkenalan dengan eksistensialisme* [Introduction to existentialism]. Jakarta: Pustaka Jaya.

Hawadi, R. A. (2001). *Psikologi perkembangan anak* [Child development psychology]. Jakarta: Gramedia.

Mangunsong, F. (1998). *Psikologi anak luar biasa* [Psychology of the exceptional child]. Jakarta: Lembaga Pengembangan Sarana Pengukuran dan Pendidikan Psikologi, University of Indonesia.

Munandar, A. S. (2001). *Psikologi industri dan organisasi* [Industrial and organizational psychology]. Jakarta: University of Indonesia Press.

Munandar, S. C. U. (2002). *Kreativitas dan keberbakatan* [Creativity and giftedness]. Jakarta: Gramedia.

Poerwandari, E. K. (2001). *Pendekatan kualitatif dalam penelitian psikologi* [Qualitative approaches to psychological research]. Jakarta: Lembaga Pengembangan Sarana Pengukuran dan Pendidikan Psikologi, University of Indonesia.

Radikun, T. B. S. (2002). *Kiat penulisan efektif pemeriksaan psikologi* [Tips for effective psychological assessment writing]. Jakarta: Lembaga Pengembangan Sarana Pengukuran dan Pendidikan Psikologi, University of Indonesia.

Sarwono, S. W. (1999). *Psikologi sosial: Psikologi kelompok dan aplikasi psikologi social* [Social psychology: Group psychology and applied psychology]. Jakarta: Balai Pustaka.

Sarwono, S. W. (2000). *Berkenalan dengan tokoh-tokoh dan aliran-aliran psikologi* [introducing authors and schools in psychology]. Jakarta: Bulan Bintang.

Sarwono, S. W. (2002). *Psikologi sosial: Individu dan teori-teori psikokogi sosial* [Social psychology: Individuals and theories of social psychology]. Jakarta: Balai Pustaka.

Sukaji, S. (2002). *Psikologi pendidikan dan psikologi sekolah* [Educational psychology and school psychology]. Jakarta: Lembaga Pengembangan Sarana Pengukuran dan Pendidikan Psikologi, University of Indonesia.

CHAPTER 28

Psychology in the Philippines

CRISTINA JAYME MONTIEL AND LOTA A. TEH

Cristina Jayme Montiel is a professor in the Psychology Department at the Ateneo de Manila University and a research associate at the Institute of Philippine Culture. She has carried out teaching and research visits to universities in the United States (University of Hawaii, Ohio State University at Marion, and Georgetown University), Germany (Technical University of Chemnitz-Zwickau), Australia (Australian National University), People's Republic of China (Xiamen University), and Malaysia (National University of Malaysia). At the 1998 annual convention of the American Psychological Association, the Division of Peace Psychology gave her an Outstanding Service Award, and Psychologists for Social Responsibility granted her the Most Distinguished Contribution Award. In 2001, Cristina Montiel received an inaugural senior fellowship from the Asian Public Intellectuals Program. During the Marcos regime, she chaired Lingap Bilanggo (Care for Prisoners), *a social movement for the general amnesty of all Filipino political prisoners. She also coordinated Philippines-wide grassroots seminars on active nonviolence and structural analysis.*

Lota A. Teh is an associate professor in the Psychology Department at Ateneo de Manila University. She received her M.A. in clinical–counseling psychology and Ph.D. in clinical psychology from the same university. Teh's research interests include extrasensory perception and continuing education of psychology teachers.

In 1997, Lota Teh was the director of a course-development project on general psychology, funded by the Commission on Higher Education. The major output of this project was the development and printing of two volumes of instructional materials for general psychology that have been distributed to various colleges and universities for use by course instructors. She has also designed and coordinated seminars and workshops on the teaching of general psychology and fundamental statistics, which the Ateneo Psychology Department has conducted for faculty from different parts of the country. She was vice president of the Psychological Association of the Philippines (PAP) in 2002 and chaired the 2002 Annual Convention of the PAP Junior Affiliates, which was attended by approximately 1,800 undergraduate psychology students from all over the country.

28.1 OVERVIEW

Historical accounts of psychology in the Philippines indicate that psychology was probably taught as early as the 17th century at two universities, namely the University of Santo Tomas in Manila and the University of San Carlos in Cebu (De Jesus, 1990; Licuanan, 1985). Philosophical psychology was brought to the Philippines by the Spanish friars (Licuanan). However, formal records of the establishment of Philippine psychology as a discipline only date back to the founding of the University of the Philippines in 1908 (Guthrie & Bulatao, 1968). Psychology was part of philosophy in the School of Education at the University of the Philippines until the Department of Psychology was established in 1926. Agustin Alonzo who received his Ph.D. in experimental psychology from the University of Chicago in 1926 became the head of the country's first department of psychology (Guthrie & Bulatao; Licuanan).

In the early 1930s, the departments of psychology of the University of Santo Tomas and Far Eastern University were established. The University of Santo Tomas has the distinction of being the first academic institution to offer undergraduate, master's, and doctoral degrees in psychology (Licuanan, 1985).

From 1928 to 1961, seven more Filipino psychologists who had undertaken advanced studies in psychology in the United States returned to the country (Licuanan, 1985). They were:

1. Sinforoso Padilla, with a Ph.D. from the University of Michigan in 1928. He established the first psychological clinic in the country at the University of the Philippines in 1932.
2. Jesus Perfinan, with a Ph.D. in psychology from Iowa State University in 1933. He chaired the Department of Psychology of Far Eastern University and set up its psychological clinic.
3. Elias Bumatay, with a Ph.D. in educational psychology from the University of Texas in 1940. He became the dean of the College of Education at National University.
4. Estefania Aldaba-Lim, with a Ph.D. in clinical psychology from the University of Michigan. She started the psychology program at Philippine Women's University in 1948. Much later, in 1962, she set up the Philippine Psychological Corporation.
5. Alfredo Lagmay, with a Ph.D. in experimental psychology from Harvard University in 1955. He headed the University of the Philippines' Psychology Department.
6. Mariano Obias, with a Ph.D. in comparative and physiological psychology from Stanford University in 1955. He led the personnel department at Caltex Philippines.
7. Jaime Bulatao, with a Ph.D. in clinical psychology from Fordham University in 1961. He established the Psychology Department of Ateneo de Manila University.

It can be seen clearly how the aforementioned seven pioneers plus Agustin Alonzo helped shape the development of academic–scientific psychology in the country. Upon their return from the United States, they established psychology departments, set up psychological clinics, or were made heads of psychology departments. In addition, except for Bumatay, these pioneers founded the Psychological Association of the Philippines (PAP) in 1962 (Psychological Association of the Philippines [PAP], 2002). The constitution and by-laws of the association enumerated four main purposes, which can be taken as its mission statement. These were to (a) promote excellence in the teaching, research, and professional practice of psychology, (b) advance the practice of psychology as a scientific discipline, (c) promote human development and nation building, and (d) cooperate with other scientists and be instrumental in the understanding and problem-solving efforts in areas of mutual concern (PAP, 1991). For the past 40 years, the PAP has been guided by its four goals. Among other activities, since 1963, the association has held annual conventions and, since 1968, has published a journal called the *Philippine Journal of Psychology* (Tan, 1999). In the mid-1960s, the PAP joined the International Union of Psychological Science (IUPsyS) (De Jesus, 1990).

The influence of the American model of psychology that the U.S.-educated pioneers in Philippine psychology brought with them was very much evident in the psychology curriculum of many schools, as well as in the use of American research methodology, textbooks, and psychological tests. To indigenize Philippine psychology, Virgilio Enriquez from the University of the Philippines founded the *Pambansang Samahan sa Sikolohiyang Pilipino* or PSSP (National Association for Filipino Psychology) in 1975. Enriquez had obtained his Ph.D. in social psychology from Northwestern University in the United States. The PSSP is a "natural development of the indigenous tradition in the history of Philippine psychology" (De Jesus, 1990, p. 331). Sinha (1997, p. 153) has noted that "of the countries in Asia, the trend to indigenize psychology is strongest and most articulate in the Philippines." This is largely due to the efforts of the PSSP.

28.2 EDUCATION AND TRAINING

Since the first department of psychology was established in 1926, the number of schools with psychology programs has continued to increase. The 2002 Directory of Higher Education Institutions in the Philippines lists 171 colleges and universities, with a total of 249 psychology programs (Commission on Higher Education [CHED], 2002). It is interesting to note that the highest rate of increase in the number of programs occurred during the period 1990–2000. As much as 32% of the 249 psychology programs were added in the last decade. About one third of the 171 academic institutions are located in Manila. While 85% are privately owned, 15% are run by the government.

With regard to the profile of the programs that these institutions offer, 50% have a bachelor of arts (A.B.) degree in psychology, whereas 47% offer a bachelor of science (B.S.) degree in psychology. The A.B. or B.S. degrees are offered either through a separate program or in combination with other programs in psychology.

Among these 171 schools, 22% offer a master's degree (M.A. or M.S.), usually in combination with an A.B. or a B.S. degree. Only 6.4% offer a Ph.D. program.

About 60% of the M.A. or M.S. programs offered by 37 schools in the country provide specialization in the following fields: counseling psychology, clinical psychology, industrial–organizational psychology and human resources, educational psychology, social psychology, child psychology, early childhood education, guidance and counseling, and developmental psychology. For doctoral programs, the areas of specialization are limited to clinical psychology, social psychology, and guidance and counseling (CHED, 2002).

Only three psychology departments in the Philippines offer a combination of the A.B., B.S., M.A., M.S., and Ph.D. programs. These are the Ateneo de Manila University, University of the Philippines, and University of Santo Tomas. Each university offers more than one master's and doctoral program (CHED, 2002). These three universities, plus Far Eastern University that has a very large undergraduate population, and De la Salle University that has an A.B., B.S., and five M.S. tracks, train the greatest number of psychology students in the country. It is important to note that both the Ateneo de Manila University and the University of the Philippines were chosen by the government's Commission on Higher Education as Centers of Excellence in Psychology (A. M. Gonzalez-Intal, personal communication, March 12, 2003).

A majority of the institutions offering a psychology program have a distinct unit called the department of psychology, which is usually under a college of arts and sciences. Some schools that do not have a psychology department have a psychology program that is part of a department of behavioral sciences or a department of liberal arts. For many schools, both the undergraduate and graduate programs are administered by a department of psychology. In some schools, however, graduate programs are not under the administration of a department of psychology, but rather under a separate unit called the "Office of Graduate Studies."

A high percentage of psychology faculty and department heads in the Philippines are educated and trained locally. Through the years, there has been a decreasing trend in the number of Filipinos who go abroad to take up advanced studies in psychology (Licuanan, 1985). This has been largely due to the scarcity of financial resources and an increase in the number of domestic institutions that offer high-quality psychology programs. Because of the latter, Philippine universities have become a training ground for graduate psychology students who come from countries such as Indonesia, India, Malaysia, Singapore, Thailand, Cambodia, Korea, and Vietnam.

The mushrooming of institutions with psychology programs is an indicator of the popularity of psychology as an undergraduate major in many colleges and universities (Tan, 1999). With the increase in the number of students majoring in psychology came problems related to nonstandardized curricular requirements across schools, unqualified faculty, and inadequate facilities. As a response to these concerns, the PAP formed an accreditation committee that launched a comprehensive program in 1980 (De Jesus, 1990). The PAP's efforts covered four phases. The first phase was the assessment of psychology graduates from the period of 1965–1979. For the second phase, implemented in 1981, a meeting of the heads of psychology departments was held to draw up an agreement on the objectives for, and the minimum requirements of, the A.B., B.S., M.A., M.S., and Ph.D. degrees. The third phase involved a self-evaluation of psychology departments in terms of their curriculum, faculty, and facilities. The results of this self-evaluation were meant to be utilized in making decisions about the accreditation of schools that offer psychology programs. The fourth phase consisted mainly of plans for the PAP to design development programs to assist schools in developing their faculty and improving their facilities (De Jesus). However, the PAP could only do so much, given that it does not have legal authority to impose standards on accreditation of psychology programs.

The year 1994 was significant in the Philippine's history of educational reforms as this was when the Commission on Higher Education (CHED) was created to promote quality education in all tertiary educational institutions (Commission on Higher Education, n.d.). The CHED's Technical Committee for Psychology reviewed the minimum requirements for undergraduate and graduate psychology programs (A. M. Gonzalez-Intal, personal communication, March 12, 2003). In 1997, the commission promulgated the new undergraduate curriculum that was to take effect by 1998.

The new curriculum for an A.B. degree in psychology requires a total of 126 units for graduation, categorized into the following subject areas: 63 units of general education courses (which are also specified by CHED), 45 course units for the psychology major plus electives from related areas, and 18 units of other courses to be determined by the school (including foreign languages). The B.S. program has an additional 20 units of natural science electives (e.g., biology, chemistry, physics), thereby increasing the total from 126 to 146 academic units (CHED Memorandum Order no.44, 1997; A. M. Gonzalez-Intal, personal communication, March 12, 2003). It is important to note that an examination of randomly selected undergraduate curricula of 20 institutions revealed that all require their students to take more than the number of units required by the commission—by as much as 72 additional units.

The current CHED curriculum requires the students to take the following undergraduate courses: general psychology, statistics (with lab), developmental psychology, personality theories, experimental psychology (with lab), social psychology, psychological testing (with lab), two courses on research in psychology (for the thesis), and a practicum (one term for a minimum of 150 hr). A survey of 20 schools showed that all offer a practicum course, but many go beyond the minimum number of hours set by CHED, requiring as many as 250–300 hr. Some schools require two terms for a total of 400–480 hr. Students are usually placed in industrial, clinical, and educational or school settings where they are assigned tasks like testing, interviewing, counseling, teaching, and writing reports.

CHED likewise requires five seminars in psychology in any of the following: learning and cognitive psychology, abnormal psychology or clinical psychology, industrial–organizational psychology, Filipino psychology, group dynamics, physiological psychology or biopsychology, and current issues in psychology.

The commission also makes available descriptions of required courses and a reading list for each course. It is interesting to note that most of the books and readings are by foreign authors, with publication dates typically in the 1990s. In addition to the curricular requirements, CHED also specifies minimum requirements for faculty qualifications, library holdings, and laboratory facilities.

The CHED is also in the process of finalizing the policies and standards for graduate programs, and these will take effect soon (A. M. Gonzalez-Intal, personal communication, March 12, 2003). The program descriptions make a distinction between the M.A. and M.S. in psychology and the master of psychology (M.P.) degree. The former is a teaching/research degree with a thesis requirement, whereas the latter is a practitioner's degree that requires, in lieu of a thesis, an applied program or project (e.g., field practicum) in the student's chosen area of practice. Except for this difference, the other requirements in terms of core and major courses and the comprehensive exam are the same, for a total of 30 units, with the following breakdown: 9 units for the core courses, 15 units for the major courses, and 6 units for the thesis or field practicum. For the Ph.D. program, CHED requires a minimum of 45 units for those with an M.A. or M.S. degree in psychology or 69 units for those without an M.A. or M.S.

The core courses specified for the master's program are Development of Psychological Thought, Advanced Statistics I, and Advanced Research Methods I. For the doctoral program, two core courses are required: Advanced Statistics II and Advanced Research Methods II.

The policies and standards for graduate programs also specify the minimum requirements for faculty, library, laboratory, and other facilities.

For the past 7 years, CHED has done much to address the problems that beset the education and training of psychology students in the country. However, much more needs to be done. For example, the implementation of the minimum requirements for graduate programs has yet to occur. There is also a need to evaluate the new undergraduate curriculum in terms of compliance and effectiveness.

A perennial issue that faces psychologists in the Philippines is the need to professionalize and regulate the practice of psychology. In 1983, the PAP drafted and submitted the Psychology Act to Congress (De Jesus, 1990). The current version bill provides for the creation of a Professional Regulatory Board of Psychology that will administer and enforce the provisions of the Psychology Act and supervise the registration, licensure, and practice of psychologists and psychometricians in the Philippines (S.2455, 2003). However, after 20 years, the bill has yet to be passed. In the absence of a law that regulates psychological practice, Filipino psychologists must contend with problems like the definition of a psychologist and psychological specialties. For instance, it is not clear who should be called a clinical psychologist. According to the PAP, a clinical psychologist must have either a Ph.D. in clinical psychology or an M.A. or M.S. in general or clinical–counseling psychology with 3 years of clinical experience (PAP, n.d.). Some institutions, however, consider even those with bachelor's degree in psychology to be clinical psychologists (E. Magno, personal communication, February 27, 2003).

Graduates of social psychology are found in various settings ranging from the industrial to developmental and even clinical settings. This is because the scope of social psychology in the Philippines is not clear-cut (J. Perez, personal communication, March 4, 2003). One other consequence of not having a psychology act is that Filipino psychologists cannot be compelled to take courses or attend seminars and workshops for continuing education. As matters stand now, those who feel the need to engage in continuing education activities do so on their own initiative.

28.3 SCOPE OF PSYCHOLOGICAL PRACTICE

Counseling and clinical work remain the more predominant forms of psychological practice in the Philippines. Filipino therapists tend to use client-centered, cognitive, and psychoanalytic approaches in their practice (Teh, 2003). However, psychologists also incorporate religious and spiritual scripts in therapy. We should note that 85% of Filipinos are Catholics, and cultural evaluations of appropriate behaviors and mental processes tend to follow Catholic prescriptions. Therapists are also sensitive to the cultural norm of strong family ties and often apply family-based interventions (Teh). At a more basic level, supportive members of an extended family provide valuable psychological and material assistance to clients who cannot afford extensive psychological services.

Because religion plays a pivotal role in the Filipino's psyche, psychologists can also be found in church counseling centers such as the Center for Family Ministries and Our Lady of Peace Guidance Center. Centers like these are usually staffed by Catholic priests who offer counseling and therapy for the clergy and marital support for couples. Psychologists in these settings also assess applicants to the clergy and applications for church annulments, and conduct trainings for religious educators (R. Champoux, personal communication, February 28, 2003). Counselors in church-affiliated centers are usually trained in pastoral counseling. The decision of some religious members to take up psychology courses implies a trend toward religious counseling with psychological overtones.

There are many schools in the country where psychologists work as guidance counselors from grade school to the tertiary level. Their training in psychology, which guidance counselors with an educational background do not have, is considered advantageous when dealing with clients.

Clinical psychologists in the country typically do testing, evaluation, counseling, and psychotherapy. They can be found in a variety of settings, such as private clinics, hospitals, government institutions, church counseling centers, academic institutions, and prisons. Clients range from children to adults, individuals to couples and families, civilians to military personnel, and normal to abnormal populations.

Some privately owned clinics are set up with a head clinical psychologist who oversees a staff of psychologists as they administer tests, prepare psychological reports, and do therapy. In other instances, clinical psychologists either refer individual assessment and therapy cases or work as a team. Hospital-based psychologists, however, take on more defined activities. For instance, psychologists employed in the Neuropsychiatric Section of the Armed

Forces of the Philippines Hospital primarily do psychodiagnostics. They assist in screening applicants for military and civilian personnel of the armed forces by administering and interpreting the results of intelligence, personality, and projective tests. They also write psychological reports and submit these to psychiatrists or neuropsychiatric screeners for final assessment (T. Rivera, personal communication, March 7, 2003; M. Rosales, personal communication, March 5, 2003). Psychologists in the Armed Forces of the Philippines sometimes conduct critical-incident debriefings for soldiers in conflict-ridden areas. At present, however, social workers and nurses from the armed forces are also being tapped to facilitate these seminars. In military hospital settings, psychologists are also asked to accompany soldiers going into battle or those being sent to missions abroad (e.g., Kuwait). Their responsibilities include monitoring soldiers' psychological and emotional status and conducting team-building sessions (M. Rosales, personal communication, March 5, 2003).

Government institutions like the Armed Forces of the Philippines and the National Center for Mental Health delineate functions carried out by psychologists and psychiatrists. Psychologists take charge of testing and evaluation. Therapeutic interventions and patient–applicant-related decisions rest with the psychiatrist who may confer with the psychologist regarding test results. One should note that screening applicants in the Philippine military setting is a politically sensitive issue because of *bata-bata* (personalized favoritism) (E. Tapawan, personal communication, February 27, 2003). The country's Department of Social Work and Development also employs psychologists who, together with

the social workers, handle cases such as sexual abuse, incest, substance abuse, and child prostitution.

Clinical psychologists also make appearances in court as expert witnesses for annulment and criminal cases. Annulment cases are a booming industry for clinical psychologists, perhaps because there is currently no existing divorce law in the Philippines (E. Magno, personal communication, February 27, 2003; Tan, 1999). In prisons, psychologists advise inmates and train counseling personnel on therapeutic techniques. They also hold informal classes with the prisoners, teaching general and abnormal psychology, and facilitate sessions on anger management, *paghahanda sa paglaya* (preparation for freedom), and *pagkilala sa pamilya at sarili* (knowing oneself and family) (J. Saplala, personal communication, February 28, 2003).

Next to clinical psychology, industrial–organizational psychology is the second most popular professional specialization among Filipino psychologists. Historically, the practice of human resource management and development in the Philippines dealt heavily with labor–union issues and collective bargaining. As a consequence, human resource managers were often lawyers (R. Hechanova, personal communication, February 28, 2003). At present, industrial–organizational psychology is predominantly identified with personnel work, such as recruitment and assessment.

In addition to personnel–related tasks, Filipino industrial–organizational psychologists contribute to human resource management, training, and organizational development. Industrial–organizational psychologists also carry out research on topics like employee morale, work motivation, leadership and management style, career planning and development, consumer behavior, impact and training needs analyses, and coping strategies for stress management in the workplace.

Other psychologists in the Philippines find themselves in equally useful professional niches. A number of psychologists teach at the tertiary level. In fact, most of the well-known Filipino psychologists are based in academia. In addition to teaching, they usually engage in research and psychotherapy. They also serve as consultants to governmental and private agencies (M.L.A. Carandang, personal communication, March 5, 2003). With a boom in preschool education in the country, psychologists with a major in child psychology and early childhood education are very much in demand as preschool teachers. Many run their own preschools.

Social psychologists work in development agencies such as the National Economic Development Authority and the Development Academy of the Philippines and also in private organizations such as the Gaston Z. Ortigas Peace Institute and Center for Integrative and Development Studies. These psychologists also provide psychosocial help to victims of abuse, violence, and poverty through counseling and social work, and help to establish and maintain rehabilitation centers (E. Protacio-De Castro, personal communication, March 7, 2003).

Dire economic conditions in the Philippines affect the way psychology is practiced professionally. The majority of Filipinos live below the poverty line, and much interpersonal and family stress can be traced to material deprivation. Furthermore, psychological services are often considered a luxury vis-à-vis basic needs like food. Aside from economic burdens, the Philippines is saddled with political instability and violence. Filipino psychologists have been called upon to assist survivors of political detention, torture, war-rape, and other forms of militarized brutality. Psychologists are at the forefront of healing individuals affected by the ongoing internal war—providing trauma-therapy in evacuation centers and tending to the psychological needs of victims of military atrocities.

A new breed of psychologists has emerged in war-torn areas like Mindanao. Not only do these practitioners specialize in conflict resolution and crisis management, they also fulfill the multiple roles of counselor, community organizer, mediator, peace partner, and even lobbyist or advocator. They do not have a clearly defined professional identity, and find it impossible to label themselves and their field of specialization according to Western categories. Practitioners in this milieu even find it disadvantageous at times to introduce themselves as psychologists. "Calling yourself as a psychologist is not really very acceptable to some people [because] they have their own notions of what a psychologist is and that filters engagement" (J. Perez, personal communication, March 4, 2003). Instead, psychologists who engage in social and community work take on various names, from "rural sociologists, community organizers, community psychologists, researchers, [to] training specialists" (Licuanan, 1985, p. 82). As such, activities that are considered "psychological" are also deputized to nonpsychologists like medical doctors, religious leaders, teachers, and community leaders (J. Perez, personal communication, March 4, 2003).

Because of the various roles required of them, psychologists in war torn settings must adopt a multidisciplinary approach. They have to be flexible and rely on a wide variety of methodologies and intervention strategies that are culturally sensitive to the community in order to better understand and address the unique experiences of the Filipino community. As Perez (personal communication, March 4, 2003) puts it, "It is really a matter of recognizing that people have their own practice but coming from the outside, we are too eager to help and sometimes you become blind to this." Although this may be true of psychological practice in other settings, indigenizing psychology is necessitated more in the social and community settings.

In summary, the practice of psychology in the Philippines is widespread and psychologists are able to position themselves in almost any field, from schools and corporations to government institutions and hospitals. The work of psychologists varies, depending on the context. It can range from testing and evaluation, recruitment and training, counseling, and therapy and rehabilitation to teaching, social work, community-organizing, mediating, and conflict-resolution. The conduct of research is also part of psychological practice in the Philippines, although this is true to a greater extent in academic rather than in applied settings (J. Bulatao, personal communication, February 26, 2003).

Given the diversity of jobs and work settings of Filipino psychologists, it is not surprising that their salaries and fees vary considerably. For example, the starting monthly salary of a university guidance counselor can range from 11,000 Philippine pesos (PhP) (approximately $204) for someone with a bachelor's degree to 31,000 PhP (about $574) for a Ph.D. holder. The monthly salary of a university instructor of psychology can range from 14,000 PhP ($260) for someone with a baccalaureate to 32,000 PhP ($593) for a PhD holder; full professors can earn three or four times more than a beginning Ph.D. holder. In clinical settings, a psychologist's fees are usually determined by an hourly rate or per psychological report. For individual psychotherapy, the going rate per session is 600–1,500 PhP ($11–$28) (Teh, 2003). A written report can fetch 1,000–2,000 PhP ($19–$37). In business and industry, the starting monthly salary of a master's-level psychologist can range from 20,000–30,000 PhP ($370–$555), whereas a human resource manager can command 150,000 PhP ($2,800) monthly (E. Franco, personal communication, November 22, 2003).

28.4 FUTURE CHALLENGES AND PROSPECTS

With its unclear identity and dearth of local literature, the future of psychology in the Philippines poses both opportunities and challenges. Filipino psychologists face several pressing issues, which include defining the boundaries of psychology, professionalizing the discipline, establishing and maintaining local and international linkages, conducting meaningful research, indigenizing psychology, and upgrading the quality of education and training of psychologists.

Among Filipinos, the term *psychology* spans a variety of meanings. Public opinion equates psychology with counseling (J. Bulatao, personal communication, February 26, 2003; J. Saplala, personal communication, February 28, 2003), services for the mentally ill, and even faith-healing practices (J. Bulatao, personal communication, February 26, 2003). Psychology is still viewed as preparatory to medicine or law and not as its own field with a broad range of specialties (J. Saplala, personal communication, February 28, 2003).

Filipino psychologists face the challenge of establishing and maintaining a network of professionals in areas beyond metropolitan Manila (M. Onglatco, personal communication, February 21, 2003). For example, there is no existing directory of psychologists to which the general public can refer if they need to see a psychotherapist. Increased collaboration with psychologists in other regions will not only augment involvement and representation but also address sensitive issues in psychological practice that are complicated by factors of language, geography, and culture.

In addition to local networks, psychologists in the Philippines also need to develop partnerships with international psychologists for collaborative training, mentoring, sharing information, and generating resources. Apart from the Afro-Asian Psychological Association in which the PAP was a founding member, "there have been little systematic links established with other third world psychologists, particularly those from neighboring Asian countries" (Licuanan, 1985, p. 85). In recent years, however, Philippine academic institutions have organized and hosted international conventions of the Asian Association of Social Psychology, International Congress of Psychology, and the Committee for the Scientific Study of Peace of the IUPsyS.

The trend toward a multidisciplinary approach to addressing psychological issues also calls for increased coordination among counselors, psychiatrists, and psychologists, as well as openness to doing collaborative work with social scientists in other disciplines. For instance, "psychologists working together with political scientists might come up with a better understanding of Philippine political processes, or work with anthropologists can help better understand the strengths and weaknesses of informal education" (Tan, 1999, p. 35).

In order to address the larger concerns that face the Philippines, psychologists cross disciplines and work collaboratively with other social scientists. For example, on matters of resolving political violence, strengthening civil society, and building a democratic political culture, psychologists work hand-in-hand with anthropologists, philosophers, and political scientists. In clinical settings, psychologists team-up with psychiatrists, with psychologists providing assessment and psychotherapy services and psychiatrists prescribing psychotropic medication.

Another daunting challenge facing Filipino psychologists lies in the conduct of psychological research. "While scientific psychology has become more inviting, few are accepting the invitation ... the number of psychologists with advanced degrees has grown tremendously, [but] the amount of research and writing in the field has not advanced proportionately" (Licuanan, 1985, p. 83). In academia, "Findings indicate that research is not a mainstream activity [either] for the overwhelming majority of psychologists in the Philippines, even those whose primary employment is in academic departments of psychology" (Bernardo, 2002, p. 33).

This dearth in research may be attributed to several factors, including the prevailing view that research is not that important and that practitioners do not have time to do research. Many psychologists in academic settings are saddled with academic and administrative responsibilities such that research activities have to take a backseat. Some schools assign as many as 24 units a semester to their faculty. There are also those who, even if they have the time, cannot do research because they do not possess the necessary scientific knowledge and skills. More efforts are being undertaken, however, to bridge the science and practice of psychology, especially in the industrial setting where the PAP and the Personnel Managers Association of the Philippines (PMAP) recently signed a memorandum of agreement to collaborate on research (R. Hechanova, personal communication, February 28, 2003).

Even when research is conducted, findings are usually limited to the individuals and institutions involved. Research findings remain largely unshared because of the limited opportunities for psychologists to convene to discuss ideas. Bernardo (2002) also found that psychologist–practitioners in the Philippines actually do very little publishing. In his survey of the PsychInfo database published by the American Psychological Association, he found only 55 publications over the years 1991 to 2000 that involved Filipino authors. Of these, only 10 were single-authored by Philippine psychologists from three universities, i.e., University of the Philippines, Ateneo de Manila University, and De La Salle University.

Philippine psychology tends to use Western paradigms, and there is a need to localize the discipline. As mentioned earlier, Virgilio Enriquez pioneered the development of indigenous Philippine psychology through the *Pambansang*

Samahan sa Sikolohiyang Pilipino or PSSP (National Association of Philippine Psychology). Enriquez's remarkable intellectual and professional leadership created an indigenous orientation in psychological research, founded on culturally sensitive data-gathering methods and analysis (Church & Katigbak, 2002). Unfortunately, although the national association was founded 28 years ago with the aim of establishing a truly Filipino psychology, it failed to revolutionize psychological thinking in the Philippines (Tan, 1999) with its followers remaining a minority voice in the field (E. Protacio-De Castro, personal communication, March 7, 2003). In fact, "there are some areas that remain relatively untouched by the move towards indigenization and these are the applied fields of industrial psychology [where testing is a primary concern]" (Licuanan, 1985, p. 84). This is because "foreign tests have a powerful distribution system through the Philippine Psychological Corporation" (Tan, 1999, p. 31) rather than because of a shortage of psychometrically sound tests in the country.

Last but not least are the challenges related to psychology education, which continues to be plagued by problems in relation to nonstandardized undergraduate and graduate curricula (De Jesus, 1990), the lack of qualified and competent faculty (Bulatao, 1979; De Jesus, 1990), and inadequate facilities (De Jesus). A number of colleges and universities have not fully complied with the curricular requirements of the new CHED undergraduate curriculum because they do not have, as yet, laboratory facilities (e.g., computer software and hardware) to run laboratory sections in statistics and psychological testing courses. Many psychology faculty do not meet the degree requirement for graduate level teaching or, even worse, have no degree or training in psychology at all. Psychology teachers complain about the lack of updated reference materials, especially journals. Although participation in practicum is a standard requirement, each school has its own list of practicum sites. The quality of training that practicum students receive is very much dependent on the tasks assigned by a particular practicum site and on the qualifications of the on-site supervisors.

REFERENCES

Bulatao, J. C. (1979). Oh, that terrible task of teachers to teach psychology in the Philippines. *Philippine Journal of Psychology, 12,* 35–40.

Carandang, M. L. A. (1987). *Filipino children under stress: Family dynamics and theraphy.* Quezon City, Philipines: Ateneo de Manila University Press.

Church, A. T., & Katigbak, M. S. (2002). Indigenization of psychology in the Philippines. *International Journal of Psychology, 37,* 129–148.

Commission on Higher Education. (1997). Memorandum Order No. 44.

Commission on Higher Education. (n.d.). *About CHED.* Retrieved March 21, 2003, from http://www.ched.gov.ph/aboutus/index.html

Commission on Higher Education. (2002). *Directory of higher education institutions in the Philippines.* Pasig City, Philippines: Government Printing Office.

De Jesus, M. L. V. (1990). Philippines. In G. Shouksmith & E. A. Shouksmith (Eds.), *Psychology in Asia and the Pacific* (pp. 311–338). Bangkok, Thailand: UNESCO.

Enriquez, V. G. (1992). *From colonial to liberation psychology: The Philippine experience.* Quezon City, Philippines: University of the Philippines Press.

Guthrie, G. M., & Bulatao, J. C. (1968). Psychology in the Philippines. *Psychologia, 1,* 201–206.

Licuanan, P. B. (1985). Psychology in the Philippines: History and current trends. *Philippine Studies, 33,* 67–86.

Liwag, M. E. C., de La Cruz, A. S., & Macapagal, M. E. J. (1998). How we raise our daughters and sons: Child-rearing and gender socialization in the Philippines. *Philippine Journal of Psychology, 31,* 1–46.

Psychological Association of the Philippines. (1991). *Approved revised constitution.* Quezon City, Philippines: Author.

Psychological Association of the Philippines. (n.d.). *Code of ethics for clinical psychologists.* Quezon City, Philippines: Author.

Psychological Association of the Philippines. (2002, August). *Fortieth founding anniversary convention: Inspirations and aspirations.* Program of the 39th annual convention of the Psychological Association of the Philippines, Manila, Philippines.

Salazar-Clemeña, R. M. (1991). *Counseling psychology in the Philippines: Research and practice.* Manila, Philippines: De La Salle University Press.

Sinha, D. (1997). Indigenizing psychology. In J. W. Berry, Y. H. Poortinga, & J. Pandey (Eds.), *Handbook of cross-cultural psychology: Vol. 1. Theory and method* (pp. 129–169). Boston: Allyn & Bacon.

Tan, A. L. (1999). Philippine psychology: Growth and becoming. In L. A. Teh & E. J. Macapagal (Eds.), *Readings in general psychology* (Vol. 2, pp. 19–38). Unpublished manuscript, Ateneo de Manila University at Manila, Philippines.

Teh, L. A. (2003). A survey on the practice and status of psychotherapy in the Philippines. *Philippine Journal of Psychology, 36,* 112–133.

Torres, A. T. (1997). Methods, mind or meaning: Shifting paradigms in Philippine psychology. *Philippine Journal of Psychology, 30,* 17–38.

IMPORTANT PUBLICATIONS

Bernardo, A. B. I. (2002). Finding our voice(s): Philippine psychologists' contribution to global discourse in psychology. *Asian Psychologists, 3,* 29–37.

Bulatao, J. C. (1992). *Phenomena and their interpretation: Landmark essays 1957–1989.* Quezon City, Philippines: Ateneo de Manila University Press.

Carandang, M. L. (1987). *Filipino children under stress: Family dynamics and therapy.* Quezon City, Philippines: Ateneo de Manila University Press.

Church, A. T., & Katigbak, M. S. (2002). Indigenization of psychology in the Philippines. *International Journal of Psychology, 37,* 129–148.

Enriquez, V. G. (1992). *From colonial to liberation psychology: The Philippine experience.* Quezon City, Philippines: University of the Philippines Press.

Guanzon-Lapena, M. A., Church, A. T., Carlota, A. J., & Katigbak, M. S. (1998). Indigenous personality measures: Philippine examples. *Journal of Cross-Cultural Psychology, 29,* 249–270.

Ledesma, L. K., Diputado, B. V., Orteza, G. O., & Santillan, C. E. (1993). De-westernization of a dementia screening scale: The Philippine experience. *Philippine Journal of Psychology, 26,* 30–38.

Liwag, M. E. C., de la Cruz, A. S., & Macapagal, M. E. J. (1998). How we raise our daughters and sons: Child-rearing and gender socialization in the Philippines. *Philippine Journal of Psychology, 31,* 1–46.

Salazar-Clemeña, R. M. (1991). *Counseling psychology in the Philippines: Research and practice.* Manila, Philippines: De La Salle University Press.

Torres, A. T. (1997). Methods, mind or meaning: Shifting paradigms in Philippine psychology. *Philippine Journal of Psychology, 30,* 17–38.

CHAPTER 29

International Psychology: A Synthesis

MICHAEL J. STEVENS AND DANNY WEDDING

In this chapter, we attempt a synthesis of the 27 national psychologies (drawn from the nine regions of the world) that are presented in the *Handbook of International Psychology*. Needless to say, there are countless ways in which to approach a synthesis that mirrors the various purposes of such a task. Originally, we considered comparing country psychologies within and between regions using the same exhaustive outline that we asked our authors to follow. We abandoned this approach for two reasons. First, we realized that the cultural, historical, and political differences among countries, which contribute to the distinctiveness of their psychologies, made it impossible for authors to provide information on every component of the outline. Second, we believed that it would be more beneficial for our readers if we undertook a sweeping view rather than a detailed one. Consistent with previous volumes on international psychology (Gilgen & Gilgen, 1987; Sexton & Hogan, 1992), we wanted our readers to conclude their examination

of the *Handbook* with an appreciation for contemporary international psychology and how it might evolve in the future.

We begin by examining several general trends in psychology around the world. Some of these trends were first identified in previous volumes on international psychology (see Gilgen & Gilgen, 1987; Sexton & Hogan, 1992), and we try to accent the historical links between the *Handbook* and earlier works. Of course, some trends have changed since the publication of the previous books on international psychology, and others have emerged only recently. Specifically, we highlight the continued growth of the discipline and profession of psychology, the proliferation of scientific and applied specializations, regional revitalization, the expansion of psychology in developing countries, the feminization of psychology, and the emergence of new paradigms that accentuate contextual realities and challenges (e.g., multiculturalism and indigenization). We end by considering what American psychology can gain from an understanding of psychology as constituted in different countries and regions of the world. We believe that this part of our synthesis is especially important to readers who have been exposed mainly to the abstract, mechanistic, and quantitative vision of American psychology, a *Weltanschauung* with limited applicability in a world that faces enormously complex and contextually embedded challenges.

29.1 GROWTH OF PSYCHOLOGY

We launch our examination of general trends in psychology with evidence of psychology's continued growth as a discipline and profession.

29.1.1 Numbers of Psychologists and Psychology Students

Sexton and Hogan (1992) remarked upon the record increase in the number of psychologists worldwide through the early 1990s, with marked expansion in Brazil, Israel, Spain, and South Africa. In general, these trends are continuing. For example, Brazil has over 10,000 psychologists joining its workforce every year. There are about 7,000 psychologists listed in the registry of Israeli psychologists, an increase of more than 100% since the late 1990s. The number of registered psychologists in Spain was 32,100 in 2002 versus 25,200 in 1994. In South Africa, there are about 120 psychologists per million citizens, a 45% increase in density in slightly over 10 years.

Each of the 27 countries that we sampled reported evidence of growth in

psychology. Even in heavily industrialized countries, the expansion of psychology is yet to plateau. In Germany, the number of students studying psychology more than doubled in less than 30 years; in the United Kingdom, the number of applicants admitted to psychology programs in 2003 rose by 20% over that in 2002. In developing countries, the number of universities with psychology programs, the number of psychology majors, and the number of psychologists with advanced degrees is growing. Two countries illustrate the rise of psychology in the developing world: the Philippines reports that 32% of its 249 psychology programs were inaugurated in the last decade, and the number of Polish psychologists grew by 20% when the psychology graduates of 2000 entered the workforce. However, in many developing and underdeveloped countries, the growth of psychology lags behind that of other social sciences, such as economics and sociology, which are perceived as having greater value to society and hence more marketability. In addition, the proportion of psychology graduates employed in the field is very low in some countries. The unemployment and underemployment of psychologists reflects the oversupply of graduates relative to each country's needs and the resources available to support jobs in psychology. This is the case in Colombia, where 12% of psychologists are unemployed, and in Thailand, where the demand for psychologists falls below the supply of psychology graduates.

29.1.2 The Definition of a Psychologist

The definition of a psychologist varies considerably across countries. Moreover, in some countries such as Kenya, psychologists are virtually indistinguishable from counselors in their training and job responsibilities. Generally, the title of psychologist is conferred upon those who hold a baccalaureate or master's degree in psychology, who then may practice professionally, treating clients or serving as research psychologists in state and private enterprises. In many countries, the master's degree is a relatively recent curricular innovation (e.g., available in Australia only since 2000), which mirrors the increased specialization of psychology, especially in applied areas. However, many countries have begun to offer advanced training through postbaccalaureate courses and continuing education credit. The United States stands alone in its declaration of the doctorate as the entry-level degree for the professional practice of psychology, although other countries where psychology is highly developed are following suit. In the United Kingdom, the D.Clin.Psy. or Psy.D. is required for the practice of clinical psychology and other applied specialties, and in Quebec, Canada, universities have eliminated applied master's programs in response to stiffer eligibility criteria adopted by the province's professional regulatory authority, criteria that include a competency-based doctorate.

Unlike clinical psychologists, most academic psychologists around the world are expected to possess advanced degrees that reflect their research training. However, although doctorates may be required for promotion to full professor in developing countries, they are not necessary for employment at lower academic levels. In Argentina, for example, only 1.3% of academic psychologists have doctorates.

29.2 SCIENTIFIC AND APPLIED SPECIALIZATION

Aside from the increased number of psychologists and psychology students worldwide (Rosenzweig, 1999), the growth of psychology can be indexed by the proliferation of scientific and applied specialties and the formation of organizations that represent these specialties.

29.2.1 Psychology Organizations

More than 15 years ago, Gilgen and Gilgen (1987) noted a vigorous trend toward applied specialization, and argued that each country's path of specialization reflected the needs and goals of that country (e.g., raising economic productivity in developing countries vs. promoting health in developed countries). Similarly, Sexton and Hogan (1992) identified different emphases that countries place on various areas within psychology. More recently, Japan, for example, has seen a rise in the number of specialties and their interface. Although the Japanese Psychological Association has only five divisions, each subsumes a number of related specialties (e.g., one division includes perception, cognition, learning, and physiology; another brings together clinical, forensics, rehabilitation, and personality). In addition, there are 38 other organizations that attest to the growth of psychological specialization in Japan.

Since the Chinese government introduced its "one country, two systems" policy, the Chinese Psychological Society has expanded to 15 committees, each representing a distinct disciplinary area; in that time,

China also launched three organizations with narrow scientific and applied foci. Even in Nigeria, an underdeveloped country, psychological associations have been formed to convene professionals in various applied specialties (e.g., the Nigerian Association of Clinical Psychologists). With the transition to civilian government and the gradual restoration of the economy and renewal of political institutions, Nigerian psychology will surely become more specialized.

29.2.2 Education and Training

Growing specialization in scientific and applied psychology is also reflected in the formalization of training in a specialty. In Russia, there are approximately 15 paths to specialization accredited by the Ministry of Education. In 2002, the Indonesian Alliance of Psychologists created an independent regulatory entity to oversee the general and specialized preparation of psychologists. Specialization in psychology is sometimes mirrored in the codification of practice standards for specialists, particularly if a specialty is well established (Oakland, 2003). Although this is the case in industrialized countries such as the United Kingdom and the United States, where the practice of clinical, counseling, educational, and school psychology is regulated by law, it is not a given elsewhere. For example, notwithstanding psychological specialization in Turkey, the title of psychologist can be adopted by anyone with a relevant baccalaureate degree. Moreover, standard definitions of different specialties are lacking, and many Turkish psychologists want to establish clearly defined and rigorous training requirements for highly specialized jobs in psychology.

The tide of specialization can also be gauged by the shifting content of journal articles. Among the most rapidly growing specialties in Mexico are the treatment of addiction, community health, and environmental psychology. Although Mexico does not have specialized training programs in psychology or professional associations for specialists, research in the aforementioned areas appears frequently in flagship Mexican journals.

29.2.3 Advances in Communications Technology

Innovations in telecommunications have exerted a profound influence on specialization in psychology. The Internet and World Wide Web are noteworthy for the speed with which a broad spectrum of contemporary psychological literature can be accessed. The relative ease with which academic and applied psychologists can contact international colleagues has also yielded collaboration within specialties. For example, many specialty conferences solicit proposals electronically and provide electronic abstracts of cutting-edge research. Other digital resources disseminate information about opportunities for additional specialization in teaching, research, and practice (e.g., academic exchanges, clinical training, and support for travel and for organizing conferences [e.g., Stevens, 2004]).

In our sample of 27 countries, almost all reported having access to the Internet and World Wide Web. The leading universities in most developing countries are digitally wired, as are hospitals and psychology organizations, although to a lesser extent. The benefits of advanced telecommunications to psychologists in developing countries include the availability of specialization via distance learning, access to recent scholarship in scientific and applied specialties (e.g., cognitive science, capacity building), and opportunities to network with international organizations that represent specialized domains. In some underdeveloped countries, expatriates have used the Internet to cultivate mentoring and peer-consultation relationships with colleagues at home. Communications technology has its detractors, however. Mexican psychologists complain that online literature is prohibitively expensive; they observe that the Internet and World Wide Web are not equally accessible to psychologists around the world, and worry that the gap in knowledge and skills between psychologists in industrialized countries versus developing and underdeveloped countries will widen. In addition, Indonesian psychologists report that the Internet and World Wide Web are not very useful because few of them are proficient in English, the increasingly accepted language of cyberspace. Finally, Nigerian psychologists believe that the dominance of English-language materials will prolong dependence on the expertise of the West and weaken the effort to construct a more congruent indigenous psychology.

29.3 REGIONAL REVITALIZATION

Beyond the expansion of scientific and applied specialties, the growth of psychology is apparent in its rejuvenation in certain regions of the world, notably in Europe and South America.

29.3.1 Europe

Gilgen and Gilgen (1987) wrote about the gradual stagnation of European psychology by the late 1970s. The current revitalization of European psychology takes two forms: the renewal of psychology in West European countries that are member states of the European Union (EU), and in East European countries that have transitioned from communism to alternative economic and political systems.

29.3.1.1 WESTERN EUROPE

The Leonardo da Vinci program, funded by the EU and administered by the European Federation of Psychologists' Associations (EFPA), involves 12 partner states that are (a) comparing education and training requirements within and between countries, and (b) developing a common core curriculum that will render qualifications for a psychology degree equivalent across Europe (Project EuroPsyT, 2001). The search for a European educational framework stemmed from earlier directives to federalize trade and political identity (e.g., the 1957 Treaty of Rome). The framework calls for a 6-year program comprised of 3 years of undergraduate study, a 2-year postgraduate certification, and a 6th year of supervised professional practice. The EFPA has agreed to facilitate a consensus regarding the core curriculum, minimum standards, and the award of a European Diploma in psychology as early as 2004. The Europeanization of education and training in psychology clearly shows the continent's evolving identity as it distances itself from U.S. influence and harmonizes its internal differences.

A similar trend is occurring in North America, following the ratification of the North American Free Trade Agreement (NAFTA), a treaty designed to promote the movement of goods and services across Canada, Mexico, and the United States. Psychologists from these countries, working through the Trilateral Forum on Professional Issues, are reviewing national models for the preparation and credentialing of psychologists with an eye toward possible regional standardization.

29.3.1.2 EASTERN EUROPE

Since the collapse of communism, Eastern Europe has undergone a transformation unprecedented in magnitude and scope that has led to the resurgence of psychology in the region. This transformation involves a complex and unfolding interaction between "top-down" causes, mostly economic and political, and "bottom-up" influences, such as normative systems that regulate daily life (Stevens, 2002). Adopting this perspective, a multidisciplinary team of social scientists and systems analysts at the University of Warsaw studies the "local" impact of Poland's transition from communism. Innovative research at the university includes computer simulations that map the slow, radiating course of macrosocial change.

In Russia, as elsewhere in Eastern Europe, the number of applicants to psychology programs has increased dramatically, as has the number of admissions. Many private universities have opened to accommodate the high demand for education and training in psychology. Alongside these trends is a movement to restructure the relationship between psychologists and physicians by credentialing psychologists as independent providers of psychotherapy. In addition to the rekindled interest in the work of Pavlov,

Bekhterev, and Vigotsky, new areas of psychological science and practice are now recognized through the establishment of distinct academic departments (e.g., social adaptation and management training). These pedagogical developments mirror the needs of Russians and Russian society; they also constitute a clear repudiation of the ideologically driven education and training mandated by the former communist regime.

29.3.2 South America

South America has also witnessed remarkable growth in psychological science and practice, particularly in countries with relatively healthy economies and political institutions. However, economic volatility and military coups have sometimes interrupted the development of psychology in South America, demonstrating the vulnerability of the discipline and profession to conditions in which individual rights are threatened or violated (Jing, 2000; Stevens, 2002). Fortunately, many South American countries now have state or federal laws that protect the status and activities of psychologists; for example, in 1998 the governments of Chile and Paraguay legally recognized the right of psychologists to practice professionally. Unlike the EFPA, the Interamerican Society of Psychology (SIP) has not embraced political advocacy. The implementation of regional trade agreements (e.g., the Andean Pact) may give this regional organization a political agenda and enhance coordination among national psychology organizations throughout South America. This is a likely outcome because, historically, South American psychology has gained vitality through regional exchanges among psychologists. Today, many Argentine psychologists have left their country due to the economic and political crises of 2002, raising concerns about a brain drain. However, their temporary relocation to neighboring countries will yield a cross-fertilization of theories and techniques, and when they repatriate, their experiences abroad will shape the future of Argentine psychology.

Brazil is an exemplar of the renewal of South American psychology. Brazilian universities have inaugurated a variety of graduate programs, and Brazilian psychologists are at the regional forefront of unifying science and practice in the psychology curriculum. Textbooks by Brazilian psychologists balance national and international scholarship, indirectly and sometimes overtly questioning the relevance of imported psychology for Brazil. Most significantly, Brazilian psychologists have been leaders in translating and adapting psychometric tools into equivalent versions appropriate to the culture of Brazil and in refining qualitative research methods.

Like their South American colleagues, Colombian psychologists have started to pursue nontraditional activities. Rural psychology has gained prominence, with more psychologists residing in villages and working in indigenous settings. Most Colombian psychologists have abandoned liberation psychology's radical call for social change and justice; due to the country's decades-old civil unrest, they remain committed to working for peace and reconciliation, albeit apolitically.

29.4 PSYCHOLOGY IN DEVELOPING COUNTRIES

As noted earlier, the growth of psychology appears to covary with certain economic and political conditions (e.g., market-oriented forms of representative government) that combine to amplify the public's need, understanding of, and support for psychology (Jing, 2000; Oakland, 2003; Rosenzweig, 1999). Under these circumstances, government, business and industry, and the populace turn to psychology as an instrument for enhancing national development and individual welfare. Accordingly, developing countries often invest in psychology by creating jobs, allocating resources for education, research, and practice, and by enacting laws that legitimize and protect psychology. Such investment reflects the hope that psychological science and practice will address national challenges.

29.4.1 Asia

Several countries in East and South Asia may be classified as "developing" according to the Human Development Index (HDI), a formula used by the U.N. Development Program that includes Gross Domestic Product per capita, life expectancy, adult literacy, and rate of school enrollment (Jing, 2000). Two prototypic developing countries in Asia are China and India. Given their status as developing countries, their psychologies emphasize research on social aspects of human functioning and interventions that target social problems linked to modernization. Thus, psychology in the developing world is skewed toward application.

Another feature of psychology in developing countries is its reliance on imported conceptual frameworks, investigative methodologies, and applied tools. Some of the harshest criticisms of imported psychology, particularly of Western psychology, come from psychologists in developing countries (Gilgen & Gilgen, 1987). Unfortunately, Western psychology is often applied to social problems without first being adapted to indigenous cultural and historical contexts, thereby sharply reducing the probability of successful outcomes.

29.4.1.1 EAST ASIA

Chinese psychology is slowly adopting a multifaceted approach to meet the demands of China's rapid economic modernization and increased exposure to the world. Globalization has produced significant problems (e.g., crime) and challenges (e.g., educational reform) for Chinese society. Unprecedented government support has created favorable conditions for education and training, scientific research, and professional practice in psychology. Psychology has emerged as a highly popular college major, and the number of students and professors participating in international exchanges has increased. Practicing psychologists are helping people balance the adjustments required by modernization with the continued observance of cultural traditions. Concerned about the moral decline of adolescents, psychologists have developed a holistic approach to education that includes instructional methods for nurturing Confucian virtues of harmony, loyalty, and altruism. Rather than applying Western models and interventions to address the unique problems associated with modernizing a socialist economy within the framework of Chinese culture, Chinese psychologists have embraced a multidisciplinary perspective, borrowing concepts, tools, and techniques from economics, history, and politics, and have begun collaborating with other social scientists.

29.4.1.2 SOUTH ASIA

Despite impressive economic gains, India is considered an underdeveloped country, with most of the population impoverished and subsisting on agriculture. Nevertheless, because of its advanced status in science and technology, India is also viewed as a high-tech powerhouse. Contemporary Indian psychology is characterized by the imperative that indigenization, grounded in religious scripture, is the preferred route for understanding and effecting change at the individual and societal levels. At the same time, Indian psychologists struggle to free themselves from the lingering notion that "West is best." As in many developing countries, psychology has become popular, and India boasts a wide range of specialties that have research and practice agendas reflecting the needs of the country. Progress has been made in standardizing the core curriculum, integrating indigenous methods (e.g., *yoga nidra*), and "vocationalizing" specialty training. Two factors, however, curtail the advancement of Indian psychology: (1) psychology organizations are often shortlived and ineffectual due to internecine conflict, and (2) many female psychologists are so burdened by multiple roles that they lack time and energy to devote to their profession.

29.5 FEMINIZATION OF PSYCHOLOGY

More than 10 years ago, Sexton and Hogan (1992) observed that "psychology around the world tends to be a female occupation, in some cases dramatically so" (p. 469). Not only are more women than men declaring psychology as their undergraduate major, women are also pursuing graduate education and training in psychology in larger numbers. In Western countries, the percentage of female undergraduates ranges from approximately 66% in the United States to 84% in the United Kingdom, and 80% of baccalaureates in Spain are awarded to women. Likewise, women form an overwhelming majority of psychologists and psychology students in India and Pakistan. Even in the conservative Middle East, the number of women pursuing psychology degrees has risen; in Egypt for example, 66% of baccalaureates are awarded to women. In graduate psychology programs, women have been the majority for some time in the United Kingdom and recently became the majority in the United States. In other countries, however, women tend not to pursue graduate study. For example, notwithstanding the number of female baccalaureates in Egypt, few women matriculate into advanced programs. In Japan, 80% of doctorates in psychology are awarded to men. To some extent, the feminization of psychology noted in the United Kingdom and the United States parallels that occurring in other health professions. For example in 2003, for the first time, the majority of applicants to U.S. medical schools were women.

There also appears to be an imbalance between women and men in the psychology workforce. In Western countries such as United Kingdom, women are becoming dominant in most settings in which psychologists are employed. In South Africa and Israel, women constitute 60% and 70% of working psychologists, respectively. In Spain, 75% of registered psychologists are women. In the developing world, women also constitute the majority of psychologists. For example, women make up 60–70% of the psychologists in Colombia. Interestingly, several employment trends for psychologists in the early 1990s (see Sexton & Hogan, 1992) have since changed. There are now more female than male psychologists in South Africa and Australia, where the composition of the Australian Psychological Society is 72% female. However, there are several countries in the Middle East and Africa in which psychologists tend to be male; in Egypt 65% of psychologists are male, and in Nigeria 95% are male.

Although women fill a variety of positions as psychologists in diverse settings, traditional differences in specialization remain, with more women holding jobs in clinics and schools, and more men employed in academia and in business and industry. This demarcation reflects the employment status of female psychologists in many countries, regardless of cultural affiliation or degree of industrialization. In Australia, significantly more men than women are Fellows in the Australian Psychological Society, suggesting that men are dominant in academia. In Spain, although the proportion of women in all specialties is growing, they are the minority in academia, in business and industry, and in the military and police forces. Furthermore, female psychologists in Spain earn less than their male counterparts, and are more likely to be employed part-time. In Colombia, most female psychologists work in applied areas, whereas men make up the majority in academia and university administration; men also form the leadership of the Colombian Society of Psychology. In India, in spite of vastly outnumbering male students, women are less likely to pursue a career in psychology due to their tendency to marry and relocate; those who remain in the field often work in low-paying community service jobs.

Women and men who pursue psychology as a career do not differ in school backgrounds, reasons for pursuing psychology, choice of psychology courses, or plans upon graduating (Metzner, Rajecki, & Lauer, 1994). Thus, the feminization of psychology in the workplace may be more a reflection of cultural norms, in conjunction with a national need for applied psychology. Because traditional gender roles are preserved in many countries, women are expected to shoulder the burden of domestic responsibilities. The unequal division of domestic labor makes it difficult for women to pursue their careers in the same unfettered manner as men, particularly as administrators, consultants, and scientists. Likewise, discrimination in the workplace is problematic for many female psychologists, who often do not have recourse to institutionalized protection or redress and consequently find themselves frustrated vocationally.

29.6 NEW PARADIGMS

The reductionism of Western psychology tends to overlook the cultural, economic, political, and religious conditions in which human experience and action are constituted (Gergen, 2001). As a result, Western psychology has yielded fragmented and overly simplified accounts of highly complex and contextually embedded phenomena. Western psychology has also become more isolated from other social sciences, further restricting its capacity to explain phenomena that are multidetermined.

Moreover, Western psychology assumes a universal research methodology that is impervious to cultural bias (Gergen); understandably, this ethnocentric stance has evoked reactions among psychologists worldwide. Finally, the support of a powerful publishing industry ensures the continued influence of Western psychology. Because English is the language of psychology, the conceptual, empirical, and practical contributions of non-English-speaking psychologists are often neglected, as the market will not bear the cost of foreign scholarship that deviates from Western tastes (Draguns, 2001). Ironically, that scholarship has enormous potential to advance psychological science and practice.

As noted in the introductory chapter to the *Handbook*, there is growing dissatisfaction with Western psychology for all of the aforementioned reasons. The limited transnational usefulness of Western psychology has triggered paradigmatic shifts in various parts of the world. Some have occurred in specific countries whereas others are beginning to manifest themselves across regions. We now turn to three evolving perspectives that represent paradigmatic challenges to Western psychology: multiculturalism, indigenization, and the realignment of psychology according to civilization.

29.6.1 Multiculturalism

The critical and central role of culture is becoming more apparent to psychologists, and various specialties have heeded the call for greater sensitivity, understanding, and competence in studying and working with culturally diverse peoples. In cross-cultural terms, *emic* approaches, in which research and practice hinge on what is familiar and meaningful to members of a culture, seek greater balance with *etic* approaches that emphasize universals, which transcend cultural divides. Psychologists, particularly those in heterogeneous and industrialized countries, increasingly realize that their activities are imprinted by a Western *emic* and hence are received perspectives with limited utility. Thus, British psychology students now study social constructionist views of the discipline, and German psychologists advocate for ethics codes and laws that address the context of culture within which psychology is practiced.

The multicultural movement in the United States illustrates American psychology's responsiveness to charges of "cultural malpractice." American psychologists are keenly aware that the changing demography of the United States in terms of age, ethnicity, language, and race necessitates an evaluation of research procedures, assessment instruments, and intervention strategies. Multicultural psychology in the United States has a broad expanse, defining culture in terms of the worldviews shared by groups with a common sexual orientation, physical disability, or socioeconomic status. There now are U.S. psychology organizations that represent African American, American Indian, Asian American, and Hispanic American interest groups. In addition, the code of ethics of the American Psychological Association (APA) acknowledges that cultural competence is necessary for ethical professional practice.

Australian psychologists also recognize the importance of sensitivity, knowledge, and competence in working effectively with its indigenous population. Australian psychologists work with indigenous communities to promote social justice, reconciliation, and inclusion, in addition to wellness. Many endeavor to empower communities, knowing that these approaches drive transformative change and offer indigenous communities the capacity to assess their needs and to develop and deliver their own services.

Singapore, a cosmopolitan country, is becoming more heterogeneous due to its commercial infrastructure and strategic location. Consequently, the Singapore Psychological Society is contemplating the design of a program to orient practitioners to the special needs of residents from distinct cultural and religious backgrounds.

29.6.2 Indigenization

Sinha (1997) has characterized the purpose of indigenization in unmistakable terms: indigenization is a struggle for consciousness in which the search to restore a people's identity demands confronting the intellectual hegemony of the West. Sinha has also cautioned against borrowing reductionistic models from the natural sciences because these models isolate the person or group from the many contexts to which they are bound. By implication, a contextually sensitive psychology requires a multidisciplinary focus, which might orient psychologists toward neglected domains, such as spirituality. Chinese and Indian psychologists have heeded these warnings and exhortations, and are reconfiguring theory, research, practice, and pedagogy into more contextualized and multidisciplinary forms (e.g., the program in indigenous psychology at Utkal University in Bhubaneshwar, India). Interestingly, in most countries in which indigenization has gained momentum, it is rare for someone to argue that Western psychology should be eliminated, even though it may have been imported and of limited usefulness; more typically, recommendations call for an amalgam of psychologies matched to the context in which they will be used.

Sinha (1997) has stated that "of the countries in Asia, the trend to indigenize psychology is strongest and most articulate in the Philippines" (p. 153). Indeed, since 1975 the National Association for Filipino Psychology has piloted efforts to indigenize psychology. Virgilio Enriquez has written extensively on the Filipino context of understanding and inquiry, and has produced more focused works on the Filipinization of personality theory, methods of data collection and analysis, and the struggle for justice and freedom (e.g., Enriquez, 1992). In spite of these contributions, few psychologists in the Philippines are committed to indigenization; although clinical psychologists integrate their clients' strong kinship ties and religious values into therapy, the practice of other specialties such as industrial–organizational psychology, remains fully integrated with Western psychological traditions.

Indigenous approaches to healing have a rich history, especially in Asia. Naikan and Morita therapies are indigenous to Japan and have their origins in Buddhism and Zen Buddhism, respectively. Both therapies value self-observation and the acceptance of anxiety, and both minimize therapist–client interaction. In Thailand, traditional-medicine clinics have been established at provincial hospitals where patients can obtain the services of folk healers, mainly herbalists and massage therapists. Over the years, Thai psychologists have also been actively involved in training

Buddhist monks to deliver mental health services. The challenges associated with developing scientifically sound indigenous measures of personality assessment in Asian countries are discussed in a recent special section of the journal *Psychological Assessment* (e.g., Cheung, Cheung, Wada, & Zhang, 2003).

There are also cases of indigenization in Europe. In Poland, Kazimierz Twardowski originated the theory of purposeful action, which paved the way for a uniquely Polish theoretical and methodological perspective that is in its third generation, having survived the intellectual devastation of fascism and communism. The theory is discipline-wide in scope, as its fundamental tenet states that all human activity is purposeful and forever adapting to environmental changes in order to fulfill its initial purpose. The theory has stimulated basic and applied research on decision-making, emotional regulation, and the expression of temperaments.

There is also evidence of indigenization in Africa. Psychologists at Kenyan universities integrate African cosmology into education and training, careful not to compromise the canon of knowledge that is accepted as psychological. South African psychology offers a case in point of indigenization. Although South African psychology is grounded in Western epistemological tradition, the contemporary issues it faces are African. Hence, South African psychologists struggle to balance Western theories and techniques with indigenous knowledge and methods that arise from and are relevant to the Black community. South African psychologists are in a paradigmatic bind: they want to disassociate from a psychology that served the oppressive practices of apartheid, yet they fear abandoning the disciplinary and professional conventions that ensure their standing in the psychology community. Notwithstanding this conflict, indigenization proceeds apace. Postmodern approaches are taught at universities. Qualitative inquiry has gained a foothold, as it does not require participants to be proficient in English or familiar with objective assessment. Psychological practice has become oriented toward social change and includes interventions to empower communities. The prevalence of indigenous healing practices (e.g., divination and herbal remedies) reflects Black-African traditions as well as the dearth of rural practitioners of psychology, and South African psychologists are currently debating the merits of including traditional healers in the healthcare system.

29.6.3 A New World Order?

Huntington's (1997) *The Clash of Civilizations and the Remaking of the World Order* offers a provocative framework for understanding the dynamics of global change in the 21st century. Huntington proposes that cultural identity influences patterns of association, collision, and separation throughout the world. He asserts that modernization has not produced a global village, but rather an emerging civilization-based world order in which the West is declining and its pretensions to universality cause conflict with other civilizations. Huntington's vision of a new world order provides a basis for anticipating how psychology might evolve internationally. Specifically, psychology might become culturally realigned across regions that have a common language, religion, and world view. With Huntington's model in mind, we

search for evidence of early manifestations of national and regional shifts in psychology that reflect changing patterns of cultural identity. Specifically, we focus our analysis on the Islamic world and the Latin world. Before proceeding, we acknowledge several assumptions and shortcomings of our analysis. First, we appreciate that global economic and political realignment does not automatically yield a parallel shift in a discipline and profession. Second, we recognize that economic and political change often precedes more elemental changes within society; in fact, economic and political change typically meets with resistance, especially when it collides with opposing local norms (Stevens, 2002). Finally, we acknowledge that the countries we sampled in the *Handbook* and the information we asked our authors to provide were neither sufficiently representative nor comprehensive for us to draw firm conclusions.

29.6.3.1 THE ISLAMIC WORLD

Huntington (1997) speaks of an Islamic resurgence that is "a product of and an effort to come to grips with modernization in non-Western societies .... These developments undermine traditional village and clan ties, and create alienation and identity crisis. Islamist symbols, commitments, and beliefs meet these psychological needs" (p. 116). Similarly, is it possible to speak of an Islamic psychology emerging across the Muslim world, which includes countries in the Middle East, South Asia, Europe, and the Pacific Rim?

Of the 27 countries sampled in the *Handbook*, 5 have a clearly Islamic cultural identity: Egypt, Iran, Indonesia, Pakistan, and Turkey. These countries are located in four regions of the globe: the

Middle East, the Pacific Rim, South Asia, and Europe.

Egyptian psychologists are quite involved in relating the science and practice of psychology to Islam. Some have tried to fashion a psychology from the writings of early Arab and Muslim scholars, whereas others have sought to reframe contemporary psychology in Islamic terms. Nevertheless, much of Egyptian psychology reflects the assumptions, theories, research findings, and methods imported from the West, which some fear has stifled the emergence of an Islamic psychology. Egyptian psychologists have not focused on the sociocultural dimension of psychology, and therefore their research and practice sometimes appear to be insensitive to the contextual realities of the region.

Indonesia has the largest Muslim population in the world. Although Indonesian psychologists acknowledge the importance of including and standardizing nontraditional approaches in the psychology curriculum, they have yet to respond to those pressing for an Islamic psychology. This is a politically sensitive issue for the country in view of growing radicalization in the Muslim community. Indonesian psychologists are comfortable applying constructs from Eastern paradigms in their work with Asian clients, such as collectivism and spirituality, which are also central to a Muslim worldview.

Iran, an Islamic republic, has undergone profound change since the 1978 revolution. One effect of transforming the country into a theocracy was the disruption of scientific and professional psychology. The Iranian Psychology Society was banned in 1978, only to reopen in 1995. The clinical master's program at Tehran University was also closed in 1978, and reconstituted 7 years later at the Tehran Psychiatric Institute.

With its turbulent past and recent renewal, Iranian psychology has had little chance to build an Islamic psychology. However, Iranian master's-degree students are learning about Muslim perspectives on psychology, researchers are investigating the relationship between religious observance and psychological adjustment, and practitioners are reforming prisons according to Islamic law.

Of the five predominantly Muslim countries, Pakistan comes closest to having a genuine Islamic psychology. In 1988, the Society for the Advancement of Muslim Psychology was launched with the aim of crafting a psychology and psychotherapy based on the Koran and scholarly treatises on Islam. A course in Islamic studies is mandatory for undergraduates, and graduate courses on Islamic psychology have also been developed. Clinicians offer several Islamic variants of psychotherapy. For example, *Zikr Allah* is a technique based on Sufi mysticism designed to alleviate stress. Other interventions synthesize Islamic values with Western psychotherapies that are grounded in rationalism and functionalism (e.g., rational emotive behavior therapy).

The history of Turkish psychology points west, explaining why an Islamic psychology did not evolve in a country rich in Islamic culture. The forced secularization of Turkey gave more credence to Western scientific ideas and practices than the Islamic knowledge that prevailed during the Ottoman Empire. Turkish psychology appears invested in its continued integration within mainstream psychology. In spite of recent political expressions of Islam, Turkish psychologists have remained curiously disinterested in bridging their imported psychology with secular Islamic traditions. However, there are some indications of change. A new course in clinical psychology at Ankara University surveys the contributions of indigenous perspectives (e.g., Sufism) to understanding aspects of individual psychology. Research on family systems is beginning to address culturally based issues of dependence, independence, and interdependence. In the corporate world, consulting psychologists are working to harmonize the global trend toward a more egalitarian organizational climate with the paternalistic traditions of Turkish businesses.

Based on our review of five Muslim countries, we conclude that a transregional psychology along Islamic lines is in a nascent stage of development, and it is unclear whether a fully formed Islamic psychology will someday emerge out of the larger Muslim world.

29.6.3.2 THE LATIN WORLD

Huntington (1997) identifies a Latin American culture that, though originally European and linked to Europe and North America, today has its own civilization. Latin America is primarily Spanish-speaking and Catholic, and has indigenous peoples who have greatly influenced its development. Latin America also has a strong authoritarian and corporatist culture, further distinguishing it from European and North American culture. Is it possible to speak of a Latin American psychology that includes Argentina, Brazil, and Colombia, as well as Mexico?

One paradigm that is fundamentally Latin American is liberation psychology. Liberation psychology "attempts to work with people in context through strategies that enhance awareness of oppression and of the ideologies and structural inequality that have kept them subjugated and oppressed, thereby collaborating with them in developing critical analysis and engaging in a transforming praxis" (Comas-Díaz, Lykes, & Alarcón, 1998, p. 778). Liberation psychology emanates from several core elements of Latin American history: the struggle of indigenous peoples, economic and political oppression, and violent social upheaval. Because so many have been and remain poor and oppressed it is reasonable to assert that abstract and reductionistic Western psychology is ill-suited for understanding, studying, and altering people's lives. Instead, liberation psychology asks psychologists to dialogue with people as they review the conditions in which they are embedded and initiate transformative action. Simply put, the psychologist must enter the other's worldview and join in the narrative of oppression and transcendence.

Whereas Colombian psychologists were politically involved during the 1980s, they are less so today, perhaps because of the obvious dangers of activism. Argentine psychologists are also less politically active than before. Brazil, however, has a long-standing organization called the Society of Political Psychology. In pursuing the possibilities of NAFTA, Mexican psychologists seek to resolve the political impasse concerning the reciprocity of credentials that would permit the movement of psychologists across Canada and the United States.

Our review suggests that the opportunity for a reorganization of psychology along Latin American lines may have come and gone. If liberation psychology is no longer a unifying paradigm in Latin America, what happened to it and what if anything has replaced it? We note that liberation psychology remains vital in some Latin American countries (e.g., Guatemala and Peru) that have suffered more recent and severe economic, political, and social oppression. Argentina, Brazil, Colombia, and Mexico, however, must be viewed differently. During the 1980s, much of Latin America shifted from authoritarian regimes and command economies to pluralistic, market-based democracies. As a consequence, respect for human and civil rights increased. The evolution of Latin American economic and political systems, along with trade agreements with the United States, have brought the cultural identity of Latin America closer to that of Canada and the United States (Huntington, 1997). It is not unreasonable, therefore, to suggest that Latin American psychology has also moved north.

Furthermore, recent economic and political developments have reinvigorated civil institutions in Argentina, Brazil, Colombia, and Mexico. Largely due to government support, cohesive social units (e.g., volunteer organizations) are better serving the needs of the community. Thus, the push for radical social transformation has declined, along with support for liberation psychology. Moreover, regional trade agreements of the 1990s (e.g., Mercosur and the Tripartite Pact) not only promise greater economic integration and prosperity for Latin America, but also the integration of education and training, research, and professional practice in psychology. As psychologists in Argentina, Brazil, Colombia, and Mexico enter the 21st century, they already share the following agenda: broadening and standardizing the curriculum, increasing the number of graduate programs and paths of specialization, improving employment opportunities, widening access to online databases, supporting multicultural research and services, updating ethics codes to safeguard human

rights, federalizing the regulation of professional psychology, enlarging the consultative role of psychology associations within government, and promoting international partnerships.

29.7 CONTRIBUTIONS TO AMERICAN PSYCHOLOGY

From the outset, we envisioned the *Handbook of International Psychology* as a means of informing our readers, particularly American readers, about the science and practice of psychology in distinct countries and regions of the world. We believe that intellectual isolation is perhaps the single greatest obstacle to the advancement of psychology. Authoritative knowledge and skill in psychology rest on an appreciation of contextual elements as well as individual and universal variables that determine human experience and action. By exposing our readers to diverse psychologies, we hope to heighten their awareness and understanding of the foundations, current status, and evolving characteristics of psychology worldwide. We also hope that they will become more involved in organized efforts to address a number of pressing global concerns such as intergroup conflict, national transformation and development, threats to the natural environment, physical and mental health needs, and the struggles of disempowered groups.

Most chapter authors shared their views on what American psychology and psychologists might gain from becoming familiar with psychology in their countries. Below, we summarize the points that our authors made explicit or which we distilled from their writing. Because we were unable to sort these views into nonoverlapping categories, we present them in list form:

1. In many countries, studying or working abroad has become highly relevant to the professional development of psychologists, especially for those who seek academic careers. Increasingly, databases are being marketed that offer information on how to gain international experience in teaching, research, and practice. The Fulbright Scholar Program is one such opportunity that the authors, as former Fulbrighters, strongly endorse for anyone desiring a professionally transformative international experience. The Peace Corps and, to a lesser extent, Volunteers in Service to America (VISTA), offer other invaluable opportunities to gain firsthand exposure to a different culture, language, and system of values. Finally, we recommend that psychology departments establish study-abroad exchanges through which students can internationalize their education and training.

2. Psychologists in other countries are educated and trained in specialties that are virtually unknown in the United States. For example, transportation psychology is an important specialty as reflected in psychology curricula, divisions within psychology organizations, and the number of psychologists working in the area. Likewise, political psychology has more prominence abroad. We believe that psychology departments in the United States should add courses in these areas as upper-division electives or, at least integrate modules on these specialties into survey-type classes.

3. In most countries, a baccalaureate, which may require 5 years to complete, or master's degree is a prerequisite to holding the title of psychologist and practicing professional psychology. Countries that require a doctorate for entry into the profession are the minority. Do alternative international definitions of *psychologist* lessen U.S. psychology's concerns about the licensure of master's-level practitioners? Or is doctoral-level training fundamental to competent practice, given the sophistication and specialization of American psychology? These questions merit further debate.

4. Given the efforts in many countries to federalize the regulation of professional practice, perhaps the time has arrived for American psychologists to seek national standards for licensure. The APA might work legislatively to establish more uniform eligibility criteria for the title of psychologist and delineate the functions that define professional practice in psychology. These efforts would substantially reduce the confusion and frustration that many psychologists and employers experience as a result of interstate variation in licensure. The experiences of European psychologists, rapidly moving toward an EU standard for credentialing psychologists, and Canadian psychologists, whose Mutual Recognition Agreement introduced a national, competency-based approach to professional regulation, provide meaningful models for American psychologists to emulate.

5. Although the exception, psychologists in a few countries are authorized as primary-care providers, and some have

prescription privileges. In these countries, psychologists are recognized as expert treatment providers, whose services are key to illness prevention and health promotion. Implicit in their status as primary-care providers is the recognition that psychological variables mediate physical disease and well-being. We call upon American psychologists and psychology organizations to redouble their efforts to educate the public about the role of psychologists as primary healthcare providers. The recent inclusion of the word *health* in the mission statement of the APA also supports this goal.

6. Psychologists around the world tend to be tolerant of, if not receptive to, indigenous cultures. In various ways, these psychologists have integrated religious philosophy and folk tradition into their perspectives of the person. From these perspectives, psychologists conduct research and deliver services that are culturally relevant. We invite psychology departments in the United States to explore how indigenous psychologies can be integrated more fully into the curriculum. We endorse efforts to internationalize scholarship, particularly that which incorporates non-Western perspectives and methodologies. Finally, we encourage practitioners who work with non-majority clients and communities to familiarize themselves with alternative therapies and consult with nontraditional healers.

7. There have been growing calls to bridge the gap between science and practice in American psychology. Other countries serve as models of cooperation and collaboration between research and applied psychologists in the education and training of students, as well as on studies and interventions at the community and societal level. For example, most psychologists worldwide are trained according to a consumer model, in which professional practice is informed by scholarship (Oakland, 2003). Perhaps because American psychology is so specialized, psychologists have difficulty communicating and working with colleagues from across the discipline. Although American psychology will likely remain specialized, its vitality hinges on forging internal alliances and consideration of viable alternatives to the scientist–practitioner framework for training.

8. There are new opportunities for multidisciplinary collaboration in areas that traditionally have been subsumed under the rubric of psychology, such as cognitive science, as well as in domains that by custom lie outside the purview of psychology, such as environmental conservation. We encourage American psychologists to archive and share their findings with colleagues from related disciplines in order to improve the coherence and utility of knowledge in the social sciences. Furthermore, there are numerous social issues whose resolution would surely accelerate if addressed in a multidisciplinary fashion (e.g., addiction and crime). We hope to see an increase in multidisciplinary responses to psychosocial and sociocultural issues in the United States.

9. Many foreign scholars have diagnosed American psychology as fragmented, identifying the underlying cause as reductionism, in which highly complex and contextual phenomena are

isolated in laboratories and dismantled in experimental manipulations that rob them of meaning. Many American psychologists find it difficult to adapt their Western intellectual heritage to the call for disciplinary reform. American psychologists must confront the disputed external validity of their science and practice and determine how to rectify it. Like their international colleagues, American psychologists will struggle with whether to choose conceptual, methodological and technical isolation, pluralism, or unity in the discipline and in relation to the social sciences generally.

10. Psychologists worldwide are heavily involved in investigating and responding to social issues. We maintain that psychology students would be better served if given opportunities to learn how psychology can facilitate an understanding of, and solutions to, social concerns (e.g., meeting the heathcare needs of isolated rural or marginalized inner-city communities). Moreover, American psychologists can learn much from their international colleagues about participatory research methods and capacity-building interventions that have a sociopolitical agenda.

11. In many countries, social needs are the most powerful force behind the development of psychology. American psychology has an opportunity to drive social policy as never before, given the changing demography and sociocultural dynamics of the United States and the international issues that have surfaced on American soil (e.g., terrorism). There is no social policy on which psychology cannot make an informed contribution.

12. Finally, the pattern of communication between American psychologists and their international colleagues remains largely unidirectional, which limits opportunities for professional development. In the globalized world of the 21st century, communication among psychologists must become reciprocal. A major obstacle to the bidirectional flow of information is that English is the language of psychology. Most American psychologists are not fluent in a foreign language, unlike their international counterparts. We believe that undergraduate majors should be encouraged to learn a foreign language. We further believe that the language requirement must be reinstated for the doctorate, as it has been at the University of Texas-El Paso, where clinical psychology students are required to become bilingual in order to meet the needs of the community they serve. In addition, American psychology will be remiss if its journals fail to publish innovative and fertile theories, research methods, and applied practices by psychologists from around the world. Editors of American psychology journals have an obligation to disseminate knowledge that challenges U.S. norms (e.g., reductionism) and has potential value to the discipline and profession.

REFERENCES

Cheung, F. M., Cheung, S. F., Wada, S., & Xhang, J. (2003). Indigenous measures of personality assessment in Asian countries: A review. *Psychological Assessment, 15,* 280–289.

Comas-Díaz, L., Lykes, M. B., & Alarcón, R. D. (1998). Ethnic conflict and the psychology of liberation in Guatemala, Peru, and Puerto Rico. *American Psychologist, 53,* 778–792.

Draguns, J. (2001). Toward a truly international psychology: Beyond English only. *American Psychologist, 56,* 1019–1030.

Enriquez, V. G. (1992). *From colonial to liberation psychology: The Philippine experience.* Quezon City, The Philippines: University of the Philippines Press.

Gergen, K. J. (2001). Psychological science in a postmodern context. *American Psychologist, 56,* 803–813.

Gilgen, A. R., & Gilgen, C. K. (Eds.). (1987). *International handbook of psychology.* New York: Greenwood Press.

Huntington, S. P. (1997). *The clash of civilizations and the remaking of the world order.* New York: Touchstone Books.

Jing, Q. (2000). International psychology. In K. Pawlik & M. R. Rosenzweig (Eds.), *The international handbook of psychology* (pp. 570–584). Thousand Oaks, CA: Sage.

Metzner, B. S., Rajecki, D. W., & Lauer, J. B. (1994). New majors and the feminization of psychology: Testing and extending the Rajecki-Metzner model. *Teaching of Psychology, 21,* 5–11.

Oakland, T. D. (2003). International school psychology: Psychology's worldwide portal to children and youth. *American Psychologist, 58,* 983–992.

Project EuroPsyT. (2001, April 5). *Common framework: A framework for education and training in Europe.* Retrieved October 27, 2003, from http://www.europsych.org/framework/v5/

Rosenzweig, M. R. (1999). Continuity and change in the development of psychology around the world. *American Psychologist, 53,* 252–259.

Sexton, V. S., & Hogan, J. D. (Eds.). (1992). *International psychology: Views from around the world.* Lincoln, NE: University of Nebraska Press.

Sinha, D. (1997). Indigenizing psychology. In J. W. Berry, Y. H. Poortinga, & J. Pandey (Eds.), *Handbook of cross-cultural psychology: Vol. 1. Theory and method* (2nd ed., pp. 129–169). Boston: Allyn and Bacon.

Stevens, M. J. (2002). The interplay of psychology and societal transformation. *International Journal of Group Tensions, 31,* 5–30.

Stevens, M. J. (2004). International psychology information clearinghouse. In J. B. Overmier & J. A. Overmier (Eds.), *Psychology: IUPsyS global resource.* Hove, UK: Psychology Press.

APPENDIX

Sociodemography of Countries Included in the *Handbook of International Psychology*

STEPHANIE R. STEINMAN

AFRICA

Africa has a population of almost 180 million. Diverse ethnic groups and many different tribes are found throughout the various countries of Africa. Christianity dominates this region; however, indigenous religious beliefs are also represented. Agriculture is the most important activity in this area, and subsistence farming and nomadic herding are the primary economic activities.

Kenya

Kenya is located in eastern Africa, bordering the Indian Ocean and between Somalia and Tanzania. The total area of Kenya is approximately 582,650 km². Founding President Jomo Kenyatta guided Kenya toward independence until his death in 1978 when President Daniel Arap Moi took power in a constitutional succession. The country was a one-party state from 1969 until 1982 when the ruling Kenya African National Union (KANU) made itself the only legal party in Kenya. Moi yielded to internal and external pressure for political liberalization in late 1991. The opposition failed to dislodge KANU from power in the 1992 and 1997 elections; although characterized by violence and fraud, the elections are widely viewed as having reflected the will of the Kenyan people. President Moi stepped down in December 2002 following fair and peaceful elections. Mwai Kibaki from the National Rainbow Coalition defeated KANU candidate Uhuru Kenyatta and assumed the presidency following a campaign centered on an anticorruption platform. Kenya now has a republican government.

In 2003 the estimated population of Kenya was 31.6 million, with a density of 54 people per square kilometer. The population is almost equally divided between Kalnjin, Kamba, Kikuyu, Luhya, and Luo, with smaller minorities of Kisii, Meru, Asian, and Arab. The majority of the country is Protestant (40%), followed by Roman Catholic (30%), Muslim (20%), and indigenous belief systems (10%). Kenya has a diverse population, including traditional herders, rural farmers, and urban residents. The standard of living in this underdeveloped country has been declining in recent years.

Nigeria

Nigeria is found in western Africa, bordering the Gulf of Guinea and between Benin and Cameroon. The area of Nigeria spans approximately 923,768 km². A new constitution was adopted in 1999, after nearly 16 years of military rule and as a peaceful transition to civilian government was completed. The president now faces the task of rebuilding a petroleum-based economy in a country that has seen its revenues dissipated through corruption. In addition, the current administration must defuse long-standing ethnic and religious tensions if it is to build a foundation for economic growth and political stability. The 2003 elections marked the first civilian transfer of power in Nigeria's history.

The population of Nigeria in 2003 was approximately 134 million, with 145 people per square kilometer. The largest ethnic groups are the Hausa-Fulani, Igbo, and Yoruba. The religions in this country include Islam, Christianity, and indigenous African beliefs. Nigeria is the most populous country in Africa. Less than a quarter of the population lives in urban areas. Agriculture in this underdeveloped country has suffered from mismanagement and a lack of basic infrastructure.

South Africa

South Africa is found at the southern tip of Africa. The area of this country is approximately 1.2 million km². The British seized the Cape of Good Hope region in 1806. After that, many of the Dutch settlers moved north to found their own republics. The discovery of diamonds and gold in the late 1800s generated wealth and immigration that intensified the subjugation of the native inhabitants. The Boers resisted British rule but were defeated in the Anglo–Boer War at the turn of the 20th century. The resulting Union of South Africa operated under a policy of apartheid (separation of the races). The 1990s ended apartheid and brought in Black majority rule. The population in South Africa was approximately 42.8 million in 2003, with a population density of 35 persons per square kilometer. The ethnic groups in this area are represented by 78% Blacks, 10% Whites, 2% Indian, and 10% other. Most of South Africans are Christian (68%); however, indigenous beliefs and animists are represented (28%), with smaller populations of Muslims, Hindus, Jews, and traditional Africans. South Africa is a middle-income, developing country with rich natural resources. However, the country faces numerous economic and social problems that are the natural sequelae of apartheid.

NORTH AMERICA

North America extends from the Atlantic Ocean to the Pacific Ocean and from the Arctic Ocean to the Gulf of Mexico. North America's population totals almost 419 million. Its population consists of people from many different ethnic backgrounds. These countries were originally settled by Native Americans. The United States and Canada both became British colonies; Mexico was conquered by the Spaniards. Most of the population is equally divided between Roman Catholics and Protestants. Canada and the United States are significantly more developed than Mexico.

Canada

Canada is located in the northern region of North America, bordering the North Atlantic Ocean on the east, North Pacific Ocean on the west, and the Arctic Ocean on the north. The country stretches over 9.98 million km². France and Britain began to permanently settle Canada in the 1600s. Canada became self-governing in 1867, but still retained ties to the British Royal Crown. Economically and technologically, the nation has developed in tandem with the United States. Its largest political problem continues to be the relationship of the province Quebec, with its French-speaking residents and unique culture, to the remainder of the country. Canada has a federal parliamentary democracy and constitutional monarchy. The head of the government is the prime minister. In 2003 Canada's population was approximately 31.6 million. Canada has approximately 3.1 residents per kilometer. The population is almost equally divided between British

(28%) and French (23%) ethnic groups, with smaller minorities of other groups, such as European, Asian, Arab, African, indigenous American, and mixed backgrounds. Roman Catholicism (46%) and various Protestant denominations (36%) are the predominant religions. Canada is a developed country and ranks among the 10 leading manufacturing nations. It is the second-largest country in the world.

Mexico

Mexico, located south of the United States, is approximately 1.97 million km² in size. Spanish conquistadors conquered the Mayas, Aztecs, Toltecs, and other smaller tribes in the 1500s. Independence was finally established in 1824. A devaluation of the peso in 1994 put Mexico into economic turmoil, triggering the worst recession in over half a century. The nation continues to make an impressive recovery. Ongoing economic and social concerns include low wages, underemployment, and inequitable income distribution. In 2000 elections were held for the first time since the 1910 Mexican Revolution. Mexico is a federal republic.

Mexico's population exceeded 100 million in 2003, with a population density of 50.9 people per kilometer. Mexico is made up mostly people of Indian–Spanish descent, with smaller minorities of Indians, Caucasians, and others. Almost 90% of the population is Roman Catholic, but there is a small Protestant population. About 70% of the population lives in urban areas. Mexico is still a developing country facing many problems including education—one of the country's highest priorities in recent years.

United States of America

The United States is between Canada and Mexico, bordering the North Atlantic and Pacific oceans. It is approximately 9.6 million km^2, with a population density of 28.6 people per square kilometer. Natives occupied the land until the Europeans began to explore in the 15th century. England gained control over the country and ruled until the American Revolution in 1776. The United States was recognized abroad as a new nation in 1783 with the Treaty of Paris. A constitution-based federal republic with a strong democratic tradition has been in place since its founding. During the 19th and 20th centuries, 37 new states were added to the original 13 as the nation expanded across the North American continent and acquired a number of overseas possessions.

The United States is one of the world's most powerful nations. The economy is marked by steady growth, low unemployment and inflation, and rapid advances in technology. In 2003 the population of the United States was estimated to be 290 million. There are six major race groups in this country, consisting of Caucasian (approximately 77%), Black or African American (13%), Asian (4%), American Indian and Alaska Native (1.5%), Native Hawaiian and other Pacific Islander (0.5%), and other minorities (4%). The majority of the population is Protestant (56%), with smaller populations of Roman Catholic (28%), Jewish (2%), other religions (4%), and those affiliated with no religion (10%). The United States has the largest and most technologically advanced economy in the world.

SOUTH AMERICA

South America's population of nearly 257 million is smaller than North America's population. The majority of South Americans are concentrated at or near the coast, particularly on the east coast facing the Atlantic. Much of this region is made up of a mixture of individuals from European backgrounds. For over 300 years, much of South America's interactions were directed from Spain and Portugal. Almost all of the population is Roman Catholic. Much of the region is characterized by economic inequities.

Argentina

Argentina is located at the south end of South America. It is approximately 2,740,000 km^2 in size and had a population of 38.7 million in 2003. Argentina has a density of 13 inhabitants per square kilometer, according to data from the last national census. Europeans arrived in Argentina in the 1500s and established colonies. Argentina did not regain its independence until the 1800s. After World War II, a military junta overtook the government until democracy was reestablished in 1983. Approximately 85% of Argentina's population is European, mostly of Spanish and Italian descent. Roman Catholicism is the predominant religion of the country, but Argentina has the largest Jewish population in Latin America. Spanish is the national language. About 80% of the population lives in cities or towns of more than 2000 people. Argentina is a developing country, currently experiencing high unemployment. The population living in poverty has soared in recent years.

Brazil

Brazil is located in eastern South America, bordering the Atlantic Ocean. It is approximately 8.5 million km^2 in size. Brazil was claimed by Portugal in 1500, but in 1822 Brazil declared its independence. This country overcame more than half a century of military intervention by the government in order to work on industrial and agricultural growth. The country is a federative republic.

Brazil's population was around 177 million as of 2003—the largest in Latin America. The country has 20.3 residents per square kilometer. The ethnic groups represented in this country include African, German, Italian, Japanese, Portuguese, and indigenous people. About 80% of the population is Roman Catholic. Brazil is a developing country with its economy currently stagnating, in part due to its relationship with Argentina—a country currently experiencing an economic crisis. Brazil has a history of extreme socioeconomic inequities.

Colombia

Colombia is located in northern South America, bordering the Caribbean Sea and the North Pacific Ocean. It has a total land area of over 1.1 million km^2. Colombia was one of the countries that grew out of the collapse of Gran Colombia in the 1800s. Colombia is currently a republic with an executive branch dominating this structure. However, there has been a 40-year campaign to overthrow the government, and this political opposition increased in the 1990s. An anti-insurgent paramilitary army has grown over the recent years.

Colombia has a population of 41.7 million. Its population density is 36.4 people per square kilometer. There is a great deal of ethnic diversity as most of the population is a mixture of indigenous Indians, Spanish colonists, and Africans. Currently, barely 1% of the population can be identified as entirely Indian, based on language and customs. Like many of the Latin American countries, almost 95% of the population is Roman Catholic. There has been a movement in Colombia from rural to urban areas. Colombia is a developing country, benefiting from an economic recovery that began in early 2000.

EAST ASIA

East Asia's population is approximately 1.4 billion, due in large part to China's population. The predominant ethnic group in this region is Chinese. Most of this region practices Buddhism. Natural resources are unevenly distributed throughout the region. China is rich in natural resources, whereas Japan is somewhat limited. However, Japan has grown into one of the world's most important economic powers.

China

China is in eastern Asia, bordering the East China Sea, Korea Bay, the Yellow Sea, and the South China Sea, between North Korea and Vietnam. The total land area is about 9.6 million km^2. For many centuries China stood as one of the world's leading civilizations, highly advanced in the arts and sciences. During the 19th and early 20th centuries, however, China was inundated by civil unrest, major famines, military defeats, and foreign occupation. After World War II, the communists established a dictatorship that, while ensuring China's sovereignty, imposed strict controls over everyday life and cost tens of millions of people their lives. After 1978 market-oriented reforms were introduced. Output quadrupled by the year 2000. Political controls remain tight while economic controls continue to be relaxed. China remains a communist state.

In 2003 the population in China was 1.3 billion, with a density of 131.5 people per square kilometer. The major ethnic group is Han Chinese (almost 92%), with other nationalities including Buyi, Hui, Korean, Manchu, Miao, Mongolian, Tibetan, Uygur, Yi, and Zhuang. China's most widely practiced religion is Buddhism, but there are large groups practicing Taoism, Islam, and Christianity. China is concerned about its population growth and has attempted to implement a family planning policy, with mixed results. China is committed to economic reform and outreach to the outside world.

Japan

Japan is an island chain in eastern Asia between the North Pacific Ocean and the Sea of Japan, east of the Korean Peninsula. The total area of Japan is 377,835 km². After Japan's defeat in World War II, the country recovered to become an economic power and an ally of the United States.

Japan is a constitutional monarchy with a parliamentary government. Although the emperor retains the throne as a symbol of national unity, actual power rests in networks of powerful politicians, bureaucrats,

and business executives. After three decades of unprecedented growth, the economy experienced a major slowdown starting in the 1990s. In 2003 Japan's population was about 127.2 million, with a population density of 334.9 inhabitants per square kilometer. Most of the population is Japanese, with less than 1% being Korean. The predominant religions are Buddhism and Shinto, with a small Christian population. Japan is an urban country, with only 6% of the labor force involved in agriculture. Japan's economy is the second-largest in the world.

Singapore

Singapore is in southeastern Asia, between Malaysia and Indonesia. It has a total area of 692.7 km². In 1819, Singapore was founded as a British trading colony. It joined the Malaysian Federation in 1963, but separated 2 years later and became independent. It has subsequently become one of the world's most prosperous countries with strong international trading links. Singapore is a parliamentary republic.

In 2003 the population in Singapore was estimated to be 4.6 million. The population density of Singapore is 6,411.2 people per square kilometer. The ethnic groups in this country include Chinese (77%), Malays (14%), and Indians (8%). The religions represented include Buddhism, Taoism, Islam, Christianity, and Hinduism. Singapore is one of the world's most densely populated countries. Singapore has a strategic location on the major sea lanes, which gives the country tremendous economic importance.

SOUTH ASIA

South Asia's population is almost 1.2 billion, which is approximately one-fifth of all the people on Earth. The ethnic groups in this region are mostly particular to the country, and the same is true for South Asian religions. A majority of the population is very poor. This region of the world is primarily underdeveloped. These countries are trying to modernize their economies, raise the standard of living for the people, and build stable governments.

India

India is located in southern Asia, bordering the Arabian Sea and the Bay of Bengal, between Burma and Pakistan. This country is approximately 3.3 million km² in size. European traders began to arrive in the late 15th century. By the 19th century, Britain had assumed political control of almost all of India. Nonviolent resistance to British colonialism under Mahatma Gandhi and Jawaharlal Nehru led to independence in 1947. There are continuing concerns in India regarding the massive overpopulation, environmental degradation, extensive poverty, and ethnic and religious conflict, despite impressive gains in economic investment and output.

In 2003 India's population was over 1 billion, with 308.4 people per square kilometer. India represents over 15% of the world's population. Almost 32% live in urban areas. The predominant ethnic group (72%) is Indo-Aryan, the remaining quarter of the population being Dravidian, and a small proportion of Mongoloid descent. Almost 82% of the population is Hindu, with 12% being Muslim, and the remainder Buddhist, Christian, Jain, Parsi, and Sikh. The caste system that remains in effect is an important source of social identification for most Hindus. Most of the population depends on agriculture in this developing country.

Pakistan

Pakistan is located in southern Asia, bordering the Arabian Sea, between India to the east, Iran and Afghanistan to the west, and China to the north. The country's total area is 803,940 km². In 1947 British India was separated into the Muslim state of Pakistan (with two sections, East and West). In 1971 East Pakistan seceded and became a separate nation known as Bangladesh. Currently, considerable tension exists between Pakistan and India over the state of Kashmir. In response to Indian nuclear weapons testing, Pakistan conducted its own tests in 1998. Pakistan is a federal republic.

As of 2003, the population in Pakistan was estimated to be 150.6 million, with a density of 176.1 people per square kilometer. The ethnic groups of this country include Baloch, Hazara, Mujajir, Pathan (Pushtun), Punjabi, Saraiki, and Sindhi. Almost 97% of the population is Muslim, with small minorities of Christians, Hindus, and others. The majority of the population lives in the Indus River valley. Extreme poverty and underdevelopment have produced a large foreign debt in Pakistan.

Thailand

Thailand is found in southeastern Asia, bordering the Andaman Sea and the Gulf of Thailand, southeast of Burma. The area is approximately 514 km². Thailand was known as Siam until 1939. It is the only Southeast Asian country that has never been conquered by a European power. A revolution in 1932 led to a constitutional monarchy. Although Thailand formed an alliance with Japan during World War II, the country became an ally of the United States following the war.

In 2003 there were approximately 64 million people living in Thailand, and estimates for this country's population take into account the effects of excess mortality due to AIDS. The population density of the country is 119.1 people per square kilometer. About 90% of the population is Thai, with 10% from other ethnic groups. Almost 95% of the country is Buddhist, with small Muslim, Christian, Hindu, and other religious populations represented. The population is mostly rural, but the urban population is growing as Thailand continues to industrialize.

EAST EUROPE

The population in East Europe is about 304.5 million, with a population density of 16 people per square kilometer. Similar to West Europe, the ethnic groups correspond to their country of origin. With the exception of Turkey, most of the population is Roman Catholic. Turkey, however, is predominantly Muslim. East Europe has been plagued by a history of economic problems.

Poland

Poland is in central Europe, east of Germany. The country has a total of 312,685 km². Poland was partitioned by Russia, Prussia, and Austria in 1772. It regained its independence in 1918, but was taken over by Germany and the former Soviet Union during World War II. Following the war, Poland became a communist state, but had a progressive government. An independent trade union was established in 1980 due to labor problems. This union became a political force that eventually assumed control of the presidency in 1990. In the 2001 parliamentary elections, no single delegate from the union was elected to the lower house. Poland, a developed country, is a republic. The country was scheduled to become a part of the European Union in 2004.

The population in Poland was approximately 39 million in 2003. The population density is 123.6 people per square kilometer. The country's ethnic group is almost completely Polish, with a small minority population of Belarussians, Germans, Lithuanians, and Ukrainians. Approximately 90% of the country is Roman Catholic, with Eastern Orthodox, Judaism, Protestant, and Uniate also represented. The Polish economy grew rapidly in the mid-1990s, but growth has slowed in recent years.

Russia

Russia is located north of Asia, bordering the Arctic Ocean, between West Europe and the North Pacific Ocean. It has 17,075,200 km². Rioting broke out after defeats of the Russian army in World War

I. When the 300-year-old Romanov Dynasty was overthrown in 1917, the Communists seized power and formed the Union of Soviet Socialist Republics (U.S.S.R.). Stalin strengthened Russian dominance, but this cost the Soviet Union tens of millions of lives. The Soviet economy and society stagnated until Mikhail Gorbachev attempted to modernize communism; however, this ultimately resulted in the balkanization of the U.S.S.R. into 15 independent republics. Since then, Russia has struggled in its efforts to build a democratic political system and market economy to replace the strict economic, political, and social controls of the communist period. A determined guerrilla conflict still plagues Russia in Chechnya. Russia is currently characterized by a federation form of government. The population of Russia in 2003 was estimated to be 145 million, with a population density of nine inhabitants per square kilometer. The predominant ethnic group is Russian. There is a small minority of Tatars, Ukrainians, and other groups. The religions in Russia include Russian Orthodoxy, Islam, Roman Catholicism, Protestantism, Judaism, Buddhism, and other faiths. Russia is one of the largest countries in the world, and one of the most sparsely populated. Its population is mostly urban. Following the collapse of the Soviet Union, the standard of living fell dramatically, but it has been on the rise since 1999.

Turkey

Turkey is located in southwestern Europe, bordering the Black, the Aegean, and Mediterranean seas. The country's size is roughly 780,580 km^2. Turkey was created in 1923 from the Turkish remnants of the Ottoman Empire. Following its establishment, the country instituted secular laws to replace religious fiats. In 1984 the Kurdistan Workers' Party, a separatist group, initiated a revolt in southeast Turkey, often using terrorist tactics to try to establish an independent Kurdistan. The group has observed a unilateral cease-fire since September 1999, although there have been occasional clashes between Turkish military units and some of the armed Partiya Karkeren Kurdistan (PKK) militants, most of whom currently are in northern Iraq. The PKK changed its name to the Kurdistan Freedom and Democracy Congress in April 2002. The current form of government in control is a republican parliamentary democracy.

In 2003 the population in Turkey was 68 million. It has 84.1 residents per square kilometer. Turkish, Kurdish, and other ethnic groups are represented in the country. The country is 98% Muslim, with small Baha'i, Christian, and Jewish populations. More than half of Turkey's population lives in urban areas. Turkey's principal economic problem continues to be inflation, which the current economic reform program is addressing.

WEST EUROPE

Western Europe consists of 18 countries and among these, France and Germany are dominant. France and Germany's access to resources and trade routes has helped them to build productive economies. The population in Western Europe is approximately 184 million, and its density is approximately 166 people per square kilometer. Roman Catholicism is the predominant religion in this region. After World War II, Western Europeans faced what appeared to be a dismal future. However, Western Europe was able to recover and become highly urbanized. This part of the world now has one of the highest standards of living in the world.

Germany

Germany is located in central Europe, bordering the Baltic and North seas, between the Netherlands and Poland. The country's landmass includes a total of 357,021 square miles. After World War II, the country was occupied by the Allied powers, including the United States, the United Kingdom, France, and the former Soviet Union. Two German states were formed in 1949 and were not unified until 1990. Germany is a federal republic.

In 2003 the estimated population in Germany was nearly 82.4 million. The population density of Germany is 231.9 people per square kilometer. The ethnic groups represented in this country are primarily German, with a Danish minority in the north and a Sorbian (Slavic) minority in the east. There are also more than 7 million foreign residents. Protestants (27.9 million) only slightly outnumber Roman Catholics (27.3 million). There are also approximately 3.2 million Muslims. Germany has one of the world's highest levels of education, technological development, and economic productivity, and it is classified as a developed country.

Spain

Spain is located in southwestern Europe, bordering the Mediterranean Sea and North Atlantic Ocean, southwest of France. It is made up of a total of 504,782 km². Spain had a powerful empire until the 16th and 17th centuries, when England began to gain control of the seas. Spain fell behind Britain, France, and Germany during the industrial revolutions, and is still lagging behind these other European countries economically. Its government is a parliamentary monarchy.

Spain's population is approximately 40 million, with a population density of 79.2 residents per kilometer. Spain's population density is lower than that of most European countries. Distinct ethnic groups within the country include the Basques, Catalans, and Galicians. The people in Spain are predominantly Roman Catholic. Most of the rural population are moving to cities. Spain is a developed country.

United Kingdom

The United Kingdom is an island in Western Europe, including the northern one-sixth of Ireland. It is between the North Atlantic Ocean and the North Sea, and its total land area consists of 244,820 km². The United Kingdom was one of the leaders in the industrial revolution and it controlled the seas in the 19th century. Its strength decreased after World War II, but it has been rebuilding itself into a prosperous European nation. Constitutional reform is a major issue currently in this country. The country is a constitutional monarchy.

In 2003 the population in the United Kingdom was 60.1 million. It has 243.1 people per square kilometer. Its overall population density is one of the highest in the world. The major ethnic groups of the country include British, Irish, West Indian, and South Asian. The major religions include the Church of England (Anglican), Roman Catholic, the Church of Scotland (Presbyterian), and Muslim. The country's population primarily resides in urban and suburban areas. It is a developed country.

MIDDLE EAST

The Middle East's population is approximately 150 million. Most of the population lives in Egypt and Iran. The ethnic groups represented in this region are very diverse. Different forms of Islam are the predominant religions, with the exception of Israel, which is predominantly Jewish. This region has been a crossroad of conflict throughout history. Today, the Middle East receives much world attention due to its oil reserves, internal wars, and the ongoing conflict between the Arabs and Israelis. Much of this region remains to be developed.

Egypt

Egypt is located in northern Africa, bordering the Mediterranean Sea, between Libya and the Gaza Strip, and the Red Sea north of Sudan. Its land mass is over 1 million km^2. Egypt became an important transportation hub after the Suez Canal was completed in 1869, but unfortunately fell heavily into debt. To protect its investments, Britain seized control of Egypt's government in 1882, but Egypt's professed allegiance to the Ottoman Empire continued until 1914. In 1922 it was made partially independent from the United Kingdom, and the country achieved full sovereignty following World War II. Today, the rapidly growing population (the largest in the Arab world), limited arable land, and dependence on the Nile, strain resources and stress society. The government has struggled to get the economy ready for the 21st century through economic reform and investment in communications and physical infrastructure. Egypt is a republic.

The population of Egypt was approximately 74 million in 2003. The population density is approximately 64 people per square kilometer. The ethnic groups represented in Egypt include Egyptian, Bedouin Arab, and Nubian. Approximately 94% of the country is Muslim, most of them members of the Sunni sect. There are several religious minorities constituting the Coptic (Egyptian) Christians. Other minorities include followers of the Greek Orthodox Church, Eastern and Latin Rite Catholic and Protestants, in addition to a small number of Jews. Egypt is the most populous country in the Arab world and the second most populous on the African continent. Small communities are clustered around oases and historic transportation routes. Much of the population is moving to the cities in search of employment and a higher standard of living. Egypt is an underdeveloped country.

Iran

Iran is located in the Middle East, bordering the Gulf of Oman, the Persian Gulf, and the Caspian Sea, between Iraq and Pakistan. The size of the country is approximately 1.65 million km^2. Iran was known as Persia until 1935. The country became an Islamic republic in 1979 after the ruling Shah was forced into exile. Conservative clerical forces established a theocratic system of government with ultimate political authority awarded to a religious scholar. A group of Iranian students seized the U.S. Embassy in Tehran in 1979 and held it until 1981. From 1980 to 1988, Iran fought an inconclusive war with Iraq over disputed territory. During the 1990s, widespread dissatisfaction with the government, driven by demographic changes, restrictive social policies, and poor economic conditions created a powerful and enduring pressure for political reform.

The estimated population of Iran in 2003 was about 68 million. The population of the country is 39.8 people per square kilometer. Approximately half of the population is Persian, with a quarter being Azeri, and approximately equal minorities of Gilaki, Kurd, and Mazandarani, and a smaller proportion of Arab, Baloch, Lur, Turkmen, and other groups represented. Most of the population is Shi'a Muslim (89%), with a minority of Sunni Muslims, Baha'i, Christian, Jewish, and Zoroastrian groups represented. Iran remains divided into urban, market-town, village, and tribal groups. Unemployment is a major problem for this developing country.

Israel

Israel is located in the Middle East, bordering the Mediterranean Sea, between Egypt and Lebanon. The country is 20,770 km². After World War II, the British withdrew from their mandate of Palestine, and the United Nations divided the area into Arab and Jewish states. This arrangement was rejected by the Arabs. Following the arrangement, the Israelis defeated the Arabs in a series of wars without ending the tensions between the two sides. A number of territorial and other disputes with Jordan were resolved with the 1994 Israel–Jordan Treaty of Peace. In 2000 Israel

withdrew from southern Lebanon, which it had occupied since 1982. Negotiations were conducted between Israel and Palestinian representatives and Syria to achieve a permanent agreement. However, progress toward a permanent agreement has been undermined by the outbreak of Palestinian–Israeli violence that has existed since September 2000. The current form of government is a parliamentary democracy. The population of Israel was 6.4 million in 2003, with a density of 281.3 inhabitants per square kilometer. The major ethnic group is Jewish (5.2 million). The religions represented in this country include Judaism, Christianity, Druze, and Islam. Israel's economy is diversified and technologically advanced as a developed country.

PACIFIC RIM

The population in the Pacific Rim is almost 330 million, and numerous ethnic groups are represented in this region. The religions in this country are also diverse. The British, who predominated among those settling the Pacific Islands, found sparsely populated lands that were colonized easily. Some of the smaller islands have retained their traditional economies and cultures, whereas others have changed drastically because of contact with Asian and Western societies. Agriculture is the main source of livelihood in the Pacific Rim.

Australia

Australia is located between the Indian Ocean and South Pacific Ocean. It consists of approximately 7.7 million km². Australia became a commonwealth of the British Empire in 1901. The country was able to take advantage of its natural resources to develop its agricultural and manufacturing industries. Australia made a major contribution to the British effort in both world wars. A referendum to change Australia's status from a commonwealth headed by the British monarch to a republic was defeated in 1999. Australia therefore remains a democratic, federal-state system, recognizing the British monarch as sovereign.

In 2003 Australia's population was approximately 19.7 million. The population density of Australia is 2.5 people per square kilometer. Most of the population is European (about 92%); however, 6% are Asian and 2% are aboriginal. The country is almost equally divided in regard to religion, with Anglicans, Roman Catholics, and other Christians equally represented. English is the national language. Australia is one of the world's most urbanized countries, with less than 15% of the population living in rural areas. It is a fairly wealthy country, in part because of its domestic market.

Indonesia

Indonesia is located southeast of Asia, between the Indian and Pacific Oceans. The total area spans 1.9 million km². Indonesia is the world's largest archipelago.

Indonesia achieved independence from the Netherlands in 1949. The country is currently completing a transition to a popularly elected government after four decades of authoritarianism, with efforts being made to hold the military and police accountable for human rights violations. Resolving growing separatist pressures in Aceh and Papua is another challenge. Indonesia is a republic.

In 2003 the population in Indonesia was estimated to be 234 million, with a population density of 117.1 people per square kilometer. The ethnic groups represented include Javanese (45%), Sundanese (14%), Madurese (7.5%), coastal Malays (7.5%), and others. The religions in this country include Islam (87%), Protestantism (6%), Catholicism (3%), Hinduism (2%), and Buddhism (1%). Indonesia is the world's fourth most populous nation. The economy is market-based, and the government plays a significant role.

Philippines

The Philippines is located southeast of Asia, between the Philippine Sea and the South China Sea, east of Vietnam. The country spans 300,000 km². The Philippines were given by Spain to the United States in 1898, following the Spanish–American War. The Philippines attained independence in 1946 after Japanese occupation in World War II. The 21-year rule of Ferdinand Marcos ended in 1986 when a widespread popular rebellion forced him into exile. In 1992 the United States closed its remaining military bases on the islands. The Philippines has had two electoral presidential transitions since the removal of Marcos. In January 2001, the Supreme Court declared Joseph Estrada unable to rule in view of mass resignations from his government and administered the oath of office to Vice President Gloria Macapagal-Arroyo as his successor. The government continues to struggle with Muslim uprisings in the south.

In 2000 the population in the Philippines was 76.5 million. The population density of the Philippines is 270.5 residents per square kilometer. The ethnic groups of this country are Malay and Chinese. The majority of the population is Catholic (83%), with smaller proportions of Buddhists, Muslims, and Protestants represented. The economy in the Philippines has a mixed history of growth and development, with important sectors including agriculture and industry.

REFERENCES

Arreola, D. D. (2003). *World geography.* Boston: McDougal Littell.

Central Intelligence Agency. (2003, August). *The world factbook.* Retrieved September 27, 2003, from http://www.cia.gov/cia/publications/factbook/docs/profileguide.html

English, P. W. (1995). *People and places in a changing world* (2nd ed.). New York: West.

United States Department of State. (n.d.). *Countries and regions.* Retrieved May 3, 2003, from http://www.state.gov/countries/

Yahoo! Reference. (2003). *World factbook.* Retrieved September 27, 2003, from http://education.yahoo.com/reference/factbook/density/g_population.html

Index